VOID IF DETACHED FROM BOOK OR ALTERED

AMERICAN HISTORIC INNS
INCORPORATED

Certificate

redeemable for

One Free Night
at a Bed & Breakfast
or Country Inn

Advance reservations required.
See "How to Make a Reservation."

Compliments of
American Historic Inns, Inc. and
participating Bed & Breakfasts
and Country Inns.

This certificate entitles the bearer to one free night
at nearly 1,200 Bed & Breakfasts
and Country Inns when the
bearer buys the first night at the regular ra
See back for requirements.

VOID IF DETACHED FROM BOOK OR ALTEREI

D1223827

VOID IF DETACHED FROM BOOK OR ALTERED

AMERICAN
HISTORIC
I N S
INCORPORATED

Free night is provided by participating inn.
Please fax/scan redeemed certificate to (949) 481-3796 or mail to:
American Historic Inns, Inc.
PO Box 669, Dana Point, CA 92629-0669
Inns with most redeemed certificates will be featured on iLoveinns.com as one of "America's Favorite Inns."

_____
Name of Guest

_____
Guest Home Address

_____
Guest City/State/Zip

_____
Guest Email Address

_____
Name of Bed & Breakfast/Inn

_____
Signature of Innkeeper

Certificate is good for one (1) free consecutive night when you purchase the first night at the regular rate. Offer not valid at all times. Contact inn in advance for availability, rates, reservations, meal plans, cancellation policies and other requirements. If book is purchased at the inn, certificate is valid only for a future visit. Offer valid only at participating inns featured in this Bed & Breakfast Guide or online at iLoveInns.com for inns with "Free Night Participating Inn". Not valid during holidays. Minimum 2-night stay. Certificate is for no more than two people and no more than one room. Other restrictions may apply. Bed tax, sales tax and gratuities not included. American Historic Inns, Inc. is not responsible for any changes in individual inn operation or policy. By use of this certificate, consumer agrees to release American Historic Inns, Inc. from any liability in connection with their travel to and stay at any participating Inn. This certificate may not be reproduced and cannot be used in conjunction with any other promotional offers. Certificate must be redeemed at participating inn by December 31, 2014. Void where prohibited.

Certificate Expires December 31, 2014

IF BOOK IS PURCHASED AT THE INN, CERTIFICATE IS VALID ONLY FOR FUTURE VISIT

Media Comments

"…lighthouses, schoolhouses, stage coach stops, llama ranches … There's lots to choose from and it should keep B&B fans happy for years." – Cathy Stapells, Toronto Sun

"Anytime you can get superb accommodations AND a free night, well that's got to be great, and it is … I've used this book before, and I must tell you, it's super … The news, information and facts in this book are all fascinating." – On the Road With John Clayton, KKGO, Los Angeles radio

"…helps you find the very best hideaways (many of the book's listings appear in the National Register of Historic Places.)" – Country Living

"I love your book!" – Lydia Moss, Travel Editor, McCall's

"Delightful, succinct, detailed and well-organized. Easy to follow style…"
– Don Wudke, Los Angeles Times

"Deborah Sakach's Bed & Breakfasts and Country Inns *continues to be the premier Bed & Breakfast guide for travelers and tourists throughout the United States."* – Midwest Book Review

"One of the better promotions we've seen." – Baton Rouge Advocate

"…thoughtfully organized and look-ups are hassle-free…well-researched and accurate…put together by people who know the field. There is no other publication available that covers this particular segment of the bed & breakfast industry – a segment that has been gaining popularity among travelers by leaps and bounds. The information included is valuable and well thought out." – Morgan Directory Reviews

"Readers will find this book easy to use and handy to have. An excellent, well-organized and comprehensive reference for inngoers and innkeepers alike."
– Inn Review, Kankakee, Ill.

"This guide has become the favorite choice of travelers and specializes only in professionally operated inns and B&Bs rather than homestays (lodging in spare bedrooms)." – Laguna Magazine

"This is the best bed and breakfast book out. It outshines them all!"
– Maggie Balitas, Rodale Book Clubs

As I began to look through the book, my heart beat faster as I envisioned what a good time our readers could have visiting some of these very special historic bed and breakfast properties." – Ann Crawford, Military Living

"This is a great book. It makes you want to card everything." – KBRT Los Angeles radio talk show

"All our lines were tied up! We received calls from every one of our 40 stations (while discussing your book.)" – Business Radio Network

"For a delightful change of scenery, visit one of these historical inns. (Excerpts from Bed & Breakfasts and Country Inns follow.) A certificate for one free consecutive night (minimum two nights stay) can be found in the book." – Shirley Howard, Good Housekeeping

"iLoveInns.com boasts independently written reviews, elegant design, and direct links to inns' URLs." – Yahoo! Internet Magazine referring to iLoveInns.com, winner of their 2002 Best B&B Site.

Recognition for InnTouch, the iLoveInns.com iPhone app

2009 Sunset Magazine, Featured iPhone travel app; 2009 Travel & Leisure, "Best iPhone Apps for Travelers"; 2009 Apple "Staff Favorite" for InnTouch

Comments From Innkeepers

"The guests we receive from the Buy-One-Night-Get-One-Night-Free program are some of the most wonderful people. Most are first time inngoers and after their first taste of the inn experience they vow that this is the only way to travel." – Innkeeper, Mass.

"Guests that were staying here last night swear by your guide. They use it all the time. Please send us information about being in your guide." – Innkeeper, Port Angeles, Wash.

"The people are so nice! Please keep up the great program!"
– K. C, The Avon Manor B&B Inn, Avon-By-the-Sea, N.J.

"I have redeemed several certificates which have led to new loyal customers who, in turn, referred our inn to new guests!" - Manchester Inn Bed & Breakfast, Ocean Grove, N.J.

"We want to tell you how much we love your book. We have it out for guests to use. They love it! Each featured inn stands out so well. Thank you for the privilege of being in your book."
– Fairhaven Inn, Bath, Maine

"We've had guests return two or three times after discovering us through your book. They have turned into wonderful guests and friends." – Port Townsend, Wash.

"I wanted to let you know that I have been getting quite a few bookings from your guide with the certificates."
– Quill Haven Country Inn, Somerset, Pa.

"The response to your book has been terrific and the guests equally terrific! Many are already returning. Thanks for all your hard work." – Rockport, Mass.

"We love your book and we also use it. Just went to New Orleans and had a great trip."
– Gettysburg, Pa.

"Outstanding! We were offering a variety of inn guide books, but yours was the only one guests bought."
– White Oak Inn, Danville, Ohio

"This has been one of the best B&B programs we have done and the guests have been delightful. Thanks!" – Eastern Shore, Md.

"We are grateful that so many of our old friends and new guests have found us through your book. We always recommend your publications to guests who wish to explore other fine country inns of New England."
– Innkeeper, Vt.

"Of all the associations I am a member of you are the most out front and progressive of them all. I guess this is why I have been a member since 1995ish…..this is my 21st year! Bravo to you!!!!" The Lockhart Bed and Breakfast Inn

"Wow! I say it again. You guys are great! BY FAR the most effective and helpful of all the organizations. THANKS!!!!" Nancy Henderson, Sunset Hill House

Comments About
Bed & Breakfasts and Country Inns

"I purchased 8 of these books in January and have already used them up. I am ordering 8 more. I've had great experiences. This year I've been to California, Philadelphia and San Antonio and by ordering so many books enjoyed getting free night at each place. The inns were fabulous." – D. Valentine, Houston, Texas

"Our office went crazy over this book. The quality of the inns and the quality of the book is phenomenal! Send us 52 books." – M.B., Westport, Conn.

"Every time we look at this book we remember our honeymoon! Every time we make another reservation with the free night certificate we relive our honeymoon! We were married in May and visited three fabulous inns that week, in Cape May, Philadelphia and one near Longwood Gardens. They all served phenomenal food and were beautifully decorated. We went back in the summer we loved it so much. It's like our honeymoon again everytime we use this book. You get such a real feel of America's little towns this way." – S. Piniak, N.J.

"The 300 women who attended my 'Better Cents' seminar went wild for the free-night book. I brought my copy and showed them the value of the free-night program. They all wanted to get involved. Thank you so much for offering such a great value."
– R.R., Making Cents Seminars, Texas

"Thank you for offering this special! It allowed us to get away even on a tight budget."
– D.L., Pittsburgh, Pa.

"I'm ordering three new books. We've never stayed in one we didn't like that was in your book!"
– M.R., Canton, Ohio

"This made our vacation a lot more reasonable. We got the best room in a beautiful top-drawer inn for half the price." – L.A., Irvine, Calif.

"I used your book and free night offer and took my 17-year-old daughter. It was our first B&B visit ever and we loved it. (We acted like friends instead of parent vs. teenager for the first time in a long time.) It was wonderful!" – B.F., Clinton, N.J.

"Thanks! Do we love your B&B offer! You betcha! The luxury of getting a two-day vacation for the cost of one is Christmas in July for sure. Keep up the good work."
– R.R., Grapevine, Texas.

"What a great idea for gifts. I'm ordering five to use as birthday, housewarming and thank-you gifts." – J.R., Laguna Niguel, Calif.

"The best thing since ice cream – and I love ice cream!" – M.C., Cape May, N.J.

"I keep giving your books away as gifts and then don't have any for myself. Please send me three more copies." – D.T., Ridgewood, N.J.

"Out of 25 products we presented to our fund raising committee your book was No. 1 and it generated the most excitement." – H.U., Detroit, Mich.

ഇരുരുരുരുരുരുരുരു

To, Jamee Danihels & Diane Ringler
Always ready for every new wild adventure.

ഇരുരുരുരുരുരുരുരു

American Historic Inns™

Bed & Breakfasts

and Country Inns

_____

by Deborah Edwards Sakach

Published by

AMERICAN HISTORIC INNS INCORPORATED

PO Box 669
Dana Point
California
92629-0669
www.iLoveInns.com

Bed & Breakfasts and Country Inns

AUTHOR:
Deborah Sakach

COVER DESIGN:
David Sakach

COVER PHOTO EDITING:
Mai Arriola

PRODUCTION MANAGER:
Jamee Danihels and Diane Ringler

BOOK LAYOUT:
Jamee Danihels

SENIOR EDITOR
Shirley Swagerty

ASSISTANT EDITORS:
Jamee Danihels, Julie Dietzel-Glair

For the up-to-the-minute information on participating properties, please visit iLoveInns.com or the iPhone free application "InnTouch"
Participating inns are designated by "Free Night Participating Inn".

Publisher's Cataloging in Publication Data

Sakach, Deborah Edwards
American Historic Inns, Inc.
Bed & Breakfasts and Country Inns

1. Bed & Breakfast Accommodations - United States, Directories, Guide Books.
2. Travel - Bed & Breakfast Inns, Directories, Guide Books.
3. Bed & Breakfast Accommodations - Historic Inns, Directories, Guide Books.
4. Hotel Accommodations - Bed & Breakfast Inns, Directories, Guide Books.
5. Hotel Accommodations - United States, Directories, Guide Books.
I. Title. II Author. III Bed & Breakfast, Bed & Breakfasts and Country Inns.

American Historic Inns is a trademark of American Historic Inns, Inc.

ISBN: **9781888050257**
Softcover
Printed in the United States of America.
10 9 8 7 6 5 4 3 2 1

Table Of Contents

How To Make A Reservation

1 Call

The FREE Night offer **requires advance reservations** and is subject to availability.*

To use the Free Night Certificate call the inn of your choice in advance of your stay and identify yourself as holding a Free Night Certificate from American Historic Inns, Inc. and iLoveinns.com.

2 Confirm

Verify availabilty, rates and the inn's acceptance of the Free Night Certificate for your requested dates. Make a written note of the name of the reservationist and confirmation code.

This offer is subject to availability. All holidays are excluded as well as certain local event dates. A consecutive two-night minimum is required.

Ask about cancellation policies as some inns may require at least a two-week notice in order to refund your deposit. (Also, please note some locales require bed tax be collected, even on free nights.) Find out what meals are included in the rates. A few properties particiapting in this program do not offer a free breakfast.

3 Check-in

Don't forget to take this book with the Free Night Certificate with you.

The FREE Night is given to you as a gift directly from the innkeeper in the hope that you or your friends will return and share your discovery with others. The inns are not reimbursed by American Historic Inns, Inc.

IMPORTANT NOTE

*"Subject to availability" and "anytime based on availability": each innkeeper interprets availability for their own property. Just as airlines may set aside a number of seats for discounted fares, so small inns in our program may use different formulas to manage the number of rooms and the times available for the Buy-One-Night-Get-One-Night-Free program. You must call the innkeeper to see if any of their vacant rooms are available for the free night. While innkeepers have proven to be extremely generous with the program, each reservation must be made by first stating that you wish to use the Free Night Certificate toward your two-night stay. When innkeepers foresee a full house during peak times, they might not be able to accept this certificate. Our innkeepers welcome your reservation and are looking forward to your visit.

How To Use This Book

You hold in your hands a delightful selection of America's best bed & breakfasts and country inns. The innkeeper of each property has generously agreed to participate in our FREE night program.

Most knowledgeable innkeepers enjoy sharing regional attractions, local folklore, history, and pointing out favorite restaurants and other special features of their areas. They are a tremendous resource, treat them kindly and you will be well rewarded.

Accommodations

You'll find bed & breakfasts and country inns in converted schoolhouses, churches, lighthouses, 18th-century farmhouses, Queen Anne Victorians, adobe lodges, plantations and more.

Many are listed in the National Register of Historic Places and have preserved the stories and memorabilia from their participation in historical events such as the Revolutionary or Civil Wars.

The majority of inns included in this book were built in the 18th, 19th and early 20th centuries. We have stated the date each building was constructed at the beginning of each description.

A Variety of Inns

A **Country Inn** generally serves both breakfast and dinner and may have a restaurant associated with it. Many have been in operation for years; some, since the 18th century as you will note in our "Inns of Interest" section. Although primarily found on the East Coast, a few country inns are in other regions of the nation. Always check as to what meals are provided.

A **Bed & Breakfast** facility's primary focus is lodging. It can have from three to 20 rooms or more. The innkeepers usually live on the premises. Breakfast is the only meal served and can be a full-course, gourmet breakfast or a simple buffet. Many B&B owners pride themselves on their culinary skills.

As with country inns, often B&Bs specialize in providing historic, romantic or gracious atmospheres with amenities such as canopied beds, fireplaces, hot tubs, whirlpools, afternoon tea in the library and scenic views.

Some give great attention to recapturing a specific historic period, such as the Victorian or Colonial eras. Many display antiques and other furnishings from family collections.

Area Codes

Although we have made every effort to update area codes throughout the book, new ones pop up from time to time. For up-to-the-minute phone numbers, please check our Web site at iLoveInns.com.

Baths

Most bed & breakfasts and country inns provide a private bath for each guest room. We have included the number of rooms and the number of private baths in each facility.

Meals

Continental breakfast: Coffee, juice, toast or pastry.

Continental-plus breakfast: A continental breakfast plus a variety of breads, cheeses and fruit.

Country breakfast: Includes all the traditional fixings of home-cooked country fare.

Full breakfast: Coffee, juice, breads, fruit and an entree.

Full gourmet breakfast: May be an elegant four-course candlelight offering or especially creative cuisine.

Teas: Usually served in the late afternoon with cookies, crackers or other in-between-meal offerings.

Vegetarian breakfast: Vegetarian fare.

Always find out what meals, if any, are included in the rates. Not every establishment participating in this program provides breakfast, although most do. *Please do not assume meals are included in the rates featured in the book.*

Rates

Rates are usually listed in ranges, i.e., $65-175. The LOWEST rate is almost always available during off-peak periods and may apply only to the least expensive room. Rates are subject to change and are not guaranteed. Always confirm the rates when making reservations. Rates for Canadian listings usually are listed in Canadian dollars. Rates are quoted for double occupancy for two people. Rates for this program are calculated from regular rates and not from seasonal promotional offers.

Breakfast and other meals MAY or MAY NOT be included in the rates and may not be included in the discount.

Smoking

The majority of country inns and B&Bs in historic buildings prohibit smoking; therefore, if you are a smoker we advise you to call and specifically check with each inn to see if and how they accommodate smokers.

Rooms

Under some listings, you will note that suites are available. We typically assume that suites include a private bath and a separate living room. If the inn contains suites that have more than one bedroom, it will indicate as such.

Additionally, under some listings, you will note a reference to cottages. A cottage may be a rustic cabin tucked in the woods, a seaside cottage or a private apartment-style accommodation.

Minimum stays

Many inns require a two-night minimum stay on weekends. A three-night stay often is required during holiday periods.

Cancellations

Cancellation policies are individual for each bed & breakfast. It is not unusual to see 7 to 14 day cancellation periods or more. Please verify the inn's policy when making your reservation.

What if the inn is full?

Ask the innkeeper for recommendations. They may know of an inn that has opened recently or one nearby. Call the local Visitors Bureau in the town you hope to visit as an additional resource. Please let us know of any new discoveries you make.

We want to hear from you!

If you wish to participate in evaluating your inn experiences, use the **Inn Evaluation Form** in the back of this book. You might want to make copies of this form prior to departing on your journey. You can also submit reviews at iLoveinns.com by going to the inn's listing and clicking on "Write A Review".

We hope you will enjoy this book so much that you will want to keep an extra copy or two on hand to offer to friends. Many readers have called to purchase our "Buy-One-Night-Get-One-Night-Free" certificate book for host-ess gifts, birthday presents, or for seasonal celebrations. It's a great way to introduce your friends to America's enchanting country inns and bed & breakfasts.

Visit us online at iLoveInns.com!

Would you like more information about the inns listed in this book? For color photos, links to the inns' Web sites and more, search our Web site at **iLoveInns.com**. You'll find reviews of inns throughout the United States and Canada and you can also post your own review. We think you'll agree with Yahoo! Internet Magazine who named iLoveInns.com "Best B&B Site."

Have Fun with iloveInns iPhone B&B Application

Add some excitement to any road trip you take this year by downloading the free "InnTouch" bed and breakfast application to your iPhone. (If you have another smart phone, please note that iLoveInns.com is mobile compatible.) The "InnTouch" application is available free at the iPhone App Store. When traveling use the "Nearby" feature and it will pull your GPS coordinates and you'll see all the nearby inns within 60 miles of your location. You will be surprised at the inns you discover and may want to make a spontaneous visit. That's what *Travel & Leisure* noted when they chose their list of "best travel applications on the iPhone" and included InnTouch.

Because the phone is an all-in-one device, you can call the inn for reservations with one touch, not dialing each digit of the phone number. You can see the inn's address on a map, get directions, save the address in your contact list, as well as e-mail or visit the inn's Web site with single-click actions. You can read descriptions, see photos, videos and guest reviews. There are more than 6,000 inns on the iPhone application, including the 1500 that honor the Buy-One-Night-Get-the-Second Night Free certificate.

Submit an online review at iLoveInns.com

You may never have considered writing an online review but it's really very easy. Simply go to iLoveInns.com and look up the inn you visited though the easy city or name search. Then click on the "Write a Review" link and enter your thoughts.

Innkeepers want you to enjoy your stay and return home refreshed and relaxed. While you are there they want to know if there is anything they can do to meet your expectations for a wonderful getaway so be sure to let them know during your stay. If you think of something afterwards, send an email or a short note.

If you remember inns from past stays that were pleasant and for which you still hold a fond memory, be sure to make a comment about them on iLoveInns.com. We have always counted on our readers to tell us about their experiences. Our more than two and a half million Bed and Breakfast books have included review forms for this purpose. You can find this form at the back of the book . We also highly encourage you to make online reviews. Watch for our frequent rewards (such as a GPS, free books, gift certificates, etc.) to guests who complete the online review at iLoveInns.com.

How to Read an Inn Listing

Anytown

An American Historic Inn

(1) 123 S Main St
Anytown, MA 98765-4321
(123)555-1212 (800)555-1212 Fax:(123)555-1234
Internet: www.iLoveInns.com
E-mail: comments@iLoveInns.com

(2) **Circa 1897.** Every inch of this breathtaking inn offers something special. The interior is decorated to the hilt with lovely furnishings, plants, beautiful rugs and warm, inviting tones. Rooms include four-poster and canopy beds combined with the modern amenities such as fireplaces, wet bars and stocked refrigerators. Enjoy a complimentary full breakfast at the inn's gourmet restaurant. The chef offers everything from a light breakfast of fresh fruit, cereal and a bagel to heartier treats such as pecan peach pancakes and Belgium waffles served with fresh fruit and crisp bacon.

(3)

(4) Innkeeper(s): Michael & Marissa Chaco. (5) $125-195. (6) 13 rooms with PB, 4 with FP, 1 suite and 1 conference room. (7) Breakfast and afternoon tea included in rates. (8) Types of meals: Full bkfst, country bkfst, veg bkfst, early coffee/tea, picnic lunch, gourmet lunch and room service.

(9) **Certificate may be used:** December, January and February, Sunday through Wednesday night only. Good only for four rooms which have a rate of $175.

(1) **Inn address**
Mailing or street address and all phone numbers for the inn. May also include the inn's Web site and email address.

(2) **Description of inn**
Descriptions of inns are written by experienced travel writers based on visits to inns, interviews and information collected from inns.

(3) **Drawing of inn**
Many listings include artistic renderings.

(4) **Innkeepers**
The name of the innkeeper(s).

(5) **Rates**
Rates are quoted for double occupancy. The rate range includes off-season rates and is subject to change.

(6) **Rooms**
Number and types of rooms available.
PB=Private Bath   FP=Fireplace
HT=Hot Tub   WP=Whirlpool

(7) **Included Meals**
Types of meals included in the rates.

(8) **Available meals**
This section lists the types of meals that the inn offers. These meals may or may not be included in the rates.

(9) **Certificate dates**
Indicates when inn has agreed to honor the Buy-One-Night-Get-One-Night-Free Certificate™. Always verify availability of discount with innkeeper.

Alabama

Alexander City

Mistletoe Bough

497 Hillabee St
Alexander City, AL 35010
(256)329-3717 (877)330-3707
Internet: www.mistletoebough.com
E-mail: mistletoebough@charter.net

Circa 1890. When Jean and Carlice Payne purchased this three-story Queen Anne Victorian, it had been in the Reuben Herzfeld family for 103 years. Surrounded by two acres of lawns, tall oak and pecan trees as well as a tulip tree, Victorian Pearl bushes,

camellias and brilliant azaleas, the home has a three-story turret and cupola, balconies, stained-glass windows and a wraparound porch. The porch ceiling is painted sky blue. A gracious foyer features tongue-and-groove wainscoting and opens to a ladies' parlor on one side and a gentlemen's parlor on the other. Fresh flowers, antiques and lace curtains are mixed with traditional and antique Victorian and European furnishings. Upon arrival, guests are pampered with refreshments and homemade cookies (frequently with ingredients from Mistletoe's fruit trees and Carlice's herb garden). Other goodies are always on hand. A four-course breakfast is served in the formal dining room with fine china, crystal and silver. The home is in the National Register.

Innkeeper(s): JoAnn Frazier, Jesse Frazier. $90-129. 5 rooms with PB. Breakfast and snacks/refreshments included in rates. Types of meals: Full bkfst.
Certificate may be used: November-March, Sunday-Thursday; subject to availability.

Montgomery

Red Bluff Cottage B&B

551 Clay Street
Montgomery, AL 36104
(888)551-2529 Fax:(334)263-3054
Internet: www.redbluffcottage.com
E-mail: info@redbluffcottage.com

Circa 1987. "Heavenly beds! The most comfortable accommodations on our whole trip!" is one of numerous comments from guests who have discovered Red Bluff Cottage B&B. Filled with warmth, comfort and an abundance of thoughtful touches that guarantee a delightful night's sleep, the inn overlooks the Alabama River Plain in historic Cottage Hill, near the heart of Montgomery, Alabama's downtown business district. Many favorite tourist attractions are within walking distance. Yet, what sets the spacious cottage apart is genuine Southern charm and a welcoming atmosphere. Relax in clean, comfortable and cozy rooms or unwind in the peaceful gazebo on the lush grounds. After a peaceful night's rest, enjoy an amazing home-cooked breakfast. Two of Bonnie's recipes are featured in the Alabama Tourism Department's brochure, "100 Dishes to Eat in Alabama Before You Die." Guests are within walking distance of Biscuits Baseball at Riverwalk Stadium, Civil Rights Memorial, Davis Theatre, First White House of the Confederacy, Hank Williams Museum, Montgomery Performing Arts Center, Old Alabama Town, Riverfront Amphitheater, Rosa Parks Museum, State Archives, State Capitol. Other attractions within a 5-15 minute drive include Maxwell AFB, Alabama Shakespeare Festival Theatre, Capitol Hill Robert Trent Jones Golf Trail, Dexter Parsonage Museum, F. Scott and Zelda Fitzgerald Museum, Hyundai Plant, Montgomery Museum of Fine Arts and the Montgomery Zoo/Mann Wildlife Museum. Wireless Internet, fax and copier services allow business guests to work efficiently and without interruption.

Innkeeper(s): Barry Ponstein, Bonnie Ponstein. $110-155. 4 rooms with PB, 1 with WP, 1 two-bedroom suite. Breakfast included in rates. Types of meals: Full gourmet bkfst, early coffee/tea, afternoon tea and snacks/refreshments.
Certificate may be used: Monday-Thursday only.

Pell City

Treasure Island Bed & Breakfast

Treasure Island
Pell City, AL 35054
(205)525-5172
Internet: www.treasureislandbedandbreakfast.com
E-mail: info@treasureislandbedandbreakfast.com

Treasure awaits at this contemporary inn on the shores of the Coosa River overlooking Logan Martin Lake. Play pool in the game room, watch the big screen plasma TV in the great room or work out on the Universal gym. Snacks and beverages are always available. Guest bedrooms offer thoughtful amenities that include bathrobes and hair dryers. Laundry, ironing, phone and computer access are provided upon request. Savor a hearty, Plantation Breakfast with waterfront views in the dining room. Enjoy a complimentary sunset pontoon boat river cruise in the evening.

Innkeeper(s): Earl Hardy, Lillie Hardy. $100-175. 4 rooms with PB, 1 suite. Breakfast and snacks/refreshments included in rates. Types of meals: Full bkfst.
Certificate may be used: November-March, Monday-Wednesday.

Alaska

Anchorage

Big Bear Bed & Breakfast

3401 Richmond Ave
Anchorage, AK 99508-1013
(907)277-8189
Internet: www.alaskabigbearbb.com/
E-mail: bigbearbb@alaska.net

Circa 1949. Stay at the Big Bear Bed & Breakfast to experience "Old Fashioned Alaskan Hospitality" in Anchorage. Innkeeper Carol Ross is a native Alaskan and Certified Alaska Tour Guide. The four guest rooms are decorated with local themes and are available year-round. The centerpiece of the home is a stained glass window designed and built by Carol's late husband. Visitors are treated to a breakfast of Alaskan specialties including reindeer sausage, sourdough waffles with wild berry toppings, and homemade Danish bear paws. Big Bear is happy to accommodate special dietary requests and is smoke, pet, and fragrance free. Guests can wander through the garden of flowers, vegetables, and berries, or sit by the fish pond with its soothing waterfall. Conveniently located only two miles from downtown Anchorage, four and a half miles from the Alaska Native Heritage Center, and near numerous local restaurants and shops, this bed and breakfast is the ideal spot for any Anchorage vacation.
Innkeeper(s): Carol J. Ross. $85-125. 4 rooms with PB, 1 with FP, 1 with HT. Types of meals: Full bkfst, early coffee/tea, snacks/refreshments, Tea all day and box breakfast for guests leaving before 6AM.
Certificate may be used: October-March, subject to availability.

Fairbanks

7 Gables Inn & Suites

4312 Birch Ln
Fairbanks, AK 99709
(907)479-0751 Fax:(907)479-2229
Internet: www.7gablesinn.com
E-mail: gables7@alaska.net

Circa 1982. There are actually 14 gables on this modern Tudor-style inn, which is located a short walk from the University of Alaska and the Chena River. Inside the foyer, a seven-foot waterfall is an amazing welcome. A two-story, flower-filled solarium and a meeting room are wonderful gathering places. Seasonally enjoy the magnificent aurora borealis or a white world of snowflakes and dog mushing, and then relax in a steaming in-room Jacuzzi tub. In summertime the midnight sun allows canoe trips down the river for a progressive dinner from restaurant to deck to dock. The innkeepers received the

city's Golden Heart Award for exceptional hospitality.
Innkeeper(s): Paul Welton, Leicha Welton. $50-200. 30 rooms, 25 with PB, 25 with WP, 15 suites, 4 cottages. Breakfast and snacks/refreshments included in rates. Types of meals: Full gourmet bkfst.
Certificate may be used: Oct. 1-April 30.

Juneau

Pearson's Pond Luxury Inn & Adventure Spa

4541 Sawa Cir
Juneau, AK 99801-8723
(907)789-3772 (888)658-6328
Internet: www.pearsonspond.com
E-mail: book@pearsonspond.com

Circa 1990. Cruise glaciers, view bears and whales, climb the ice, mush dogs, go fishing, or take a chance at gold-panning while staying at this award-winning luxury resort. Enchanted master-planned gardens, lined with wild Alaska blueberry bushes and dotted with hot tubs and gazebos, give you an immediate feeling of serenity. Exquisitely appointed accommodations make you feel so pampered and comfortable that you won't ever want to leave. Every room has a fireplace, kitchenette, sitting area, flat panel TV, water or forest views, and much more. Near to everything, yet seeming a world apart, this is the perfect place for an Alaska adventure vacation, wedding, or romantic interlude.
Innkeeper(s): Maryann Ray, Rachael Ray, Rick Nelson. $219-799. 7 rooms, 8 with PB, 5 with FP, 2 with WP, 4 total suites, including 1 two-bedroom suite. Breakfast, hors d'oeuvres, wine and Self serve breakfast in winter included in rates. Types of meals: Full bkfst, veg bkfst, early coffee/tea, picnic lunch, afternoon tea, snacks/refreshments, room service, Expanded continental breakfast with hot entree in summer and self-serve anytime. Self-serve expanded continental breakfast in fall/winter/spring.
Certificate may be used: October-April.

Nikiski

Daniels Lake Lodge B&B

PO Box 8222
Nikiski, AK 99635
(907)776-5578 (800)774-5578
Internet: www.danielslakelodge.com
E-mail: visit@danielslakelodge.com

Circa 1955. Nine forested acres surround this secluded bed & breakfast in a cove on the shore of the area's third-largest lake. Experience fantastic views, smoke-free accommodations, privacy for romantic getaways and comfort for families. Stay in a lakeside guest bedroom or a log cabin. Most feature whirlpool tubs. All the kitchens are generously stocked with an assortment of ingredients for a self-serve breakfast. Relax in the waterfront hot tub after a day of boating, rowing or fishing for wild rainbow trout. An abundance of wildlife includes moose, eagles, ducks, loons, owls, lynx, beaver and swans. Nearby Nikiski's indoor swimming pool boasts a 136-foot water slide. Beachcomb at Captain Cook State Recreation Area. The Swanson River has a canoe landing and salmon fishing. Local restaurants offer free delivery to the lodge.

Innkeeper(s): Karen Burris, Jim Burris. $50-250. 10 rooms with PB, 3 cabins. Breakfast included in rates. Types of meals: Cont plus.
Certificate may be used: Oct. 1-Nov. 15, Jan. 7-March 30.

Palmer

Colony Inn & Cafe

325 E Elmwood
Palmer, AK 99645-6622
(907)745-3330 Fax:(907)746-3330
Internet: www.tripadvisor.ca/Hotel_Review-g31086-d113748-Reviews-Colony_Inn-Palmer_Alaska.html

Circa 1935. Historic buildings are few and far between in Alaska, and this inn is one of them. The structure was built to house teachers and nurses in the days when President Roosevelt was sending settlers to Alaska to establish farms. When innkeeper Janet Kincaid 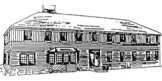 purchased it, the inn had been empty for some time. She restored the place, including the wood walls, which now create a cozy ambiance in the common areas. The 12 guest rooms are nicely appointed, and 10 include a whirlpool tub. Meals are not included, but the inn's restaurant offers breakfast and lunch. The inn is listed in the National Register.

Innkeeper(s): Janet Kincaid. $110. 12 rooms with PB. Types of meals: Lunch and Dinner on Friday night with Live music and Sunday Brunch. Restaurant on premises.
Certificate may be used: Oct. 1-May 1.

Sitka

Alaska Ocean View Bed & Breakfast Inn

1101 Edgecumbe Dr
Sitka, AK 99835-7122
(907)747-8310 Fax:(907)747-3440
Internet: www.sitka-alaska-lodging.com
E-mail: info@sitka-alaska-lodging.com

Circa 1986. Alaska Ocean View Bed & Breakfast Inn is a red-cedar executive home is located in a quiet neighborhood one block from the seashore and the Tongass National Forest in Sitka. Witness spectacular sunsets over stunning Sitka Sound and on clear days view majestic Mt. Edgecumbe, an extinct volcano located offshore on Kruzoff Island. Binoculars are kept handy for guests who take a special interest in looking for whales and eagles. Guest bedrooms are named after popular local wildflowers. Explore the scenic area after a hearty breakfast.

Innkeeper(s): Carole & Bill Denkinger. $129-249. 3 rooms with PB, 2 with FP, 1 conference room. Breakfast, afternoon tea and snacks/refreshments included in rates. Types of meals: Full gourmet bkfst, veg bkfst, early coffee/tea, hors d'oeuvres and room service.
Certificate may be used: Sunday-Wednesday, October-March, Sunday-Wednesday, April-May 7. Subject to availability. Anytime at the last minute.

Arizona

Amado

Amado Territory Inn

3001 E. Frontage Road
Amado, AZ 85645
(520) 398-8684 (888) 398-8684 Fax:(520)398-8186
Internet: www.amadoterritoryinn.com
E-mail: info@amadoterritoryinn.com

Circa 1986. Spanning 25 acres in the heart of cattle country in the Santa Cruz River Valley, this modern ranch with an old-west ambiance and rustic elegance is a desert delight. Amado means beloved and the name fits perfectly with the inn's goal to extend enjoyment, rest and recreation. Nature trails and buildings blend into the landscape that includes a riparian habitat where more than fifty birds have been sighted. The inn offers a traditional high tea in the Atrium. Come dressed in period clothing; hats and feather boas are provided. There are two on-site restaurants, conference facilities and outdoor events at Grasslands or The Oasis with views of Elephant Head and the Santa Rita Mountains. Explore the night sky at the state-of-the-art astronomy center. Ask about special packages for Mystery by Design Dinner Theater.

Innkeeper(s): Cara Williams, Ricky Williams. $129-139. 11 rooms with PB, 1 guest house, 1 conference room. Breakfast, snacks/refreshments, wine and We offer a twilight wine and cheese included in rates. Types of meals: Afternoon tea. Restaurant on premises.

Certificate may be used: June-July only.

Bisbee

Gardens At Mile High Ranch

901 Tombstone Cyn
Bisbee, AZ 85603
(520)432-3866
Internet: www.gardensatmilehighranch.com
E-mail: info@gardensatmilehighranch.com

Circa 1920. Three high-desert country acres in a lush setting just one mile from the Historic District of Bisbee, Arizona provide the backdrop for a peaceful getaway or vacation. Mature shade trees, 150-year cottonwoods, earthy garden walls and a goldfish pond with flowers and lily pads combine to invite wildlife and bird watching in a peaceful environment. Meditation, picnics and nature walks are popular activities. Stay in a spacious and private apartment-like accommodation with a kitchenette and generous amenities. Children and pets are welcome. A healthy continental breakfast is delivered to each unit daily. Spa treatments, body detoxification products and services are offered from an extensive menu.

Innkeeper(s): Maggie Kohanek. $70-115. 7 rooms with PB, 3 with FP. Breakfast included in rates. Types of meals: Cont.

Certificate may be used: Aug. 1-Sept. 15, Sunday-Thursday. Subject to availability.

Flagstaff

Abineau Lodge Bed and Breakfast

1080 Mountainaire Rd
Flagstaff, AZ 86001-9569
(928) 525-6212 (888) 715-6386 Fax:(928)255-5577
Internet: www.abineaulodge.com
E-mail: info@abineaulodge.com

Circa 1997. Outdoor enthusiasts will savor each moment spent at this contemporary mountain lodge, nestled in the sunny mountains of the Southwest. The scent of the north woods entices one to venture out on the many hiking and biking trails surrounding the property. At the end of the day, relax in a private bath or the indoor sauna. Built on the site of the original settlement of Mountainaire, the inn shares the property with the original log cabin that was the first residence in the area. The Arcadian ambiance makes it hard to believe that urban Flagstaff is just a few miles away, providing shops and entertainment to fill the serene, moonlit nights.

Innkeeper(s): Wendy White. $94-159. 9 rooms, 8 with PB, 2 with FP, 1 two-bedroom suite, 1 conference room. Breakfast included in rates. Types of meals: Country bkfst, veg bkfst, early coffee/tea, lunch, wine, Saturday afternoon wine tasting and weekend dinner menu.

Certificate may be used: September-Febuary, Sunday-Friday. No holidays, subject to availability.

Starlight Pines Bed & Breakfast

3380 E Lockett Rd
Flagstaff, AZ 86004-4039
(928)527-1912 (800)752-1912
Internet: www.starlightpinesbb.com
E-mail: romance@starlightpinesbb.com

Circa 1996. Tall pine trees and nearby mountains create a peaceful ambiance at this Victorian-styled home. Relax on the wraparound porch with a swing or curl up with a book in front of the fireplace in the parlor. Guest bedrooms include amenities such as a fireplace and/or antique clawfoot tub. Country antiques are placed on oak-plank floors and luxurious spreads top the beds. Bathrobes and bubble baths are found in the private baths. The innkeepers pamper with fresh flowers, gourmet breakfasts, enjoyable conversation and friendly pet Shih Tzus, Mooshu and Taz.

Innkeeper(s): Richard Svends'en & Michael. $159-189. 4 rooms with PB, 1 with FP, 1 suite. Breakfast included in rates. Types of meals: Full gourmet bkfst, veg bkfst, early coffee/tea, Refreshments and special occasions receive

a complementary bottle of wine. Must ask for it when reserving.
Certificate may be used: November-May. Sunday-Friday or Anytime, Last Minute-Based on Availability.

Hereford

Casa De San Pedro

8933 S Yell Ln
Hereford, AZ 85615-9250
(520)366-1300 (888)257-2050 Fax:(520)366-0701
Internet: www.bedandbirds.com
E-mail: info@bedandbirds.com

Circa 1996. Built around a courtyard and fountain, this Territorial hacienda-style bed & breakfast inn is furnished with hand-carved wood furnishings and accent tiles from Mexico. Its care for the environment as well as its location on ten acres of high prairie grassland adjacent to the San Pedro River and Riparian Reserve create a world-class hideaway for naturalists and ecotourism. Relax by the fire in the Great Room, or research birds on the computer. Romantic guest bedrooms offer quiet privacy and the warm hospitality includes quality concierge services. Experience the made-to-satisfy breakfast that will include old favorites and wonderful new recipes. Special dietary needs are easily accommodated.

Innkeeper(s): Karl Schmitt, Patrick Dome. $169. 10 rooms with PB, 6 with FP, 1 conference room. Breakfast, afternoon tea, snacks/refreshments, Full served breakfast each morning featuring fresh seasonal fruit, fresh baked muffins/scones and egg entre' with optional meats. Vegetarian and special diets supported included in rates. Types of meals: Full gourmet bkfst, veg bkfst and early coffee/tea.
Certificate may be used: Anytime, subject to availability.

Payson

Verde River Rock House Bed and Breakfast

602 W. Eleanor Drive
Payson, AZ 85541
(928)472-4304 Fax:(480)444-0235
Internet: verderiverrockhouse.com
E-mail: verderiverbnb@aol.com

Circa 1949. Feel mesmerized by the picturesque views of Payson Rim Country from this secluded hilltop setting along the banks of the East Verde River in Tonto National Forest. The inn is poised to offer comfort and charm amid casual elegance. Sit on a glider or hammock on the creekside deck and gather for evening appetizers and beverages. Relax in the four-person Canadian cedar sauna then soak in the Jacuzzi hot tub/spa. Massage and spa services can be arranged. Stay in a private suite with a den, fireplace and extensive Blue-Ray DVD library. Linger over a gourmet breakfast. Fishing gear and a gas barbecue grill are available as well as kitchen usage. Rent bikes, ATVs and paddle boats right at the inn.

Innkeeper(s): Steve Evans, Maggie Evans. $185-245. Call inn for details. The Basic Daily Weekend Rate of $225 (based on double occupancy) is inclusive of, fresh Belgium chocolate dipped strawberries upon arrival (in season), Evening Hors d'oeuvres with Beverage (wine/beer or non-alcoholic selections), Full Breakfast in the morning and snacks/beverages included in rates. Types of meals: Full gourmet bkfst, early coffee/tea, gourmet lunch, picnic lunch, snacks/refreshments, wine, gourmet dinner, Evening Hors d'oeuvres, full menu of dinner entrees (call or visit website for details), wine tastings and belgium chocolate strawberries and "to die for desserts."
Certificate may be used: December-March, Monday-Thursday, excluding holi-

days, rack rates apply, cannot be used in conjunction with any other discounts, subject to availability.

Phoenix

Maricopa Manor Bed & Breakfast Inn

15 W Pasadena Ave
Phoenix, AZ 85013
(602)264-9200 (800)292-6403 Fax:(602)264-9204
Internet: www.maricopamanor.com
E-mail: res@maricopamanor.com

Circa 1928. Secluded amid palm trees on an acre of land, this Spanish-style house features four graceful columns in the entry hall, an elegant living room with a marble mantel and a music room. Completely refurbished suites are very spacious and distinctively furnished with style and good taste. Relax on the private patio or around the pool while enjoying the soothing sound of falling water from the many fountains.

Innkeeper(s): Scott and Joan Eveland. $129-239. 6 rooms, 4 with FP, 4 with WP, 6 total suites, including 2 two-bedroom suites, 1 conference room. Breakfast and snacks/refreshments included in rates. Types of meals: Cont plus and Breakfast delivered to suite.
Certificate may be used: Anytime, subject to availability.

Sedona

Apple Orchard Inn

656 Jordan Rd
Sedona, AZ 86336
(928)282-5328 (800)663-6968 Fax:(928)204-0044
Internet: www.appleorchardbb.com
E-mail: info@appleorchardbb.com

Circa 1953. Ideally located on two private acres looking out at Sedona red rocks and surrounded by pinon trees, shaggy-barked juniper and Arizona spruce, historic Apple Orchard Inn is a haven for romance, retreat and relaxation in Sedona, Arizona. This home away from home offers a friendly atmosphere, world-class service and unforgettable memories. Innkeepers Peg and Marc will gladly take care of concierge needs. Pleasant guest rooms include refrigerators with complimentary beverages and some boast whirlpool tubs, fireplaces and patios. Marco and Silvia create a gourmet three-course breakfast served in the dining room or patio. Stroll out the front door of this B&B for a ten-minute walk to uptown shops or enjoy a hike among the scenic beauty. Every afternoon the inn's signature homemade chocolate chip cookies are a delightful treat.

Innkeeper(s): Jean. $130-225. 7 rooms with PB, 2 with FP. Breakfast included in rates. Types of meals: Country bkfst, early coffee/tea and World famous chocolate chip cookies.
Certificate may be used: Sunday-Thursday in July and August, excluding holidays.

Lodge at Sedona-A Luxury Bed and Breakfast Inn

125 Kallof Place
Sedona, AZ 86336-5566
(800) 619-4467 (800) 619-4467 Fax:(928)204-2128
Internet: www.lodgeatsedona.com
E-mail: info@lodgeatsedona.com

Circa 1959. Elegantly casual, this newly renovated mission-style B&B sits on three secluded acres with expansive red rock views, mature juniper, sculpture gardens, fountains and a private labyrinth. Enjoy Sunset Snacks in the Fireplace Lounge,

Celebration Porch or outdoor terrace. Artfully decorated king suites feature romantic fireplaces, spa tubs, sitting areas, private decks and entrances. Linger over a five-course breakfast. Massage therapy is available. Exclusive receptions, weddings and executive meetings are accommodated. The lodge offers health club privileges, including access to two swimming pools. The Grand Canyon is a two-hour day trip, and the area includes hiking trails, Jeep tours and hot air balloons.

Innkeeper(s): Innkeeper. $115-349. 15 rooms, 14 with PB, 13 with FP, 2 with HT, 8 with WP, 9 suites, 2 conference rooms. Breakfast, Sunday brunch, afternoon tea, snacks/refreshments and hors d'oeuvres included in rates. Types of meals: Full gourmet bkfst, veg bkfst, early coffee/tea, gourmet lunch, dinner, room service and dinners or special events can be catered.

Certificate may be used: Anytime, subject to availability. Holidays excluded.

Snowflake

The Heritage Inn

161 North Main
Snowflake, AZ 85937
(928) 536-3322 (866) 486-5937 Fax:(928)536-4834
Internet: www.heritage-inn.net
E-mail: heritageinn@live.com

Circa 1890. A loving heritage surrounds this restored inn boasting two-story brick buildings. The decor is Victorian, and the antique furnishings can be purchased. Visit the adjacent antique shop to find more treasures. For solitude or socializing, ample common rooms include the parlor with DVD, library and reception room. Gas-log stoves highlight guest bedrooms and a honeymoon suite. Several rooms feature romantic spa tubs for two. Linger over a hearty gourmet breakfast in the dining room. French or cowboy steak-dinner parties can be arranged. After a day of touring historic pioneer homes, relax in the large hot tub.

Innkeeper(s): Craig Guderian, JoAnne Guderian. $95-145. 10 rooms. Breakfast and snacks/refreshments included in rates. Types of meals: Full gourmet bkfst, early coffee/tea, gourmet lunch, gourmet dinner, We are flexible with our menu, just let us know in advance your dietary requirements. We also offer evening meals as long as we are given advance notice. We will cater to large groups up to 100 as long as the banquet room is rented. We also offer group lunches and brunches and meals. Restaurant on premises.

Certificate may be used: Sunday-Thursday.

Tucson

Casa Tierra Adobe B&B Inn

11155 W Calle Pima
Tucson, AZ 85743-9462
(520)578-3058 (866)254-0006 Fax:(520)578-8445
Internet: www.casatierratucson.com
E-mail: info@casatierratucson.com

Circa 1988. The Sonoran Desert surrounds this secluded, adobe retreat. The mountain views and brilliant sunsets are spectacular. The interior arched courtyard, vaulted brick ceilings and Mexican furnishings create a wonderful Southwestern atmosphere. Each guest room has a private entrance and patios that overlook the desert landscape. The rooms open up to the courtyard. Freshly ground coffee and specialty teas accompany the full vegetarian breakfast. Old Tucson, the Desert Museum and a Saguaro National Park are nearby. The inn also provides a relaxing hot tub and telescope.

Innkeeper(s): Dave Malmquist. $135-325. 4 rooms with PB, 1 suite. Breakfast and snacks/refreshments included in rates. Types of meals: Full gourmet bkfst, veg bkfst and early coffee/tea.

Certificate may be used: April 15-June 15, Aug. 15-Nov. 15.

Williams

Grand Living Bed and Breakfast

701 Quarter Horse Rd
Williams, AZ 86046-9520
(928)635-4171 (800)210-5908 Fax:(928)635-2920
Internet: www.grandlivingbnb.com
E-mail: job@grandlivingbnb.com

Circa 1992. Taste the romantic Old West at this two-story log home near the Grand Canyon. Relax in the Great Room by the fireplace. The wraparound veranda has inviting porch rockers that melt away any stress. Stroll to the rustic gazebo and the rest in the garden swings by the trees. A barbecue arbor adds to the amenities. Guest bedrooms feature fireplaces and two-person jetted or clawfoot tubs. Breakfast is a social experience with recipes frequently requested and gladly shared. Trip planning and excursion ideas are helpful resources available to make the most of all there is to see and do in this scenic area.

Innkeeper(s): Gloria Job, Bill Job. $140-290. 6 rooms, 5 with PB, 6 with FP, 1 with WP, 1 two-bedroom suite. Breakfast included in rates. Types of meals: Full gourmet bkfst, veg bkfst, early coffee/tea, room service and chocolates in room.

Certificate may be used: November and February only, anytime.

Winkelman

Across the Creek at Aravaipa Farms

89395 E. Aravaipa Road
Winkelman, AZ 85292
(520)357-6901
Internet: www.aravaipafarms.com
E-mail: carol@aravaipafarms.com

A desert paradise is waiting for you in Arizona. Share a secluded retreat with more than 100 different species of butterflies. Sit on the patio to watch darting hummingbirds, blue heron, or migrating cardinal. Colorful and completely harmless lizards may join you by the pool. The organic garden, greenhouse, orchard, and henhouse provide many ingredients for meals at this inn. A plentiful continental breakfast is available en-suite, a picnic lunch can be enjoyed on a canyon hike, and a full dinner will leave you completely satisfied. Five individual casitas are decorated with the innkeeper's eclectic style and have private entrances, covered patios, and wood-burning fireplaces. There are no televisions and cell phones rarely find a signal so guests can truly escape on this vacation (a telephone is available in the dining room for those that wish to make a call). Splash through the cool creek as you hike past prickly pear cactus on the 300-acre property.

Innkeeper(s): Carol Steele. Call for rates. Call inn for details. Breakfast, snacks/refreshments, wine and dinner included in rates.

Certificate may be used: July-August, Tuesday-Thursday, subject to availability.

Arkansas

Eureka Springs

All Seasons Inns

165 Spring St
Eureka Springs, AR 72632-3151
(479) 253-2001 (866) 336-2001
Internet: www.allseasonsluxuryproperties.com
E-mail: innkeeper@allseasonsluxuryproperties.com

Circa 1880. All Seasons Luxury Properties welcomes guests to their small village in the heart of Eureka Springs. Five of the most unique lodging establishments in town are offered from the oldest lodging home, The 1880 Piedmont House, to a restored parsonage and church, and now brand new tree houses comprise the village. The inn's versatility, convenience to downtown and activities, group discounts and gathering places as well as excellent customer service and generous amenities offer amazing value for guest budgets. Park your car in your reserved spot for the entire time, or in the covered motorcycle garage, and enjoy walking to shops, dining, entertainment. Or just stroll through the wonderful tree lined streets and gardens. All of rooms have access to porches to simply relax and enjoy the ongoing parade of people and wildlife that visit and make Eureka Springs home.

Innkeeper(s): Pat Fitzsimmons. $79-210. 32 rooms with PB, 7 with FP, 28 with WP, 3 total suites, including 2 two-bedroom suites and 2 three-bedroom suites, 1 conference room. Breakfast and snacks/refreshments included in rates. Types of meals: Full bkfst, veg bkfst, early coffee/tea and Candy and Snacks are available to all our guests - at no additional cost.

Certificate may be used: Tuesday and Wednesdays only, does not include Tree Houses. Cannot be used during festivals or holidays.

Benton Place Inn

32 Benton St
Eureka Springs, AR 72632-3502
(479)253-7602
Internet: www.bentonplaceinn.com
E-mail: bentonplace@sbcglobal.net

Circa 1940. Eureka Springs, Arkansas is truly the perfect destination for a leisurely vacation or a quick getaway and this intimate inn boasts a romantic ambiance throughout the year. Surrounded by Ozark woods, the grounds are accented with lush greenery, rock formations, a koi pond and a stone walled waterfall. Sip a glass of champagne or nonalcoholic wine in the garden gazebo sheltered among shade trees. Each secluded guest suite features an elegant decor with Victorian furnishings, two-person Jacuzzi, kitchenette and sitting area. The Benton Suite includes a full kitchen and a private deck. Cuddle in front of the fire in the Memories Suite. Antique prints and colorful Tiffany-style lamps

highlight the Cliffside Suite. Beverages and a continental breakfast are provided. Local attractions are easily accessible with the trolley depot only 100 yards away.

Innkeeper(s): Rebecca Pope. $110-155. 3 rooms with PB, 2 with FP, 3 with HT. Types of meals: Orange juice, coffee and locally baked pastries,complimentary champagne or sparkling grape juice.

Certificate may be used: Sunday-Thursday, November-March.

Cliff Cottage Inn - Luxury B&B Suites & Historic Cottages

42 Armstrong Street
Eureka Springs, AR 72632
(479) 253-7409
Internet: www.cliffcottage.com
E-mail: cliffcottage@sbcglobal.net

Circa 1880. The Cliff Cottage Inn is the only B&B in the heart of Historic Downtown with an elf who delivers full-gourmet breakfasts to each suite and puts a complimentary bottle of Champagne or white wine in the fridge. Comprised of three  houses in a row, the inn is just steps to the shops and restaurants of Main Street in Eureka Springs, Arkansas. An 1880 Eastlake Victorian, Sears' first kit home, is a State and National Landmark. It features suites with private front porches and decks tucked into the three-story high rock bluff. The Place Next Door is a Victorian replica boasting two upstairs suites with balconies. The Artist's Cottage is a renovated 1910 Craftsman. Two elegant suites include pure-air whirlpool tubs, a porch and a deck.

Innkeeper(s): Sandra CH Smith . $129-230. 8 rooms with PB, 4 with FP, 2 with HT, 6 with WP, 6 suites, 5 cottages, 5 guest houses, 1 conference room. Breakfast, snacks/refreshments, wine and The two stand-alone Cottages have fully-equipped kitchens so breakfast not available to these two cottages. Award-winning Full-Gourmet hot breakfast is delivered to all suites on silver tray included in rates. Types of meals: Full gourmet bkfst, veg bkfst, early coffee/tea, room service, All suites/cottages have coffeemakers with large selection of imported teas, coffee, hot chocolate, chai, granola/dry cereals and cookie samplers and complimentary bottle of Champagne or white wine chilled in your fridge.

Certificate may be used: Queen suites only for stays completed Monday-Thursday, excluding May, ,June, October and holidays. Subject to availability and not valid with other promotions.

Kingston

Fool's Cove Ranch B&B

360 Madison 2729
Kingston, AR 72742-2729
(479)665-2986 (866)665-2986 Fax:(479)665-2986
E-mail: foolscoveranch@aol.com

Circa 1979. Situated in the Ozark's Boston Mountain range, this 6000 sq. ft. farmhouse, part of a family farm, offers 130 acres of meadows and forests. Guests may angle for bass or catfish in one of several ponds on the property. Favorite gathering spots are the roomy parlor with large screen TV and the outside deck with a great view of the mountains. Area attractions include the Buffalo National River with canoeing and elk watching, several fine fishing areas and great sightseeing opportunites. The inn is fairly close to Branson, Missouri and Eureka Springs, Arkansas.

Innkeeper(s): Mary Jo Sullivan, Bill Sullivan. $65-110. 4 rooms, 2 with PB, 1 with WP. Breakfast included in rates. Types of meals: Full bkfst, early coffee/tea and snacks/refreshments.

Certificate may be used: May 15 to Dec. 15, Anytime, subject to availability.

Mountain View

Ozark Country Inn

219 South Peabody
Mountain View, AR 72560-1201
(870)269-8699 (800)379-8699
Internet: www.ozarkcountryinn.com
E-mail: ozarkcountryInn@gmail.com

Circa 1906. Tucked in the unspoiled Ozark Mountains is the charming town of Mountain View with this historic Victorian inn. Reserve the Anniversary Package in the deluxe Victoria room with a king-size bed for a romantic getaway complete with cheesecake and flowers. Up to 16 people can be housed at the inn for a reunion with plenty of space to spread out and private bathrooms in each guest room. Early risers will find coffee waiting in the parlor before the family-style breakfast each morning. Sit back and celebrate a quiet evening in a rocking chair on the wraparound porch or take a short walk to the town square. Enjoy country, rock and roll, folk music, or a night of comedy in the intimate Backstreet Theater directly behind the inn. Nearby Blanchard Springs Caverns offers a leisurely underground stroll along the Dripstone Trail and the opportunity to crawl and climb through undeveloped areas on the Wild Cave Tour.

Innkeeper(s): Debbie Jadrich, Leonard Jadrich. $79-105. 6 rooms with PB, 1 cabin. Breakfast included in rates. Types of meals: Country bkfst and early coffee/tea.

Certificate may be used: December-February, excluding holidays, subject to availability.

California

Albion

Fensalden Inn

33810 Navarro Ridge Rd
Albion, CA 95410-0099
(707) 937-4042 (800) 959-3850
Internet: www.fensalden.com
E-mail: inn@fensalden.com

Circa 1860. Originally a stagecoach station, Fensalden looks out over the Pacific Ocean as it has for more than 100 years. The Tavern Room has witnessed many a rowdy scene, and if you look closely you can see bullet holes in the original redwood ceiling. The inn provides 20 acres for walks, whale-watching, viewing deer and bicycling. Relax with wine and hors d'oeuvres in the evening.

Innkeeper(s): Chris & Molli Hamby. $139-253. 8 rooms with PB, 8 with FP, 1 with HT, 2 suites, 1 cottage, 1 conference room. Breakfast, wine, Full three course breakfast each morning and with champagne and mimosas on Sundays - complimentary wine in room upon arrival included in rates. Types of meals: Full bkfst.

Certificate may be used: Anytime: Jan. 2-May 15, Midweek: May 16-Jan. 1, Subject to availability, Excludes holidays.

Aptos

Historic Sand Rock Farm

6901 Freedom Blvd
Aptos, CA 95003
(831)688-8005 Fax:(831)688-8025
Internet: www.sandrockfarm.com
E-mail: staff@sandrockfarm.com

Circa 1910. Cradled in the foothills, this Arts and Crafts country estate sits on 10 acres of spectacular gardens, fountains and woodland. Built as one of the region's first wineries, the ivy-covered ruins are located near the giant saw that milled the redwood trees onsite for the home's frame and finished woodwork. Lovingly restored with hand-printed wallpaper, vintage lighting and antique furnishings, this bed & breakfast offers gracious hospitality. The well-appointed guest bedrooms and suites feature down comforters for comfort and Internet connections for convenience. Indulge your senses with the culinary talent of renown chef Lynn Sheehan. Lounge on the deck under a moss-covered heritage oak or on the rose garden hammock.

Innkeeper(s): Kristine Sheehan. $185-225. 5 rooms with PB, 3 with HT, 2 total suites, including 1 two-bedroom suite. Breakfast included in rates. Types of meals: Full gourmet bkfst, veg bkfst, early coffee/tea, gourmet lunch, picnic lunch, afternoon tea, snacks/refreshments, wine, gourmet dinner and room service.

Certificate may be used: January-March, Monday-Thursday.

Ben Lomond

Fairview Manor

245 Fairview Ave
Ben Lomond, CA 95005-9347
(831)336-3355
Internet: www.fairviewmanor.com
E-mail: FairviewBandB@comcast.net

Circa 1924. The Santa Cruz Mountains serve as a backdrop at this private and restful getaway. The inn is surrounded by nearly three acres of park-like wooded gardens. The Redwood County inn offers comfort and relaxation. The deck off the Great Room overlooks the San Lorenzo River. Built in the early 1920s, the decor reflects that era. Each of the cozy guest bedrooms boasts a private bath and delightful garden view. Enjoy a full country breakfast and afternoon snacks. The inn is an excellent place for family get-togethers as well as small meetings and outdoor weddings. Beaches, thousands of acres of state parks and many wineries are nearby.

Innkeeper(s): Gael Glasson Abayon/Jack Hazelton. $149-159. 5 rooms with PB, 1 conference room. Breakfast, snacks/refreshments, hors d'oeuvres, wine, Raves for our new Breakfast Menu that could include German Apple Pancakes, Eggs Benedict, Citrus Slices in ginger or Blueberry Panckes and just to name a few included in rates. Types of meals: For a nominal charge and we can assist with picnic lunches and such.

Certificate may be used: Sunday-Thursday.

Big Bear

Gold Mountain Manor Historic B&B

1117 Anita
Big Bear, CA 92314
(909)585-6997 (800)509-2604 Fax:(909)585-0327
Internet: www.goldmountainmanor.com
E-mail: info@goldmountainmanor.com

Circa 1928. This spectacular log mansion was once a hideaway for the rich and famous. Ten fireplaces provide a roaring fire in each room in fall and winter. The Presidential Suite offers a massive rock fireplace embedded with fossils and quartz, facing the two-person Jacuzzi rock tub and four-poster bed. In the Clark Gable room is the fireplace Gable and

Carole Lombard enjoyed on their honeymoon. Gourmet country breakfasts and afternoon hors d'oeuvres are served. In addition to the guest rooms, there are home rentals.

Innkeeper(s): Cathy Weil. $149-269. 7 rooms with PB, 7 with FP, 3 with WP, 3 suites, 1 conference room. Afternoon tea and snacks/refreshments included in rates. Types of meals: Full gourmet bkfst and early coffee/tea.

Certificate may be used: Monday-Thursday, March 24-Dec.13, no holidays, subject to availability.

Big Bear Lake

Alpenhorn Bed & Breakfast

601 Knight Ave
Big Bear Lake, CA 92315
(909)866-5700 (888)829-6600 Fax:(909)878-3209
Internet: www.alpenhorn.com
E-mail: contactz@alpenhorn.com

Circa 1999. Experience informal elegance in a modern, mountain setting at this spacious cedar inn boasting front and rear decks. The bed & breakfast sits on almost two acres, with the gardens and surrounding forest creating a park-like atmosphere. Generous amenities and a cordial ambiance impart a delightful appeal. Guest bedrooms reflect a casual luxury featuring marble, brick, stack-stone or river-rock fireplaces, hypoallergenic featherbeds on firm mattresses, two-person spa tubs, tiled showers, Aveda bath products, soft robes and private balconies. Evening turndown service is offered, and an extensive video library is available for in-room use. Honey-baked grapefruit, homemade granola with vanilla yogurt, oatmeal banana brulee, turkey sausage, cinnamon French toast with fresh strawberries and cinnamon syrup are typical breakfast treats. Evening wine and hors d'oeuvres are equally mouthwatering. Services include full concierge and shuttle service to Snow Summit ski resort.

Innkeeper(s): Timothy & Linda Carpenter. $184-312. 9 rooms with PB, 8 with FP, 7 with HT, 8 suites, 1 cottage, 1 guest house. Breakfast, afternoon tea, snacks/refreshments, hors d'oeuvres and wine included in rates. Types of meals: Full gourmet bkfst and early coffee/tea.

Certificate may be used: November-April, excludes Dec. 20-Jan. 5 and holiday weekends.

Eagle's Nest B&B

41675 Big Bear Blvd, Box 1003
Big Bear Lake, CA 92315
(909)866-6465 (888)866-6465 Fax:(909)866-6025
Internet: www.eaglesnestlodgebigbear.com
E-mail: stay@eaglesnestlodgebigbear.com

Circa 1983. Poised amid the tall pines of the San Bernardino Mountains in Big Bear Lake, California, Eagle's Nest Bed and Breakfast Lodge and Cottage Suites offers four seasons of relaxing comfort and hospitality. Accommodations in the Ponderosa-style log lodge include guest rooms with gas or electric fireplaces. Gather for a hearty breakfast in the dining area each morning. The secluded log cabin cottage suites boast river rock fireplaces, microwaves, mini-refrigerators and other amenities for a pleasing stay. This B&B is conveniently located near the lake, shops, restaurants and local ski resorts. Take day trips to the many Southern California attractions.

Innkeeper(s): Mark Tebo, Vicki Tebo. $110-130. 5 rooms with PB, 3 with FP. Breakfast and snacks/refreshments included in rates. Types of meals: Country bkfst.

Certificate may be used: Anytime except holidays and weekends from Dec. 15-April 15, subject to availability.

Bodega

Sonoma Coast Villa Inn & Spa

16702 Coast Highway One
Bodega, CA 94922
(707)876-9818 (888)404-2255 Fax:(707)876-9856
Internet: www.scvilla.com
E-mail: reservations@scvilla.com

Circa 1976. Experience a taste of the Mediterranean and Old World Tuscany after a drive past the ocean, vineyards and rural countryside through the cypress tree-lined, 200-foot drive to this amazing terra cotta stucco villa. Secluded and luxurious, this red-tile roofed B&B resort offers 60 acres of pleasurable serenity. Choose a standard country or deluxe villa room with a private deck or courtyard, fireplace and double-size jetted tub. Classic junior suites also are available. A nine-hole putting green prepares the golfer for a game nearby. Play billiards, ping pong or read a book in the Tower Library. Swim in the pool, or relax in the courtyard spa.

Innkeeper(s): Johannes Zachbauer. $175-365. 18 rooms with PB, 18 with FP, 2 conference rooms. Breakfast and snacks/refreshments included in rates. Types of meals: Country bkfst, wine, gourmet dinner and room service. Restaurant on premises.

Certificate may be used: Sunday-Thursday (Junior Suite $245) offer cannot be combined with any other offers or discounts.

Calistoga

Chelsea Garden Inn

1443 2nd St
Calistoga, CA 94515-1419
(707)942-0948 (800)942-1515 Fax:(707)942-5102
Internet: www.chelseagardeninn.com
E-mail: innkeeper@chelseagardeninn.com

Circa 1940. Located in the heart of Napa Valley, this delightfully different California-style inn features two-room suites with fireplaces and private entrances. The romantic ground-level Palm Suite has a large sitting room with fireplace, additional Queen bed and library. The adjoining Lavender Suite is perfect for couples traveling together. Named for its view of the mountains, the second-floor Palisades Suite boasts a four-poster bed and a small balcony overlooking the pool. A full gourmet breakfast is served in the dining room or garden with fresh-brewed coffee from a local roastery. Enjoy afternoon hors d'oeuvres. Explore the extensive gardens with grapevines, flowers, fruit and nut trees. Swim in the pool (seasonal) or relax by the fire in the social room. Visit local shops, wineries, museums, spas, art galleries and restaurants just two blocks away.

Innkeeper(s): Dave DeVries, Susan DeVries. $165-375. 5 guest houses with PB, 5 with HT, 4 total suites, including 3 two-bedroom suites, 1 cabin, 1 conference room. Breakfast included in rates. Types of meals: Country bkfst, veg bkfst, early coffee/tea and snacks/refreshments.

Certificate may be used: November-April, Monday-Wednesday. Valid only on rooms at $225 or more.

Cottage Grove Inn

1711 Lincoln Ave
Calistoga, CA 94515
(707) 942-8400 (800) 799-2284 Fax:(707)942-2653
Internet: www.cottagegrove.com
E-mail: cottage@sonic.net

Circa 1996. There are 16 cottages at this inn, each with a wood-burning fireplace and luxury double Jacuzzi tub. Each cottage has a rich, luxurious decor with beds covered with down comforters and pillows. Many thoughtful amenities have been provided, including stereos with CD players, a refrigerator, coffeemaker with gourmet coffee and a wet bar. For business travelers, there is a phone with modem jacks. Wine and cheese are served in the afternoons. Continental fare is served in the mornings. Wineries, horseback riding, biking and the famous Calistoga hot springs are nearby.

Innkeeper(s): Donna Johnson. $250-425. 16 cottages, 16 with FP. Breakfast, hors d'oeuvres and wine included in rates. Types of meals: Full bkfst, early coffee/tea and Complimentary wine and cheese every afternoon.

Certificate may be used: November-March, subject to availability.

Mount View Hotel & Spa

1457 Lincoln Ave.
Calistoga, CA 94515
(707) 942-6877 (800) 816-6877 Fax:(707)942-6904
Internet: www.mountviewhotel.com
E-mail: relax@mountviewhotel.com

Circa 1912. Relax and refresh in a luxury suite or private cottage after pampering yourself at the award-winning spa. Pure bliss can be found with a couples massage, facial, and dip in the outdoor heated pool. This inn promotes the art of relaxation with a mineral whirlpool, breakfast in bed, and Friday evening wine tastings. Guest rooms are boldly decorated with elegance and comfort in mind. A bottle of wine awaits you in rooms hosted by a local vintner. Winery artist cottages have private patios with Jacuzzi tubs; if the life of luxury sparks your creativity step out into a vineyard with the available easel, paints, and canvas. Savor local ingredients at JoLe Restaurant or your favorite Italian dishes at Barolo Restaurant; both establishments are on-site. Ask about special packages for romance, girlfriend getaways, and babymoons. Located at the tip of Napa Valley, the quaint town of Calistoga is known for its hot springs, fine restaurants, and unique wineries.

Innkeeper(s): Andrea Hoogendoorn. $189-449. 31 rooms with PB, 3 with HT, 3 with WP, 10 total suites, including 2 two-bedroom suites, 3 cottages, 1 conference room. Continental breakfast included in rates. Types of meals: Cont, picnic lunch, wine and room service. Restaurant on premises.

Certificate may be used: December-January, Sunday-Thursday, subject to availability.

Carlsbad

Pelican Cove Bed & Breakfast

320 Walnut Ave
Carlsbad, CA 92008-3151
(760)434-5995 (888)PEL-COVE Fax:(760) 434-7649
Internet: www.pelican-cove.com
E-mail: pelicancoveinn@pelican-cove.com

Circa 1985. Just 200 yards from the ocean, this bed and breakfast inn is a short stroll away from village activities.

Surrounded by gardens of flowers and trees, the setting is refreshing. Play cards or relax in the spacious lobby. Well-appointed guest bedrooms are named after Southern California beaches and feature gas fireplaces and European-style feather beds with down comforters. Many rooms boast spa tubs and four-poster beds. For families or friends traveling together, the Balboa and Coronado rooms have a connecting door. Linger over a pleasant breakfast in the parlor, on a tray in the room, on the garden patio, sun deck or gazebo.

Innkeeper(s): Nancy & Kris Nayudu. $105-235. 10 rooms with PB, 10 with FP. Breakfast included in rates. Types of meals: Full bkfst, picnic lunch and special dietary needs.

Certificate may be used: Sept. 3-May 23, Sunday-Thursday.

Coronado

Cherokee Lodge

964 D Avenue
Coronado, CA 92118
(619)437-1967 Fax:(619)437-1012
Internet: www.cherokeelodge.com
E-mail: stay@cherokeelodge.com

Circa 1896. Experience the delights of Coronado Island while staying at this bed and breakfast located just one block from downtown and four blocks from the beach. Named after the Cherokee roses that framed the property in the late 1800s, it is steeped in history. There are common areas to relax in and one offers a computer to use as well as wireless high-speed Internet. Enjoy comfortable, smoke-free accommodations with a choice of twelve guest bedrooms that feature VCRs and refrigerators. A washer and dryer are available. A continental breakfast is provided daily. Walk to nearby bistros and restaurants.

Innkeeper(s): Vicki. $135. 12 rooms with PB. Free continental breakfast at a local diner included in rates. Types of meals: Cont and Breakfast vouchers are provided for a free continental breakfast at a local diner. Coffee and tea are in each room.

Certificate may be used: October-May, anytime subject to availability, no holidays.

Crowley Lake

Rainbow Tarns B&B at Crowley Lake

505 Rainbow Tarns Road
Crowley Lake, CA 93546
(760)935-4556 (888)588-6269
Internet: www.rainbowtarns.com
E-mail: innkeeper@rainbowtarns.com

Circa 1940. Just south of Mammoth Lakes, at an altitude of 7,000 feet, you'll find this secluded retreat amid three acres of ponds, open meadows and the High Sierra Mountains.

 Country-style here includes luxury touches, such as a double Jacuzzi tub, queen-size bed, down pillows, comforters and a skylight for star-gazing. In the '50s, ponds on the property served as a "U-Catch-Em." Folks rented fishing poles and paid 10 cents an inch for the fish they caught. Nearby Crowley Lake is still one of the best trout-fishing areas in California. Romantic country weddings are popular here. Guests are free to simply

relax in the peaceful setting, but hiking, horseback riding and skiing all are available in the area. In the afternoons, guests are treated to snacks and wine.

Innkeeper(s): Brock Thoman, Diane Thoman. $100-155. 3 rooms with PB. Breakfast, snacks/refreshments, hors d'oeuvres and wine included in rates. Types of meals: Full gourmet bkfst, veg bkfst, early coffee/tea and lunch.

Certificate may be used: Anytime, November-March, subject to availability.

Dana Point

Blue Lantern Inn

34343 Street of the Blue Lantern
Dana Point, CA 92629
(949)661-1304 (800)950-1236 Fax:(949)496-1483
Internet: www.bluelanterninn.com
E-mail: bluelanterninn@foursisters.com

Circa 1990. Blue Lantern Inn is situated high on a blufftop overlooking a stunning coastline and the blue waters of Dana Point harbor with its pleasure craft, fishing boats and the tall ship, Pilgrim. Each guest bedroom of this four-diamond inn features both a fireplace and a whirlpool tub and many offer private sun decks. Afternoon tea, evening turndown service and bicycles are just a few of the amenities available. In the evening, wine and hors d'oeuvres are served. Shops, restaurants and beaches are nearby, and popular Laguna  Beach, California is just a few miles to the north. Blue Lantern is one of the Four Sisters Inns.

Innkeeper(s): Lin McMahon. $175-600. 29 rooms with PB, 29 with FP, 2 conference rooms. Breakfast, afternoon tea, snacks/refreshments, hors d'oeuvres and wine included in rates. Types of meals: Full gourmet bkfst.

Certificate may be used: Sunday-Thursday, December-February, based on promotional discount availability and excludes special event periods, holidays and certain room types. First night must be at full rack rate to receive second night free.

Elk

Greenwood Pier Inn

5926 S Highway 1
Elk, CA 95432
(707) 877-3800 Fax:(707) 877-1802
Internet: www.greenwoodpierinn.com
E-mail: greenwoodpierinn@yahoo.com

Feel immersed in the expansive views of the Mendocino Coast and the Pacific Ocean while staying at Greenwood Pier Inn in Elk, California. The grounds are accented with colorful gardens and include a hot tub on a cliff for a relaxing soak. Walk along the wide sandy beach of the nearby state park. Schedule in advance an in-room therapeutic or herbal facial massage. Stay in a guest room or suite in the main house or multi-level accommodations in a redwood cabin or converted high rise water tower. Amenities may include a two-person Jacuzzi, private deck, water view and kitchenette. Some rooms are designated pet friendly. A continental breakfast is delivered to each room every morning. Browse the garden shop and country store and linger over a meal in the Greenwood Pier Cafe.

Innkeeper(s): Kathleen. $100-350. 15 rooms with PB, 14 with FP. Breakfast

included in rates. Types of meals: Country bkfst, veg bkfst and dinner. Restaurant on premises.

Certificate may be used: Nov. 1-March 30, Sunday-Thursday, no holidays, subject to availability.

Eureka

Carter House Inns

301 L St
Eureka, CA 95501
(707)444-8062 (800)404-1390 Fax:(707)444-8067
Internet: www.carterhouse.com
E-mail: reserve@carterhouse.com

Circa 1884. Superior hospitality is offered in these Victorian inns that grace the historic district. Perched alongside Humboldt Bay, blissfully relax amid appealing views. Carter House Inns in Eureka, California boasts luxurious guest rooms and suites that feature fireplaces, antique furnishings and spas. Begin each morning with a highly acclaimed breakfast. Renowned for regional, seasonal cuisine, many ingredients are grown in the garden or bought from local purveyors.  Restaurant 301 boasts a coveted international Wine Spectator Grand Award, maintaining in its cellars an extensive collection of the world's finest vintages.

Innkeeper(s): Audrey Archibald - mgr. $155-615. 32 rooms with PB, 11 with FP, 7 with HT, 6 with WP, 9 total suites, including 2 two-bedroom suites, 2 cottages, 1 conference room. Breakfast, afternoon tea, hors d'oeuvres and wine included in rates. Types of meals: Full gourmet bkfst, early coffee/tea, snacks/refreshments, gourmet dinner and room service. Restaurant on premises.

Certificate may be used: Anytime, November-April, subject to availability.

Fallbrook

Santa Margarita Inn

1634 Riverview Drive
Fallbrook, CA 92028
(760)731-9222
Internet: www.santamargaritainn.com/
E-mail: arlene@santamargaritainn.com

Circa 1990. Perched atop the canyon overlooking the gorgeous Santa Margarita River, the Inn is a perfect retreat from everyday life.

Innkeeper(s): Arlene Yates. Call for rates. 5 rooms with PB, 2 suites.
Certificate may be used: Anytime, subject to availability.

Ferndale

Gingerbread Mansion Inn

400 Berding St
Ferndale, CA 95536-1380
(707) 786-4000 (855) 786-4001 Fax:(707)786-4381
Internet: www.gingerbread-mansion.com
E-mail: innkeeper@gingerbread-mansion.com

Circa 1899. Elegant romance and storybook luxury can be found at this opulent Victorian inn. Eastlake and Queen Anne styles were uniquely combined to create a significant architectural landmark, well known to photographers. Guest rooms are richly decorated with antique furnishings, goose down comforters, and embroidered bath robes. You can each have your own claw foot tub in the glamorous blue and gold-toned Fountain Suite or choose the Rose Suite where the water will never grow cold when you bathe beside the fireplace. Another choice offers the opportunity to fill your dreams with the serene images from the murals in the Veneto. The breakfast table is laden with artfully displayed spicy eggs and cheese souffle or stuffed French toast made with regional ingredients. Explore Ferndale then recount your adventures over wine, tea, pastries, and hors d'oeuvres each afternoon. The romantic inn offers meticulously maintained gardens with statues, fountains, and shaped hedges. Experience the Gingerbread Mansion with friends or family and receive a discount when at least three separate rooms are booked.

Innkeeper(s): Linda Elderkin. $150-400. 11 rooms with PB, 5 with FP, 5 suites. Breakfast and afternoon tea included in rates. Types of meals: Full bkfst and early coffee/tea.

Certificate may be used: Sunday-Thursday, subject to availability.

Shaw House B&B Inn

703 Main Street
Ferndale, CA 95536-1369
(707)786-9958 (800)557SHAW
Internet: www.shawhouse.com
E-mail: stay@shawhouse.com

Circa 1854. The owners of Ferndale's most historic structure note that the Shaw House was opened to the public in 1860 (six years after its construction) "to serve man and beast." A carpenter Gothic house with gables, bays and balconies it is set back on an acre of garden. An old buckeye tree frames the front gate, and in the back, a secluded deck overlooks a creek. Nestled under the wallpapered gables are several guest rooms filled with antiques and fresh flowers.

Innkeeper(s): Paula Bigley. $125-275. 8 rooms with PB, 2 with FP, 2 suites. Breakfast and afternoon tea included in rates. Types of meals: Cont plus, early coffee/tea, picnic lunch, hors d'oeuvres and wine.

Certificate may be used: January.

Fish Camp

Tin Lizzie Inn

7730 Laurel Way
Fish Camp, CA 93623
(559)641-7731 Fax:(559) 641-7731
Internet: www.tinlizzieinn.com
E-mail: modelttours@yahoo.com

Circa 2006. Recently opened and newly built, Tin Lizzie Inn is a replica of an 1890's Victorian mansion. This B&B offers an elegant and intimate setting just two miles from the south entrance of Yosemite National Park, across from Tenaya Lodge in Fish Camp, California. Tour the town in an original Model T Ford. Relax with a beverage on the front porch; sit by the waterfall or bronze fountain. Enjoy evening treats by the firepit. Stay in the romantic Tin Lizzie Suite that spans the entire sec-

ond floor and includes a fireplace, clawfoot massage tub and body spray shower. The first-floor Lady Suite features a Jacuzzi tub. Linger over a gourmet breakfast on the attached private balcony or patio. Bass Lake and the surrounding area is known for its incredible beauty.

Innkeeper(s): David & Sheran Woodworth. $250-400. 3 rooms, 2 with PB, 2 with FP, 1 with WP, 1 suite, 1 cottage. Breakfast, afternoon tea and snacks/refreshments included in rates. Types of meals: Full gourmet bkfst, veg bkfst, early coffee/tea, picnic lunch and Evening Treats. **Certificate may be used:** October, Sunday-Thursday, subject to availability.

Fort Bragg

Country Inn

632 N Main St
Fort Bragg, CA 95437-3220
(707) 964-3737 (800) 831-5327 Fax:(707)964-3737
Internet: www.beourguests.com
E-mail: info@beourguests.com

Circa 1890. The Union Lumber Company once owned this two-story townhouse built of native redwood. It features rooms with slanted and peaked ceilings, and several rooms have fireplaces. Camellia trees, flower boxes, and a picket fence accent the landscaping, while two blocks away a railroad carries visitors on excursions through the redwoods.

Innkeeper(s): Christine Churchill. $90-180. 7 rooms with PB, 7 with HT, 2 guest houses. Breakfast, snacks/refreshments, hors d'oeuvres and wine included in rates. Types of meals: Full gourmet bkfst, early coffee/tea and room service.

Certificate may be used: Sunday-Thursday.

Glass Beach B&B

726 N Main St
Fort Bragg, CA 95437-3017
(707)964-6774
Internet: www.glassbeachinn.com
E-mail: glassbeachinn@hotmail.com

Circa 1920. Each of the guest rooms at this Craftsman-style home is decorated in a different theme and named to reflect the decor. The Malaysian and Oriental Jade rooms reflect Asian artistry, while the Forget-Me-Not and Victorian Rose rooms are bright, feminine rooms with walls decked in floral prints. Antiques are found throughout the home and the back cottage, which includes three of the inn's nine guest rooms. The inn also offers a hot tub for guest use. Breakfasts are served in the inn's dining room, but guests are free to take a tray and enjoy the meal in the privacy of their own room.

Innkeeper(s): Nancy Cardenas, Richard Fowler. $60-195. 9 rooms with PB, 4 with FP, 1 suite, 1 cottage. Breakfast and snacks/refreshments included in rates. Types of meals: Country bkfst, afternoon tea and room service.

Certificate may be used: Jan. 5-June 4, Oct. 1-Dec. 31, Sunday-Thursday. Most holidays excluded.

Geyserville

Hope-Merrill House

21253 Geyserville Ave.
Geyserville, CA 95441-9637
(707) 857-3356 (800) 825-4233 Fax:(707)857-4673
Internet: www.hope-inns.com
E-mail: moreinfo@hope-inns.com

Circa 1870. The Hope-Merrill House is a classic example of the Eastlake Stick style that was so popular during Victorian times. Built entirely from redwood, the house features original wainscoting and silk-screened wallcoverings. A swimming pool, vineyard and gazebo are favorite spots for guests to relax. The Hope-Bosworth House, on the same street, was built in 1904 in the Queen Anne style by an early Geyserville pioneer who lived in the home until the 1960s. The front picket fence is covered with roses. Period details include oak woodwork, sliding doors, polished fir floors and antique light fixtures.

Innkeeper(s): Cosette & Ron Scheiber. $149-289. 8 rooms with PB, 4 with FP, 2 with WP, 1 suite. Breakfast included in rates. Types of meals: Full gourmet bkfst, veg bkfst, early coffee/tea, picnic lunch, wine and Gluten free.
Certificate may be used: From Dec. 1-March 31 anyday, Monday-Thursday April 1-Nov. 30.

Groveland

Hotel Charlotte

18736 Main Street
Groveland, CA 95321
(209)962-6455 Fax:(209)962-6254
Internet: www.HotelCharlotte.com
E-mail: Stay@HotelCharlotte.com

Circa 1921. Gracing one acre in the Sierra Nevada Mountains of California, the Hotel Charlotte is on the way to Yosemite near Stanislaus National Forest. Find entertainment in the game room or relax on the balcony overlooking the gold rush town of Groveland. Beverages are usually available at any time. Listed in the National Register, this bed and breakfast hotel provides comfortable and convenient accommodations. Air-conditioned guest bedrooms feature new, soundproof windows and a variety of sleeping arrangements. Several rooms boast a clawfoot tub, one room with a spa tub. Enjoy a buffet breakfast in the morning. Cafe Charlotte, the onsite full-service restaurant and bar, offers good food and spirits.

Innkeeper(s): Jenn Edwards, Doug Edwards. $99-199. 12 rooms, 10 with PB, 1 with FP, 1 with WP, 2 two-bedroom suites, 7 guest houses. Hot buffet breakfast included in rates. Types of meals: Country bkfst, veg bkfst, early coffee/tea, lunch, snacks/refreshments, wine, dinner and On-site restaurant with "garden-to-table" style cuisine.
Certificate may be used: Oct. 1-April 30, Sunday-Thursday.

The Groveland Hotel at Yosemite National Park

18767 Main St.
Groveland, CA 95321-0289
(209) 962-4000 (800) 273-3314 Fax:(209)962-6674
Internet: www.groveland.com
E-mail: guestservices@groveland.com

Circa 1849. Located 23 miles from Yosemite National Park, the 1992 restoration features both an 1849 adobe building with 18-inch-thick walls constructed during the Gold Rush and a 1914 building erected to house workers for the Hetch Hetchy Dam. Both feature two-story balconies. There is a Victorian parlor, a gourmet restaurant and a Western 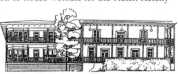 saloon. Guest rooms feature European antiques, down comforters, some feather beds, in-room coffee, phones with data ports, and hair dryers. The feeling is one of casual elegance.

Innkeeper(s): Peggy Mosely, Grover Mosley. $145-285. 17 rooms with PB, 3 with FP, 3 with WP, 3 suites, 1 conference room. Breakfast and Full Breakfast included in rates. Types of meals: Country bkfst, veg bkfst, early coffee/tea, picnic lunch, wine, gourmet dinner, room service and Cellar Door Restaurant features gourmet California cuisine. . Restaurant on premises.
Certificate may be used: Oct. 15-April 15, Sunday-Thursday, excluding holidays.

Yosemite Rose Bed & Breakfast

22830 Ferretti Rd
Groveland, CA 95321
(209)962-6548 (866)962-6548
Internet: www.yosemiterose.com
E-mail: info@yosemiterose.com

Circa 1890. A quiet retreat on a 210-acre ranch, Yosemite Rose Bed & Breakfast is located off an old stage coach run. The "Italianate Victorian" in Groveland, California, has a parlor, a library full of leather bound classics, and a billiard room for a friendly game of pool. Each of the six guest rooms have private baths, soothing views of the gardens or majestic trees, and include a full country breakfast. Those looking for a little more privacy can reserve the one-bedroom cabin that has served as a church and a caretaker's cottage in the past. In-room massages are available to sooth muscles afters a long day of hiking. Astronomers and novice star gazers can set up telescopes on a knoll 2000 feet above the Toulumne River. Guests can share their fish tales after casting a line in the Yosemite Rose Bass Pond. Scenic Yosemite National Park is only 20 short minutes away. Wineries, golf courses, Mercer Cavern, and Moaning Cavern are all conveniently located near Yosemite Rose.

Innkeeper(s): Katherine Davalle, Donald Davalle. $145-275. 8 rooms, 6 with PB. Breakfast, afternoon tea and snacks/refreshments included in rates. Types of meals: Country bkfst, veg bkfst, early coffee/tea and Special dietary requests - with 48 hours notice.
Certificate may be used: January-February, excluding holidays, subject to availability.

Gualala

Breakers Inn

39300 Old Highway 1
Gualala, CA 93445
(707)884-3200
Internet: www.breakersinn.com
E-mail: info@breakersinn.com

Breathtaking views of the water are seen from these accommodations that are poised on a bluff overlooking the Gualala River and the Pacific Ocean. The location is great for a visit to Sonoma and the Mendocino Coast in scenic Northern California. Elegantly furnished and custom designed with a European flair, there is radiant floor heat, artwork and private decks. Stay in a delightful guest room that boasts a regional theme and features a whirlpool spa, fireplace, DVD player, wet bar, microwave and a refrigerator. Start each day with a continental breakfast in the lobby before embarking on the day's adventures. Peruse the local menus available to help choose a restaurant for dinner.

Innkeeper(s): Jim Moseley, Kim Moseley. Call for rates. 28 rooms with PB, 27 with FP, 25 with WP, 4 suites. Afternoon tea included in rates. Types of meals: Early coffee/tea and snacks/refreshments.

Certificate may be used: Nov. 15-Feb. 28, Sunday-Thursday, holiday weeks excluded.

Guerneville

Fern Grove Cottages

16650 Highway 116
Guerneville, CA 95446-9678
(707)869-8105 (888)243-2674
Internet: www.ferngrove.com
E-mail: innkeepers@ferngrove.com

Clustered in a village-like atmosphere and surrounded by redwoods, these craftsman cottages have romantic fireplaces, private entrances, and are individually decorated. The cottages were built in the 1920s and served as little vacation houses for San Francisco families visiting the Russian River. Some units have a kitchen or wet bar, some have double whirlpool tubs and other cottages are suitable for families. Guests enjoy use of the swimming pool. The cottages are just a few blocks from shops and restaurants, as well as a swimming beach on the river. Visit a nearby redwood state reserve or the Russian River Valley wineries for wine tasting and tours.

Innkeeper(s): Mike Kennett, Margaret Kennett. $99-279. 20 cottages with PB, 14 with FP, 1 conference room. Breakfast included in rates. Types of meals: Cont plus and Wines By The Fireside during winter months: on non-event Saturdays.

Certificate may be used: November-March, event and holidays excluded, subject to availability.

Half Moon Bay

Landis Shores Oceanfront Inn

211 Mirada Rd
Half Moon Bay, CA 94019
(650)726-6642 Fax:(650)726-6644
Internet: www.landisshores.com
E-mail: luxury@landisshores.com

Circa 1999. Luxuriate in pampered pleasure at this Contemporary Mediterranean bed & breakfast inn overlooking Miramar Beach. Guest bedrooms boast impressive extras that include binoculars, private balconies, fireplaces, robes, radiant heated floors, a generous assortment of personal grooming amenities and mini-refrigerators with bottled water. Marble or granite bathrooms feature whirlpools and separate showers except for the ADA San Francisco Bay room, with a large limestone shower. Enjoy in-room entertainment centers and business services. Choose a movie selection from the library. Savor a gourmet breakfast in the dining room at a table for two or on a tray delivered to the door. The restaurant has a sommelier and an award-winning wine list. Exercise in the fully equipped fitness center or jog along the coastline trail. Guest services can arrange horseback riding or bike rentals.

Innkeeper(s): Ken Landis, Ellen Landis. $295-345. 8 rooms with PB, 8 with FP, 1 conference room. Breakfast, hors d'oeuvres and wine included in rates. Types of meals: Full gourmet bkfst and early coffee/tea.

Certificate may be used: Sunday-Thursday, except holidays.

Old Thyme Inn

779 Main Street
Half Moon Bay, CA 94019-1924
(650) 726-1616 (800) 720-4277 Fax:(650)726-6394
Internet: www.oldthymeinn.com
E-mail: innkeeper@oldthymeinn.com

Circa 1898. Spend enchanted nights in this "Princess Anne" Victorian inn located on the historic Main Street of Old Town, Half Moon Bay. Its lush, aromatic English flower and herb garden with a bubbling fountain provides a perfect backdrop for casual conversations or romantic tete-a-tetes. Just 28 miles from San Francisco and less than one hour from San Jose and the Silicon Valley, the inn is within walking distance of a crescent-shaped beach, art galleries, shops and fine dining. Furnished in antiques and adorned with the innkeeper's art collection, it offers seven freshly decorated guest rooms, each with a queen bed and hypoallergenic featherbed and down comforter. Two rooms have both Jacuzzis and fireplaces. Savor the inn's tantalizing full breakfast before a day of relaxing or sightseeing.

Innkeeper(s): Rick & Kathy Ellis. $159-349. 7 rooms with PB, 7 with HT, 3 cottages, 3 guest houses. Breakfast, hors d'oeuvres and wine included in rates. Types of meals: Full gourmet bkfst, veg bkfst and early coffee/tea.

Certificate may be used: Nov. 1 to April 30, Sunday-Thursday (except for Thanksgiving, year-end holidays and Valentine's/President's Day weekends), valid for the Garden or Thyme room only, subject to availability.

Healdsburg

Camellia Inn

211 North St
Healdsburg, CA 95448-4251
(707)433-8182 (800)727-8182 Fax:(707)433-8130
Internet: www.camelliainn.com
E-mail: info@camelliainn.com

Circa 1869. Just two blocks from the tree-shaded town plaza, this Italianate Victorian townhouse elegantly graces a half-acre of award-winning grounds. Architectural details include ceiling medallions, ornate mahogany and Palladian windows. Gather in the double parlor with twin marble fireplaces and antiques. Spacious guest bedrooms feature inlaid hardwood floors with Oriental rugs and chandeliers. Many feature whirlpool tubs for two, gas-log fireplaces, canopy beds, sitting areas and private entrances. The Memento can be used as a family suite with an adjoining room. Savor a hearty breakfast buffet fireside in the main dining room. Relax in the swimming pool, and enjoy the more than 50 varieties of camellias.

Innkeeper(s): Lucy Lewand. $139-299. 10 rooms, 9 with PB, 4 with FP, 1 two-bedroom suite, 1 conference room. Breakfast and wine included in rates. Types of meals: Full bkfst.

Certificate may be used: Sunday-Thursday, November-April; excludes weekends, holiday periods and special events.

Healdsburg Inn on The Plaza

112 Matheson St.
Healdsburg, CA 95448-4108
(707)433-6991 (800)431-8663 Fax:(707)433-9513
Internet: www.healdsburginn.com
E-mail: Healdsburginn@foursisters.com

Circa 1900. Located in a former Wells Fargo building, the
Healdsburg Inn on the
Plaza is a renovated brick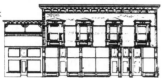
gingerbread overlooking
the plaza in historic
downtown Healdsburg,
California. Ornate bay
windows, embossed
wood paneling and broad, paneled stairs present a welcome
entrance. Relax by a fireplace and the halls are filled with sunlight
from vaulted, glass skylights. A solarium is the setting for breakfast and evening wine and hors d'oeuvres. A large covered balcony extends along the entire rear of the building. Shops on the
premises sell gifts, toys, quilts and fabric as well as an antique
shop and art gallery to browse through. The surrounding area is
full of things to do, including vineyards and wine-tasting rooms.
Innkeeper(s): Wanda & Kristen. $295-395. 10 rooms with PB, 9 with FP, 1
conference room. Breakfast and snacks/refreshments included in rates. Types
of meals: Full gourmet bkfst and early coffee/tea.

Certificate may be used: Sunday-Thursday, December-February, based on
promotional discount availability and excludes special event periods, holidays
and certain room types. First night must be at full rack rate to receive second
night free.

Hope Valley

Sorensen's Resort

14255 Hwy 88
Hope Valley, CA 96120
(530)694-2203 (800)423-9949
Internet: www.sorensensresort.com
E-mail: info@sorensensresort.com

Circa 1876. Where Danish sheepherders settled in this 7,000-
foot-high mountain valley, the Sorensen family built a cluster of
fishing cabins. Thus began a
century-old tradition of valley
hospitality. The focal point of
Sorensen's is a "stave" cabin
— a reproduction of a 13th-
century Nordic house. Now
developed as a Nordic ski
resort, a portion of the
Mormon-Emigrant Trail and Pony Express Route pass near the
inn's 165 acres. In the summer, river rafting, fishing, pony
express re-rides and llama treks are popular Sierra pastimes.
Lake Tahoe lies 20 miles to the north. Breakfast is included in
the rates for bed & breakfast units only. All other cabins are
equipped with kitchens.
Innkeeper(s): John Brissenden, Patty Brissenden. $115-425. 33 rooms, 31
with PB, 23 with FP, 28 cottages, 2 conference rooms. Types of meals: Full
bkfst, early coffee/tea, lunch, picnic lunch, snacks/refreshments and gourmet
dinner. Restaurant on premises.

Certificate may be used: Monday-Thursday, non-holiday, excluding February,
July, August and October.

Ivanhoe

Hummingbird Cottage at Seven Sycamores Ranch

32985 Road 164
Ivanhoe, CA 93235
(559)798-0557
Internet: www.sevensycamoresfarmstay.com/
E-mail: mikka@sevensycamores.com

Circa 1927. Five of the original seven sycamore trees still shade
this cottage and bunkhouse in the San Joaquin Valley 30 minutes
from the Sequoia National Forest. Nestled among the orange
groves, the three-bedroom Hummingbird Cottage offers all the
comforts of home. The beauty of the mountains is brought
indoors with original Albert Marshall paintings. The pantry and
refrigerator are well-stocked and guests may pick as much fresh
fruit as they wish from the orchards. Enjoy your own home-
cooked meals on the back porch or patio overlooking the landscaped grounds. The smaller, intimate Bunkhouse can sleep up
to four people and has a convenient kitchenette. Take a hayride
through the orange groves, pack a bag of fruit to bring home,
and test your navigation skills in the world's only orange grove
maze. Hold a lovely wedding in the Glass Barn with a private
bridal dressing room then preserve your memories with photographs in the gardens with natural granite walkways.
Innkeeper(s): Mikka. $145-350. 4 rooms, 2 with PB, 2 with HT, 2 total
suites, including 1 three-bedroom suite, 2 cottages, 2 guest houses, 1 conference room. Breakfast and Guests are provided with the ingredients to prepare
the breakfast of their choice and a basket of fresh locally grown fruit of the
season included in rates.

Certificate may be used: Sunday-Thursday, subject to Availability.

Jamestown

1859 Historic National Hotel

18183 Main St,
Jamestown, CA 95327-0502
(209)984-3446 (800)894-3446 Fax:(209)984-5620
Internet: www.national-hotel.com
E-mail: info@national-hotel.com

Circa 1859. Located between Yosemite National Park and Lake
Tahoe, in Gold Country, this is one of the 10 oldest continuously operating hotels in the state. The inn maintains its original redwood bar where thousands of dollars in gold dust were
once spent. Original furnishings, Gold Rush period antiques,
brass beds, lace curtains and regal comforters grace the guest
bedrooms. A soaking room is an additional amenity, though all
rooms include private baths. Enjoy a daily bountiful buffet
breakfast. Arrange for romantic dining at the on-site gourmet
restaurant, considered to be one of the finest in the Mother
Lode. Order a favorite liquor or espresso from the saloon, or try
the area's wine tasting. Favorite diversions include gold pan-
ning, live theatre and antiquing, golf and shopping.
Innkeeper(s): Stephen Willey. $140-175. 9 rooms with PB, 1 conference
room. Breakfast and Buffet breakfast in dining room for hotel guests included
in rates. Types of meals: Country bkfst, Sun. brunch, early coffee/tea,
gourmet lunch, picnic lunch, snacks/refreshments, hors d'oeuvres, wine,
gourmet dinner, room service, Banquets, meetings, seminars, weddings and
receptions. Restaurant on premises.

Certificate may be used: (24 hour)Last minute availability only, no weekends.

Americas Best Value Inn & Suites Royal Carriage

18239 Main St
Jamestown, CA 95327-0219
(209)984-5271 Fax:(209)984-1675
Internet: www.abvijamestown.com
E-mail: info@abvijamestown.com

Circa 1922. Guests can experience a bit of the Old West at the Royal Hotel, which was built in the early '20s to provide luxurious lodging for travelers. The hotel originally had a ballroom and restaurant, and for those who preferred to ignore Prohibition, there was a secret "back bar." Rooms are decorated in Victorian style with turn-of-the-century antiques. In addition to the hotel guest rooms, there are secluded cottages. Jamestown is California's second oldest gold mining town and has been the site of more than 150 movies and television shows. Jamestown offers shops, antique stores, restaurants and gold mining attractions. The innkeepers can arrange for theater and golf packages.
$95-150. 6 rooms, 17 with PB, 2 suites, 3 cottages, 1 conference room. Breakfast included in rates. Types of meals: Cont plus and early coffee/tea.
Certificate may be used: January, Sunday-Thursday, subject to availability.

The Victorian Gold Bed and Breakfast

10382 Willow St
Jamestown, CA 95327-9761
(209)984-3429 (888)551-1852 Fax:(209)984-4929
Internet: www.victoriangoldbb.com
E-mail: innkeeper@victoriangoldbb.com

Circa 1890. Enjoy Gold Country at this Victorian, which was home to Albert and Amelia Hoyt, publishers of the Mother Lode Magnet. In the 1890s, the home served as a boarding house. Today, it offers eight guest rooms with lacy curtains, fresh flowers, clawfoot tubs, marble showers and robes. A full breakfast is served each morning along with The Palm's special blend of coffee. The inn is located two-and-a-half hours from San Francisco and about an hour from Yosemite Valley, and it is within walking distance of Main Street, boutiques, galleries, restaurants and Railtown State Park.
Innkeeper(s): Ken spencer, Anita Spencer. $110-185. 8 rooms with PB. Breakfast included in rates. Types of meals: Full gourmet bkfst and early coffee/tea.
Certificate may be used: Anytime, November-March, subject to availability.

Julian

Butterfield B&B

2284 Sunset Dr
Julian, CA 92036
(760)765-2179 (800)379-4262 Fax:(760)765-1229
Internet: butterfieldbandb.com
E-mail: info@butterfieldbandb.com

Circa 1935. On an ivy-covered hillside surrounded by oaks and pines, the Butterfield is a peaceful haven of hospitality and country comfort. Overlooking the countryside, several of the charming guest bedrooms feature fireplaces and fluffy feath-

erbeds. A delicious gourmet breakfast is served in the gazebo during summer or by a warm fire in cooler months. The parlor is a delightful place to enjoy hot beverages and afternoon treats. Whether it is scheduling an in-room massage, or making dinner reservations, the innkeepers are always happy to oblige.
Innkeeper(s): Ed Glass, Dawn Glass. $135-185. 5 rooms with PB, 3 with FP, 1 cottage. Breakfast and snacks/refreshments included in rates. Types of meals: Full gourmet bkfst, veg bkfst and early coffee/tea.
Certificate may be used: Jan. 7-Aug. 31, Sunday-Thursday, last minute based on projected availability.

Kenwood

Birmingham Bed and Breakfast

8790 Sonoma Hwy
Kenwood, CA 95452
(707)833-6996 (800)819-1388 Fax:(707)833-6398
Internet: www.birminghambb.com
E-mail: info@birminghambb.com

Circa 1915. Set amongst vineyards, this two-acre Prairie-style country estate with breathtaking views was given historic designation by Sonoma County. A fireplace, library and game table are located in the Victorian breakfast parlor. The sitting parlor offers a reading nook and small visitors center. Romantic guest bedrooms and suites feature four-poster and sleigh beds. The spacious Red Room boasts a soaking tub with shower and a private balcony overlooking the pond and hazelnut trees. Fresh produce from the orchard and garden provides ingredients for seasonal breakfast recipes like artichoke cheese frittata, scones and poached pears. Relax on the wraparound porch facing mountain vistas.
Innkeeper(s): Nancy Fischman, Jerry Fischman. $160-295. 5 rooms, 4 with PB, 1 two-bedroom suite, 1 cottage, 1 conference room. Breakfast and afternoon tea included in rates. Types of meals: Full gourmet bkfst, veg bkfst and early coffee/tea.
Certificate may be used: November-March, anytime subject to availability.

Kernville

Kern River Inn B&B

119 Kern River Dr
Kernville, CA 93238
(760)376-6750 (800)986-4382
Internet: www.kernriverinn.com
E-mail: kernriverinn@gmail.com

Circa 1991. Kern River Inn overlooks the river in Kernville, California amid the Southern Sierra Nevada Mountains.

Relaxing and comfortable, this B&B has an inviting front porch and fireside gathering room for pleasant conversation. Stay in a delightful guest room with picturesque water and mountain views, a wood-burning fireplace or spa shower. The first-floor Piute Room is wheelchair accessible and meets ADA requirements. Savor a bountiful breakfast that may include the inn's renowned waffles, egg and cheese dishes or stuffed French toast; then explore the Kern River Valley and Lake Isabella. Whitewater rafting and fly fishing are popular outdoor sports. The local area offers many seasonal annual events and year-round activities. Ask about inn specials available.

Innkeeper(s): Virginia McLaughlin. $142-165. 5 rooms with PB, 5 with HT, 3 guest houses. Breakfast, afternoon tea and snacks/refreshments included in rates. Types of meals: Full bkfst, veg bkfst, early coffee/tea, picnic lunch and Birder breakfasts.

Certificate may be used: Anytime, subject to availability.

Klamath

Historic Requa Inn

451 Requa Rd
Klamath, CA 95548-9342
(707) 482-1425 (866) 800-8777
Internet: www.requainn.com
E-mail: innkeeper@requainn.com

Situated in the midst of the Redwood national and state parks in Klamath, California, this award-winning inn is less than a mile from the Pacific Ocean and overlooks the river. Simple yet comfortable and inviting accommodations on the second floor feature antique furnishings. Some may include a clawfoot tub or walk-in shower and an electric fireplace. Linger over a substantial home-cooked breakfast made with locally produced foods and organic ingredients. Seasonal dinner options are offered at an additional charge. The beverage bar is available at any time and baked treats are provided each afternoon. Sip wine in the fireside living room. Watch TV, play the piano or read in one of the spacious common rooms. The inviting gazebo and swing sit alongside the river. Take a leisurely hike through the woods then enjoy a relaxing soak in the hot tub.

Innkeeper(s): Jan Wortman, Marty Wortman . $139-169. 12 rooms with PB, 2 with FP, 1 two-bedroom suite. Breakfast and snacks/refreshments included in rates. Types of meals: Full gourmet bkfst, veg bkfst, early coffee/tea, wine and gourmet dinner.

Certificate may be used: November-April, excluding weekends, subject to availability.

Lemon Cove

Plantation B&B

33038 Sierra Drive (hwy 198)
Lemon Cove, CA 93244-1700
(559) 597-2555 Fax:(559)597-2551
Internet: www.theplantation.net
E-mail: relax@plantationbnb.com

Circa 1908. The history of orange production is deeply entwined in the roots of California, and this home is located on what once was an orange plantation. The original 1908 house burned in the 1960s, but the current home was built on its foundation. In keeping with the home's plantation past, the innkeepers decorated the bed and breakfast with a "Gone With the Wind" theme. The comfortable, country guest rooms sport names such as the Scarlett O'Hara, the Belle  Watling, and of course, the Rhett Butler. A hot tub is located in the orchard, and there also is a heated swimming pool.

Innkeeper(s): Scott Munger, Marie Munger. $99-179. 8 rooms with PB, 2 with FP, 1 with WP, 3 suites. Breakfast and snacks/refreshments included in rates. Types of meals: Full gourmet bkfst and early coffee/tea.

Certificate may be used: Sept. 7-May 15, subject to availability, not valid holidays and special events.

Mendocino

Alegria Oceanfront Inn & Cottages

44781 Main St
Mendocino, CA 95460
(707)937-5150 (800)780-7905 Fax:(707)937-5151
Internet: www.oceanfrontmagic.com
E-mail: inn@oceanfrontmagic.com

Circa 1861. Sitting in the historic village on a bluff overlooking an ocean cove, this inn lightens the sprits just as the name Alegria means when translated. The main house was built in 1861 as a saltbox and recently renovated. Stay in one of the guest bedrooms or a private cottage. They all feature generous amenities and some include wood-burning stoves. The second-floor Pacific Suite boasts a microwave and wet bar sink. The ocean view dining room is the perfect spot for an incredible breakfast that is made with organically grown produce when possible. The ever-changing perennial garden includes antique roses and a relaxing hot tub. Take the trail 200 footsteps from the garden's edge down to Big River Beach.

Innkeeper(s): Eric and Elaine Wing Hillesland. $159-299. 6 rooms, 10 with PB, 1 suite, 4 cottages. Breakfast included in rates. Types of meals: Full gourmet bkfst, veg bkfst and early coffee/tea.

Certificate may be used: November-February, Sunday-Thursday, excluding holidays, subject to availability.

Brewery Gulch Inn

9401 North Highway One
Mendocino, CA 95460-9767
(707)937-4752 (800)578-4454 Fax:(707)937-1279
Internet: www.brewerygulchinn.com
E-mail: guestservices@brewerygulchinn.com

Circa 2001. Brewery Gulch Inn is located on three acres with coastal spruce, mature pine and redwood trees, hundreds of rhododendrons and many native plants in Mendocino, California. This extraordinary inn features ancient virgin redwood timbers eco-salvaged from Big River. Guest rooms, eight with private decks, are furnished to provide the ultimate in comfort. Each room has a fireplace, quality Sferra Italian linens, a cozy seating area with leather club chairs, a desk, excellent lighting and an ocean view framed by trees. Additional amenities include LCD flat screen TVs with cable and DVD, iHome clock radios, complimentary local and domestic long distance service and Wi-fi high-speed Internet. Indulge in an outstanding cooked-to-order breakfast each morning. The evening wine hour features bountiful hors d'oeuvres and carefully chosen wines from Mendocino County wineries.

Innkeeper(s): Jo Ann Stickle, GM. $210-465. 11 rooms, 10 with PB, 10 with FP, 2 with HT, 2 with WP, 1 two-bedroom suite. Breakfast, snacks/refreshments, hors d'oeuvres, wine, Full and cooked to order breakfast; evening wine hour includes light dinner buffet included in rates. Types of meals: Full gourmet bkfst, veg bkfst, early coffee/tea, gourmet lunch, picnic lunch and room service.

Certificate may be used: November-April, Sunday-Thursday, subject to availability, except during holidays or local special events.

Headlands Inn

10453 Howard Street
Mendocino, CA 95460
(707)937-4431 (800)354-4431 Fax:(707)937-0421
Internet: www.headlandsinn.com
E-mail: innkeeper@headlandsinn.com

Circa 1868. A historic setting by the sea in the village of Mendocino complements this New England Victorian Salt Box. The quaintness of the past combines with amenities of the present. Meet new friends sharing afternoon tea and cookies in the parlor. Almost all of the romantic guest bedrooms feature fireplaces, comfortable feather beds with down comforters, fresh flowers and bedside chocolates. Some have white-water ocean views. A cottage provides more spacious privacy. Indulge in a full breakfast delivered to the room with homemade treats and creative entrees. The front porch is also an ideal spot for ocean views. Lawn seating gives ample opportunity to enjoy the year-round English garden. Many unique shops and fine restaurants are within walking distance.

Innkeeper(s): Denise & Mitch. $99-249. 7 rooms with PB, 6 with FP, 1 suite, 1 cottage. Breakfast, afternoon tea and snacks/refreshments included in rates. Types of meals: Full gourmet bkfst and veg bkfst.

Certificate may be used: November-February, Monday-Thursday, excluding holiday periods. Strauss, Cottage or Barry rooms only.

MacCallum House Inn

45020 Albion St
Mendocino, CA 95460
(707)937-0289 (800)609-0492
Internet: www.maccallumhouse.com
E-mail: innkeeper@maccallumhouse.com

Circa 1882. Choose from a variety of accommodations with ocean views and upscale amenities at this Mendocino inn on the coast of northern California. Winner of the iLoveInns.com Top 10 Romantic Inns of 2009, MacCallum House was built in 1882 and includes a renowned restaurant situated in the sun porch, library and dining rooms of this vintage Victorian. The menus showcase regional organic products and a gourmet breakfast is included in your room fee. Surrounding the main house, cottages feature wood stoves and decks, some with private hot tubs. The original barn was restored and boasts river stone fireplaces in each guest bedroom. Properties also include the MacCallum Suites, a luxury mansion on two hilltop acres and the Mendocino Village Inn, an historic three-story 1882 mansion. Massage and Spa services are available, as well as limousine tours of Anderson Valley wine country.

Innkeeper(s): Herman Seidell, Sarah Mitchell. $149-399. 30 rooms with PB, 20 with FP, 9 with HT, 16 with WP, 13 suites, 7 cottages, 1 conference room. Breakfast and Daily "Food and Wine" Credits included in rates. Types of meals: Full gourmet bkfst, veg bkfst, Sun. brunch, early coffee/tea, gourmet lunch, picnic lunch, afternoon tea, snacks/refreshments, hors d'oeuvres, wine, gourmet dinner, Executive Chef Alan Kantor showcases regional North Coast wines, seafood and meats and produce with an emphasis on organics and quality purveyors. We change our menus seasonally. Restaurant on premises.

Certificate may be used: November-April, Sunday-Thursday, non holiday.

Sea Gull Inn

44960 Albion St
Mendocino, CA 95460
(707)937-5204 (888)937-5204
Internet: www.seagullbb.com
E-mail: seagull@mcn.org

Circa 1883. Shaded by a giant holly tree, this house built in 1878 was one of the area's first bed & breakfast inns. Relax on the front porch or in the lush private garden. Stay in a spacious upstairs or first-floor guest bedroom or a private cottage with antiques, fresh flowers and original artworks. A variety of amenities are offered from sitting areas to ocean views. A light breakfast is delivered to the room at a prearranged time and a morning newspaper is available upon request. Walk to the village shops and art galleries. Visit the Mendocino Art Center or the botanical coastal gardens. Tour Anderson Wine Valley and take the Skunk Train at Fort Bragg through the mountains and redwoods.

Innkeeper(s): Jim and Ayla Douglas. $135-198. 9 rooms with PB, 1 with FP, 1 cottage. Breakfast included in rates. Types of meals: Cont plus.

Certificate may be used: Nov. 1-March 31.

The Inn at Schoolhouse Creek

7051 N Hwy 1
Mendocino, CA 95460
(707)937-5525 (800)731-5525 Fax:(707)937-2012
Internet: www.schoolhousecreek.com
E-mail: innkeeper@schoolhousecreek.com

Circa 1860. The Inn at School House Creek offers both private cottages and rooms on its 8 acres of rose gardens, forests and meadows. (The inn's gardens have been featured in several magazines.) Many cottages include views of the ocean and all have a fireplace. The inn offers a quiet getaway, while still being close to all of the fun in Mendocino two miles away. Private beach access to Buckhorn Cove allows guests to enjoy whale watching, sea lions and the crashing waves of the Pacific. Organize your day to include a picnic lunch (available by advance notice) to enjoy at a secluded waterfall in the redwoods. Be sure to take a sunset soak in the inn's ocean view hot tub.

Innkeeper(s): Sandy Van Derbes, Kevin Van Derbes. $130-399. 19 rooms with PB, 19 with FP, 4 with HT, 6 with WP, 1 total suite, including 2 two-bedroom suites, 12 cottages, 2 conference rooms. Afternoon tea, snacks/refreshments, hors d'oeuvres and wine included in rates. Types of meals: Early coffee/tea, picnic lunch and Lunch by request.

Certificate may be used: Nov. 1-Feb. 28, Sunday-Thursday, holidays and local festivals excluded.

Middletown

Backyard Garden Oasis B&B

24019 Hilderbrand Dr
Middletown, CA 95461-1760
(707)987-0505
Internet: www.backyardgardenoasis.com
E-mail: greta@backyardgardenoasis.com

Circa 1997. Be renewed by the blend of simple elegance and rustic ambiance in the Collayomi Valley of North Calistoga over Mt. St. Helens. Stay in one of the individual cottages that feature air conditioning, skylight, gas fireplaces, a refrigerator and coffeemaker and access to the video collection. The private redwood decks overlook the Manzanita grove, pond and waterfall.

One cottage is wheelchair accessible. Gather in the dining room of the main house for a hearty country breakfast that begins with fresh-squeezed orange juice. Schedule a massage with a certified therapist then soak under the stars in the hot tub. Harbin Hot Springs is ten minutes away and it is a two-hour drive to San Francisco or Sacramento. Take a wine tasting tour of nearby Lake County wineries.

Innkeeper(s): Greta Zeit. $139-159. 3 cottages with PB, 3 with FP, 1 suite. Breakfast included in rates. Types of meals: Early coffee/tea and full country breakfast.

Certificate may be used: Anytime, subject to availability.

Mill Creek

St. Bernard Lodge

44801 Hwy 36E
Mill Creek, CA 96061
(530) 258-3382
Internet: www.stbernardlodge.com
E-mail: stbernardlodge@citlink.net

Circa 1920. Located in the center of Northern California near Lake Almanor and Mount Lassen Volcanic National Park, this inn-like B&B lodge sits in Mill Creek where the year-round highway divides the Cascade and the Sierra Nevada Mountains. Relax on the deck overlooking the tout pond and soak in the hot tub with views of the mountains and a stream. Historic memorabilia, vintage artwork and antique furnishings accent the rustic warmth of the upstairs guest rooms whose names reflect their decor. The restaurant features a creative breakfast, lunch and dinner menu. Gather for cocktails, meals and snacks in the warm and friendly tavern that has a fully stocked bar. Watch TV, play cribbage, shoot darts or billards on the custom-made Olhausen pool table. Overnight boarding can be reserved for horses. Hike or ride the trails, go cross-country skiing or snowmobiling.

Innkeeper(s): Sharon L. Roberts. $99. 7 rooms. Breakfast and hors d'oeuvres included in rates. Types of meals: Full gourmet bkfst, veg bkfst, lunch, wine and dinner. Restaurant on premises.

Certificate may be used: Oct. 15-May 15, based on availability, not valid holidays.

Montara

The Goose & Turrets B&B

835 George St.
Montara, CA 94037-0937
(650) 728-5451 Fax:(650)728-0141
Internet: www.gooseandturretsbandb.com
E-mail: gooseandturretsbandb@gmail.com

Circa 1908. Now a haven focusing on comfort and hospitality, this classic bed & breakfast once served as Montara's first post office, the town hall, and a country club for Spanish-American War veterans. Large living and dining room areas are filled with art and collectibles. Sleep soundly in one of the tranquil guest bedrooms then linger over a leisurely four-course breakfast. Stimulating conversation comes easily during afternoon tea. There are plenty of quiet spots including a swing and a hammock, to

enjoy the fountains, orchard, rose, herb and vegetable gardens.

Innkeeper(s): Raymond & Emily Hoche-Mong. $175-230. 5 rooms with PB. Breakfast, afternoon tea and Four-course breakfast included in rates. Types of meals: Full gourmet bkfst and veg bkfst.

Certificate may be used: Monday-Thursday September-May. Major holidays excluded.

Monterey

The Jabberwock

598 Laine St
Monterey, CA 93940-1312
(831)372-4777 (888)428-7253 Fax:(831)655-2946
Internet: www.jabberwockinn.com
E-mail: innkeeper@jabberwockinn.com

Circa 1911. Set in a half-acre of gardens, this Craftsman-style inn provides a fabulous view of Monterey Bay with its famous barking seals. When you're ready to settle in for the evening, you'll find huge Victorian beds complete with lace-edged sheets and goose-down comforters. Three rooms include Jacuzzi tubs. In the late afternoon, hors d'oeuvres and aperitifs are served on an enclosed sun porch. After dinner, guests are tucked into bed with homemade chocolate chip cookies and milk. To help guests avoid long lines, the innkeepers have tickets available for the popular and nearby Monterey Bay Aquarium.

Innkeeper(s): Dawn Perez & John Hickey. $169-299. 7 rooms with PB, 4 with FP, 3 with HT. Breakfast, afternoon tea, snacks/refreshments, hors d'oeuvres and wine included in rates. Types of meals: Full gourmet bkfst, veg bkfst, early coffee/tea, picnic lunch and evening wine.

Certificate may be used: Sunday-Thursday, Nov. 1-April 30, excluding holidays. Subject to availability.

Morro Bay

Bayfront Inn

1148 Front Street
Morro Bay, CA 93442
(805)772-5607 (877)772-0072 Fax:(805)772-0101
Internet: www.bayfront-inn.com
E-mail: bayfrontinn@sbcglobal.net

Circa 1892. Stay in the closest inn to Morro Rock at this European style bed and breakfast in Morro Bay. Request a room on the second floor for spectacular views of Morro Bay, the Rock, and local sea life. Stay in a pet-friendly room if you want to bring a furry or winged family member on the trip. Watch the fishing boats in the morning while enjoying a continental breakfast of fruit, cinnamon rolls, oatmeal, and waffles. Visit a Central Coast winery and bring back a bottle to sip while the sun sets in breathtaking style. Go kayaking, rock-climbing, deep-sea fishing, or surf next to Morro Rock. Play the Morro Bay Golf Course, considered by many to be an inexpensive Pebble Beach. Walk along the Embarcadero for shops, entertainment, and restaurants or take a nature walk or docent led tour at the Museum of Natural History. Some of the best bird watching is in the winter months when 70,000 migratory birds travel to the Bay.

Innkeeper(s): Jayne Behman. Call for rates. 5 rooms with PB.

Certificate may be used: Monday-Thursday, January-February.

Marina Street Inn

305 Marina St
Morro Bay, CA 93442
(805)772-4016 (888)683-9389
Internet: www.marinastreetinn.com
E-mail: vfoster105@aol.com

Circa 199. The Marina Street Inn is a friendly bed and breakfast in the seaside village of Morro Bay, California. The Garden Room Suite brings a touch of the outdoors with a birdhouse nightstand and a four-poster willow bed. The Dockside Suite has views of the ocean and sports a maritime decor. Socialize with other guests over a gourmet breakfast and wine in the afternoon. The kitchen is available for everyone to use; walk to the Saturday Farmer's Market and create a dinner masterpiece. Spend a quiet evening on the patio amidst the gardens or play with Trapp, the resident dog. The Embarcadero shops and restaurants are a short five-minute stroll from the inn. Hop onboard a tour boat to watch magnificent humpback whales breach right outside the Bay entrance or meditate on spectacular Morro Rock, an extinct volcano and last of the Nine Sisters. The landmark site is now a bird sanctuary and home to nesting peregrine falcons.
Innkeeper(s): Claudia. Call for rates. 4 rooms.
Certificate may be used: Anytime, subject to availability.

Moss Beach

Seal Cove Inn

221 Cypress Ave
Moss Beach, CA 94038
(650)728-4114 (800)995-9987 Fax:(650)728-4116
Internet: www.sealcoveinn.com
E-mail: info@sealcoveinn.com

Circa 1991. Considered a European sanctuary on the California coast, Seal Cove Inn in Moss Beach is a serene hideaway with a border of cypress trees and a wildflower meadow. The inn overlooks acres of a county park and the Pacific Ocean beyond. Stroll the tree-lined trail along the waterfront bluffs. Gorgeous guest bedrooms are delightful, spacious retreats with a fireplace, towel warmer and private balcony or terrace. Located just 24 miles south of San Francisco, the surrounding area offers many activities from wine tasting to whale watching. Horseback riding is available on Half Moon Bay and two golf courses are nearby.
$235-350. 10 rooms with PB, 2 with WP. Breakfast, afternoon tea and hors d'oeuvres included in rates. Types of meals: Full bkfst, veg bkfst, early coffee/tea and snacks/refreshments.
Certificate may be used: Sunday-Thursday, December-February, based on promotional discount availability and excludes special event periods, holidays and certain room types. First night must be at full rack rate to receive second night free.

Napa

Belle Epoque

1386 Calistoga Ave
Napa, CA 94559-2552
(707)257-2161 (800)238-8070 Fax:(707)226-6314
Internet: www.napabelle.com
E-mail: georgia@napabelle.com

Circa 1893. This luxurious Victorian inn has won awards for "best in the wine country" and "best breakfast in the nation." Enjoy the experience in the wine cellar and tasting room where  guests can casually sip Napa Valley wines. The inn, which is one of the most unique architectural structures found in the wine country, is located in the heart of Napa's Calistoga Historic District. Beautiful original stained-glass windows include a window from an old church. Six guest rooms offer a whirlpool tub. A selection of fine restaurants and shops are within easy walking distance, as well as the riverfront, art museums and the Wine Train Depot.
Innkeeper(s): Georgia Jump Innkeeper/Manager. $199-419. 9 rooms with PB, 6 with FP, 3 suites, 1 conference room. Breakfast, snacks/refreshments, hors d'oeuvres and wine included in rates. Types of meals: Full gourmet bkfst and early coffee/tea.
Certificate may be used: Nov. 15 - April 1, Sunday - Thursday.

Blackbird Inn

1755 1st Street
Napa, CA 94559
(707) 226-2450 (888) 567-9811 Fax:707-258-6391
Internet: www.blackbirdinnnapa.com
E-mail: blackbirdinn@foursisters.com

Circa 2001. Blackbird Inn in Napa, California is a meticulously restored hideaway, built with Greene and Greene-type architecture. It is within an easy walk to town and the surrounding area is picturesque and inviting. The stone pillared porch, leaded glass and blackbird vines are a welcome setting for the wonderful atmosphere found inside. True to the Craftsman-style furnishings and decor, the period lighting accents the subdued colors and warm ambiance. Double-paned windows offer quiet views of the garden fountain. Many of the guest bedrooms feature private decks, spa tubs and fireplaces. Wine and hors d' oeuvres are served in the afternoon.
Innkeeper(s): Gina Massolo. $185-300. 8 rooms with PB, 6 with FP. Breakfast, afternoon tea, snacks/refreshments, hors d'oeuvres and wine included in rates. Types of meals: Full gourmet bkfst, veg bkfst and early coffee/tea.
Certificate may be used: Sunday-Thursday, December-February, based on promotional discount availability and excludes special event periods, holidays and certain room types. First night must be at full rack rate to receive second night free.

Candlelight Inn, a Napa Valley Bed & Breakfast

1045 Easum Drive
Napa, CA 94558-5524
(707) 257-3717 (800) 624-0395 Fax:(707) 257-3762
Internet: www.candlelightinn.com
E-mail: mail@candlelightinn.com

Circa 1929. Located on a park-like acre with gardens, this elegant English Tudor-style house is situated beneath redwood groves and towering trees that shade the banks of Napa Creek. Six rooms feature a marble fireplace and two-person marble Jacuzzi inside the room. The Candlelight Suite offers cathedral ceilings, stained-glass windows and a private sauna. The inn's breakfast room has French doors and windows overlooking the garden. Breakfast is served by candlelight.

Innkeeper(s): Sam Neft. $239-499. 10 rooms with PB, 6 with FP, 6 with WP, 1 cottage. Breakfast and snacks/refreshments included in rates. Types of meals: Full gourmet bkfst, early coffee/tea and wine.

Certificate may be used: December-February, Sunday-Thursday, holiday periods excluded, subject to availability.

Hennessey House-Napa's 1889 Queen Anne Victorian B&B

1727 Main St
Napa, CA 94559-1844
(707)226-3774 Fax:(707)226-2975
Internet: www.hennesseyhouse.com
E-mail: inn@hennesseyhouse.com

Circa 1889. Colorful gardens greet you at this gracious Victorian. It was once home to Dr. Edwin Hennessey, a Napa County physician and former mayor. Pristinely renovated, the inn features stained-glass windows and a curving wraparound porch. A handsome hand-painted, stamped-tin ceiling graces the dining room. The inn's romantic rooms are furnished in antiques. Some offer fireplaces, feather beds and spa tubs. The bathrooms all feature marble floors 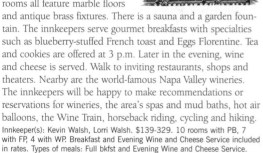 and antique brass fixtures. There is a sauna and a garden fountain. The innkeepers serve gourmet breakfasts with specialties such as blueberry-stuffed French toast and Eggs Florentine. Tea and cookies are offered at 3 p.m. Later in the evening, wine and cheese is served. Walk to inviting restaurants, shops and theaters. Nearby are the world-famous Napa Valley wineries. The innkeepers will be happy to make recommendations or reservations for wineries, the area's spas and mud baths, hot air balloons, the Wine Train, horseback riding, cycling and hiking.

Innkeeper(s): Kevin Walsh, Lorri Walsh. $139-329. 10 rooms with PB, 7 with FP, 4 with WP. Breakfast and Evening Wine and Cheese Service included in rates. Types of meals: Full bkfst and Evening Wine and Cheese Service.

Certificate may be used: Nov. 18-March 13, Sunday-Thursday. Holidays and Dec. 26-Dec 31 excluded.

The Beazley House Bed & Breakfast Inn

1910 1st Street
Napa, CA 94559-2351
(707)257-1649 (800)559-1649 Fax:707-257-1518
Internet: www.beazleyhouse.com
E-mail: innkeeper@beazleyhouse.com

Circa 1902. Nestled in green lawns and gardens, this graceful shingled mansion is frosted with white trim on its bays and balustrades. Stained-glass  windows and polished-wood floors set the atmosphere in the parlor. There are five rooms in the main house, and the carriage house features five more, all with fireplaces and whirlpool tubs. The venerable Beazley House was Napa's first bed & breakfast inn.

Innkeeper(s): Jim Beazley, Carol Beazley. $179-340. 11 rooms with PB, 6 with FP, 5 with WP. Breakfast, afternoon tea, snacks/refreshments and wine included in rates. Types of meals: Full bkfst, veg bkfst, early coffee/tea and hors d'oeuvres.

Certificate may be used: December-March, Sunday-Thursday, excludes holidays, subject to availability.

Nevada City

Emma Nevada House

528 E Broad St
Nevada City, CA 95959-2213
(530)265-4415 (800)916-3662 Fax:(530)265-4416
Internet: www.emmanevadahouse.com
E-mail: mail@emmanevadahouse.com

Circa 1856. The childhood home of 19th-century opera star Emma Nevada now serves as an attractive Queen Anne Victorian inn. English roses line the white picket fence in front, and the forest-like back garden has a small stream with benches. The Empress' Chamber is the most romantic room with ivory linens atop a French antique bed, a bay window and a massive French armoire. Some rooms have whirlpool baths and TV. Guests enjoy relaxing in the hexagonal sunroom and on the inn's wraparound porches. Empire Mine State Historic Park is nearby.

Innkeeper(s): Susan Howard, Andrew Howard. $149-249. 6 rooms with PB, 2 with FP, 2 with WP, 1 two-bedroom suite. Breakfast and afternoon tea included in rates. Types of meals: Full gourmet bkfst, early coffee/tea and snacks/refreshments.

Certificate may be used: Jan. 2 to April 30, Monday-Thursday, no holidays.

Nice

Featherbed Railroad Company B&B

2870 Lakeshore Blvd
Nice, CA 95464
(707)274-8378 (800)966-6322
Internet: www.featherbedrailroad.com
E-mail: room@featherbedrailroad.com

Circa 1988. On the shores of Clear Lake in Northern California, Featherbed Railroad Company Bed & Breakfast Resort spans five park-like acres. Luxuriously refurbished railroad cabooses provide unusual yet inviting accommodations. Each one is individually furnished and decorated around a theme with its own feather bed and upscale amenities. Most feature Jacuzzi tubs for two. Swim in the pool or explore the scenic area on a tanden bike. This lakefront resort also boasts a private dock and boat launch.

Innkeeper(s): Tony Barthel, Peggy Barthel. $99-220. 9 rooms with PB, 9 with HT, 7 with WP. Breakfast and snacks/refreshments included in rates. Types of meals: Full bkfst, veg bkfst and early coffee/tea.

Certificate may be used: Sunday-Thursday, Oct. 15-April 15.

Oakhurst

Vulture's View

39045 John West Rd
Oakhurst, CA 93644
(559)683-8470
Internet: www.yosemitevulturesviewbandb.com
E-mail: jalex@sti.net

Vulture's View is a family-run bed and breakfast in Madera County, California, offering excellent service in a relaxed setting on more than two acres. Feel at peace while watching deer and birds or viewing the clear 180-degree vista of the mountains surrounding Oakhurst basin. At night the star-filled sky can be seen while sitting by the outdoor firepit. A three-tiered waterfall provides a soothing interlude near the wisteria-covered arbor. Stay in a guest bedroom accented with antique furnishings, a fireplace, microwave, refrigerator and coffee pot. A private spa boasts a 60-mile visual range. Start the day with a continental breakfast before exploring Yosemite National Park or Bass Lake. Chukchansi Gold Casino is close by.

Innkeeper(s): Judy Alexander. $159-199. 3 rooms with PB, 1 with FP, 1 with HT. Snacks/refreshments included in rates. Types of meals: Cont plus.

Certificate may be used: September-October, subject to availability.

Pacific Grove

Gosby House Inn

643 Lighthouse Ave
Pacific Grove, CA 93950-2643
(831)375-1287 (800)527-8828 Fax:(831)655-9621
Internet: www.gosbyhouseinn.com
E-mail: gosbyhouseinn@foursisters.com

Circa 1887. Built as an upscale Victorian inn for those visiting the old Methodist retreat in Pacific Grove, California, this sunny yellow mansion features an abundance of gables, turrets and bays. During renovation the innkeeper slept in all the guest bedrooms to determine just what antiques were needed and how the beds should be situated. Many of the romantic rooms include fireplaces and offer canopy beds. The Carriage House rooms include fireplaces, decks and spa tubs. Savor a delicious breakfast before visiting nearby attractions. The Monterey Bay Aquarium and Carmel are nearby. Historic Gosby House Inn, which has been open for more than a century, is in the National Register and is one of the Four Sisters Inns.

$185-300. 22 rooms with PB, 11 with FP. Breakfast, afternoon tea, snacks/refreshments, hors d'oeuvres and wine included in rates. Types of meals: Full gourmet bkfst and early coffee/tea.

Certificate may be used: Sunday-Thursday, December-February, based on promotional discount availability and excludes special event periods, holidays and certain room types. First night must be at full rack rate to receive second night free.

Green Gables Inn

301 Ocean Avenue
Pacific Grove, CA 93950
(831)375-2095 (800)722-1774 Fax:(831)375-5437
Internet: www.greengablesinnpg.com
E-mail: greengablesinn@foursisters.com

Circa 1888. Green Gables Inn, a half-timbered Queen Anne Victorian in Pacific Grove, California, appears as a fantasy of gables overlooking spectacular Monterey Bay. The parlor has stained-glass panels framing the fireplace and bay windows looking out to the sea. A favorite focal point is an antique carousel horse. Most of the guest rooms have panoramic views of the ocean, fireplaces, gleaming woodwork, soft quilts and teddy bears, and four rooms have spa tubs. After a bountiful breakfast borrow a bike from the inn and ride along cross the paved oceanfront cycling path across the street. Green Gables Inn is one of the Four Sisters Inns.

Innkeeper(s): Honey Spence. $145-300. 11 rooms, 8 with PB, 6 with FP, 5 suites. Breakfast, afternoon tea, snacks/refreshments, hors d'oeuvres and wine included in rates. Types of meals: Full gourmet bkfst and early coffee/tea.

Certificate may be used: Sunday-Thursday, December-February, based on promotional discount availability and excludes special event periods, holidays and certain room types. First night must be at full rack rate to receive second night free.

Martine Inn

255 Ocean View Blvd
Pacific Grove, CA 93950
(831)373-3388 (800)852-5588 Fax:(831)373-3896
Internet: www.martineinn.com
E-mail: don@martineinn.com

Circa 1899. This turn-of-the-century oceanfront manor sits atop a jagged cliff overlooking the coastline of Monterey Bay, just steps away from the water's edge. Bedrooms are furnished with antiques, and each room contains a fresh rose. Thirteen rooms also boast fireplaces. Some of the museum-quality antiques were exhibited in the 1893 Chicago World's Fair. Other bedroom sets include furniture that belonged to Edith Head, and there is an 1860 Chippendale Revival four-poster bed with a canopy and side curtains. Innkeeper Don Martine has a collection of vintage MGs, six on display for guests. Twilight wine and hors d'oeuvres are served, and chocolates accompany evening turndown service. The inn is a beautiful spot for romantic getaways and weddings.

Innkeeper(s): Don Martine. $209-499. 5 rooms, 25 with PB, 13 with FP, 2 total suites, including 1 two-bedroom suite, 6 conference rooms. Breakfast, snacks/refreshments, hors d'oeuvres and wine included in rates. Types of meals: Full gourmet bkfst and early coffee/tea.

Certificate may be used: November-February, subject to availability. Not on Valentine's, between Christmas and New Year's, Thanksgiving or 3 day holiday weekends.

Palm Springs

Sakura, Japanese B&B Inn

1677 N Via Miraleste at Vista Chino
Palm Springs, CA 92262
(760)327-0705 Fax:(760)327-6847
Internet: www.sakurabedandbreakfast.com
E-mail: george@sakurabedandbreakfast.com

Circa 1945. An authentic Japanese experience awaits guests of this private home, distinctively decorated with Japanese artwork and antique kimonos. Guests are encouraged to leave their shoes at the door, grab kimonos and slippers and discover what real relaxation is all about. Futon beds, and in-room refrigerators and microwaves are provided. Guests may choose either American or Japanese breakfasts, and Japanese or vegetarian dinners also are available. The Palm Springs area is home to more than 100 golf courses and hosts annual world-class golf and tennis charity events. A favorite place for celebrity watching, the area also is the Western polo capital and offers the famous 9,000-foot aerial tram ride that climbs through several temperature zones. There are cycling trails, theater, horseback riding in the canyons and fine dining, skiing and antiquing. During the summer months, the innkeepers conduct tours in Japan.

Innkeeper(s): George Cebra. $75-125. 3 rooms, 2 with PB, 1 suite. Breakfast included in rates. Types of meals: Full bkfst, early coffee/tea, picnic lunch, afternoon tea and dinner.

Certificate may be used: Anytime, Sunday-Thursday.

Paso Robles

Belvino Viaggio

1985 Peachy Canyon Road
Paso Robles, CA 93446
(805)237-8895
Internet: www.belvinoviaggio.com
E-mail: lois@belvinoviaggio.com

Circa 2008. Huge windows frame views of the surrounding vineyards from the moment you step into this Tuscan bed and breakfast two miles from downtown Paso Robles, California. The inn's hilltop location and 40 acres make you feel a world away. Each of the seven luxurious guest rooms is decorated to represent a wine region of the world. The king-size bed in the Chile room is covered in warm sunset colors or you can choose the elegant safari decor of the South Africa room. Start the day on the loggia with a three-course breakfast including bananas foster pancakes or artichoke heart cheese frittata. The inn strives to be eco-friendly and uses local and organic ingredients. The Paso Robles wine region has more than 200 wineries; ask about inn packages that include tours. The area offers many different activities; ride in an authentic stage coach, sample olive oil in local tasting rooms, play golf at the four courses, or shop for antiques.

Innkeeper(s): Lois Fox. Call for rates. 7 rooms with PB, 6 with FP. Breakfast and wine included in rates. Types of meals: Full bkfst, veg bkfst and early coffee/tea.

Certificate may be used: January-February, Monday-Thursday, excluding holidays and subject to availability.

Placerville

Albert Shafsky House Bed & Breakfast

2942 Coloma St
Placerville, CA 95667
(530)642-2776 (877)BNBINNS Fax:(503)642-2109
Internet: www.shafsky.com
E-mail: stay@shafsky.com

Circa 1902. Gold Country hospitality is offered at this Queen Anne Victorian Bed and Breakfast located just a stroll to the historic district and the shops of Old Hangtown. Enjoy a welcome snack and refreshments in the elegant living room. Pleasantly decorated guest bedrooms are furnished with antiques and offer individually controlled heat and air conditioning as well as feather beds and goosedown comforters during winter. The two-room Lighthouse Suite also boasts a sitting room for a private breakfast. Arrangements can be made for special occasions, or a personalized bouquet of flowers.

Innkeeper(s): Rita Timewell, Stephanie Carlson. $135-185. 3 rooms with PB. Breakfast, snacks/refreshments and wine included in rates. Types of meals: Full gourmet bkfst, veg bkfst, early coffee/tea and hors d'oeuvres.

Certificate may be used: Sunday-Thursday, subject to availability.

Point Reyes Station

The Black Heron Inn

51 Cypress Road
Point Reyes Station, CA 94956
(415)663-1894OFFICE Fax:415-663-1805
Internet: www.blackheroninn.com
E-mail: stay@blackthorneinn.com

Circa 1978. Historic Point Reyes Station is the gateway to the Point Reyes National Seashore and Tomales Bay. Point Reyes National Seashore offers over 70,000 acres of beaches, forests, trails, horseback riding, bird watching, majestic Tule Elk and unlimited spectacular scenery. It is the hub of West Marin County and is located only one hour from the Golden Gate Bridge and 45 minutes from Napa Valley. Though small in size, this town features a diverse and eclectic mixture of shops, restaurants, Saturday farmer's market, oysters and wine tasting near the inn. Luxury guest suites and rooms provide the utmost of upscale comfort and amenities. Tomales Bay is a mecca for small boats and sailboats, as well as a number of kayak touring companies.

Innkeeper(s): Bill Wigert. $165-195. 3 rooms with PB, 1 suite. Breakfast included in rates.

Certificate may be used: Anytime, excluding all holidays and weekends.

Sacramento

Inn and Spa at Parkside

2116 6th Street
Sacramento, CA 95818
(916)658-1818 (800)995-7275 Fax:(800)995-1809
Internet: www.innatparkside.com
E-mail: info@innatparkside.com

Circa 1936. Swedish, deep tissue, and hot stone massage are available at this mansion overlooking Southside Park. Indulge in a citrus body wrap at the spa and lounge in the courtyard. A Couples Retreat package is the ultimate in romance and relaxation. Add chocolate-covered strawberries, roses, or sparkling cider to any room as a special surprise. Choose a themed guest room named to reflect feelings. Soak in the Jacuzzi tub in Refresh, enjoy breathtaking views in Spirit, be playful in Kiss, or light candles in Passion. Snuggle in a robe and enjoy a two-course breakfast in bed. Join others for cheese and beverages in the main living room. Ask about the special for first-time guests. Walk to the Capitol Building, downtown, or historic Sacramento, California.

Innkeeper(s): Erin Tignor. $169-259. 11 rooms with PB, 7 with FP, 7 with WP.
Certificate may be used: January-December, Sunday-Thursday, subject to availability.

San Miguel

Work Family Guest Ranch

75893 Ranchita Canyon Rd
San Miguel, CA 93451
(805)467-3362
Internet: www.workranch.com
E-mail: info@workranch.com

Five generations' strong, starting with John Work in the late 1800s, this ranch in the Cholame Hills of Central California offers an authentic Western experience. Spread over 12,000 acres of impressive country, the rolling hills and expansive views are breathtaking. The Guest Cabin bunks eight and is fully equipped with kitchen and bath facilities or choose one of the guest bedrooms of the ranch house. Share delicious home-cooked meals with the Work family, and encounter the daily activities of cattle and grain farming. A guided trail ride on horseback (priced separately) is not to be missed.

Innkeeper(s): Elaine J. Work, Ben Work, Kelly Work. $175-225. 4 rooms, 2 with PB, 1 cottage, 1 guest house. Breakfast, dinner and Breakfast and dinner included in price. included in rates.
Certificate may be used: Anytime, subject to availability.

Santa Barbara

A White Jasmine Inn

1327 Bath St
Santa Barbara, CA 93101-3630
(805)966-0589
Internet: www.whitejasmineinnsantabarbara.com
E-mail: stay@whitejasmineinnsantabarbara.com

Circa 1885. A Craftsman Bungalow, Victorian Cottage and an Artisan Cottage comprise A White Jasmine Inn, located in the theatre and arts district of Santa Barbara, California.

Accommodations include guest rooms and elegant suites with antiques and rich wood trim. Some rooms also have fireplaces, mini refrigerators or whirlpools tubs. Each cottage has private gardens, but everyone is welcome in the main house common areas that include the parlor and secluded garden hot tub. Homemade breakfasts in a basket are delivered to each room. It's a three-block walk to restaurants, shops and the shuttle to the beach.

Innkeeper(s): Marlies Marburg, John Cicekli. $154-309. 12 rooms with PB, 12 with FP, 2 with HT, 8 with WP, 4 suites, 3 cottages. Breakfast, afternoon tea, snacks/refreshments, hors d'oeuvres, wine and Various treats included in rates. Types of meals: Full gourmet bkfst, veg bkfst, early coffee/tea, In-room, full and hot breakfast is standard. This may be taken in various other areas. Continental breakfast also available.

Certificate may be used: Sunday-Thursday, November-December and January-May, valid on rooms priced at $209 or higher. Excludes holiday weeks.

Cheshire Cat Inn & Spa

36 W Valerio St
Santa Barbara, CA 93101-2524
(805) 569-1610 Fax:(805)682-1876
Internet: www.cheshirecat.com
E-mail: cheshire@cheshirecat.com

Circa 1894. This elegant inn features three Queen Anne Victorians, a Coach House and three cottages surrounded by fountains, gazebos and lush flower gardens. The guest bedrooms and suites are furnished with English antiques, Laura Ashley fabrics and wallpapers or oak floors, pine furniture and down comforters. Some boast fireplaces, Jacuzzi tubs, private balconies, VCRs and refrigerators. Wedgewood china set in the formal dining room or brick patio enhances a delicious breakfast. Local wine and hors d'oeuvres are served in the evening. Spa facilities offer massage and body treatments.

Innkeeper(s): Connie, Bharti, Cynthia. $169-399. 18 rooms with PB, 3 with FP, 3 with HT, 4 two-bedroom suites, 4 cottages, 1 conference room. Breakfast, hors d'oeuvres and wine included in rates. Types of meals: Cont plus, early coffee/tea and room service.

Certificate may be used: Anytime, subject to availability.

The Country House

1323 De La Vina St
Santa Barbara, CA 93101-3120
(805) 962-0058 (800) 727-0876
Internet: www.countryhousesantabarbara.com
E-mail: innkeeper@uphamhotel.com

Circa 1898. Gracing Santa Ynez wine country in a picturesque Santa Barbara, California neighborhood, this classic Victorian features a steep front gable and Colonial diamond-paned bay windows. A veranda and balcony invite relaxation. Gather for afternoon wine and appetizers and indulge in homemade cookies in the evening. Romantic, upscale accommodations boast modern conveniences amid well-placed antique furnishings. Stay in a spacious guest room or the Penthouse Suite with a living room, fireplace, whirlpool tub, waterfall shower and private terrace. After breakfast, take a short walk to the theater district or browse through local shops. Several packages are available with a variety of activities included. Hop on the electric shuttle to savor the urban wine trail to sample the harvest from local vintners. Save time to take a day trip to tour the stunning Hearst Castle.

Innkeeper(s): Jan Martin Winn. $200-475. 8 rooms with PB, 5 with FP, 5 with WP. Breakfast, snacks/refreshments and wine included in rates. Types of meals: Full bkfst and early coffee/tea.

Certificate may be used: Sunday-Thursday, subject to availability. Not valid July and August. No holidays.

The Upham Hotel

1404 De La Vina St
Santa Barbara, CA 93101-3027
(805)962-0058 (800)727-0876 Fax:(805)963-2825
Internet: www.uphamhotel.com
E-mail: innkeeper@uphamhotel.com

Circa 1871. Antiques and period furnishings decorate each of the inn's guest rooms and suites. The inn is the oldest continu-

ously operating hostelry in Southern California. Situated on an acre of gardens in the center of downtown, it's within easy walking distance of restaurants, shops, art galleries and museums. The staff is happy to assist guests in discovering Santa Barbara's varied attractions. Garden cottage units feature porches or secluded patios and several have gas fireplaces.

Innkeeper(s): Jan Martin Winn. $235-475. 6 rooms, 50 with PB, 8 with FP, 1 with WP, 3 total suites, including 1 two-bedroom suite, 2 cottages, 3 conference rooms. Breakfast, snacks/refreshments and wine included in rates. Types of meals: Cont plus and early coffee/tea.

Certificate may be used: Sunday-Thursday, subject to availability.

Santa Cruz

Cliff Crest Bed & Breakfast Inn

407 Cliff St
Santa Cruz, CA 95060-5009
(831)427-2609 (831)252-1057 Fax:(831)427-2710
Internet: www.cliffcrestinn.com
E-mail: Innkpr@CliffCrestInn.com

Circa 1887. Warmth, friendliness and comfort characterize this elegantly restored Queen Anne Victorian home. An octagonal solari-

um, tall stained-glass windows, and a belvedere overlook Monterey Bay and the Santa Cruz Mountains. The mood is airy and romantic. The spacious gardens were designed by John McLaren, landscape architect for Golden Gate Park. Antiques and fresh flowers fill the rooms, once home to William Jeter, lieutenant governor of California.

Innkeeper(s): Constantin Gehriger, Adriana Gehriger Gil. $95-245. 6 rooms with PB, 2 with FP, 1 with HT, 1 four-bedroom suite, 1 guest house. Healthy full gourmet breakfast and everything made from scratch included in rates. Types of meals: Full gourmet bkfst, early coffee/tea and lunch/dinner events made to order.

Certificate may be used: Sunday-Thursday, subject to availability.

The Darling House A B&B Inn By The Sea

314 W Cliff Dr
Santa Cruz, CA 95060-6145
(831) 458-1958 Fax:(831)458-0320
Internet: www.darlinghouse.com
E-mail: info@darlinghouse.com

Circa 1911. Overlook the Monterey Bay while staying in lavish accommodations in Santa Cruz, California. Relax amid the peaceful elegance of this ocean-side inn with beveled glass, Tiffany lamps, open hearths and warm hearts. Verandas on the first and second floors are inviting sitting areas. Stay in a guest room that features a fireplace, antique furnishings, fresh flowers, an ice bucket, wine glasses, turndown service and other pampering amenities. Gather for a hearty breakfast then take an easy stroll to Lighthouse Point, Steamer Lane, Cowell's Beach and the Boardwalk. Ask about special packages that can include gourmet wine dinners and house concerts.

Innkeeper(s): Denise Darling. $195-225. 7 rooms. Breakfast included in rates. Types of meals: Cont plus.

Certificate may be used: Sunday-Thursday, Oct. 15-May 15, excluding Dec. 23-Jan. 2 and holidays.

West Cliff Inn

174 West Cliff Drive
Santa Cruz, CA 95060
(831)457-2200 (800)979-0910 Fax:(831)457-2221
Internet: www.westcliffinn.com
E-mail: westcliffinn@foursisters.com

Circa 1877. Boasting seaside serenity in Santa Cruz, California, West Cliff Inn sits on a bluff across from the beach. Originally built in 1877 as a private home, this renovated and stately three-story Victorian Italianate has become a Four Sisters Inn. The coastal decor is inviting with a clean and fresh ambiance. Feel the ocean breeze while relaxing on the wraparound porch. Gather for afternoon wine and appetizers. Stay in a guest bedroom with a marble tile bathroom, fireplace and jetted spa tub. A second-story room boasts a private outdoor hot tub and the two top-floor suites include sitting areas. Breakfast is a satisfying way to begin each day's adventures. Explore the local surfing museum or hit the waves and hang ten. Stroll along the famous beach boardwalk. Seasonal packages are offered.

$195-400. 9 rooms with PB, 9 with FP. Breakfast, afternoon tea, snacks/refreshments, wine and Afternoon wine and Hors d'oeuvres included in rates. Types of meals: Full gourmet bkfst and hors d'oeuvres.

Certificate may be used: Sunday-Thursday, December-February, based on promotional discount availability and excludes special event periods, holidays and certain room types. First night must be at full rack rate to receive second night free.

Santa Rosa

Melitta Station Inn

5850 Melitta Rd
Santa Rosa, CA 95409-5641
(707)538-7712 (800)504-3099
Internet: www.melittastationinn.com
E-mail: info@melittastationinn.com

Circa 1885. Originally built as a stagecoach stop, this inn was

the focus for the little town of Melitta. Still located down a country lane with walk-in access to a state park, the station has been charmingly renovated. Oiled-wood floors, a rough-beam cathedral ceiling and French doors opening to a balcony are features of the sitting room. Upon arrival, enjoy English tea and homemade scones. Three inviting guest bedrooms feature antique clawfoot tubs. Linger over a hearty country breakfast in the great room. Wineries and vineyards stretch from the inn to the town of Sonoma. Basalt stone, quarried from nearby hills, was sent by rail to San Francisco where it was used to pave the cobblestone streets.

Innkeeper(s): Jackie Thresh, Tim Thresh. $149-219. 6 rooms with PB, 1 two-bedroom suite, 1 conference room. Breakfast, afternoon tea, snacks/refreshments, Full gourmet 3-course cooked breakfast and complimentary water and sodas included in rates. Types of meals: Full gourmet bkfst, veg bkfst, early coffee/tea and Complimentary water/sodas.

Certificate may be used: Monday-Thursday, November-April, excludes holidays.

Sonoma

Inn at Sonoma

630 Broadway
Sonoma, CA 95476
(707)939-1340 (888)568-9818 Fax:(707)939-8834
Internet: www.innatsonoma.com
E-mail: innatsonoma@foursisters.com

Circa 2002. Located within walking distance to the historic Sonoma Plaza, this delightful new inn is sure to please. Inn at Sonoma reflects a casual California decor. The well-furnished guest bedrooms feature fireplaces and some offer private balconies. Start the day with a sumptuous breakfast then grab a bicycle to explore the local area. Hors d'oeuvres and afternoon wine are a welcome respite, and the rooftop Jacuzzi is a soothing relaxer. Take time to tour the nearby wineries of Somona and Napa Valley in the wine country of Northern California.

Innkeeper(s): Rachel Retterer. $205-300. 19 rooms with PB, 19 with FP. Breakfast, snacks/refreshments and Afternoon wine included in rates. Types of meals: Full bkfst, early coffee/tea and Afternoon wine.

Certificate may be used: Sunday-Thursday, December-February, based on promotional discount availability and excludes special event periods, holidays and certain room types. First night must be at full rack rate to receive second night free.

South Pasadena

Bissell House

201 Orange Grove Ave
South Pasadena, CA 91030-1613
(626) 441-3535
Internet: www.bissellhouse.com

Circa 1887. Adorning famous Orange Grove Avenue on historic Millionaire's Row, this restored three-story Victorian mansion is a cultural landmark that offers an elegant ambiance and inviting hospitality. Spacious guest bedrooms feature antique furnishings, tasteful decor and modern conveniences that include DSL. Linger over a scrumptious full breakfast in the formal dining room served with crystal glassware, vintage silver

and fresh flowers. Apricot bread pudding, egg strata, ginger scones, creme brulee and lemon souffle French toast are some of the popular specialties. Swim in the pool surrounded by lush foliage or relax in the gorgeous English garden. Visit nearby Old Town Pasadena with a small-town atmosphere and big-city entertainment, boutiques, and upscale restaurants.

Innkeeper(s): Janet Hoyman . $159-350. 7 rooms with PB, 1 with WP. Breakfast, afternoon tea and snacks/refreshments included in rates. Types of meals: Full gourmet bkfst, veg bkfst, early coffee/tea and 24 hour tea table with afternoon dessert.

Certificate may be used: Last minute availability, excludes weekends and Dec. 15-Jan. 15.

Sutter Creek

Grey Gables B&B Inn

161 Hanford St
Sutter Creek, CA 95685-1687
(209)267-1039 (800)473-9422
Internet: www.greygables.com
E-mail: reservations@greygables.com

Circa 1897. The innkeepers of this Victorian home offer poetic accommodations both in the delightful decor and by the names  of their guest rooms. The Keats, Bronte and Tennyson rooms afford garden views, while the Byron and Browning rooms include clawfoot tubs. The Victorian Suite, which encompasses the top floor, affords views of the garden, as well as a historic churchyard. All of the guest rooms boast fireplaces. Stroll down brick pathways through the terraced garden or relax in the parlor. A proper English tea is served with cakes and scones. Hors d'oeuvres and libations are served in the evenings.

Innkeeper(s): Roger Garlick, Susan Garlick. $153-236. 8 rooms with PB, 8 with FP. Breakfast, afternoon tea, hors d'oeuvres and wine included in rates. Types of meals: Full gourmet bkfst, veg bkfst and early coffee/tea.

Certificate may be used: Sunday-Thursday, excludes all holidays, some black-out dates.

Templeton

Bike Lane Inn

749 Gough Ave.
Templeton, CA 93465
(805)434-0409
Internet: www.bikelaneinn.com/
E-mail: info@bikelaneinn.com

Cycle to wineries while staying at this inn, a perfect starting point for exploring the picturesque vineyards of Paso Robles and Templeton, California. Walk around town, enjoy the view, and relax amid the quiet residential setting just two blocks from the park where a weekly farmer's market is held. Comfortable second-floor accommodations include Wifi, a local newspaper, DVD library and iPod docking stations. Savor a satisfying homemade breakfast before embarking on the day's adventures. Relax on the patio or play a game in the fireside lounge. Indulge in a day of pampering at a nearby spa or salon. RV parking is available.

Innkeeper(s): Scott McElmury, Elaine McElmury. $89-99. Call inn for details.

Certificate may be used: January-March, Monday-Wednesday only.

Carriage Vineyards Bed and Breakfast

4337 S. El Pomar Road
Templeton, CA 93465
(805) 227-6807 (800) 617-7911 Fax:(805)226-9969
Internet: www.carriagevineyards.com
E-mail: Stay@CarriageVineyards.com

Circa 1995. Named after the owners' horse-drawn carriage collection, this 100-acre ranch is tucked away in the country of the Central Coast. Enjoy vineyards, orchards, pastures, gardens and a creek. Hike the hillsides to be immersed in the peaceful scenery of the area. Tastefully decorated guest bedrooms are furnished with well-placed antiques. The Victoria Room is a second-story master suite featuring an oversize shower and Jacuzzi tub for two. Savor a hot gourmet breakfast served daily. Overnight horse facilities are available.

Innkeeper(s): Larry Smyth. $140-230. 4 rooms with PB, 2 with WP. Breakfast included in rates. Types of meals: Full gourmet bkfst, veg bkfst, early coffee/tea, afternoon tea and snacks/refreshments.

Certificate may be used: Sunday-Thursday excludes holidays and the months of May and October. No other discounts, Please make reservations online.

Ukiah

Vichy Hot Springs Resort & Inn

2605 Vichy Springs Rd
Ukiah, CA 95482-3507
(707)462-9515 Fax:(707)462-9516
Internet: www.vichysprings.com
E-mail: vichy@vichysprings.com

Circa 1854. This famous spa, now a California State Historical Landmark (#980), once attracted guests Jack London, Mark Twain, Robert Louis Stevenson, Ulysses Grant and Teddy Roosevelt. Eighteen rooms and eight cottages comprise the property. Some of the cottages are historic and some are new. The 1860s naturally warm and carbonated mineral baths remain unchanged. A hot soaking pool and historic Olympic-size pool await your arrival. A magical waterfall is a 30-minute walk along a year-round stream.

Innkeeper(s): Gilbert Ashoff, Marjorie Ashoff. $195-390. 26 rooms with PB, 8 with FP, 1 suite, 8 cottages, 3 conference rooms. Breakfast and Sunday brunch included in rates. Types of meals: Country bkfst.

Certificate may be used: Sunday-Thursday; April-September, Sunday-Friday; October-March, excludes holidays.

Westport

Howard Creek Ranch

40501 N Hwy One
Westport, CA 95488
(707)964-6725 Fax:(707)964-1603
Internet: www.howardcreekranch.com
E-mail: Please Call 707-964-6725

Circa 1871. First settled as a land grant of thousands of acres, Howard Creek Ranch in Westport, California is now a 60-acre farm with sweeping views of the Pacific Ocean, sandy beaches and rolling mountains. A 75-foot bridge spans a creek that

flows past barns and outbuildings to the beach 200 yards away. The farmhouse is surrounded by green lawns, an award-winning flower garden, and grazing cows, horses and llama. This rustic rural location offers antiques, a hot tub, sauna and heated pool. A traditional ranch breakfast is served each morning.

Innkeeper(s): Charles Grigg, Sally Grigg. $105-198. 13 rooms with PB, 13 with FP, 2 suites, 3 cabins. Breakfast included in rates. Types of meals: Country bkfst and early coffee/tea.

Certificate may be used: Oct. 15-May 15, Sunday-Thursday, excluding holiday periods. (coupons good only in certain rooms).

Woodlake

Wicky-Up Ranch B&B

22702 Avenue 344
Woodlake, CA 93286
(559)564-8898 Fax:(559)564-3981
Internet: www.wickyup.com
E-mail: innkeeper@wickyup.com

Circa 1902. Surrounded by 20 acres of organic orange groves, this turn-of-the-century Craftsman-style home was built by President Warren Harding's family. Now five generations strong, the historical integrity has been preserved. Treasures that include heirlooms, antiques, Oriental rugs and fine arts are cherished and shared. Experience a slower pace of living while here, whether staying in one of the beautifully appointed guest bedrooms or the private country cottage. French toast naranjo, Mexican souffle, omelettes and pancakes are some of the hearty breakfast specialties served. Relax on the wraparound veranda or the Sunset Deck. A stroll through the many gardens with fountains and cooing doves imparts a peaceful tranquility.

Innkeeper(s): Monica R. Pizura, Jack Pizura. $90-150. 3 rooms, 2 with PB, 1 two-bedroom suite, 1 cottage, 1 conference room. Breakfast included in rates. Types of meals: Full gourmet bkfst, veg bkfst and afternoon tea.

Certificate may be used: November-March, Sunday-Thursday except holidays.

Yountville

Lavender

2020 Webber Ave
Yountville, CA 94599
(707) 944-1388 (800) 522-4140 Fax:(707)944-1579
Internet: www.lavendernapa.com
E-mail: lavender@foursisters.com

Circa 1999. Stroll through lavender and flower gardens or relax on the veranda of this French farmhouse located in California's Napa Valley wine country. Privacy and elegant country comfort are the order of the day in guest bedrooms decorated in bold natural colors. Each cottage boasts a private entrance, patio and two-person bathtubs. The farm breakfast is an all-you-can-eat buffet with a variety of courses sure to please the most discriminating palate. Gather for afternoon teatime with wine, cheese, crackers and baked goods. Walk through the small town of Yountville with vintage 1870 shopping center, cafes and historic residential homes. Check out a bicycle and explore the area. Take the Wine Train tour and visit nearby Calistoga.

Innkeeper(s): Gina Massolo. $225-325. 8 rooms with PB, 8 with FP, 3 with HT, 3 with WP, 6 cottages. Breakfast, hors d'oeuvres and wine included in rates. Types of meals: Full bkfst and early coffee/tea.

Certificate may be used: Sunday-Thursday, December-February, based on promotional discount availability and excludes special event periods, holidays and certain room types. First night must be at full rack rate.

Maison Fleurie

6529 Yount St
Yountville, CA 94599-1278
(707)944-2056 (800)788-0369 Fax:(707)944-9342
Internet: www.maisonfleurienapa.com
E-mail: maisonfleurie@foursisters.com

Circa 1894. Vines cover the two-foot thick brick walls of the Bakery, Carriage House and the Main House of this French country inn. One of the Four Sisters Inns, it is reminiscent of a bucolic setting in Provence. Guest bedrooms are decorated in a warm, romantic style, some with vineyard and garden views. Accommodations in the Old Bakery have fireplaces. After a satisfying breakfast go for a swim in the pool and soak in the outdoor hot tub. Bicycles are available for wandering the surrounding countryside. In the evenings, wine and hors d'oeuvres are served. Yountville, just north of Napa, California, offers close access to the multitude of wineries and vineyards in the valley.

Innkeeper(s): Gina Massolo. $235-300. 13 rooms with PB, 7 with FP, 7 with WP. Breakfast, afternoon tea and wine included in rates. Types of meals: Full gourmet bkfst.

Certificate may be used: Sunday-Thursday, December-February, based on promotional discount availability and excludes special event periods, holidays and certain room types. First night must be at full rack rate to receive second night free.

Colorado

Avon

West Beaver Creek Lodge

220 W Beaver Creek Blvd
Avon, CO 81620
(970)949-9073 (888)795-1061
Internet: wbclodge.com
E-mail: info@wbclodge.com

Circa 1996. Feel rejuvenated by the personalized service and award-winning accommodations at the newly built West Beaver Creek Lodge in picturesque Vail Valley in Avon, Colorado. Relax on the patio or deck with complimentary snacks and beverages or soak in the hot tub. Watch a movie in the lounge area, read in the loft, play a game of pool or sit by the fire in the Great Room. Contemporary Western-style decor and furnishings accent the guest bedrooms and suites. Indulge in a healthy, hearty breakfast each morning. Concierge services, laundry facilities, ski equipment storage and discount lift tickets are available. A shuttle to Beaver Creek or Vail leaves just outside the front door every 20 minutes.

Innkeeper(s): Bob Borg, Terry Borg. $99-129. 9 rooms with PB. Breakfast and snacks/refreshments included in rates. Types of meals: Full bkfst and All-day coffee/tea/cocoa.

Certificate may be used: April-June and Oct. 1-Dec.15, subject to availability.

Bennett

Willow Tree Country Inn

49990 E. 64th Ave.
Bennett, CO 80102
(303)644-5551 (800)257-1241 Fax:(303)644-3801
Internet: www.willowtreebb.com
E-mail: willowtreeinn@tds.net

Circa 1920. A peaceful setting permeates this English Tudor inn that sits on 60 acres with magnificent views of the Rocky Mountains. The country decor and antique furnishings are tastefully blended in an uncluttered and inviting way. Enjoy a light supper upon arrival. Watch a glorious sunset from the large covered porch. Read in the sunroom or watch a video by the fire in the parlor. Delightful guest bedrooms boast snow-capped mountain vistas, robes, slippers, a snack basket and a stocked refrigerator. Feel pampered with a complimentary hydrotherapy foot bath and herbal foot massage. Breakfast in the dining room may start with just-baked cinnamon rolls, a fruit plate and green chili strata. Soak in the hot tub after playing croquet, badminton or horseshoes.

Innkeeper(s): Deborah Toczek, Gerald Toczek. $69-139. 3 rooms with PB. Breakfast, afternoon tea, snacks/refreshments and dinner included in rates.

Types of meals: Full gourmet bkfst, veg bkfst, early coffee/tea and room service.
Certificate may be used: Anytime, subject to availability.

Carbondale

Ambiance Inn

66 N 2nd St
Carbondale, CO 81623-2102
(970)963-3597 (800)350-1515 Fax:(970)963-1360
Internet: www.ambianceinn.com
E-mail: ambiancein@aol.com

Located in the gorgeous Crystal Valley between Aspen and Glenwood Springs, this contemporary chalet-style home offers all-season accommodations for a wonderful getaway. Relax with one of the books or magazines in the second-floor New Orleans Library, or plan the next day's activities. Themed guest bedrooms include sitting areas and soft robes. The Aspen Suite features a ski lodge decor with knotty pine paneling and snow-shoes hung on the walls. It is the perfect size for two couples or a large family traveling together. In the morning, savor a lavish breakfast at the oak table in the dining room before exploring the scenic area.

Innkeeper(s): Norma Morris, Robert Morris. Call for rates. 5 rooms. Breakfast included in rates. Types of meals: Full gourmet bkfst, veg bkfst, early coffee/tea and gourmet lunch.

Certificate may be used: Excludes holidays, Christmas week and peak summer weekends.

Colorado Springs

Black Forest B&B Lodge & Cabins

11170 Black Forest Rd
Colorado Springs, CO 80908-3986
(719)495-4208 (800)809-9901 Fax:(719)495-0688
Internet: www.blackforestbb.com
E-mail: blackforestbb@msn.com

Circa 1984. Surrounded by the scenic beauty of the Pikes Peak region of Colorado, Black Forest Bed and Breakfast Lodge and Cabins in Colorado Springs sits at the highest point east of the Rocky Mountains. Ponderosa Pines, golden Aspens and fragrant meadows highlight the 20 scenic acres that boast panoramic views. The rustic mountain setting includes a log pavilion and cabins. Stay in a guest bedroom or suite with a stocked kitchen or kitchenette, fireplace, and whirlpool tub. Select a movie to watch from the video collection. A breakfast tray is delivered to the room each morning. There is an abundance of outdoor activities to enjoy in the area.

Innkeeper(s): Susan Redden. $75-350. 7 rooms with PB, 4 with FP, 1 with WP, 2 two-bedroom, 1 three-bedroom and 1 four-bedroom suites, 1 guest house, 2 cabins, 2 conference rooms. Breakfast and snacks/refreshments included in rates. Types of meals: Cont plus, early coffee/tea, All rooms have full kitchens or kitchenettes stocked with, coffee/tea/milk/cocoa/juice, cereals/oatmeal and microwave popcorn.

Certificate may be used: Anytime, subject to availability.

Holden House-1902 Bed & Breakfast Inn

1102 W Pikes Peak Avenue
Colorado Springs, CO 80904-4347
(719) 471-3980 (888) 565-3980 Fax:(719) 471-4740
Internet: www.HoldenHouse.com
E-mail: mail@HoldenHouse.com

Circa 1902. Built by the widow of a prosperous rancher and businessman, this Victorian inn has rooms named after the Colorado towns in which the Holden's owned mining interests.

The main house, adjacent carriage house and Victorian house next door include the Cripple Creek, Aspen, Silverton, Goldfield and Independence suites. The inn's suites boast fireplaces and oversized tubs for two. Guests can relax in the living room with fireplace, front parlor, veranda with mountain views or garden with gazebo and fountains. There are friendly cats in residence.

Innkeeper(s): Sallie & Welling Clark. $145-160. 7 rooms, 5 with PB, 5 with FP, 5 suites. Breakfast, snacks/refreshments, hors d'oeuvres and wine included in rates. Types of meals: Full gourmet bkfst, veg bkfst, early coffee/tea, afternoon tea and Breakfast ensuite for additional $15 charge.

Certificate may be used: Oct. 15-April 30, Sunday-Thursday, excludes holidays.

Old Town GuestHouse

115 S 26th St
Colorado Springs, CO 80904
(719)632-9194 (888)375-4210 Fax:(719)632-9026
Internet: www.oldtown-guesthouse.com
E-mail: luxury@oldtown-guesthouse.com

Circa 1997. Serving as the gateway to Old Colorado City, this recently built urban inn is surrounded by galleries, boutiques and restaurants. The three-story brick Federal-style design is in keeping with the 1859 period architecture of the historic area. Enjoy the breathtaking views of Pike's Peak and Garden of the Gods. It is entirely handicap accessible, soundproof, has an elevator, sprinklers and a security system, and boasts a four-diamond rating. International videoconferencing is available with WIFI 802.11 wireless fidelity hot spot. Play pool or work out on equipment in the game room and plan to join the innkeepers for a daily social hour. Elegant guest bedrooms are named after flowers and offer luxurious comfort with fireplaces, steam showers or hot tubs on private porches. Linger over breakfast in the indoor/outdoor fireside dining room.

Innkeeper(s): Shirley & Don Wick. $99-215. 8 rooms with PB, 5 with FP, 4 with HT, 1 two-bedroom suite, 1 conference room. Breakfast and snacks/refreshments included in rates. Types of meals: Full bkfst, early coffee/tea and evening reception with wine/beer/sodas/snacks.

Certificate may be used: Last minute subject to availability, not valid Fridays.

Empire

Mad Creek B&B

167 Park Avenue
Empire, CO 80438-0404
(303) 569-2003
Internet: www.madcreekbnb.net
E-mail: madmadam@aol.com

Circa 1881. There is just the right combination of Victorian dÃ©cor with lace, flowers, antiques and gingerbread trim on the facade of this mountain town cottage. The home-away-from-home atmosphere is inviting and the Eastlake furnishings comfortable. Relax in front of the rock fireplace while watching a movie, peruse the library filled with local lore, or plan an adventure with local maps and guide books. Empire was once a mining town, conveniently located within 20 to 60 minutes of at least six major ski areas.

Innkeeper(s): Myrna Payne. $85-105. 3 rooms with PB. Breakfast, afternoon tea, snacks/refreshments and Full breakfast at your choice of time. We cater to special needs included in rates. Types of meals: Full bkfst and early coffee/tea.

Certificate may be used: Oct. 15-Nov. 20, Sunday-Thursday; April 16-May 20, Sunday-Thursday.

The Peck House

83 Sunny Ave.
Empire, CO 80438-0428
(303)569-9870 Fax:(303)569-2743
Internet: www.thepeckhouse.com
E-mail: thepeckhouse@yahoo.com

Circa 1862. Built as a residence for gold mine owner James Peck, this is the oldest hotel still in operation in Colorado. Many pieces of original furniture brought here by ox cart remain in the inn, including a red antique fainting couch and walnut headboards. Rooms such as the Conservatory provide magnificent views of the eastern slope of the Rockies, and a panoramic view of Empire Valley can be seen from the old front porch.

Innkeeper(s): Gary & Sally St. Clair. $75-135. 11 rooms, 9 with PB, 1 suite. Breakfast included in rates. Types of meals: Cont, hors d'oeuvres, wine and gourmet dinner. Restaurant on premises.

Certificate may be used: January-May and October-November, Sunday-Thursday, subject to availability.

Estes Park

Romantic RiverSong Inn

1766 Lower Broadview Rd
Estes Park, CO 80517
(970) 586-4666
Internet: www.romanticriversong.com
E-mail: theromantictraveler@gmail.com

Circa 1928. This Craftsman-style country inn sits on a private wildlife habitat of 27 acres adjacent to Rocky Mountain National Park. Each of the enchanting guest bedrooms, appropriately named after ten local wildflowers, exudes a romantic charm. They all feature fireplaces, large antique, jetted, sunken or whirlpool tubs and unique showers such as a rock wall waterfall and a rooftop shower for two. Stargaze through skylights, and enjoy spectacular views from private decks. Start the day with RiverSong coffee or Mexican hot chocolate. A generous breakfast includes a fruit starter, a savory, potato or sweet main entree, and perhaps John Wayne casserole with sour cream peach muffins. Outdoors, the breath-taking scenery is enhanced by extensive varieties of birds, trout streams and deer. Close by are some of the nation's best hiking and snowshoeing trails. RiverSong's forte is offering fantastic wedding packages.

Innkeeper(s): Gary. $165-350. 10 rooms with PB, 10 with FP, 6 with WP, 9 suites, 6 cottages. Breakfast, afternoon tea and snacks/refreshments included in rates. Types of meals: Full gourmet bkfst, veg bkfst, early coffee/tea, picnic lunch, dinner and room service.

Certificate may be used: Oct. 25-April 1 on Mondays, Tuesdays, and Wednesdays only. Holidays excluded subject to availability.

Evergreen

Highland Haven Creekside Inn

4395 Independence Trail
Evergreen, CO 80439
(303)674-3577 (800)459-2406 Fax:(303)674-9088
Internet: www.highlandhaven.com
E-mail: info@highlandhaven.com

Circa 1884. Feel rejuvenated at this classic Colorado style inn situated just 30 miles west of Denver in the foothills of the Rocky Mountains. Winner of the iLoveInns.com Top 10 Romantic Inns of 2009, Highland Haven Creekside Inn borders Bear Creek and is accented with blue spruce and columbine. Guest bedrooms, suites and cottages feature a casual elegance, mountain ambiance and intimate balance of romance and professionalism. Select from accommodations with a private entrance, whirlpool tub, fireplace, walk-out balcony or secluded deck. A hearty breakfast is served in the historic Dailey Cabin, a restored log structure from 1884. Nearby Evergreen Lake offers boating or winter ice skating. Visit Creekside Cellars, the local winery or Tall Grass, the day spa. Browse through art galleries, museums and eclectic shops in nearby downtown.

Innkeeper(s): Blake & Roxy. $155-550. 17 rooms, 18 with PB, 10 with FP, 3 with WP, 4 with HT, 7 two-bedroom suites, 5 cottages, 2 conference rooms. Breakfast included in rates. Types of meals: Full bkfst and Friday night Port Night.

Certificate may be used: January-May 19, Sunday-Thursday only in rooms $290 and above in price, Excludes Tree House.

Manitou Springs

Avenue Hotel, A Victorian B&B

711 Manitou Ave
Manitou Springs, CO 80829-1809
(719) 685-1277 (800) 294-1277
Internet: www.AvenueHotelBandB.com
E-mail: info@avenuehotelbandb.com

Circa 1886. Sitting on a hillside with a terraced back garden and scenic views of Pikes Peak, this historic Queen Anne Victorian has been recently renovated to offer the utmost of modern comfort and vintage style. A parlor and fireside living room grace either side of the three-story turned staircase which leads to spacious guest rooms and two-room suites. Many include an antique clawfoot tub and

shower. Private accommodations in the two-level Carriage House feature fully equipped kitchens and are ideal for longer visits, business travel or romantic getaways. The secluded garden-level bungalow is ideal for families. Hosts Gwenn and Randy generously provide thoughtful amenities that make each stay a pampering delight. A hot beverage area with muffins and fresh cookies, and a snack station with a refrigerator stocked with bottled water enhance the relaxed setting. Savor a hearty breakfast in the dining room and feel satisfied until dinner time. Explore the picturesque area then soak in the hot tub on the patio. Spa services can be scheduled in advance.

Innkeeper(s): Gwenn David. $95-145. 9 rooms, 7 with PB, 3 with FP, 3 total suites, including 2 two-bedroom suites, 2 cottages. Breakfast, snacks/refreshments and wine included in rates. Types of meals: Full bkfst, veg bkfst, early coffee/tea and hors d'oeuvres.

Certificate may be used: Nov. 1 to April 30, Sunday-Thursday, excluding holidays and special events.

Pagosa Springs

Canyon Crest Lodge

580 Yeoman Dr
Pagosa Springs, CO 81147
(970) 731-3773 Fax:(970)731-5502
Internet: www.canyoncrestpagosa.com
E-mail: canyoncrest@pagosa.net

Circa 1999. Canyon Crest Lodge sits on 35 acres of tall pine trees and mountainous rocky terrain with magnificent views of America's newest National Monument "Chimney Rock," Pagosa Peak and the Mountains of the Great Divide. This English Country House is a traditional rock structure with 18-inch thick walls. Guest suites are named after famous castles, and can be accessed from inside or from the private upper deck. Each suite includes a comfortable sitting area with a TV and a walk-in closet. There are also three Barn Studio Units set apart from the Lodge. Breakfast for Lodge guests is served in the dining room and other meals can be arranged in advance. Be sure to set aside time to gather by the large fireplace in the lounge and enjoy the relaxing ambiance.

Innkeeper(s): Valerie Green. $65-200. 6 rooms, 1 with FP, 6 suites, 1 conference room. Breakfast and wine included in rates. Types of meals: Country bkfst, veg bkfst, early coffee/tea, picnic lunch, afternoon tea, gourmet dinner and room service.

Certificate may be used: January-May, excludes holidays, subject to availability.

Paonia

The Bross Hotel B&B

312 Onarga Ave.
Paonia, CO 81428
(970) 527-6776 Fax:(970)527-7737
Internet: www.paonia-inn.com
E-mail: brosshotel@paonia.com

Circa 1906. This turn-of-the-century western hotel was restored to its original splendor with a front porch and balcony while being updated with late-century amenities in the mid-1990s. Wood floors and trim, dormer windows and exposed brick walls all add to the Victorian decor. For pleasure, relax in the sitting area or library/TV/game room. A conference room and communications center is perfect for business. Guest bedrooms feature antiques and handmade quilts. Some rooms can be adjoined into suites. Breakfast is an adventure in seasonal culinary delights that cover the antique back bar in the dining room. Visit Black Canyon of the Gunnison National Park, Grand Mesa, West Elk and Ragged Wilderness areas and Fort Uncompaghre-a Living History Museum.

Innkeeper(s): Linda Lentz. $125-145. 10 rooms with PB, 1 conference room. Breakfast included in rates. Types of meals: Full gourmet bkfst, veg bkfst and early coffee/tea.

Certificate may be used: November-March, subject to availability or anytime, at the last minute.

Red Feather Lakes

Sundance Trail Guest Ranch

17931 Red Feather Lakes Rd
Red Feather Lakes, CO 80545-9410
(970)224-1222 (800)357-4930 Fax:(970)224-1222
Internet: www.sundancetrail.com
E-mail: ride@sundancetrail.com

Circa 1965. Granite outcroppings, whispering aspens, stately pines, open meadows and breathtaking mountain vistas are found in the Roosevelt National Forest, only two hours from Denver International Airport. This dude ranch in the summer and mountain lodge country inn the rest of the months, boasts horseback riding and hiking year round. Fishing, rock climbing, white-water rafting, evening campfires and other summer activities are planned every two hours. Off season means horseback riding and romantic tranquility. The dining room and parlor have rock fireplaces. Decks invite stargazing or breathing the fresh morning air, coffee in hand. Cabins and suites boast private entrances, decks, refrigerators, coffee makers and hair dryers among other amenities. The recreation barn is always open with a Jacuzzi, billiards, foosball table and board games. No television and no cell phone service equal an escape from stress.

Innkeeper(s): Dan Morin, Ellen Morin. $149-219. 7 rooms, 1 with FP, 7 total suites, including 3 two-bedroom suites and 1 three-bedroom suite, 3 cabins, 1 conference room. Breakfast, lunch, snacks/refreshments and dinner included in rates. Types of meals: Country bkfst and veg bkfst.

Certificate may be used: November-March, except during Christmas holiday.

Steamboat Springs

Alpine Rose B&B

724 Grand St
Steamboat Springs, CO 80477
(970)879-1528 Fax:(970)879-4976
Internet: www.alpinerosesteamboat.com
E-mail: bnb@alpinerosesteamboat.com

Providing the perfect setting for a mountain vacation, this elegant three-story contemporary home sits in the historic Olde Town district of Steamboat Springs, Colorado. Relax and soak up the view on the redwood deck or sit in the hot tub that overlooks Strawberry Park. Watch a movie in the upstairs living room or downstairs hearth room. Stay in a comfortable guest suite or room with pleasing amenities. Wake up and savor a gourmet breakfast of house specialties served in the sunny dining room. Take a leisurely walk to downtown. A world-class ski resort is just two miles away. The scenic area offers many activities.

Innkeeper(s): Bob Riley, Jo Riley. Call for rates. 5 rooms, 3 with PB.

Breakfast included in rates. Types of meals: Full gourmet bkfst, veg bkfst, early coffee/tea and gourmet dinner.

Certificate may be used: April-June, Sunday-Thursday, excluding holidays, subject to availability.

Woodland Park

Bristlecone Lodge

510 N. Hwy 67
Woodland Park, CO 80863
(719)687-9518
Internet: www.bristleconebb.com/
E-mail: BristleconeLodge@gmail.com

Circa 1995. Spread out in a private cabin with a living room, kitchenette, and separate bedroom. Sleep easy on a king or queen-size bed in an airy room with vaulted ceilings. Another couple or kids can use the comfortable queen-size futon in the living room. Sally's Cabin has two bedrooms and can sleep seven people. Two permanently placed camper rentals are also available. Don't let the name "cabin" fool you; there is wireless Internet and cable television and cool mountain air and ceiling fans keep the cabins at a comfortable temperature. There is space for 44 RVs in the attached resort. Downtown Woodland Park is within walking distance. Start the day with waffles in the main lodge, then cook your favorite lunch or dinner on the charcoal grill. Spend the day hiking or skiing and finish the day with a soak in the hot tub under the stars. Reserve all of the cabins for a class reunion and use the large message board to keep activities organized.

Innkeeper(s): Joyce Mehlhaff, Ivan Mehlhaff. $89-150. 8 cabins, 8 suites. Breakfast included in rates.

Certificate may be used: First two weeks in June.

Connecticut

Haddam

Nehemiah Brainerd House B&B

988 Saybrook Rd.
Haddam, CT 06438
(860)345-8605 Fax:(860)345-8879
Internet: www.brainerdhousebb.com
E-mail: innkeeper@brainerdhousebb.com

Look out over the bluff to the Connecticut River from this historic home in Haddam, Connecticut. Fully restored in 2002, it has been featured on "If Walls Could Talk" on HGTV. The Library Suite has built-in bookcases and a queen-size four-poster bed. Walk up the maroon carpeted stairs to the soothing green Victorian Room and romantic Toile Room. Stay in the private Laurel Cottage with river views all year long. Play the baby grand piano in the parlor or watch the boats from the porch. A country breakfast is served in the dining room. Sample wines at the 19 vineyards along the Connecticut Wine Trail. Buy tickets for an evening production or simply tour the Goodspeed Opera House. Wander the halls of the 24-room medievel-style Gillette Castle.

Innkeeper(s): Maryan Muthersbaugh, Jeff Muthersbaugh. $140-200. 4 rooms, 5 with PB, 1 with FP, 1 two-bedroom suite, 1 cottage.

Certificate may be used: Sunday-Thursday, February-March, subject to availability, excluding holidays.

Lakeville

A Meadow House

67 White Hollow Road
Lakeville, CT 06039
(860)248-1799
Internet: www.ameadowhouse.com
E-mail: tr7terry@hotmail.com

Circa 1840. Built in 1850, this historic country farmhouse offers scenic privacy across from Lime Rock Park. Relax on white wicker chairs that surround the fire pit, nap in the hammock for two, soak in the hot tub under the stars, hike on the trails and sled down the hillside. A Meadow House offers many year-round activities in the picturesque location of Lakeville, Connecticut. Wake up to a continental breakfast after a good night's rest, or feel right at home in the kitchen if cooking is a favorite pastime. Warm and inviting, feel free to do as much or as little as desired at this bed and breakfast inn.

Innkeeper(s): Therese A. (Terry) Dunne. $30-90. 3 rooms, 2 with PB, 1 two-bedroom suite. Types of meals: Cont.

Certificate may be used: Anytime, excluding five main auto racing weekends. (call to inquire when those are).

Madison

Tidewater Inn

949 Boston Post Road
Madison, CT 06443-3236
(203)245-8457 Fax:(203)318-0265
Internet: www.TheTidewater.com
E-mail: escape@thetidewater.com

Circa 1900. Experience the pleasures of coastal living at this recently renovated French farmhouse-style inn with comfortable yet elegant antiques and estate furnishings from the 1930s. A beamed sitting room features a large fireplace. Guest bedrooms boast floral wallpaper, four-poster or canopy beds. The Cottage suite also offers a sitting room, Jacuzzi for two, refrigerator, VCR and private patio. Favorite breakfast items include a melon boat, California egg puff, tomato salad, bacon, apple coffee cake and Top of the Mountain French toast with sausages and maple syrup. Appreciate the two nicely landscaped acres from backyard Adirondack chairs, front porch rockers or under an umbrella in the English garden.

Innkeeper(s): Victoria Kolyvas. $100-300. 9 rooms with PB, 2 with FP. Breakfast, afternoon tea and snacks/refreshments included in rates. Types of meals: Full gourmet bkfst and early coffee/tea.

Certificate may be used: Sunday-Thursday, November-April, excludes Curtis Cottage Suite, Madison Suite and holidays.

Mystic

The Whaler's Inn

20 E Main St
Mystic, CT 06355-2646
(860) 536-1506 Fax:(860)572-1250
Internet: www.whalersinnmystic.com
E-mail: sales@whalersinnmystic.com

Circa 1901. This classical revival-style inn is built on the historical site of the Hoxie House, the Clinton House and the U.S. Hotel. Just as these famous 19th-century inns offered, the Whaler's Inn has the same charm and convenience for today's visitor to Mystic. Once a booming ship-building center, the town's connection to the sea is ongoing, and the sailing schooners still pass beneath the Bascule Drawbridge in the center of town. More than 75 shops and restaurants are within walking distance.

Innkeeper(s): Richard Prisby. $79-259. 49 rooms with PB, 8 with FP, 8 with WP, 1 conference room. Types of meals: Cont plus, gourmet lunch and gourmet dinner. Restaurant on premises.

Certificate may be used: Nov. 28-April 30, excluding holidays.

Niantic

Inn at Harbor Hill Marina

60 Grand St
Niantic, CT 06357
(860)739-0331 Fax:(860)691-3078
Internet: www.innharborhill.com
E-mail: info@innharborhill.com

Circa 1890. Arise each morning to panoramic views of the Niantic River harbor at this traditional, late-19th-century inn. Travel by boat or car to neighboring cities and enjoy the finest culture New England has to offer. This three-story, harbor-front inn offers rooms filled with antiques and seaside decor. Some have balconies and fireplaces. Experience true adventure at sea on a chartered fishing trip, or spend the day in town shopping or relaxing on the beach, all within walking distance. During the summer, guests can listen to outdoor concerts in the park while overlooking Long Island Sound. Whatever the day has in store, guests can start each morning the right way with a fresh, continental breakfast on the wraparound porch overlooking the marina and gardens.

Innkeeper(s): Sue Labrie, Dave Labrie. $135-325. 16 rooms with PB, 12 with FP, 1 suite, 2 conference rooms. Breakfast, afternoon tea and snacks/refreshments included in rates. Types of meals: Cont plus, early coffee/tea and wine.

Certificate may be used: Nov. 1-March 31, Sunday-Thursday, not valid on holidays.

Norfolk

Blackberry River Inn

538 Greenwoods Road W
Norfolk, CT 06058
(860)542-5100 Fax:(860)542-1763
Internet: www.blackberryriverinn.com
E-mail: bri@blackberryriverinn.com

Circa 1763. In the National Register, the Colonial buildings that comprise the inn are situated on 27 acres. A library with cherry paneling, three parlors and a breakfast room are offered for guests' relaxation. Guest rooms are elegantly furnished with antiques. Guests can choose from rooms in the main house with a fireplace or suites with a fireplace or Jacuzzi. The Cottage includes a fireplace and Jacuzzi. A full country breakfast is included.

Innkeeper(s): Jeanneth Angel. $155-289. 15 rooms, 14 with PB, 2 with FP, 2 two-bedroom suites, 1 cottage, 1 conference room. Breakfast and afternoon tea included in rates. Types of meals: Full bkfst.

Certificate may be used: May-November only, Sunday-Thursday, subject to availability.

Manor House

69 Maple Ave
Norfolk, CT 06058-0447
(860)542-5690 (866)542-5690 Fax:(860)542-5690
Internet: www.manorhouse-norfolk.com
E-mail: innkeeper@manorhouse-norfolk.com

Circa 1898. Poised in the heart of the Green Woods, The Manor House sits in the New England Village of Norfolk, Connecticut. This romantic bed and breakfast is accented with many gables, exquisite cherry paneling, a grand staircase, Moorish arches and

Tiffany windows. Relax on a private porch or sip hot-mulled cider by the fire after a sleigh ride or horse and carriage drive along nearby country lanes. Stay in a guest room with a Jacuzzi tub for two. Schedule a spa treatment or in-room masssage. After a made-to-order breakfast, take a bike ride or arrange a fly fishing or river canoe and kayak guided tour.

Innkeeper(s): Michael Sinclair, Holly Kelsey. $130-255. 9 rooms with PB, 4 with FP, 1 suite, 1 conference room. Breakfast and afternoon tea included in rates. Types of meals: Full gourmet bkfst, early coffee/tea and room service.

Certificate may be used: Weekdays, excluding holidays and month of October.

Mountain View Inn

67 Litchfield Road, Rt 272
Norfolk, CT 06058
(860)542-6991 (866)792-7812
Internet: www.mvinn.com
E-mail: innkeepers@mvinn.com

Circa 1900. Sitting on more than three scenic hillside acres in Norfolk, Connecticut, this Gilded Age Victorian bed and breakfast offers the New England tradition of gracious hospitality and treasured privacy. Listen to classical music with a glass of sherry in the main parlor or sit by the fire in the great room. Relax in the elegance and comfort of a spacious guest bedroom with antique furnishings or stay in the two-bedroom guest house with fireplace, kitchen and dining area. A farm-fresh breakfast is served fireside or on the sunny garden porch. Browse through the vintage boutique, admire the work in the art gallery and ask about Mountain View Photography. The quiet country surroundings in the foothills of the Berkshire Mountains and the warm ambiance inspire creativity.

Innkeeper(s): Dean Johnson, Jean Marie Johnson. $100-400. 8 rooms, 7 with PB, 1 guest house. Breakfast and Afternoon Sherry and Evening Port included in rates. Types of meals: Full gourmet bkfst, early coffee/tea, Breakfast in Bed, Afternoon Sherry and Evening Port.

Certificate may be used: September, November-April, excluding holidays and holiday weekends, subject to availability.

North Stonington

High Acres Bed and Breakfast

222 Northwest Corner Road
North Stonington, CT 06359
(860)887-4355
Internet: www.highacresbb.com
E-mail: highacres@99main.com

Circa 1743. Experience the relaxed and enjoyable atmosphere of this 18th century hilltop estate with150 acres of private walking trails, meadows, woodlands and expansive lawns with inviting seating areas and a patio. The 1743 historic Colonial home is furnished with English antiques and large family portraits. Comfortable guest bedrooms feature canopy beds with down comforters. Stay in Jane?s Room with a clawfoot tub. Start each day with a hearty breakfast in the country kitchen with views in three directions or in the fireside dining room. It is an easy drive to Mohegan Sun and Foxwoods Casinos, museums and art galleries.

Innkeeper(s): Peter Agnew, Liz Agnew . $129-169. 4 rooms with PB. Breakfast, afternoon tea, snacks/refreshments and wine included in rates. Types of meals: Country bkfst, veg bkfst, early coffee/tea and picnic lunch.

Certificate may be used: August, no Saturdays.

Inn at Lower Farm

119 Mystic Rd
North Stonington, CT 06359
(860) 535-9075 (866) 535-9075
Internet: www.lowerfarm.com
E-mail: info@lowerfarm.com

Circa 1740. Fully restored, this 1740 center-chimney Georgian Colonial boasts six working fireplaces. The bed and breakfast is located on more than four acres of lawns, gardens and cattail marshes. Enjoy the scenic surroundings while relaxing in the hammock or on the comfortable outdoor furniture scattered throughout the property. Swing on the porch swing and breathe in the fresh country air. Well-appointed guest bedrooms feature queen-size beds, en-suite private baths and bright sitting areas with recliner chairs. Three rooms have fireplaces and a fourth includes a whirlpool tub. Wake up to a full country breakfast served by candlelight in front of the original open hearth and beehive oven. In the afternoon gather for tea and homemade cookies.

Innkeeper(s): MaryWilska , Jon Wilska. $100-180. 4 rooms with PB, 3 with FP, 1 with WP, 1 two-bedroom suite, 1 conference room. Breakfast, afternoon tea and snacks/refreshments included in rates. Types of meals: Full gourmet bkfst, veg bkfst and early coffee/tea.

Certificate may be used: November-May, Sunday-Thursday.

Norwalk

Silvermine Tavern

194 Perry Ave
Norwalk, CT 06850-1123
(203)847-4558
Internet: www.silverminetavern.com
E-mail: SilvermineTavernInn@gmail.com

Circa 1790. The Silvermine consists of the Old Mill, the Country Store, the Coach House and the Tavern itself. Primitive paintings and furnishings, as well as family heirlooms, decorate the inn. Guest rooms and dining rooms overlook the Old Mill, the waterfall and swans gliding across the millpond. Some guest rooms offer items such as canopy bed or private decks. In the summer, guests can dine al fresco and gaze at the mill pond.

Innkeeper(s): Frank Whitman, Marsha Whitman. Call for rates. 11 rooms, 10 with PB, 1 suite. Breakfast included in rates. Types of meals: Cont, lunch and dinner. Restaurant on premises.

Certificate may be used: No Friday nights, no September or October. No holidays.

Old Saybrook

Deacon Timothy Pratt Bed & Breakfast Inn C.1746

325 Main Street
Old Saybrook, CT 06475
(860)395-1229 Fax:(860)395-4748
Internet: www.pratthouse.net
E-mail: stay@pratthouse.net

Circa 1746. Built prior to the Revolutionary War, this slate blue house is an outstanding example of center chimney Colonial-style architecture. Listed in the National Register, the inn's original features include six working fireplaces, hand-hewn beams, wide board floors, a beehive oven and built-in cupboard. Four-poster and canopy beds, Oriental rugs and period furnishings accentuate the New England atmosphere. Fireplaces and Jacuzzi tubs invite romance and relaxation. On weekends a multi-course, candlelight breakfast is served in the elegant dining room. Enjoy homemade muffins or scones, fresh fruit and entrees such as heart-shaped blueberry pancakes or eggs Benedict. Among the variety of local historic house museums to visit, the William Hart house is across the street. The area offers many shopping and dining opportunities as well as galleries to explore. Beaches, a state park and river cruises also are available.

Innkeeper(s): Patricia McGregor. $100-220. 7 rooms with PB, 7 with FP, 7 with HT, 7 with WP, 3 total suites, including 1 two-bedroom suite. Breakfast, afternoon tea and snacks/refreshments included in rates. Types of meals: Veg bkfst, early coffee/tea, Full gourmet breakfast on weekends; home-baked goods breakfast on week days. Complimentary tea, coffee, cookies and port wine and spring water is always available in dining room.

Certificate may be used: Monday-Thursday, November-April only.

Preston

Roseledge Country Inn & Farm Shoppe

418 route 164
Preston, CT 06365-8112
(860) 892-4739
Internet: www.roseledge.com
E-mail: roseledgefarm@aol.com

Circa 1720. Hearth-cooked New England breakfasts of eggs, bacon and homemade breads are served in this colonial inn, one of the oldest homes in Preston. Wide floor boards original to the home create a feeling of reverence for the finely maintained historic home. There are pegged mortise and tenon beams and scrolled moldings on the stair treads. Canopy beds with floaty bed curtains add a romantic touch. There is a stone tunnel connecting the street with the barn's basement, and ancient stone walls divide the rolling meadows in view of the inn's four acres. Guests are invited to help with the farm animals, including gathering eggs.

Innkeeper(s): Derek and Gail Beecher. $149-159. 3 rooms with PB, 2 with FP, 1 suite, 1 conference room. Breakfast, afternoon tea, wine and Garden lunch and dessert teas are by reservation please included in rates. Types of meals: Early coffee/tea, picnic lunch, snacks/refreshments, dinner and Full breakfast using the herbs and eatable flowers we grow.

Certificate may be used: Anytime, subject to availability.

Southbury

Cornucopia At Oldfield

782 Main St North
Southbury, CT 06488-1898
(203)267-6772 Fax:(203)267-6773
Internet: cornucopiabnb.com
E-mail: innkeeper@cornucopiabnb.com

Circa 1818. Cornucopia at Oldfield is surrounded by acres of rolling lawns and gardens that are bordered by huge sugar and Norway maples and the original stone walls. Experience country elegance in a relaxed setting at this stately Georgia Federal home in the historic district. The fireside public rooms include the Keeping Room for watching a DVD, video or playing games. The front parlor offers a more reserved, quiet ambiance. A desk and a library of books, magazines and CDs are on the second floor. Inviting guest bedrooms feature fleece robes and all the modern amenities. Stay in a room with a clawfoot tub, fireplace or balcony. A full hot breakfast is served daily. In summertime, sit by the lily pond, relax in the shady gazebo or nap in a hammock or take a refreshing dip in the swimming pool. In winter, curl up with a book or play a game by our fireplace.

Innkeeper(s): Christine Edelson, Ed Edelson. $160-275. 6 rooms, 5 with PB, 4 with FP, 1 with WP, 1 two-bedroom suite, 2 conference rooms. Breakfast, snacks/refreshments and wine included in rates. Types of meals: Full gourmet bkfst, veg bkfst, early coffee/tea, picnic lunch and afternoon tea.

Certificate may be used: Sunday-Thursday, Jan. 1-May 30, subject to availability, no holidays.

Westbrook

Angels' Watch Inn

902 Boston Post Rd
Westbrook, CT 06498-1848
(860)399-8846 Fax:(860)399-2571
Internet: www.angelswatchinn.com
E-mail: info@angelswatchinn.com

Circa 1830. Appreciate the comfortable elegance and tranquil ambiance of this stately 1830 Federal bed and breakfast that is situated on one acre of peaceful grounds in a quaint New England village along the Connecticut River Valley Shoreline. Romantic guest bedrooms are private retreats with canopy beds, fireplaces, stocked refrigerators, strawberries dipped in chocolate, fresh fruit and snack baskets, whirlpools or two-person clawfoot soaking tubs. Maintaining a fine reputation of impeccable standards, the inn caters to the whole person. After breakfast choose from an incredible assortment of spa services that include massage therapy, yoga, intuitive guidance, as well as mind, body and spirit wellness. Go horseback riding then take a sunset cruise. Ask about elopement/small wedding packages and midweek or off-season specials.

$115-195. 4 rooms, 5 with PB, 5 with FP, 4 with HT. Breakfast, afternoon tea, snacks/refreshments and wine included in rates. Types of meals: Full gourmet bkfst, veg bkfst, early coffee/tea, picnic lunch and dinner.

Certificate may be used: Sunday-Thursday year-round, holidays and special events excluded. Full season rates, double occupancy only.

Captain Stannard House

138 South Main Street
Westbrook, CT 06498-1904
(860)399-4634 Fax:(860)399-0072
Internet: www.stannardhouse.com
E-mail: stay@stannardhouse.com

Circa 1872. Abundant in history, space and charm, Captain Stannard House is a sea captain's manor located on the Connecticut shore in quaint Westbrook. Experience this all-season home away from home for a romantic winter getaway, spring renewal, autumnal adventure or summer love at the beach. Stay in a delightfully furnished guest bedroom with individual climate control, desk and sitting area. Anticipate a satisfying candlelit breakfast in the warm and inviting dining room. Linger with morning coffee or an evening glass of wine by the fire in the great room or on the huge south porch overlooking landscaped grounds. Add a piece to the ongoing jigsaw puzzle in the Captain's Room. Visit the nearby casinos, go to the theater and take a wine-tasting tour of Chamard Vineyard. Ask about specials and packages.

Innkeeper(s): Jim Brewster, Mary Brewster. $150-220. 9 rooms with PB. Breakfast and snacks/refreshments included in rates. Types of meals: Full gourmet bkfst, early coffee/tea and Early Riser Station w/seasonal fresh fruit/yogurt selection/homemade granola/cereal variety/nutritional bars/homemade baked goods.

Certificate may be used: November-May, subject to availability.

Wethersfield

Chester Bulkley House B&B

184 Main St
Wethersfield, CT 06109-2340
(860) 563-4236 Fax:(860)257-8266
Internet: www.chesterbulkleyhouse.com
E-mail: ChesterBulkley@aol.com

Circa 1830. Offering the best of both worlds, this renovated Greek Revival structure is ideally located in the historic village of Old Weathersfield with its quaint sites, museums and shops, yet the inn also boasts a 10-minute drive to downtown Hartford with ballet, Broadway shows, opera and the symphony. Hand-carved woodwork, wide pine floors, working fireplaces and period pieces enhance the comfortable ambiance. Cut flowers, pillow chocolates and other thoughtful treats ensure a pleasant and gracious stay for business or leisure.

Innkeeper(s): Tom Aufiero. $105-165. 5 rooms, 3 with PB, 1 suite. Breakfast and afternoon tea included in rates. Types of meals: Full gourmet bkfst, veg bkfst and early coffee/tea.

Certificate may be used: January-August, Sunday-Thursday.

Woodstock

B&B at Taylor's Corner

880 Route 171
Woodstock, CT 06281
(860) 974-0490 (888) 974-0490
Internet: www.taylorsbb.com
E-mail: info@taylorsbb.com

Circa 1731. Traditional lodging and hearthside cooking is part of the historic yet romantic ambiance of this restored 18th-century central-chimney Colonial and attached Connecticut cottage, listed in the National Register. It boasts two beehive ovens, eight fireplaces, original wide-floor boards, moldings, gunstock beams, mantels and stair rails. Relax by the fireside in the keeping room, parlor or in an Adirondack chair on the patio. Spacious guest bedrooms are furnished with antiques and reproductions. Besides a daily breakfast in the dining room, light snacks and beverages are available. Ask about getaway specials. Popular Old Sturbridge Village is 15 miles away.

Innkeeper(s): Kevin, Brenda . $125-145. 3 rooms with PB, 3 with FP. Breakfast and snacks/refreshments included in rates. Types of meals: Full bkfst, veg bkfst, early coffee/tea and Gluten-free breakfast available upon request.

Certificate may be used: November-April, subject to availability.

Delaware

Milford

The Towers B&B

101 NW Front St
Milford, DE 19963-1022
(302) 422-3814
Internet: www.mispillion.com

Circa 1783. Once a simple colonial house, this ornate Steamboat Gothic fantasy features every imaginable Victorian architectural detail, all added in 1891. This winner of the iLoveInns.com Top 10 Romantic Inns of 2009 has 10 distinct styles of gingerbread as well as towers, turrets, gables, porches and bays. Inside, chestnut and cherry woodwork, window seats and stained-glass windows

are complemented with American and French antiques. The back garden boasts a sunroom and swimming pool. Ask for the splendid Tower Room or Rapunzel Suite.

Innkeeper(s): Christopher Clausen, David Rule. $135-175. 4 rooms with PB, 1 two-bedroom suite. Breakfast and Full gourmet breakfast. Please advise innkeeper of any dietary restrictions. Complimentary sherry available in Music Room included in rates. Types of meals: Full bkfst and veg bkfst.

Certificate may be used: Any night of the week throughout the year, except NASCAR Race weekends and holidays.

Rehoboth Beach

Bewitched & BEDazzled

67 Lake Ave
Rehoboth Beach, DE 19971-2107
(302) 226-3900 (866) 732-9482
Internet: www.bewitchedbnb.com
E-mail: innkeeper@bewitchedbandb.com

Circa 1900. Though less than ten years old, this Victorian bed & breakfast is complete with turret, wraparound porch, nine-foot ceilings and period antiques. Discriminating travelers appreciate this smoke-free inn, situated in a quiet downtown neighborhood, close to the ocean, boutiques and restaurants. Savor afternoon tea or evening dessert in the parlor. Each guest bedroom boasts a fireplace. The Sunrise Suite also features a Jacuzzi and small private balcony. The windows of Suite William are adorned with gold sheers and burgandy velvet curtains. French doors lead to a clawfoot tub and shower. Linger over amazing culinary creations for breakfast in the formal dining room. There is room for two to swing in the back yard, or relax in the sunken hot tub.

Innkeeper(s): Inez Conover . $69-355. 17 rooms, 17 with FP, 4 with WP, 17 suites. Breakfast, afternoon tea, snacks/refreshments, Chef Patrick provides a mouth watering breakfast, and he always bakes a unique afternoon snack. Ice tea and lemonaid and as well as coffee and Hot Tea service 24/7 included in rates. Types of meals: Full gourmet bkfst, veg bkfst, early coffee/tea, gourmet lunch, picnic lunch, hors d'oeuvres, wine, gourmet dinner and room service. Restaurant on premises.

Certificate may be used: Nov. 1-March 15 excluding New Years.

Florida

Apalachicola

Coombs House Inn

80 6th St
Apalachicola, FL 32320
(850) 653-9199 (888) 244-8320 Fax:(850)653-2785
Internet: www.coombshouseinn.com
E-mail: info@coombshouseinn.com

Circa 1905. Located in the antebellum fishing village of
Apalachicola on Florida's unspoiled Gulf Coast, this exquisitely
restored historic inn consists of three stately mansions. A member of Select Registry, it is known for its grace and elegance
with fine antiques, oil paintings and oriental carpets. There are
seventeen original fireplaces, gleaming wood paneling and
hardwood floors. Lavish guest suites are equipped with modern
amenities including private baths, sumptuous bedding, and
plush robes. Savor a delicious breakfast each morning. Spacious
Camellia Gardens and a gazebo are ideal for weddings, while
broad wraparound verandas with comfortable wicker chairs are
a perfect setting for afternoon teas or wine tastings.
Complimentary provisions include bicycles for touring the historic district as well as beach chairs and umbrellas for enjoying
the pristine beaches of nearby St. George Island.

Innkeeper(s): Estella and Destinee. $109-269. 23 rooms with PB, 7 with
WP, 3 suites, 3 guest houses, 1 conference room. Breakfast, afternoon tea,
snacks/refreshments, hors d'oeuvres, wine and Weekend wine and cheese
receptions 6-7 PM included in rates. Types of meals: Full bkfst, veg bkfst and
early coffee/tea.

Certificate may be used: Sunday-Thursday, December-January.

Brandon

Behind The Fence B&B Inn

1400 Viola Dr
Brandon, FL 33511-7327
(813)685-8201
Internet: www.behindthefencebb.com
E-mail: behindthefence.carolyn@gmail.com

Circa 1976. Warm and welcoming, this Colonial salt box replica
features New England antiques and Amish country furniture to
provide a realistic view of life as it once was with simple needs
and sacred values. Experience the historically accurate ambiance
and folklore at this quiet retreat from today's stressful schedules.
The oak-shaded property features accommodations in the main
house or in the Caretakers Cabin with two porches. One faces
the in-ground swimming pool and the other overlooks the private wooded setting. Gather for a continental-plus breakfast each
morning with homemade Amish sweet rolls, fresh fruit, cereal,
toast, coffee, tea and orange juice. Brandon, Florida is within five
minutes of downtown Tampa and Ybor City.

Innkeeper(s): Larry Yoss, Carolyn R. Yoss. $79-99. 5 rooms, 3 with PB, 1
suite, 1 cottage, 1 conference room. Breakfast and afternoon tea included in
rates. Types of meals: Cont plus, early coffee/tea and snacks/refreshments.

Certificate may be used: Anytime, subject to availability.

Gainesville

Camellia Rose Inn

205 S. E. 7th Street
Gainesville, FL 32601
(352)395-7673 Fax:(352)378-8030
Internet: www.camelliaroseinn.com
E-mail: info@camelliaroseinn.com

Circa 1903. Recently renovated, Camellia Rose Inn offers modern technology and pleasing amenities wrapped in a warm and
cozy ambiance that reflects its Queen Anne-era beginning in historic Gainesville, Florida. Relax on the wraparound porch with a
beverage or snack. More than forty different varieties of camellias, azaleas, crape myrtle, oak and red bud trees adorn the
grounds. Stay in one of the spacious guest bedrooms with freshly pressed bed linens. Most feature a fireplace and spa shower.
The Anticipation master suite boasts a corner bubble tub while
Southern Charm has a clawfoot. On the second floor, Stardust
includes a private balcony overlooking the gardens. A detached
cottage offers even more privacy. Wake up and indulge in a
delicious three-course breakfast in the dining room.

Innkeeper(s): Tom & Patricia McCants. $125-250. 7 rooms, 6 with PB, 1
cottage. Breakfast, snacks/refreshments, hors d'oeuvres and wine included in
rates. Types of meals: Full bkfst, early coffee/tea, Fresh baked cookies and
evening happy hour.

Certificate may be used: June-August, anytime subject to availability.

Magnolia Plantation Cottages and Gardens

309 SE 7th Street
Gainesville, FL 32601-6831
(352)375-6653 Fax:(352)338-0303
Internet: www.magnoliabnb.com
E-mail: info@magnoliabnb.com

Circa 1885. This restored French Second
Empire Victorian is in the National Register.
Magnolia trees surround the house and
the gardens include a reflecting pond
with waterfalls and gazebo. Five guest
rooms are filled with family heirlooms
and the bathrooms feature clawfoot

tubs and candles. There are also private historic cottages available with Jacuzzis. Some of the cottages are pet friendly. The innkeepers offer bicycles and evening wine and snacks are included. The inn is two miles from the University of Florida.

Innkeeper(s): Joe Montalto, Cindy Montalto. $135-335. 5 rooms with PB, 5 with FP, 5 with WP, 7 cottages, 6 guest houses. Breakfast and afternoon tea included in rates. Types of meals: Full bkfst.

Certificate may be used: Sunday-Thursday, all year or anytime, last minute.

Green Cove Springs

River Park Inn

103 S Magnolia Ave
Green Cove Springs, FL 32043-4100
(904)284-2994 (888)417-0363
Internet: www.riverparkinn.com
E-mail: Riverparkinn@comcast.net

Circa 1885. Experience small-town charm while staying at this frame, vernacular-style inn located in the city's waterfront district. It was originally built for those partaking of the medicinal warm mineral springs which still flow, supplying the chemical-free community pool. The overflow then feeds a gentle stream winding through the park before emptying into the mighty St. John's River. The decor befits the 1800s era with period antiques and tasteful furnishings. Comfortable guest bedrooms offer modern conveniences for business and pleasure. Savor a wholesome breakfast before taking a self-guided historic walking tour. A porch swing and double rocker invite relaxation on the two verandas.

Innkeeper(s): Pat and Dale. $94-169. 5 rooms with PB, 5 with FP, 1 cottage. Breakfast and snacks/refreshments included in rates. Types of meals: Full bkfst and early coffee/tea.

Certificate may be used: July 15-Sept. 15th, Sunday-Thursday, Subject to Availability.

Gulfport

The Historic Peninsula Inn & Spa

2937 Beach Blvd
Gulfport, FL 33707
(727)346-9800 (888)9000-INN Fax:(727)343-6579
Internet: www.innspa.net
E-mail: inn_spa@yahoo.com

Circa 1905. Combining the architectural styles of New England and Southern Vernacular, this boutique inn is a landmark in the waterfront historic district. Reminiscent of a Raj, the old-world atmosphere exudes British Colonial ambiance and decor and is embellished by hosting the foreign office of the Kingdom of Mandalay. Well-appointed suites and guest bedrooms are found on the second and third floors. On the first floor, savor gourmet dishes at the highly acclaimed Six Tables, or enjoy more casual fare in our Palm Lounge which offers a full service bar adjacent to a covered veranda and private, open-air alcove. Play croquet on the north side lawn. Relaxing and rejuvenating spa services offered here on the premises include massage, reflexology and skin care. Customized packages are popular at this premier location for special functions and intimate weddings.

Innkeeper(s): Jim Kingzett, Alexandra Kingzett. $110-189. 11 rooms with PB. Breakfast included in rates. Types of meals: Cont plus, early coffee/tea, gourmet lunch, afternoon tea and gourmet dinner. Restaurant on premises.

Certificate may be used: Sunday-Thursday, subject to availability.

Indialantic

Windemere Inn By The Sea

815 S Miramar Ave
Indialantic, FL 32903
(321)728-9334
Internet: www.windemereinn.com
E-mail: stay@windemereinn.com

Circa 1994. This island-pink inn fits perfectly among the palm trees and tropical plants of Indialantic, Florida. Located directly on a natural beach where turtles nest, the inn provides towels, chairs, and umbrellas so guests need to only think about fun in the sun. With the Main House, Cottage, and Carriage House Suite there is a perfect room for everyone. Choose a room with an ocean-view balcony, private entrance, or Jacuzzi tub. Let the sound of the waves calm your soul or just sit and relax by the koi pond. In the morning, wake to a gourmet breakfast in the bright breakfast room with intimate tables. The romantic pergola gives a beachside ambiance to an intimate wedding without the sandy shoes. Receive a 15% discount at the Spessard Holland Golf Course when the inn books your tee time or plan a getaway during a shuttle launch to see the bright lights of the Kennedy Space Center in the distance.

Innkeeper(s): Bonnie L. De Lelys. $175-275. 11 rooms with PB, 4 with WP, 2 suites, 1 conference room. Breakfast, hors d'oeuvres and wine included in rates. Types of meals: Full bkfst, veg bkfst, early coffee/tea and picnic lunch.

Certificate may be used: Sunday-Thursday, August-September for Seabreeze or Melbourne room. Subject to availability.

Inverness

Magnolia Glen

7702 E Allen Dr
Inverness, FL 34450-2622
(352) 726-1832
Internet: www.magnoliaglen.com
E-mail: ykuntz@earthlink.net

Circa 1985. Discover another side of Florida in Inverness. Magnolia Glen is surrounded by magnolia and moss-draped oak trees with rolling hills and lakes filling the countryside. Choose the fresh pink and burgundy Savannah Room or the Lake Room with a rustic feel with dark green and wood accents. Find romance and dressed-up class in the Trafalger Room where you can snuggle up by the fireplace in the cozy living room on chilly nights. Fresh baked muffins will draw you to the Admiral Nelson dining room for fresh fruit and a hot entree each morning. Those interested in sailing will enjoy studying the model sailboats at the inn. Enjoy the Florida sunshine with a game of golf or tennis or bike or walk along the 46-mile Withlacoochee Trail through small towns and natural beauty. Go antiquing in the Inverness Historic Square. The Gulf of Mexico is a short 17-mile drive away for those who wish to go swimming at a beach.

Innkeeper(s): Bonnie Kuntz. $79-100. 3 rooms with PB, 1 with HT. Breakfast included in rates.

Certificate may be used: December-Jan. 15.

Lake Wales

Chalet Suzanne Country Inn & Restaurant

3800 Chalet Suzanne Dr
Lake Wales, FL 33859-7763
(863)676-6011 (800)433-6011 Fax:(863)676-1814
Internet: www.chaletsuzanne.com
E-mail: info@chaletsuzanne.com

Circa 1924. Situated on 70 acres adjacent to Lake Suzanne, this country inn's architecture includes gabled roofs, balconies, spires

and steeples. The superb restaurant has a glowing reputation and offers a six-course candlelight dinner. Places of interest on the property include the Swiss Room, Wine Dungeon,  Gift Boutique, Autograph Garden, Museum, Ceramic Salon, Airstrip and the Soup Cannery. The inn has been transformed into a village of cottages and miniature chateaux, one connected to the other seemingly with no particular order.

Innkeeper(s): Eric Hinshaw, Dee Hinshaw. $129-189. 26 rooms with PB. Breakfast included in rates. Types of meals: Full bkfst, lunch and Call for days and times of gourmet dinner.

Certificate may be used: Anytime, subject to availability. Excludes weekends and holidays.

Orlando

The Courtyard at Lake Lucerne

211 N Lucerne Circle E
Orlando, FL 32801-3721
(407)648-5188 (800)444-5289 Fax:(407)246-1368
Internet: www.orlandohistoricinn.com
E-mail: orlandohistoricinn@hotmail.com

Circa 1883. This award-winning inn, precisely restored with attention to historical detail, consists of four different architec-

 tural styles. The Norment-Parry House is Orlando's oldest home. The Wellborn, an Art-Deco Modern Building, offers one-bedroom suites with kitchenettes. The I.W. Phillips is an antebellum-style manor where breakfast is served in a large reception room with a wide veranda overlooking the courtyard fountains and lush gardens. The Grand Victorian Dr. Phillips House is listed in the National Register of Historic Places. For an enchanting treat, ask for the Turret Room.

Innkeeper(s): David Messina. $99-225. 30 rooms with PB, 3 with FP, 8 with WP, 15 suites, 4 guest houses, 3 conference rooms. Breakfast included in rates. Types of meals: Cont plus.

Certificate may be used: Anytime except New Year's Eve and Valentines Day weekend.

Port Charlotte

Tropical Paradise

19227 Moore Haven Court
Port Charlotte, FL 33948
(941)626-8940 Fax:941-624-4533
Internet: www.tropicalparadisebb.com
E-mail: tropicalparadisebb@msn.com

Gracing the southwest waterfront on Charlotte County's Bluewater Trails, this quiet haven boasts a wall mural and furnishings that evoke the ambiance of a private tropical island. Take a relaxing swim in the screened-in, heated pool or lounge on the lanai near a waterfall into a fish pond accented with water lilies. Stay in a sound-insulated guest room or The Island Suite which features a whirlpool tub and private poolside exit. Savor breakfast each morning then go fishing from the grounds or by boat with access to the harbor and the Gulf of Mexico. Kayaking and canoeing are popular activities on the creeks with coves.

Innkeeper(s): Joanne McMahon, Clift McMahon. Call for rates. 2 rooms with PB, 1 with WP.

Certificate may be used: May-January.

Port Saint Joe

Cape San Blas Inn

4950 Cape San Blas Road
Port Saint Joe, FL 32456-4406
(850)229-7070 (800)315-1965 Fax:(850)229-7056
Internet: www.capesanblasinn.com
E-mail: innkeeper@capesanblasinn.com

Circa 1999. Situated on picturesque St. Joseph Bay across the street from the turquoise waters and secluded beaches of the Gulf of Mexico, this peaceful bed and breakfast was built in 1999. Inviting guest bedrooms feature Select Comfort beds, mini-refrigerators and DVDs. Start each day with a complimentary gourmet breakfast. Wine is provided for anniversaries. Enjoy canoeing, kayaking and biking year-round.

Innkeeper(s): George Weber, Betty Weber. $95-225. 7 rooms with PB, 1 with FP. Breakfast included in rates. Types of meals: Full gourmet bkfst and early coffee/tea.

Certificate may be used: November-February, Sunday-Thursday, excluding holidays.

Saint Augustine

Alexander Homestead B&B

14 Sevilla St
Saint Augustine, FL 32084-3529
(904)826-4147 (888)292-4147 Fax:(904)823-9503
Internet: www.alexanderhomestead.com
E-mail: bonnie@alexanderhomestead.com

Circa 1888. Green pastel hues dotted with white create a fanciful, tropical look at this Victorian bed & breakfast. Polished wood floors, colorful rugs and a mix of antiques and family pieces set the stage for a nostalgic getaway. Oversized tubs, lace, scented sachets and fresh flowers are just a few treats awaiting guests. The plentiful breakfasts are served in the elegant dining room. In the evening, guests also may enjoy a cordial in the Victorian parlor. The inn is located in St. Augustine's downtown historic area, so there is plenty of nearby activity.

Innkeeper(s): Bonnie Alexander. $119-229. 5 rooms with PB, 3 with FP. Breakfast and afternoon tea included in rates. Types of meals: Country bkfst, early coffee/tea, picnic lunch, snacks/refreshments and room service.

Certificate may be used: Monday-Thursday only.

Bayfront Marin House Bed & Breakfast

142 Avenida Menendez
Saint Augustine, FL 32084-5049
(904)824-4301 (866)256-5887 Fax:(904)824-1502
Internet: www.bayfrontmarinhouse.com
E-mail: info@bayfrontmarinhouse.com

Circa 1880. Romantic luxury is the theme at this extraordinary waterfront bed & breakfast inn. Bask in the tropical setting overlooking Matanzas Bay and the Bridge of Lions while relaxing on one of the porches, decks, patios, gazebo or courtyard. Adorning the historic district, recent renovations ensure modern comfort and conveniences while retaining the original coquina walls from the 1790 colonial house as well as details from the Victorian sections built during the 1800s. Gorgeous guest bedrooms and suites feature double Jacuzzis, candles, robes, personal products and a daily newspaper. Linger over a buffet breakfast; in the evening enjoy wine and dessert. An ice machine, snacks and refreshments are available any time. Bikes, discount tickets and access to the Anastasia Athletic Club are also provided.

Innkeeper(s): Sandy Wieber, Mike Wieber. $119-269. 15 rooms with PB, 10 with FP, 10 with WP, 1 two-bedroom suite, 1 conference room. Breakfast, snacks/refreshments, and Beer/wine happy hour in the evening. Dessert included in rates. Types of meals: Full gourmet bkfst and early coffee/tea.

Certificate may be used: August-September, no weekends.

Casa de Solana, B&B Inn

21 Aviles St
Saint Augustine, FL 32084-4441
(904) 824-3555 Fax:(904)824-3316
Internet: www.casadesolana.com
E-mail: stay@casadesolana.com

Circa 1763. Poised inside a private walled courtyard surrounded by tropical gardens in the historic district of St. Augustine Antigua, Florida, this bed and breakfast inn is an easy walk

along brick-paved streets to all the sites and attractions of America's oldest city. Casa de Solana B&B Inn has been recently renovated to be an oasis of comfort. Sit on the second-floor balcony with horse-drawn carriages passing below. Gather for beverages and appetizers at the inn's evening social. Antique-filled guest bedrooms and suites feature pleasing amenities. Many of the romantic rooms include a fireplace, whirlpool tub, writing desk and refrigerator. Two homemade hot entrees, just-baked pastries, fresh fruit and special blend coffees accent a satisfying breakfast. There are facilities for small group functions and weddings. Various special packages are available.

Innkeeper(s): Jeff , Amelia, Hilde, Luis. $149-279. 10 rooms with PB, 7 with FP, 7 with WP. Breakfast, afternoon tea, wine, Lunch served from 11:30 am to 2:30 pm Tuesday and Wednesday and $10 pp included in rates. Types of meals: Full gourmet bkfst, veg bkfst, room service, Social hour 4:30-5:30

PM, daily with wine. Rotating Breakfast Menu, We request that you notify us at least two days prior to arrival with any dietary needs..

Certificate may be used: Anytime, subject to availability.

Casablanca Inn on The Bay

24 Avenida Menedez
Saint Augustine, FL 32084
(904)829-0928 (800)826-2626 Fax:904-826-1892
Internet: www.casablancainn.com
E-mail: innkeeper@casablancainn.com

Circa 1914. Casablanca Inn on The Bay is a lovingly restored Mediterranean revival bed and breakfast inn gracing the premium bayfront location of historic St. Augustine, Florida. Listed in the National Register, elegant suites and rooms boast panoramic Matanzas Bay views, whirlpools, rainfall showers, private porches and sundecks, antiques, decorative fireplaces, luxurious bedding and large flat screen TVs. Secret Garden rooms are pet friendly. Be pampered with a two-course gourmet breakfast. View the historic Fort Castillo de San Marcos from the sprawling verandas, watch the horse and carriage tours, or sink into a hammock while the tropical palms sway in the breeze. The Tini Martini Bar is surrounded by colorful art, intimate porch seating, tables under the stars and exotic concoctions or a complimentary glass of wine or beer.

$99-349. 23 rooms with PB, 11 with FP, 17 with HT, 17 with WP, 2 suites. Afternoon tea, snacks/refreshments and two-course gourmet sit-down breakfast served daily from 8:15 to 10:00 AM included in rates. Types of meals: Full gourmet bkfst and early coffee/tea.

Certificate may be used: June-November, Sunday-Thursday.

Castle Garden B&B

15 Shenandoah St
Saint Augustine, FL 32084-2817
(904)829-3839
Internet: www.castlegarden.com
E-mail: castlegarden@bellsouth.net

Circa 1860. This newly-restored Moorish Revival-style inn was the carriage house to Warden Castle. Among the seven guest rooms are three bridal rooms with in-room Jacuzzi tubs and sunken bedrooms with cathedral ceilings. The innkeepers offer packages including carriage rides, picnic lunches, gift baskets and

other enticing possibilities. Guests enjoy a homemade full, country breakfast each morning.

Innkeeper(s): Bruce & Brian Kloeckner. $99-229. 7 rooms with PB, 3 suites. Breakfast included in rates. Types of meals: Full bkfst, early coffee/tea and picnic lunch.

Certificate may be used: Sunday-Thursday. Other times if available.

St. Francis Inn

279 Saint George St
Saint Augustine, FL 32084-5031
(904)824-6068 (800)824-6062 Fax:(904)810-5525
Internet: www.stfrancisinn.com
E-mail: info@stfrancisinn.com

Circa 1791. St. Francis Inn reflects the rich culture and heritage of St. Augustine, America's oldest city. Gracious and inviting, it boasts a tranquil garden courtyard and pleasing amenities. This Florida bed and breakfast is centrally located amid a quiet setting in the historic district. Bikes are provided to easily explore the surrounding area. Take a relaxing swim in the pool and later, gather for evening socials with homemade desserts. Stay in a delightful guest room or suite infused with a perfect blend of romance, old world charm and modern comforts. Each accommodation provides unique

amenities and many include a fireplace, balcony, kitchenette and whirlpool, clawfoot or Jacuzzi tub. Wake up refreshed and savor a satisfying gourmet breakfast before visiting the local attractions. Ask about specials and packages available.

Innkeeper(s): Joe Finnegan. $129-279. 17 rooms with PB, 8 with FP, 1 with HT, 11 with WP, 4 suites, 1 cottage, 1 conference room. Breakfast, snacks/refreshments and hors d'oeuvres included in rates. Types of meals: Full gourmet bkfst, picnic lunch, evening social with desserts, Bloody Marys & Mimosas with breakfast on weekends/holidays, Inn-baked cookies and apples.

Certificate may be used: May 1 to Feb.10, Sunday-Thursday, excluding holiday periods.

Saint Petersburg

Beach Drive Inn

532 Beach Drive NE
Saint Petersburg, FL 33701
(727) 822-2244 Fax:(813)354-4702
Internet: www.beachdriveinn.com
E-mail: info@beachdriveinn.com

Circa 1910. Gracing the downtown waterfront district of St. Petersburg, Florida, Beach Drive Inn Bed & Breakfast is just across from Tampa Bay. Built in 1910 in the Key West style, this historic home was nationally designated The Vinoy House. Surrounded by palm trees and other lush plants, the setting is truly tropical. Stay in one of the delightful guest bedrooms or a spacious suite with a whirlpool, entertainment center and attached private sunroom with kitchenette. A made-to-order breakfast is served daily. Walk to Bayside Beach and the many popular local attractions and cultural sites.

Innkeeper(s): Roland Martino/Heather Martino. $129-275. 6 rooms with PB, 2 suites. Breakfast, afternoon tea, snacks/refreshments and wine included in rates. Types of meals: Full gourmet bkfst and hors d'oeuvres.

Certificate may be used: June-September, last minute subject to availability.

Georgia

Dahlonega

Long Mountain Lodge Bed and Breakfast

144 Bull Creek Road
Dahlonega, GA 30533
(706)864-2337
Internet: www.longmountainlodge.com
E-mail: innkeeper@longmountainlodge.com

Circa 2006. Incredible beauty surrounds this newly built Adirondack-style mountain lodge that sits on eight scenic acres with ponds, waterfalls, gardens and walking trails. Long Mountain Lodge Bed and Breakfast is just seven miles from historic Dahlonega Square in Georgia and boasts an upscale rustic décor. Relax in the Great Room with a two-story stone wood-burning fireplace. Enjoy snacks and beverages in the library/game room and gather each afternoon for a wine reception. Watch the sunset over the Blue Ridge Mountains from the large wraparound porch. Guest bedrooms and suites feature majestic views, whirlpool tubs and satellite TV. Most have a private entrance, fireplace and patio or deck. A wonderfully satisfying breakfast is made by innkeeper Dianne, a former restaurant owner and chef and is served in the dining room or on the screened porch.

Innkeeper(s): Tim Quigley, Dianne Quigley. $129-199. 6 rooms with PB, 5 with FP, 5 with WP, 5 suites, 1 cabin, 1 conference room. Breakfast, snacks/refreshments and wine included in rates. Types of meals: Full bkfst and hors d'oeuvres.

Certificate may be used: November-August, Sunday-Thursday, excluding holidays.

Lookout Mountain

Garden Walk Inn B&B

1206 Lula Lake Rd
Lookout Mountain, GA 30750
(706)820-4127 (800)617-0502 Fax:(706)820-7671
Internet: www.gardenwalkinn.com
E-mail: gardenwalk@gardenwalkinn.com

Circa 1940. A fanciful garden setting surrounds this cottage-style inn that sits on two acres among 100-year-old pines. Themed guest bedrooms and suites with scenic mountain vistas offer a choice of romance, fantasy or nostalgia. Jacuzzi suites are available, and some rooms feature fireplaces. Accommodations also include cottages. Start the day with a delicious meal served in seasonal summer and winter breakfast rooms. Enjoy the peaceful atmosphere, outdoor pool and hot tub. Stroll down garden paths to the sound of a gentle waterfall.

Innkeeper(s): Ed Caballero, Erma Caballero. $90-195. 11 rooms with PB, 2

with FP, 5 suites, 9 cottages, 1 conference room. Breakfast included in rates. Types of meals: Full bkfst and early coffee/tea.

Certificate may be used: January-June, August-September, excluding weekends.

Perry

New Perry Hotel

800 Main Street
Perry, GA 31069-3332
(478) 224-1000
Internet: www.newperryhotel.com
E-mail: manager@newperryhotel.com

Circa 1924. This registered national historic landmark has hosted travelers for more than 100 years. The grand inn makes a striking first impression with its columned balcony on the front façade. Southern elegance can be found throughout from the grand piano to the brilliant chandelier. The main building features a honeymoon suite with a private balcony along with other guest rooms of all sizes. The pool-side building pays homage to old Hollywood royalty with rooms dedicated to Audrey Hepburn, James Dean, Marilyn Monroe, and John Wayne. The restaurant is open for breakfast, lunch, and dinner; children can order from a menu just for them and adults can enjoy country classics like chicken and dumplings followed by pecan pie for dessert. Sip a nightcap at The Tavery, a full service bar. Take a refreshing dip in the saltwater pool after exploring downtown Perry, Georgia. The inn is just minutes from the Georgia National Fairgrounds and the Warner Robins Air Force Base.

Innkeeper(s): Dianne Phillips . $59-125. 30 rooms, 26 with PB, 5 total suites, including 6 two-bedroom suites, 2 conference rooms. Types of meals: Country bkfst, veg bkfst, early coffee/tea, lunch, hors d'oeuvres, wine and dinner. Restaurant on premises.

Certificate may be used: August, no weekends.

Rabun Gap

Sylvan Falls Mill

156 Taylors Chapel Rd
Rabun Gap, GA 30568
(706)746-7138
Internet: www.sylvanfallsmill.com
E-mail: linda3010@windstream.net

Circa 1840. The Sylvan Falls Mill Site has been the location of a working gristmill for more than 150 years. The mill was constructed in 1840 from wormy chestnutwood. The original waterwheel was replaced in 1950 by a steel waterwheel from Tennessee. The mill is still powered by the waterfall that cascades over one side of the property that overlooks picturesque

Wolffork Valley. The property has been a home since then, offering four unique guest rooms with private baths. Refreshments are served at check-in and a full, gourmet breakfast is served in the morning. Outdoor activities are the highlight of the inn. Guests will delight in hiking the Bartram Trail or rafting down the Chattooga River.

Innkeeper(s): Michael & Linda Johnson. $115-145. 4 rooms with PB, 1 with FP. Breakfast, snacks/refreshments and wine included in rates. Types of meals: Full gourmet bkfst, veg bkfst, early coffee/tea, picnic lunch, afternoon tea, gourmet dinner, gourmet gift baskets in rooms, cakes for special occasions and Homemade candies.

Certificate may be used:

Saint Marys

Goodbread House

209 Osborne St
Saint Marys, GA 31558-8415
(912)882-7490
Internet: www.goodbreadhouse.com
E-mail: info@goodbreadhouse.com

Circa 1870. In the heart of Saint Marys Historic District, this Victorian inn rests behind a white picket fence, a three-minute walk from the Cumberland Island Ferry. There are five antique-filled guest rooms, three with fireplaces. Visitors will enjoy the original wood trim, high ceilings, wide-plank pine floors and a two-story veranda with swings. Breakfast is served in the dining room and in

the evening, wine is served in the parlor. The historic fishing village has many points of interest to explore, and the Cumberland Island Sea Shore, Kings Bay Naval Submarine Base and Crooked River State Park are close by. Okefenokee Swamp is 30 minutes away. Activities in the area include kayaking, fishing and boating on the Intracoastal Waterway.

Innkeeper(s): Margie. $89-149. 6 rooms, 3 with FP, 6 suites, 1 cottage, 1 guest house. wine, brunch, lunch, snacks/refreshments, picnic lunches and afternoon tea included in rates. Types of meals: Full gourmet bkfst, veg bkfst, early coffee/tea, snacks/refreshments and daily social hour with libations and homemade desserts.

Certificate may be used: August-September, Sunday-Thursday, Subject to Availability.

Saint Simons Island

Village Inn and Pub

500 Mallery St
Saint Simons Island, GA 31522
(912)634-6056 (888)635-6111 Fax:(912)634-1464
Internet: www.villageinnandpub.com
E-mail: kristy@villageinnandpub.com

Circa 1930. Between the parks and oceanfront village, this award-winning island B&B inn sits under ancient live oaks. Restored and carefully expanded, the 1930 beach cottage hous-

es the reception, sitting and breakfast areas as well as the Village Pub, a solid mahogany olde English bar and original stone fireplace. Standard and deluxe guest bedrooms are named after historical people with local significance and feature upscale amenities, soothing color palettes, crown molding and custom-built armoires that hold large TVs. Most rooms include a balcony with a view of the pool and flower-filled courtyard or the neighborhood. A generous continental breakfast is available on the sun porch.

Innkeeper(s): Kristy Murphy. $99-220. 28 rooms with PB. Breakfast included in rates. Types of meals: Cont plus, wine and Pub on property.

Certificate may be used: August-February, Sunday-Thursday, based on availability.

Talmo

Mt. Creek Manor

2005 Mt. Creek Church Rd.
Talmo, GA 30575
(706)693-2721 (706)693-2721
Internet: www.mtcreekmanor.com/
E-mail: kcjernigan1@windstream.net

Circa 1975. Rolling hills and pastures surround this elegant brick manor in rural Talmo, Georgia. Get away from it all on 80 acres of land. Hike trails through the woods or lounge by the pool. Enjoy an energetic tennis match or shoot pool with a friend. Enjoy breakfast in the sunroom and afternoon tea on the front porch. Rest comfortably in one of guest rooms or spacious suite. Mt. Creek Manor hosts bridal luncheons, baby showers, or small weddings. Make dreams come true for a special young lady with a children's birthday tea party; china cups, face painting, and a photographer are all included. Stroll through the historic town or take a day trip to Atlanta or Athens. Sample fruit-infused wines at Chateau Elan Winery. Spend a day shopping in one of the nearby antique stores or flea markets.

Innkeeper(s): Karen Jernigan, Bob Jernigan. $119-129. 3 rooms, 2 with PB. Breakfast, afternoon tea and snacks/refreshments included in rates. Types of meals: Full bkfst and early coffee/tea.

Certificate may be used: Sunday-Thursday, based on availability.

Washington

Washington Plantation

15 Lexington Avenue
Washington, GA 30673
(706)678-2006 (877)405-9956 Fax:(706)678-3454
Internet: www.washingtonplantation.com
E-mail: info@washingtonplantation.com

Circa 1828. Period antiques and reproductions furnish this restored 1828 Greek Revival plantation home. Enjoy the seven acres of natural beauty with rose gardens, fountains, a waterfall, stream and koi pond. Scattered seating with tables are shaded by magnolia, oak, dogwood, pecan, hickory, elm and crape myrtle. Relax on a porch rocker or wicker chair. Large, bright guest bedrooms feature lavish draperies, Oriental rugs, brass and crystal chandeliers and fireplaces. Generous upscale amenities pamper and please. Early risers partake of juice and goodies before a full-service Southern breakfast is provided daily. Lunch and dinner can be ordered in advance for an extra charge.

Innkeeper(s): Tom Chase, Barbara Chase. $162-232. 5 rooms with PB, 5 with FP, 1 with WP. Breakfast, snacks/refreshments and wine included in rates. Types of meals: Full gourmet bkfst, veg bkfst, early coffee/tea, picnic lunch, hors d'oeuvres and gourmet dinner.

Certificate may be used: June-August anytime, September-May, Sunday-Thursday, except April 1-10.

Waverly

Horse Stamp Inn

#2418 Horse Stamp Church Road
Waverly, GA 31565
(912)882-6280
Internet: www.HorseStampInn.com
E-mail: tom@horsestampinn.com

Circa 2006. Drive through the gate, up the stately driveway, and around the fountain to this luxurious inn. Climb the grand staircase or take the European-style elevator to the five guest rooms, each named after a famous horse. The handsomely decorated rooms have private baths, king-sized beds, and views of the green pastures. Guests may board their own horse in the rustic four-stall barn. Walk through the lush fields or fish for trout in the artesian pond. The waters of the private salt water pool are inviting and refreshing. Start the day with a farm-to-table breakfast and end it by socializing or cuddling by the bonfire. Let the staff assist in planning an unforgettable wedding in front of the magnificent fountain, country barn, peaceful pond, or stone fireplace. Waverly, Georgia, is a short distance from Jekyll Island and St. Simon Island where guests can relax on the beach, take a sea turtle walk, play golf, and go fishing.

Innkeeper(s): Tom Hutcheson, Kris Hutcheson. $175-325. 5 rooms, 1 with WP, 5 suites, 3 conference rooms. Breakfast, snacks/refreshments, hors d'oeuvres and wine included in rates. Types of meals: Full gourmet bkfst, veg bkfst, early coffee/tea and room service.

Certificate may be used: January-February, June-September.

Hawaii

Hana

Hana Maui Botanical Gardens B&B

470 Ulaino Road
Hana, HI 96713
(808) 248-7725
Internet: ecoclub.com/hanamaui
E-mail: JoLoyce@aol.com

Circa 1976. This Hawaiian country farm features a ranch house and duplex with two studio apartments set on 27 acres that include a public botanical garden, fruit trees and flowers. The Flower and Marine studio have a private bath, kitchen, lanai and carport. Also offered is Volcano Heart Chalet near Volcano National Park on the Big Island. The chalet features two keyed rooms, each decorated in an individual theme, private half baths, a shared shower and a shared kitchenette and sitting room with a gas fireplace.

Innkeeper(s): JoLoyce Kaia. $100-125. 3 rooms, 2 suites, 1 cottage. Coffee/tea, box juice and pastry included in rates. Types of meals: Cont.

Certificate may be used: Anytime, subject to availability. Reservations may be made only one month in advance to qualify for one night free.

Honaunau

A Dragonfly Ranch B&B

84-5146 Keala O Keawe Road
Honaunau, HI 96726
(808)328-2159
Internet: www.dragonflyranch.com
E-mail: info@dragonflyranch.com

Circa 1977. Enter this tropical country estate to experience the world of Aloha at Dragonfly Ranch Bed and Breakfast in Honaunau, on the Big Island of Hawaii. This upscale eco-spa treehouse-style expansion mansion is a romantic retreat with healthy pleasures. The Healing Arts Center features an inviting hammock on a sunset lanai, a labyrinth in a rainbowed illuminarium and a far infrared sauna. Schedule a lomilomi massage and experience flower essence therapy. Stay in a guest suite or room with a screened-in bed under a pavilion roof and an outdoor shower. The Honeymoon Suite also boasts a double bathtub sunken in lava and adjoining indoor redwood room. The private round deck overlooks gardens, rock walls, a meadow and Honaunau Bay. Breakfast includes fresh produce from the organic garden. Visit nearby Place of Sanctuary and Kailua-Kona town is just a half-hour drive.

Innkeeper(s): Barbara Moore. $100-300. 5 rooms with PB, 2 with HT, 1 two-bedroom suite.

Certificate may be used: September-October, excluding holidays.

Volcano

A'Alani Volcano Heart Hawaii

470 Ulaino Rd
Volcano, HI 96713
(808)248-7725 Fax:(808)248-7725
Internet: ecoclub.com/hanamaui
E-mail: joloyce@aol.com

Circa 1987. This comfortable cedar home can be your base for visiting one of Hawaii's most fascinating landscapes. The entrance to Volcano National Park is just two miles away from this inn, which is nestled in a natural setting of tree ferns and ohia trees. The park features hiking trails around Kilauea volcano crater and through landscape that changes from forest to arid to tropical. The Volcano Art Center, volcano exhibit and observatory are a must for everyone and provide great insight into the Hawaiian culture.

Innkeeper(s): Danette Kekahio, Newton Kekahio. $100-125. 3 rooms. Types of meals: Cont.

Certificate may be used: Reservations may be made only one month in advance to qualify for one free night.

Idaho

Athol

Cedar Mountain Farm

25249 N Hatch Rd
Athol, ID 83801-8683
(208)683-0572 (866)683-0572
Internet: www.cedarmountainfarm.com
E-mail: info@cedarmountainfarm.com

Circa 1998. Expect down-home peaceful hospitality at Cedar Mountain Farm in Athol, the heart of Northern Idaho. This working family farm spans 440 acres of field, creek, mountains and forest; perfect for vacations, reunions, retreats, seminars and weddings. Enjoy hiking, biking, sledding, cross-country skiing or snowshoeing. Fish in Sage Creek, watch for birds and wildlife and pet the farm animals. The library invites relaxation and the game closet is well-stocked. Stay in a guest suite or log cabin with kitchen and laundry facilities. The Forest Suite boasts an electric fireplace, and the Bunkhouse offers more space and privacy. Wheelchair-accessible Granny's Woods features a jetted tub, two-headed walk-in shower and can be adjoined with Spring, both located in one wing of the main cabin. Savor a hearty breakfast served family style.

Innkeeper(s): Al and Daryl Kyle. $115-150. 4 rooms with PB, 1 with FP, 1 with WP, 3 two-bedroom suites, 2 cabins, 1 conference room. Breakfast and snacks/refreshments included in rates. Types of meals: Country bkfst, veg bkfst and early coffee/tea.

Certificate may be used: November-March, subject to availability or anytime, last minute-based on availability.

Coeur D'Alene

The Roosevelt Inn

105 E Wallace Ave
Coeur D'Alene, ID 83814-2947
(208)765-5200 (800)290-3358 Fax:(208)664-4142
Internet: www.therooseveltinn.com
E-mail: info@therooseveltinn.com

Circa 1905. Elegant yet comfortable, this grand four-story red brick Coeur d' Alene bed and breakfast was named for President Roosevelt and is the town's oldest schoolhouse. Relax in the front or back parlor and play a game or read a book. Listed in the National Register, The Roosevelt Inn offers elegant yet comfortable guest suites and rooms that boast a nostalgic ambiance. The Bell Tower Suite and the Honeymoon Suite are popular favorites. Breakfast is always such a delight that the inn sells a cookbook that includes the often-requested recipes. Lake Coeur d' Alene provides a variety of fun activities and the area features the world's longest floating boardwalk and Tubb's

Hill Nature Park. Shops and restaurants are within a five-minute stroll from the inn. The natural surroundings offer mountain biking, boating, skiing and hiking.

Innkeeper(s): John & Tina Hough. $89-319. 15 rooms, 12 with PB, 3 with FP, 6 total suites, including 4 two-bedroom suites, 2 conference rooms. Breakfast, afternoon tea and snacks/refreshments included in rates. Types of meals: Full gourmet bkfst, veg bkfst, early coffee/tea, Murder Mystery Dinners and Special party dinners for groups.

Certificate may be used: September-May, Sunday-Thursday.

Gooding

Gooding Hotel Bed & Breakfast

112 Main St
Gooding, ID 83330-1102
(208)934-4374
Internet: www.goodinghotelbandb.com
E-mail: goodingbandb@yahoo.com

Circa 1906. An early Gooding settler, William B. Kelly, built this historic hotel, which is the oldest building in town. Each

of the guest rooms is named in honor of someone significant in the history of Gooding or the hotel. A buffet breakfast is served every morning in the William Kelly Room. The area offers many activities, from golfing and fishing to exploring ice caves or visiting wineries and museums.

Innkeeper(s): Dean Gooding, Judee Gooding. $64-80. 11 rooms, 2 with PB, 3 suites. Breakfast included in rates. Types of meals: Full gourmet bkfst and room service.

Certificate may be used: Labor Day through April 1, upon availability.

Grangeville

Gateway Inn

700 W Main St
Grangeville, ID 83530
(208) 983-2500 (877) 983-1463 Fax:208-983-1458
Internet: idahogatewayinn.com
E-mail: stay@idahogatewayinn.com

Circa 1978. Comfortable and convenient, this renovated inn in Grangeville, Idaho, is located near the downtown area attractions, retailers, restaurants and historic landmarks. Three major rivers make fishing, hunting and seasonal sports easily accessible. Swim in the heated outdoor pool or use the indoor pool at nearby Super 8 Motel. Guest rooms feature Direct TV and wifi and may include a kitchenette. Wake up each day to gather in the breakfast room for the morning meal before exploring the area.

Innkeeper(s): Ted Lindsley. $49-72. 6 rooms, 26 with PB. Breakfast included in rates. Types of meals: Cont and Coffee and Espresso shop on Property!.

Certificate may be used: November-April, subject to availablity.

Saint Maries

St. Joe Riverfront Bed & Breakfast

816 Shepherd Rd.
Saint Maries, ID 83861
(208) 245-8687
Internet: stjoeriverbb.com
E-mail: info@stjoeriverbb.com

Circa 2003. A modern Bed and Breakfast along the shores of the river that flows into the Coeur d'Alene Lake. The Tuscan charm is fantastic for couples seeking a romantic getaway who need to relax, drink good wine, rekindle a romance, but it is also convenient, comfortable and offers corporate rates for those traveling on business.

Innkeeper(s): Val Day. $119-209. 5 rooms, 3 with PB. Breakfast, Wonderful gourmet breakfast featuring local foods, homemade breads and muffins and seasonal fruits included in rates. Types of meals: Full gourmet bkfst, picnic lunch and For four or more guests we will offer a wonderful dinner dining outdoors on deck or in the SunRoom with water views. Please check for rates.

Certificate may be used: November-March, subject to availability, no weekends or holidays.

Salmon

Greyhouse Inn B&B

1115 Hwy 93 South
Salmon, ID 83467
(208)756-3968 (800)348-8097
Internet: www.greyhouseinn.com
E-mail: greyhouse@greyhouseinn.com

Circa 1894. The scenery at Greyhouse is nothing short of wondrous. In the winter, when mountains are capped in white and the evergreens are shrouded in snow, this Victorian appears as a safe haven from the chilly weather. In the summer, the rocky peaks are a contrast to the whimsical house, which looks like something out of an Old West town. The historic home is known around town as the old maternity hospital, but there is nothing medicinal about it now. The rooms are Victorian in style with antique furnishings. The parlor features deep red walls and floral overstuffed sofas and a dressmaker's model garbed in a brown Victorian gown. Outdoor enthusiasts will find no shortage of activities, from facing the rapids in nearby Salmon River to fishing to horseback riding. The town of Salmon is just 12 miles away.

Innkeeper(s): David & Sharon Osgood. $89-124. 7 rooms with PB. Breakfast included in rates. Types of meals: Country bkfst, veg bkfst, early coffee/tea, picnic lunch and dinner.

Certificate may be used: Anytime, subject to availability.

Illinois

Algonquin

Victorian Rose Garden Bed & Breakfast

314 Washington St
Algonquin, IL 60102
(847) 854-9667
Internet: victorianrosegarden.com
E-mail: innkeeper@victorianrosegarden.com

Circa 1886. Sit back and let the innkeepers pamper you at this quaint inn 45 miles from Chicago. Walk into downtown Algonquin for dinner then return to continue your conversation on the front porch swing or on the quiet brick patio. Bring a bike or jog along the nearby Fox River Regional Bike Trail. In the evening you might want to gather around the grand piano in the parlor as someone plays a joyful tune. Hints of nostalgia can be found throughout the inn including the old-time barber corner, claw foot tub in the Presidential Chamber, and oak sewing machine in Lady Teresa's Room. Finger sandwiches and scones are served during Jane Austen themed teatimes for 10-32 guests. In the morning, start the day with a full breakfast in the formal dining room or sleep in and nibble on scones and juice anytime before checkout. Cat lovers may get some snuggle time with the resident kitty in the common rooms.
Innkeeper(s): Sherry Brewer. $104-159. 4 rooms with PB, 1 with FP.
Certificate may be used: November-March, excluding holidays, subject to availability.

Alton

Beall Mansion, An Elegant B&B

407 E. 12th St.
Alton, IL 62002-7230
(618)474-9100 (866)843-2325
Internet: www.beallmansion.com
E-mail: bepampered@beallmansion.com

Circa 1903. An eclectic blend of Neoclassic, Georgian and Greek Revival styles, the mansion was designed as a wedding gift by world renown architect, Lucas Pfeiffenberger. Original woodwork, eleven and a half-foot ceilings, leaded-glass windows, pocket doors, crystal chandeliers and imported marble and bronze statuary reflect the era's opulence. Elegantly appointed guest bedrooms are unique in size and decor. Each includes a private bath with shower and clawfoot tub or whirlpool for two, imported marble floor and chandelier. Voted "Illinois Best Bed & Breakfast" by Illinois Magazine's Readers Poll.
Innkeeper(s): Jim Belote, Sandy Belote. $119-358. 5 rooms with PB, 2 with FP, 4 with WP, 1 suite, 2 conference rooms. Plans are available with your choice of self-serve continental breakfast or gourmet breakfast in bed (or the

formal dining room). All stays include our famous 24 hour "all you can eat" chocolate buffet included in rates. Types of meals: Full gourmet bkfst, veg bkfst, early coffee/tea, snacks/refreshments, room service and 24 Hour "All You Can Eat" Chocolate Buffet.
Certificate may be used: Sunday-Thursday night stays for the standard everyday rate. Not available with any other certificate, discount or coupon. Blackout dates apply, subject to availability. Not valid if booked through a third party. Restrictions apply.

Bloomington

Vrooman Mansion B&B

701 E Taylor St
Bloomington, IL 61701-5425
(309)828-8816 (877)346-6488 Fax:(309)828-2596
Internet: www.vroomanmansion.com
E-mail: information@vroomanmansion.com

Circa 1869. Located in the heart of Bloomington/Normal, Illinois, this historic estate is situated in the quiet neighborhood of Dimmitt's Grove. Exquisite decor and furnishings include rich textiles, oak wood accents, as well as stained glass and leaded beveled glass windows in the foyer. Gather in one of the spacious common areas that include the music room, fireside parlor, safe room and library. Offering privacy and luxury with pampering amenities, each themed guest suite represents part of the legacy of the Bloomington family who once lived in the red brick Italianate home. Wake up to indulge in a satisfying gourmet breakfast in the dining room. Leisurely explore the nearby area by antiquing in downtown and browsing the farmer's market on a sunny Saturday morning. Take a wine-tasting tour of the local vineyards.
Innkeeper(s): Robin. $100-275. 5 rooms with PB, 1 cottage. Types of meals: Full bkfst, veg bkfst, early coffee/tea and Afternoon Tea upon request.
Certificate may be used: Anytime, subject to availability.

Chicago

Hansen House Mansion, The Centennial Houses of Lincoln Park

164 W. Eugenie St.
Chicago, IL 60614
(773) 871-6020 Fax:(773)871-0412
Internet: HansenMansion.net
E-mail: HansenMansion@aol.com

Circa 1886. This elegant urban inn boasts a perfect downtown location a few blocks or less from many city attractions and the lake. All public transportation is within 1/2 to 2 blocks. Hansen House Mansion, a Historically Significant Building in Chicago, Illinois, has retained all its original Victorian detail, even Giannini and Hilgart stained glass. The carefully selected 19th century furnishings reflect the home's original charms, and the 21st century conveniences such as central air conditioning, high-speed Internet, WiFi and free local calls all provide complete comfort. Select a single deluxe room with private bath, a suite with private deck, or the entire inn, all with use of the living room, dining room and fully-equipped kitchen. Plan a special event with the renowned chef or architectural docent.

Innkeeper(s): Frances Ramer, Quincy Stringham. Call for rates. 4 rooms, 2 with PB, 1 total suite, including 1 two-bedroom suite and 1 four-bedroom suite, 1 conference room. Breakfast, Continental breakfast of coffee, decaf and fine teas and homemade biscotti included in rates. Types of meals: Full gourmet bkfst, veg bkfst, Sun. brunch, early coffee/tea, gourmet lunch, picnic lunch, afternoon tea, snacks/refreshments, hors d'oeuvres, gourmet dinner and Any of the above may be arranged with sufficient notice.

Certificate may be used: All bookings subject to availability. Reservations accepted no more than two weeks in advance and must be mentioned at the time of the request.

Dixon

Crawford House Inn

204 E Third St
Dixon, IL 61021
(815)288-3351
Internet: www.crawfordhouseinn.com
E-mail: crawfordinn@grics.net

Circa 1854. In 1854, Joseph Crawford, who counted Abraham Lincoln among his friends, built this Italianate Victorian house that bears his name. Now a B&B, Crawford House offers a glimpse into small-town America. Guest bedrooms feature feather beds. Breakfasts are served with white linens, china and stemware in the dining room. Gourmet breakfasts include juice, coffee, an egg entree, fresh baked goods and seasonal fruits. The streets of Dixon are lined with colorful flower beds. The area is popular for cycling and scenic country trails offer opportunities for walking, horseback riding and cross-country skiing. Visit the Ronald Reagan boyhood home, John Deere Historical Site or local antique stores. Rock River is two blocks away for boating, fishing and canoeing.

Innkeeper(s): Lyn Miliano. $95-135. 4 rooms, 1 with PB. Breakfast included in rates. Types of meals: Full gourmet bkfst.

Certificate may be used: Anytime, subject to availability.

Galena

Hellman Guest House

318 Hill St
Galena, IL 61036-1836
(815)777-3638
Internet: www.hellmanguesthouse.com
E-mail: hellman@hellmanguesthouse.com

Circa 1895. A corner tower and an observatory turret rise above the gabled roof line of this Queen Anne house built of Galena brick. The house was constructed from designs drawn by Schoppel of New York. An antique telescope in the parlor is a favorite of guests who wish to view the town. Stained glass, pock-

et doors and antique furnishings add to the inn's charms. The Tower Room with its brass bed, fireplace and village views is recommended.

Innkeeper(s): Rita Wadman. $99-159. 4 guest houses with PB, 1 suite. Breakfast included in rates. Types of meals: Full bkfst and early coffee/tea.

Certificate may be used: January-April, Sunday-Thursday for Pauline or Irene Room, subject to availability.

The Steamboat House Bed and Breakfast

605 S. Prospect
Galena, IL 61036
(815)777-2317 Fax:(815)776-0712
Internet: www.thesteamboathouse.com
E-mail: glenchar@thesteamboathouse.com

Circa 1855. Truly elegant as well as historic, this brick Gothic Revival, pre-Civil War mansion was built for a renowned Mississippi River steamboat captain. The inn exudes luxury while imparting a welcome, friendly ambiance. Main-floor parlors include a library and billiards room. A central parlor on the second floor offers early-morning Gevalia coffee and tea. Enjoy midweek afternoon treats or wine and cheese on the weekends. Each guest bedroom features a fireplace, heirloom furniture, vintage photographs and original artwork. The formal dining room is set with antique china, crystal and silver for a breakfast that is sure to please. Relax on the front porch overlooking roses.

Innkeeper(s): Glen Carlson, Char Carlson. $105-160. 5 rooms with PB, 5 with FP, 1 suite. Breakfast and Wine time included in rates. Types of meals: Full gourmet bkfst, early coffee/tea, snacks/refreshments and wine.

Certificate may be used: Bess or Amanda Room, November-February, Monday-Thursday, subject to availability.

Maeystown

Corner George Inn

1101 Main
Maeystown, IL 62256
(618)458-6660 (800)458-6020
Internet: www.cornergeorgeinn.com
E-mail: cornrgeo@htc.net

Circa 1884. This inn is located in a restored hotel listed in the National Register of Historic Places. The inn originally served as both a hotel and saloon, but eventually served as a general store. Rooms in the inn are named after prominent local citizens and include Victorian appointments and antiques. The Summer Kitchen, a rustic cottage, once served as a smoke house, bakery and kitchen for the hotel's earliest owners. The cottage features original limestone walls and exposed beams. Another suite is also available in an 1859 rock house, and it includes two bedrooms. Breakfasts include entrees such as baked Victorian French toast, fresh fruit and homemade muffins or coffeecake.

Innkeeper(s): David Braswell, Marcia Braswell. $89-169. 7 rooms with PB, 3 suites, 1 cottage, 1 conference room. Breakfast included in rates. Types of meals: Full bkfst.

Certificate may be used: Anytime, Wednesday-Saturday, subject to availability.

Mossville

Old Church House Inn

1416 E Mossville Rd.
Mossville, IL 61552
(309)579-2300
Internet: www.oldchurchhouseinn.com
E-mail: oldchurchhouseinn@frontier.com

Circa 1869. Take sanctuary at this lovingly restored 1869 brick Colonial country church situated on Peoria's north side. The inn offers warm hospitality and comfortable elegance. Relax by a wood-burning fire with afternoon tea or sit on a bench among colorful garden blooms. Each guest bedroom features pampering amenities and distinctive details that may include an antique carved bedstead, handmade quilts and lacy curtains. Chocolates are a pleasant treat with turndown service in the evening.

Innkeeper(s): Dean & Holly Ramseyer. $139-179. 1 two-bedroom suite. Breakfast included in rates. Types of meals: Cont plus, veg bkfst, early coffee/tea, picnic lunch, afternoon tea, room service and Gourmet Continental Plus Breakfast.

Certificate may be used: Monday-Thursday all year or anytime with reservations within 48 hours of requested date.

Nauvoo

Nauvoo Grand-A Bed & Breakfast Inn

2015 Parley Street
Nauvoo, IL 62354
(217)453-2767
Internet: www.bbonline.com/il/nauvoogrand

Circa 1904. Across from the state's oldest winery, this historic treasure boasts intricately detailed brick, Victorian trim, etched and stained glass, carved woodwork, copper hardware and pressed metal ceilings. Experience the tranquil ambiance of the past in the elegant parlor with ebonized oak furniture. In the evening, dessert is enjoyed in the exquisite library. Spacious guest bedrooms on three floors feature antique furnishings and modern amenities like DVD players. Some boast jetted tubs and scenic views overlooking the one-acre grounds and surrounding orchards and vineyards. In the formal dining room savor a complete gourmet breakfast served on Spode china.

Innkeeper(s): Brenda Logan, Kim Orth. $129. 5 rooms with PB. Breakfast and snacks/refreshments included in rates. Types of meals: Full gourmet bkfst.

Certificate may be used: November-April except for Eagle Days & Civil War ReEnactment.

Oregon

Pinehill Inn

400 Mix St
Oregon, IL 61061-1113
(815)732-2067 (800)851-0131 Fax:(815)732-1348
Internet: www.pinehillbb.com
E-mail: info@pinehillbb.com

Circa 1874. Pinehill Inn Bed & Breakfast is a stunning red brick, Italianate country mansion located in Oregon, Illinois. The inn was built in 1874 and is listed in the National Register. Relax on the wraparound porch and veranda surrounded by century-old pine trees. Snacks and refreshments are always available in the Butler's Pantry/Guest Kitchen. Sit by the fire in the parlor and enjoy the art collection. Some of the guest bedrooms boast marble fireplaces, French silk-screened mural wallpaper and whirlpool tubs. Savor a delicious breakfast in the dining room.

Innkeeper(s): Chris Williams, Ken Williams. $99-199. 6 rooms with PB, 4 with FP, 3 with WP, 2 conference rooms. Breakfast and snacks/refreshments included in rates. Types of meals: Full gourmet bkfst, veg bkfst, early coffee/tea, picnic lunch and Free snacks and drinks 24/7.

Certificate may be used: Monday-Thursday, November-March.

Sheffield

Chestnut Street Inn

301 E Chestnut St
Sheffield, IL 61361
(815)454-2419 (800)537-1304
Internet: www.chestnut-inn.com
E-mail: monikaandjeff@chestnut-inn.com

Circa 1854. This inn is an award winning bed and breakfast featuring gourmet Mediterranean cuisine using locally grown foods. The four elegantly appointed guests suites offer signature toiletries, satellite TV, a VCR/DVD with more than 1000 titles and snacksand beverages. The innkeeper serves a full hot breakfas. This inn is near antiquing, shopping, hiking and biking and fishing. Nearby are also several historical sites, theater, golf, wineries and more. Experience big city dining in a small town atmosphere.

Innkeeper(s): Monika Sudakov, Jeff Sudakov. $109-179. 4 rooms with PB, 1 with FP, 2 total suites, including 1 two-bedroom suite, 1 conference room. Breakfast and snacks/refreshments included in rates. Types of meals: Full gourmet bkfst, veg bkfst, early coffee/tea, gourmet lunch, afternoon tea, hors d'oeuvres, wine, gourmet dinner, 4-Course Fixed Price Menu served daily by reservation only and Beer and Wine license on premises. Restaurant on premises.

Certificate may be used: Anytime, subject to availability.

Taylorville

Market Street Inn

220 E Market St
Taylorville, IL 62568-2212
(217)824-7220 (800)500-1466
Internet: www.marketstreetinn.com
E-mail: innkeeper@marketstreetinn.com

Circa 1892. Carefully and lovingly renovated, this vintage 1892 Queen Anne Victorian home and Carriage House in Taylorville is perfectly located in central Illinois, in the heart of historic Lincolnland. The common area with a kitchenette is on the third floor. Most of the well-appointed guest bedrooms feature double whirlpool tubs and either gas or electric fireplaces. Stay in one of the two romantic suites in the Carriage House with pampering amenities. Wake up each day to enjoy a satisfying fireside breakfast. There are many local attractions and activities to enjoy and plan to take a day trip to St. Louis, Missouri, 93 miles away.

Innkeeper(s): Myrna Hauser. $145-235. 10 rooms with PB, 10 with FP, 7 with WP, 2 suites, 1 cottage, 1 conference room. Breakfast, wine, complimentary social hour 4 to 6 pm, wine and fruit & cheese included in rates. Types of meals: Country bkfst, veg bkfst, early coffee/tea, There are restaurants nearby and within walking distance.

Certificate may be used: Anytime, subject to availability.

Indiana

Berne

Historic Schug House Inn

706 W Main St
Berne, IN 46711-1328
(260)589-2303
E-mail: schughouseinn@comcast.net

Circa 1907. This Queen Anne home was built in 1907 by Emanuel Wanner. It was constructed for the Schug family, who occupied the home for 25 years, and whom the innkeepers chose the name of their inn. Victorian features decorate the home, including inlaid floors, pocket doors and a wraparound porch. Guest rooms boast walnut, cherry and oak furnishings. Fruit, cheeses and pastries are served on antique china each morning in the dining room. Horse-drawn carriages from the nearby Old Order Amish community often pass on the street outside.
Innkeeper(s): John Minch. $50-60. 9 rooms with PB, 1 conference room. Breakfast included in rates. Types of meals: Cont.
Certificate may be used: Jan. 2-Dec. 20, except July 20-27 and Aug. 23-30.

Bremen

Scottish Bed and Breakfast

2180 Miami Trail
Bremen, IN 46506
(574)220-6672
Internet: www.scottishbb.com
E-mail: info@scottishbb.com

Circa 1999. Close to the Amish region, this year-round bed and breakfast sits on two park-like acres in the country. Practice golf on the putting green. Stay in a comfortable guest bedroom or suite with a Jacuzzi tub, TV and DVD player. The King Suite boasts a private entrance to the indoor swimming pool. Start the day with a hot continental-plus breakfast and enjoy evening refreshments. An assortment of pleasing packages is offered from theater to romance or create a customized getaway.
Innkeeper(s): Homer Miller, Brenda Miller. $99-169. 4 rooms with PB, 2 with FP, 1 with WP, 1 two-bedroom suite, 1 cottage, 1 guest house, 1 conference room. Breakfast and snacks/refreshments included in rates. Types of meals: Full gourmet bkfst, veg bkfst, early coffee/tea, picnic lunch, afternoon tea, homemade soup and sandwich dinner extra cost and advance reservation only.
Certificate may be used: November-April, Sunday-Thursday, subject to availability. Excluding holidays.

Chesterton

The Gray Goose

350 Indian Boundary Rd
Chesterton, IN 46304-1511
(219)926-5781 (800)521-5127 Fax:(219)926-4845
Internet: www.graygooseinn.com
E-mail: graygoose350@gmail.com

Circa 1939. Situated on 100 wooded acres, just under one hour from Chicago, this English country inn overlooks a private  lake. Guests can see Canadian geese and ducks on the lake and surrounding area. Rooms are decorated in 18th-century English, Shaker and French-country styles. Some of the rooms feature fireplaces, Jacuzzi and poster beds. Complimentary snacks, soft drinks, coffee and tea are available throughout the day. Strains of Mozart or Handel add to the ambiance.
Innkeeper(s): Tim Wilk. $110-195. 8 rooms with PB, 3 with FP, 3 suites, 1 conference room. Breakfast, afternoon tea and snacks/refreshments included in rates. Types of meals: Full gourmet bkfst, veg bkfst and early coffee/tea.
Certificate may be used: November to April.

Indianapolis

The Old Northside Bed & Breakfast

1340 North Alabama St.
Indianapolis, IN 46202
(317)635-9123 (800)635-9127 Fax:(317)635-9243
Internet: www.oldnorthsideinn.com
E-mail: garyh@hofmeister.com

Circa 1885. This Romanesque Revival mansion is fashioned out of bricks, and the grounds are enclosed by a wrought-iron fence. Border gardens and an English side garden complete the look. Rooms are decorated with a theme in mind. The Literary Room, which includes a fireplace and Jacuzzi tub, is decorated to honor Indiana authors. Another room honors the Hollywood's golden years. The home has many modern conveniences, yet still retains original maple floors and hand-carved, mahogany woodwork. Full breakfasts are served in the formal dining room or on the patio. Guests can walk to many city attractions.
Innkeeper(s): Gary Hofmeister. $135-215. 7 rooms with PB, 5 with FP, 7 with WP, 1 suite. Breakfast, afternoon tea and snacks/refreshments included in rates. Types of meals: Full bkfst.
Certificate may be used: August, September, October, November, Sunday-Friday.

Jeffersonville

Market Street Inn

330 West Market Street
Jeffersonville, IN 47130
(812)285-1877 (888)284-1877 Fax:(812)218-0926
Internet: www.innonmarket.com
E-mail: info@innonmarket.com

Circa 1881. One block from the Ohio River, Market Street Inn is a stately, three-story Second Empire mansion built in 1881 and recently restored in downtown Jeffersonville, Indiana. Sit on the front porch or relax on the third-floor deck by the fountain and outdoor fireplace. Guest bedrooms feature fireplaces and each suite also includes a double Jacuzzi tub, separate shower, two sinks, bidet and wet bar. Savor a magnificent breakfast made by a professional chef and served in one of the two dining rooms. Browse through the antique and gift shop for treasures to take home.

Innkeeper(s): Carol Stenbro, Steve Stenbro. $79-199. 7 rooms with PB, 7 with FP, 6 with WP, 3 suites, 1 conference room. Breakfast and snacks/refreshments included in rates. Types of meals: Full gourmet bkfst, veg bkfst, early coffee/tea, lunch, picnic lunch, afternoon tea and gourmet dinner.

Certificate may be used: Anytime except during Thunder, Derby and holidays.

La Porte

Arbor Hill Inn

263 W Johnson Rd
La Porte, IN 46350-2026
(219) 362-9200
Internet: www.arborhillinn.com
E-mail: info@arborhillinn.com

Circa 1910. Built with classic Greek Revival architecture, this premiere bed and breakfast is furnished in an upscale designer decor. The back of the grounds sits on the third hole green of Beacon Hills Golf Course. Accommodations in the main inn or in the guest house include guest bedrooms and suites with an assortment of amenities. Choose a room with single or double whirlpool tub, fireplace, oversized shower or private balcony. Browse the video library. A bountiful breakfast is served daily at a pre-arranged time. Evening dining can be scheduled with advance notice. Special events, meetings and retreats are welcome and business support services are provided. Ask about available packages.

Innkeeper(s): Laura Kobat & Kris Demoret. $79-259. 12 rooms with PB, 9 with FP, 9 with WP, 9 suites, 1 conference room. Full hot breakfast, fresh baked cookies every evening and some packages include special snacks or dinners included in rates. Types of meals: Full bkfst, veg bkfst, early coffee/tea, lunch, hors d'oeuvres, dinner, room service, Lunches and dinners and catered affairs served with 48-hour notice (menus can be viewed online).

Certificate may be used: Midweek only (Sunday-Thursday) Not available holiday and specialty days. No packages or discounts apply.

Ligonier

Solomon Mier Manor Bed Breakfast

508 South Cavin Street
Ligonier, IN 46767-1802
(260)894-3668
Internet: www.smmanor.com
E-mail: stay@smmanor.com

Circa 1899. This turn-of-the-century Queen Anne-Italianate manor boasts hand-painted ceilings, intricate woodwork and stained-glass windows. The ornate carved staircase is especially appealing with its staircase library. Antiques fill the guest rooms and common areas. The home is eligible to be on the National Register and originally was home to Solomon Mier, one of the area's first Jewish residents who came to the Ligonier area in search of religious tolerance and word of the railroad to come. Guests will find many areas of interest, such as the Shipshewana Flea Market & Auction and the on-site antique shop.

Innkeeper(s): Amanda Moser. $79-129. 4 rooms with PB, 4 with FP, 1 total suite, including 2 two-bedroom suites, 1 conference room. Breakfast, afternoon tea and snacks/refreshments included in rates. Types of meals: Full gourmet bkfst, veg bkfst and early coffee/tea.

Certificate may be used: Anytime, November-March, subject to availability; October - Monday through Thursday, subject to availability.

Middlebury

Country Victorian Bed & Breakfast

435 S Main St
Middlebury, IN 46540
(574)825-2568 (800)262-7829 Fax:(574)822-9465
Internet: www.countryvictorian.com
E-mail: stay@countryvictorian.com

Circa 1894. Built in 1894, Country Victorian Bed & Breakfast in Middlebury, Indiana has been recently renovated to provide country comfort while remaining true to its original Victorian splendor. Located in the heart of Amish country, sit on the front porch and watch the buggies go by. Relax inside by the fire with a good book. Guest bedrooms and a guest suite are furnished with antiques. Some feature whirlpools and one has a clawfoot soaking tub. Wake up each morning to enjoy a different breakfast menu that starts with the signature Country Victorian Breakfast Blend Coffee. Ask about special getaway packages available.

Innkeeper(s): Lori Schumacher, Arnie Schumacher. $109-159. 4 rooms with PB, 3 with FP, 1 with WP. Breakfast and hors d'oeuvres included in rates. Types of meals: Full bkfst, veg bkfst and early coffee/tea.

Certificate may be used: December-April, Sunday-Thursday.

Nappanee

Homespun Country Inn

302 N Main St
Nappanee, IN 46550
(574)773-2034 (800)311-2996 Fax:(574)773-3456
Internet: www.homespuninn.com
E-mail: homespun@kcaccess.com

Circa 1902. Windows of stained and leaded glass create colorful prisms at this Queen Anne Victorian inn built in 1902. Quarter-sawn oak highlights the entry and first-floor common rooms. Comfortable antiques and family heirlooms accent the inn. Two parlors offer areas to read, do a jigsaw puzzle or watch satellite TV or a movie. Each guest bedroom displays photos of the home's original occupants. Early risers enjoying a cup of coffee or tea might see a passing horse and buggy while sitting on the porch swing. Breakfast is served in the dining room. Ask about the assortment of special packages and how to add a Homespun Memory Gift Bag to a reservation.

Innkeeper(s): Dianne & Dennis Debelak. $89. 5 rooms with PB. Breakfast and snacks/refreshments included in rates. Types of meals: Full bkfst and early coffee/tea.

Certificate may be used: Any day January-April. Discount based on regular room rates. No other discount applies.

South Bend

Oliver Inn

630 W Washington St
South Bend, IN 46601-1444
(574)232-4545 (888)697-4466 Fax:(574)288-9788
Internet: www.oliverinn.com
E-mail: oliver@michiana.org

Circa 1886. This stately Queen Anne Victorian sits amid 30 towering maples and was once home to Josephine Oliver Ford, daughter of James Oliver, of chilled plow fame. Located in South Bend's historic district, this inn offers a comfortable library and nine inviting guest rooms, some with built-in fireplaces or double Jacuzzis. The inn is within walking distance of downtown and is next door to the Tippecanoe Restaurant in the Studebaker Mansion.

Innkeeper(s): Tom Erlandson, Alice Erlandson. $95-329. 10 rooms, 8 with PB, 6 with FP, 4 with WP, 4 total suites, including 2 two-bedroom suites, 1 guest house, 1 conference room. Breakfast and snacks/refreshments included in rates. Types of meals: Full gourmet bkfst, veg bkfst, early coffee/tea. Adjacent to Tippecanoe Place Restaurant.

Certificate may be used: January-December, Sunday-Thursday.

Valparaiso

Inn at Aberdeen

3158 South SR 2
Valparaiso, IN 46385
(219)465-3753 (866)761-3753 Fax:(219)465-9227
Internet: www.innataberdeen.com
E-mail: inn@innataberdeen.com

Circa 1856. An old stone wall borders this inn, once a dairy farm, horse farm and then hunting lodge. Recently renovated and expanded, this Victorian farmhouse is on more than an acre. An elegant getaway, there's a solarium, library, dining room and parlor for relaxing. The inn offers traditional Queen Anne furnishings in the guest rooms. The Timberlake Suites include fireplaces, two-person Jacuzzi tubs and balconies. The Aberdeen Suite includes a living room and fireplace, while the Alloway Suite offers a living room, kitchenette and a balcony. A conference center on the property is popular for executive meetings and special events, and there is a picturesque gazebo overlooking the inn's beautifully landscaped lawns and English gardens. Golf packages and mystery weekends have received enthusiastic response from guests. There is a golf course, spa and microbrewery adjacent to the inn.

Innkeeper(s): Bill Simon, Val & Chris Urello, Audrey Slingsby, Mandy Wiley, John & Lyn Johnson. $106-201. 11 rooms, 10 with FP, 11 with HT, 11 with WP, 11 suites, 1 conference room. Breakfast, snacks/refreshments, Evening dessert, Flavia Coffee Bar, Hot tea, Cocoa, Snacks and Beverages included in rates. Types of meals: Full gourmet bkfst, early coffee/tea and The inn's chef can be used for special functions.

Certificate may be used: Anytime, subject to availability.

Iowa

Amana

Die Heimat Country Inn

4434 V Street
Amana, IA 52236
(319)622-3937
Internet: www.dieheimat.com
E-mail: dieheimat@southslope.net

Circa 1854. The Amana Colonies is a German settlement listed in the National Register. This two-story clapboard inn houses a collection of hand-crafted Amana furnishings of walnut and cherry. Country-style quilts and curtains add personality to each guest room. Nearby, you'll find museums, wineries and a woolen mill that imports wool from around the world.
Innkeeper(s): Joy Miller. $36-63. 19 rooms with PB. Types of meals: Full bkfst.
Certificate may be used: Anytime, subject to availability.

Ames

Iowa House

405 Hayward Avenue
Ames, IA 50014
(515)292-2474
Internet: www.iowahouseames.com
E-mail: IowaHouse@mchsi.com

Circa 1924. Massive renovation transformed a fraternity house in this delightful historic hotel just three blocks from the central campus of Iowa State University and convenient to the Memorial Union, Knapps-Storms Dining, The Iowa State Center, Jack Trice Stadium, Hilton Coliseum and Campustown shops and restaurants. Listed in the National Register, unique architectural details include a double facade facing two different streets, a steeply pitched complex hip roof intersected by lower gables and a covered coach entrance. Gather in the living room, dining room or former frat Chapter Room to enjoy warm hospitality and pleasing amenities amid an eclectic mix of vintage and modern furnishings. Guest rooms feature flat-screen TVs, whirlpool tubs, pillow-top beds covered with white hypoallergenic comforters and award-winning hand-stitched quilts. Most rooms have refrigerators and microwaves. Lofts are air-conditioned. Indulge in gourmet country breakfasts served daily.
Innkeeper(s): Monte Parrish. $94-155. 15 rooms, 2 suites. Types of meals: Gourmet country breakfast.
Certificate may be used: Sunday-Thursday.

Bellevue

Mont Rest

300 Spring St
Bellevue, IA 52031-1125
(563)872-4220 (877)872-4220 Fax:(563)872-5094
Internet: www.montrest.com
E-mail: innkeeper@montrest.com

Circa 1893. Built with an unusual mix of architectural designs, the 1893 mansion was labeled Gothic Steamboat Revival and underwent an extensive restoration in 1997. Inside the inn a splendid Victorian atmosphere is enhanced by vintage woodwork, chandeliers and antique furnishings. The welcome begins with homemade cookies. In the early evening mingle at the hors d'oeuvres party. Enjoy parlor games or sing to the 1905 player grand piano. The guest kitchen provides complimentary beverages. Luxurious guest bedrooms and suites feature fresh flowers, chocolates, robes, heated towel bars and many include fireplaces and Jacuzzis. Arrange for an in-room therapeutic massage or reflexology. Stay in one of the Moon River Cabins on the banks of the Mississippi.
Innkeeper(s): Naomi. $149-199. 12 rooms with PB, 10 with FP, 9 with WP, 4 cabins, 2 conference rooms. Breakfast, snacks/refreshments and Complimentary non-alcoholic beverages are available in main floor kitchen included in rates. Types of meals: Full gourmet bkfst, veg bkfst, early coffee/tea, picnic lunch, afternoon tea, hors d'oeuvres, gourmet dinner and room service.
Certificate may be used: Anytime subject to availability. Not valid in October, holidays or holiday weekends.

Bentonsport

Mason House Inn and Caboose Cottage of Bentonsport

21982 Hawk Dr
Bentonsport, IA 52565
(319)592-3133 (800)592-3133
Internet: www.masonhouseinn.com
E-mail: stay@masonhouseinn.com

Circa 1846. A Murphy-style copper bathtub folds down out of the wall at this unusual inn built by Mormon craftsmen who stayed in Bentonsport for three years on their trek to Utah. More than half of the furniture is original to the home, including a nine-foot walnut headboard and a nine-foot mirror. The Caboose Cottage, a self-contained apartment within a real railroad caboose, is the newest lodging addition. It features a kitchen, dining area and Queen bed. This is the oldest operating pre-Civil War steamboat inn in Iowa. Guests can imagine the days when steamboats made their way up and down the Des Moines River, while taking in the scenery. A full breakfast is served in the main house dining room, but if guests crave a mid-day snack, each room is equipped with its own stocked cookie jar.

Innkeeper(s): Chuck & Joy Hanson. $84-105. 9 rooms with PB, 1 two-bedroom suite, 1 cottage. Breakfast included in rates. Types of meals: Country bkfst and early coffee/tea.

Certificate may be used: Anytime, subject to availability.

Dubuque

The Hancock House

1105 Grove Ter
Dubuque, IA 52001-4644
(563)557-8989 Fax:(563)583-0813
Internet: www.TheHancockHouse.com
E-mail: chuckdbq@mchsi.com

Circa 1891. Victorian splendor can be found at The Hancock House, one of Dubuque's most striking examples of Queen Anne architecture. Rooms feature period furnishings and offer views of the Mississippi River states of Iowa, Illinois and Wisconsin. The Hancock House, listed in the National Register, boasts several unique features, including a fireplace judged blue-ribbon best at the 1893 World's Fair in Chicago. Guests can enjoy the porch swings, wicker furniture and spectacular views from the wraparound front porch.

Innkeeper(s): Chuck Huntley, Susan Huntley. $80-175. 9 rooms with PB, 3 with FP, 4 with WP, 4 suites. Breakfast and snacks/refreshments included in rates. Types of meals: Full bkfst, veg bkfst and early coffee/tea.

Certificate may be used: Sunday-Thursday, excluding holidays.

The Mandolin Inn

199 Loras Blvd
Dubuque, IA 52001-4857
(563)556-0069 (800)524-7996
Internet: www.mandolininn.com
E-mail: innkeeper@mandolininn.com

Circa 1908. This handicapped-accessible three-story brick Edwardian with Queen Anne wraparound veranda boasts a mosaic-tiled porch floor. Inside are inlaid mahogany and rosewood floors, bay windows and a turret that starts in the parlor and ascends to the second-floor Holly Marie Room, decorated in a wedding motif. This room features a seven-piece Rosewood bedroom suite and a crystal chandelier. A gourmet breakfast is served in the dining room with a fantasy forest mural from the turn of the century. There is an herb garden outside the kitchen. Located just 12 blocks away, is the fabulous National Mississippi River Museum and Aquarium. The inn can equally accommodate both business and pleasure travel.

Innkeeper(s): Amy Boynton. $85-150. 8 rooms, 6 with PB, 1 with FP, 1 two-bedroom suite, 2 conference rooms. Breakfast included in rates. Types of meals: Full gourmet bkfst and early coffee/tea.

Certificate may be used: Sunday-Thursday, no holidays.

Guttenberg

Court House Inn

618 S River Park Dr
Guttenberg, IA 52052
(888) 224-2188
Internet: www.thecourthouseinn.biz
E-mail: lodging@thecourthouseinn.biz

Circa 1878. Located in the quaint historic area of Guttenberg, named one of "America's 20 Prettiest Towns," the Court House Inn offers a quiet and unique stay in one of the area's oldest cities and is in the National Register of Historical Places. The exterior has been restored. Located in Front Street Historical District, it is the perfect place to relax and enjoy the scenery and you can walk to restaurants and shopping just minutes away. Rooms are tastefully decorated with a mixture of old world charms and modern convenience and there are three fully furnished and equipped townhouses. An enclosed patio offers an outdoor dining table and barbecue. Sit back and breathe in the fresh country air or basque in the sunshine or stroll down to the river and walk on the two-mile long river walk. You can enjoy a picnic, cook under an open grill, or simply rest in the shade on one of the numerous park benches that dot the landscape. While there, take in the sites of the barges going through the locks of the Mississippi River or look for Bald Eagles that often soar overhead. You can enjoy the angler's paradise with numerous species of river fish or launch your boat for an afternoon of sailing pleasure.

Innkeeper(s): Brenda Landwehr, Mike Landwehr. $80-125. 2 rooms.

Certificate may be used: November-March, subject to availability.

Ionia

The Dairy Barn B&B

1436 210th Street
Ionia, IA 50645
(866)394-6302 Fax:(641)394-5376
Internet: www.thedairybarn.com
E-mail: gerrie.etter@gmail.com

Circa 1939. The Dairy Barn Bed and Breakfast in Ionia, Iowa is the perfect getaway in the countryside. The stress of city life immediately disappears. Feel welcomed the first night with a farmhand's supper. Ride a bike through the scenic area or stroll along the walking trails. Picnic lunches can be arranged in advance. Guest bedrooms are named after the dairy cows that resided there before renovations took place. The first-floor rooms are handicap accessible. Rooms in the hayloft are accented by a mural. Mabel's and Rosie's Rooms have entrances to a private outside balcony. Linger over Gerrie's hearty breakfast made with farm-fresh ingredients and from recipes collected in the B&B's cookbook available for purchase.

Innkeeper(s): Gerrie Etter. $108. 8 rooms with PB. Breakfast and Supper included in rates.

Certificate may be used: Anytime, subject to availabilty, excluding holidays, weekends and special events.

Keokuk

The Grand Anne

816 Grand Ave
Keokuk, IA 52632-5030
(319)524-6310 (800)524-6310 Fax:(319)524-6310
Internet: www.bbonline.com/ia/grandanne
E-mail: grandannekeokuk@yahoo.com

Circa 1897. Situated high on a hill overlooking the Mississippi River, this exquisitely restored Queen Anne Victorian, listed in the National Register, is a dramatic testimony to the craftsmanship of the renowned architect, George F. Barber. Signature details include the candle-snuffer porch and tower rooms with bent-glass windows, an oak-paneled reception hall with coffered ceiling and staircase with hand-turned spindles. A conservatory and two spacious parlors feature wainscoting and intricate moldings. A refrigerator is stocked with soda. Enjoy a full breakfast in the formal dining room. One of the parlors opens to a screened porch viewing formal gardens and expansive lawns. Innkeeper can be reached on cell at 319-795-6990.
Innkeeper(s): Cretia Hesse, Rick Hesse. $114-159. 5 rooms with PB. Breakfast included in rates. Types of meals: Full bkfst.

Certificate may be used: November-April except for Eagles Days and Civil War Reenactment.

Maquoketa

Squiers Manor B&B

418 W Pleasant St
Maquoketa, IA 52060-2847
(563)652-6961 Fax:(563)652-5995
Internet: www.squiersmanor.com
E-mail: innkeeper@squiersmanor.com

Circa 1882. Innkeepers Virl and Kathy Banowetz are ace antique dealers, who along with owning one of the Midwest's largest antique shops, have refurbished this elegant, Queen Anne Victorian. The inn is furnished with period antiques that are beyond compare. Guest rooms boast museum-quality pieces such as a Victorian brass bed with lace curtain wings and inlaid mother-of-pearl or an antique mahogany bed with carved birds and flowers. Six guest rooms include whirlpool tubs, and one includes a unique Swiss shower. The innkeepers restored the home's original woodwork, shuttered-windows, fireplaces, gas and electric chandeliers and stained- and engraved-glass windows back to their former glory. They also recently renovated the mansion's attic ballroom into two luxurious suites. The Loft, which is made up of three levels, features pine and wicker furnishings, a sitting room and gas-burning wood stove. On the second level, there is a large Jacuzzi, on the third, an antique queen-size bed. The huge Ballroom Suite boasts 24-foot ceilings, oak and pine antiques, gas-burning wood stove and a Jacuzzi snuggled beside a dormer window. Suite guests enjoy breakfast delivered to their rooms. Other guests feast on an array of mouth-watering treats, such as home-baked breads, seafood quiche and fresh fruits. Evening desserts are served by candlelight.
Innkeeper(s): Virl Banowetz, Kathy Banowetz. $80-195. 8 rooms with PB, 3 suites. Breakfast included in rates. Types of meals: Full gourmet bkfst.

Certificate may be used: Anytime based on projected availability, not valid in October, Valentines week or holidays.

Marion

Victorian Lace Bed & Breakfast

300 E Main St
Marion, IA 52302-9343
(319) 377-5138 (888) 377-5138 Fax:319 3773560
Internet: www.victorian-lace-iowa.com
E-mail: viclacebb@aol.com

Circa 1900. Enjoy this peaceful and romantic Victorian refuge that is perfect for a weekend getaway or a memorable wedding event. Jim Condit, the innkeeper, is also a reverend who performs many ceremonies each year. Stay in the inviting Summer Kitchen or Cottage or the third-floor Holiday Suite with four rooms, including one that is hidden. Both accommodations feature stocked refrigerators with beer, wine, soda, cheese, chocolates and evening dessert. After breakfast, grab a pair of binoculars and a bike to explore the surrounding area. In the afternoon, relax on the terrace with a good book and take a refreshing swim in the heated in-ground pool.
Innkeeper(s): Jim Condit, Renee Condit. Call for rates. 2 rooms, 2 with WP, 2 suites, 1 cottage. Breakfast, afternoon tea, snacks/refreshments, hors d'oeuvres and wine included in rates. Types of meals: Full gourmet bkfst, veg bkfst, early coffee/tea and room service.

Certificate may be used: Sunday-Thursday only.

Saint Ansgar

Blue Belle Inn B&B

PO Box 205, 513 W 4th St
Saint Ansgar, IA 50472-0205
(641)713-3113 (877)713-3113Internet:
www.bluebelleinn.com
E-mail: innkeeper@bluebelleinn.com

Circa 1896. This home was purchased from a Knoxville, Tenn., mail-order house. It's difficult to believe that stunning features, such as a tin ceiling, stained-glass windows, intricate woodwork and pocket doors could have come via the mail, but these original items are still here for guests to admire. Rooms are named after books special to the innkeeper. Four of the rooms include a whirlpool tub for two, and the  Never Neverland room has a clawfoot tub. Other rooms offer a skylight, fireplace or perhaps a white iron bed. During the Christmas season, every room has its own decorated tree. The innkeeper hosts a variety of themed luncheons, dinners and events, such as the April in Paris cooking workshop, Mother's Day brunches, the "Some Enchanted Evening" dinner, Murder Mysteries, Ladies nights, Writer's Retreats, quilting seminars and horse-drawn sleigh rides.
Innkeeper(s): Sherrie Hansen. $45-375. 11 rooms, 8 with PB, 2 with FP, 3 with WP, 5 total suites, including 2 two-bedroom suites and 1 three-bedroom suite, 1 cottage, 1 guest house, 2 conference rooms. Breakfast and snacks/refreshments included in rates. Types of meals: Full gourmet bkfst, veg bkfst, early coffee/tea, gourmet lunch, afternoon tea, dinner, room service and Visit website for a quarterly schedule of events/menus with weekly specials. Restaurant on premises.

Certificate may be used: Nov. 1-April 30, Monday-Thursday nights only, holidays excluded, Dec. 26-31 excluded, subject to availability.

Kansas

Abilene

Abilene's Victorian Inn B&B

820 NW 3rd St
Abilene, KS 67410
(785) 263-7774 (888) 807-7774
Internet: www.AbilenesVictorianInn.com
E-mail: AbilenesInn@yahoo.com

Circa 1887. Experience the peaceful luxury of Abilene's
Victorian Inn Bed & Breakfast. It is just a short walk to downtown Abilene, Kansas from this B&B's tree-lined neighborhood. Relax on the wicker porch swing while the songbirds serenade or sit by the fire in one of the parlors and play the
upright or parlor grand piano. Refreshments and a small refrigerator stocked with beverages are available in the dining room.
Combining Victorian elegance and modern convenience, the
guest bedrooms and suites are enchanting and comfortable. Sip
early-morning coffee on a balcony before indulging in the
morning meal. Chef Adrian prepares a wholesome and delightful breakfast from a gourmet menu that is not to be missed.
Ask about packages available for special events. Visit the
Dwight D. Eisenhower Presidential Library and Museum as
well as his nearby childhood home.

Innkeeper(s): Adrian Potter. $79-129. 6 rooms with PB, 3 total suites,
including 1 two-bedroom suite and 1 three-bedroom suite. Breakfast and
snacks/refreshments included in rates. Types of meals: Full gourmet bkfst,
veg bkfst, early coffee/tea, gourmet lunch, picnic lunch, afternoon tea, hors
d'oeuvres, gourmet dinner and room service.

Certificate may be used: November, January-February, subject to availabilty.

Emporia

The White Rose Inn

901 Merchant St
Emporia, KS 66801-2813
(620)343-6336
Internet: www.whiteroseinnemporia.com
E-mail: whiteroseinnemporia@gmail.com

Circa 1904. Emporia is a Midwest college town, and the White
Rose Inn is a mere three blocks from Emporia State University.
This Queen Anne Victorian home offers three private suites for
its guests, all with a sitting room and queen beds. Each morning, guests will be treated to a different and delicious menu.
Guests who so desire may have breakfast in bed, and the
innkeepers will happily arrange for a massage, manicure or
pedicure. The inn also hosts weddings and family reunions.

Innkeeper(s): Matthew Lowery, Scarlett Lowery. $79-149. 4 total suites,
including 1 two-bedroom suite. Breakfast included in rates. Types of meals:

Full gourmet bkfst.

Certificate may be used: Sunday-Thursday, November-February, excluding
holidays. Subject to Availability.

Fort Scott

Lyons' Twin Mansions B&B Hotel & Spa/Nate's Place, Restaurant & Lounge

742 & 750 S National Ave
Fort Scott, KS 66701-1319
(620) 223-3644 (800) 784-8378
Internet: www.LyonsTwinMansions.com
E-mail: FallinLove@LyonsTwinMansions.com

Circa 1876. For a business trip, vacation or romantic getaway,
this landmark Victorian mansion is a luxurious choice. This
gracious home has parlors to gather and Paradise, a full service
spa. Extreme Media TV, 42" Plasma in one, 50" flat screen in
another. All guest rooms have full cable with movie channels.
Spacious guest bedrooms offer king-size beds, refined comfort
and modern technology with refreshment centers and high-
speed Internet. The baths feature oversized jetted whirlpools
that are made to look like antique clawfoot tubs. Enjoy a hearty
breakfast in the grand dining room, unless a breakfast basket
delivered to the door is preferred. The grounds are showcased
by a gazebo, fish ponds, picnic areas and an enclosed starlit hot
tub. Ask about the creative specialty packages offered such as
mystery, private dining and couples and ladies spa packages.

Innkeeper(s): Pat & Larry Lyons and Nate Lyons. $119-225. 8 rooms, 7 with
PB, 3 with FP, 4 with WP, 1 two-bedroom suite, 1 cottage, 1 guest house, 3
conference rooms. Breakfast and snacks/refreshments included in rates.
Types of meals: Veg bkfst, picnic lunch, hors d'oeuvres, wine, gourmet dinner,
room service and full breakfast off menu at restaurant.

Certificate may be used: Anytime, last minute-based on availability.

Oberlin

The Landmark Inn at The Historic Bank of Oberlin

189 S Penn
Oberlin, KS 67749
(785)475-2340 (888)639-0003
Internet: www.landmarkinn.com
E-mail: info@landmarkinn.com

In 1886, this inn served as the Bank of Oberlin, one of the
town's most impressive architectural sites. The bank lasted only
a few years, though, and went through a number of uses, from
county courthouse to the telephone company. Today, it serves as
both inn and a historic landmark, a reminder of the past with

rooms decorated Victorian style with antiques. One room includes a fireplace; another has a whirlpool tub. In addition to the inviting rooms, there is a restaurant serving dinner specialties such as buttermilk pecan chicken and roasted beef with simmered mushrooms. The inn is listed in the National Register.

Innkeeper(s): Gary Anderson. Call for rates. 7 suites. Breakfast included in rates. Types of meals: Full gourmet bkfst, early coffee/tea, gourmet lunch, afternoon tea, snacks/refreshments, gourmet dinner and room service. Restaurant on premises.

Certificate may be used: January-April, Sunday-Thursday, subject to availability.

Wichita

Serenity Bed and Breakfast Inn

1018 North Market Street
Wichita, KS 67214
(316) 266-4666 (888) 788-0884
Internet: www.SerenityBedAndBreakfastInn.com
E-mail: SerenityBedAndBreakfastInn@yahoo.com

Circa 1889. Completely renovated and redecorated, this historic brick home offers elegant, quiet and comfortable surroundings with a wide assortment of upscale amenities. Schedule a massage or facial, select a romantic movie from the extensive collection or work out in the fitness room. Guest bedrooms and a two-bedroom suite provide a retreat with plush Eqyptian cotton robes and towels, whirlpool tubs and one features a fireplace. Wake up and linger over a deluxe breakfast that includes made-to-order eggs, specialty dishes, baked goods, pancakes, potatoes, fresh fruit, oatmeal and beverages. Experience the local flavor of Wichita and Sedgewick County. Near the heart of downtown, Serenity Bed and Breakfast Inn is a short walk to many fun and interesting attractions.

Innkeeper(s): Ken Elliott. $89-149. 3 rooms, 1 with FP, 1 with HT, 3 total suites, including 1 two-bedroom suite, 1 conference room. Breakfast and snacks/refreshments included in rates. Types of meals: Country bkfst, veg bkfst, early coffee/tea, gourmet lunch, picnic lunch, hors d'oeuvres, wine, gourmet dinner, room service. Serenity Inn also offers guests sack lunches and box lunches to-go. We also provide fully-stocked picnic baskets complete with glasses, wine (optional), hors d'oeurves, cheese and napkins and more to create a memorable day at the park or lake.

Certificate may be used: Sunday-Thursday, excluding holidays, subject to availability.

Winfield

Iron Gate Inn

1203 E 9th Ave
Winfield, KS 67156
(888)788-0884
Internet: www.irongateinnks.com
E-mail: IronGateInn@yahoo.com

Circa 1892. Two-story columns and tall trees create a grand welcome for guests of this inn situated on two city lots. Classic details including imported European parquet floors, a hand-carved walnut staircase and ornate Victorian fireplaces. Five guest suites have canopy or sleigh beds, pillow-top mattresses with monogrammed Egyptian cotton linens and individual climate controls. The gourmet breakfast looks almost too good to eat and is served either in the main dining room or as breakfast-in-bed. Outside, there's a child's playhouse in the backyard with its own front porch. Consider adding an extra package to celebrate a special anniversary with an elegant candlelit dinner for two and a guest room filled with rose petals and votive candles or stay on a Murder Mystery Saturday for an evening of camaraderie and fun. The inn also specializes in picture-perfect weddings to fit any style and budget.

Innkeeper(s): Ken Elliott. Call for rates. Call inn for details.

Certificate may be used: Sunday-Thursday, excluding holidays, subject to availability.

Kentucky

Bardstown

Red Rose Inn

209 E Stephen Foster Ave
Bardstown, KY 40004-1513
(502)349-3003 Fax:(502)349-7322
Internet: www.redroseinnbardstown.com
E-mail: redroseinn@bardstown.com

Circa 1820. This late Victorian style home in the National
Register, is located in the historic district a block and a half
from Courthouse Square. Some of the rooms offer fireplaces,
all have cable TV and VCRs. The inn's fireplaces were made by
Alexander Moore, the master craftsman of "My Old Kentucky
Home." Full gourmet country breakfasts are served, often on
the outdoor terrace in view of the gardens, Koi pond and
fountain. Smoking is not permitted.

Innkeeper(s): Audrey A. Simek. $99-139. 4 rooms with PB, 4 with FP, 1
conference room. Breakfast and snacks/refreshments included in rates. Types
of meals: Full gourmet bkfst and early coffee/tea.

Certificate may be used: November-March, subject to availability.

Bellevue

Christopher's B&B

604 Poplar St
Bellevue, KY 41073
(859) 491-9354 (888) 585-7085
Internet: www.christophersbb.com
E-mail: christophers@twc.com

Circa 1889. The former home of Bellevue Christian Church,
this unique inn sits in one of the area's three historic districts.
The spacious building was transformed into a delightful residence and B&B featuring the original hardwood floors and
stained-glass windows. Tastefully decorated and furnished in a
Victorian style, the gracious guest bedrooms and suite feature
Jacuzzi tubs and VCRs.

Innkeeper(s): Brenda Guidugli. $125-189. 3 rooms with PB, 3 with WP, 1
suite. Breakfast and snacks/refreshments included in rates.

Certificate may be used: JR Jacuzzi Room, Sunday-Friday, subject to
availability.

Bloomfield

Springhill Plantation B&B

3205 Springfield Rd
Bloomfield, KY 40008
(502)252-9463 Fax:502-252-9463
Internet: www.springhillwinery.com
E-mail: wineshop@springhillwinery.com

Circa 1857. Poised on five acres of rolling hills and vineyards
in the Bardstown area of central Kentucky in Bloomfield,
Springhill Plantation Bed & Breakfast is a stately, historic antebellum mansion boasting Federal and Victorian architecture
with Greek and Egyptian influences. Relax on the patio or take
a complimentary wine-tasting tour. Visit the gift store featuring
the inn's award-winning wines and locally made arts, crafts and
food products. Themed guest suites are named after types of
wines and accented with fresh flowers seasonally. Early risers
appreciate coffee and tea available outside each room in the
morning before enjoying a hearty country breakfast. The surrounding Bluegrass region offers popular activities from horse
racing to the Bourbon Trail.

Innkeeper(s): Eddie O'Daniel, Carolyn O'Daniel. $115-152. 6 rooms, 4 with
PB. Breakfast, Complimentary wine tasting in the gift shop and Coffee & tea
served outside suite each morning included in rates.

Certificate may be used: November-March, Monday-Thursday.

Louisville

1853 Inn at Woodhaven

401 South Hubbard Lane
Louisville, KY 40207-4074
(502)895-1011 (888)895-1011 Fax:(502)896-0449
Internet: www.innatwoodhaven.com
E-mail: woodhavenb@aol.com

Circa 1853. This Gothic Revival, painted in a cheerful shade of
yellow, is still much the same as it was in the 1850s, when it
served as the home on a prominent local farm. The rooms still
feature the outstanding carved woodwork, crisscross window
designs, winding staircases, decorative mantels and hardwood
floors. Guest quarters are tastefully appointed with antiques,
suitable for their 12-foot, nine-inch tall ceilings.
Complimentary coffee and tea stations are provided in each
room. There are several common areas in the Main House and
Carriage House, and guests also take advantage of the inn's
porches. Rose Cottage is octagon shaped and features a 25-foot
vaulted ceiling, a king bed, fireplace, sitting area, double
whirlpool, steam shower and wraparound porch. The National

Register home is close to all of Louisville's attractions.

Innkeeper(s): Marsha Burton. $95-225. 8 rooms with PB, 3 with FP, 6 suites, 1 cottage. Breakfast included in rates. Types of meals: Full gourmet bkfst.

Certificate may be used: Sunday-Thursday, January-March.

Petersburg

First Farm Inn

2510 Stevens Rd
Petersburg, KY 41080
(859) 586-0199
Internet: www.firstfarminn.com
E-mail: info@firstfarminn.com

Circa 1870. Elegantly updated, this 1870s farm house and historic wooden barn with tobacco rails are located just outside Cincinnati and surrounded by 21 acres of rolling hills, ponds stocked with bass, centuries-old maple trees, gardens and horses. Situated above the Ohio River, where Kentucky joins Ohio and Indiana, city sites and country pleasures are equally accessible. Spend two hours learning about horses and riding one of the friendly equines. Lessons begin with grooming, working in the arena, then graduating to a trail ride around the farm, along the pond and through the woods. Schedule a massage with a licensed therapist in a spacious guest bedroom furnished with antique oak heirlooms. Indulge in a bountiful homemade breakfast of fresh fruit, assorted breads and an entree served family style around the big dining room table. Sit by the fire or play the grand piano. Relax in the outdoor hot tub; swing or rock on the veranda.

Innkeeper(s): Jen Warner, Dana Kisor. $90-162. 2 rooms with PB, 1 with FP. All-you-can eat healthy balanced breakfast included in rates. Types of meals: Full gourmet bkfst, veg bkfst, early coffee/tea, Swiss Rosti, FFI Pasta Carbonara, Multi-grain pancakes, Latkes, Quiches, Carmel-walnut French toast and more conventional breakfasts.

Certificate may be used: Monday-Tuesday, December-March, last minute subject to availability.

Princeton

Cadiz Street Bed & Breakfast

209 Cadiz Street
Princeton, KY 42445
(270)625-1314
Internet: www.cadizstreetbedandbreakfast.com
E-mail: inquiries@cadizstreetbedandbreakfast.com

The green roof of this inn is a welcome sight for travelers in Princeton, Kentucky. Lovingly restored, the hardwood floors and crown molding are new but the ten-foot ceilings and claw foot tubs are original. Named after sisters that were longtime residents of the town, both guest rooms have queen size beds and private bathrooms. Choose the bright and airy Miss Sula Room or slip into the Miss Eliza Room from an entrance off the screened porch. Add that special touch to a romantic getaway with roses or chocolate covered strawberries. A full breakfast including fresh-made treats is available in the dining room or can be delivered to the room for guests that enjoy that extra quiet time in the morning. The area is known for its quilt shows and attendees who stay three or more nights during a show receive a discount. Walk into town to browse through antique shops and explore museums.

Innkeeper(s): Charles Pratt, Helen Pratt. Call for rates. Call inn for details.

Certificate may be used: Anytime, subject to availability.

Springfield

1851 Historic Maple Hill Manor B&B

2941 Perryville Rd (US 150 EAST)
Springfield, KY 40069-9611
(859) 336-3075 (800) 886-7546 Fax:(859) 336-3076
Internet: www.maplehillmanor.com
E-mail: maplehillmanorbb@aol.com

Circa 1851. In a tranquil country setting on 14 acres, this Greek Revival mansion with Italianate detail is considered a Kentucky Landmark home and is listed in the National Register of Historic Places.
Numerous architectural features include 14-foot ceilings, nine-foot windows, 10-foot doorways and a grand cherry spiral staircase. Guest bedrooms provide spacious serenity, and some boast fireplaces and or Jacuzzis. Enjoy a full country breakfast, and then take a peaceful stroll through flower gardens and the fruit orchard, or relax on a patio swing or porch rocker. The local area has a rich abundance of attractions including Bardstown, Shaker Village, Bourbon, historic Civil War areas and Lincoln Trails. Lexington and Louisville are within an hour's drive.

Innkeeper(s): Todd Allen & Tyler Horton. $129-189. 7 rooms with PB, 4 with FP, 2 with WP, 4 suites, 1 conference room. Breakfast, afternoon tea and snacks/refreshments included in rates. Types of meals: Full gourmet bkfst, veg bkfst, early coffee/tea, lunch, picnic lunch, wine, gourmet dinner and 24-hour beverages.

Certificate may be used: April-October, Sunday-Thursday, Anytime November-March, subject to availability.

Cinnamon House B&B

202 Lincoln Park Road
Springfield, KY 40069
(859)336-7367
Internet: www.cinnamonhouseky.com
E-mail: info@cinnamonhouseky.com

Circa 1900. The colors on the inside and outside of this inn are just as spicy and playful as the name. Enjoy views of downtown Springfield, Kentucky, from the Nancy Hanks Lincoln room, the large family-friendly Elizabeth Maddox Roberts room, or the private en suite bathroom in the Marithelma Kelly room. Deluxe roll-away beds are available and children are welcome. A full breakfast made with local ingredients is included and the cafe next door offers a discount to Cinnamon House guests. Choose a book, movie, or game from the inn library then sit in a rocking chair on the front porch to read or explore the small town just steps away. You will never be out of touch as the entire town has free Wi-Fi. All seven stops along the Kentucky Bourbon Trail are within one hour of this quaint town. Study the nation's great history by visiting civil war and Mary Lincoln Legacy sites.

Innkeeper(s): Eric Amon, Cynthia Cain. $75-119. 3 rooms, 1 with PB. Breakfast included in rates. Types of meals: Full gourmet bkfst, veg bkfst, Sun. brunch, early coffee/tea, gourmet lunch, picnic lunch, afternoon tea, snacks/refreshments, hors d'oeuvres, wine, gourmet dinner, room service, A fully certified restaurant/cafe adjacent to the B&B can serve a sumptuous meal for two of local lamb from a farm that you can visit, served with locally sourced vegetables, or an elegant meal for up to thirty friends and family. Cynthia is becoming renowned in the community for her delicious all home-made soups, quiches, paninis, and desserts. Ask us about gluten-free and vegetarian friendly options. Learn more about our sustainable and communi-ty-friendly cafe at www.littleredhencafe.blogspot.com or on Facebook at The Little Red Hen Cafe. Restaurant on premises.

Certificate may be used: November-March, subject to availability.

Taylorsville

Millview Bed and Breakfast

139 Elk Creek Road
Taylorsville, KY 40071
(502)477-8049
Internet: millviewbedandbreakfast.com/Home_Page.html
E-mail: millviewbandb7@gmail.com

Circa 1897. Old world charm is alive and well in the original woodwork and fireplace mantels of this country Queen Anne Victorian. A single five-room suite allows guests to enjoy the historic ambiance in privacy. Explore one of the 13 annual festivals then return to the quiet of a queen-size bed lit by a chandelier and bedside lamps. A second couple can doze on the queen sleeper sofa by the fireplace in the drawing room. Read a book in the sitting room with a warm cup of tea. Enjoy a soak in the antique claw foot tub or the gentle breezes that flow through the wrap around porch. Local ingredients and a sun-filled dining room are on the agenda for breakfast each morning. The refrigerator is stocked with beverages and a microwave is available for quick snacks. Numerous restaurants, antique stores, and a golf course provide nourishment and entertainment while visiting Taylorsville.

Innkeeper(s): Larry Dennison, Rita Dennison. $140. 1 suite.

Certificate may be used: February-March.

Versailles

Montgomery Inn Bed & Breakfast

270 Montgomery Ave
Versailles, KY 40383
(859)251-4103 Fax:(859)251-4104
Internet: www.montgomeryinnbnb.com
E-mail: innkeeper@montgomeryinnbnb.com

Circa 1911. Located in the horse capital of the world, Montgomery Inn Bed & Breakfast is a restored 1911 Victorian in the Kentucky Bluegrass region of Versailles. This family-operated inn offers concierge service and many upscale amenities with Southern hospitality. Munch on fresh-baked cookies in the Library upon check-in, swing on the wraparound porch or nap in the double hammock. Snacks, beverages, and access to a microwave and refrigerator are in the Media Room. Play the antique baby grand piano in the front parlor. Stay in a guest bedroom or spa suite with a two-person whirlpool tub, cotton sateen sheets, oversized Egyptian cotton towels and terry robes. A hearty gourmet breakfast is served in the GardenSide Dining Room. Dinner is available by reservation.

Innkeeper(s): Pam Matthews. $119-189. 10 rooms, 8 with FP, 10 with HT, 10 with WP, 10 total suites, including 2 two-bedroom suites, 1 conference room. Breakfast and snacks/refreshments included in rates. Types of meals: Full gourmet bkfst, early coffee/tea, gourmet lunch, picnic lunch, afternoon tea, hors d'oeuvres, wine and gourmet dinner.

Certificate may be used: Not valid during Equestrian Events, subject to availability.

Warsaw

Riverside Inn Bed & Breakfast

85 US Highway 42 East
Warsaw, KY 41095
(859) 567-1329 (877) 313-7298
Internet: www.riversideinnbb.com
E-mail: riversideinn@zoomtown.com

Circa 1869. Escape to a relaxing oasis along the Ohio River. Luxurious guest rooms have crown molding, soft carpeting or elegant hardwood floors, and are decorated in soothing neutral tones. None of the guest rooms share walls providing the ultimate in quiet and privacy. A breakfast buffet is served each morning and local vineyards are featured during afternoon wine and cheese hours. Grab a book from the library and sit on the screened gazebo with a view of the river. Or inside, tickle the ivories on the baby grand piano in the music parlor or try your luck at a game in the billiards room; both rooms have a romantic fireplace for chilly evenings. You can also explore the area on a complimentary bicycle or play a rousing game of croquet on the manicured lawn. Halfway between Louisville, Kentucky and Cincinnati, Ohio, this bed and breakfast is near wineries and the Kentucky Speedway. If you bring a group ask about the discount for booking three or more rooms.

Innkeeper(s): Chef Kurt Doerflinger, Kathy Doerflinger. $125-269. 7 rooms with PB, 3 with FP, 1 total suite, including 2 two-bedroom suites, 1 conference room. Chef on staff. Full breakfast with hot entree, snacks/refreshments included in rates.

Certificate may be used: Monday-Thursday. No holidays. Cannot be combined with other offers. Subject to availability.

Louisiana

Baton Rouge

Stockade Bed & Breakfast

8860 Highland Road
Baton Rouge, LA 70808
(225)769-7358 (888)900-5430
Internet: www.thestockade.com
E-mail: stay@thestockade.com

The gated entrance near the road is a reminder that this large Spanish-style hacienda was once a Civil War stockade. It is listed in the National Register of Historic Places as an archeological site. Sit by the large wood-burning fireplace in the great room that has a baby grand piano, custom-sculpted copper fountain and floor-to-ceiling glass wall. Nicely appointed guest bedrooms include an assortment of comfortable amenities. Select a room with a sitting area or balcony. The Red and Blue Rooms can be adjoined into a suite. Enjoy a hearty southern breakfast or lighter fare in the dining room with an entrance to a covered patio with a view of the bayou wilderness beyond. Garlic cheese grits, egg souffle and hickory smoked bacon are favorites.

Innkeeper(s): Janice DeLerno. $135-216. 6 rooms, 5 with PB, 1 with WP, 1 two-bedroom suite. Breakfast and snacks/refreshments included in rates. Types of meals: Full gourmet bkfst.

Certificate may be used: December-January, Sunday-Thursday.

New Orleans

Avenue Inn Bed and Breakfast

4125 Saint Charles Ave
New Orleans, LA 70115
(504) 269-2640 (800) 490-8542 Fax:(504)269-2641
Internet: www.avenueinnbb.com
E-mail: info@avenueinnbb.com

Circa 1891. Set among timeless oaks on famous St. Charles Street is this 1891 Thomas Sully mansion. The inn has high ceilings and hardwood floors, and its 17 guest rooms are furnished with period pieces. Come during Mardi Gras and you can sit on the big front porch and watch the 18 Mardi Gras parades that come down St. Charles Avenue. The French Quarter, Central Business District, Convention Center as well as Tulane and Loyola Universities are all within 1-3/4 miles. Antique shops, restaurants and night spots are within walking distance.

Innkeeper(s): Joe & Bebe Rabhan. $89-399. 17 rooms with PB, 5 with FP. Breakfast included in rates. Types of meals: Cont.

Certificate may be used: Subject to availability, excludes holidays and special events.

Fairchild House

1518 Prytania Street
New Orleans, LA 70130-4416
(504)524-0154 (800)256-8096 Fax:(504)568-0063
Internet: www.fairchildhouse.com
E-mail: info@fairchildhouse.com

Circa 1841. Situated in the oak-lined Lower Garden District of New Orleans, this Greek Revival home was built by architect L.H. Pilie. The house and its guest houses maintain a Victorian ambiance with elegantly appointed guest rooms. Wine and cheese are served upon guests' arrival. The bed & breakfast, which is on the Mardi Gras parade route, is 17 blocks from the French Quarter and 12 blocks from the convention center. Streetcars are just one block away, as are many local attractions, including paddleboat cruises, Canal Place and Riverwalk shopping, an aquarium, zoo, the St. Charles Avenue mansions and Tulane and Loyola universities.

Innkeeper(s): Rita Olmo & Beatriz Aprigliano-Ziegler. $65-145. 5 rooms, 9 with PB, 1 suite. Breakfast included in rates. Types of meals: Cont plus.

Certificate may be used: June 1-Aug. 31. Please call during other seasons.

HH Whitney House on the Historic Esplanade

1923 Esplanade Avenue
New Orleans, LA 70116-1706
(504)948-9448 (800)924-9448
Internet: www.hhwhitneyhouse.com
E-mail: stay@hhwhitneyhouse.com

Circa 1865. The Civil War had barely ended when builders broke ground on this elegant Italianate mansion. More than a century later, much of its original charm has been maintained. The intricate molding and plasterwork are of the highest quality. Common rooms with Victorian furnishings and appointments complement the architecture. Distinctive antiques include an early 20th-century player piano. A decorative fireplace is featured in each guest bedroom. The Bride's Room, with a lace-draped canopy bed, makes a spacious two- or three-bedroom suite when combined with the Solarium or Groom's rooms. The romantic Honeymoon Suite in the former servants' quarters offers total privacy. Located in the Esplanade Ridge historic district, the French Quarter is just a half-mile walk.

Innkeeper(s): Glen Miller/Randy Saizan. $75-259. 5 rooms, 3 with PB, 5 with FP. Breakfast and snacks/refreshments included in rates. Types of meals: Full bkfst.

Certificate may be used: Last minute bookings, subject to availability.

Terrell House

1441 Magazine St.
New Orleans, LA 70130
(504)237-2076 (866)261-9687 Fax:(504)247-0565
Internet: www.terrellhouse.com
E-mail: lobrien@terrellhouse.com

Circa 1858. Gracing the Lower Garden District in an historic area near the French Quarter, Terrell House is a grand three-story Italianate stucco-over-brick antebellum mansion in New Orleans, Louisiana. Relax in elegance and comfort on a porch, in the den or double parlors with period English and American antiques. Air-conditioned guest bedrooms with generous upscale amenities in the main house and the adjacent carriage house look out or open onto the courtyard with lush gardens, fountains and shaded sitting areas. The carriage house is furnished with locally handcrafted cypress furniture. Linger over a satisfying breakfast that reflects warm southern hospitality before exploring the popular sites of the city.

Innkeeper(s): Ed O'Brien, Linda O'Brien. $125-250. 9 rooms, 8 with PB, 1 two-bedroom suite. Breakfast included in rates. Types of meals: Full bkfst, early coffee/tea, snacks/refreshments and hors d'oeuvres.

Certificate may be used: October-June, Sunday-Thursday, subject to availability.

Maine

Bar Harbor

Shore Path Cottage on the Ocean

24 Atlantic Avenue
Bar Harbor, ME 04609
(207)288-0643
Internet: www.shorepathcottage.com/
E-mail: stay@shorepathcottage.com

Circa 1880. Gracing a quiet neighborhood on the Bar Harbor oceanfront, this classic example of Maine coast architecture and its desirable location is just a five-minute drive or bike ride to Acadia National Park, one of the area's popular destinations. Relax on the inviting wraparound porch or sit by the fire in the evening. Guest rooms are named after the children who grew up in the home and some boast clawfoot tubs, fireplaces, ocean views, oriental rugs, paintings, books and pleasing amenities. Several function as suites for families or friends traveling together. A hearty, healthy breakfast includes an assortment of local fruit, homemade organic granola, breads, egg recipes, yogurts, and beverages. Gather for afternoon refreshments and treats.
Innkeeper(s): Roberta Chester. $140-260. 9 rooms. Types of meals: Full bkfst, early coffee/tea, snacks/refreshments, wine and Lemonade and Cookies.
Certificate may be used: Oct. 22-Nov. 15.

Bath

Inn At Bath

969 Washington St
Bath, ME 04530-2650
(207)443-4294 Fax:(207)443-4295
Internet: www.innatbath.com
E-mail: innkeeper@innatbath.com

Circa 1835. Located in the heart of Bath's Historic District, this Greek Revival home is surrounded by fabulous gardens. Well-appointed, spacious guest bedrooms are furnished with antiques. Some feature two-person Jacuzzis, wood-burning fireplaces, sofas, writing desks and private entrances. Breakfast includes buttermilk blueberry pancakes, green chili egg puff, pecan waffles with fresh fruit, homemade granola and organic yogurt. Walk to the Kennebec River, the Chocolate Church Arts Center or local shops, galleries and restaurants. Visit the Maine Maritime Museum. Innkeeper Elizabeth will assist with arranging guided fishing trips; spotting bald eagles, ospreys and seals; taking a lighthouse tour; finding the perfect lobster roll on a dock or booking a sailing excursion.
Innkeeper(s): Elizabeth Knowlton. $150-190. 8 rooms with PB, 4 with FP, 1 suite. Breakfast included in rates. Types of meals: Full bkfst, veg bkfst and early coffee/tea.

Certificate may be used: Nov. 1-May 15, Sunday-Thursday, excludes holiday weeks, school weekends and graduations.

Belfast

The Jeweled Turret Inn

40 Pearl St
Belfast, ME 04915-6330
(207) 338-2304 (800) 696-2304
Internet: www.jeweledturret.com
E-mail: info@jeweledturret.com

Circa 1898. This grand Victorian is named for the staircase that winds up the turret, lighted by stained- and leaded-glass panels and jewel-like embellishments. It was built for attorney James Harriman. Dark pine beams adorn the ceiling of the den, and the fireplace is constructed of bark and rocks from every state in the Union. Elegant antiques furnish the guest rooms. Guests can relax in one of the inn's four parlors, which are furnished with period antiques, wallpapers, lace and boast fireplaces. Some rooms have a ceiling fan and whirlpool tub or fireplace. The verandas feature wicker and iron bistro sets and views of the historic district. The inn is within walking distance of the town and its shops, restaurants and the harbor.
Innkeeper(s): Cathy Heffentrager, Carl Heffentrager. $130-169. 7 rooms with PB, 1 with FP, 1 with WP. Breakfast and afternoon tea included in rates. Types of meals: Full gourmet bkfst, early coffee/tea, Crackers and cheese and sherry served during social hour 5:30-6:30 pm.
Certificate may be used: April, May and November, holidays excluded.

Boothbay Harbor

Harbour Towne Inn on The Waterfront

71 Townsend Ave
Boothbay Harbor, ME 04538-1158
(207) 633-4300 (800) 722-4240
Internet: www.harbourtowneinn.com
E-mail: info@harbourtowneinn.com

Circa 1840. This Victorian inn's well-known trademark boasts that it is "the Finest B&B on the Waterfront." The inn's 12 air-conditioned rooms offer outside decks, and the Penthouse has an outstanding view of the harbor from its private deck. Breakfast is served in the inn's Sunroom, and guests also may relax in the parlor, which has a miniature antique library and a beautiful antique fireplace. A conference area is available for meetings. The inn's meticulous

grounds include flower gardens and well-kept shrubs and trees. A wonderful new addition is a dock and float for sunning, sketches/painting, reading or hopping aboard a canoe, kayak or small boat. It's a pleasant five-minute walk to the village and its art galleries, restaurants, shops and boat trips. Special off-season packages are available. Ft. William Henry and the Fisherman's Memorial are nearby.

Innkeeper(s): Stefanie McElman, Patricia Richardson. $99-399. 8 rooms with PB, 1 two-bedroom suite. Breakfast and afternoon tea included in rates. Types of meals: Full gourmet bkfst, early coffee/tea, picnic lunch, snacks/refreshments and wine.

Certificate may be used: Anytime, subject to availability.

Camden

Blue Harbor House, A Village Inn

67 Elm St
Camden, ME 04843-1904
(207)236-3196 (800)248-3196 Fax:(207)236-6523
Internet: www.blueharborhouse.com
E-mail: info@blueharborhouse.com

Circa 1810. Blue Harbor House is a classic village inn on the coast of Maine. This Camden bed and breakfast is comfortably elegant yet refreshingly casual. Historic charms  blend well with modern comforts. Relax in the parlor or on a front-porch rocker. Stroll to the picturesque harbor, dine on lobster and seafood chowder in the wonderful local restaurants, browse the art galleries and shop in the boutiques. Inviting guest rooms or suites boast four-poster beds with soft linens, fireplaces, Jacuzzi tubs, robes and WiFi. Begin each day with a delicious breakfast offering popular specialties that may include hazelnut waffles, blueberry pancakes with maple syrup and blueberry butter or portabella mushroom and gruyere omelet with Irish soda bread. Go on a windjammer cruise or take a day trip to Acadia National Park. Ask about special packages available.

Innkeeper(s): Annette Hazzard, Terry Hazzard. $95-185. 11 rooms with PB, 3 with FP, 1 with HT, 4 total suites, including 2 two-bedroom suites, 1 conference room. Breakfast and afternoon tea included in rates. Types of meals: Full gourmet bkfst, early coffee/tea and wine.

Certificate may be used: Anytime, November-March, subject to availability.

Captain Swift Inn

72 Elm St
Camden, ME 04843-1907
(207)236-8113 (800)251-0865 Fax:(207)230-0464
Internet: www.swiftinn.com
E-mail: swiftinn@roadrunner.com

Circa 1810. This inviting Federal-style home remains much as it did in the 19th century, including the original 12-over-12 windows and a beehive oven. The home's historic flavor has been diligently preserved and the original five fireplaces, handsome wide pine floors, restored moldings and exposed beams add to the warm and cozy interior. Air-

conditioned guest bedrooms feature warm quilts on comfortable beds and private baths. On the first floor a guest bedroom is entirely handicapped accessible. A full and hearty breakfast is offered daily and includes specialties such as Blueberry French Toast or Sausage and Brie Casserole. Situated in Camden, the Captain Swift Inn is centrally located on the Mid-Coast of Maine to easily explore all that this scenic state has to offer.

Innkeeper(s): Norm & Linda Henthorn. $99-245. 8 rooms with PB, 4 with FP, 2 with WP, 2 suites. Breakfast and snacks/refreshments included in rates. Types of meals: Full bkfst, veg bkfst and early coffee/tea.

Certificate may be used: November-April, subject to availability.

Lord Camden Inn

24 Main Street
Camden, ME 04843
(207) 236-4325 (800) 336-4325 Fax:(207)236-7141
Internet: www.lordcamdeninn.com
E-mail: info@lordcamdeninn.com

Circa 1893. Lord Camden Inn, a fine luxury boutique inn, has been extensively renovated to offer pampering new amenities while retaining its classic, richly elegant heritage. Adorning the coastal village of Camden, Maine, it boasts award-winning hospitality and comfort. Work out in the Fitness Room and schedule in-room spa services. An assortment of lavish guest bedrooms and suites offer modern-day comfort and a warm and inviting ambiance. Sleep in a Suite Dreams Bed by a gas fireplace and private balcony overlooking the Megunticook River or Camden Harbor and Penobscot Bay. Some rooms are ADA accessible, child and pet friendly. Linger over a breakfast buffet before embarking on the scenic sites and historic attractions of the area. This B&B is a popular choice for intimate weddings and romantic or family getaways.

Innkeeper(s): Erick Anderson. $99-299. 36 rooms with PB, 11 with FP, 2 with WP, 7 suites, 1 conference room. Breakfast and snacks/refreshments included in rates. Types of meals: Full bkfst, early coffee/tea and wine.

Certificate may be used: Nov. 1-June 15.

Dexter

The Brewster Inn

37 Zion's Hill Rd
Dexter, ME 04930-1122
(207) 924-3130 Fax:(207)924-9768
Internet: www.brewsterinn.com
E-mail: innkeeper@brewsterinn.com

Circa 1860. Once the home of Senator and Governor Ralph Owen Brewster, this historic inn allows guests to walk in the footsteps of famous visitors including Presidents Truman and Taft. Featured on HGTV's "If Walls Could Talk," there are covered porches, a rose garden, event space, and nine guest rooms. Natural wood paneling adds a warm ambiance to the three-room Honeymoon Suite with a queen-size bed and whirlpool tub for two. The whimsical Game Room is decorated like a ski chalet and can comfortably sleep four people. For a minimal fee, friends and relatives can join guests on the patio for the continental breakfast which includes a hot dish; guest favorites include orange and raspberry croissants and an apple and cranberry bake. Request the romance package with roses, champagne, and strawberries for a special getaway for two. If you travel with friends, receive a 30% discount off select rooms when you stay two nights or more.

Innkeeper(s): Mark Stephens. $69-149. 9 rooms with PB, 2 with FP, 2 with WP, 1 two-bedroom suite, 1 conference room. Breakfast included in rates. Types of meals: Full bkfst, veg bkfst, early coffee/tea, wine, Gluten free, Vegetarian, nut free and lactose free.

Certificate may be used: Anytime, subject to availability, excludes holidays.

Eliot

Farmstead Bed and Breakfast

999 Goodwin Road
Eliot, ME 03903
(207)748-3145 Fax:(207)748-3659
Internet: www.farmstead-bb.com
E-mail: farmsteadb@aol.com

Circa 1704. New England is known for its quaint, colonial towns. This bed and breakfast in Eliot, Maine combines that nostalgic ambiance with modern amenities. Quilts cover the comfortable beds in the six charming guest rooms. A large picture window allows plentiful sunshine into the breakfast room where guests can enjoy homemade syrup and blueberry pancakes made on the griddle. No trip to Maine would be complete without lobster and the inn has a large pot and gas grill on the shady lawn if guests want to cook their own for a picnic. Let the cool breezes envelop you as you laze away on the hammock. Visit in winter to see the pine trees covered in pristine white snow. Experience the Seacoast area's history of farming at the Raitt Homestead Farm Museum. The historic town of Portsmouth, New Hampshire is only 12 minutes away; the walkable city is filled with cafes, restaurants, jazz clubs, and art galleries.

Innkeeper(s): John Lippincott, Marian Lippincott. $72-95. 6 rooms with PB. Breakfast included in rates.

Certificate may be used: Sunday-Thursday, subject to availability.

Greenville

Greenville Inn at Moosehead Lake

40 Norris Street
Greenville, ME 04441-1194
(207)695-2206 (888)695-6000
Internet: www.greenvilleinn.com
E-mail: innkeeper@greenvilleinn.com

Circa 1885. Lumber baron William Shaw built this inn, which sits on a hill overlooking Moosehead Lake and the Squaw Mountains. The inn includes many unique features. Ten years were needed to complete the embellishments on the cherry and mahogany paneling, which is found throughout the inn. A spruce tree is painted on one of the leaded-glass windows on the stairway landing. The inn's  six fireplaces are adorned with carved mantels, English tiles and mosaics. The inn's dining room is ideal for a romantic dinner. Fresh, seasonal ingredients fill the ever-changing menu, and the dining room also offers a variety of wine choices.

Innkeeper(s): Terry Johannemann, Jeff Johannemann. $100-450. 14 rooms with PB, 6 with FP, 1 with WP, 4 two-bedroom suites, 6 cottages, 2 conference rooms. Breakfast included in rates. Types of meals: Country bkfst, veg bkfst, early coffee/tea, picnic lunch, wine and gourmet dinner. Restaurant on premises.

Certificate may be used: Nov. 1-April 30.

Hallowell

Maple Hill Farm B&B Inn

11 Inn Road
Hallowell, ME 04347
(207) 622-2708 (800) 622-2708 Fax:(207)622-0655
Internet: www.MapleBB.com
E-mail: stay@MapleBB.com

Circa 1906. See much of Maine from Maple Hill Farm Bed & Breakfast Inn and Conference Center in the four-season location of Hallowell, near Augusta. This award-winning, eco-friendly B&B spans 130 acres of wildflower fields, pastures, woods, a pond and more than 800 neighboring acres of public land. Ask for a trail map to hike, walk, run, snowshoe or cross-country ski. Relax on a hammock or chair in the shade of a maple tree or on the front porch. Sit by the fire in the living room, sip a locally brewed beer in the full-service bar and use the well-equipped guest kitchen. This renovated Victorian house boasts guest rooms that may include a double whirlpool tub, fireplace and secluded deck. A custom country breakfast uses fresh eggs from the farm. Maple Hill is a certified environmental leader with comprehensive renewable energy systems and daily green practices.

Innkeeper(s): Scott Cowger, Vince Hannan. $99-209. 8 rooms with PB, 5 with FP, 4 with WP, 3 conference rooms. Breakfast and afternoon tea included in rates. Types of meals: Country bkfst, veg bkfst, early coffee/tea, snacks/refreshments, wine and Custom catering and private events on request.

Certificate may be used: May-October, Sunday-Wednesday. November-April, anytime, but not both Friday and Saturday. Discount is off rack rates. Please inquire.

Harpswell

Harpswell Inn

108 Lookout Point Rd
Harpswell, ME 04079
(207)833-5509 (207)800-8435509 Fax:(207)833-2437
Internet: www.harpswellinn.com
E-mail: reservations@harpswellinn.com

Circa 1761. Originally the cookhouse of the shipyard, Harpswell Inn was built in 1761 as a three-story Colonial at Lookout Point on a knoll overlooking the cove in Harpswell, Maine. Now completely renovated, this inn is furnished with antiques and offers pleasant surroundings on more than two acres with oak-shaded lawns. Watch the sunsets over Middle Bay from the front porch. Play pool in the Billiards Room or do a jigsaw puzzle in the Great Room. The Middle Bay Room is perfect for special events and meetings. Stay in a gracious guest bedroom or suite that may include a gas fireplace, private ocean-view deck, Jacuzzi or clawfoot tub and skylights. Start each day with Chef Moseley's famous breakfast in the dining room.

Innkeeper(s): Anne and Richard Moseley. $135-259. 12 rooms, 10 with PB, 5 with FP, 2 with WP, 3 suites, 4 cottages, 1 conference room. Breakfast included in rates. Types of meals: Full bkfst and Evening meals for overnight function room guests.

Certificate may be used: mid-October though mid-May, subject to availability and discount must be mentioned when making the actual reservation.

Kennebunkport

Maine Stay Inn & Cottages

34 Maine Street
Kennebunkport, ME 04046-6174
(207) 967-2117 (800) 950-2117
Internet: www.mainestayinn.com
E-mail: innkeeper@mainestayinn.com

Circa 1860. In the National Register, this inn is a square-block Italianate contoured in a low hip-roof design. Later additions reflecting the Queen Anne period include a suspended spiral

staircase, crystal windows, ornately carved mantels and moldings, bay windows and porches. A sea captain built the handsome cupola that became a favorite spot for making taffy. In the 1920s, the cupola was a place from which to spot off-shore rumrunners. Guests enjoy afternoon tea with stories of the Maine Stay's heritage. Two suites and one room in the main building and six of the cottage rooms have working fireplaces.

Innkeeper(s): Judi Hauer, Walter Hauer. $129-369. 17 rooms with PB, 9 with FP, 6 with WP, 3 total suites, including 1 two-bedroom suite, 11 cottages. Breakfast and afternoon tea included in rates. Types of meals: Full gourmet bkfst, early coffee/tea and Limited In-Room menu.

Certificate may be used: Dec. 15-March, Sunday-Thursday, excludes holidays.

The Captain Lord Mansion

Corner Pleasant & Green, PO Box 800
Kennebunkport, ME 04046
(207)967-3141 (800)522-3141 Fax:(207)967-3172
Internet: www.captainlord.com
E-mail: innkeeper@captainlord.com

Circa 1812. In the National Register, the Captain Lord Mansion was built during the War of 1812 and is one of the finest examples of Federal architecture on the coast of Maine. The home rests at the edge of the village green within view of the Kennebunk River and within walking distance of the town's many historic sites. The romantically appointed guest rooms include roomy four-poster beds, gas fireplaces and heated marble and tile floors in the bathrooms. Some rooms include a double Jacuzzi tub. Guests are further pampered with fresh flowers, a full breakfast and afternoon treats.

Innkeeper(s): Bev Davis, Rick Litchfield. $199-499. 8 rooms, 16 with PB, 16 with FP, 8 with WP, 1 suite, 2 conference rooms. Breakfast, afternoon tea and snacks/refreshments included in rates. Types of meals: Full bkfst and early coffee/tea.

Certificate may be used: November-June, Sunday-Thursday, excluding holidays, subject to availability. Deluxe rooms only. Cannot be combined with any other coupon, discount or 3rd party gift certificates.

Kittery

Enchanted Nights B&B

29 Wentworth St
Kittery, ME 03904-1720
(207)439-1489
Internet: www.enchantednights.org

Circa 1890. The innkeepers bill this unique inn as a "Victorian fantasy for the romantic at heart." Each of the guest rooms is unique, from the spacious rooms with double whirlpool tubs and fireplaces to the cozy turret room. A whimsical combination of country French and Victorian decor permeates the interior. Wrought-iron beds and hand-painted furnishings add to the ambiance. Breakfasts, often with a vegetarian theme, are served with gourmet coffee in the morning room on antique floral china.

Innkeeper(s): Nancy Bogenberger & Peter Lamandia. $52-300. 8 rooms, 6 with PB, 4 with FP, 2 conference rooms. Breakfast included in rates. Types of meals: Full gourmet bkfst, veg bkfst and early coffee/tea.

Certificate may be used: Nov. 1-April 30, Sunday-Thursday. No holidays.

Naples

Augustus Bove House

11 Sebago Rd
Naples, ME 04055
(207)693-6365 (888)831-2039
Internet: www.naplesmaine.com
E-mail: augbovehouse@roadrunner.com

Circa 1820. A long front lawn nestles up against the stone foundation and veranda of this house, once known as the Hotel Naples, one of the area's summer hotels in the 1800s. In the 1920s, the inn was host to a number of prominent guests, including Enrico Caruso, Joseph P. Kennedy and Howard Hughes. The guest rooms are decorated in a Colonial style and modestly furnished with antiques. Many rooms provide a view of Long Lake. A fancy country breakfast is provided.

Innkeeper(s): David Stetson, Arlene Stetson. $99-250. 10 rooms with PB, 3 suites. Breakfast and afternoon tea included in rates. Types of meals: Full bkfst and early coffee/tea.

Certificate may be used: Sunday-Thursday, must mention certificate before making reservation.

Ogunquit

Yardarm Village Inn

406 Shore Road
Ogunquit, ME 03907-0773
(207)646-7006 (888)927-3276
Internet: www.yardarmvillageinn.com
E-mail: yardarm@maine.rr.com

Circa 1892. In the quiet part of town, just south of the entrance to Perkins Cove, this three-story classic New England inn offers a delightful selection of accommodations. The large veranda is the perfect spot for relaxing on a white wicker rocker. Comfortable guest bedrooms and two-room suites are furnished and decorated in a Colonial-country style. Start the day with homemade blueberry muffins, fruit and beverages. Take an afternoon or evening charter on the Inn's private sailboat past the three-mile beach or along the rocky coast. The on-site wine and cheese shop is well-stocked to satisfy the most discriminating palate.

Innkeeper(s): Scott Drury, Beverlee Drury. $100-175. 10 rooms with PB, 4 suites. Breakfast included in rates. Types of meals: Continental breakfast of homemade blueberry muffins, fresh fruit, juice, beer/wine, cheese and gift shop.

Certificate may be used: In season rates apply;Sunday-Thursday, May-June, Sept. 14-30 and October 1-9 and 14-23, excluding holidays. Anytime, within one week of arrival. Not to be combined with any other special promotions. In season rates apply.

Old Orchard Beach

Atlantic Birches Inn

20 Portland Ave Rt 98
Old Orchard Beach, ME 04064-2212
(207)934-5295 (888)934-5295 Fax:(207)934-3781
Internet: www.atlanticbirches.com
E-mail: info@AtlanticBirches.com

Circa 1903. The front porch of this Shingle-style Victorian and 1920s bungalow are shaded by white birch trees. The houses are a place for relaxation and enjoyment, uncluttered, simple havens filled with comfortable furnishings. The guest rooms are decorated with antiques and pastel wallcoverings. Maine's coast offers an endless amount of activities, from boating to whale watching. It is a five-minute walk to the beach and the pier.

Innkeeper(s): Ray Deleo, Heidi Deleo. $101-216. 10 rooms with PB, 3 two-bedroom suites. Breakfast included in rates. Types of meals: Cont plus and early coffee/tea.

Certificate may be used: Nov. 1-May 15, no holidays.

Rockland

Winding Way Bed and Breakfast

39 Union Street
Rockland, ME 04841
(207) 542-5540
Internet: www.windingwaybedandbreakfast.com
E-mail: windway@midcoast.com

Circa 1855. Relax while sitting in a rocking chair with a beverage on the enclosed front porch of this restored Victorian home. The welcome area, gift shop, sunroom, kitchen and art gallery are downstairs. Gather to play a game or read in the second-floor sitting lounge. Stay in one of the two comfortable guest rooms with fine linens, fluffy towels and pleasing amenities. Start each day with a continental-plus breakfast buffet that may include homemade scones, lobster quiche, granola, and Keurig beverages among other delights. Onsite parking is provided. From the downtown Rockland location, take a short walk to the Harbor boardwalk. Visit the nearby Farnsworth Museum and other local sights of midcoast Maine, then sit in one of the small gardens with refreshments.

Innkeeper(s): Anne McMath. $125-175. 2 rooms with PB, 2 with HT. Breakfast, afternoon tea, snacks/refreshments and Ice cream available to guests included in rates. Types of meals: Cont plus and early coffee/tea.

Certificate may be used: Anytime, subject to availability.

Rumford

The Perennial Inn

141 Jed Martin Road
Rumford, ME 04276
(207)369-0309 Fax:(207)369-8016
Internet: Perennialinn.com
E-mail: info@perennialinn.com

Circa 1884. Encompassing 42 acres of scenic beauty in the Blue Mountains, this historic 1884 Victorian farmhouse is surrounded by grassy fields, ponds, streams and pine forests. The renovated New England home with a wraparound porch and huge red barn offers secluded comfort and convenient access to Route 2. Read a book from the library in the cheery parlor or watch a DVD by the fieldstone fireplace in the Gathering Room. Play pool on a maple table in the billiard parlor. Genuine hospitality is extended with thoughtful details to pamper and please. Romantic guest bedrooms and a two-room suite feature wide pine floors, high ceilings, sunny windows and sitting areas with family heirlooms and fine furnishings. A hearty country breakfast is served in the dining room. Soak in the hot tub under the stars.

Innkeeper(s): Jenna, Darlene Ginsberg. $85-175. 7 rooms, 4 with PB, 1 two-bedroom suite. Breakfast, afternoon tea, snacks/refreshments and wine included in rates. Types of meals: Country bkfst and early coffee/tea.

Certificate may be used: Sunday-Thursday, May-June and September-Dec. 15.

South Thomaston

Weskeag Inn B&B at the Water

14 Elm St.
South Thomaston, ME 04858-0213
(207)596-6676 (800)596-5576
Internet: www.weskeag.com
E-mail: innkeeper@weskeag.com

Circa 1830. The backyard of this three-story house stretches to the edge of Weskeag River and Ballyhac Cove. Fifty yards from the house, there's reversing white-water rapids, created by the 10-foot tide that narrows into the estuary. Guests often sit by the water's edge to watch the birds and the lobster fishermen. Sea kayakers can launch at the inn and explore the nearby coves and then paddle on to the ocean. The inn's furnishings include a mixture of comfortable antiques. Featherbed eggs are a house specialty.

Innkeeper(s): Gray Smith and Hazel Giberson. $95-150. 8 rooms, 6 with PB, 1 two-bedroom suite. Breakfast included in rates. Types of meals: Full bkfst and early coffee/tea.

Certificate may be used: Oct. 16 through June 14.

Southwest Harbor

Penury Hall Bed & Breakfast

374 Main St
Southwest Harbor, ME 04679-4245
(207)244-7102 (866)473-6425 Fax:(207)244-5651
Internet: www.penuryhall.com
E-mail: tstrong@penuryhall.com

Circa 1830. Located by Acadia National Park on Mount Desert Island in Southwest Harbor is a Victorian home that originated in 1830 when the first part of the house was built. Little by little, the house was added to. Eventually, the three homes had been combined into this one rambling structure, a common occurrence in New England in the 1800s. Today the asymmetrical roofline reveals that history. The seven garden areas have perennial and annual flowers as well as vegetables and herbs. The home is decorated with fine art, antiques and memorabilia that reflects the innkeepers' interests in gardening, music and sailing. At Penury Hall, every effort is made to make guests feel at home. Guests may store food items in the fridge, wash clothes in the laundry room and play games or listen to music in the library. Retire in one of the three guest rooms, then awake to a gourmet breakfast that offers such courses as eggs Benedict, "Penurious Omelets" or cinnamon-raisin French toast. Then take out the inn's canoe to explore nearby lakes or else rent mountain bikes and carracks next door and head out for bike trails. Or, enjoy sauntering through the antique shops or the 14 local museums. End the day by relaxing in the sauna.

Innkeeper(s): Gretchen Strong. $100-145. 3 rooms with PB. Breakfast and afternoon tea included in rates. Types of meals: Full gourmet bkfst and early coffee/tea.

Certificate may be used: Anytime, November-March, subject to availability.

The Birches Bed and Breakfast

44 Fernald Point Road
Southwest Harbor, ME 04679
(207) 244-5182 Fax:(207)244-5182
Internet: www.thebirchesbnb.com
E-mail: dick@thebirchesbnb.com

Circa 1916. Overlooking the Atlantic Ocean and Acadia National Park, enjoy the relaxed, casual atmosphere of this year-round, historic bed and breakfast in coastal Maine. Originally built as a summer house, extensive renovations make this an inviting place in any season. Sit on the large front porch with island views or on the wind-protected sundeck. Stroll the gardens or play croquet on the court. The Birches is just 350 yards from the first tee at the golf course. Stay in a large, airy guest bedroom and wake up to a satisfying breakfast. A daily rotating menu features Maine blueberry pancakes on Sundays, omelets on Saturdays, and waffles, egg dishes and French toast on the days in between. Entrees are accompanied by fresh fruit, cereals, juices and hot beverages.

Innkeeper(s): Susi Homer. $129-249. 3 rooms with PB, 1 cottage. Breakfast, afternoon tea, snacks/refreshments, wine and Picnics can be arranged by prior arrangements. Please inquire when making your reservation included in rates.

Certificate may be used: Novemer-March, subject to availbility.

Sullivan

Taunton River Bed and Breakfast

19 Taunton Drive
Sullivan, ME 04664
(207)422-2070
Internet: www.tauntonriverbnb.com/
E-mail: dottiemace@aol.com

Circa 1845. Ocean views, lighthouses, blueberry fields, and this lovely inn can be found along the Schoodic Scenic Byway. Let serenity fill your soul as you sit on a porch swing or Adirondack chair looking out over the water. Three cozy guest rooms offer a queen bed, sitting area, and comfortable robes

while mornings bring a full breakfast to keep you satisfied as you explore Acadia National Park. Flowers decorate the lawn in summer and a crackling fire keeps everything warm in winter. Lobster boats and clamming are still part of the tradition in this unspoiled part of Maine. A golfer's paradise, there are nine courses within 30 miles of the bed and breakfast. Artists showcase paintings, sculptures, and hand-woven textiles in local galleries and studios. Stay for a weekend or spend a whole week; the innkeeper has a 7 Trips in 7 Days plan ready to help you create your perfect itinerary.

Innkeeper(s): Dottie Mace. $115-125. 3 rooms.

Certificate may be used:

Vinalhaven

Payne Homestead at the Moses Webster House

14 Atlantic Ave
Vinalhaven, ME 04863
(207)863-9963 (888)863-9963
Internet: www.paynehomestead.com
E-mail: Donna@paynehomestead.com

Circa 1873. Make your inn visit an adventure by taking a short ferry ride to this island mansion off the coast of Rockland. The handsome Second Empire French Victorian is at the edge of town. Enjoy a game room, reading nooks and a parlor. The Coral Room boasts a view of Indian Creek, while shadows of Carver's Pond may be seen through the windows of Mama's Room. A favorite selection is the Moses Webster Room that features a marble mantel, tin ceiling and a bay window looking out at the town. Breakfast usually offers fresh fruit platters and egg dishes with either French toast or pancakes. Restaurants and Lane Island Nature Conservancy are close. Take scenic walks past private fishing boats, ponds and shoreline, all part of the hideaway quality noted by National Geographic in "America's Best Kept Secrets."

Innkeeper(s): Lee Payne, Donna Payne. $90-265. 4 rooms, 1 with PB, 1 two-bedroom suite. Breakfast included in rates. Types of meals: Full bkfst and early coffee/tea.

Certificate may be used: June-August, Monday-Thursday.

Walpole

Brannon-Bunker Inn

349 S St Rt 129
Walpole, ME 04573
(207)563-5941 (800)563-9225
Internet: www.brannonbunkerinn.com
E-mail: brbnkinn@lincoln.midcoast.com

Circa 1820. This Cape-style house has been a home to many generations of Maine residents, one of whom was captain of a ship that sailed to the Arctic. During the '20s, the barn served as a dance hall. Later, it was converted into comfortable guest rooms. Victorian and American antiques are featured, and there are collections of WWI military memorabilia.

Innkeeper(s): Joe Hovance, Jeanne Hovance. $90-100. 7 rooms, 5 with PB, 1 suite. Breakfast included in rates. Types of meals: Cont plus.

Certificate may be used: September-June, except holiday weekends, subject to availability.

Maryland

Annapolis

Gibson's Lodgings

110 Prince George St
Annapolis, MD 21401-1704
(410) 268-5555 (877) 330-0057
Internet: www.gibsonslodgings.com
E-mail: gibsonslodgings@starpower.net

Circa 1774. This Georgian house in the heart of the Annapolis Historic District was built on the site of the Old Courthouse, circa 1680. Two historic houses make up the inn, and there was a new house built in 1988. All the rooms, old and new, are furnished with antiques. Only a few yards away is the City Dock Harbor and within two blocks is the Naval Academy visitor's gate.

Innkeeper(s): Meredith Lauer & Peggy Summers. $99-319. 21 rooms, 18 with PB, 1 with WP, 6 total suites, including 3 two-bedroom suites, 1 conference room. Breakfast included in rates. Types of meals: Cont plus.

Certificate may be used: Sunday-Thursday, no holidays or special events.

Reynolds Tavern

7 Church Circle
Annapolis, MD 21401
(410)295-9555 Fax:(410)295-9559
Internet: www.reynoldstavern.org
E-mail: reynoldstavern@comcast.net

Circa 1737. Prominently positioned on Church Circle in Annapolis, Maryland, Reynolds Tavern is wonderfully restored to reflect its 1737 origins and is one of America's oldest taverns. The stately red brick inn with Georgian architecture offers gracious hospitality. Play darts in the English-style Sly Fox Pub and Restaurant in the cellar with a large open fireplace and Rumford Broiler. Spacious guest suites feature period antiques and a soft elegance. Casual alfresco dining is available in the courtyard. Besides serving tea, the Reynolds Tea Room offers lunch and dinner. The location is convenient to the local sites and historic area attractions.

Innkeeper(s): Wes Burge, Marilyn Burge. $220-295. 3 rooms with PB, 2 two-bedroom suites. Breakfast, snacks/refreshments and Cream Tea included in rates. Types of meals: Full gourmet bkfst, veg bkfst, Sun. brunch, early coffee/tea, afternoon tea, hors d'oeuvres, wine and gourmet dinner. Restaurant on premises.

Certificate may be used: Dec. 1-Feb. 28, excludes all holidays.

Baltimore

1840s Carrollton Inn

50 Albemarle Street
Baltimore, MD 21202
(410)385-1840 Fax:(410)385-9080
Internet: www.1840scarrolltoninn.com
E-mail: info@1840scarrolltoninn.com

Circa 2007. Stay at historic 1840s Carrollton Inn for a romantic getaway or an executive retreat. Interconnected row homes surrounding a brick courtyard feature antiques and decorator furnishings. This boutique B&B graces the center of Heritage Walk in Baltimore, Maryland and is perfectly suited for relaxation or activity. Walk to Inner Harbor, Little Italy and experience the local nightlife. Lavish comfort is found in guest rooms and suites with whirlpools, fireplaces with marble and oak mantles, fresh flowers, robes, handcrafted Kingsdown mattresses and other upscale amenities to meet most every need. Linger over a gourmet breakfast before exploring the surrounding area or taking care of business.

Innkeeper(s): Tim Kline. $150-350. 13 rooms with PB, 13 with FP, 13 with WP, 4 two-bedroom suites, 1 conference room. Breakfast included in rates. Types of meals: Full gourmet bkfst.

Certificate may be used: Sunday-Thursday.

4 East Madison Inn

4 E Madison St
Baltimore, MD 21202
(410) 332-0880
Internet: www.4eastmadisoninn.com
E-mail: 4eastinn@gmail.com

Circa 1840. Feel refreshed while staying at this historic boutique hotel that exudes an elegant ambiance. Poised in the center of the Mt. Vernon Cultural District in Baltimore, Maryland, many popular attractions are nearby including the Peabody Conservatory, Lyric Theater, Walters Art Gallery and local universities. Penn Station is 20 minutes away. Marble fireplaces, ornate plaster and woodwork accent the two spacious parlors off the hallway that boasts mahogany doors, wainscoting and a sweeping marble staircase under vintage stained-glass skylight. Luxury guest rooms with individual climate controls feature soft cotton sheets, large towels and numerous other thoughtful amenities. Gather each morning for a splendid homemade breakfast served in the dining room that has handicap-accessible French doors leading to the formal side garden. Take a day trip to explore Washington, DC.

Innkeeper(s): Betty Loafman. $155-210. 9 rooms with PB. Breakfast included in rates. Types of meals: Full bkfst, early coffee/tea and dinner. Restaurant on premises.

Certificate may be used: Anytime, last minute-based on availability.

Chesapeake City

The Blue Max Inn Bed & Breakfast

300 Bohemia Ave.
Chesapeake City, MD 21915-1244
(410)885-2781 (877)725-8362 Fax:(410)885-2809
Internet: www.bluemaxinn.com
E-mail: innkeeper@bluemaxinn.com

Circa 1854. Known as "the house with generous porches," this is one of the town's largest residences, built with Georgian architecture by the owner of the sawmill. This elegant inn has working fireplaces and a parlor with a grand player piano. Elaborate upscale amenities in the romantic suites and guest bedrooms include robes, flowers, chocolates and luxurious linens. Whirlpool tubs, a private balcony and second-floor verandas are also featured. Mouth-watering dishes like peaches and kiwi with amaretto cream sauce, apple crisp pancakes and country bacon, and eggs Benedict souffle are enjoyed in the fireside dining room or in the solarium overlooking gardens and a fish pond. A waterfall and gazebo highlight lush landscaping.
Innkeeper(s): Christine Mullen. $90-300. 9 rooms with PB, 2 suites. Breakfast, afternoon tea and snacks/refreshments included in rates. Types of meals: Full gourmet bkfst, early coffee/tea and picnic lunch.
Certificate may be used: November-April weekday/weekend. May-September weekdays only (Monday-Thursday). Subject to availability and not valid holidays or special events.

Chestertown

Great Oak Manor

10568 Cliff Rd
Chestertown, MD 21620-4115
(410) 778-5943 (800) 504-3098
Internet: www.greatoakmd.com
E-mail: info@greatoakmd.com

Circa 1938. This elegant Georgian mansion anchors vast lawns at the end of a long driveway. Situated directly on the

Chesapeake Bay, it is a serene and picturesque country estate. A library with fireplace, den and formal parlors are available to guests. With its grand circular stairway, bayside gazebo, private beach and nearby marina, the Manor is a remarkable setting for events such as weddings and reunions. Chestertown is eight miles away.
Innkeeper(s): Jenn Donisi. $159-315. 12 rooms with PB, 5 with FP, 3 suites, 2 conference rooms. Breakfast and snacks/refreshments included in rates. Types of meals: Country bkfst, veg bkfst, early coffee/tea and hors d'oeuvres.
Certificate may be used: Nov. 1-March 31, Sunday-Thursday, gold rooms only.

The Inn at Mitchell House

8796 Maryland Pkwy
Chestertown, MD 21620-4209
(410)778-6500
Internet: www.innatmitchellhouse.com
E-mail: innkeeper@innatmitchellhouse.com

Circa 1743. This pristine 18th-century manor house sits as a jewel on 12 acres overlooking Stoneybrook Pond. The guest rooms and the inn's several parlors are preserved and appointed in an authentic Colonial mood, heightened by handsome polished wide-board floors. Eastern Neck Island National Wildlife Refuge, Rock Hall, Chesapeake Farms, St. Michaels, Annapolis and nearby Chestertown are all delightful to explore. The Inn at Mitchell House is a popular setting for romantic weddings and small corporate meetings.
Innkeeper(s): Tracy Stone, Jim Stone. $109-239. 6 rooms, 5 with PB, 4 with FP, 1 cottage. Breakfast, snacks/refreshments and wine included in rates. Types of meals: Full gourmet bkfst, veg bkfst and early coffee/tea.
Certificate may be used: Sunday-Thursday, excluding holidays.

Elkton

Elk Forge Bed & Breakfast Inn, Spa, Events, Tea Room & Shop

807 Elk Mills Rd
Elkton, MD 21921
(410) 392-9007 (877) ELKFORG Fax:(410)392-2954
Internet: www.elkforge.com
E-mail: reservations@elkforge.com

Circa 1761. Rich in history and gorgeous surroundings, this Colonial manor house with Victorian elegance offers warm hospitality and maximum comfort. This five-and-a-half-acre estate features a variety of common areas. Some are perfect for intimate weddings, family reunions or business meetings. Appealing guest bedrooms and suites boast numerous amenities for a pleasurable stay. A well-prepared breakfast may include fresh fruit, Belgian waffles, an egg dish and daily organic selections. Create memorable moments playing badminton or croquet, walking in the woods or strolling the gardens before afternoon tea. Plan tri-state excursions from a hammock or lawn swing. Browse through the quaint gift shop, and enjoy an evening reception with sumptuous desserts. Be pampered with a Swedish massage or other spa services.
Innkeeper(s): LeAnn Lenderman, Seth Whitley, Andrew Whitley. $109-289. 14 rooms with PB, 14 with FP, 11 with HT, 5 two-bedroom and 1 three-bedroom suites, 2 cottages, 2 conference rooms. Breakfast, afternoon tea and snacks/refreshments included in rates. Types of meals: Full gourmet bkfst, veg bkfst, early coffee/tea, picnic lunch, wine and room service. Restaurant on premises.
Certificate may be used: December-January, Sunday-Thursday, subject to availability.

Havre De Grace

Vandiver Inn, Kent & Murphy Homes

301 S Union Ave
Havre De Grace, MD 21078-3201
(410)939-5200 (800)245-1655 Fax:(410)939-5202
Internet: www.vandiverinn.com
E-mail: vandiverinn@comcast.net

Circa 1886. Three acres surround this three-story historic Victorian mansion. A chandelier lights the entrance. Some of the rooms offer gas fireplaces and clawfoot tubs, and all are furnished with Victorian antiques. For instance, a king-size Victorian bed, original to the house, is one of the features of the

Millard E. Tydings Room, also offering a decorative fireplace and sitting area. The innkeeper creates gourmet breakfasts with freshly baked scones or muffins. Spend some time in the garden where a summer gazebo is supported by 12 cedar tree trunks.
Innkeeper(s): John and Susan Muldoon. $109-159. 19 rooms with PB, 4 with FP. Breakfast included in rates. Types of meals: Full gourmet bkfst, veg bkfst, early coffee/tea, picnic lunch and dinner.

Certificate may be used: Sunday-Thursday, September-April. Not valid on holidays and other blackout dates.

Princess Anne

The Alexander House Booklovers B&B

30535 Linden Ave
Princess Anne, MD 21853
(410)651-5195
Internet: BookloversBnB.com
E-mail: Alexanderbookloverbnb1@verizon.net

Circa 1885. Cradled between Chesapeake Bay and the beach, this Queen Anne Victorian graces the historic district with an inviting, wicker-furnished wraparound front porch and a veranda with a flower garden shaded by a large magnolia tree. The bed and breakfast is filled with literary memorabilia and portraits that honor writers and their books. Sit by the fire in the Mark Twain Reading Parlor. Each guest bedroom realistically reflects a famous author. Select the 1920s jazzy Harlem Renaissance of the Langston Hughes Room or the romantic Jane Austen Room with a clawfoot tub and ambiance of Regency England. The Robert Louis Stevenson Room offers 19th-century high-seas adventure. Linger over a gourmet breakfast in the French Cafe Colette where afternoon tea and evening liqueur are also served. A stocked refrigerator and microwave is available for guest use.
Innkeeper(s): Elizabeth Alexander, Peter Alexander. $85-140. 3 rooms with PB. Breakfast, afternoon tea, snacks/refreshments, Afternoon tea and pastry and Evening liqueurs and teas included in rates. Types of meals: Breakfast Buffet.

Certificate may be used: Monday-Thursday in October and April.

Rock Hall

Inn at Osprey Point

20786 Rock Hall Ave.
Rock Hall, MD 21661
(410) 639-2194
Internet: www.ospreypoint.com
E-mail: innkeeper@ospreypoint.com

Circa 1993. Spread over 30 acres on the Eastern Shore, this inn and restaurant are open year-round with a marina accessible during boat season. A casual and friendly ambiance accents modern luxury and colonial sophistication. Swim in the pool, play volleyball, pitch horseshoes and take a nature walk. Picnic areas, bicycles and kayaks are available to use. Accommodations include guest suites and rooms in the main inn and annex with contemporary amenities and classic style. Some rooms boast a balcony, porch, fireplace or whirlpool tub. A generous expanded continental breakfast is provided daily. Savor fine dining creations in the restaurant. Ask about special packages and events happening in Rock Hall, Maryland.

Innkeeper(s): Terry Nelson. $80-280. 15 rooms, 13 with PB, 1 with FP, 1 with WP, 1 two-bedroom suite. Breakfast included in rates.

Certificate may be used: Anytime, November-March, subject to availability. Cannot be combined with any other offers or discounts. Night free is least expensive.

Saint Michaels

Hambleton Inn

202 Cherry St
Saint Michaels, MD 21663
(410) 745-3350 (866) 745-3350 Fax:(410)745-5709
Internet: www.hambletoninn.com
E-mail: innkeeper@hambletoninn.com

Circa 1805. Relax at year-round accommodations on the harbor overlooking the Miles River and the Chesapeake Bay in scenic St. Michaels, Maryland. Gracious amenities hallmark this elegant and historic shipbuilder's home in the popular Eastern Shore area. Walk to local galleries, boutiques, antique shops and meander across the Honeymoon Bridge to the Maritime Museum. Hop on a bike to explore nearby towns of Tilghman Island, Easton and Oxford. Sit on one of the two porches with fabulous views. Stay in a spacious air-conditioned guest room or suite with modern conveniences and wake up to savor a gourmet breakfast. Gather for sherry and port wine in the evening amid the distinctive character and ambiance of this wonderful inn. Weddings and special events are memorable experiences in this picturesque and hospitable setting.
Innkeeper(s): Sherry Manning. $245-265. 5 rooms with PB.

Certificate may be used: October 15-March 15, Last minute, subject to availability.

Parsonage Inn

210 N Talbot St
Saint Michaels, MD 21663-2102
(410)745-8383
Internet: www.parsonage-inn.com
E-mail: parsinn@atlanticbb.net

Circa 1883. A striking Victorian steeple rises next to the wide bay of this brick residence, once the home of Henry Clay Dodson, state senator, pharmacist and brickyard owner. The  house features brick detail in a variety of patterns and inlays, perhaps a design statement for brick customers. Porches are decorated with filigree and spindled columns. Waverly linens, late Victorian furnishings, fireplaces and decks add to the creature comforts. Six bikes await guests who wish to ride to Tilghman Island or to the ferry that goes to Oxford. Gourmet breakfast is served in the dining room.
Innkeeper(s): Kathy Robertson. $100-195. 8 rooms with PB, 3 with FP. Breakfast and afternoon tea included in rates. Types of meals: Full bkfst.

Certificate may be used: Sunday-Thursday, Nov.1-May 1.

Stevenson

Gramercy Mansion

1400 Greenspring Valley Rd
Stevenson, MD 21153-0119
(410)486-2405 Fax:(410)486-1765
Internet: www.gramercymansion.com
E-mail: info@gramercymansion.com

Circa 1902. Dreams come true at this English Tudor mansion and gardens that crown 45 acres of woodlands. A superb grand staircase, high ceilings, artwork, antiques and Oriental carpets exude historic elegance.

Retire to handsome guest suites decorated with lavish comfort and style. Comparable to a master suite, they feature wood-burning fireplaces and whirlpool tubs. Wake up to birds singing and the aroma of a multi-course gourmet breakfast. Dine by the fire in the dining room or at a private table on the flower-filled porch by the Olympic-size swimming pool. The terraced lower garden, "Our Special Place," overlooking historic Greenspring Valley is long remembered. Downtown Baltimore is a 20-minute drive.

Innkeeper(s): Anne Pomykala & Cristin Kline. $125-375. 11 rooms with PB, 7 with FP, 9 with WP, 2 two-bedroom suites, 7 conference rooms. Breakfast, snacks/refreshments and All-inclusive package available including dinner with wine at nearby restaurant inquire for details included in rates. Types of meals: Full gourmet bkfst, veg bkfst, early coffee/tea, In-room dinner basket available by special order and Wine dinners hosted once a month (dates listed at www.gramercymansion.com).

Certificate may be used: Monday-Thursday, No Holidays.

Taneytown

Antrim 1844

30 Trevanion Rd
Taneytown, MD 21787-2347
(410) 756-6812 (800) 858-1844 Fax:(410)756-2744
Internet: www.antrim1844.com
E-mail: amanda@antrim1844.com

Circa 1844. Antrim 1844 is luxury, history and location combined in one delightful setting in Taneytown, Maryland. The grounds are activity rich, with formal gardens, a swimming pool, putting green, croquet and tennis courts. Books, games, cards and reading materials are found in the second-floor mansion library. Elegant and inviting guest rooms and suites, some with fireplaces, double Jacuzzis, private decks and more, are offered in an assortment of accommodations on the grounds. Feel pampered with a continental breakfast delivered to each door, then gather for a formal breakfast. Afternoon tea is a pleasant treat to enjoy later in the day. Make reservations for six-course world-class gourmet dining at the inn's Smokehouse Restaurant. The onsite Pickwick Pub is perfect for sipping late-night cognac. Three metropolitan areas make easy day trips.

Innkeeper(s): Lance. $160-400. 40 rooms with PB, 30 with FP, 32 with WP, 8 suites, 1 cottage, 8 guest houses, 8 conference rooms. Breakfast, afternoon tea and hors d'oeuvres included in rates. Types of meals: Country bkfst, veg bkfst, wine and gourmet dinner. Restaurant on premises.

Certificate may be used: Sunday-Thursday, subject to availability, excludes some holidays.

Massachusetts

Amherst

Allen House Victorian Inn

599 Main St
Amherst, MA 01002-2409
(413)253-5000
Internet: www.allenhouse.com
E-mail: allenhouse@webtv.net

Circa 1886. This stick-style Queen Anne is much like a Victorian museum with guest rooms that feature period reproduction wallpapers, pedestal sinks, carved golden oak and

brass beds, painted wooden floors and plenty of antiques. Among its many other treasures include Eastlake fireplace mantels. Unforgettable breakfasts include specialties such as eggs Benedict or French toast stuffed with rich cream cheese.

Afternoon tea is a treat, and the inn offers plenty of examples of poetry from Emily Dickinson, whose home is just across the street from the inn.

Innkeeper(s): Alan Zieminski, Ann Zieminski. $75-195. 7 rooms with PB. Breakfast, afternoon tea and snacks/refreshments included in rates. Types of meals: Full bkfst and early coffee/tea.

Certificate may be used: Jan. 1-April 1, Sunday-Thursday.

Barnstable

Lamb and Lion Inn

2504 Main Street (Rt. 6A)
Barnstable, MA 02630-0511
(508)362-6823 (800)909-6923 Fax:(508) 362-0227
Internet: www.lambandlion.com
E-mail: info@lambandlion.com

Circa 1740. This rambling collection of Cape-style buildings sits on four acres overlooking the Old King's highway. Newly decorated, the inn offers a feeling of casual elegance. The Innkeeper's Pride is a romantic suite with sunken tub, fireplace, kitchenette and a deck overlooking a garden and woods. The Barn-stable is one of the original buildings and now offers three

sleeping areas, a living and dining area and French doors to a private patio. A large central courtyard houses a generous sized

heated pool and hot tub spa.

Innkeeper(s): Ali & Tom. $165-250. 10 rooms with PB, 8 with FP, 2 with HT, 2 with WP, 6 total suites, including 1 two-bedroom suite and 1 three-bedroom suite, 1 cottage, 1 guest house, 1 cabin, 1 conference room. Breakfast included in rates. Types of meals: Cont plus, early coffee/tea, picnic lunch, Our breakfast is far from "continental" and every day is a surprise.

Certificate may be used: Oct. 31-May 18, Sunday-Friday, excluding holidays.

The Acworth Inn

4352 Main Street
Barnstable, MA 02637
(508)362-3330 (800)362-6363 Fax:(508)375-0304
Internet: www.acworthinn.com
E-mail: acworthinn@acworthinn.com

This inn, located on the scenic Olde Kings Highway on the north side of Cape Cod, offers a strategic midway point for those exploring the area. The historic Cape-style house features five beautifully decorated guest rooms, including a luxury suite. Hand-painted, restored furniture adds charm to the inn's interior. Guests select from the Cummaquid, Chatham, Yarmouth Port, Barnstable and Orleans rooms, all named for Cape Cod villages.

Innkeeper(s): Lisa Callahan. Call for rates. 5 rooms. Breakfast included in rates. Types of meals: Early coffee/tea, afternoon tea and full service breakfast each morning.

Certificate may be used: Nov. 1-May 15, excluding holidays.

Boston

Clarendon Square Bed and Breakfast

198 West Brookline Street
Boston, MA 02118-1280
(617) 536-2229
Internet: www.clarendonsquare.com
E-mail: stay@clarendonsquare.com

Circa 1860. Business travelers and discriminating tourists to Boston will appreciate the impeccable service at this luxuriously renovated Boston townhouse bed and breakfast in the South End. The side street location allows easy access to all that Boston offers, without the noise of the city intruding. Each elegantly furnished room, many with original local artwork, provides a spacious seating/working area as well as a private bathroom, complete with plush robes and high-end toiletries. There is a satellite flat screen TV, wireless Internet access and a docking station for your IPod and CD/DVD player in addition to new pillow-top mattresses. A special treat is the city view available from the hot tub on the roof deck. Each morning enjoy a variety of appetizing and substantial continental breakfasts.

Innkeeper(s): Stephen Gross. $135-455. 3 rooms with PB. Breakfast included in rates. Types of meals: Expanded continental breakfast.

Certificate may be used: Sunday-Thursday, November-March for last minute availability in Deluxe Queen or Luxury Suites.

College Club

44 Commonwealth Ave
Boston, MA 02116
(617) 536-9510 Fax:(617)247-8537
Internet: www.thecollegeclubofboston.com
E-mail: accommodations@thecollegeclubofboston.com

Circa 1800. Established in 1890, the oldest women's college club in America was formed in the heart of historic Back Bay in Boston, Massachusetts. Open year-round, College Club offers accommodations and hosts events in a classic Victorian Brownstone. Snacks and tea are available throughout the day. Period antiques, reproductions and artwork accent the inviting guest bedrooms. Some boast decorative fireplaces and private baths. A complimentary continental breakfast buffet is provided daily in the dining room. The Drawing Room and the Members Room are elegant venues for weddings, concerts, business meetings or other special events. Onsite catering is available. The bed and breakfast is one block from the Public Garden, Newberry Street and Boylston Street, near Beacon Hill. Take a walking tour of the city and be immersed in a rich heritage.

Innkeeper(s): Edith Toth, General Manager. $129-275. 11 rooms, 6 with PB, 2 conference rooms. Breakfast, afternoon tea and snacks/refreshments included in rates. Types of meals: Cont and early coffee/tea.

Certificate may be used: Anytime, November-March via telephone/email reservations only.

Brewster

Old Sea Pines Inn

2553 Main St.
Brewster, MA 02631-1959
(508)896-6114 Fax:(186)644-44552
Internet: www.oldseapinesinn.com
E-mail: info@oldseapinesinn.com

Circa 1900. Formerly the Sea Pines School of Charm and Personality for Young Women, this turn-of-the-century mansion sits on three-and-one-half acres of trees and lawns. Recently

renovated, the inn displays elegant wallpapers and a grand sweeping stairway. On Sunday evenings, mid June through mid September, enjoy a dinner show in conjunction with Cape Cod Repertory Theatre. Beaches and bike paths are nearby, as are village shops and restaurants.

Innkeeper(s): Michele Rowan, Stephen Rowan. $85-165. 24 rooms, 16 with PB, 3 with FP, 2 suites, 2 conference rooms. Breakfast included in rates. Types of meals: Full bkfst, early coffee/tea, afternoon tea, snacks/refreshments and room service.

Certificate may be used: Sunday-Thursday April 1-June 15 and Sept. 15-Dec. 1.

Cambridge

A Bed & Breakfast In Cambridge

1657 Cambridge St
Cambridge, MA 02138-4316
(617) 868-7082 (800) 795-7122 Fax:(617)876-8991
Internet: www.cambridgebnb.com
E-mail: doaneperry@yahoo.com

Circa 1897. Located minutes from Harvard Square, this colonial revival house reflects the rich ambiance of the Cambridge historical district. Surround yourself in the finest New England culture, located walking distance from the house. Visit museums, theaters and fine restaurants. Rest under the voluminous trees in the park across the street, or hop on the Red Line for an excursion to Boston. After an active day of sight seeing, return to the warmth of turn-of-the-century antique decor at this three-story home away from home. Enjoy a savory breakfast featuring such delights as home-baked, sesame-orange spice bread and cranberry brody, and spend the afternoon relaxing in an overstuffed chair or Grandmother's cane rockers with some tea or sherry.

Innkeeper(s): Doane Perry. $95-160. 3 rooms. Breakfast and afternoon tea included in rates. Types of meals: Full gourmet bkfst, veg bkfst and early coffee/tea.

Certificate may be used: Jan. 7-Feb. 11, Feb. 23-March 4, Dec. 8-18, based on availability.

Chatham

Chatham Old Harbor Inn

22 Old Harbor Rd
Chatham, MA 02633-2315
(508)945-4434 (800)942-4434 Fax:(508)945-7665
Internet: www.chathamoldharborinn.com
E-mail: info@chathamoldharborinn.com

Circa 1932. This pristine New England bed & breakfast was once the home of "Doc" Keene, a popular physician in the area. A meticulous renovation has created an elegant, beautifully appointed inn offer-ing antique furnishings, designer linens and lavish amenities in an English country decor. A buffet breakfast, featuring Judy's homemade muffins, is served in the sunroom or on the deck. The beaches, boutiques and galleries are a walk away and there is an old grist mill, the Chatham Lighthouse and a railroad museum. Band concerts are offered Friday nights in the summer at Kate Gould Park.

Innkeeper(s): Judy Braz, Ray Braz. $149-329. 8 rooms with PB, 2 with FP, 1 with WP, 1 suite, 1 conference room. Breakfast, afternoon tea and snacks/refreshments included in rates. Types of meals: Full bkfst, veg bkfst and early coffee/tea.

Certificate may be used: Nov. 1-April 30, Sunday-Thursday.

Concord

Hawthorne Inn

462 Lexington Rd
Concord, MA 01742-3729
(978) 369-5610 Fax:(978)287-4949
Internet: www.concordmass.com
E-mail: inn@concordmass.com

Circa 1870. Share the joy of history, literature, poetry and art-work at this intimate New England bed & breakfast. For 25 years, the inn's ambiance has imparted the spirit of writers and philosophers such as the Alcotts, Emerson, Hawthorne and Thoreau, who once owned and walked the grounds. Antique fur-  nishings, weavings, hardwood floors, a welcoming fireplace and stained-glass windows all exude a wonderful warmth and gentility. Enjoy afternoon tea on a rustic garden bench in the shade of aged trees and colorful plants. The area offers woods to explore, rivers to canoe, a quaint village with museums, infamous Sleepy Hollow Cemetery, and untold treasures.

Innkeeper(s): Marilyn Mudry, Gregory Burch. $139-359. 7 rooms with PB, 1 with FP, 1 conference room. Breakfast and afternoon tea included in rates. Types of meals: Full bkfst, early coffee/tea, snacks/refreshments, wine and special platters with wine package upgrades.

Certificate may be used: January-March, Sunday-Thursday (premium rooms only).

Dennis Port

Joy House Inc., B&B

181 Depot Street
Dennis Port, MA 02639
(508)760-3663 (877)569-4687 Fax:(508)760-6618
Internet: www.joyhousecapecod.com
E-mail: sales@joyhousecapecod.com

Circa 1730. Remodeled for comfort and privacy, this Pre-Revolutionary War, Antique Colonial house is an ideal place to be pampered and served with joy. An old sea captain's home with wide pumpkin pine floors, the foyer gives access to a large common room and fireside sitting area. Listen to classical music or watch cable TV. Attractive guest bedrooms offer a restful stay. Sleep on a four-poster bed under a skylight in the romantic Lighthouse Suite with a decorative fireplace. Wake up to Chef Barbara's breakfast in the dining room. Splendidly landscaped gardens are resplendent with hollies, hydrangeas, roses, rhododendrons and cherry trees.

Innkeeper(s): Barbara Bach, Peter Bach. $120-180. 3 rooms with PB, 2 with FP, 1 two-bedroom suite. Breakfast and snacks/refreshments included in rates. Types of meals: Cont plus and early coffee/tea.

Certificate may be used: Anytime, except July and August.

East Orleans

Ship's Knees Inn

186 Beach Rd
East Orleans, MA 02643
(508) 255-1312 (888) 744-7756 Fax:(508)240-1351
Internet: www.shipskneesinn.com
E-mail: info@shipskneesinn.com

Circa 1820. This 180-year-old restored sea captain's home is a three-minute walk to the ocean. Rooms are decorated in a nautical style with antiques. Several rooms feature authentic ship's knees, hand-paint-  ed trunks, old clipper ship models and four-poster beds. Some rooms boast ocean views, and the Master Suite has a working fireplace. The inn offers swimming and tennis facilities on the grounds. About three miles away, the innkeepers also offer three rooms, a bedroom efficiency apartment and two heated cottages on the Town Cove. Head into town, or spend the day basking in the beauty of Nauset Beach with its picturesque sand dunes.

Innkeeper(s): Pete Butcher, Denise Butcher. $100-350. 18 rooms, 14 with PB, 2 with FP, 2 suites, 2 guest houses. Breakfast included in rates. Types of meals: Cont plus.

Certificate may be used: Nov. 1-March 31.

The Nauset House Inn

143 Beach Rd, PO Box 774
East Orleans, MA 02643
(508)255-2195 (800)771-5508
Internet: www.nausethouseinn.com
E-mail: info@nausethouseinn.com

Circa 1810. Located a 1/2 mile from Nauset Beach, this inn is a renovated farmhouse set on three acres, which include an  old apple orchard. A Victorian conservatory was purchased from a Connecticut estate and reassembled here, then filled with wicker furnishings, Cape flowers and stained glass. Hand-stenciling, handmade quilts, antiques and more bouquets of flowers decorate the rooms. The breakfast room features a fireplace, brick floor and beamed ceiling. Breakfast includes treats such as ginger pancakes or waffles with fresh strawberries. Wine and cranberry juice are served in the evenings.

Innkeeper(s): Diane Johnson, John Vessella, Cindy Vessella. $85-195. 14 rooms, 8 with PB, 1 cottage. Breakfast, snacks/refreshments, hors d'oeuvres and wine included in rates. Types of meals: Full bkfst, early coffee/tea and afternoon tea.

Certificate may be used: Sunday-Thursday, excludes July-September and Holidays.

Eastham

Inn at the Oaks

3085 State Highway
Eastham, MA 02642
(508) 255-1886 (877) 255-1886 Fax:(508)240-0345
Internet: www.InnAtTheoaks.com
E-mail: reservations@InnAtTheOaks.com

Circa 1870. Originally an 1870 sea captain's home, this Queen Anne Victorian listed in the National Register, graces the Eastham Center Historic District in Massachusetts. Inn at the Oaks offers family-friendly amenities and packages. Children  enjoy the outdoor playground and Little Acorns Play Room inside. Play pool, chess, checkers, games, puzzles and use the computer with Internet access in the Billiard Room. Relax on a porch rocker or hammock and read by the fire in the parlor. Select a Suite, Getaway Room or Traditional Room. Some include a fireplace, porch or clawfoot tub. The Carriage House offers two pet-friendly rooms. Savor a country breakfast with specialty entrees in the Gathering Room or on the porch. The signature dish is Abelskivers, Danish pancakes. Spa services feature a two-person hot tub and massage therapy.

Innkeeper(s): Samantha Stone. $95-305. 13 rooms with PB, 2 with FP, 4 suites, 1 conference room. Breakfast and snacks/refreshments included in rates. Types of meals: Cont and early coffee/tea.

Certificate may be used: September-June, Sunday-Thursday only. July and August, subject to availability.

Fairhaven

Baggins End Guest House

2 West Street
Fairhaven, MA 02719
(508)326-2567 Fax:(508)992-5608
Internet: www.bagginsendguesthouse.com
E-mail: info@bagginsendguesthouse.com

Relaxing and comfortable waterfront accommodations are accented by the beautiful setting. Sit on the stone patio deck or dock and enjoy the 180 degree view of the working harbor. Baggins End Guest House offers spacious yet intimate guest rooms and a continental breakfast to linger over while watching the swans go by. This Fairhaven, Massachusetts bed and breakfast is also for weddings and tented events. Take a harbor tour, or visit the New Bedford Whaling Museum. Ferry boats go to Martha's Vineyard and Nantucket. Wi-fi is available for exploring the world from indoors.

Innkeeper(s): Diane Tomassetti. $130-150. 2 rooms, 1 conference room. Breakfast and wine included in rates. Types of meals: Cont plus, veg bkfst and early coffee/tea.

Certificate may be used: November-January, Monday-Thursday.

Falmouth

Bailey's By the Sea

321 Grand Ave
Falmouth, MA 02540
(508)548-5748 (866)548-5748 Fax:(508)548-6974
Internet: www.baileysbythesea.com
E-mail: info@baileysbythesea.com

Circa 1874. Open year-round, this renovated 1874 Victorian bed and breakfast offers a non-smoking environment on the oceanfront in the Falmouth Heights area of Cape Cod. Bailey's By the Sea overlooks Martha's Vineyard Island. Enjoy the spectacular view from the deck and landscaped yard. Sit by the fire in the living room that is furnished with oriental and American antiques. Inviting guest bedrooms feature gracious amenities that include waffle robes to lounge in. Adjoining rooms are available upon request. Breakfast is a creative meal with daily changing menus and is served on the enclosed wraparound porch.

Innkeeper(s): Liz Bailey. $165-310. 6 rooms with PB, 1 with WP. Breakfast, afternoon tea, snacks/refreshments, wine and Full breakfast included in rates.

Certificate may be used: September-October, no weekends.

Greenfield

The Brandt House

29 Highland Ave
Greenfield, MA 01301-3605
(413) 774-3329 (800) 235-3329 Fax:(413)772-2908
Internet: www.brandthouse.com
E-mail: info@brandthouse.com

Circa 1890. Three-and-a-half-acre lawns surround this impressive three-story Colonial Revival house, situated hilltop. The library and poolroom are popular for lounging, but the favorite gathering areas are the sunroom and the covered  north porch. Ask for the aqua and white room with the fireplace, but all the rooms are pleasing. A full breakfast often includes homemade scones and is sometimes available on the slate patio in view of the expansive lawns and beautiful gardens. A full-time staff provides for guest needs. There is a clay tennis court and nature trails, and in winter, lighted ice skating at a nearby pond. Historic Deerfield and Yankee Candle Company are within five minutes.

Innkeeper(s): Sean Warren. $105-359. 9 rooms, 7 with PB, 2 with FP, 1 suite, 1 conference room. Breakfast included in rates. Types of meals: Full bkfst and early coffee/tea.

Certificate may be used: Sunday-Thursday only.

Haydenville

Penrose Victorian Inn

133 Main Street
Haydenville, MA 01060
(413)268-3014 (888)268-7711 Fax:(413)268-9232
Internet: www.penroseinn.com
E-mail: zimmer@penroseinn.com

Circa 1820. Experience Victorian elegance at this distinctive
Queen Anne that sits on two resplendent acres across from the
river. Recently renovated, the inn's antique furnishings and period decor offer a warm hospitality. Common rooms include the
music room and parlor. Most of the well-appointed guest bedrooms feature fireplaces. Savor Penrose French toast with fresh
seasonal fruit, juice and hot beverages by candlelight. Stroll the
perennial and rose gardens with fountain, relax on the porch or
go for a swim. Explore Emily Dickens House, Old Deerfield and
Calvin Coolidge House, each less than 10 miles away.

Innkeeper(s): Nancy Zimmer, Dick Zimmer. $125-165. 3 rooms with PB.
Breakfast included in rates. Types of meals: Full gourmet bkfst and veg bkfst.

Certificate may be used: Nov. 30-May 1.

Hyannis Port

The Simmons Homestead Inn

288 Scudder Ave
Hyannis Port, MA 02647
(508)778-4999 (800)637-1649 Fax:(508)790-1342
Internet: www.simmonshomesteadinn.com
E-mail: simmonshomestead@aol.com

Circa 1805. The only bed and breakfast in Hyannis Port,
Massachusetts, The Simmons Homestead Inn is a relaxing and
pleasant place for a getaway or vacation. Sit on a porch and sip
wine during the
social hour. On
cooler evenings,
gather in the fire-
side common
room. Bikes are
available for exploring Cape Cod, and beach chairs and towels
are provided too. Take a nap in a backyard hammock. A billiard room offers more entertainment. Animal-themed guest
rooms and a two-bedroom family suite feature optional air
conditioning and some rooms boast canopy or brass beds.
Breakfast is a fresh and filling way to start each day. Ask about
the inn's pet-friendly policy.

Innkeeper(s): Bill Putman. $120-320. 14 rooms with PB, 2 with FP, 2 suites.
Breakfast included in rates. Types of meals: Full bkfst and early coffee/tea.

Certificate may be used: Anytime, November-May except holiday weekends, subject to availability. June-October, Sunday-Thursday only, subject
to availability.

Lee

1800 Devonfield Inn, an English Country Estate

85 Stockbridge Rd
Lee, MA 01238-9308
(413)243-3298 (800)664-0880 Fax:(413)243-1360
Internet: www.devonfield.com
E-mail: innkeeper@devonfield.com

Circa 1800. 2009 Winner - Travelers' Choice for Romance.
Devonfield is a gracious English-Style country house built in
the late 1800s.
Overlooking a pastoral
meadow shaded by grace-
ful birch trees with the
rolling tapestry of the
Berkshire Hills beyond,
the B&B sits on 29 acres.
In the main house, a fire-
side living room is complete with grand piano, library and
stereo. Relax in the television room and on the porch. A guest
pantry is always stocked with coffee, tea, hot chocolate, popcorn and fresh-baked cookies. Browse through the movie
library. Many spacious guest bedrooms have wood-burning fireplaces; some boast Jacuzzis and terry robes. All rooms have
complimentary cognac, locally hand-made chocolates and bottled water. A hearty country breakfast proudly features foods
locally grown and or prepared. A tennis court and heated
swimming pool offers pleasant onsite activities.

Innkeeper(s): Ronnie Singer, Bruce Singer. $200-350. 10 rooms with PB, 4
with FP, 4 suites, 1 cottage. Breakfast, snacks/refreshments, Fully stocked
guest pantry with coffee/tea/hot chocolate/popcorn/fresh baked cookies,
cognac, hand-made chocolates and bottled water included in rates. Types of
meals: Early coffee/tea, afternoon tea, A fireside (fall/winter) candlelit
gourmet breakfast is served on fine china accompanied by classical music
and a bountiful buffet followed by a specially selected hot entree served
table-side each day.

Certificate may be used: Nov. 15-May 15, Rooms 6 and 7 only, Sunday-
Thursday. Holidays excluded.

Lenox

Gateways Inn & Restaurant

51 Walker Street
Lenox, MA 01240
(413)637-2532 (888)492-9466 Fax:(413)637-1432
Internet: www.gatewaysinn.com
E-mail: innkeeper@gatewaysinn.com

Circa 1912. Infused with European charm and generous hospitality, the elegant Proctor Mansion is perfect for an enchanting getaway in the Berkshire Hills. Recently restored guest bedrooms feature antique canopy, sleigh and brass beds as well as
fireplaces. The suite also boasts an Italian marble-tiled bathroom with Jacuzzi tub, plush terry robes, a sitting room with
French doors and mahogany library with dry bar. Linger over a
relaxed breakfast inside or al fresco on the Venetian blue
canopied terrace. In the elegant three-star restaurant's main
dining room and more intimate Rockwell Room, seasonal culinary masterpieces are available for dinner.

Innkeeper(s): Michele Gazit, Eiran Gazit. $150-600. 12 rooms with PB, 9
with FP, 1 suite. Breakfast included in rates. Types of meals: Full gourmet

bkfst, veg bkfst, early coffee/tea, afternoon tea, wine, gourmet dinner and Room service by previous reservation. Restaurant on premises.

Certificate may be used: November-March, weekdays only, no holidays. Excludes Miranda Suite.

Marblehead

Fox Pond B&B

31 Arthur Ave.
Marblehead, MA 01945
(781)631-1630
Internet: www.foxpondbnb.com
E-mail: foxpond@comcast.net

Circa 1950. Nestled amongst tall oaks and settled in expansive gardens, Fox Pond provides a welcome retreat for guests wishing to relax and escape the noise and traffic in the town center. Understated elegance and luxurious details are the signature ingredients that are found throughout this beautifully renovated and expanded cape building. Each designer bedroom and suite includes amenities not found except in the most distinctive boutique hotels including a double Jacuzzi in the Canton suite, marble floors, artist edition sinks, wall mounted HDTV's, period antiques, oil paintings, custom vanities, a Canton vessel sink, marble showers/bath, and the highest quality fixtures throughout. A hot breakfast is enjoyed in the dining room or on the patio. The servings include a variety of hot recipes together with fruits and a side of hot muffins. The house has many surprises and an architecture that is both inviting as well as beautiful and serves as a showcase for the owner's architectural business. Guest rooms are accessed by the front door and stairway and have been designed for privacy and comfort. Every room was remodeled and reconfigured to meet the highest standards and is a welcomed surprise for the discriminating traveler.

Innkeeper(s): Ted Baker. $90-235. 3 rooms with PB, 1 with HT, 1 with WP, 1 total suite, including 2 two-bedroom suites. 8:30-9:30 Hot breakfast, fresh muffins, melon ~ (topped with fruit/granola/French Vanilla yogurt) and coffee/juice included in rates. Types of meals: Full bkfst and early coffee/tea.

Certificate may be used: November-March, Monday-Thursday.

Harborside House B&B

23 Gregory Street
Marblehead, MA 01945
(781)631-1032
Internet: www.harborsidehouse.com
E-mail: stay@harborsidehouse.com

Circa 1850. Enjoy the Colonial charm of this home, which overlooks Marblehead Harbor on Boston's historic North Shore. Rooms are decorated with antiques and period wallpaper. A third-story sundeck offers excellent views. A generous continental breakfast of home-baked breads, muffins and fresh fruit is served each morning in the well-decorated dining room or on the open porch. The village of Marblehead provides many shops and restaurants. Boston and Logan airport are 30 minutes away.

Innkeeper(s): Susan Livingston. $90-125. 2 rooms. Breakfast, afternoon tea and snacks/refreshments included in rates. Types of meals: Cont plus, veg bkfst, early coffee/tea and homemade cookies.

Certificate may be used: January-April.

Middleboro

On Cranberry Pond B&B

43 Fuller St
Middleboro, MA 02346-1706
(508)946-0768 Fax:(508)947-8221
Internet: www.oncranberrypond.com
E-mail: OnCranberryPond@Gmail.com

Circa 1989. Nestled in the historic "cranberry capital of the world," this 8,000 square-foot modern farmhouse rests on a working cranberry bog. There are two miles of trails to meander, and during berry picking season guests can watch as buckets of the fruit are collected. Rooms are comfortable and well appointed. The Master Suite includes a whirlpool bath for two. A 93-foot deck overlooks the cranberry bog. Innkeeper Jeannine LaBossiere creates gourmet breakfasts and yummy homemade snacks at night. Honeymoons and anniversaries are popular here. There is a spacious conference room with plenty of business amenities. Borrow a fishing rod or one of the innkeeper's mountain bikes for an afternoon's adventure you will long remember. Plymouth, Mass. is nearby and whale watching is a popular activity.

Innkeeper(s): Jeannine LaBossiere- Krushas, Ken Krushas and son Tim. $95-180. 6 rooms, 4 with PB, 2 suites, 2 conference rooms. Breakfast and snacks/refreshments included in rates. Types of meals: Full gourmet bkfst, veg bkfst, early coffee/tea and lunch.

Certificate may be used: Anytime subject to availability.

Nantucket

Martin House Inn

61 Centre Street
Nantucket, MA 02554
(508)228-0678 Fax:(508)325-4798
Internet: www.martinhouseinn.net
E-mail: info@martinhouseinn.net

Circa 1803. Take the ferry from Martha's Vineyard, Hyannis or Harwich to begin an island holiday on Nantucket at Martin House Inn in Massachusetts. Open year round, this Greek Revival mariner's mansion is a comfortable, refreshing blend of old-world flair and new-world luxury. Relax on the wicker-filled veranda or sit by the fire in the living room. Afternoon tea and treats are served daily. The inn is accented by a revolving collection of original paintings from local artists. Inviting guest rooms and a suite boast canopy and four-poster beds; some include fireplaces. Indulge in a bountiful continental breakfast that features homemade granola, cereals, fruit, scones and other creations made by the pastry chef. Walk to the beach or browse the galleries, museums and shops along the famous cobblestone Main Street.

Innkeeper(s): Skye Schuyler. $95-395. 13 rooms, 9 with PB, 5 with FP, 1 suite. Breakfast, afternoon tea, snacks/refreshments, hors d'oeuvres and wine included in rates. Types of meals: A bountiful continental breakfast prepared by pastry chef is served each morning featuring her famous homemade granola/scones, cereals, fruit, juices, gourmet coffee/tea and homemade afternoon treats.

Certificate may be used: Oct. 15-May 15, excluding Christmas Stroll and Daffodil weekend, subject to availability.

Petersham

Clamber Hill Inn & Restaurant

111 N Main St
Petersham, MA 01366-9501
(978)724-8800 (888)374-0007 Fax:(978)724-8829
Internet: www.clamberhill.com
E-mail: relax@clamberhill.com

Circa 1927. Sitting in the midst of 33 peaceful and secluded wooded acres this statuesque 1927 European country estate is just minutes from Quabbin Reservoir. The local forests, known for their dramatic seasonal color changes, draw many leaf peepers to the inn. Furnished with antiques and Oriental carpets, guest bedrooms are inviting retreats. Stay in a suite with a sitting room and fireplace. Breakfast is a gourmet delight with fresh fruit, homemade cinnamon rolls, muffins, waffles with strawberries, peach-filled French toast and wild blueberry pancakes. High tea is available by arrangement. A full-service restaurant serves dinner Friday, Saturday and Sunday. Stroll through the colorful gardens and bird watch. Visit the Fisher Museum just three miles away at the 3,000-acre Harvard Forest.

Innkeeper(s): Mark Ellis, Deni Ellis. $165-235. 5 rooms with PB, 4 with FP, 2 total suites, including 1 two-bedroom suite, 2 conference rooms. Breakfast and snacks/refreshments included in rates. Types of meals: Full gourmet bkfst, veg bkfst, early coffee/tea, afternoon tea and wine. Restaurant on premises.

Certificate may be used: Sunday-Thursday, Nov. 1-April 30, excluding holidays.

Winterwood at Petersham

19 N Main St
Petersham, MA 01366
(978)724-8885 Fax:(978)724-8884
Internet: www.winterwoodinn.net
E-mail: winterwoodatpetersham@verizon.net

Circa 1842. The town of Petersham is often referred to as a museum of Greek Revival architecture. One of the grand houses facing the common is Winterwood. It boasts fireplaces in almost every room. Private dining is available for groups of up to 70 people. The inn is listed in the National Register.

Innkeeper(s): Jean Day, Robert Day.
$159-209. 6 rooms with PB, 5 with FP, 1 with WP, 1 two-bedroom suite. Breakfast included in rates. Types of meals: Cont plus.

Certificate may be used: Sunday-Thursday, Not valid in October or any holiday.

Provincetown

Gabriel's at the Ashbrooke Inn

102 Bradford St
Provincetown, MA 02657
(508) 487-3232
Internet: www.gabriels.com
E-mail: info@gabriels.com

Circa 1830. Experience Gabriel's heavenly setting and cozy hospitality that have been enjoyed by many since 1979. Restored homes are graced with sky-lit common areas to gather in as a group or an individual. Each guest bedroom and suite is distinguished by the name and character of a famous personality. Most feature fireplaces, many boast Jacuzzi tubs and some include kitchenettes, skylights, sleeping lofts and semi-private porches. Modern amenities include high-speed Internet access and computers, voice mail, VCRs and a video library. Savor a full breakfast each morning. Lounge on a sun deck with afternoon wine and cheese. Conveniently located in the heart of quaint Provincetown, the beach is only one block away.

Innkeeper(s): Elizabeth Brooke. $125-400. 16 rooms, 14 with PB, 13 with FP, 10 with WP, 3 total suites, including 2 two-bedroom suites, 1 conference room. Breakfast, afternoon tea and snacks/refreshments included in rates. Types of meals: Full gourmet bkfst, veg bkfst and early coffee/tea.

Certificate may be used: Nov. 1 to April 1 excludes some weekends, holidays and special events.

Rehoboth

Gilbert's B&B

30 Spring St
Rehoboth, MA 02769-2408
(508) 252-6416
Internet: www.gilbertsbb.com
E-mail: jg@gilbertsbb.com

Circa 1835. This country farmhouse sits on 17 acres of woodland that includes an award-winning tree farm. Cross-country skiing and hiking are found right outside the door. If they choose to, guests can even help with the farm chores, caring for horses and gardening. Three antique-filled bedrooms share a second-floor sitting room and bathroom. There are two first-floor rooms with a working fireplace and private bath. The nearby town of Rehoboth is 360 years old.

Innkeeper(s): Jeanne Gilbert, Donald Beardsworth. $84-109. 5 rooms, 2 with PB, 2 with FP, 1 two-bedroom suite, 1 conference room. Breakfast, afternoon tea and snacks/refreshments included in rates. Types of meals: Country bkfst, veg bkfst, early coffee/tea and Vegetarian and gluten-free breakfasts are available upon request. Request should be made a day before arrival.

Certificate may be used: Sunday-Thursday, Dec. 1-April, subject to availability.

Rockport

Emerson Inn By The Sea

One Cathedral Avenue
Rockport, MA 01966
(978)546-6321 (800)964-5550 Fax:(978)546-7043
Internet: www.emersoninnbythesea.com
E-mail: info@emersoninnbythesea.com

Circa 1846. This Greek Revival inn's namesake, Ralph Waldo Emerson, once called the place, "thy proper summer home." As it is the oldest continuously operated inn on Cape Ann, decades of travelers agree with his sentiment. The guest rooms are comfortable, yet tastefully furnished, and some boast ocean views. The grounds include a heated swimming pool as well as landscaped gardens. Breakfast is included in the rates. Guests also can enjoy dinner at The Grand Cafe, the inn's award winning restaurant.

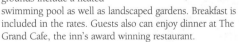

Innkeeper(s): Bruce Coates, Michele Coates. $99-399. 36 rooms with PB, 2 with FP, 2 two-bedroom suites, 2 cottages, 3 conference rooms. Breakfast and afternoon tea included in rates. Types of meals: Full gourmet bkfst, early cof-

fee/tea, snacks/refreshments, wine and gourmet dinner. Restaurant on premises.
Certificate may be used: October-May, Sunday-Thursday, subject to availability.

Linden Tree Inn

26 King St
Rockport, MA 01966-1444
(978)546-2494 (800)865-2122 Fax:(978)546-3297
Internet: www.lindentreeinn.com
E-mail: lindentreeinn@gmail.com

Circa 1870. The breakfasts at this Victorian-style inn keep guests coming back year after year. Guests feast on home-baked treats such as scones, coffee cakes or Sunday favorites, French toast bread pudding, asparagus frittatas and spinach quiche. Each of the bedchambers features individual decor, and the innkeepers offer a formal living room and sun room for relaxation. The cupola affords a view of Mill Pond and Sandy Bay.

Innkeeper(s): Tobey Shepherd, John Shepherd. $105-162. 16 rooms with PB, 1 two-bedroom suite. Breakfast, afternoon tea and Full breakfast served buffet style included in rates. Types of meals: Full bkfst, early coffee/tea, Breakfast served buffet style and afternoon tea available through out day and evening.
Certificate may be used: Anytime, November-March, subject to availability.

Pleasant Street Inn

17 Pleasant St
Rockport, MA 01966-2152
(978)546-3915 (800)541-3915 Fax:(978)546-3907
Internet: www.pleasantstreetinn.net
E-mail: pleasantstreetinn@verizon.net

Poised to overlook Rockport, Massachusetts, a quaint New England seacoast village on Boston's North Shore, Pleasant Street Inn offers year-round ocean views. Sit on a country swing or porch accented by a folk-art mural. Play croquet on the front lawn or pitch horseshoes. Renovated for maximum comfort, this Victorian B&B features air-conditioned accommodations. Each floor has a compact refrigerator. An ice maker is located on the first-level hallway. The Whirlpool Room boasts cottage wicker furniture; a staircase leads up to the Turret Room loft. The entire second story of the Carriage House Apartment Suite is perfect for families with a private deck, fully equipped kitchen, two bedrooms and a living room. Savor a continental-plus breakfast in the elegantly understated dining room.

Innkeeper(s): Lynne Norris. $115-150. 8 rooms with PB, 1 cottage, 1 guest house. Types of meals: Cont.
Certificate may be used: Anytime, subject to availability, excludes holidays.

Sally Webster Inn

34 Mount Pleasant St
Rockport, MA 01966-1713
(978) 546-9251 Fax:978 546 9251
Internet: www.sallywebster.com
E-mail: sallywebsterinn@hotmail.com

Circa 1832. William Choate left this pre-Civil War home to be divided by his nine children. Sally Choate Webster, the ninth child, was to receive several first-floor rooms and the attic chamber, but ended up owning the entire home. The innkeepers have filled the gracious home with antiques and period reproductions, which complement the original pumpkin pine floors,

antique door moldings and six fireplaces. Shops, restaurants, the beach and the rocky coast are all within three blocks of the inn. Whale watching, kayaking, antique shops, music festivals, island tours and museums are among the myriad of nearby attractions. In addition to these, Salem is just 15 miles away, and Boston is a 35-mile drive.

Innkeeper(s): Suzan & Dean. $130-160. 7 rooms with PB, 3 with FP, 1 suite. Breakfast, snacks/refreshments and Hot Full Breakfast Buffet from 8:30-10:00 am included in rates. Types of meals: Full bkfst, early coffee/tea, Refrigeration services for cold teas and water, Keurig Machine for coffee, hot tea and and hot cocoas.
Certificate may be used: Sunday-Friday, Nov. 15-March, excluding holidays.

Seven South Street Inn

7 South Street
Rockport, MA 01966-1799
(978)546-6708 (888)284-2730
Internet: www.sevensouthstreetinn.com
E-mail: theinn@sevensouth.net

Circa 1766. Relax in the friendly and gracious atmosphere of this family-owned inn, open year-round. The 1766 Colonial with antiques and reproductions was recently renovated to provide a warm haven of peace and privacy. Gather in the fireside living room, library or sitting room to watch a movie, play games or chat. An outdoor deck is surrounded by colorful, well-kept gardens. Guest bedrooms, a two-room suite and an efficiency suite are inviting accommodations for vacations or extended stays. Enjoy fine linens, towels and robes. Two gourmet breakfast seatings are offered each morning for well-presented, elegant dining that tastes as great as it looks. Swim in the seasonal pool, or ride a bike to explore the scenic area. Make whale watching reservations and visit the local Circles Day Spa.

Innkeeper(s): Debbie Benn, Nick Benn. $79-179. 8 rooms with PB, 1 two-bedroom suite. Breakfast and snacks/refreshments included in rates. Types of meals: Full gourmet bkfst, veg bkfst and early coffee/tea.
Certificate may be used: Oct. 1-May 20, subject to availability.

Rowe

Maple House Bed & Breakfast

51 Middletown Hill Rd
Rowe, MA 01367-9702
(413)339-0107
Internet: www.maplehousebb.com
E-mail: info@maplehousebb.com

Circa 1784. Sitting on a hilltop in the Berkshires, this 200-year-old Colonial homestead farm is also known as The House on the Hill with a View of Yesteryear. Twenty scenic acres provide an assortment of activities. Hike, cross-country ski, nap on a hammock or feed the animals. Relax in the solarium by the brick fireplace. Recently renovated guest bedrooms and a suite feature the original hand-hewn beams and knotty pine flooring with antique furnishings and colorful quilts. Savor a hearty, home-grown and homemade breakfast with choices of baked goods, fruited pancakes, Maple House Granola, fresh egg dishes and much more. Lunch and dinner are available by request for groups of 8 or more. Walk or bike to Rowe Town Forest and play tennis, volleyball or basketball. Swim, fish or canoe at Pelham Lake Park.

Innkeeper(s): Rebecca Bradley, Michael Bradley. $60-125. 5 rooms, 3 with PB, 1 suite, 2 conference rooms. Breakfast, afternoon tea and snacks/refreshments included in rates. Types of meals: Country bkfst, veg bkfst, early coffee/tea, gourmet lunch, picnic lunch and gourmet dinner.

Certificate may be used: Sunday-Thursday.

Salem

The Salem Inn

7 Summer St
Salem, MA 01970-3315
(978)741-0680 (800)446-2995 Fax:(978)744-8924
Internet: www.saleminnma.com
E-mail: reservations@saleminnma.com

Circa 1834. Located in the heart of one of America's oldest cities, the inn's 41 individually decorated guest rooms feature an array of amenities such as antiques, Jacuzzi baths, fireplaces and canopy beds. Comfortable and spacious one-bedroom family suites with kitchenettes are available. A complimentary continental breakfast is offered. Nearby are fine restaurants, shops, museums, Pickering Wharf and whale watching boats for cruises.

Innkeeper(s): Jennifer MacAllister. $129-370. 40 rooms with PB, 18 with FP, 11 suites. Breakfast included in rates. Types of meals: Cont plus.

Certificate may be used: Anytime, at the last minute based on projected availability. Excludes October and May-September weekends.

Sandwich

1830 Quince Tree House

164 Main Street
Sandwich, MA 02563
(508)833-8496 (866)933-8496 Fax:(508)833-8568
Internet: www.quincetreehouse.com
E-mail: stay@quincetreehouse.com

Circa 1600. Centrally located in the historic village of Sandwich, Massachusetts, this Georgian Colonial inn on Cape Cod is within walking distance to the town beach, boardwalk and salt marsh as well as shops, art galleries and restaurants. Beach towels and tote bags are provided. Relax with snacks and refreshments on the mahogany deck overlooking the gardens or sit under the grape arbor in the yard. Make use of the guest refrigerator and computer. Wireless Internet is available throughout the inn. An elegant guest room with a rainfall shower and spacious two-room suites boast a working fireplace and many luxurious amenities. Some accommodations feature a canopy bed and the Robert Tobey Suite has a whirlpool tub. Indulge in a satisfying three-course breakfast served in the dining room. This New England vacation destination offers numerous indoor and outdoor attractions to explore.

Innkeeper(s): Richard Pratt, Cecily Denson. $125-275. 3 rooms with PB, 3 with FP, 2 total suites, including 1 two-bedroom suite. Breakfast, afternoon tea, snacks/refreshments and wine included in rates. Types of meals: Full gourmet bkfst, early coffee/tea, complimentary bottled water & sodas, Wine and sun tea in late afternoon, coffee, tea, hot chocolate & cookies, after dinner port, sherry and brandy.

Certificate may be used: November-May, excluding holidays.

Sheffield

Birch Hill Bed & Breakfast

254 S Undermountain Rd
Sheffield, MA 01257-9639
(413)229-2143 (800)359-3969 Fax:(413)229-3405
Internet: birchhillbb.com
E-mail: birchhill@roadrunner.com

Circa 1780. A slice of history is felt at this Colonial home that was built during the American Revolution. Graciously situated on 20 scenic acres in the Berkshires, it is adjacent to the Appalachian Trail. The Chestnut Room has a fantastic view and invites gathering to play the piano or games in front of the fire, listening to a CD or watching TV. Guest bedrooms and suites offer  total relaxation. Some feature sitting areas and fireplaces. Creative, mouth-watering breakfasts begin a day of serendipity. Swim in the pool, try croquet and kayak or canoe in the lake across the street. Bicycles are available to explore the local area.

Innkeeper(s): Wendy Advocate, Michael Advocate. $125-250. 7 rooms, 5 with PB, 3 with FP, 1 suite, 1 conference room. Breakfast and afternoon tea included in rates. Types of meals: Full gourmet bkfst, veg bkfst and early coffee/tea.

Certificate may be used: Anytime, subject to availability, Sunday-Thursday, excluding July and August.

South Egremont

The Ergemont Village Inn

17 Main Street
South Egremont, MA 01258
(413)528-9580 (800)528-9580 Fax:(413)528-1713
Internet: theegremontvillageinn.com/
E-mail: innkeeper@.theegremontvillageinn.com

Circa 1785. The original post-and-beam New England farmhouse with its beehive oven was added on to throughout its history. It has been restored to combine today's modern amenities with the charm of the inn's historic past. The inn's historic architectural features include broad plank floors, tree trunk supports and granite columns. A full breakfast is offered every morning.

Innkeeper(s): Dee. $95-275. 10 rooms, 8 with PB, 2 two-bedroom suites. Breakfast included in rates. Types of meals: Country bkfst, afternoon tea, snacks/refreshments and wine.

Certificate may be used: Nov.1-March 31, excluding holidays and holiday periods, subject to availability.

South Lee

Historic Merrell Inn

1565 Pleasant St, Rt 102
South Lee, MA 01260
(413)243-1794 (800)243-1794
Internet: www.merrell-inn.com
E-mail: info@merrell-inn.com

Circa 1794. This elegant stagecoach inn was carefully preserved under supervision of the Society for the Preservation of New England Antiquities. Architectural drawings of Merrell Inn

have been preserved by the Library of Congress. Eight fireplaces in the inn include two with original beehive and warming ovens. An antique circular birdcage bar serves as a check-in desk. Comfortable rooms feature canopy and four-poster beds with Hepplewhite and Sheraton-style antiques. The Riverview Suite is tucked on the back wing of the building and has a private porch which overlooks the Housatonic River.

Innkeeper(s): George Crockett. $100-295. 10 rooms with PB, 4 with FP. Breakfast included in rates. Types of meals: Full bkfst.

Certificate may be used: November-April, Except Holiday Weekends.

Stockbridge

1862 Seasons On Main B&B

47 Main St
Stockbridge, MA 01262
(413) 298-5419 (855) 223-1862 Fax:(413)298-3514
Internet: www.seasonsonmain.com
E-mail: innkeeper@seasonsonmain.com

Circa 1862. Seasons on Main was built during the Civil War. The historic Greek Revival home includes a sweeping veranda where guests can relax on wicker chairs and loveseats. The interior is Victorian in style, and two of the rooms include a fireplace. Breakfasts include items such as fresh fruit, muffins or coffeecake and entrees such as baked French toast strata. The inn offers close access to Tanglewood, the Norman Rockwell Museum, Berkshire Botanical Gardens, Edith Wharton's home, hiking, skiing and biking.

Innkeeper(s): Camilo Manrique. $185-365. 8 rooms, 5 with PB, 3 with FP, 1 with WP, 1 conference room. Breakfast, afternoon tea, snacks/refreshments, hors d'oeuvres and wine included in rates. Types of meals: Full bkfst.

Certificate may be used: Sunday-Thursday, Nov. 1-May 1, subject to availability, holidays excluded. Cannot be combined with any other discount.

Sturbridge

Sturbridge Country Inn

530 Main Street
Sturbridge, MA 01566-0060
(508)347-5503 Fax:(508)347-5319
Internet: www.sturbridgecountryinn.com
E-mail: info@sturbridgecountryinn.com

Circa 1840. Shaded by an old silver maple, this classic Greek Revival house boasts a two-story columned entrance. The attached carriage house now serves as the parlor and displays the original post-and-beam construction and

exposed rafters. All guest rooms have individual fireplaces and whirlpool tubs and include breakfast with champagne. They are appointed gracefully in colonial style furnishings, including queen-size and four-posters. A patio and gazebo are favorite summertime retreats. A five-star restaurant and outdoor heated pool are also on the premesis.

Innkeeper(s): Kevin MacConnell, Patricia Affenito. $99-199. 16 rooms with PB, 16 with FP, 15 with WP, 2 total suites, including 1 two-bedroom suite, 1 conference room. Breakfast, snacks/refreshments and Continental Breakfast: Midweek Basket or Weekend Buffet included in rates. Types of meals: Cont, early coffee/tea and room service.

Certificate may be used: Sunday-Thursday, subject to management approval, limited availability.

Sudbury

Inn on The Horse Farm

277 Old Sudbury Road
Sudbury, MA 01776
(978)443-7400 (800)272-2426
Internet: www.InnOnTheHorseFarm.com
E-mail: joanbeers@aol.com

Circa 1880. Secluded on nine wooded acres with a horse farm, this 1880 Queen Anne Victorian offers the ultimate in privacy and romance. This inn is the perfect retreat to celebrate birthdays, anniversaries or other special occasions. The three-room Tanah Suite with a canopy bed, two-person Jacuzzi and fireplace is a honeymoon favorite. A stay in the two-room Orlanda Suite featuring a draped four-poster bed, two-person Jacuzzi and huge balcony is also a popular pleaser. A complete breakfast is made at a flexible time to suit every taste with delicious entrees and accompaniments. Enjoy the meal in the Ye Old Worlde Cafe, on the veranda under the pergola or in-room. Lunch or dinner can be arranged with advance reservation. Tours are gladly given of the original four-story barn with post and beam ceiling and huge cupola.

Innkeeper(s): Joan Beers, Rick Beers. $129-319. 3 rooms with PB, 1 with FP, 2 with WP, 1 cottage. Breakfast included in rates. Types of meals: Full gourmet bkfst, veg bkfst, early coffee/tea and You can reserve brunch/lunch/dinner or afternoon tea/cookies with 48 hours notice.

Certificate may be used: Anytime, subject to availability.

Vineyard Haven

Hanover House at Twin Oaks

28 Edgartown Rd
Vineyard Haven, MA 02568
(508)693-1066 (800)696-8633 Fax:(508)696-6099
Internet: www.twinoaksinn.net
E-mail: innkeeper@hanoverhouseinn.com

Circa 1906. When visiting Martha's Vineyard, Twin Oaks offers two pleasurable places to choose from that are within walking distance to the beach, ferry or downtown shops. Stay at the award-winning Clark House, a classic bed & breakfast or the Hanover House, an elegant three-diamond country inn just next door. Gather on one of the porches, the large backyard or private brick patio and gazebo. Complimentary bikes and high-speed Internet access are available on a first come first serve basis. Each of the comfortable guest bedrooms offer Internet access. Join the "breakfast party" for a bountiful continental-plus morning meal.

Innkeeper(s): Steve and Judy Perlman. $99-285. 15 rooms. Breakfast and snacks/refreshments included in rates. Types of meals: Cont plus.

Certificate may be used: Post Columbus Day through the Thursday prior to Memorial Day. Subject to availability. Cannot combine with any other discount or program.

Wellfleet

The Inn at Duck Creeke

Inn at Duck Creeke
Wellfleet, MA 02667
(508) 349-9333
Internet: www.innatduckcreeke.com
E-mail: info@innatduckcreeke.com

Circa 1815. The five-acre site of this sea captain's house features both a salt-water marsh and a duck pond. The

Saltworks house and the main house are appointed in an old-fashioned style with antiques, and the rooms are comfortable and cozy. Some have views of the nearby salt marsh or the pond. The inn is favored for its two restaurants; Sweet Seasons and the Tavern Room. The latter is popular for its jazz performances.

Innkeeper(s): Bob Morrill, Judy Pihl. $115-165. 27 rooms, 19 with PB. Breakfast included in rates. Types of meals: Cont. Restaurant on premises.
Certificate may be used: Sunday-Thursday, Aug. 25-29, Monday-Thursday, September-October, subject to availability.

Yarmouth Port

One Centre Street Inn

1 Center St
Yarmouth Port, MA 02675-1342
(508)362-9951 (866)362-9951
Internet: www.onecentrestreetinn.com
E-mail: sales@onecentrestreetinn.com

Circa 1824. Originally a church parsonage, this Greek Revival-style inn is listed in the National Register. Located one mile from Cape Cod Bay, the classic elegance enhances the comfort and amenities offered, including luxurious linens, robes, flat screen TV, in-room WiFi, CD players and refrigerators.

After a restful night's sleep, indulge in a gourmet breakfast featuring hot coffee, specialty teas, fresh baked muffins and seasonal fresh fruit served with entrees such as Lemon Ricotta Pancakes, One Centre Street Inn

Eggs Benedict or Oven Baked Stuffed French Toast, served on the screened porch or in the sun-filled dining room. A short drive away is the Cape Playhouse, Cape Cod Melody Tent, whale watching tours, golf courses, deep sea fishing, and ferries to Nantucket or Martha's Vineyard. Take day trips to Provincetown, Chatham, and the National Seashore beaches as well as Boston, Plymouth and Newport Rhode Island.

Innkeeper(s): Mary Singleton. $135-250. 5 rooms, 4 with PB, 1 with FP, 1 suite. Breakfast included in rates. Types of meals: Full gourmet bkfst, early coffee/tea, afternoon tea and snacks/refreshments.
Certificate may be used: Oct. 1-May 15, subject to availability.

Michigan

Allegan

Castle In The Country Bed and Breakfast

340 M 40 S
Allegan, MI 49010-9609
(269)673-8054 (888)673-8054
Internet: www.castleinthecountry.com
E-mail: info@castleinthecountry.com

Circa 1906. Reflecting its nickname and castle-like appearance, a three-story turret and wide wraparound porch accent this 1906 Queen Anne Victorian adorning five acres of scenic countryside. Gather in one of the several common rooms or sitting areas. A Guest Refreshment Center has a coffee pot and refrigerator. Romantic guest bedrooms and a suite feature fresh flowers, candles, terry robes, handmade bath products, a video library and VCR. Several rooms include whirlpool tubs, fireplaces and CD players. Breakfast is specially prepared and served on fine china and vintage crystal. Innkeepers Herb and Ruth enjoy providing personalized service that ensures a pleasant stay. Ask for an Adventure Map, a helpful tool to enjoy local activities and sites. Many special packages are regularly offered.
Innkeeper(s): Herb Boven, Ruth Boven. $129-319. 10 rooms with PB, 10 with FP, 8 with WP, 8 suites, 1 conference room. Breakfast included in rates. Types of meals: Full gourmet bkfst, veg bkfst, early coffee/tea, picnic lunch, afternoon tea, snacks/refreshments, wine, dinner and room service.
Certificate may be used: Sunday-Thursday, Nov. 1-May 31 (excluding holidays).

Alma

Saravilla

633 N State St
Alma, MI 48801-1640
(989)463-4078
Internet: www.saravilla.com
E-mail: Ljdarrow@saravilla.com

Circa 1894. This 11,000-square-foot Dutch Colonial home with its Queen Anne influences was built as a magnificent wedding gift for lumber baron Ammi W. Wright's only surviving child, Sara. Wright spared no expense building this mansion for his daughter, and the innkeepers have spared nothing in restoring the home to its former prominence. The foyer and dining room boast imported English oak woodwork. The foyer's hand-painted canvas wallcoverings and the ballroom's embossed wallpaper come from France. The home still features original leaded-glass windows, built-in bookcases, window seats and light fixtures. In 1993, the innkeepers added a sunroom with a hot tub that overlooks a formal garden. The full, formal breakfast includes such treats as homemade granola, freshly made coffeecakes, breads, muffins and a mix of entrees.
Innkeeper(s): Linda Darrow, Jon Darrow. $99-169. 7 rooms with PB, 3 with FP, 2 with WP, 2 conference rooms. Breakfast and snacks/refreshments included in rates. Types of meals: Full bkfst, early coffee/tea and room service.
Certificate may be used: Sunday-Thursday, Jan. 2 to Dec. 30, excluding holidays.

Bellaire

Grand Victorian Bed & Breakfast Inn

402 North Bridge Street
Bellaire, MI 49615-9591
(231)533-6111 (877)438-6111
Internet: www.grandvictorian.com
E-mail: innkeeper@grandvictorian.com

Circa 1895. Featured in Country Inns and Midwest Living magazines, this Queen Anne Victorian mansion boasts three original fireplaces, hand-carved mantels, intricate fretwork and numerous architectural details. Relax with a glass of wine before the fire in the formal front parlor, or listen to music while playing cards and games in the back parlor. Guest bedrooms offer an eclectic mix of antique furnishings including Victorian Revival, Eastlake and French Provincial. Soak in an 1890s clawfoot tub, or enjoy the park view from a private balcony. Be pampered with an incredible stay in one of the country's most remarkable and unique inns. The gazebo is a perfect spot to while away the day, or take advantage of the area's many nearby activities.
Innkeeper(s): Ken Fedraw, Linda Fedraw. $105-235. 6 rooms with PB, 4 with FP, 2 with WP. Breakfast and snacks/refreshments included in rates. Types of meals: Full gourmet bkfst.
Certificate may be used: November 15-May 31.

Brooklyn

Dewey Lake Manor

11811 Laird Rd
Brooklyn, MI 49230-9035
(517)467-7122 Fax:517 467 2356
Internet: www.deweylakemanor.com
E-mail: deweylk@frontier-net.net

Circa 1868. This Italianate house overlooks Dewey Lake and is situated on 18 acres in the Irish Hills. The house is furnished in a country Victorian style with antiques. An enclosed porch is a favorite spot to relax and take in the views of the lake while having breakfast. Favorite pastimes include lakeside bonfires in the summertime and ice skating or cross-country skiing in the winter. Canoe and paddleboats are available to guests.

Innkeeper(s): Barb Phillips, Joe Phillips. $89-139. 5 rooms with PB, 5 with FP, 1 with WP, 1 conference room. Breakfast, snacks/refreshments and certain specials have meals included in rates. Types of meals: Country bkfst, early coffee/tea and picnic lunch.

Certificate may be used: November-April, subject to availability, special events excluded.

Fennville

J. Paules' Fenn Inn

2254 S 58th St
Fennville, MI 49408-9461
(269) 561-2836 (877) 561-2836
Internet: www.jpaulesfenninn.com
E-mail: jpaules@accn.org

Circa 1900. This traditional bed and breakfast is peacefully situated in the countryside. Choose from a variety of impressive guest bedrooms, some with sun decks. There is a two-bedroom suite that is perfect for families. Starting with a gourmet breakfast, the hospitality continues throughout the day. Hot beverages, baked goods and fruit are available in the main dining room. Popcorn is offered as the perfect companion while watching a video. Pets are welcome.

Innkeeper(s): Paulette Clouse . $100-150. 6 rooms with PB, 3 with FP, 3 with WP, 1 two-bedroom suite. Breakfast, afternoon tea, snacks/refreshments and wine included in rates. Types of meals: Full gourmet bkfst, veg bkfst, early coffee/tea and dinner.

Certificate may be used: November-March, subject to availability.

Grand Rapids

Prairieside Suites Luxury B&B

3180 Washington Ave SW
Grand Rapids, MI 49418
(616)538-9442 Fax:(616) 538-9440
Internet: www.prairieside.com
E-mail: cheri@prairieside.com

Circa 1920. 2009 Winner - Travelers' Choice for Romance. Stay at this luxury bed and breakfast in Grandville, Michigan. Spacious guest suites feature pampering details that include heated towel bars, heated toilet seats and tile floors, Jacuzzis, Fireplace, coffee makers, refrigerators, microwaves, CD players and VCRs. Special amenities are offered for business travelers in three suites that boast executive business centers. The European Shower Experience in three of the private baths has body massaging sprays, and has hand held shower heads. Evening snacks are available. full breakfast in the dining room or a deluxe continental breakfast packed in the refrigerator in your room plus cookies and baked goods. Swim in the heated outdoor pool with a waterfall, relax in the pergola's double slider, or wander the perennial gardens accented by a fountain. Special arrangements and personal services are gladly taken care of at Prairieside Suites.

Innkeeper(s): Cheri Antozak, Paul Antozak. $199-269. 7 rooms with PB, 7 with FP, 7 with WP, 1 conference room. Breakfast, afternoon tea, snacks/refreshments, cookies, homemade cocoa, micro popcorn, in-room coffee makers/tea service and soda is waiting in your refrigerator upon arrival included in rates. Types of meals: Veg bkfst, early coffee/tea, and full hot candle light breakfast in dining room every morning or full hot breakfast delivered to your room.

Certificate may be used: Anytime for any suite if booked the day you are arriving. Or for advance reservations anytime Monday-Thursday during November-May [excludes holidays].

Lakeside

Lakeside Inn

15251 Lakeshore Rd
Lakeside, MI 49116-9712
(269)469-0600 Fax:(269)469-1914
Internet: www.lakesideinns.com
E-mail: reservationslk@lakesideinns.com

Circa 1890. Totally renovated in 1995, the Lakeside Inn features original wood pillars and rustic stone fireplaces in the

lobby and ballroom. The inn overlooks Lake Michigan located just across the street, and was featured in a USA Today article "Ten Great Places to Sit on the Porch" because of its 100-foot-long veranda. Each individually decorated room combines the special ambiance of comfortable antique furnishings with modern amenities like TVs, air conditioning and private baths. Many of the rooms are on the lake side, and some offer Jacuzzi tubs. Besides board games or cards for indoor recreation, the inn offers an exercise room and dry sauna. Cycling, horseback riding, swimming, antique shops, art galleries and a state park are nearby.

Innkeeper(s): Connie Williams. $90-185. 31 rooms with PB, 1 suite, 1 conference room.

Certificate may be used: Nov. 1 through the Wednesday before Memorial Day Weekend.

Ludington

The Inn at Ludington

701 E Ludington Ave
Ludington, MI 49431-2224
(231)845-7055 (800)845-9170
Internet: www.inn-ludington.com
E-mail: innkeeper@inn-ludington.com

Circa 1890. Experience an informal elegance at this Victorian bed and breakfast in the Great Lakes region near Lake Michigan beach that offers a fine blend of the past and the present. Built in 1890, it has been locally awarded for retaining its historical integrity during replicate restoration. Lounge by one of the four fireplaces and savor afternoon refreshments. Choose from one of the seven ethnically-themed guest bedrooms. Early risers can enjoy fresh coffee, cereal, yogurt and nut bread. A personally tailored meal is offered at an agreed-upon, predetermined time. Ask about seasonal getaway or family packages,

special events and murder mystery weekends.

Innkeeper(s): Kathy Kvalvaag, Ola Kvalvaag. $90-225. 7 rooms, 1 with PB, 2 with FP, 1 with HT, 3 suites. Breakfast included in rates. Types of meals: Full bkfst and early coffee/tea.

Certificate may be used: November-April, anytime; May, June, September, October, Sunday-Thursday as available at last minute.

Petoskey

Terrace Inn & Restaurant

1549 Glendale Ave.
Petoskey, MI 49770
(231) 347-2410 (800) 530-9898
Internet: www.theterraceinn.com
E-mail: info@theterraceinn.com

Circa 1911. Poised in the picturesque Victorian village of Bay View, Petoskey, the 1911 Terrace Inn is located just 45 minutes south of Mackinac Island near sandy Lake Michigan beaches in scenic Northwest Michigan.

This year-round bed and breakfast inn is a National Historic Landmark. Feel refreshed by the warm and friendly service perfectly blended with privacy. Sit in a
rocker on the wide veranda or relax by the fire in the lobby. Accommodations include themed guest bedrooms, from cottage style to deluxe rooms with fireplaces to whirlpool suites. After a hearty continental breakfast play croquet, then visit the nearby sophisticated downtown area for recreational and cultural activities. The inn's restaurant with owner and chef Mo Rave, offers in-season dinners.

Innkeeper(s): Mo Rave, Patty Rasmussen-Rave. $79-189. 6 rooms, 7 with FP, 6 with WP, 6 suites, 1 conference room. Breakfast, Dinner/Lodging packages offered, picnic lunch peak/fall color season and romance packages may include wine included in rates. Types of meals: Full bkfst, early coffee/tea, lunch, afternoon tea, hors d'oeuvres, wine, gourmet dinner. Inn offers open dining in the summer months (June-August), dinner is served Tuesday-Saturday 5PM-9PM Fri/Sat through October then weekends until March. Reservations recommended. Restaurant on premises.

Certificate may be used: Weekdays year-round. Standard Rooms. Upgrade if available on Deluxe Room and Suites Only.

Saugatuck

Bayside Inn

618 Water St
Saugatuck, MI 49453
(269)857-4321 Fax:(269) 857-1870
Internet: www.baysideinn.net
E-mail: info@baysideinn.net

Circa 1926. Located on the edge of the Kalamazoo River and across from the nature observation tower, this downtown inn was once a boathouse. The common room now has a fireplace and view of the water. Each guest room has its own deck. The inn is near several restaurants, shops and beaches. Fishing for

salmon, perch and trout is popular.

Innkeeper(s): Kathy Wilson, Frank Wilson. $90-305. 10 rooms with PB, 4 with FP, 3 with WP, 6 total suites, including 1 two-bedroom suite.

Breakfast and snacks/refreshments included in rates. Types of meals: Cont plus and early coffee/tea.

Certificate may be used: Nov. 1-March 31, Sunday-Thursday, subject to availability.

Hidden Garden Cottages & Suites

247 Butler St
Saugatuck, MI 49453
(269) 857-8109 (888) 857-8109
Internet: www.hiddengardencottages.com
E-mail: Indakott@AOL.com

Circa 1879. Perfect for a secluded bed breakfast experience, these elegantly furnished cottages are designed for two. Tucked away in the downtown area, the quiet location is convenient to all of the local shopping, dining and attractions. Each luxurious cottage features a gorgeous canopy or four-poster bed, down comforter and exquisite bed linens. Relax in the romantic seating area by the fireplace with color cable TV, VCR, CD stereo system and a phone. The luxurious bathroom has a whirlpool for two, plush robes and complete bath amenities. A mini-kitchen includes a refrigerator, icemaker and microwave oven. Overlook the intimate courtyard garden and fountains from a private porch that completes the tranquil setting. A continental breakfast is offered each morning. Take a boat cruise on Lake Michigan, play golf or ride the dunes.

Innkeeper(s): Gary Kott, Jonathan Schreur. $135-250. 4 rooms with PB, 4 with FP, 4 with WP. Breakfast and snacks/refreshments included in rates. Types of meals: Cont plus.

Certificate may be used: Sunday-Thursday, November-May.

Kingsley House

626 W Main St
Saugatuck, MI 49408-9442
(269) 561-6425 (866) 561-6425
Internet: www.kingsleyhouse.com
E-mail: romanticgetaways@kingsleyhouse.com

Circa 1886. Experience the elegance of this Victorian Queen Anne mansion located near the resort towns of Saugatuck, Holland and South Haven. Restored and opened as a bed and

breakfast, this relaxing retreat specializes in thoughtful hospitality and generous amenities. Sip lemonade on the wraparound front porch. Savor afternoon tea by the fire in the parlor. Indulge in a treat from the dining room cookie jar. Tastefully appointed and well-decorated guest bedrooms feature an assortment of pleasing comforts. Stay in the Jonathan Room with a two-person Hydromassage tub and gas log fireplace. The Northern Spy is a popular honeymoon suite on the entire third floor, with a double whirlpool tub, fireplace and sitting area in the turret. Royal Doulton china, heirloom silver and vintage linens accent a plentiful gourmet breakfast. Bikes are provided for an easy ride to Hutchins Lake or the winery. Drive to the nearby beaches of Lake Michigan.

Innkeeper(s): Terrie Hunter. $69-299. 8 rooms with PB, 8 with FP, 4 with WP, 4 suites. Breakfast, afternoon tea and snacks/refreshments included in rates. Types of meals: Full gourmet bkfst, veg bkfst, early coffee/tea, picnic lunch and gourmet dinner.

Certificate may be used: November-April, Sunday-Thursday, excluding holidays.

The Beachway Resort & Hotel

106 Perryman
Saugatuck, MI 49453
(269)857-3331
Internet: www.beachwayresort.com
E-mail: info@beachwayresort.com

Circa 1900. Overlooking the Kalamazoo River, The Beachway Resort & Hotel is a relaxing destination in Saugatuck, Michigan. Lake Michigan's award-winning Oval Beach is popular nearby. Swim in the large, heated pool and relax on a sundeck. Browse through the movie and game library for inside entertainment. Accommodations offer something for everyone from romantic waterfront suites that may include a balcony, fireplace and Jacuzzi, to family-friendly cottages or more economic B&B-style guest rooms. Start each day with coffee, fruit and donuts before exploring the area attractions and seasonal festivals.

Innkeeper(s): Kathy Wilson, Frank Wilson. $60-600. 40 rooms with PB, 2 with FP, 2 with WP, 11 total suites, including 2 two-bedroom suites and 2 four-bedroom suites, 4 cottages, 3 guest houses. Types of meals: Early coffee/tea.

Certificate may be used: May, September-October, Sunday-Thursday, no holidays. Closed November-April.

Twin Oaks Inn

PO Box 818, 227 Griffith St
Saugatuck, MI 49453-0818
(269)857-1600 (800)788-6188 Fax:(269)857-7446
Internet: www.twinoaksinn.com
E-mail: twinoaks@sirus.com

Circa 1860. This large Queen Anne Victorian inn was a boarding house for lumbermen at the turn of the century. Now an old-English-style inn, it offers a variety of lodging choices, including a room with its own Jacuzzi. There are many diversions at Twin Oaks, including a collection of videotaped movies numbering more than 700. Guests

may borrow bicycles or play horseshoes on the inn's grounds.

Innkeeper(s): Willa Lemken. $110-150. 6 rooms with PB, 1 conference room. Types of meals: Full bkfst, early coffee/tea and snacks/refreshments.

Certificate may be used: Nov. 1-April 30, Sunday through Thursday.

South Haven

Martha's Vineyard Bed and Breakfast

473 Blue Star Hwy
South Haven, MI 49090
(269)637-9373 Fax:(269)639-8214
Internet: www.marthasvy.com
E-mail: adamson@marthasvy.com

Circa 1852. In a park-like setting of more than four acres, this 1852 Federal style estate offers a quiet respite for all of its guests. Stroll the beautifully landscaped gardens or private vineyard, sit by the pond or one of its waterfalls, or stroll along the golf course. You will be pampered by its luxurious accommodations and the hosts extravagant hospitality. Each guest bedroom boasts a fireplace, steeped with charm and your comfort in mind, guest bathrobes provided. A four-course breakfast with antique china, silver settings, and cloth napkins may include the inns signature caramel apple pancakes. Indulge in special packages designed as personally requested. Choose golf, massage or an assortment of getaway amenities. Lou and Ginger look forward to having you as their guests.

Innkeeper(s): Lou & Ginger Adamson. $99-205. 11 rooms with PB, 11 with FP, 7 with WP, 1 guest house. Breakfast, afternoon tea and snacks/refreshments included in rates. Types of meals: Full bkfst, veg bkfst, early coffee/tea, picnic lunch and room service.

Certificate may be used: Sunday-Thursday, November-April.

Traverse City

Grey Hare Inn Vineyard B&B

1994 Carroll Rd.
Traverse City, MI 49686
(231) 947-2214 (800) 873-0652 Fax:(231)947-2401
Internet: www.greyhareinn.com
E-mail: greyhareinn@hughes.net

Circa 1997. Near Traverse City, this elegant country vineyard estate is a glorious retreat. Relax on the trellised stone patio or by the limestone fireplace in the great room and library. Hike, sail, golf, bike and ski amid this Old Mission Peninsula region that boasts cherry trees and numerous related seasonal festivals. Stay in a guest room or suite that features European-styled dÃ©cor, a clawfoot or Jacuzzi tub, gas fireplace and expansive views of the bay, vineyard and orchards. Daily breakfasts boast a gourmet Northern Michigan fusion with a Tuscan and Provence flair. Wine-inspired cuisine whets the appetite for local tastings. Special packages may include wonderful activities, events and upgrades.

Innkeeper(s): Cindy Ruzak, Jay Ruzak. $135-275. 3 rooms with PB, 1 with FP, 1 with HT, 1 with WP, 1 two-bedroom suite. Breakfast, hors d'oeuvres and room turndown treat included in rates. Types of meals: Full gourmet bkfst, veg bkfst, early coffee/tea, gourmet lunch, picnic lunch, wine and nightly room turndown treat.

Certificate may be used: Sunday-Thursday, November-March, excludes Dec. 20-Jan. 2.

Oviatt House Bed and Breakfast

244 E. 8th St
Traverse City, MI 49684
(231)675-6709 Fax:(231)421-5225
Internet: oviatthouse.com
E-mail: franny@oviatthouse.com

Circa 1900. Just cross the street from this classic historic home, centrally located in Old Town, and take the Boardman River Walkway two blocks to Downtown Traverse City, Michigan. Bikes are provided to explore the surrounding urban area. Enjoy the privacy and comforts of home with a house key to come and go. Relax in the fireside living room with early American furnishings from the federalist era or on the garden deck with an evening glass of local wine. Hot and cold beverages are available anytime. Antiques accent guest rooms with sitting areas and feature a sleigh or four-poster canopy bed. Indulge in a hearty breakfast made with fresh organic ingredients. Take a wine-tasting tour of nearby wineries, and pick fruit in the cherry orchards of the Grand Traverse Bay area.

Innkeeper(s): Franny Bluhm. $125-175. 6 rooms, 2 with PB. Breakfast, afternoon tea, snacks/refreshments, hors d'oeuvres and wine included in rates. Types of meals: Full gourmet bkfst, veg bkfst and early coffee/tea.

Certificate may be used: Sunday-Thursday, November-March.

Wakefield

Regal Country Inn

1602 E Hwy 2
Wakefield, MI 49968-9581
(906)229-5122 Fax:(906)229-5755
Internet: www.regalcountryinn.com
E-mail: info@regalcountryinn.com

Circa 1973. Choose from four types of accommodations at this quaint, smoke-free bed & breakfast. Historical rooms feature antique furnishings, scrapbooks and literature documenting nearby towns. Relax on rocker/recliners in a comfortable study bedroom. The Victorians include quilt-topped beds. Country rooms are ideal for families. Savor treats from the 1950s as well as a limited menu and delicious desserts at the inn's Old Tyme Ice Cream Parlour and Soda Fountain. Room service and meals are offered for an added charge. Gather for conversation in the Fireside Room. Hike, fish, ski, golf, snowmobile, visit waterfalls and lighthouses in this scenic Upper Peninsula region. Cultural events and local festivals are held throughout the year.

Innkeeper(s): Richard Swanson. $70-145. 17 rooms with PB. Types of meals: Early coffee/tea, Fresh baked breakfast rolls/muffins and hot chocolate.

Certificate may be used: Anytime subject to availability. Not valid July 1-6. Cannot be used with any other discounts. Only one discount per stay.

Whitehall

Cocoa Cottage Bed and Breakfast

223 S. Mears Avenue
Whitehall, MI 49461
(231) 893-0674 (800) 204-7596
Internet: www.cocoacottage.com
E-mail: innkeeper@cocoacottage.com

Circa 1912. Historically restored, this authentic 1912 Arts and Crafts bungalow is accented with period furniture, pottery, wallpaper and copper work. Several common areas, including an intimate fireplace room, sunny screened-in porch and lush gardens with a pergola and patio, offer peaceful surroundings that enhance relaxation and conversation. Reflecting the inn's delicious theme, each tempting guest bedroom is named after chocolates. Lavish amenities will pamper and please. Soak in the large whirlpool bath in the Ghirardelli Room. Pillow-topped mattresses invite sleep on a brass bed in the Godiva or on the Cadbury's white wrought iron. Evening port, handmade confections and turndown service are thoughtful touches. Indulge in a bountiful, award-winning breakfast that may feature Cottage eggs, Lemon-ricotta pancakes, stuffed French toast and other popular favorites. Bikes are available to explore the scenic area.

Innkeeper(s): Larry Robertson, Lisa Tallarico. $145-195. 4 rooms with PB, 1 with WP. Breakfast, hors d'oeuvres and Check-in reception of wine/cheese/chocolate provided between 5-6:00pm only-Not available for early or late arrivals included in rates. Types of meals: Full gourmet bkfst, veg bkfst, early coffee/tea, gourmet lunch, picnic lunch, afternoon tea, Gluten free/Diabetic/Low Sodium meals available and Dinner/lunch available seasonally at an additional cost.

Certificate may be used: January-May 25, anytime. May 25-Oct. 31, Sunday-Thursday only. Nov. 1-Dec. 31, anytime. Subject to availability. Can not be combined with other promotions or 3rd party gift certificates.

White Swan Inn

303 S Mears Ave
Whitehall, MI 49461-1323
(231)894-5169 (888)948-7926
Internet: www.whiteswaninn.com
E-mail: info@whiteswaninn.com

Circa 1884. Maple trees shade this sturdy Queen Anne home, a block from White Lake. A screened porch filled with white wicker and an upstairs coffee room are leisurely retreats. Parquet floors in the dining room, antique furnishings and chandeliers add to the comfortable decor. Chicken and broccoli quiche is a favorite breakfast recipe. Cross the street for summer theater or walk to shops and restaurants nearby.

Innkeeper(s): Cathy & Ron Russell. $109-179. 4 rooms with PB, 2 with FP, 1 with WP. Breakfast and snacks/refreshments included in rates. Types of meals: Full bkfst, veg bkfst, early coffee/tea and dinner upon request.

Certificate may be used: May 25-Oct. 25, Sunday-Thursday and Oct. 26-May 24 anytime.

Wolverine

Silent Sport Lodge

8300 Trout Lily Trail
Wolverine, MI 49799
(231) 525-6166
Internet: www.silentsportlodge.com
E-mail: info@silentsportlodge.com

Circa 1997. Experience peaceful tranquility amid this 30-acre north woods setting on the Sturgeon River, a Blue Ribbon trout stream in Wolverine, Michigan. Nap in a hammock, relax in a swing or sit on the waterfront deck. Ponds connect to a stream with waterfalls by the bonfire pit. Stroll through the gardens, ski or snowshoe the grounds and soak in the outdoor hot tub. The wilderness log lodge is a green facility with sustainable practices. Stay in a pleasantly themed, spacious guest room or the separate River Cabin. The River Room boasts a private balcony and The Cedar Room includes a two-person whirlpool tub. Hearty breakfasts include signature recipes made with local, seasonal and organic ingredients. The area has many attractions from elk viewing to casinos. Be sure to visit Mackinac Island. Custom romance packages are available.

Innkeeper(s): John Smit, Rhonda Smit. $110-125. 4 rooms with PB, 1 with FP, 1 with WP, 1 cabin. Breakfast and other meals included in specialty package pricing included in rates. Types of meals: Full bkfst, veg bkfst and other meals included in specialty packages.

Certificate may be used: Anytime, subject to availability.

Wyandotte

Bishop Brighton Bed and Breakfast

2709 Biddle Street
Wyandotte, MI 48192
(734) 284-7309 (877) 284-7309
Internet: www.bishop-brightonbedandbreakfast.com/
E-mail: info@bishop-brightonbedandbreakfast.com

Circa 1902. To love arts and crafts is to love Bishop-Brighton Bed and Breakfast in Wyandotte, Michigan. The English Tudor revival has been decorated using an artistic eye including stencils done by the innkeeper. The nationally known Wyandotte Art Fair is held nearby each July. Each of the three guest rooms is painted in a muted color and has a private bath with antique claw-foot tub. For those traveling as a family, two of the rooms have separate sitting rooms with a sofa bed. Relax on the wrap-around porch with a refreshment from the butler's pantry and a book or magazine from the library. Enjoy a gourmet breakfast before venturing to the boardwalk at Bishop Park directly behind the inn. The park also hosts outdoor concerts and is an ideal spot to watch freighters traveling on the Detroit River. Walk two blocks to downtown Wyandotte for restaurants and shops or drive 15 miles to Ford Motor Headquarters and downtown Detroit.

Innkeeper(s): Gerry Lucas, Vicki Lucas. $100-135. 3 rooms with PB, 2 suites. Types of meals: Full gourmet bkfst, veg bkfst, snacks/refreshments, Breakfast available for Celiac, diabetic and Vegan.

Certificate may be used: November-March, subject to availability.

Minnesota

Afton

The Historic Afton House Inn

3291 S. St. Croix Trail
Afton, MN 55001
(651)436-8883 Fax:(651)436-6859
Internet: www.aftonhouseinn.com
E-mail: reservations@aftonhouseinn.com

Circa 1867. Located on two acres of waterfront on the St. Croix River, this historic inn reflects an old New England-style architecture. Guest rooms offer Jacuzzi tubs, fireplaces, water-front balconies and are deco-rated with American country antiques. A restaurant on the premises provides candle-light dining in the Wheel Room. Ask for Bananas Foster, a house specialty, or any flaming dessert. Or you might prefer to dine in the Catfish Saloon & Cafe, which has a more casual menu. Champagne Brunch cruises are offered on the Grand Duchess May-October. Three charter vessels are available for private cruises for weddings, birthdays, anniver-saries, corporate getaways or for groups of 10-350. Visit the inn's web site for online availability.

Innkeeper(s): Gordy & Kathy Jarvis. $85-285. 25 rooms with PB, 19 with FP, 21 with WP, 3 total suites, including 2 two-bedroom suites, 2 conference rooms. Continental plus breakfast included in rates. Types of meals: Cont plus, veg bkfst, Sun. brunch, early coffee/tea, lunch, snacks/refreshments, hors d'oeuvres, wine, gourmet dinner and room service. Restaurant on premises.

Certificate may be used: Anytime, Sunday-Thursday and available weekends on last minute availability.

Duluth

Fitger's Inn

600 E Superior St
Duluth, MN 55802-2222
(218)722-8826 (800)726-2982 Fax:(218)722-8826
Internet: www.fitgers.com
E-mail: fitgers@fitgers.com

Circa 1858. Gracing the shore of majestic Lake Superior, in Duluth, Minnesota, this premiere historic hotel is located with-in the renovated Fitger's Brewery, and is listed on the National Register. Feel pampered by classic European-style service, gra-cious hospitality, fine cuisine, and luxurious accommodations. Guest rooms and suites boast a wide array of character and per-sonality. Many of the amenities available include balconies, fire-places, skylights, whirlpool tubs for two, multiple windows, split-levels, 16-foot ceilings and spectacular views of the water. Enjoy a complimentary continental breakfast daily in the priva-cy of the original board room. The large complex is also home to three great restaurants, two night clubs, a micro brewery, day spa and salon, and many unique retail shops. In addition, the convenient downtown location offers direct access to the lakewalk and Canal Park.

Innkeeper(s): James Makitalo. $130-370. 62 rooms with PB, 4 with FP, 10 with HT, 10 with WP, 10 suites, 4 conference rooms. Types of meals: Midi Restaurant, Mexico Lindo and Fitger's Brewhouse Brewery & Grill. Restaurant on premises.

Certificate may be used: Anytime, Nov. 1-April 30 except Dec. 31 and Sunday-Thursday only May 1-Oct. 31.

Jordan

Nicolin Mansion Bed & Breakfast

221 Broadway Street South
Jordan, MN 55352
(952) 492-6441 (800) 683-3360
Internet: www.nicolinmansion.com
E-mail: innkeeper@nicolinmansion.com

Circa 1888. Nicolin Mansion Bed & Breakfast is a Victorian retreat in the historic district of Jordan, Minnesota. Listed in the National Register, the mansion boasts imported stained glass, rich wood and brick from Frank Nicolin's quarry. Play the piano in the double parlor, sit on a swing or wicker rocker on one of the porches and relax on a bench by a pond and fountain in the courtyard. Browse through the book and movie library. Modern amenities enhance every stay. Luxurious air-conditioned guest rooms feature Euro pillow-top mattresses, and soaps are handcrafted onsite. Savor a leisurely three-course breakfast on the weekends and a midweek breakfast buffet in the dining room. Packages and specials are available to enhance every stay.

Innkeeper(s): Kevin and Terri Knox. $99-189. 5 rooms with PB, 5 with FP, 3 with WP. Breakfast and snacks/refreshments included in rates. Types of meals: Full gourmet bkfst, veg bkfst, early coffee/tea and wine.

Certificate may be used: Oct. 6-December, Sunday-Thursday. Must call to reserve.

Lanesboro

Anna V's B&B

507 Fillmore Ave S
Lanesboro, MN 55949-9707
(507)467-2686
Internet: www.annavbb.com

Circa 1908. Relax, refresh, and renew on the wraparound porch of this Victorian inn four blocks from downtown Lanesboro, Minnesota. A queen or king-size bed and private bathroom await guests in each of the four rooms. Guests that want a truly private getaway may have a continental breakfast in the newest room, the third-floor Brooklyn Suite. The aroma of coffee and fresh-baked muffins fills the dining room each morning as guests gather for a multi-course breakfast made from local ingredients including some from the inn's garden. A gentlemen's and a ladies' parlor set the scene for laughter and stories. Walk to the Root River to bike along 60 miles of paved trails amid 300-foot scenic bluffs. The local Commonweal Theatre has over 200 performances each year. The Scenic Valley Winery, with a downtown tasting room and gift shop, offers unique bottles of rhubarb, cranberry, and raspberry wine.
Innkeeper(s): Steve Harris , Suzie Harris. Call for rates. 3 rooms.
Certificate may be used: November to March, no weekends or holidays.

Stone Mill Suites

100 Beacon Street East
Lanesboro, MN 55949
(507)467-8663 (866)897-8663
Internet: www.stonemillsuites.com
E-mail: stonemillsuites@hotmail.com

Circa 1885. Combining a historical heritage with modern conveniences, this nineteenth-century stone building was built using limestone quarried from the area's surrounding bluffs. The original clay ceilings and stair railings accent the decor. Themed suites and guest bedrooms reflect local history and its undeniable charm. Relaxing amenities feature a fireplace, whirlpool tub, microwave and refrigerator. Children are welcome, ask about family packages. A generous continental breakfast may include English muffins, bakery items from Lanesboro Pastries, cereal, fruit, beverages and French toast topped with strawberries, blueberries and whipped cream. A variety of museums and the Laura Ingalls Wilder Site are all within a 30-minute drive.
Innkeeper(s): Dorothy Amanda (Mandy) Smith. $80-180. 11 rooms with PB, 4 with FP, 5 with WP, 7 suites. Breakfast included in rates. Types of meals: Cont plus and early coffee/tea.
Certificate may be used: Sunday-Thursday, Anytime, Last Minute-Based on Availability. One certificate per customer per year.

New Ulm

Deutsche Strasse (German Street) B&B

404 South German Street
New Ulm, MN 56073
(507) 354-2005 (866) 226-9856
Internet: www.deutschestrasse.com
E-mail: info@deutschestrasse.com

Circa 1884. Overlooking the Minnesota River Valley, this stately 1884 home located in the historic district blends Craftsman or Arts and Crafts architecture with a Victorian flair. Common rooms offer a variety of relaxing settings. Play games in the formal dining room, watch the fish in the huge aquarium, sit by the candlelit fireplace in the living room, or play the piano in the Welcome Room. Guest bedrooms exude Old World charm and are furnished with antiques and decorative accents. Breakfast is served on fine crystal and china in the All-Season Sun Porch. Accompanied by the inn's special blend coffee, signature dishes may include homemade granola, German sauteed apples with cinnamon-swirl French toast and Deutsche Strasse Potato Hash.
Innkeeper(s): Gary Sonnenberg, Ramona Sonnenberg. $109-189. 5 rooms with PB, 4 with FP, 1 with HT, 1 with WP, 1 suite, 1 conference room. Breakfast, snacks/refreshments and wine included in rates. Types of meals: Full gourmet bkfst, veg bkfst, early coffee/tea and Breakfast menus will be modified to accommodate special dietary restrictions - advance notice please. Catered Dinners available upon arrangement.
Certificate may be used: Sunday-Thursday anytime, weekends Dec. 15-April 15, excludes festivals and holidays.

Spicer

Spicer Castle Inn

11600 Indian Beach Rd
Spicer, MN 56288-9694
(320)796-5870 (800)821-6675 Fax:(320)796-4076
Internet: www.spicercastle.com
E-mail: stay@spicercastle.com

Circa 1895. On the scenic shores of Green Lake, this Tudor castle with English Country decor is listed in the National and State Registers of Historic Places. Air conditioned suites and guest bedrooms feature a variety of delightful amenities. Choose Amy's Room, boasting a clawfoot tub and balcony overlooking gardens, woods and a lagoon. Stay in the masculine Mason's or romantic Eunice's Room each with a double whirlpool tub. John's Cottage also offers a refrigerator, microwave and coffeemaker. A lumberjack built Raymond's Cabin with rustic logs and a stone fireplace chimney. Hospitality includes full breakfast and afternoon tea. A Murder Mystery Dinner, Belle Dinner Cruise, and holiday festivities are some of the special events to ask about.
Innkeeper(s): Mary Swanson. $99-187. 18 rooms, 7 with PB, 10 with FP, 12 with WP, 2 suites, 1 cottage, 1 cabin, 3 conference rooms. Breakfast and afternoon tea included in rates. Types of meals: Full gourmet bkfst, veg bkfst, Sun. brunch, early coffee/tea, gourmet lunch, picnic lunch, snacks/refreshments, hors d'oeuvres, wine, gourmet dinner, room service and Dinner restaurant hours are Tuesday through Saturday from 5:00 to 9:00 pm. Private lunch or dinner parties of 10 or more any day of the week. Restaurant on premises.
Certificate may be used: November-June, not valid on Friday and Saturday.

Stillwater

Aurora Staples Inn

303 N 4th St
Stillwater, MN 55082
(651)351-1187 (800)580-3092 Fax:(651)351-9061
Internet: www.aurorastaplesinn.com
E-mail: info@aurorastaplesinn.com

Circa 1892. This historic Queen Anne Victorian Inn was built in the 1890s for Isaac Staple's daughter, Aurora. Her husband, Adolphus Hospes, was a Civil War veteran and survivor of the famous first Minnesota charge at Gettysburg. The inn is elegantly decorated to reflect the Victorian era with five guest rooms offering a variety of amenities such as double whirlpool tubs, private baths and fireplaces. The Carriage House is also open as a guest room. A full breakfast is served, as well as wine and hors d'oeuvres during check-in. Enjoy our formal gardens or walk through the scenic St. Croix Valley.

Innkeeper(s): Cathy & Jerry Helmberger. $119-249. 5 rooms with PB, 5 with FP, 5 with HT, 5 with WP, 2 suites, 1 cottage. Breakfast included in rates. Types of meals: Full bkfst.

Certificate may be used: Sunday-Thursday, Anytime, based on projected availability, carriage house not part of program. No holidays.

Two Harbors

Northern Rail Traincar Inns

1730 Hwy 3
Two Harbors, MN 55616
(218)834-0955 (877)834-0955 Fax:(218)834-0957
Internet: www.northernrail.net/
E-mail: info@northernrail.net

Ride the rails without leaving the station in Two Harbors, Minnesota. A depot-style main building greets guests at this unique travel experience. There you will find a book and game lending library and continental breakfast each morning. Walk down the enclosed platform between two rows of authentic train boxcars that have been renovated into 17 elegant guest rooms. King and Queen Conductor suites encompass an entire car to include a master bedroom, living room, and electric fireplace. Porter Suites share boxcars but don't skimp on comfort with queen beds and private showers. Choose the decorative style that you enjoy most whether it is Northwoods, Victorian, Oriental, or Safari. Deer and other North Shore creatures have been known to drop by for a visit. Get the second night half off when you stay Sunday through Thursday. Enjoy the scenery at Lake Superior or travel 23 minutes into Duluth. Hike nearby Gooseberry Falls State Park to see spectacular waterfalls.

Innkeeper(s): Cyndi. $87-199. 4 suites.

Certificate may be used: November-April, no weekends or holidays, subject to availability.

Winona

Alexander Mansion Historic Bed & Breakfast

274 East Broadway St
Winona, MN 55987
(507)474-4224
Internet: www.alexandermansionbb.com
E-mail: alexandermansion@gmail.com

Circa 1886. Indulge in a pampering stay at this renovated, historic Victorian that graces a scenic bluff in the Mississippi River town of Winona, Minnesota. Distinctive surroundings include inviting gardens with benches and statuaries. Wicker furnishings adorn the veranda. Gather for wine and cheese socials, peruse the book collection in the cherry wood library or relax in the balcony music room. Feel pampered by the gracious amenities, European-quality linens and period antiques. Spacious guest suites feature soaking tubs and fireplaces. Early risers savor hot beverages in the breakfast room. Linger over a hearty four-course gourmet breakfast made with fresh local ingredients accented by Watkins spices in the formal candlelit dining room or dine alfresco. Browse the gift shop for J.R. Watkins Natural Apothecary personal products and other items to take home as souvenirs.

Innkeeper(s): Richard Grabow. $99-199. 4 rooms with PB, 2 with FP, 2 suites. Breakfast, snacks/refreshments and wine included in rates. Types of meals: Full gourmet bkfst, veg bkfst and early coffee/tea.

Certificate may be used: November-March, Sunday-Thursday.

Mississippi

Clarksdale

Delta Bohemian Guest House

1114 Seminole Street
Clarksdale, MS 38614
(662) 313-9222 (662) 624-8794
Internet: www.deltabohemianguesthouse.com
E-mail: madge@deltabohemian.com

Circa 1917. Originally the cook's house, this one-of-a-kind lodging gem is located only three blocks from downtown Clarksdale, Mississippi. The recently renovated two-bedroom guest house is a private retreat available year-round. Color fills the interior, even the staircase is green. The first floor has a living room with a widescreen television; a fully-equipped kitchen stocked with fruit, cereals, breads, coffee and juice, and a dining area. Green Acres and Delta Princess bedrooms and a bathroom fill the second floor. Added amenities include a combination washer and dryer, phone docking/charging stations, wifi, and covered parking. Sit on the back patio by the fountain or people watch from the front yard. Relax amid the residential neighborhood, just minutes from restaurants, museums, live music venues, the library, and business district. Experience authentic Delta culture and blues.

Innkeeper(s): Billy Howell, Madge Howell. $215. 2 rooms, 1 guest house. Continental Breakfast stocked Kitchen included in rates. Types of meals: Cont and early coffee/tea.
Certificate may be used: Sunday-Thursday.

Jackson

Fairview Inn & Sophia's Restaurant

734 Fairview Street
Jackson, MS 39202-1624
(601) 948-3429 (888) 948-1908 Fax:(601)948-1203
Internet: www.fairviewinn.com
E-mail: fairview@fairviewinn.com

Circa 1908. Built in 1908, the Fairview Inn is a small luxury hotel with a four-diamond AAA rating. This historic Colonial Revival mansion is one of the few architecturally designed homes of that period remaining, which exudes the rich history of Jackson, Mississippi. The Inn boasts eighteen luxurious guest rooms, Sophia's Restaurant serving lunch, dinner, and

Sunday brunch, nomiSpa for relaxation, a game room, private guest lounge, 24-hour guest kitchen and a gift shop. An oasis for leisure and business travelers alike, the Inn provides a tranquil setting with more than an acre of grounds featuring pristine gardens, outdoor decks and a gazebo. The Fairview Inn offers the charm, ambiance, and hospitality of a bed and breakfast with the service and amenities of a small luxury hotel. Come see why the Fairview Inn is Jackson's best kept secret.

Innkeeper(s): Tamar Sharp, Peter Sharp . $159-329. 18 rooms with PB, 9 with FP, 13 with WP, 13 total suites, including 1 two-bedroom suite, 7 conference rooms. Breakfast and snacks/refreshments included in rates. Types of meals: Full bkfst, Sun. brunch, early coffee/tea, lunch, wine, gourmet dinner and room service. Restaurant on premises.
Certificate may be used: Jan. 1 to Dec. 31, except for Thanksgiving and Christmas Day.

Vicksburg

Annabelle

501 Speed St
Vicksburg, MS 39180-4065
(601) 638-2000 (800) 791-2000
Internet: www.annabellebnb.com
E-mail: annabelle@vicksburg.com

Circa 1868. From the outside, Annabelle looks like a friendly mix of Victorian and Italianate architecture set on an unassuming lawn of magnolias and pecan trees. It is the gracious interior and hospitality that has earned this bed & breakfast consistently high ratings. Walls are painted in deep, rich hues, highlighting the polished wood floors, Oriental rugs and beautiful antiques. Some of the furnishings are family heirlooms, and some rooms include a whirlpool tub.

$99-195. 7 rooms with PB, 1 suite, 1 cottage. Breakfast and afternoon tea included in rates. Types of meals: Full gourmet bkfst, early coffee/tea and room service.
Certificate may be used: Tuesday-Thursday, November-January, except holidays.

Missouri

Clarksville

Cedarcrest Manor at Overlook Farm

901 S Highway 79
Clarksville, MO 63336
(573) 242-3310 Fax:(573)242-3433
Internet: www.overlookfarmmo.com
E-mail: philip@overlookfarmmo.com

Circa 1842. Luxurious accommodations await your arrival at Overlook Farm and offer you an incomparable experience of country living. Cedarcrest Manor is set in a cluster of towering cedars and tucked away just up the hill from The Station Restaurant. Built in 1842 by Captain Benjamin Clifford, a prominent riverboat captain, Cedarcrest began its life as a plantation home, and quickly became the archetype for a number of houses built in the Mississippi River Valley. It was acquired and renovated in 2005 by Nathalie Pettus, and today, its neo-classic interior, heated Romanesque pool, and stunning views of the Mississippi offer peace, quiet and a restful place to relax and recharge. Rich with amenities, this enchanting Missouri inn is adorned with antiques and features a fireplace in every room. You can also book a room at Rackheath House, as both properties are part of Overlook Farm. Check-in for each of the inns is located at The Station Restaurant.
Innkeeper(s): Nathalie Pettus. $200-300. 6 rooms with PB, 6 with FP. Breakfast coupon provided for the Farm Cafe Monday - Friday and Breakfast coupon provided for the Station Saturday - Sunday included in rates. Types of meals: Full gourmet bkfst, early coffee/tea, gourmet lunch, picnic lunch, hors d'oeuvres, wine and gourmet dinner. Restaurant on premises.
Certificate may be used: Anytime, subject to availability.

Rackheath House at Overlook Farm

901 S Highway 79
Clarksville, MO 63336
(573) 242-9677 Fax:(573)242-3455
Internet: www.overlookfarmmo.com
E-mail: philip@overlookfarmmo.com

Circa 1860. Rackheath House is perched atop the hills of the Mississippi River Valley, and situated just a short walk from the Overlook Farm - one of the highest spots along the river. Built in 1860 and restored in 2006 by Nathalie Pettus, this Greek revival-style manor features sprawling grounds, a spacious veranda, and a romantic, flourishing garden filled with walking paths. Its accessible, state-of-the art kitchen and elegant dining room provide guests with the ideal place to uncork a bottle of wine - or enjoy a fresh, seasonally inspired meal, prepared exclusively by The Station's award-winning chef, Timothy Grandinetti. Prepare to lose yourself in rich country warmth, enchanting amenities, and strikingly serene landscapes at Rackheath or at its sister property Cedarcrest Manor. Each of the two inns offer quiet corners and cozy spots to relax, enjoy a lively conversation, or get lost in a good book. Oversized Jacuzzi tubs and plush, comfy bathrobes are a feature in every room, offering the utmost in relaxation. In-suite coffee makers provide instant access to your morning pick-me-up. Check-in for each of the inns is located at The Station Restaurant.
Innkeeper(s): Nathalie Pettus. $225-350. 3 rooms with PB. Breakfast coupon provided Monday-Friday at the Farm Cafe and Breakfast coupon provided Saturday-Sunday at the Sation included in rates. Types of meals: Full gourmet bkfst, gourmet lunch, picnic lunch, hors d'oeuvres, wine and gourmet dinner. Restaurant on premises.
Certificate may be used: Anytime, subject to availability.

Excelsior Springs

The Inn on Crescent Lake

1261 Saint Louis Ave
Excelsior Springs, MO 64024-2938
(816) 630-6745 (866) 630LAKE
Internet: www.crescentlake.com
E-mail: info@crescentlake.com

Circa 1915. Located on 22 acres of lush grounds with woodland and bucolic ponds, this three-story, Georgian-style house is just a half-hour drive from downtown Kansas City and the airport. Spacious suites and guest rooms all have private baths, and guests can choose to have either a whirlpool or clawfoot tub. Enjoy a delicious hot breakfast in the sun-filled solarium. Relax in the outdoor hot tub after a refreshing dip in the pool. Try the paddle boats, or borrow a fishing rod and take out the bass boat.
Innkeeper(s): Beverly Delugeau. $120-250. 10 rooms with PB, 3 with FP, 1 with HT, 6 with WP, 3 suites, 1 cottage. Breakfast included in rates. Types of meals: Country bkfst, veg bkfst and wine.
Certificate may be used: November-April, Sunday-Thursday, higher rates prevail.

Fulton

Loganberry Inn

310 W Seventh St
Fulton, MO 65251-2608
(573)642-9229 (888)866-6661
Internet: www.loganberryinn.com
E-mail: info@loganberryinn.com

Circa 1899. Adorning the historic district, this 1899 grand Victorian is an award-winning inn on one acre surrounded by extensive gardens accented by a gazebo. The English country decor also boasts some well-placed French antiques. All of the pampering guest bedrooms feature fireplaces and entertainment centers. The Garden Room includes a spa tub. A Corporate Cottage is perfect for business travelers. Complimentary refreshments are provided and a celebrity chef creates bountiful breakfasts served on fine china and crystal in the elegant dining room. A sample menu might offer cinnamon pears with raspberry coulis, crab and roasted artichoke quiche, banana pecan waffles, maple pepper bacon as well as an extensive assortment of coffees, teas and juices. Hike or bike the easily accessible Katy Trail. Special packages are available.

Innkeeper(s): Carl & Cathy McGeorge. $89-189. 6 rooms with PB, 6 with FP. Breakfast and snacks/refreshments included in rates. Types of meals: Full gourmet bkfst, veg bkfst, early coffee/tea, picnic lunch and afternoon tea.

Certificate may be used: Sunday-Thursday, no holidays.

Hannibal

Robards Mansion Bed and Breakfast

215 N 6th St
Hannibal, MO 63401-3412
(573)248-1218
Internet: www.thegildedage.net

Circa 1871. Walk in the footsteps of Mark Twain at this historic mansion built as a family home for one of his lifelong friends. The famed author is known to have visited Robard's ailing granddaugter, a fan of his writing, in the Blue Bonnie Room. The classic Italianate inn has been carefully restored and guests will find marble fireplaces, patterned wood floors, pocket doors, and a flying staircase. The original library is now a guest room with built-in bookcases and a writing desk. The large Robards Suite with two bedrooms and a living room is perfect for a getaway with girlfriends or a family vacation. Ask for a tour of the home to see the view of the Mississippi River from the cupola. Breakfast is served each morning in the first floor dining room. Hannibal, Missouri, is home to many Mark Twain landmarks including the Mark Twain Boyhood Home and Garden and the Huckleberry Finn House.

Innkeeper(s): Nedra McClellan, Leon McClellan. $80-120. 4 rooms with PB, 1 suite. Types of meals: Full bkfst.

Certificate may be used: Jan. 5-Feb. 4.

Hermann

Harbor Haus Inn & Suites

113 Market St
Hermann, MO 65041
(573)486-2222
Internet: www.harborhaus.net
E-mail: harborhaus@yahoo.com

Circa 1894. Enjoy grand river views from a private balcony while staying in the heart of historic Hermann. The quirky tree covered with shoes in the lobby reminds guests to kick off their own shoes for a rejuvenating getaway. Comfortable queen or king-size beds allow for sweet dreams and restful nights. Many guest rooms offer relaxing jet tubs or romantic fireplaces. The breakfast area, with a complimentary buffet, gives the nostalgic feel of a general store where the walls are covered in small mirrors and eclectic pictures. Tell stories around the outdoor fireplace and indulge in a childhood favorite with complimentary marshmallows to roast. With seven wineries within 15 min-

utes, guests can sample a variety of national and international award-winning wines. Lots of free parking is available or the convenient train station is four minutes away. The inn is one block from downtown Hermann and two miles from the scenic Katy Trail.

Innkeeper(s): Frank Van Kamp, Donna Nestle. Call for rates. Call inn for details.

Certificate may be used: November-February, excluding holidays, Sunday-Thursday, subject to availability.

Wohlt House Bed & Breakfast

415 E 1st St
Hermann, MO 65041-1117
(573)486-2394
Internet: www.wohlthouse.com
E-mail: wohltbb@ktis.net

Circa 1884. Scenic views of the Missouri River are the hallmark of this historic and grand brick home open all year. Walk to the nearby shops and restaurants of Hermann. Relax on the outdoor deck overlooking the water. Watch movies and browse the books and magazines in the Victorian sitting room, an inviting common area. Homemade cookies are a daily indulgence each afternoon. Luxurious accommodations include robes, a refrigerator and a Jacuzzi or clawfoot tub. Linger over a sumptuous breakfast in the dining room before exploring the area attractions. Visit the Hermannhof Winery or other local vineyards for a tasting tour.

Innkeeper(s): Judy Gregresen. $120-160. 3 rooms with PB. Breakfast and snacks/refreshments included in rates. Types of meals: Full bkfst and homemade cookies served in afternoon.

Certificate may be used: January.

Hollister

Cameron's Crag

738 Acacia Club Road
Hollister, MO 65672
(417) 334-4720 (800) 933-8529 Fax:(417)335-8134
Internet: www.camerons-crag.com
E-mail: stay@camerons-crag.com

Circa 1986. Sitting high on a bluff, this contemporary bed and breakfast overlooks Lake Taneycomo and the Branson, Missouri skyline. Cameron's Crag offers breathtaking panoramic views of spectacular Ozark scenery, warm hospitality and spacious accommodations. Stay in a guest suite that includes a separate entrance, entertainment center with movie library and private deck area with hot tub. Suites in the detached guest house also offer full kitchens and deluxe whirlpool tubs for two. Innkeeper Glen serves delicious breakfasts using the traditionally southern, local cuisine that blends the influence of early German, French, English and Scandinavian settlers.

Innkeeper(s): Janet Miller, Managing Innkeeper. $125-165. 4 rooms, 4 with HT, 2 with WP, 4 suites. Breakfast included in rates. Types of meals: Full bkfst and accommodate dietary restrictions when possible.

Certificate may be used: April-December, Sunday-Thursday or January-March; Holidays excluded.

Independence

Serendipity B&B

116 S Pleasant St
Independence, MO 64050
(816)833-4719 (800)203-4299
Internet: www.serendipitybedandbreakfast.com
E-mail: Please call the inn

Circa 1887. This three-story brick home offers guests the ultimate Victorian experience. Antique furnishings and period appointments create an authentic period ambiance. Victorian children's books and toys, antique pictures, china figurines and a collection of antique colored glassware add to the home's charm. Stereoscopes and music box tunes are other special touches. A full breakfast is served by candlelight in the formal dining room. Outside gardens include arbors, Victorian gazing balls, birdhouses, birdbaths, a hammock, swing and fountain. If time and weather permit, guests may request a ride in an antique car and tour of the house.

Innkeeper(s): Susan Walter, Doug Walter. $95. 3 total suites, including 1 two-bedroom suite. Types of meals: Full bkfst.

Certificate may be used: Sunday-Thursday, excluding holidays and local festivals, subject to availability.

Lake Ozark

Bass & Baskets Bed & Breakfast

1117 Dogwood Road
Lake Ozark, MO 65049
573-964-5028
Internet: www.bassandbaskets.com
E-mail: efranko@charter.net

Poised on the shore of the Lake of the Ozarks in the hills of mid-Missouri, this highly regarded inn was named for the innkeepers' love of bass fishing and Longaberger baskets. Open all year for four-season enjoyment, swim and fish off the dock or relax in one of the common areas. Movies, games and music are available for further entertainment. Inviting guest rooms reflect a tastefully themed decor and boast pleasing amenities that include luxury linens, gas fireplaces, DVD and CD players, wifi, whirlpool tubs for two and decks that overlook the water. Award-winning breakfasts beckon and are a satisfying indulgence that won't be regretted. Venture out to explore the local sights and attractions and ask about specials and packages available.

Innkeeper(s): Debbie Franko. Call for rates. 4 rooms.

Certificate may be used: November-March, Sunday-Thursday.

Louisiana

Eagle's Nest

221 Georgia
Louisiana, MO 63353-1715
(573)754-9888
Internet: www.theeaglesnest-louisiana.com
E-mail: info@theeaglesnest-louisiana.com

Circa 1859. Experience small-town America just a block from the Mississippi River at this inn that was originally an old bank. Four adjacent historic buildings are being restored for expansion to include a cooking school and conference facilities. Lavish guest bedrooms and suites feature Jacuzzi tubs and plush robes. Linger over a scrumptious breakfast in the Bistro. Sip an afternoon beverage and fresh cookies from the bakery on the patio. Soak in the solarium hot tub for a truly stress-free stay.

Innkeeper(s): Lynn Dempsey. $95-125. 16 rooms, 7 with PB, 3 with WP, 1 two-bedroom suite, 2 conference rooms. Breakfast and Sunday brunch included in rates. Types of meals: Full gourmet bkfst, veg bkfst, gourmet lunch, picnic lunch, snacks/refreshments, wine and gourmet dinner. Restaurant on premises.

Certificate may be used: Anytime except New Years, Valentines and during Local Festivals. Not valid on Saturday nights or last minute based on availability with an additional fee of $10.00 pp for a Saturday night.

Marshfield

The Dickey House B&B

331 S Clay St
Marshfield, MO 65706-2114
(417)468-3000 Fax:(417)859-5478
Internet: www.dickeyhouse.com
E-mail: info@dickeyhouse.com

Circa 1908. This Greek Revival mansion is framed by ancient oak trees and boasts eight massive two-story Ionic columns.

Burled woodwork, beveled glass and polished hardwood floors accentuate the gracious rooms. Interior columns soar in the parlor, creating a suitably elegant setting for the innkeeper's outstanding collection of antiques. A queen-size canopy bed, fireplace and sunporch are featured in the Heritage Room. Some rooms offer amenities such as Jacuzzi tubs and a fireplace. All rooms include cable TV and a VCR. The innkeepers also offer a sun room with a hot tub.

Innkeeper(s): Larry Stevens, Michaelene Stevens. $89-169. 3 rooms with PB, 4 suites. Breakfast included in rates. Types of meals: Full gourmet bkfst, veg bkfst, early coffee/tea, snacks/refreshments and Friday and Saturday evening dinners by advance reservations only. Limited seating.

Certificate may be used: Jan. 10 to April 30, Sunday-Thursday, excluding Valentines Day.

Marthasville

Concord Hill Bed & Breakfast

16469 Concord Hill Road
Marthasville, MO 63357-1417
(636)782-2042
Internet: www.concord-hill.com
E-mail: info@concord-hill.com

Circa 1850. An idyllic small town of 40 people waits for you in Missouri. Feel yourself relax the moment you enter the quiet, agricultural community where you can look out over the countryside or gaze at the star-filled sky from the hot tub. Explore the farmhouse property with an original smokehouse, occupied chicken coop, and carriage house. The Sunrise and Sunset rooms are aptly named for their respective dazzling views. Add the Loft to the Sunset Room to accommodate larger groups. Find romance in the Carriage House with a wrought-iron queen bed and claw foot tub and take advantage of the opportunity to reserve an in-room massage to ease any lingering stress from everyday life. Sample wines at Blumenhof Winery or visit the wine cellar in the inn then while sipping your wine enjoy live music in the Great Room. Pick your own fruit at Thierbach Orchards and Berry Farm. Bike along a portion of the Katy Trail or consider if you want to plan ahead and traverse the entire 237-mile trail.

Innkeeper(s): Maggie Fendelman, George McVicker . $100-125. 5 rooms, 3 with PB. Breakfast included in rates. Types of meals: Country bkfst, early coffee/tea, dinner. Book in advance for prepared dinners and wine cellar.

Certificate may be used: Anytime, subject to availability.

Morrison

The Nesting Box Bed & Breakfast

525 Main Street
Morrison, MO 65061
(573)252-4402
Internet: www.thenestingboxbedandbreakfast.com
E-mail: the_nestingbox@yahoo.com

Circa 1917. Relax in an inviting living room or on the front porch swing in Morrison, Missouri. The delightful small town registered 139 people during the 2010 census. The inn's welcoming committee includes Peggy, the one-legged pet chicken. Celebrate the Wild West in the Cowboy room with dark wood. Native American art graces the walls of the Indian room. Romance is in the air in the flowery Victorian room. A buffet breakfast, including seasonal vegetables and farm-fresh eggs, is served on the back deck. Schedule an in-room deep muscle massage. Find the perfect gift in the local antique and specialty shops. The historic German city of Hermann is a short drive away. Explore the banks of the Missouri River or sample wines at local vineyards. Enjoy the many annual festivals held in the area.

Innkeeper(s): David Rose, Fran Rose. $50-80. 5 rooms with PB. Breakfast, afternoon tea and snacks/refreshments included in rates. Types of meals: Full bkfst and early coffee/tea.

Certificate may be used: January-February, Subject to Availability.

Osage Beach

Inn at Harbour Ridge

6334 Red Barn Road
Osage Beach, MO 65065
(573)302-0411 (877)744-6020
Internet: www.harbourridgeinn.com
E-mail: info@harbourridgeinn.com

Circa 1999. Romantic and inviting, the Inn at Harbour Ridge Bed and Breakfast boasts a contemporary setting with modern and French decor. Poised on a ridge overlooking Lake of the Ozarks in Central Missouri, there are almost two well-landscaped acres with oak trees, goldfish ponds and an herb garden. A gazebo near the waterfall is the perfect place for a wedding. Osage Beach is conveniently located between Kansas City and St. Louis. Select a delightful guest bedroom that may feature a fireplace, whirlpool, private deck or a patio with a hot tub. An early-morning coffee tray is delivered to each room. Indulge in an incredible breakfast in the solarium dining room. Swim in the cove or sun on the dock. Special requests are granted with pleasure.

Innkeeper(s): Sue Westenhaver. $129-199. 5 rooms with PB, 5 with FP, 3 with HT, 3 with WP, 1 cottage. Breakfast and snacks/refreshments included in rates. Types of meals: Full gourmet bkfst and early coffee/tea.

Certificate may be used: November-March, Monday-Thursday excluding holidays, anytime at the last minute.

Saint Louis

Eastlake Inn Bed & Breakfast

703 N Kirkwood Rd
Saint Louis, MO 63122-2719
(314)965-0066
Internet: www.eastlakeinn.com
E-mail: info@eastlakeinn.com

Circa 1920. Nestled among established trees and perennial gardens in historic Kirkwood, Missouri, this historic colonial inn's golden retrievers extend a friendly greeting with tails wagging and a welcome bark. Once inside, feel at home in the comfortable surroundings of much-loved antique Eastlake furnishings. Relax in the comfortable living room, enjoy a good book by the fireplace or in the sun-filled library. Descend the stairs to a guest room with a king bed, fireplace and two-person Jacuzzi. All rooms have private baths. An antique chandelier warms the dining room where a gourmet breakfast is served daily. The specialty is Peach French Toast Cobbler featuring tree-ripened peaches from Murray's Orchard in Calhoun County Illinois. Visit all the great attractions that St. Louis has to offer, just twenty minutes away.

Innkeeper(s): Lori Murray, Allen Rector. $120-200. 3 rooms with PB, 1 with FP, 1 with WP. Breakfast and wine included in rates. Types of meals: Full gourmet bkfst and early coffee/tea.

Certificate may be used: Jan. 1-March 31, Sunday-Thursday, subject to availability.

Lehmann House B&B

10 Benton Place
Saint Louis, MO 63104-2411
(314) 422-1483 Fax:(314)621-5449
Internet: www.lehmannhouse.com
E-mail: marie@lehmannhouse.com

Circa 1893. This National Register manor's most prominent resident, former U.S. Solicitor General Frederick Lehmann, hosted Presidents Taft, Theodore Roosevelt and Coolidge at this gracious home. Several key turn-of-the-century literary figures also visited the Lehmann family. The inn's formal dining room, complete with oak paneling and a fireplace, is a stunning place to enjoy the formal breakfasts. Antiques and gracious furnishings dot the well-appointed guest rooms. The home is located in St. Louis' oldest historic district, Lafayette Square.

Innkeeper(s): Marie Davies. $99-179. 5 rooms with PB, 3 with FP. Breakfast included in rates. Types of meals: Full bkfst, veg bkfst and early coffee/tea.

Certificate may be used: Nov. 1-March 1, Sunday-Thursday only, holidays and special events excluded. Anytime, Last Minute-Based on Availability.

Sainte Genevieve

Inn St. Gemme Beauvais

78 N Main St
Sainte Genevieve, MO 63670-1336
(573) 883-5744 (800) 818-5744 Fax:(573)880-1953
Internet: www.stgem.com
E-mail: stgemme@brick.net

Circa 1848. This three-story, Federal-style inn is an impressive site on Ste. Genevieve's Main Street. The town is one of the oldest west of the Mississippi River, and the St. Gemme Beauvais is the oldest operating Missouri bed & breakfast. The rooms are nicely appointed in period style, but there are modern amenities here, too. The Jacuzzi tubs in some guest rooms are one relaxing example. There is an outdoor hot tub, as well. The romantic carriage house includes a king-size bed, double Jacuzzi tub and a fireplace. Guests are pampered with all sorts of cuisine, including full breakfasts served at individual candle-lit tables with a choice of eight entrees. Later, tea, drinks, hors d'oeuvres and refreshments are also served.

Innkeeper(s): Janet Joggerst. $89-179. 9 rooms, 5 with FP, 1 with WP, 9 suites, 1 cottage. Breakfast, afternoon tea, snacks/refreshments and wine included in rates. Types of meals: Full gourmet bkfst and veg bkfst. Restaurant on premises.

Certificate may be used: Sunday-Thursday, Nov. 1-April 30.

Montana

Bozeman

Olive Branch Inn at the Lindley House

202 Lindley Pl
Bozeman, MT 59715-4833
(406)640-1710 (866)587-8403 Fax:(406)582-8112
Internet: theolivebranchinn.com
E-mail: cecjohnson@gmail.com

Circa 1889. The beautiful Montana scenery is a perfect backdrop for this romantic bed & breakfast listed in the National
Register. The pampering begins in the
guest rooms, which offer plenty of soft,
down comforters, feather pillows, fluffy
robes and a collection of soaps and oils
for a long soak in the tub. Each of the
rooms is distinct and memorable. The
Madison Suite boasts a fireplace, sitting
room, clawfoot tub and balcony. Other
rooms include items such as wicker
furnishings, bay windows, lacy curtains,
dramatic wall coverings, a French bistro table or brass bed. An
organic continental breakfast offered, along with a voucher for
breakfast at the locally-owned Nova Cafe.

Innkeeper(s): Cecily Johnson. $100-180. 5 rooms with PB, 3 total suites,
including 1 two-bedroom suite. Breakfast included in rates. Types of meals:
Early coffee/tea, all organic continental breakfast and voucher for free breakfast
at nearby cafe.

Certificate may be used: Nov. 1-April 30, Sunday-Wednesday.

Voss Inn

319 S Willson Ave
Bozeman, MT 59715-4632
(406)587-0982 Fax:(406)585-2964
Internet: www.bozeman-vossinn.com
E-mail: vossinn@bresnan.net

Circa 1883. The Voss Inn is a restored two-story Victorian
mansion with a large front porch and a
Victorian parlor. Antique furnishings
include an upright piano and
chandelier. Two of the inn's
six rooms include air conditioning. A full breakfast is
served, with freshly baked

rolls kept in a unique warmer that's built into an ornate
1880s radiator.

Innkeeper(s): Bruce Muller, Frankee Muller. $120-159. 6 rooms with PB, 3
with FP, 1 suite, 1 conference room. Breakfast and afternoon tea included in
rates. Types of meals: Full gourmet bkfst, veg bkfst and Early Coffee.

Certificate may be used: Sunday-Thursday, January-April and October-Dec.
15, subject to availability.

Hamilton

Deer Crossing B&B

396 Hayes Creek Rd
Hamilton, MT 59840-9744
(406)363-2232 (800)763-2232
Internet: www.deercrossingmontana.com
E-mail: info@deercrossingmontana.com

Circa 1980. This Western-style ranch bed & breakfast is located
on 25 acres of woods and pastures. One suite includes a double
Jacuzzi tub and another has a private balcony. In addition to the
suites and guest rooms, travelers also can opt to stay in the
bunkhouse, a historic homestead building with a wood-burning
stove. A new creekside log cabin includes a covered porch, fireplace and full kitchen especially appealing to families with small
children or long-term guests who want to regroup while enjoying a scenic setting. The area offers many activities, including
horseback riding, hiking, fly fishing and historic sites.

Innkeeper(s): Stu Dobbins, Linda Dobbins. $75-149. 5 rooms, 4 with PB, 2
suites, 2 cabins. Breakfast and snacks/refreshments included in rates. Types
of meals: Full bkfst and early coffee/tea.

Certificate may be used: Oct. 1-May 1.

Whitefish

Good Medicine Lodge

537 Wisconsin Ave
Whitefish, MT 59937-2127
(406)862-5488 (800)860-5488 Fax:(406)862-5489
Internet: www.goodmedicinelodge.com
E-mail: info@goodmedicinelodge.com

Circa 1976. Fashioned from square cedar logs, this modern
Montana-style lodge bed and breakfast boasts a Western decor
with comfortable furnishings and textiles reminiscent of Native
American themes. Relax by the fire in one of the common areas.
Guest bedrooms feature natural cedar walls and ceilings with
exposed cedar beams. Two rooms have a fireplace. A European-
style breakfast buffet includes homemade baked goods and granola, cereals, yogurt, a specialty entree, fresh fruit, brewed coffee
and juices. The bed and breakfast is located in a mountain setting near Glacier Park, golf courses, cross country and alpine skiing, water sports, fishing and Big Mountain Resort.

Innkeeper(s): Betsy Cox, Woody Cox. $125-295. 9 rooms, 6 with PB, 2 with
FP, 2 with WP, 3 total suites, including 2 two-bedroom suites, 1 conference
room. Full breakfast and hors d'oeuvres included in rates.

Certificate may be used: Oct. 1-April 30.

Nebraska

Lincoln

Westview B&B

7000 NW 27th Street
Lincoln, NE 68524
(402)470-6000 Fax:(402)470-0006
Internet: www.westviewbb.com
E-mail: westviewbb@inebraska.com

Circa 1916. Completely renovated, this historic landmark was built in the prairie-style and is surrounded by ten landscaped acres and open land. The delightful interior setting is perfect for small events. Larger gatherings are memorable occasions outdoors. Stay in the Westview Sunset Suite on the northwest first floor wing with French doors, a private porch, entertainment center, fireplace, living room, kitchen, whirlpool and clawfoot tub. Thoughtful details and pleasing amenities add to the distinctively pampered ambiance. Start each weekday with a generous continental breakfast and an expanded meal is provided on weekends. This Lincoln, Nebraska location is only ten minutes from golf, the university, stadium, air museum and Historic Haymarket. Also nearby, the Branched Oak and Pawnee State Recreation Areas offer lake activities, hiking and biking.
Innkeeper(s): Colleen Burden, Jim Burden. $109-139. 5 rooms, 1 with PB, 1 with FP, 1 with WP, 1 suite. Breakfast included in rates. Types of meals: Full gourmet bkfst, veg bkfst, early coffee/tea, snacks/refreshments, Ice Cream Treats, Fruit Juices, Soda, V-8 Juice, Hot Chocolate, Cider, Tea, Coffee, Mixed Nuts, Candy, Granola Bars and Popcorn and much more - FREE with Stay.
Certificate may be used: Sunday-Thursday.

North Platte

Knoll's Country Inn

6132 South Range Rd
North Platte, NE 69101
(308)368-5634 (877)378-2521
Internet: www.knollscountryinn.com
E-mail: knollscountryinn@yahoo.com

The quiet countryside of Nebraska sets the scene for a relaxing getaway at this family-friendly inn with five guest rooms. Once the home for a family of eight, the inn is cozy and comfortable. Snuggle under an heirloom bedspread as fresh breezes flow through open windows. Bedside lamps cast a warm glow over queen-size beds with extra pillows to support the perfect reading position or enjoy the night sky as a canopy of twinkling stars over the outdoor hot tub. Two lean-tos provide overnight accommodations for traveling horses and electric and water hookups are available for campers. The innkeepers are happy to

arrange tickets for a custom vacation package exploring North Platte and Hershey. The nearby wetlands are a favorite stopover point for migrating sandhill cranes along with hundreds of other bird species. Golfers can practice driving, chipping, and putting on the four local golf courses while train buffs will want to explore the artifacts at the Cody Park Railroad Museum.
Innkeeper(s): Bob Knoll, Arlene Knoll. $79-89. 5 rooms, 2 with PB.
Certificate may be used: November-March, subject to availability.

Ravenna

Cedar Hills Vineyard Guesthouse

48970 375th Road
Ravenna, NE 68869-4019
(308)452-3181
Internet: www.cedarhillsvineyard.com
E-mail: info@cedarhillsvineyard.com

A winery, a farm, and a private one-bedroom apartment are blended in perfect harmony in Nebraska. After choosing a favorite wine during the complimentary tasting, retire to the full kitchen to create a perfectly matched meal. Be sure to order a fresh baked pie for dessert. The views of the rolling hills expand far into the horizon offering stunning sunrises and sunsets. Breakfast is available for overnight guests of the inn. Sit on the top of the hill overlooking the South Loup River and keep a camera handy for visiting eagles, quail, turkey, and deer. Tour the farm and sample raspberries, strawberries, and grapes before they are made into wine, jams, or jellies. You can settle in on the porch outside the tasting room sipping on Raspberry Passion, Annevar Blush, or Rhubarb wine. With more than ten different wines available, there is something for everyone. Drive into the small town of Ravenna for shops and restaurants.
Innkeeper(s): Joyce Sears, Paul Sears. $75. 1 room with PB. Types of meals: Full bkfst, wine and reservations include a free wine tasting.
Certificate may be used: December-February.

Nevada

Alamo

A Cowboys Dream

95 Hand Me Down Rd
Alamo, NV 89001
(775) 725-3500 (877) 885-2236 Fax:(775)725-3565
Internet: www.cowboysdream.com
E-mail: info@cowboysdream.com

Circa 2009. Escape to the serene desert in Alamo, Nevada, to experience A Cowboy's Dream, a unique bed and breakfast. Watch the sun set from the private porch of one of the eight guest suites. Soak in a claw foot tub and doze on custom bedding. Guests can shoot a game of pool, play the piano, or socialize in the Great Room. This desert hideaway is built for relaxation or business with high-speed Internet and audio-visual capabilities. Reserve the dance hall and wedding pavilion for a cowboy celebration. Lincoln County is home to the Pahranagat National Wildlife Refuge. Visitors can fish, hunt, and bird watch in this essential part of the Great Pacific Migratory Route. Alamo has an early history of horse thievery but is now a family friendly town. Area 51 enthusiasts will be happy to note that Alamo is one of the closest inhabited places to this secretive government installation. Plus, the flashing neon lights of Las Vegas are only 90 miles away. Winner - 2013 Top 10 Romantic Inn.

Innkeeper(s): Jessica Canning, Wes Canning. $159-399. 8 rooms with PB, 1 conference room. Breakfast included in rates. Types of meals: Country bkfst, early coffee/tea, snacks/refreshments, wine, gourmet dinner and Chef Prepared Dinners (addt'l charge)-must reserve in advance.

Certificate may be used: June-August, subject to availability. No other discouts apply.

Virginia City

B Street House Bed and Breakfast

58 North B Street
Virginia City, NV 89440
(775) 847-7231
Internet: www.BStreetHouse.com
E-mail: innkeepers@BStreetHouse.com

Circa 1875. Set on an idyllic small town street in the Old West town of Virginia City, the B Street House is a Victorian home with comforts and amenities galore. Recently renovated in 2007, the home is the only B&B in Virginia City with a listing in the National Register of Historic Places. Spring and summer guests will enjoy a beautiful garden with butterflies and quail, and in colder weather the parlor and library are great places to relax out of the cold. The inn's guest rooms all feature private baths, satellite TV and high speed internet, and many have huge windows with picturesque views. The inn's location allows guests to experience all of the sights, sounds and outdoor activities of Reno, Lake Tahoe and Carson City.

Innkeeper(s): Chris, Carolyn. $99-139. 3 rooms with PB. Breakfast, afternoon tea and Full gourmet breakfast; snacks and fresh fruit available 24/7 included in rates.

Certificate may be used: May-October, subject to availability.

New Hampshire

Bethlehem

Adair Country Inn and Restaurant

80 Guider Lane
Bethlehem, NH 03574
(603) 444-2600 (888) 444-2600 Fax:(603)444-4823
Internet: www.adairinn.com
E-mail: innkeeper@adairinn.com

Circa 1927. Representing all that a New England country inn is hoped to be, enjoy relaxation and tranquility on more than 200 picturesque acres with mountain views and perennial gardens. This four-diamond-rated inn was originally a wedding gift

from Frank Hogan to his daughter, Dorothy Adair Hogan. Dorothy hosted many famed guests here, including presidential candidates, Supreme Court justices and actors. Just-baked popovers start the morning fare, followed by fresh fruit, yogurt

and specialty dishes such as pumpkin pancakes with Vermont bacon. Homemade cakes and cookies are served during the complimentary afternoon tea service. Flavorful food, made with only the freshest ingredients and artfully presented, is a point of pride at Adair. The intimate dining room with fireplace and wonderful views of gardens, both front and back, is filled with enticing aromas morning and night. Make reservation at Adair's gourmet restaurant for a dinner to remember.

Innkeeper(s): Kimberly and Barry Hunter. $195-375. 9 rooms with PB, 7 with FP, 1 with WP, 1 suite. Breakfast, afternoon tea and snacks/refreshments included in rates. Types of meals: Full gourmet bkfst, veg bkfst, Sun. brunch, early coffee/tea, picnic lunch, hors d'oeuvres, wine, gourmet dinner and Fine New England Style Cuisine. Restaurant on premises.

Certificate may be used: Anytime, subject to availability, Not valid during holidays or foliage season.

Bear Mountain Lodge

3249 Main Street
Bethlehem, NH 03574
(603)869-2189 (888)869-2189
Internet: www.bearmountainlodge.net
E-mail: info@bearmountainlodge.net

Circa 2005. Newly built, Bear Mountain Lodge is surrounded by The White Mountain National Forest. This log lodge B&B spans 26 wooded acres in Bethlehem, New Hampshire, just a 15-minute drive to Franconia Notch State Park. Enjoy a cup of early-morning coffee on the huge deck by the rustic firepit and watch the sunrise. A wood soapstone stove and Western furni-

ture enhance the warm and inviting setting in the great room. Browse through the reading materials in the loft area and select a hot or cold beverage and a snack from the guest pantry. Several of the romantic guest bedrooms feature views of Mt. Washington, gas fireplaces, two-person Jacuzzi tubs or steam showers. Savor a generous homemade breakfast in the dining room. Special packages are offered.

Innkeeper(s): Carol Kerivan, Michael Kerivan. $175-360. 9 rooms with PB, 4 with FP, 3 with WP. Breakfast and snacks/refreshments included in rates. Types of meals: Country bkfst.

Certificate may be used: Sunday-Thursday, November-May 15 (non-holiday periods).

Bristol

A Newfound Bed & Breakfast

94 Mandi Lane
Bristol, NH 03222
(603)744-3442 (877)444-3442 Fax:(603)744-9548
Internet: anewfoundbnb.com
E-mail: sondra@anewfoundbnb.com

Circa 1985. This pristine inn offers mountainside views of Newfound Lake and Cardigan Mountain. Room choices include some with fireplaces, flat screen TVs, and large baths. All are supplied with fine linens and Turkish towels. Acres of woodland surround the property with an abundance of trails and a small brook. The inn's grounds offer vegetable gardens, a frog pond and even a handsome chicken coop from which fresh eggs are gathered for breakfast dishes which are finely crafted each morning. The lake provides boating and swimming in summer and in winter there are snowmobile trails right from the property. A huge fireplace in the common room invites relaxing in the evening after daytime excursions.

Innkeeper(s): Sondra J. Keene. $199-250. 4 rooms with PB, 4 with FP, 1 with HT, 1 with WP, 1 two-bedroom suite, 1 conference room. Breakfast, snacks/refreshments and hors d'oeuvres included in rates. Types of meals: Full gourmet bkfst, veg bkfst, early coffee/tea, picnic lunch, Outdoor gas grill, kitchen available to guests any time after breakfast and can accommodate diet restrictions upon request. In room breakfasts upon request.

Certificate may be used: Sunday-Thursday.

Henry Whipple House Bed & Breakfast

75 Summer Street
Bristol, NH 03222
(603)744-6157 Fax:(603)744-6569
Internet: www.thewhipplehouse.com
E-mail: info@thewhipplehouse.com

Circa 1904. Centrally located in scenic New England, this Queen Anne is a grand example of a typical Victorian-era home. Stained-glass windows, oak woodwork, chandeliers and hardwood floors all add to the historic charm. Bedchambers in the main house and two carriage house suites are furnished with antiques, candles, personal spa amenities and plush towels. Several rooms feature bronze-engraved fireplaces. Locally grown produce and high-quality meats from Edwards of Surrey, Virginia are used to make a gourmet breakfast of homemade scones or baked goods, eggs Benedict, potato cakes with warm apple sauce, asparagus frittata, crispy bacon and gruyere omelets, tipsy orange French toast and apple pecan pancakes. Enjoy the year-round beauty and activities available nearby.

Innkeeper(s): Sandra Heaney. $110-165. 8 rooms with PB, 2 suites, 2 guest houses. Breakfast included in rates. Types of meals: Full gourmet bkfst, veg bkfst and early coffee/tea.

Certificate may be used: Anytime, subject to availability.

Pleasant View Bed and Breakfast

22 Hemp Hill Road
Bristol, NH 03222
(603)744-5547 (888)909-2700 Fax:(603)744-9757
Internet: www.pleasantviewbedandbreakfast.com
E-mail: theinnwench@metrocast.net

Circa 1832. Gracing the heart of the state's Lakes Region on a scenic rural road, this bed and breakfast was built as a farmhouse prior to 1832 for a local blacksmith with land extending to the shores of Newfound Lake. Relax in country elegance in the great room or on the patio. Play games or read a book from the library by a warm fire. Comfortable guest bedrooms include turndown service. After a satisfying breakfast take a bike ride to enjoy the surrounding beauty.

Innkeeper(s): Heidi Milbrand. $110-150. 6 rooms with PB, 1 cottage. Breakfast, afternoon tea and snacks/refreshments included in rates. Types of meals: Country bkfst, early coffee/tea and picnic lunch.

Certificate may be used: Anytime, Sunday-Thursday, not applicable for cottage, Anytime, Last Minute-Based on Availability.

Campton

Mountain-Fare Inn

Mad River Rd, PO Box 553
Campton, NH 03223
(603)726-4283 Fax:(603)726-8188
Internet: www.mountainfareinn.com
E-mail: info@mountainfareinn.com

Circa 1830. Located in the White Mountains between Franconia Notch and Squam Lake, this white farmhouse is surrounded by flower gardens in the summer and unparalleled  foliage in the fall. Mountain-Fare is an early 19th-century village inn in an ideal spot from which to enjoy New Hampshire's many offerings. Each season brings with it different activities, from skiing to biking and hiking or simply taking in the beautiful scenery. Skiers will enjoy the inn's lodge atmosphere during the winter, as well as the close access to ski areas. The inn is appointed in a charming New Hampshire style with country-cottage decor. There's a game room with billiards and a soccer field for playing ball. The hearty breakfast is a favorite of returning guests.

Innkeeper(s): Susan & Nick Preston. $85-145. 10 rooms with PB. Breakfast

and afternoon tea included in rates. Types of meals: Full bkfst.

Certificate may be used: Sunday-Thursday, excluding Dec. 15-Jan. 2 and Sept. 15-Oct. 20.

Chocorua

Brass Heart Inn

88 Philbrick Neighborhood Road
Chocorua, NH 03817
(603)323-7766 (800)833-9509 Fax:(603)323-8769
Internet: www.thebrassheartinn.com
E-mail: info@thebrassheartinn.com

Circa 1778. The main building of Harte's, home to a prosperous farm family for over 150 years, is Federal style. It became a guest house in the 1890s. An old apple orchard and sugar house remain, and there's a kitchen garden. A rocky brook still winds through the rolling fields, and in the adjacent woods, there's a natural swimming hole. Guest rooms are furnished in antiques and replicas.

Innkeeper(s): DJ Harte, Sheena Harte. $80-260. 17 rooms, 6 with PB, 1 with FP, 6 suites, 5 cottages, 1 conference room. Breakfast included in rates. Types of meals: Country bkfst, veg bkfst and early coffee/tea. Restaurant on premises.

Certificate may be used: Anytime, subject to availability.

Riverbend Inn Bed & Breakfast

273 Chocorua Mountain Highway
Chocorua, NH 03817-0288
(603) 323-7440 (800) 628-6944
Internet: www.riverbendinn.com
E-mail: info@riverbendinn.com

Circa 1968. Sitting on 15 scenic acres, this secluded country estate is conveniently located between the White Mountains and Lakes Region. Recently renovated, a luxurious decor is accented by antique furnishings. Enjoy afternoon drinks by the fire. Air conditioned guest bedrooms feature cotton linens, mahogany beds, terry robes and cable TV. One room boasts a private deck and entrance. Breakfast is a multi-course delight that may include  favorites like fresh fruit compote and maple yogurt with roasted granola or grapefruit sections with rum-raisin sauce, cinnamon plum cake or cranberry-bran muffins, eggs florentine or Creme Brulee French Toast. Wander through the gorgeous gardens, meadows and be refreshed by the Chocorua River that runs through the grounds. Relax on the deck or in a hammock.

Innkeeper(s): Craig Cox, Jerry Weiss. $100-250. 10 rooms, 6 with PB. Breakfast included in rates. Types of meals: Full gourmet bkfst and snacks/refreshments.

Certificate may be used: November-May, subject to availability, or anytime at the last minute.

Hanover

The Trumbull House Bed & Breakfast

40 Etna Road
Hanover, NH 03755
(603)643-2370 (800)651-5141 Fax:(603)643-0079
Internet: www.trumbullhouse.com
E-mail: Trumbull.House@gmail.com

Circa 1919. This handsome two-story farmhouse was built by
Walter Trumbull using treasures he gathered from old
Dartmouth College buildings and fraternity houses. Presiding
over 16 acres with stands of maple and a meandering brook,
the inn offers a cozy refuge for all, including cross-country
skiers and Dartmouth College alumni and parents. The parlor
features comfortable Country English chairs and sofas.

Innkeeper(s): Hilary Pridgen. $150-315. 6 rooms with PB, 1 with FP, 2 with
WP, 1 two-bedroom suite, 1 cottage. Sumptuous breakfast served whenever
you wish included in rates. Types of meals: Full gourmet bkfst, early
coffee/tea and Tea or coffee throughout the day.

Certificate may be used: November-March.

Hebron

Coppertoppe Inn & Retreat Center

8 Range Road
Hebron, NH 03241
(603)744-3636 (866)846-3636 Fax:603-744-5036
Internet: www.coppertoppe.com
E-mail: info@coppertoppe.com

Circa 1999. Poised on 15 acres at the top of Tenney
Mountain Ridge in the foothills of the White Mountains,
Coppertoppe Inn & Retreat Center overlooks Newfound
Lake. The modern setting is in the timeless New England
town of Hebron, New Hampshire. Can host up to 150 people
for weddings. Feel pampered and appreciated at this intimate
and secluded luxury retreat. Beverages and snacks are available all day. Common areas include the living room, library
and fitness area. Guest bedrooms and a suite are named after
colorful gemstones and boast balconies, large whirlpool tubs
and two-person European-style showers. Make a reservation
for an in-room spa service. Breakfast is served family-style or
as a buffet in the elegant dining room with balcony access.

Innkeeper(s): Sheila Oranch, Bill Powers. $125-275. 4 rooms with PB, 1
with FP, 2 with WP, 2 two-bedroom suites, 2 conference rooms. Breakfast,
afternoon tea, snacks/refreshments, wine, Meal plans including lunch and
dinner may be arranged at reasonable cost. Kitchen and charcoal grill are
available for guests. Kosher and vegetarian and vegan menus available.
Allergy avoidance is a specialty and special requests will be accommodated if
possible included in rates. Types of meals: Full gourmet bkfst, veg bkfst, Sun.
brunch, early coffee/tea, gourmet lunch, picnic lunch, hors d'oeuvres,
gourmet dinner, room service, Gourmet coffee, espresso, cappuccino, tea variety, fresh fruits, fresh baked goods. We customize food service for each guest.
Gourmet chefs are available in the area, if you want to plan a dinner party.
We use organic or local foods whenever possible. You pick it or catch it and
we'll make it. Allergy avoidance is a specialty here.

Certificate may be used: June-September, Sunday-Thursday; October-May;
all subject to availability.

Jackson

Inn at Ellis River

17 Harriman Road
Jackson, NH 03846
(603)383-9339 (800)233-8309 Fax:(603)383-4142
Internet: www.InnAtEllisRiver.com
E-mail: stay@InnAtEllisRiver.com

Circa 1893. Imagine a romantic getaway or relaxing vacation at
an award-winning New England bed and breakfast, then make
that vision a reality by visiting Inn at Ellis River in Jackson,
New Hampshire. Surrounded by the White Mountains, the inn
has a trout stream flowing
by and nearby hiking
trails. Enjoy the intimate
ambiance while soaking
in the atrium-enclosed
hot tub looking out on
the river or reading in the
sunny sitting room.

Gather for afternoon refreshments in the game room and pub,
sit in the sauna or swim in the seasonal outdoor heated pool.
Period furnishings along with traditional and modern amenities
are featured in the guest bedrooms and separate cottage. Many
rooms boast two-person Jacuzzis and/or balconies. Most
include gas or woodburning fireplaces. Savor a gourmet country breakfast made with local and regional foods.

Innkeeper(s): Frank Baker, Lyn Norris-Baker. $129-299. 3 rooms, 21 with
PB, 17 with FP, 9 with WP, 1 suite, 1 cottage, 1 conference room. Breakfast
and snacks/refreshments included in rates. Types of meals: Full gourmet bkfst,
veg bkfst, early coffee/tea, gourmet lunch, picnic lunch, wine and cheese.

Certificate may be used: Sunday-Thursday; January, March, April, May, June
and November (non-holiday periods).

North Conway

1785 Inn & Restaurant

3582 White Mountain Hwy
North Conway, NH 03860-1785
(603)356-9025 (800)421-1785
Internet: www.the1785inn.com
E-mail: info@the1785inn.com

Circa 1785. The main section of this center-chimney house
was built by Captain Elijah Dinsmore of the New Hampshire
Rangers. He was granted the
land for service in the American
Revolution. Original hand-hewn
beams, corner posts, fireplaces,
and a brick oven are still visible
and operating. The inn is located at the historical marker pop-
ularized by the White Mountain
School of Art in the 19th century.

Innkeeper(s): Becky Mallar, Charlie Mallar. $69-219. 17 rooms, 12 with PB, 1
suite, 3 conference rooms. Breakfast included in rates. Types of meals: Country
bkfst, veg bkfst, early coffee/tea, afternoon tea, snacks/refreshments, hors d'oeuvres, wine, gourmet dinner and room service. Restaurant on premises.

Certificate may be used: Anytime, non-holiday, November-June, subject to
availability.

Cabernet Inn

3552 White Mountain Highway
North Conway, NH 03860
(603)356-4704 (800)866-4704
Internet: www.cabernetinn.com
E-mail: info@cabernetinn.com

Circa 1842. The Cabernet Inn is a vintage bed and breakfast in North Conway, New Hampshire secluded amid towering pines in the heart of White Mountain National Forest. Enjoy a short stroll to see an incredible view of Mt. Washington. This romantic New England inn caters to couples who will enjoy an intimate getaway in a completely refurbished 1842 country cottage. Experience the warm and elegant setting that boasts modern conveniences and pampering amenities. Select a delightful guest room that includes a double Jacuzzi and a fireplace. Savor a hearty country breakfast that is made to order and served in the dining room or al fresco when weather permits. Choose the chef's special of the day or an entree from the extensive menu. Special packages are available.

Innkeeper(s): Bruce Zarenko, Jessica Zarenko. $99-239. 11 rooms with PB, 7 with FP, 5 with HT, 1 suite. Breakfast, afternoon tea and snacks/refreshments included in rates. Types of meals: Full gourmet bkfst, veg bkfst, early coffee/tea, Full cook to order gourmet breakfast and Afternoon refreshments and snacks.

Certificate may be used: November-June, Sunday-Thursday, subject to availability.

Old Red Inn & Cottages

2406 White Mountain Highway
North Conway, NH 03860-0467
(603)356-2642 (800)338-1356 Fax:(603)356-6626
Internet: www.oldredinn.com
E-mail: oldredinn@roadrunner.com

Circa 1810. Guests can opt to stay in an early 19th-century home or in one of a collection of cottages at this country inn. The rooms are decorated with handmade quilts and stenciling dots the walls. Several rooms include four-poster or canopy beds. Two-bedroom cottages feature a screened porch. A hearty, country meal accompanied by freshly baked breads, muffins and homemade preserves starts off the day. The inn is near many of the town's shops, restaurants and outlets.

Innkeeper(s): Susan & Richard LeFave. $79-198. 15 rooms with PB, 13 with FP, 1 two-bedroom suite, 10 cottages, 10 cabins. Breakfast included in rates. Types of meals: Country bkfst, early coffee/tea, afternoon tea and snacks/refreshments.

Certificate may be used: Jan. 2-June 1, Sunday-Thursday, (inn rooms only), non-holiday or vacation weeks.

Sanbornton

Lake House at Ferry Point

100 Lower Bay Rd
Sanbornton, NH 03269
(603) 524-0087
Internet: www.new-hampshire-inn.com
E-mail: innkeeper@lakehouseatferrypoint.com

Circa 1800. Picturesque Lake Winnisquam is the setting for this gracious Victorian bed & breakfast that was built as a summer retreat for the Pillsbury family. Antique furnishings, Oriental rugs and hardwood floors enhance a pleasant sentimental ambiance. Guest bedrooms boast high back beds for comfort and continuous lake views. Gourmet house specialties are found in the dining room. Indulge in stuffed French toast, crepes, cheese-baked apples, poached pears in raspberry sauce and eggs Benedict. A 60-foot porch invites relaxation on white wicker furniture. Romance is inspired in the waterfront gazebo, or stroll through the enchanting gardens that highlight the two-acre estate.

Innkeeper(s): John Becker, Cindy Becker. $145-260. 10 rooms with PB, 2 with WP, 1 two-bedroom suite. Breakfast, snacks/refreshments, Enjoy a gourmet breakfast between 8am and 9:30am each morning, Fresh Inn-made cookies available 24/7, Coffee, Hot chocolate and Hot Cider available 24/7 included in rates. Types of meals: Full gourmet bkfst, early coffee/tea. Can accommodate some special diets if requested prior to arrival.

Certificate may be used: November-April, Sunday-Thursday.

Sugar Hill

A Grand Inn-Sunset Hill House

231 Sunset Hill Rd
Sugar Hill, NH 03586
(603)823-5521 (800) 786-4455 Fax:(603)823-5523
Internet: www.sunsethillhouse.com
E-mail: innkeeper@sunsethillhouse.com

Circa 1882. This Second Empire luxury inn has views of five mountain ranges. Three parlors, all with cozy fireplaces, are favorite gathering spots. Afternoon tea is served here. The inn's lush grounds offer many opportunities for recreation or relaxing, and guests often enjoy special events here, such as the Fields of Lupine Festival. The Cannon Mountain Ski Area and Franconia Notch State Park are nearby, and there is 30 kilometers of cross-country ski trails at the inn. Be sure to inquire about golf and ski packages. In the fall, a Thanksgiving package allows guests to help decorate the inn for the holidays as well as enjoy Thanksgiving dinner together. NH Magazine just named Sunset Hill House — A Grand Inn the "Very Best in NH for a Spectacular Meal."

Innkeeper(s): Lon, Nancy, Mary Pearl, Adeline, Yani, Tad Henderson. $99-499. 28 rooms with PB, 10 with FP, 12 with WP, 2 two-bedroom suites, 3 conference rooms. Breakfast and afternoon tea included in rates. Types of meals: Full gourmet bkfst, veg bkfst, early coffee/tea, lunch, picnic lunch, snacks/refreshments, hors d'oeuvres, wine, gourmet dinner, room service, Award winning fine dining restaurant, Chaine Des Rotisseurs property, Wine spectator award and casual tavern. Restaurant on premises.

Certificate may be used: Not valid weekends Sept. 15-Oct. 15.

Warner

The Maples at Warner

69 East Main Street
Warner, NH 03278
(603) 456-6275
Internet: www.themaplesatwarner.com
E-mail: innkeeper@themaplesatwarner.com

Circa 1790. A classic New England village, tall maple trees, and a meandering stream define this inn. Rent the entire house or a single room as a bed and breakfast. The five guest rooms are free of telephones and televisions to ensure rest and comfort. Furry friends are welcome and a pet daycare is next door for when you go sightseeing. Take time each morning to enjoy a breakfast entree, muffins, fruit, and gourmet coffee. The bed and breakfast has had a long history as an inn and it is rumored that the spirit of one of the original caretakers still roams the halls. Take a short walk to restaurants, shops, and museums in the charming small town. The ski slopes at Mount Sunapee are 15 minutes away. Celebrate the ability to communicate over long distances at the New Hampshire Telephone Museum. Think about visiting on Columbus Day weekend for a festival celebrating the fall foliage.

Innkeeper(s): Cheryl Johnson. $99-139. 5 rooms, 4 with PB. Breakfast and snacks/refreshments included in rates. Types of meals: Full bkfst, veg bkfst and early coffee/tea.

Certificate may be used: January-February, April, subject to availability.

Waterville Valley

Snowy Owl Inn

41 Village Rd
Waterville Valley, NH 03215
(603)236-8383 (800)766-9969 Fax:(603)236-4890
Internet: www.snowyowlinn.com
E-mail: snowy@snowyowlinn.com

Circa 1974. Snowy Owl Inn is poised in the center of Waterville Valley and the White Mountain National Forest in New Hampshire. This four-season New England country inn is perfect for family getaways, corporate retreats and romantic destination weddings. Enjoy the many recreational activities and resort amenities that include a fitness center, men's and women's saunas, brook-side lawn and shuttle to ski areas. Swim in the indoor and outdoor pools and soak in one of the Jacuzzis. Some of the air-conditioned guest rooms and suites at this traditional natural wood lodge feature fireplaces, wet bars, Jacuzzi tubs and fully equipped kitchens. Handicapped accessible and pet-friendly rooms are also available. Start each day with a continental breakfast and gather for the afternoon wine and cheese social.

Innkeeper(s): Steve Hodges. $99-265. 82 rooms with PB, 1 with FP, 40 with HT, 1 two-bedroom suite, 2 conference rooms. Breakfast included in rates. Types of meals: Full gourmet bkfst, veg bkfst, picnic lunch, snacks/refreshments and wine. Restaurant on premises.

Certificate may be used: Sunday-Thursday, subject to availability, no holidays.

New Jersey

Avon By The Sea

The Avon Manor B&B & Cottage Rentals

109 Sylvania Ave
Avon By The Sea, NJ 07717-1338
(732)776-7770 Fax:(732)776-7476
Internet: www.avonmanor.com
E-mail: gregmav@aol.com

The Avon Manor was built as a private summer residence in the Colonial Revival style. The handsome facade is graced by a 100-foot wraparound veranda. Light, airy bedrooms are decorated with antiques, wicker and period pieces. Guests breakfast in a sunny dining room or on the veranda.

Innkeeper(s): Greg Dietrich. Call for rates. Call inn for details. Breakfast and afternoon tea included in rates. Types of meals: Full bkfst.

Certificate may be used: Oct. 1-May 10, not valid holidays or special events.

Barnegat Light

Minerva's By The Sea

13 W 7th Street
Barnegat Light, NJ 8006
(609)494-1000
Internet: www.minervasbandb.com
E-mail: MinervasBandB@gmail.com

Circa 2003. Let your creative juices flow at an inn named for the goddess of medicine, healing, crafts, poetry, and music. Located two blocks from the beach on the northern tip of Long Beach Island, the bed and breakfast is a wheelchair accessible, quiet retreat. Eat breakfast on the deck with views of the Barnegat Lighthouse, or "Old Barney" as it is affectionately called. There's a diverse library for a book to read at the beach. You can ride around town using the complimentary bicycles. Feel like you have your own private family apartment in the Emperor Penguin suite with a full kitchen, bedroom with queen bed, and room for three people to sleep in the living room. All five guest rooms have their own bathroom. Plan your family reunion in Barnegat Light; up to 20 family members can stay at the inn. Get away from it all in this un-commercialized and rarely crowded part of the Jersey Shore.

Innkeeper(s): Emma Lapsansky. $99-292. Call inn for details. Breakfast included in rates. Types of meals: Full gourmet bkfst and veg bkfst.

Certificate may be used: November-March or Anytime, last minute-based on availability.

Belmar

The Inn at The Shore Bed & Breakfast

301 4th Ave
Belmar, NJ 07719-2104
(732)681-3762 Fax:(732)280-1914
Internet: www.theinnattheshore.com
E-mail: tomandrosemary@theinnattheshore.com

Circa 1880. This child friendly country Victorian actually is near two different shores. Both the ocean and Silver Lake are within easy walking distance of the inn. From the inn's wraparound porch, guests can view swans on the lake. The innkeepers decorated their Victorian home in period style. The inn's patio is set up for barbecues.

Innkeeper(s): Rosemary Volker, Tom Volker. $145-295. 10 rooms, 4 with PB, 4 with FP, 1 conference room. Breakfast, afternoon tea and snacks/refreshments included in rates. Types of meals: Full gourmet bkfst.

Certificate may be used: Anytime, subject to availability, except weekends in June, July and August.

Cape May

Albert Stevens Inn

127 Myrtle Ave
Cape May, NJ 08204-1237
(609)884-4717 (800)890-2287 Fax:(609)884-8320
Internet: www.albertstevensinn.com
E-mail: AlbertStevensInn@hotmail.com

Circa 1898. Dr. Albert Stevens built this Queen Anne Free Classic house for his home and office. Carved woodwork and Victorian antiques enhance the delightful architectural details. The floating staircase and tower lead to spacious air-conditioned guest bedrooms. Enjoy a complete breakfast as well as afternoon tea and refreshments. Relax in the comfortably heated sunroom, or on the inviting veranda. Free on-site parking is convenient for shopping, restaurants and the beach a short walk away. Bicycles, beach towels and chairs are gladly provided.

Innkeeper(s): Jim & Lenanne Labrusciano. $100-265. 10 rooms with PB, 2 with FP, 1 with WP, 3 total suites, including 2 two-bedroom suites. Breakfast, afternoon tea and wine included in rates. Types of meals: Full bkfst and early coffee/tea.

Certificate may be used: Oct. 30-April 26, Sunday-Thursday, except weeks that contain a holiday (based on season high rate).

Bedford Inn

805 Stockton Ave
Cape May, NJ 08204-2446
(609)884-4158 (866)215-9507 Fax:(609)884-6320
Internet: www.bedfordinn.com
E-mail: info@bedfordinn.com

Circa 1883. The Bedford, decked in gingerbread trim with verandas on both of its two stories, has welcomed guests since its creation in the 19th century. Electrified gaslights, period wallcoverings and rich, Victorian furnishings create an air of nostalgia. The inn is close to many of Cape May's shops and restaurants, as well as the beach, which is just half a block away. Guests are pampered with breakfasts of quiche, gourmet egg dishes, French toast and freshly baked breads.

Innkeeper(s): Archie Kirk, Stephanie Kirk. $120-265. 11 rooms, 10 with PB, 3 total suites, including 1 two-bedroom suite. Breakfast and afternoon tea included in rates. Types of meals: Full bkfst and early coffee/tea.

Certificate may be used: October-June, Sunday-Thursday, excluding holidays, based on availability.

Fairthorne B&B

115 Ocean St
Cape May, NJ 08204-2319
(609) 884-8791 (800) 438-8742
Internet: www.fairthorne.com
E-mail: info@fairthorne.com

Circa 1880. Antiques abound in this three-story Colonial Revival. Lace curtains and a light color scheme complete the charming decor. There is a new, yet historic addition to the B&B. The innkeepers now offer guest quarters (with fireplaces) in The Fairthorne Cottage, a restored 1880s building adjacent to the inn. The signature breakfasts include special daily entrees along with an assortment of home-baked breads and muffins. A light afternoon tea also is served with refreshments. The proximity to the beach will be much appreciated by guests, and the innkeepers offer the use of beach towels, bicycles and sand chairs. The nearby historic district is full of fun shops and restaurants.

Innkeeper(s): Diane Hutchinson, Ed Hutchinson. $225-295. 4 rooms with PB, 4 with FP, 2 with WP. Breakfast and snacks/refreshments included in rates. Types of meals: Full bkfst and early coffee/tea.

Certificate may be used: Nov. 1-May 31, Sunday-Thursday, except holidays.

Gingerbread House

28 Gurney St
Cape May, NJ 08204
(609)884-0211
Internet: gingerbreadinn.com
E-mail: info@gingerbreadinn.com

Circa 1869. The Gingerbread is one of eight original Stockton Row Cottages, summer retreats built for families from Philadelphia and Virginia. It is a half-block from the ocean and breezes waft over the wicker-filled porch. The inn is listed in the National Register. It has been meticulously restored and decorated with period antiques and a fine collection of paintings. The inn's woodwork is especially notable, guests enter through handmade teak double doors.

Innkeeper(s): Fred & Joan Echevarria. $110-330. 6 rooms, 3 with PB, 1 suite. Breakfast and Coffee/Tea & innkeepers choice of snacks available throughout the day included in rates. Types of meals: Full bkfst and afternoon tea.

Certificate may be used: Oct. 1-May 25, Sunday-Thursday.

John Wesley Inn & Carriage House

30 Guerney Ave
Cape May, NJ 08204
(609)884-1012 (800)616-5122
Internet: www.johnwesleyinn.com
E-mail: info@johnwesleyinn.com

Circa 1869. Just one-half block from the beach, this American classic features Carpenter Gothic architecture and adorns the serene primary Historic District. The inn has undergone meticulous Victorian restorations with extensive attention paid to details. Sip afternoon tea on a veranda rocker while watching a horse and carriage go by. Gather by the fire in the family parlor or in the spacious third-floor sun parlor. Delightful guest bedrooms offer a variety of choices. The Stockton room features a private front porch. Share lively conversation over a bountiful homemade breakfast in the dining room.

Innkeeper(s): Bonnie Pontin, Lance Pontin. $150-325. 6 rooms with PB, 6 with FP, 1 with WP, 2 suites, 2 cottages. Breakfast, afternoon tea, snacks/refreshments, Iced peach and/or raspberry tea freshly brewed daily all summer long, hot Earl Grey and/or the flavor of your choice, piping hot all winter and cookies baked daily included in rates. Types of meals: Full gourmet bkfst, early coffee/tea, Belgium waffles with whipped cream and fresh strawberries, specialty of the house and served every Sunday.

Certificate may be used: November through April, midweek only.

Rhythm of The Sea

1123 W. Beach Ave
Cape May, NJ 08204-2628
(609)884-7788
Internet: www.rhythmofthesea.com
E-mail: stay@rhythmofthesea.com

Circa 1915. The apt name of this oceanfront inn describes the soothing sounds of the sea that lull many a happy guest into a restful night's sleep. Watching sunsets, strolling the beach, bird watching and whale watching are popular activities. Many of the features of a Craftsman home are incorporated in this seaside inn, such as light-filled spacious rooms, adjoining dining and living areas and gleaming natural wood floors. Mission oak furnishings compliment the inn's architecture. For guests seeking an especially private stay, ask for the three-room suite and arrange for a private dinner prepared by the innkeeper Wolfgang Wendt, a European trained chef. Full breakfasts are provided each morning. Guests are given complimentary beach towels and chairs. There is free parking and complimentary use of bicycles.

Innkeeper(s): Robyn, Wolfgang Wendt. $225-399. 9 rooms, 7 with PB, 2 with FP, 1 suite. Breakfast and snacks/refreshments included in rates. Types of meals: Full bkfst and dinner.

Certificate may be used: November-April, Sunday-Thursday, not valid on holidays or with any other promotional offer. Based on regular rack rate.

The Carroll Villa B&B

19 Jackson St
Cape May, NJ 08204-1417
(609)884-9619 (877)275-8452 Fax:(609)884-0264
Internet: www.carrollvilla.com
E-mail: manager@carrollvilla.com

Circa 1882. This Victorian hotel is located one-half block from the ocean on the oldest street in the historic district of Cape May. Breakfast at the Villa is a memorable event, featuring dishes acclaimed by the New York Times and Frommer's. Homemade fruit breads, Italian omelets and Crab Eggs Benedict are a few specialties. Meals are served in the Mad Batter Restaurant on a European veranda, a secluded garden terrace or in the sky-lit Victorian dining room. The restaurant serves breakfast, lunch, dinner and cocktails daily. The decor of this inn is decidedly Victorian with period antiques and wallpapers.
Innkeeper(s): Mark Kulkowitz, Pamela Ann Huber. $110-299. 21 rooms with PB, 2 conference rooms. Breakfast included in rates. Types of meals: Full bkfst, lunch and dinner.

Certificate may be used: Sept. 19-May 19, Sunday-Thursday, no holidays, weekends or Christmas week.

The Henry Sawyer Inn

722 Columbia Ave
Cape May, NJ 08204-2332
(609)884-5667 (800)449-5667
Internet: www.henrysawyerinn.com
E-mail: henrysawyerinn@verizon.net

Circa 1877. This fully restored, three-story peach Victorian home boasts a gingerbread embellished veranda, brick-colored shutters and brown trim. Inside, the parlor features Victorian antiques, a marble fireplace, polished wood floors, an Oriental rug, formal wallcoverings, a crystal chandelier and fresh flowers. Guest rooms have been decorated with careful attention to a romantic and fresh Victorian theme, as well. One room includes a whirlpool tub, one includes a private porch, and another a fireplace.
Innkeeper(s): Mary Morris, Barbara Morris. $150-295. 5 rooms with PB, 1 with FP, 2 suites. Breakfast and afternoon tea included in rates. Types of meals: Full bkfst and early coffee/tea.

Certificate may be used: November-April, subject to availability, Anytime, Last Minute-Based on Availability.

The Queen Victoria

102 Ocean St
Cape May, NJ 08204-2320
(609)884-8702
Internet: www.queenvictoria.com
E-mail: stay@queenvictoria.com

Circa 1881. 2009 Winner - Travelers' Choice for Romance. This nationally acclaimed inn, a block from the ocean and shops in the historic district, is comprised of two beautiful Victorian homes, restored and furnished with antiques. "Victorian Homes" magazine featured 23 color photographs of The Queen Victoria, because of its decor and luxurious amenities. Guest rooms offer handmade quilts, antiques, air conditioning, mini-refrigerators and all have private baths. Luxury suites and many rooms have a whirlpool tub and some with handsome fireplace. Afternoon tea is enjoyed while rocking on the porch in summer or before a warm fireplace in

winter. Breakfast is hearty buffet style and the inn has its own cookbook. The innkeepers keep a fleet of complimentary bicycles available for guests and there are beach chairs and beach towels as well. The inn is open all year with special Christmas festivities and winter packages.
Innkeeper(s): Doug McMain, Anna Marie McMain. $110-425. 34 rooms with PB, 6 with FP, 14 with WP, 6 suites, 2 cottages. Breakfast, afternoon tea and snacks/refreshments included in rates. Types of meals: Full bkfst and early coffee/tea.

Certificate may be used: Monday-Thursday, November-March, except holidays, Christmas week and special events.

Flemington

Main Street Manor Bed and Breakfast

194 Main Street
Flemington, NJ 08822
(908)782-4928 Fax:(908)782-7229
Internet: www.mainstreetmanor.com
E-mail: innkeeper@mainstreetmanor.com

Circa 1901. Located in the quaint village of Flemington, this bed and breakfast has been welcoming guests for 13 years. Elegantly restored, the Queen Anne Victorian adorns the historic district. Sip lemonade on the front porch, converse by the fire in the formal front parlor or catch up on reading in the intimate side parlor. Visit local wineries, dine in great restaurants and explore the many shops. All guest bedrooms feature private baths; one room boasts a balcony and another has a claw-foot tub. Each morning a delicious gourmet breakfast is served in the block-paneled dining room. Feel spoiled in the delightful setting so filled with comfort it will be hard to leave.
Innkeeper(s): Donna Arold, Ken Arold . $155-220. 5 rooms with PB, 1 with FP, 1 with HT, 1 conference room. Breakfast, afternoon tea, snacks/refreshments, hors d'oeuvres and wine included in rates. Types of meals: Full gourmet bkfst, veg bkfst, Sun. brunch, early coffee/tea, gourmet lunch, picnic lunch, gourmet dinner, room service, All food is prepared on premesis and no preservatives of any kind are used. Fresh-baked goods are always offered for guests to enjoy. Full gourmet breakfasts include fresh and seasonal fruit and ingredients from our local organic farm. The Inn's herb garden helps to supply the fresh herbs which are incorporated into all meals prepared at Main Street Manor.

Certificate may be used: July, August, February and March, Monday-Thursday excluding certain rooms, holidays and special event dates, based on availabilty.

Mannington

Barrett's Plantation House

203 Old Kings Hwy
Mannington, NJ 08079
(856) 935-0812
Internet: barrettsplantationhouse.com/
E-mail: barrettsplantationhouse@comcast.net

Circa 1735. Step into a stately brick home with pumpkin pine floors and original woodwork. The historic charm of this Salem County inn is maintained with period antiques and several fireplaces. Spread out in one of two suites with a queen-size canopy bed and sitting area then curl up in a spa robe after showering in a private bathroom. Return after a day of sightseeing to a complimentary cocktail and snacks hour and share stories of the day and learn about new places to visit tomorrow. Start each day with breakfast in the bright parlor. Enjoy the high-speed wireless Internet to share pictures with loved ones back home. Keep your eyes open for birds, including Bald

Eagles, in the colorful gardens. Learn about the history of the area at the Salem County Historical Society Museum or the Finns Point Lighthouse then sample wines and take a tour at Auburn Road Vineyard and Winery or Heritage Vineyards.

Innkeeper(s): Gay Schneeman, Craig Schneeman. $105-135. 2 suites. Breakfast, hors d'oeuvres and wine included in rates. Types of meals: Full gourmet bkfst, veg bkfst and early coffee/tea.

Certificate may be used: January-December, Sunday-Thursday only, weekends last minute.

Ocean City

Inn The Gardens Bed & Breakfast

48 Wesley Rd
Ocean City, NJ 08226-4462
(609)399-0800
Internet: www.innthegardens.com
E-mail: innthegardens@aol.com

Circa 1923. Adorning the quiet, residential Gardens neighborhood on the New Jersey Shore, this relaxing bed and breakfast is only eight miles from Atlantic City. Enjoy the ocean breeze while sitting on a porch with a beverage or on the backyard patio surrounded by gardens. Complimentary beach tags are also provided. Comfortable guest bedrooms feature refrigerators and the Daybreak Room boasts a private balcony. Indulge in an extensive continental breakfast each morning. A computer is available to check e-mail. Ask about specials and packages offered.

Innkeeper(s): Jennifer Torres. $139-189. 7 rooms with PB. Breakfast included in rates. Types of meals: Scrumptious Continental Plus buffet served between 8-10 AM.

Certificate may be used: November-April, excluding holidays.

Ocean Grove

The Majestic Hotel

19 Main Avenue
Ocean Grove, NJ 07756
(732)775-6100 Fax:(732)775-6108
Internet: www.majesticoceangrove.com
E-mail: info@majesticoceangrove.com

Circa 1870. The beach is waiting in this historical New Jersey town. Built as a hotel in the late 1800s, the Majestic Hotel celebrates its history in renovated luxury. The enclosed widow's walk offers sunny panoramic views all year long. The fragrance of the salty sea fills the front porch and second floor balcony. Double, queen, and king-size rooms are available, all with private marble and tile bathrooms, terrycloth bathrobes, and kitchenettes. Feel like royalty in the Penthouse Suite with a king-size bedroom, private living room, and two-person Jacuzzi tub. The bed and breakfast is also ADA compliant. Dine in the European-style bistro, Bia, which is open seasonally. Feel the sand between your toes during an intimate seaside wedding then relax in the cozy lobby with friends and family. Show your special someone how much you care with a Romance Package including a fruit and cheese assortment and dinner voucher.

Innkeeper(s): Jim Shanahan. $105-500. 1 suite. Breakfast included in rates. Types of meals: Cont plus.

Certificate may be used: October-April, Sunday-Thursday.

Plainfield

The Pillars of Plainfield Bed and Breakfast Inn

922 Central Ave
Plainfield, NJ 07060
(908)753-0922 (888)PIL-LARS
Internet: www.pillars2.com
E-mail: info@pillars2.com

Circa 1870. Victorian and Georgian influences are mingled in the design of this grand historic mansion, which boasts majestic columns and a wraparound porch. An acre of well-manicured grounds and gardens surrounds the home, which is located in Plainfield's Van Wyck Historic District. Guest rooms and suites are appointed with traditional furnishings, and each room has its own special decor. The romantic Van Wyck Brooks Suite includes a fireplace and a canopy bed topped with a down quilt. A wicker table and chairs are tucked into the bay window alcove of the Clementine Yates room. Another spacious room includes a full kitchen. Business travelers will appreciate the private in-room phones with voice mail and wi-fi. Swedish home cooking highlights the morning meal, which is accompanied by freshly ground coffee. Plainfield, the first inland settlement in New Jersey, offers many historic attractions, including the Drake House Museum.

Innkeeper(s): Nancy Fiske, Lamont Blowe. $125-190. 7 rooms with PB, 2 with FP. Snacks/refreshments and Full Gourmet Breakfast included in rates. Types of meals: Full bkfst, veg bkfst and early coffee/tea.

Certificate may be used: Last minute bookings, booked within one week of arrival date.

Point Pleasant Beach

The Tower Cottage

203 Forman Ave
Point Pleasant Beach, NJ 08742
(877)766-2693
Internet: www.thetowercottage.com
E-mail: stay@thetowercottage.com

Stay in deluxe, environmentally-friendly accommodations at The Tower Cottage in Point Pleasant Beach, New Jersey. Newly remodeled, this luxury bed and breakfast inn is a Queen Anne Victorian in a residential neighborhood just two blocks from a sandy beach and an easy walk to shopping, dining and other activities. Complimentary beach badges and towels are thoughtful details amid the seaside setting. Health club passes are available upon request. Savor afternoon refreshments in one of the common rooms. Spacious guest rooms and a suite boast gas fireplaces, generous upscale amenities including aromatherapy toiletries and microfiber robes. Most rooms feature views of Little Silver Lake. Gather in the second-floor breakfast room for a gourmet morning meal before exploring the surrounding area.

Innkeeper(s): Maureen Haddad, Anthony Haddad. Call for rates. 5 rooms with PB, 5 with FP, 4 with WP, 1 suite. Breakfast, afternoon tea, snacks/refreshments, hors d'oeuvres, Late night snacks such as cookies, cakes, specialty breads, scones, included in rates. Types of meals: Full gourmet bkfst, veg bkfst, early coffee/tea, gourmet lunch, picnic lunch, fruit /cheese platters, cookies/scones/coffee cake and 24-hour coffee/tea service.

Certificate may be used: January-March, anytime.

Sea Girt

Beacon House

100 & 104 Beacon Blvd
Sea Girt, NJ 08750-1609
(732)449-5835 (866)255-0005 Fax:732-282-0974
Internet: www.beaconhouseinn.com
E-mail: info@beaconhouseinn.com

Circa 1879. Built in classic Victorian style, this recently renovated inn has been a relaxing getaway for more than a century. Splendidly furnished parlors with fireplaces, crystal chandeliers and oak floors are pleasurable places to while away time. The two main houses, a cottage and a carriage house offer the best in casual elegance. Encounter wicker, brass and chintz in the sunny guest bedrooms. Some boast oceanview balconies, fireplaces and Jacuzzi tubs. Morning is a celebration when a memorable gourmet breakfast is served in the candle-lit dining room. Enjoy the colorful landscape from a rocker on one of the wraparound porches, lounge by the swimming pool, or take a bike ride to the popular boardwalk in this quaint seaside community.
Innkeeper(s): Candace Kadimik. $89-365. 18 rooms with PB, 7 with FP, 2 with WP, 2 two-bedroom suites, 3 cottages, 1 conference room. Breakfast included in rates. Types of meals: Full gourmet bkfst, veg bkfst, early coffee/tea and snacks/refreshments.
Certificate may be used: October and April, subject to availability and excluding holiday weekends.

Spring Lake

White Lilac Inn

414 Central Ave
Spring Lake, NJ 07762-1020
(732)449-0211 (866)449-0211
Internet: www.whitelilac.com
E-mail: mari@whitelilac.com

Circa 1880. The White Lilac looks like a sweeping Southern home with wide wraparound private and semi-private porches decorating its three stories. The first story veranda is lined with wicker rockers and baskets of flowering plants hang from the ceiling, creating an ideal spot for relaxation. Inside, the Victorian decor contains period furnishings,  antiques, double whirlpool tubs, fireplaces, air conditioning in every room and queen beds. Breakfast is served fireside on intimate tables for two in the Garden Room and on the enclosed porch. The ocean is less than five blocks from the inn.
Innkeeper(s): Mari Kennelly. $99-319. 9 rooms, 8 with PB, 10 with HT, 1 total suite, including 1 two-bedroom suite and 1 four-bedroom suite, 5 cottages, 10 guest houses. Breakfast, snacks/refreshments, Tea and soda and guest refrigerator always accessible to guests included in rates. Types of meals: Full bkfst, early coffee/tea and Victorian Treasure has the option of a full breakfast delivered to their sitting room.
Certificate may be used: Sunday-Thursday, September-May; subject to availability, holidays excluded.

Stanhope

Whistling Swan Inn

110 Main St
Stanhope, NJ 07874-2632
(973)347-6369 (888)507-2337 Fax:(973)347-6379
Internet: www.whistlingswaninn.com
E-mail: info@whistlingswaninn.com

Circa 1905. This Queen Anne Victorian has a limestone wraparound veranda and a tall, steep-roofed turret. Family antiques fill the rooms and highlight the polished ornate woodwork, pocket doors and winding staircase. It is a little more than a mile from  Waterloo Village and the International Trade Center.
Innkeeper(s): Rosalind. $119-259. 9 rooms with PB, 9 with FP, 4 with WP, 4 suites. Breakfast and snacks/refreshments included in rates. Types of meals: Full bkfst.
Certificate may be used: Sunday-Thursday, excluding August-October and holidays. Not available for suites.

Ventnor City

Carisbrooke Inn

105 S Little Rock Ave
Ventnor City, NJ 08406-2840
(609)822-6392 Fax:(609)822-9710
Internet: www.carisbrookeinn.com
E-mail: info@carisbrookeinn.com

Circa 1918. Relaxation is easy at this enticing seaside bed & breakfast just a few steps away from the world-famous boardwalk and only one mile from Atlantic City. Delight in the ocean view from the front deck or the tranquility of the back patio. Afternoon refreshments are enjoyed in the sunny Main Parlor, or by the warmth of a winter fire. Pleasant guest bedrooms feature comfortable amenities and the romantic accents of plants, fresh flowers and lacy curtains. The innkeepers offer a huge breakfast that may include homemade waffles and fresh berries, banana pecan pancakes, Italian frittata with fresh herbs and cheese, Quiche Lorraine and French toast, accompanied by fruit and just-baked muffins and breads. Beach towels and tags are provided for fun in the sun at the shore.
Innkeeper(s): John Battista. $85-360. 9 rooms with PB. Breakfast, snacks/refreshments, hors d'oeuvres and wine included in rates. Types of meals: Full gourmet bkfst, veg bkfst and early coffee/tea.
Certificate may be used: Nov. 1-April 30, Sunday-Thursday, holidays excluded. Other black out days may apply, subject to availability.

Vernon

Alpine Haus B&B

217 State Rt 94
Vernon, NJ 07462
(973)209-7080 (877)527-6854 Fax:(973)209-7090
Internet: www.alpinehausbb.com
E-mail: alpinehausbb@gmail.com

Circa 1885. A private hideaway in the mountains, this former farmhouse is more than 100 years old. The renovated Federal-style inn with Victorian accents offers comfortable guest bedrooms named after mountain flowers with a decor reflecting that theme. Antiques also highlight the inn. The adjacent Carriage House has two suites with four-poster beds, stone fireplace and Jacuzzi. A generous country breakfast is enjoyed in the dining room or a continental breakfast on the second-story covered porch with majestic views. The family room and formal sitting room with fireplace are wonderful gathering places for games or conversation. Located next to Mountain Creek Ski and Water Park.

Innkeeper(s): Jack Smith, Allison Smith. $110-225. 10 rooms with PB, 3 with FP, 2 suites, 1 conference room. Breakfast included in rates. Types of meals: Country bkfst, veg bkfst, early coffee/tea and snacks/refreshments.

Certificate may be used: Anytime, except Friday-Saturday for the periods Dec. 15-March 15 and June 15-Sept. 7, not valid holiday periods.

New Mexico

Albuquerque

Bottger Mansion of Old Town

110 San Felipe St., NW
Albuquerque, NM 87104
(505)243-3639 (800)758-3639
Internet: www.bottger.com
E-mail: info@bottger.com

Circa 1910. Gracing the historic district of Old Town Albuquerque, Bottger Mansion of Old Town B&B is a Victorian delight listed in the National Register. Sitting amid the vibrant southwestern culture and distinct architecture of New Mexico, this elegant B&B focuses on comfort and convenience while offering gracious hospitality. Enjoy the inn's signature chocolate chip cookies and other afternoon treats in the parlor or relax in the courtyard shaded by massive ancient Chinese elms. Accommodations boast pleasing color schemes and furnishings and vary from an intimate sun porch room to a two-bedroom suite with living area. Indulge in a gourmet breakfast before taking a day trip to Santa Fe, the lava tubes, Salinas National Monument, the Turquoise Trail, or Bopsque del Apache National Wildlife Refuge. Special packages are available.
Innkeeper(s): Steve & Kathy Hiatt. $99-179. 7 rooms with PB, 1 with WP, 1 two-bedroom suite. Breakfast and snacks/refreshments included in rates. Types of meals: Full gourmet bkfst, veg bkfst and early coffee/tea.
Certificate may be used: Anytime, subject to availability. Week of International Balloon Fiesta is excluded.

Inn At Paradise & Golf Club

10035 Country Club Ln NW
Albuquerque, NM 87114
(505)898-6161
Internet: www.innatparadise.com
E-mail: info@innatparadise.com

Poised atop the west mesa with a landscaped water garden, accommodations overlook the Rio Grande Valley and scenic Sandia Mountains. Located on the first tee of Desert Greens Golf Club, visit the pro shop, schedule a massage and relax in the restaurant and lounge. Stay in a newly remodeled guest room or spacious suite with original local artwork on consignment, a fireplace and kitchen. A fiesta breakfast is served daily at the onsite Full Moon Saloon. Albuquerque, New Mexico offers many attractions that have contributed to the state being called the Land of Enchantment. The colorful balloon festival is a popular international event. Ask about golf packages available.
Innkeeper(s): Antoni Niemczak, Natalia L. Niemczak. Call for rates. 15 rooms.
Certificate may be used: Anytime, excluding October.

The Mauger

701 Roma Ave NW
Albuquerque, NM 87102-2038
(505) 242-8755 (800) 719-9189 Fax:(505)842-8835
Internet: www.maugerbb.com
E-mail: maugerbb@aol.com

Circa 1897. Now an elegantly restored Victorian, this former boarding house is listed in the National Register. Guest bedrooms offer amenities that include satellite television, refrigerators, a basket with snacks, voice mail and European down comforters on the beds. The inn is located four blocks from the convention center/business district and Historic Route 66. Old Town is less than one mile away. There are many interesting museums to visit locally, featuring topics from Native American culture to the atomic age.
Innkeeper(s): Tammy Walden. $89-209. 10 rooms, 8 with PB, 1 suite, 2 guest houses, 1 conference room. Breakfast, snacks/refreshments and wine included in rates. Types of meals: Full bkfst, veg bkfst, early coffee/tea and Breakfast to-go for early departures.
Certificate may be used: Nov. 15-March 1, except Thanksgiving and Christmas, Subject to availability.

Algodones

Hacienda Vargas

PO Box 307
Algodones, NM 87001-0307
(505)867-9115 (800)261-0006 Fax:(505)867-0640
Internet: www.haciendavargas.com
E-mail: stay@haciendavargas.com

Circa 1840. Nestled among the cottonwoods and mesas of the middle Rio Grande Valley, between Albuquerque and Santa Fe, Hacienda Vargas has seen two centuries of Old West history. It once served as a trading post for Native Americans as well as a 19th-century stagecoach stop between Santa Fe and Las Cruces.

The grounds contain an adobe chapel, courtyard and gardens. The main house features five kiva fireplaces, Southwest antiques, Spanish tile, a library and suites with private Jacuzzis.

Innkeeper(s): Cynthia Spence, Richard Spence. $79-149. 7 rooms with PB, 6 with FP, 4 suites. Breakfast included in rates. Types of meals: Full bkfst.

Certificate may be used: Sunday-Thursday except holidays or Balloon Fiesta.

Cedar Crest

Elaine's, A B&B

72 Snowline Rd
Cedar Crest, NM 87008-0444
(505)281-2467 (800)821-3092 Fax:(505)281-1384
Internet: www.elainesbnb.com
E-mail: elaine@elainesbnb.com

Circa 1979. Ideally located on the historic Turquoise Trail adjacent to the Cibola National Forest, this three-story log home is situated on four acres of evergreens in the forests of the Sandia Peaks. Over one hundred varieties of birds, including three types of hummingbirds, visit the property. Enchanting mountain views from one of the three balconies are unforgettable. Furnished with European country antiques, several of the guest bedrooms feature private fireplaces and Jacuzzis. Start the day off right with a substantial breakfast of favorite comfort foods. Visit the historic sites, shops and galleries in Albuquerque and Santa Fe, only minutes away from this secluded inn.

Innkeeper(s): Elaine O'Neil. $105-159. 5 rooms, 2 with FP, 5 suites. Breakfast included in rates. Types of meals: Full gourmet bkfst, veg bkfst, early coffee/tea and snacks/refreshments.

Certificate may be used: Jan. 15-April 15, excluding holidays.

Chama

Parlor Car Bed & Breakfast

311 Terrace Ave
Chama, NM 87520
(575) 756-1946 Fax:(575)756-1057
Internet: www.parlorcar.com/
E-mail: wendybonsall@yahoo.com

Circa 1924. Reflecting the distinctive luxury of historic parlor cars, this is the perfect getaway destination to experience the Spirit of the West in the Northern New Mexico Rocky Mountains. Pan for gold, go fossil hunting, take a walking tour, chow down on a chuck wagon dinner and listen to a cowboy poetry reading. Relax in a common room accented with original artwork, oriental rugs and antiques, or enjoy the outside sitting areas that invite bird watching. Delightful guest rooms are named after men who gained notoriety through their involvement in the railroad era. The Chama Valley offers horseback riding, hiking, water sports and hunting.

Innkeeper(s): Bonsall Johnson, Wendy Johnson. $79-159. 3 rooms with PB, 1 with WP. Breakfast, snacks/refreshments and bedtime treats included in rates. Types of meals: Full bkfst, vegetarian breakfast on request and bedtime treats.

Certificate may be used: Anytime, sunject to availability.

Chimayo

Casa Escondida Bed & Breakfast

64 County Road 0100
Chimayo, NM 87522
(505) 351-4805
Internet: www.casaescondida.com
E-mail: info@casaescondida.com

Circa 1970. Secluded on six acres in an historic mountain village, this Adobe-style inn features Spanish Colonial architecture. Tongue and groove ceilings, heavy beams known as vigas, French doors, wood, brick and Saltillo tile floors all add to the warm ambiance. The air is scented with the fragrance of pinon wood from kiva fireplaces. A library offers quiet entertainment. Inviting guest bedrooms include bathrobes to relax in. Some rooms boast gorgeous views, oversized tubs, fireplaces, private access to a deck or patio, and can be made into an adjoining suite. Enjoy a leisurely gourmet breakfast in the sunny dining room, or alfresco. Surrounded by trees, an outside hot tub is the perfect spot to relax.

Innkeeper(s): Belinda Bowling. $109-169. 8 rooms with PB, 3 with FP, 1 suite. Breakfast and snacks/refreshments included in rates. Types of meals: Full bkfst and coffee/tea and snacks 24/7.

Certificate may be used: May-October, Sunday-Thursday, Any day November-April. Excluding holiday periods and special events all year. Anytime, Last Minute-Based on Availability.

Kingston

The Black Range Lodge

119 Kingston Main Street
Kingston, NM 88042
(575) 895-5652 (800) 676-5622
Internet: www.blackrangelodge.com
E-mail: cat@blackrangelodge.com

Circa 1884. Ivy covers the three-story high vigas (log-beamed ceilings) and stone walls of this old hotel, a remnant of the bustling days when silver was discovered nearby and the town  mushroomed to 7,000 people. Now only a few dozen citizens populate the hamlet, tucked in a mountain valley of the Gila National Forest. Cavalry soldiers are said to have headquartered here while protecting miners from the Indians. Hosts Catherine and Mike pursue movie script writing careers. Furnishings from the '40s fill the guest rooms on the second floor. There is a room with pool table and free video games. Pets and children are welcome.

Innkeeper(s): Catherine E. Wanek. $95-149. 15 rooms, 7 with PB, 4 two-bedroom suites, 1 cottage, 2 guest houses, 2 conference rooms. Breakfast included in rates. Types of meals: Full bkfst, veg bkfst, early coffee/tea and snacks/refreshments.

Certificate may be used: Anytime, except holidays, subject to availability.

Las Cruces

DreamCatcher Inn Bed & Breakfast de Las Cruces

10201Starfly Rd.
Las Cruces, NM 88011
(575)522-3035 (866)298-1935 Fax:(575)373-1615
Internet: dreamcatcherinn.com
E-mail: dreamcatcherinn@yahoo.com

Escape to a tranquil desert hideaway at the base of the picturesque Organ Mountains. Start the morning off right with a full country breakfast in the great room and dining room. Perhaps you or another guest will serenade everyone with a tune on the piano. A guest kitchen with a refrigerator, stove, and microwave is available so you never have to leave the 10-acre retreat. The Southwest decor blends wonderfully with the quiet atmosphere. All guest rooms have a private entrance and large bathroom, king or queen-size bed, and the entire inn is wheelchair-friendly. Sit by the outdoor fireplace beneath a star-filled sky. During the day enjoy the clean desert air as you watch for jackrabbits and hummingbirds. Marvel at the sparkling gypsum sand dunes at White Sands National Monument. Las Cruces is home to many challenging golf courses. The inn is also a convenient home base for those visiting New Mexico State University. Pets and children are welcome.

Innkeeper(s): Ken McLeod, Anita McLeod. Call for rates. 3 rooms with PB, 1 with WP. Breakfast included in rates. Types of meals: Full bkfst, early coffee/tea and Full Guest Kitchen available for your pleasure 24/7.

Certificate may be used: September-January, Tuesday-Thursday, Queen beds only.

Santa Fe

Alexander's Inn

529 E Palace Ave
Santa Fe, NM 87501-2200
(505)986-1431 Fax:(505)982-8572
Internet: www.alexanders-inn.com
E-mail: info@alexanders-inn.com

Circa 1903. Alexander's Inn offers the distinctive southwestern flavor of a Santa Fe hotel with great value and a memorable experience in New Mexico. This inn recently changed from a bed & breakfast to more of a private vacation rental with upscale services. Traditional casitas provide a relaxing oasis and the welcome warmth of a kiva fireplace after a great day of skiing.

New Mexican furnishings and decor, full kitchens and patios are perfect for family vacations or romantic holidays. Comfort and convenience is found in the heavenly beds, fine linens, down comforters, feather pillows, daily maid service and luxuriously soft robes. A basket filled with homemade cookies, fresh fruit, coffee & teas, bottled water, chips & salsa is provided upon arrival. Packages, facials, various massages and rose petal baths are available at the inn's Absolute Nirvana Spa.

Innkeeper(s): Carolyn Lee. $170-240. 4 cottages, 4 with FP. Each unit

stocked with locally roasted organic coffee/teas/sweeteners/creamer and Welcome basket of fruit/coffee/bottled water/chips & salsa and homemade cookies included in rates.

Certificate may be used: Nov. 1-Feb. 28, Sunday-Thursday, no holidays.

El Paradero Bed and Breakfast Inn

220 W Manhattan Ave
Santa Fe, NM 87501-2622
(505)988-1177 (866)558-0918 Fax:(505)988-3577
Internet: www.elparadero.com
E-mail: info@elparadero.com

Circa 1820. This historic bed and breakfast was originally a two-bedroom Spanish farmhouse that doubled in size to a Territorial style in 1860, was remodeled as a Victorian in 1912 and became a Pueblo Revival in 1920. All styles are present today and provide a walk through many years of history. Located in historic downtown Santa Fe, the inn is within easy walking distance to the Plaza and Canyon Road.

Innkeeper(s): Sue Jett. $110-200. 15 rooms, 13 with PB, 7 with FP, 2 suites, 1 conference room. Breakfast and afternoon tea included in rates. Types of meals: Full gourmet bkfst and early coffee/tea.

Certificate may be used: Nov. 1-March 31, excluding weekends and holidays (Nov. 24-28, Dec. 20-31).

Hacienda Nicholas Bed & Breakfast

320 East Marcy Street
Santa Fe, NM 87501
(505)992-8385 (888)284-3170 Fax:(505)982-8572
Internet: www.haciendanicholas.com
E-mail: info@haciendanicholas.com

Circa 1930. Tranquility surrounds Hacienda Nicholas, a historic Santa Fe B&B inn that boasts eco-friendly lodging in New Mexico. Experience the extreme comfort and modern conveniences with a minimal environmental impact. Thick Adobe walls and an interior courtyard provide a quiet, peaceful retreat. Guest rooms feature upscale amenities for total relaxation and pampering. Linger over an organic breakfast that includes vegetarian options. Indulge in homemade treats served at teatime and gather for the fireside wine and cheese hour. The inn's luxurious Absolute Nirvana Spa in the back garden offers Asian spa rituals, rose petal baths and a selection of massages and facials. Ask about special packages available. Fitness privileges are offered at the El Gaucho Health Club.

Innkeeper(s): Anna Tenaglia. $100-249. 11 rooms, 7 with PB, 3 with FP, 3 suites, 1 conference room. Breakfast and afternoon tea included in rates. Types of meals: Full gourmet bkfst, veg bkfst, early coffee/tea, snacks/refreshments, hors d'oeuvres, wine, Local dishes featured at breakfast and during happy hour, utilizing natural and organic ingredients in all cooking and baking, bottomless plates of cookies and pastries available all afternoon and nightly wine & appetizer hour in front of the roaring fire or outside on the garden patio.

Certificate may be used: Nov. 1-Feb. 28, Sunday-Thursday, no holidays.

The Madeleine Bed and Breakfast Inn

106 Faithway St
Santa Fe, NM 87501
(505)982-3465 (888)877-7622 Fax:(505)982-8572
Internet: www.madeleineinn.com
E-mail: info@madeleineinn.com

Circa 1886. Gracing a quiet neighborhood in Santa Fe, New Mexico, this historic and romantic bed and breakfast combines Asian and Victorian decor. Guests are invited for complimentary tea, wine and cheese at Hacienda Nicholas, just across the street. Each delightful guest bedroom is a warm and inviting retreat that features generous upscale amenities to please and pamper both business and leisure travelers. After a satisfying breakfast indulge the senses at the Madeleine's Absolute Nirvana Spa, Tea Room and Gardens. Select a

therapeutic massage or treatment from the spa menu. Schedule a facial, bathe in a sea of rose petals and be sure to visit the blissful gardens and the tea room for delectable treats. Ask about special packages.

Innkeeper(s): Carolyn Lee. $110-210. 7 rooms with PB, 4 with FP, 2 cottages. Breakfast, afternoon tea and nightly wine & appetizer hour included in rates. Types of meals: Full gourmet bkfst, early coffee/tea, hors d'oeuvres and wine.
Certificate may be used: Nov. 1-Feb. 28, Sunday-Thursday, no holidays.

Taos

Adobe and Stars B&B Inn

PO Box 2285
Taos, NM 87571
(575)776-2776 (800)211-7076 Fax:(575)776-2872
Internet: www.TaosAdobe.com
E-mail: jsalathiel@yahoo.com

Circa 1996. Sangre de Christo Mountains provide breathtaking views while staying at the Adobe and Stars Bed and Breakfast Inn located in Taos, New Mexico. It's a few minutes from either the historic Taos Plaza or the Taos Ski Valley slopes. The guest room decor complements the Southwestern adobe exterior. Kiva fireplaces, wood beam ceilings, hand-carved furnishings and artwork complete the look. Radiant heat floors, terra cotta tiles and a Jacuzzi tub or double shower are pleasant amenities. Several rooms boast a mountain or mesa view. Hearty country breakfasts include a changing daily entree and homemade baked goods, fruit, juice and coffee served in the dining room or on the patio. Soak in the hot tub under a starry sky after rafting down the Rio Grande. Bike or hike in the national forest or ski local slopes. Shops, galleries and restaurants are nearby.

Innkeeper(s): Judy Salathiel. $95-205. 8 rooms with PB, 8 with FP, 5 with WP. Breakfast and snacks/refreshments included in rates. Types of meals: Full bkfst.
Certificate may be used: April 15-May 15; Nov. 3-21, subject to availabilty.

Casa Benavides Inn

137 Kit Carson Rd
Taos, NM 87571-5949
(575) 758-1772 (800) 552-1772 Fax:(575)758-5738
Internet: www.taos-casabenavides.com
E-mail: casabena@newmex.com

Circa 1860. Translated, the name of this historic inn located one-half block east of Taos Plaza, means The House of Good Life. The adobe architecture of the buildings includes high ceilings, vigas, cedar latillas, Mexican tiles, handmade wood-burning fireplaces, wrought iron chandeliers, flagstone and original oak floors. Relax by the fireplace in the formal lobby on hand-carved furniture with leather cushions. Indian artifacts, Kit Carson's piano and a collection of early Taos artists' paintings are displayed. Guest bedrooms feature upscale amenities, luxury linens, down comforters and Natural Beginnings personal products. Breakfast in the colorful dining room may include yogurt, fresh fruit, Barbara's homemade "drop dead" granola, baked goods, and an entree such as eggs smothered in red chili with cheese, accompanied by tortillas, waffles, French toast or blueberry pancakes. Walk to nearby museums, galleries, and gift shops. Soak in one of the two outdoor hot tubs.

Innkeeper(s): Tom McCarthy, Barbara McCarthy. $105-300. 38 rooms with PB, 24 with FP, 5 with HT, 20 suites, 1 cottage, 2 conference rooms. Breakfast included in rates. Types of meals: Full gourmet bkfst, early coffee/tea and afternoon tea.
Certificate may be used: November-March, subject to availability.

The Historic Taos Inn

125 Paseo Del Pueblo Norte
Taos, NM 87571-5901
(575) 758-2233 (800) 826-7466 Fax:(575)758-5776
Internet: www.taosinn.com
E-mail: taosinn@newmex.com

Circa 1936. Voted by National Geographic Traveler as one of "America's 54 Great Inns", The Taos Inn is a historic landmark with sections dating back to the 1600s. The inn's authentic adobe pueblo architecture enhances the inviting wood-burning fireplaces (kivas), vigas and wrought iron accents. Handsomely decorated rooms include reflections of the area's exotic tri-cultural heritage of Spanish, Anglo and Indian in the hand-loomed Guatamalan Indian bedspreads, antique armoires and Taos furniture. The Doc Martin's well reviewed restaurant includes the legendary Adobe Bar. Ancient Taos Pueblo and the historic taos Plaza are nearby.

Innkeeper(s): Douglas Smith, Carolyn Haddock. $75-250. 44 rooms with PB, 3 with FP, 3 suites. Types of meals: Full gourmet bkfst, veg bkfst, early coffee/tea, gourmet lunch, snacks/refreshments and gourmet dinner. Restaurant on premises.
Certificate may be used: All year, Sunday-Thursday, subject to availability. Holiday period exclusions apply. Call for availablity and reservations.

Touchstone Inn, Spa & Gallery

110 Mabel Dodge Ln
Taos, NM 87571
(575)779-8712
Internet: www.touchstoneinn.com
E-mail: touchstoneinn@gmail.com

Circa 1800. Touchstone Inn is a quiet, historic adobe estate secluded among tall trees at the edge of Taos Pueblo lands. The grounds have an unobstructed view of Taos Mountain. USA Today calls it "the place to stay in Taos." The inn, connected to a spa and a gallery, features cozy rooms with fireplaces, luxurious textiles, intimate patios and exquisite tiled baths (four of which have Jacuzzi tubs). The inn offers full gourmet vegetarian and continental breakfasts. The spa offers massages, yoga and art classes, facials and therapeutic baths and wraps. Guests enjoy the outdoor hot tub with choice vistas of Taos Mountain. Taos Ski valley is 18 miles to the north.

Innkeeper(s): Brad Gordon, Amber Gordon. $135-350. 9 rooms with PB, 3 with FP, 4 with WP, 1 suite, 1 conference room. Breakfast and snacks/refreshments included in rates. Types of meals: Full gourmet bkfst, We have vegetarian breakfasts available upon request. If you book a large party like a birthday bash, girls weekend away and or reunions then we can cater for you. Call us to ask our classically trained Chef for details. 575-779-8712.

Certificate may be used: Monday-Wednesday, November-April excluding holidays and fiestas. Subject to availability. Free night does not include breakfast. Not valid on Groups and Destination Spa Packages.

Tijeras

Heavenly Lodge

33 Big Dipper Rd
Tijeras, NM 87059
(505) 474-8359
Internet: www.heavenlylodge.us
E-mail: heavenlylinda@gmail.com

Circa 1975. Perfect for weddings and special events as well as corporate conferences and spiritual retreats, this peaceful three-story gabled lodge is located in Tijeras, New Mexico. Heavenly Lodge Conference and Retreat Center sits on six acres with pines and a reflecting pond in the East Mountains just 30 minutes from Albuquerque International Airport. Groups can gather in the two large living rooms with fireplaces. The sunroom and second-floor balcony are break-out areas. Accommodations include pleasant guest bedrooms that can sleep 6 to 12 people. Delicious meals are prepared by a certified chef and served in the open dining area, or plan to cook together in the fully equipped kitchen. A nearby park boasts jogging trails, basketball and badminton courts. Take a day trip to Santa Fe.

Innkeeper(s): Linda Dunnill. $69-138. 4 rooms, 1 cottage, 1 guest house, 1 conference room. Types of meals: Meals can be cooked and served to groups of 8 or more. Prices and menus upon request.

Certificate may be used: Anytime, last minute-based on availability

New York

Adirondack

Adirondack Pines Bed & Breakfast & Vacation Cabin's

1257 Valentine Road
Adirondack, NY 12808
(518)494-5249
Internet: www.adirondackpines.com
E-mail: stay@adirondackpines.com

Circa 1837. Surrounded by year-round scenic beauty, there is much to experience while staying at this historic 1837 Country Farmhouse, just two minutes from Schroon Lake's beach and boat launch. Relax in the living room with cable TV. Antiques and handmade quilts accent the pleasant decor of the air-conditioned guest bedrooms. The Master Suite boasts wide plank flooring, a refrigerator, gas stove and a two-person Jacuzzi tub. The spacious Balsam Room offers a Queen and a twin bed. A small room with a twin bed accommodates a fourth person. Linger over a candlelit country breakfast in the dining room by the wood stove. A private, newly renovated three-bedroom house with a gas fireplace is also available. Soak up nature while strolling the 100 acres of grounds. Ski nearby Gore Mountain or hike Pharaoh Mountain for breathtaking views.

Innkeeper(s): Dan Lindsley-Freebern, Nancy Lindsley-Freebern. $65-175. 3 rooms, 2 with PB, 1 with FP, 2 guest houses. Breakfast and snacks/refreshments included in rates. Types of meals: Country bkfst.

Certificate may be used: Sunday-Thursday, subject to availability.

Allegany

Gallets House B&B

1759 Four Mile Rd
Allegany, NY 14706-9724
(716) 373-7493 Fax:(716)806-0384
Internet: www.galletshouse.com
E-mail: info@galletshouse.com

Circa 1896. Built by the innkeeper's great uncle Joseph Gallets, who was an oil producer, lumberman and farmer, this historic Victorian home features a third-floor museum with original family photos and heirlooms to browse through. Relax by the fireplaces in the parlor and common room. Enjoy refreshments on the 100-foot porch. Elegant air-conditioned guest bedrooms feature private baths and robes. Two rooms boast whirlpool tubs. Perfect for families and pets, the Carriage House Apartment has three bedrooms, two baths and a full kitchen. Fruits, homemade breads and biscuits are a prelude to sumptuous hot entrees and Joan's memorable French toast or apple cinnamon

pancakes for breakfast in the formal dining room. The B&B is near ski resorts, Allegany State Park, St. Bonaventure University, golf courses and a main snowmobile trail. Ask about romance packages and monthly murder mysteries.

Innkeeper(s): Joan & Gary Boser & Cheri Stady. $79-140. 6 rooms with PB, 2 with FP, 2 with WP, 2 two-bedroom and 1 three-bedroom suites, 1 cottage, 3 guest houses, 1 conference room. Breakfast and snacks/refreshments included in rates. Types of meals: Full gourmet bkfst, veg bkfst, early coffee/tea, afternoon tea and Murder mystery dinner package.

Certificate may be used: Anytime, subject to availability.

Amenia

Hilltop House

43 Depot Hill Rd
Amenia, NY 12501-5602
(845) 789-1354 Fax:845 789 1355
Internet: www.hilltophousebb.com
E-mail: info@hilltophousebb.com

Circa 1909. Offering elegant style and classic comfort in the Berkshire foothills of the Hudson Valley, this Dutch Colonial boasts Victorian flair. Relax on wicker furnishings on the porch, sit in the gazebo or by the stone fireplace in the living room and gather for afternoon tea. Cheerful guest rooms and a suite are accented with antiques and quilts. Hearty gourmet country breakfasts are served to start each day right. Mountain bikes are available to ride on the Harlem Valley Rail Trail. Nearby Western Stables boast 5,000 acres for horseback riding. The area surrounding Armenia, New York features many cultural attractions and regional outdoor activities.

Innkeeper(s): Sandy Johnson, West Johnson. $145-225. 5 rooms, 3 with PB, 1 two-bedroom suite. Breakfast and afternoon tea included in rates. Types of meals: Country bkfst, veg bkfst, early coffee/tea, High nutrient smoothies available, fresh baked cookies and lemonade.

Certificate may be used: November-March, Sunday-Thursday.

Auburn

10 Fitch

10 Fitch Avenue
Auburn, NY 13021
(315)255-0934 Fax:(315)255-1660
Internet: www.10Fitch.com
E-mail: innkeeper@10Fitch.com

Circa 1920. Stay at this romantic, adults-only Colonial Revival mansion for a truly luxurious setting in the Finger Lakes region of Auburn, New York. Elegant and fully restored to preserve its character while adding amenities, the spacious yet intimate ambiance reflects upscale boutique accommodations in a quiet neighborhood amid the historic district. Relax in the expansive back yard with perennial gardens, screened-in gazebo, koi ponds and waterfalls. Sitting rooms include the library, formal living room and sunroom. Guest suites are professionally decorated with designer fabrics, original artwork, a mix of antiques, modern and handcrafted furnishings, fireplaces, premium spa bedding, European rain showers and Jacuzzi tubs. Breakfast is served daily in the dining room, or order room service in advance. Explore Owasco Lake and nearby wineries from this central location between Syracuse and Rochester.

Innkeeper(s): Cheryl Barber. $200-330. 3 rooms, 3 with FP, 1 with WP, 3 suites. Breakfast and snacks/refreshments included in rates. Types of meals: Full bkfst, veg bkfst, early coffee/tea, picnic lunch, hors d'oeuvres, Breakfast in suite, romantic in-suite picnic dinner for two and picnic lunch basket.

Certificate may be used: November-April, no holiday weeks, subject to availability, not valid with any other gift card, certificate, promo or offer..

Averill Park

La Perla at the Gregory House, Country Inn & Restaurant

Rt 43 PO Box 401
Averill Park, NY 12018-0401
(518)674-3774 Fax:(518)674-8916
Internet: www.gregoryhouse.com
E-mail: innkeeper@gregoryhouse.com

Circa 1830. Stockbroker Elias Gregory built what is now the restaurant, as his Colonial home in the 1800s. The newer B&B inn, just twelve years old, blends well with the original house to retain the ambiance of its Victorian heritage. Gather by the dramatic fireplace in the common room which boasts vaulted ceilings, comfy furniture and a big-screen TV. The decor of each well-appointed guest bedroom is inviting. Award-winning La Perla offers Italian continental cuisine and is personally run by innkeeper Alfonso. This rural country town is surrounded by the Adirondacks, Berkshires, Hudson River, Saratoga and Albany with a variety of historic and scenic attractions.

Innkeeper(s): Anna Maria, Alfonso Acampora. $100-125. 12 rooms with PB, 1 conference room. Breakfast included in rates. Types of meals: Cont. Restaurant on premises.

Certificate may be used: November-April, Sunday-Thursday.

Avon

White Oak Bed and Breakfast

277 Genesee Street
Avon, NY 14414
(585)226-6735
Internet: whiteoakbandb.com
E-mail: avon-bnb@frontiernet.net

Circa 1860. Built as a summer home in the 1860s, this distinctive Second Empire Victorian with a mansard roof and wraparound porch has been recently renovated to retain its original charm and traditional decor. A private den/parlor with TV/VCR and board games is a convenient gathering place. Well-placed period furnishings accent the guest bedrooms and spacious Pine Suite. Enjoy the expansive view from the dining room while savoring home-baked breads, fresh fruit, and perhaps a broccoli cheddar omelette with home fries and bacon for breakfast. The one acre of gardens, with flowers for every

season, include private sitting areas to chat. Visit nearby Genesee Country Village, a living history village or take day trips to explore the scenic Finger Lakes Region.

Innkeeper(s): Barbara Herman. $105-125. 3 rooms with PB. Breakfast and snacks/refreshments included in rates. Types of meals: Country bkfst, veg bkfst, early coffee/tea and picnic lunch.

Certificate may be used: Nov. 1-April 30, subject to availability.

Bainbridge

Berry Hill Gardens B&B

242 Ward Loomis Rd.
Bainbridge, NY 13733
(607)967-8745 (800)497-8745 Fax:(607)967-2227
Internet: www.berryhillgardens.com
E-mail: info@berryhillgardens.com

Circa 1820. Located off the beaten path on a secluded lane, this country bed and breakfast graces the heart of Central New York.

Two different B&B experiences are offered on 300 acres of gardens, lakes, ponds, woods and meadows. Berry Hill Gardens Inn is situated on a hilltop overlooking miles of rural beauty; the Buckthorn Lodge is poised in a sunny glen deep in the woods. Find comfortable antiques, fireplaces and all-natural luxury linens. Delicious breakfasts are served in a friendly, healthy informal atmosphere. Conveniently centered between Bainbridge, Afton and Oxford, the scenic Leatherstocking Region features museums, sporting facilities, artisans and fascinating history.

Innkeeper(s): Jean Fowler. $115-190. 8 rooms with PB, 3 with FP, 1 guest house. Breakfast and snacks/refreshments included in rates. Types of meals: Country bkfst and early coffee/tea.

Certificate may be used: Jan. 2-April 30, anytime. May 1-Dec. 20, Sunday through Thursday only. Holidays and special events excluded.

Bloomfield

Abner Adams House Bed and Breakfast

2 Howard Ave.
Bloomfield, NY 14469
(585) 657-4681 (888) 657-4682
Internet: www.abneradamshouse.com
E-mail: innkeeper@abneradamshouse.com

Circa 1810. Three scenic acres surround historic Abner Adams House Bed and Breakfast in Bloomfield. This upstate New York B&B sits in the Finger Lakes region near Canandaigua and Rochester, amid the wine trails. Take a nap in the hammock under a shade tree, sit on a rocker on the screened porch or walk along wooded trails with inviting benches. Comfortable furniture, books, games and movies are enjoyed in the Keeping Room with original beehive oven. The dining room features a guest amenity cabinet with utensils, microwave, snacks and refrigerator stocked with beverages. Select a guest room with amenities that may include a fireplace, sitting area, balcony overlooking the gardens and a balneotherapy or champagne massage clawfoot tub for two. Indulge in a hearty country breakfast each morning.

Innkeeper(s): Bob Dobberstein, Lynda Dobberstein. $159-179. 3 rooms with PB, 3 with FP, 2 with WP, 1 two-bedroom suite. Breakfast and snacks/refreshments included in rates. Types of meals: Country bkfst, veg bkfst, early

coffee/tea, Lactose free and gluten free and vegetarian available upon request.
Certificate may be used: Sunday-Thursday, November-April, subject to availability, holidays and holiday weekends excluded.

Blooming Grove

The Dominion House

50 Old Dominion Road
Blooming Grove, NY 10914
(845)496-1826 Fax:(845)496-3492
Internet: www.thedominionhouse.com
E-mail: kathy@thedominionhouse.com

Circa 1880. At the end of a country lane in the scenic Hudson Valley, this Victorian Farmhouse has been adorning four-and-a-half acres since 1880. Original marble mantels, ornate cornice work, wide-plank floors, large pocket doors and eleven-foot ceilings with plaster medallions reflect a well-maintained elegance. The library offers a large book selection or relax by the fire in the oak den. Play a game of pool on the slate-top table and listen to music in the parlor. Large guest bedrooms and a private Honeymoon Cottage are furnished with antiques. A hearty breakfast is served in the dining room with specialty dishes that may include caramel sticky buns, featherlight scones, stuffed croissants, peach French toast and sausage. Swim in the inground pool, play horseshoes or relax on the wraparound porch.

Innkeeper(s): Kathy Spear, Joe Spear. $150-199. 4 rooms, 1 with PB, 1 cottage. Breakfast and snacks/refreshments included in rates. Types of meals: Country bkfst and early coffee/tea.

Certificate may be used: Sunday-Thursday, November-April, subject to availability. Excludes holidays.

Brockport

The Victorian B&B

320 S Main St
Brockport, NY 14420-2253
(585)637-7519 Fax:(585)637-7519
Internet: www.victorianbandb.com
E-mail: sk320@aol.com

Circa 1889. Within walking distance of the historic Erie Canal, this Queen Anne Victorian inn is located on Brockport's Main Street. Visitors select from five second-floor guest rooms, all with phones, private baths and TVs. Victorian furnishings are found throughout the inn. A favorite spot is the solarium, with its three walls of windows and fireplace, perfect for curling up with a book or magazine. Two first-floor sitting areas with fireplaces also provide relaxing havens for guests. Lake Ontario is just 10 miles away, and visitors will find much to explore in Brockport and Rochester. Brockport is home to the State University of New York and Niagara Falls is an hour away.

Innkeeper(s): Sharon Kehoe. $79-150. 5 rooms with PB. Breakfast and afternoon tea included in rates. Types of meals: Country bkfst, veg bkfst and early coffee/tea.

Certificate may be used: Oct. 1 to April 30, no holidays or special events.

Brooktondale

Eagles Rest at White Church

637 White Church Road
Brooktondale, NY 14817-0115
(607) 539-6810 (800) 862-7846
Internet: eaglesrestbb.com
E-mail: reservations@eaglesrestbb.com

Circa 1895. Surround yourself with the quiet countryside of the White Church Valley. Enjoy homemade breads, muffins, organic eggs, and French toast in a 19th-century farmhouse. Play a Mozart symphony or Chopsticks on the baby grand piano in the living room. A combination of antiques and modern furniture grace the rooms with original pine floors. Look to the west to see the beaver in the pond then look to the east to see woods full of deer and wild turkeys. Reserve one of the three guest rooms in the house or the unique Coachmen R.V. Suite. The suite offers private accommodations for up to four adults and two children. Use this bed and breakfast as a home base for visiting Cornell University and Ithaca College. Explore the forests, waterfalls, farmlands, and abandoned railroad beds of the valley or join in supporting the lively art scene at local galleries. Sample wines, limoncella, and grappa at Six Mile Creek Vineyard.

Innkeeper(s): Dorann Martin, John Martin. $69-175. 3 rooms, 1 two-bedroom suite. Breakfast, snacks/refreshments and Homemade breads & muffins included in rates. Types of meals: Full bkfst and veg bkfst.

Certificate may be used: October-April, Anytime; May-September, Sunday-Wednesday.

Campbell

Halcyon Place Bed & Breakfast

11 Maple Lane
Campbell, NY 14821
(607) 583-4311
Internet: www.plus.google.com/116292912529660026060/about?gl=US&hl=en
E-mail: halcyonplbb@gmail.com

Circa 1850. Named after a Greek word that means peace and tranquility, this circa 1840 Greek Revival inn is a landmark Steuben County home surrounded by two acres of open fields and scenic vistas. Its classic six-over-six windows, graceful columns, pine floors and detailed woodwork are accented by period antique furnishings. Relax by the fire in the parlor or sit on the wicker-filled porch. Browse the new herb and antique shop in the former harness shop. Gorgeous guest bedrooms with ample space feature four-poster, canopy and tiger maple beds, toile fabrics and rich paint colors. A gourmet breakfast is served in the dining room with favorites like rum sticky buns or pear gingerbread and satisfying seasonal entrees. Explore the Keuka Lake Wine Trail, or nearby Corning.

Innkeeper(s): Yvonne Allen. $135-185. 4 rooms, 2 with PB, 1 with FP, 1 two-bedroom suite. Breakfast included in rates. Types of meals: Full gourmet bkfst and veg bkfst.

Certificate may be used: November-April, subject to availability. Excludes holidays.

Canandaigua

1792 Filigree Inn

5406 Bristol Valley Rd.(RT.64S.)
Canandaigua, NY 14424
(585)229-5460 (888)560-7614
Internet: www.filigreeinn.com
E-mail: filigree@filigreeinn.com

Circa 1792. Escape to 1792 Filigree Inn, a four-season country retreat in the Finger Lakes wine country region of New York. Relax on 180 breathtaking acres in Bristol Hills of Canandaigua. Renovated guest suites boast air-conditioned comfort, feather beds, whirlpool tubs, fully equipped kitchens, entertainment centers and a private deck. Each refrigerator is stocked with breakfast foods to enjoy when desired. Ski and snowboard at local Bristol Mountain Resort or try cross-county trails at the nearby Cumming Nature Center. Weddings are popular at this bed and breakfast amid a gorgeous setting and a peaceful ambiance. Ask about special promotions and packages available.
Innkeeper(s): Don Simmons, Connie Simmons. $100-180. 8 rooms with PB, 8 with FP, 8 with WP, 4 two-bedroom suites. Breakfast and snacks/refreshments included in rates. Types of meals: Full bkfst.

Certificate may be used: Sunday-Thursday only, subject to availability.

Candor

The Edge of Thyme, A B&B Inn

6 Main St
Candor, NY 13743-0048
(607)659-5155 (800)722-7365 Fax:(607)659-5155
Internet: www.edgeofthyme.com
E-mail: innthyme@twcny.rr.com

Circa 1840. Originally the summer home of John D. Rockefeller's secretary, this two-story Georgian-style inn offers gracious accommodations a short drive from Ithaca. The inn sports many interesting features, including an impressive stair-

way, marble fireplaces, parquet floors, pergola (arbor) and windowed porch with leaded glass. Guests may relax in front of the inn's fireplace, catch up with reading in its library or watch television in the sitting room. An authentic turn-of-the-century full breakfast is served, and guests also may arrange for special high teas.
Innkeeper(s): Frank Musgrave. $95-145. 5 rooms, 3 with PB, 2 suites. Breakfast included in rates. Types of meals: Full gourmet bkfst, veg bkfst, early coffee/tea and High Tea by appointment.

Certificate may be used: Sunday-Thursday. Not valid in May, excluding specific weekends, Anytime, Last Minute-Based on Availability.

Cazenovia

Brae Loch Inn

5 Albany St
Cazenovia, NY 13035-1403
(315)655-3431 Fax:(315)655-4844
Internet: www.braelochinn.com
E-mail: thebraelochinn@gmail.com

Circa 1805. Hunter green awnings accentuate the attractive architecture of the Brae Loch. Since 1946 the inn has been owned and operated by the same family. A Scottish theme is evident throughout, including in the inn's restaurant. Four of the oldest rooms have fireplaces (non-working). Stickley, Harden and antique furniture add to the old-world atmosphere, and many rooms offer canopy beds. Guest rooms are on the second floor above the restaurant.
Innkeeper(s): Jim Barr, Val Barr. $85-155. 12 rooms with PB, 3 with FP, 3 with WP, 1 conference room. Breakfast and You can have a getaway package that includes dinner or brunch included in rates. Types of meals: Cont, Sun. brunch, wine and gourmet dinner. Restaurant on premises.

Certificate may be used: Sunday-Thursday.

Clarence

Asa Ransom House

10529 Main St
Clarence, NY 14031-1684
(716)759-2315 (800)841-2340 Fax:(716)759-2791
Internet: www.asaransom.com
E-mail: innfo@asaransom.com

Circa 1853. Set on spacious lawns, behind a white picket fence, the Asa Ransom House rests on the site of the first

grist mill built in Erie County. Silversmith Asa Ransom constructed an inn and grist mill here in response to the Holland Land Company's offering of free land to anyone who would start and operate a tavern. A specialty of the dining room is "Veal Perrott" and "Pistachio Banana Muffins."
Innkeeper(s): innkee. $120-185. 10 rooms with PB, 9 with FP, 2 with WP, 2 two-bedroom suites, 1 conference room. Breakfast included in rates. Types of meals: Full gourmet bkfst, early coffee/tea, lunch, afternoon tea, snacks/refreshments, wine and dinner. Restaurant on premises.

Certificate may be used: March-June, September-Dec. 15, Sunday-Thursday.

Cold Spring

Pig Hill Inn

73 Main St
Cold Spring, NY 10516-3014
(845) 265-9247 Fax:(845)265-9154
Internet: www.pighillinn.com
E-mail: pighillinn@aol.com

Circa 1808. The antiques at this stately three-story inn can be purchased, and they range from Chippendale to chinoiserie style. Rooms feature formal English and Adirondack decor with special touches such as four-poster or brass beds, painted rockers and, of course, pigs. The delicious breakfasts can be shared with guests in the Victorian conservatory dining room or a tri-level garden, or it may be served in the privacy of your room. The inn is about an hour out of New York City, and the train station is only two blocks away.

Innkeeper(s): Kyle R. Gibbs. $150-250. 9 rooms with PB, 6 with FP, 2 with WP, 1 conference room. Breakfast, afternoon tea and Refreshments or Afternoon Tea included in rates. Types of meals: Full gourmet bkfst, wine and room service.

Certificate may be used: Monday-Thursday, Nov. 1-April 30, excluding holidays.

Corinth

Agape Farm B&B and Paintball

4839 Rt 9N
Corinth, NY 12822-1704
(518)654-7341 Fax:(518)654-7341
Internet: www.agape-farm.com/
E-mail: agapefarmbnb@roadrunner.com

Circa 1870. Amid 33 acres of fields and woods, this Adirondack farmhouse is home to chickens and horses, as well as guests seeking a refreshing getaway. Visitors have their choice of six guest rooms, all with ceiling fans, phones, private baths and views of the tranquil surroundings. The inn's wraparound porch lures many visitors, who often enjoy a  glass of icy lemonade. Homemade breads, jams, jellies and muffins are part of the full breakfast served here, and guests are welcome to pick berries or gather a ripe tomato from the garden. A trout-filled stream on the grounds flows to the Hudson River, a mile away.

Innkeeper(s): Fred Koch, Sigrid Koch. $120-150. 3 rooms with PB, 1 conference room. Breakfast and snacks/refreshments included in rates. Types of meals: Full gourmet bkfst, veg bkfst and early coffee/tea.

Certificate may be used: Sept. 15-June 1, no holidays, premium rooms.

Corning

Rosewood Inn

134 E 1st St
Corning, NY 14830-2711
(607)962-3253
Internet: www.rosewoodinn.com
E-mail: stay@rosewoodinn.com

Circa 1855. Rosewood Inn was originally built as a Greek Revival house. In 1917, the interior and exterior were remodeled in an English Tudor style. Original black walnut and oak woodwork grace the interior, decorated with authentic wallpapers, period draperies and fine antiques. It is within walking distance to historic, restored Market Street and museums.

Innkeeper(s): Stewart Sanders, Suzanne Sanders. $109-289. 7 rooms with PB, 2 suites. Breakfast, afternoon tea and afternoon refreshments included in rates. Types of meals: Full bkfst.

Certificate may be used: November-March, subject to availability. Not valid on holiday weekends.

Cornwall

Cromwell Manor Inn B&B

174 Angola Rd
Cornwall, NY 12518
(845) 534-7136
Internet: www.cromwellmanor.com
E-mail: cmi@hvc.rr.com

Circa 1820. Listed in the National Register of Historic Places, this stunning Greek Revival mansion sits on seven lush acres with scenic Hudson Valley views. It is elegantly furnished with period antiques and fine reproductions. The Chimneys Cottage, built in 1764, features romantic bedrooms  with a more rustic colonial decor. Awaken to the aroma of a gourmet breakfast served in the country dining room or outside veranda. More than 4,000 acres of hiking trails are steps from the front door. Arrange for a picnic or enjoy a fireside massage. Nap in the hammock, sip wine on the patio next to the classic fountain and watch the sunset from the rear lawn. The farm next door offers unique gifts and treats. Each season has plenty to explore.

Innkeeper(s): Eileen Hartmann. $165-380. 13 rooms, 12 with PB, 7 with FP, 3 total suites, including 1 two-bedroom suite, 1 conference room. Breakfast and afternoon tea included in rates. Types of meals: Full gourmet bkfst, early coffee/tea, picnic lunch, snacks/refreshments and room service.

Certificate may be used: Anytime, Sunday-Thursday, subject to availability, holidays excluded.

Dryden

The Turret House B&B

9 Library Street
Dryden, NY 13053
(607)708-8034
Internet: www.theturrethouse.com
E-mail: nancyw@twcny.rr.com

Circa 1897. Be part of a small-town community with a stay at this quaint Finger Lakes inn. Strike up a conversation while sitting on the wrap-around porch or meet the locals while dining at the volunteer operated Dryden Community Cafe. Gather your girlfriends for a getaway to take a wine and women trip along the Cayuga Wine Trail. The Lavender Oasis offers two twin beds. Get lost in a book while sitting on the window seat in the Dusty Rose Retreat. The Golden Luxury Suite is a romantic haven for honeymooners with a private sitting room, marble shower, and sunken tub. The Queen Anne Victorian inn is listed in the National Register of Historic Places but also includes modern amenities including wireless Internet, cable television, and air conditioning. Nibble on egg casserole, blueberry pancakes, or homemade scones in the cozy dining room each morning. The bed and breakfast is minutes from Ithaca and Cortland.

Innkeeper(s): Nancy Werany. $85-185. 3 rooms, 1 with PB, 1 suite. Types of meals: Full gourmet bkfst and early coffee/tea.

Certificate may be used: December, Sunday-Thursday.

Dundee

Sunrise Landing B&B

4986 Apple Road Extension
Dundee, NY 14837
(607)243-7548 (866)670-5253
Internet: www.sunriselandingbb.com
E-mail: relax@sunriselandingbb.com

Circa 2004. Poised on a wooded hillside on the west shore of Seneca Lake in Dundee, Sunrise Landing Bed & Breakfast is a perfect upstate New York getaway. A large dock, paddle boat and canoe make it easy to fully enjoy the scenic surroundings. Locally handcrafted furnishings and family heirlooms accent the contemporary architecture of this small country inn. Relax on a deck or patio or sit by the fire in the great room. Stay in one of the spacious guest suites that may feature a private balcony or patio, kitchen or mini-fridge stocked with beverages and snacks. Linger over a satisfying breakfast in the garden-view dining room. This Finger Lakes B&B is located on the wine trail with easy access to many local events and activities.

Innkeeper(s): Robert Schiesser, Barbara Schiesser. $155-255. 3 rooms, 4 with PB, 4 with HT, 4 total suites, including 1 four-bedroom suite, 2 guest houses. Full gourmet breakfast and homemade cookies every afternoon included in rates.

Certificate may be used: November and April only, No weekends.

East Marion

Arbor View House B&B

8900 Main Road
East Marion, NY 11939-0226
(631)477-8440 (800)963-8777
Internet: www.Arborviewhouse.com
E-mail: innkeeper@arborviewhouse.com

Circa 1820. Elegant and romantic in Long Island's North Fork Wine Country, this bed and breakfast was originally built with Federal architecture and was later renovated with Victorian design. Relax with afternoon tea and refreshments or sit by the fireplace with a good book. Luxurious guest bedrooms offer an assortment of pleasing amenities that include bottles of spring water, plush robes, entertainment centers and other comforts. Indulge in the spacious Champagne Suite with a whirlpool bath. An optional private deck can be reserved. The Merlot Room boasts a cast iron tub. A four-course brunch-style breakfast is served by candlelight in the formal dining room or al fresco when weather permits. Walk to the beach, tour a local winery or schedule a massage from an extensive spa services menu.

Innkeeper(s): Veda Daley Joseph, Wilfred Joseph. $195-325. 4 rooms with PB, 2 with WP, 1 suite. Breakfast, Sunday brunch, afternoon tea, snacks/refreshments and hors d'oeuvres included in rates. Types of meals: Full gourmet bkfst, early coffee/tea and picnic lunch.

Certificate may be used: Monday-Thursday, except February-March 15 and May-November.

Quintessentials B&B and Spa

8985 Main Rd
East Marion, NY 11939-1537
(631)477-9400 (800)444-9112
Internet: www.quintessentialsinc.com
E-mail: innkeeper@quintessentialsinc.com

Feel rejuvenated at this historic 1840's Victorian bed and breakfast in a sea captain's mansion with a Widow's Walk. Situated between the villages of Greenport and Orient on North Fork's East End of Long Island, it is an easy walk to the beach. Complimentary passes and towels are provided. Relax with afternoon tea on the wraparound porch. A second-floor office/sitting area features a computer, high-speed Internet access, fax, desk and refrigerator. Choose to stay in a guest bedroom with a fireplace, private sun deck, clawfoot tub or whirlpool bath and wireless Internet access. Each room boasts upscale amenities, fine linens, fresh flowers, monogrammed robes, mineral water and chocolates on pillows. Savor a lavish brunch-style breakfast and the famous afternoon high tea. Stroll the Japanese meditation garden and schedule a massage or European skin treatment at the on-site, full-service day spa.

Innkeeper(s): Sylvia Daley. $249-359. 5 rooms with PB, 2 suites. Breakfast, afternoon tea and snacks/refreshments included in rates.

Certificate may be used: Sunday-Thursday, December-March, Monday-Thursday, April-November excludes holidays and special events.

Geneva

Geneva On The Lake

1001 Lochland Rd, Rt 14S
Geneva, NY 14456
(315)789-7190 (1-8)00-3-GENEVA Fax:(315)789-0322
Internet: www.genevaonthelake.com
E-mail: info@genevaonthelake.com

Circa 1911. This opulent world-class inn is a replica of the Renaissance-era Lancellotti Villa in Frascati, Italy. It is listed in the National Register. Although originally built as a residence, it became a monastery for Capuchin monks. Now it is one of the finest resorts in the U.S.

Renovated under the direction of award-winning designer William Schickel, there are 10 two-bedroom suites, some with views of the lake. Here, you may have an experience as fine as Europe can offer, without leaving the country. Some compare it to the Grand Hotel du Cap-Ferrat on the French Riviera. The inn has been awarded four diamonds from AAA for more than two decades. Breakfast is available daily and on Sunday, brunch is served. Dinner is served each evening, and in the summer lunch is offered on the terrace.

Innkeeper(s): William J. Schickel. $165-795. 29 rooms with PB, 3 with FP, 23 suites, 3 conference rooms. Breakfast included in rates. Types of meals: Cont, gourmet dinner and room service. Restaurant on premises.

Certificate may be used: Sunday-Thursday, Nov. 1-June 20.

Granville

The Sheldon Mansion Inn Bed and Breakfast

48 North Street
Granville, NY 12832
(518) 642-0000
Internet: www.sheldonmansion.com
E-mail: information@sheldonmansion.com

Circa 1906. Visit Lake George, Saratoga, the Adirondacks, and Vermont from this historic and rare red-slate estate in Granville, New York. It served as a family home, hospital, and assisted-living facility before becoming a B&B. View the Green Mountains while enjoying breakfast in the solarium. Sip coffee while relaxing in a cushioned Adirondack chair on the verandah. Read a book or play a game in the sitting room, restored to its original purple hue based on Mrs. Sheldon's love of hydrangeas and lilacs. An original sketch of the mansion graces the walls of The Granville Suite. Fans of Norman Rockwell will enjoy the books and knickknacks in The Arlington Room. Celebrate the Saratoga Race Course with original items in The Saratoga Room. Host a special dinner or meeting in the formal dining room. Use WiFi and the copier in the English study for business.

Innkeeper(s): Stephen Lynch, Marianne Lynch. $100-150. 1 two-bedroom suite. Types of meals: Full gourmet bkfst, veg bkfst, early coffee/tea, afternoon tea and snacks/refreshments.

Certificate may be used: Anytime, subject to availability.

Greenport

Stirling House Bed & Breakfast

104 Bay Avenue
Greenport, NY 11944
(631)477-0654 (800)551-0654 Fax:(631)477-2885
Internet: www.stirlinghousebandb.com
E-mail: info@stirlinghousebandb.com

Circa 1880. Located in the heart of the village in the historic district, this water-view bed and breakfast offers old-world southern charm combined with modern luxuries. Attention to detail is given all year round. Unwind on the wraparound porch with changing views of Shelter Island. Explore quaint shops, museums and art galleries, all a few steps from the resort. Richly appointed guest bedrooms are inviting and pampering retreats. Dine on bold, contemporary cuisine at one of the award-winning area restaurants. Discover world-class Long Island Wine Country vineyards on a tasting tour or take to the water on an exclusive lighthouse cruise.

Innkeeper(s): Clayton Sauer. $199-395. 3 rooms with PB, 3 with FP, 1 with WP, 1 total suite, including 2 two-bedroom suites. Breakfast, afternoon tea, snacks/refreshments, wine and The only B&B on the North Fork of Long Island licensed by the State of New York to serve and sell wine. Wine and cheese are now served as alternating weekend snack and on request included in rates. Types of meals: Full gourmet bkfst, early coffee/tea, Homemade special home-baked treats on weekend afternoons and Wine & Cheese Hour announced during stay. Complimentary wine at check-in.

Certificate may be used: Nov. 1-April 30, Sunday-Thursday, subject to availability. Cannot be combined with other offers. Not valid for holidays or special events.

Haverstraw

Bricktown Inn

112 Hudson Avenue
Haverstraw, NY 10927
(845)429-8447
Internet: www.bricktowninnbnb.com
E-mail: michelle@bricktowninnbnb.com

Circa 1885. Surrounded by thousands of acres of scenic parkland, Bricktown Inn in Haverstraw, Rockland County, New York, is near the many historic sites and attractions of the Hudson River. Built in 1885, this brick Mansard Colonial home has been recently renovated to offer modern technology while retaining its original heritage. Furnished with antiques and family heirlooms, the Victorian B&B has many common areas to enjoy. The front porch boasts wicker, rockers and a swing. Conversation flows easily in the parlor or the garden room has a movie library and Internet access. Cookies and beverages are available at the hospitality station. Gather for breakfast after a restful sleep in a comfortable guest bedroom. New York City is only 40 minutes away.

Innkeeper(s): Michelle Natale, Joe Natale . $115-165. 4 rooms with PB. Breakfast, snacks/refreshments, Hospitality station with cookies, soda, coffee and tea included in rates. Types of meals: Full bkfst and early coffee/tea.

Certificate may be used: Anytime, subject to availability. Not valid during West Point graduation week.

Herkimer

Bellinger Rose Bed & Breakfast

611 W German St
Herkimer, NY 13350
(315)867-2197 (866)867-2197 Fax:(315)867-2197
Internet: www.bellingerrose.com
E-mail: bellingerrose@hotmail.com

Circa 1865. Originally built in 1865 by the prominent Bellinger family, this recently renovated inn exudes Victorian grace and charm. The exquisite decor and splendid antique furnishings invite pleasantries and relaxation. The common rooms include a formal parlor with a vintage player piano and a sitting room offering modern entertainment such as videos or DVD with surround sound. Both areas provide the warmth and ambiance of wood-burning marble fireplaces. In keeping with the name, a romantic theme of roses adorns the two unique guest bedrooms with spacious sitting areas. A full breakfast is served daily in the elegant dining room. The pampering continues with plush robes, a year-round hot tub, and a chair massage that is included with each night's stay.

Innkeeper(s): Chris Frost, Leon Frost. $129-169. 4 rooms with PB, 3 with FP, 2 with WP. Breakfast included in rates. Types of meals: Full bkfst and snacks/refreshments.

Certificate may be used: Sunday-Thursday, excludes July 25-28, subject to availability.

Hudson

Thyme In The Country

671 Fish & Game Road
Hudson, NY 12534
(518) 672-6166
Internet: www.thymeinthecountrybandb.com
E-mail: mary@thymeinthecountrybandb.com

Circa 1875. Find peace and comfort in an eco-friendly farmhouse inn in Hudson, New York. Life on the five pastoral acres is quiet and wholesome and the fresh scent of sun-dried linens promotse sweet dreams on an organic mattress. Try the inn's historic charm in the Sumac Room with a claw foot tub in the wainscoted bathroom or celebrate a girls weekend away in the Lavender Room and adjoining Chamomile Room. You can curl up in the recliner in the Rose Room with a book or a hot cup of tea. All guest rooms offer air conditioning, and Wi-Fi access. Look out over fields where cows graze around the solar panels that help support sustainable living habits. Fresh eggs and seasonal ingredients are combined each morning to create a delectable breakfast. Drive to the town's main thoroughfare, Warren Street, to browse through numerous antique shops.

Innkeeper(s): Mary Koch, Bill Koch. $130-180. 4 rooms, 3 with PB, 1 with FP, 1 two-bedroom suite, 1 cabin. Breakfast and snacks/refreshments included in rates. Types of meals: Full gourmet bkfst, veg bkfst, Sun. brunch, early coffee/tea, picnic lunch, afternoon tea, gourmet dinner, Made from scratch foods, most of it organic and local. Often from the back yard. Afternoon drinks are made from fresh fruits in the summer months and hot cider and ginger and local teas in the winter. Freshly baked goodies and breads are made from organic ingredients.

Certificate may be used: November to March, Sunday-Thursday.

Ithaca

Log Country Inn - B&B of Ithaca

PO Box 581
Ithaca, NY 14851
(607) 589-4771 (800) 274-4771 Fax:(607)589-4709
Internet: www.logtv.com/inn
E-mail: wanda@logtv.com

Circa 1969. As the name indicates, this bed & breakfast is indeed fashioned from logs and rests in a picturesque country setting surrounded by 100 wooded acres. The cozy rooms are rustic with exposed beams and country furnishings. There is also a Jacuzzi, fireplace and sauna. The decor is dotted with a European influence, as is the morning meal. Guests enjoy a full breakfast with blintzes or Russian pancakes. The innkeeper welcomes children and pets.

Innkeeper(s): Wanda Grunberg. $85-250. 9 rooms, 3 with PB, 1 suite. Breakfast included in rates. Types of meals: Full bkfst, veg bkfst and Wanda's famous cheese blintzes and Russian pancakes and potato pancakes.

Certificate may be used: Jan. 15-May 1, Sunday-Thursday.

Jay

Book and Blanket B&B

Rt 9N, PO Box 164
Jay, NY 12941-0164
(518)946-8323
Internet: www.bookandblanket.com
E-mail: bookinnjay@aol.com

Circa 1860. This Adirondack bed & breakfast served as the town's post office for many years and also as barracks for state troopers. Thankfully, however, it is now a restful bed & breakfast catering to the literary set. Guest rooms are named for authors and there are books in every nook and cranny of the house. Guests may even take a book home with them. Each of the guest rooms is comfortably furnished. The inn is a short walk from the Jay Village Green and the original site of the Historic Jay covered bridge.

Innkeeper(s): Kathy, Fred, Sam & Zoe the Basset Hound. $85-105. 3 rooms, 1 with PB. Breakfast, afternoon tea and snacks/refreshments included in rates. Types of meals: Full bkfst, veg bkfst and early coffee/tea.

Certificate may be used: Jan. 15 to June 20, Sunday-Thursday.

Keene Valley

Snow Goose Bed and Breakfast

1433 Route 73
Keene Valley, NY 12943
(518)576-9460
Internet: www.thesnowgoose.com
E-mail: snowgoosebnb@gmail.com

Circa 1900. All four seasons at this woodland retreat offer stress-free relaxation, adventure and scenic beauty. Gracing 13 acres at the foot of the Adirondack High Peaks and surrounded by hiking trails this is the perfect location for a wilderness experience, serene contemplation, artistic inspiration or relationship reconnection. Winter and summer sports are popular with the convenience of nearby Lake Placid, Whiteface Mountain and local Keene Valley attractions. The less active appreciate the art galleries, shops and fine dining opportunities. Watch movies in the TV Room or sit and read on the spacious porch with a hammock and Adirondack chairs. Stay in a guest room on the second floor accented with antiques and a fireplace with an electric insert among other pleasing amenities. The first-floor Legacies also includes a kitchenette and private entrance. A delicious breakfast is made with local organic ingredients when possible and served by the fireplace.

Innkeeper(s): Wayne Stoner, Amy Stoner. $100-140. 3 rooms with PB, 2 with FP.

Certificate may be used: Sunday-Thursday, November-March, subject to availability, excludes holidays.

Lewiston

Sunny's Roost Bed & Breakfast

421 Plain Street
Lewiston, NY 14092
(716)754-1161
Internet: www.sunnysroost.com
E-mail: sunny@sunnysroost.com

Circa 1900. Formerly a church rectory, Sunny's Roost now nurtures visitors to this area from it's Historic District location. From the inn, guests love to meander the streets and take in the shops, museums and special restaurants. In the summer there are midweek concerts in the park, but often guests just find their way to the back garden and listen amidst the flowers and lawns. Sunny is known for her scones - blueberry, pecan praline and cranberry-orange to name a few.

Innkeeper(s): Sunny and Bob. $125. 4 rooms, 3 with PB. Types of meals: Full bkfst.

Certificate may be used: November-March, subject to availability.

Livingston Manor

Guest House

408 Debruce Rd
Livingston Manor, NY 12758
(845)439-4000 Fax:(845)439-3344
Internet: www.theguesthouse.com
E-mail: andrea@theguesthouse.com

Circa 2000. This 40-acre estate near New York City boasts the best private fly fishing on the Willowemoc River. The inn has five guest bedrooms and three private cottages, one is located on the edge of the woods and across a footbridge that spans the river. This cottage has two bedrooms, a living room, an outdoor Jacuzzi, covered porches and even an enclosed dog run at the back. Guests in the main house and the cottages have views of the pond, woods, river and gardens. Breakfast is a sumptuous beginning to an active, or perhaps, a leisurely day. It includes items such as freshly pressed orange or grapefruit juice, eggs, French toast, pancakes, Belgian waffles and blueberry, corn or oat muffins. Near the inn are golf courses, many tennis courts, hiking, riding and biking trails, cross-country skiing, ice skating and a dozen antique stores.

Innkeeper(s): Andrea Plunket. $176-245. 6 cottages with PB, 4 with FP, 2 with HT, 2 with WP. Breakfast and "Cocktail hour" with hosts (complimentary) included in rates. Types of meals: Room service.

Certificate may be used: Mid-week all months except July and August. No holidays. Subject to availability.

Marcellus

Blakeslee House

3708 S Street Rd
Marcellus, NY 13108
(315)673-2881
Internet: www.blakesleehouse.com
E-mail: antiki@twcny.rr.com

Set among rolling hills, the Blakeslee House in Marcellus, New York, is a charming retreat. Relax in the sunroom and watch for deer or turkeys or wrap up in a comfy robe and listen to the sound of the wind rustling the leaves outside your window. The three guest rooms have queen or double beds, cable television, and central air conditioning. If friends or family are in the area, they are welcome guests for the home-style country breakfast. Spend the evening watching the sun set or taking a swim in the onsite pool. Hike in the woods right outside the inn. Play a round of golf at The Links at Sunset Ridge. Nearby Marcellus Park has horseshoes, beach volleyball, skateboarding, and summer concerts. Go ice skating, skiing, or snowshoeing during winter months. Take a day trip to Syracuse or the Finger Lakes wine country.

Innkeeper(s): Bev Blakeslee, Dave Blakeslee. $85-150. 3 rooms, 1 with PB, 1 with WP. Types of meals: Full bkfst.

Certificate may be used: January-February, Monday-Thursday, subject to availability.

Mount Tremper

Four Corners Country Inn

1564 Wittenberg Rd
Mount Tremper, NY 12457
(845) 688-3054
Internet: www.fourcornerscountryinn.com
E-mail: contact@FourCornersCountryInn.com

Circa 1850. Lavish grounds and the rolling hills of the Catskills set the backdrop in Mount Tremper, New York. The welcoming wrap-around porch is an enchanting place to relax. This inn is filled with antiques and pleasing amenities. Enjoy breakfast in bed during the week and a full buffet on the weekends. The onsite restaurant is open on the weekends and features year-round favorites and weekly specials with local ingredients. Light fare and specialty cocktails are served at the historic bar imported from Brooklyn. Fish for trout in Esopus Creek or hike the trails of surrounding mountains. Explore Saugerties, Phoenicia and Woodstock. Visit during the winter months for top-notch downhill ski slopes.

Innkeeper(s): Sibyle and Frank. $100-150. 8 rooms with PB. Breakfast included in rates. Types of meals: Country bkfst, Sun. brunch, picnic lunch, wine and dinner. Restaurant on premises.

Certificate may be used: January-April, Monday-Wednesday, no holidays, subject to availability.

New Lebanon

Shaker Meadows

14209 State Route 22
New Lebanon, NY 12125
(518)794-9385 Fax:(518)794-9381
Internet: www.shakermeadows.com
E-mail: shakermeadows@surfbest.net

Circa 1795. Bordering the original Shaker settlement in Lebanon Valley at Mount Lebanon, New York, Shaker Meadows Bed & Breakfast spans fifty acres of meadows and woods in the Berkshire Hills. Built in 1795 and boasting recent renovations, the B&B offers rustic charm and modern conveniences. Relax on a porch, in the library or by the lily pond. Saunter along the peaceful, mile-long walking trail. Enjoy access to a private, sandy beach on Queechy Lake with towels and chairs provided. Delightful guest bedrooms in the farmhouse and spacious suites in the creamery have pastoral and mountain views. Savor a complete breakfast in the dining room. Picnic areas are inviting spots for lunch.

Innkeeper(s): Sean Cowhig, Jean Cowhig. $85-195. 9 rooms, 6 with PB, 3 total suites, including 1 two-bedroom suite, 1 cottage, 1 guest house, 1 conference room. Breakfast, Rates include a full breakfast each morning in the Creamery Dining Room (Weekly Farmhouse rates do not include breakfast as most weekly guests prefer to prepare their own; however and breakfast can be requested for any morning at a rate of $10.00 per adult and $6.00 per child) included in rates. Types of meals: Full bkfst, early coffee/tea, picnic lunch, Lunch or dinner in the dining room will be provided for your family or workshop group of up to 50 people with previous arrangement. Rehearsal dinners, BBQs and tented parties on the 100'x24' outdoor tenting site can be arranged.

Certificate may be used: Any Sunday-Thursday night and any weekend last minute (one week ahead).

Newburgh

Stockbridge Ramsdell House

158 Montgomery St
Newburgh, NY 12550
(845)562-9310
Internet: www.stockbridgeramsdell.com
E-mail: sbramsdell@gmail.com

Circa 1870. This child-friendly gem in Newburgh, New York, overlooks the Hudson River and boasts original tapestries and period furniture and sits in the historic district of town. A brick Victorian, it was originally the home of the Erie Railroad president. Now you can wake each morning in a comfortable guest room with river views. The aroma of freshly brewed coffee leads the way to a full hot breakfast each morning. Afterwards walk to restaurants, a spa or tour boats at the Newburgh Marina. Spend a day at Dia:Beacon, the world's largest contemporary art museum. The country's largest sculpture garden is also nearby at Storm King Art Center. A shop and stay discount package is available for those who wish to look for deals in the 200 stores at Woodbury Common Premium Outlets. Weekend retreats for up to ten quilters are offered on a regular basis or plan a visit during one of the many local festivals.

Innkeeper(s): Nancy Russell. $95-175. 5 rooms with PB, 2 with FP. Breakfast and afternoon tea included in rates. Types of meals: Full bkfst and early coffee/tea.

Certificate may be used: Dec. 1-March 31, excluding holidays, subject to availability.

Potsdam

Siam Classic Inn & Spa

62 Elm Street
Potsdam, NY 13676
(315)265-1893 (866)223-7293 Fax:(315)265-3494
Internet: www.siamclassicinnandspa.com/
E-mail: siamclassicinnandspa@gmail.com

Circa 1883. Travel through the Thai heritage without leaving North America. Each guest room at this historic Victorian home in Potsdam, New York, is renovated to reflect an era of the Siam Kingdom with furnishings, artwork and photographs. Snuggle in a cotton robe by a Tiffany lamp in a room filled with Thai-inspired scents. A full Thai breakfast is served in the garden on the weekends; enjoy an American breakfast with an ethnic twist during the week. Located in the heart of town, walk to SUNY Potsdam or Clarkson University. Explore the natural beauty of the Adirondack Mountains or watch ocean-going vessels travel through the locks and canals of the St. Lawrence Seaway.

Innkeeper(s): John Lindsey, Amornrat Lindsey. $119-190. 3 rooms, 1 with WP, 1 two-bedroom suite. Breakfast, afternoon tea and Thai welcome drink (Upon arrival) included in rates. Types of meals: Full gourmet bkfst, early coffee/tea, room service and Monday-Friday full American style breakfast with a Thai twist. Weekends full authentic Thai breakfast.

Certificate may be used: Sunday-Thursday in April.

Prattsburgh

Feather Tick 'N Thyme B&B

7661 Tuttle Rd
Prattsburgh, NY 14873-9520
(607)522-4113
Internet: www.bbnyfingerlakes.com
E-mail: info@bbnyfingerlakes.com

Circa 1890. Feel revived and refreshed after a stay in the peaceful valley that surrounds this 1890's Victorian Country bed and breakfast inn. Prattsburgh is situated in the New York Finger Lakes wine country between Keuka Lake and Canandaigua Lake. Soak up the scenic view from the wrap-around porch. Stroll among the flower gardens by the creek. Enjoy a restful sleep in an ornate iron bed, a four-poster rice bed or a sleigh bed depending upon the room selected. Breakfast is served family style in the dining room with heirloom recipes accented by the collection of depression glass. Feather Tick 'N Thyme B&B offers special weekend packages for a romantic getaway.

Innkeeper(s): Maureen Kunak, John Kunak. $100-125. 4 rooms, 2 with PB. Breakfast and snacks/refreshments included in rates. Types of meals: Full bkfst, picnic lunch and hors d'oeuvres.

Certificate may be used: December-May, Sunday-Thursday, subject to availability.

Rochester

Reen's Bed and Breakfast

44 Magee Avenue
Rochester, NY 14613
(585)458-9306
Internet: www.stayatreens.com
E-mail: reen@stayatreens.com

Circa 1910. Gracing the Maplewood neighborhood in Rochester, New York, Reen's Bed and Breakfast is just three miles from downtown and four miles from Lake Ontario. The list of amenities seems endless at this very comfortable B&B that was built in 1910 in the Edwardian style and boasts leaded and stained-glass windows, hardwood floors and oak woodwork. Relax in the living room or fireside den. Air-conditioned guest bedrooms are named after the children who grew up in this house. Start each day with a hearty breakfast in the dining room, front porch or back patio. Tour the George Eastman House, visit the planetarium or history museum. Ask about special packages available.

Innkeeper(s): Irene Zaremski-Saltrelli. $70-130. 3 rooms. Breakfast included in rates. Types of meals: Full gourmet bkfst and veg bkfst.

Certificate may be used: January-February.

The Edward Harris House B&B Inn

35 Argyle Street
Rochester, NY 14607
(585)473-9752 (800)419-1213 Fax:(585)473-9752
Internet: www.edwardharrishouse.com
E-mail: innkeeper@edwardharrishouse.com

Circa 1896. Acclaimed as one of the finest early examples of architect Claude Bragdon's work, this restored Georgian mansion is one of the iLoveInns.com Top 10 romantic Inns for 2009. Its history only enhances the rich warmth, and the immense size reflects a cozy ambiance. Relax in a leather chair in the traditional library. Antiques and collectibles combine well with florals and chintz for a touch of romance. Two guest bedrooms and the Garden Suite boast fireplaces. Four-poster rice beds and hand-painted furniture add to the individual decorating styles. A gourmet candlelight breakfast is served in the formal dining room on crystal and china or on the brick garden patio. Enjoy afternoon tea on the wicker-filled front porch. Walk one block down tree-lined streets to the urban village of Park Avenue. A plethora of historic sites, including The George Eastman House and Strong Museum, are within a one-mile range.

Innkeeper(s): Susan Alvarez. $169-189. 5 rooms with PB, 4 with FP, 3 total suites, including 1 two-bedroom suite, 1 cottage, 1 conference room. Breakfast, afternoon tea, snacks/refreshments and Afternoon tea provided upon request. Please contact the Innkeeper included in rates. Types of meals: Full bkfst, veg bkfst, early coffee/tea, picnic lunch, hors d'oeuvres, room service and Catering can be arranged easily for lunch or dinner. Please call the Inn for more information.

Certificate may be used: Sunday-Thursday, subject to availability, holiday and special events may be excluded. Anytime, at the last minute. Please call the Inn.

Saratoga Springs

Union Gables

55 Union Avenue
Saratoga Springs, NY 12866
(518) 584-1558 Fax:(518)583-0649
Internet: www.uniongables.com
E-mail: stay@uniongables.com

Circa 1901. Be greeted by roses and fountains in Saratoga Springs, New York just two blocks from Historic Congress Park and Saratoga Thoroughbred Racetrack. The large wrap-around porch beckons. Tour each inviting guest room; see the hand-painted mural in the Michael room, the octagon-shaped Linda room, and the Library accented with antiques. Reserve the separate Pond Cottage for a private getaway with a gated patio and gas fireplace. All rooms have a refrigerator, wireless Internet, private bathroom and complimentary breakfast. This one-acre estate is within strolling distance of downtown. Explore nearby Lake George or the Adirondack Mountains.

Innkeeper(s): Candace and Paul. $140-450. 15 rooms with PB, 13 with FP, 1 with HT, 1 with WP, 3 total suites, including 1 two-bedroom suite, 1 cottage, 1 guest house, 1 conference room. Breakfast and snacks/refreshments included in rates.

Certificate may be used: Anytime, November-March; Sunday - Thursday Sept.9 -July 14, subject to availability.

Sharon Springs

Edgefield

153 Washington Street
Sharon Springs, NY 13459
(518)284-3339
Internet: www.edgefieldbb.com
E-mail: info@edgefieldbb.com

Circa 1865. This home has seen many changes. It began as a farmhouse, a wing was added in the 1880s, and by the turn of  the century, sported an elegant Greek Revival facade. Edgefield is one of a collection of nearby homes used as a family compound for summer vacations. The rooms are decorated with traditional furnishings in a formal English-country style. In the English tradition, afternoon tea is presented with cookies and tea sandwiches. Sharon Springs includes many historic sites, and the town is listed in the National Register.

Innkeeper(s): Daniel Marshall Wood. $150-250. 5 rooms with PB. Breakfast, afternoon tea, hors d'oeuvres and wine included in rates. Types of meals: Full gourmet bkfst and early coffee/tea.

Certificate may be used: Anytime, subject to availability.

Sodus

Maxwell Creek Inn Bed & Breakfast

7563 Lake Rd
Sodus, NY 14551-9309
(315) 483-2222
Internet: www.maxwellcreekinn-bnb.com
E-mail: mcinnbnb@gmail.com

Circa 1846. Located on the South shore of Lake Ontario, halfway between Rochester and Syracuse, this historic cobblestone house is secluded on six acres surrounded by woodland wildlife preserve and apple orchards. There is a 1794 grist mill on the grounds and the buildings are rumored to have been a part of the Underground Railroad. The tranquil setting is peaceful and relaxing. Stay in one of the five spacious guest bedrooms in the main house or in one of the efficiency suites in the cobblestone carriage house, perfect for groups or families. Indulge in a full gourmet breakfast by candlelight.

Innkeeper(s): Patrick McElroy, Belinda McElroy. $135-155. 7 rooms, 5 with PB, 3 suites, 1 cottage. Breakfast, coffee and tea throughout day included in rates. Types of meals: Full gourmet bkfst, veg bkfst, early coffee/tea and afternoon tea.

Certificate may be used: July-October, Sunday-Wednesday, subject to availability.

Southampton

Hampton's House of Gardens Bed and Breakfast

534 North Magee Street
Southampton, NY 11968
(631)283-2414
Internet: www.hamptonshouseofgardens.com/
E-mail: msimmons12@gmail.com

Find rejuvenation inside the inn and outside in the gardens at this Feng Shui designed Southampton retreat. Step into a luxurious guest room with fresh flowers, quality bath products, and WiFi access. Candlelight paint helps the Enlightenment Room walls glow with the morning sun. Find your muse in the Inspiration Room decorated with whimsical musical notes. The other three guest rooms stimulate Transition, Restoration, and Transformation. Stroll through the garden to let the scent of sweet blossoms calm your senses then take a relaxing dip in the salt water pool or the mineral water hot tub. Read a book while swinging on a hammock. In the morning, breakfasts made with fresh, local ingredients will feed your body and mind. Beach passes are provided for all of the 11 town beaches. Those with an adventurous spirit can go wake surfing in Sag Harbor Cove or sailing in the harbor. Shops, wineries, and restaurants are just minutes away.

Innkeeper(s): Michelle Simmons. Call for rates. 5 rooms, 1 with PB, 1 suite, 1 guest house. Breakfast included in rates. Types of meals: Full gourmet bkfst, veg bkfst and early coffee/tea.

Certificate may be used: January, anytime. February, Sunday-Thursday.

Southold

Shorecrest Bed & Breakfast

54300 County Road 48
Southold, NY 11971-1360
(631)765-1570 Fax:(631)765-5373
Internet: www.shorecrestbedandbreakfast.com
E-mail: marilyn@shorecrestbedandbreakfast.com

Built as a seaside mansion in 1897 using American Four Square style architecture, this bed and breakfast sits on a crest in wine and farm country on the North Fork of Long Island. It has been renovated with modern comforts. Relax on the wicker-filled screened porch or in the living room by the fireplace. Cheerful guest bedrooms are nicely furnished with antiques, feather beds and pillow top mattresses. The Rose Room with a blue and white motif boasts a lace canopy bed. Early morning coffee is served in the library, then gather for a generous gourmet breakfast in the formal dining room. Beach passes, towels and chairs are provided. Rent bikes and kayaks nearby.

Innkeeper(s): Marilyn Marks. $200-425. 5 rooms with PB, 5 with FP, 1 suite, 1 guest house. Breakfast and snacks/refreshments included in rates. Types of meals: Full gourmet bkfst and early coffee/tea.

Certificate may be used: Sunday-Thursday, excludes holidays and June 20-Labor Day.

Troy

Olde Judge Mansion B&B

3300 6th Ave
Troy, NY 12180-1206
(518) 274-5698
Internet: www.oldejudgemansion.com
E-mail: Oldejudgemansion@gmail.com

Circa 1892. Experience the Victorian splendor of oak woodwork, 12-foot ceilings, pocket doors and embossed tin walls at this Gothic Italianate built in 1892. In the oak archway entry, view the photos displayed of historic Troy. Gather in the formal parlor to converse by the glow of kerosene lamps. An inviting Lazy Boy is perfect for video watching in the TV room. A sunny sitting room features reading materials and a chest stocked with forgotten conveniences. Kitchen privileges and laundry facilities are available. A stained-glass Newel Post Lamp on the ornate staircase leads to the comfortable guest bedrooms which are all on the second floor. Enjoy a casual, self-serve expanded continental breakfast buffet in the dining room. Shoot pool, play traditional feather, baseball or electric darts in the recreation/game room.

Innkeeper(s): Christina A. Urzan. $60-95. 5 rooms, 3 with PB, 1 guest house. Breakfast, afternoon tea, snacks/refreshments, No breakfast is included with Monthly discount plan. It is in the Weekly discount plan and Weekly is 7 days or more included in rates. Types of meals: Full bkfst, veg bkfst, early coffee/tea. Kitchen available for very light cooking and use of microwave and refrigerator.

Certificate may be used: Anytime, subject to availability.

Warrensburg

Glen Lodge B&B

1123 State Route 28
Warrensburg, NY 12885-5606
(518)494-4984 (800)867-2335 Fax:(518)494-7478
Internet: www.TheGlenLodge.com
E-mail: info@TheGlenLodge.com

Feel rejuvenated after a visit to this newly built bed and breakfast that reflects an authentic Adirondack lodge. Relax on one
of the large porches or in the quiet sitting room. Furnished
entirely with cedar log furniture, watch satellite TV in the Great
Room by the stone fireplace. Comfortable guest bedrooms are
carpeted and boast private baths. Start each day with classic
breakfast favorites such as pancakes, French toast, eggs, bacon,
sausage and muffins. Browse through the country store.
Situated in the scenic North Country area of upstate New York,
activities abound. Ski at nearby Gore and Whiteface Mountains
or swim at Lake George. Ask about available packages that
include rafting on the Hudson River.
Innkeeper(s): Aimee Azaert, Douglas Azaert. Call for rates. Call inn for
details. Breakfast included in rates. Types of meals: Country bkfst, veg bkfst
and early coffee/tea.
Certificate may be used: October-April, last minute, subject to availability.

The Cornerstone Victorian B&B

3921 Main Street
Warrensburg, NY 12885-1149
(518)623-3308 Fax:(518)623-3979
Internet: www.cornerstonevictorian.com
E-mail: stay@cornerstonevictorian.com

Circa 1904. Replete with gleaming woodwork and polished interior columns, this large wood and stone Victorian home has a
wraparound porch overlooking Hackensack Mountain. Inside are
stained-glass windows, Victorian furnishings, three terra-cotta
fireplaces and a beautiful cherry staircase. Awake each morning
to a candlelight breakfast complete with homemade morning
cakes, Louise's famous granola and other gourmet entrees.
Simply ask the innkeepers, with their 25-year experience in the
hospitality field, and they can help you plan your leisure activities in the Lake George/Adirondack and Saratoga Springs area.
Innkeeper(s): Doug Goettsche, Louise Goettsche. $98-194. 5 rooms with PB,
1 with FP, 1 conference room. Breakfast and snacks/refreshments included in
rates. Types of meals: Full gourmet bkfst and early coffee/tea.
Certificate may be used: January-March, Sunday-Thursday, excluding holidays, subject to availability.

Warwick

Warwick Valley Bed & Breakfast

24 Maple Ave
Warwick, NY 10990-1025
(845)987-7255 (888)280-1671 Fax:(845)988-5318
Internet: www.wvbedandbreakfast.com
E-mail: loretta@warwick.net

Circa 1900. This turn-of-the-century Colonial Revival is located in Warwick's historic district among many of the town's
other historic gems. The B&B includes five guest rooms decorated with antiques and country furnishings. Breakfasts are a
treat with entrees such as eggs Benedict, apple pancakes or a
savory potato, cheese and egg bake. Wineries, antique shops
and many outdoor activities are nearby, and innkeeper Loretta
Breedveld is happy to point guests in the right direction.
Innkeeper(s): Loretta Breedveld. $149-199. 6 rooms with PB. Breakfast
included in rates. Types of meals: Full gourmet bkfst and early coffee/tea.
Certificate may be used: Anytime. BOGO is based on number of available
rooms and lead time. Generally, no weekends; however, you are encouraged
to inquire with the owner Loretta Breedveld.

Wilmington

Willkommen Hof

5367 NYS Rt 86
Wilmington, NY 12997
(518)-946-SNOW (800) 541-9119 Fax:(518)946-7669
Internet: www.willkommenhof.com
E-mail: willkommenhof@whiteface.net

Circa 1890. This farmhouse was constructed around 1890 and
30 years later served as an inn during the 1920s, but little else
is known about its past. The innkeepers have created a cozy

atmosphere, perfect for
relaxation after a day exploring the Adirondack
Mountain area. A large
selection of books and a
roaring fire greet guests who
choose to settle down in
the reading room. The innkeepers also offer a large selection of
movies. Relax in the sauna or outdoor spa or simply enjoy the
comfort of your bedchamber.
Innkeeper(s): Heike Yost, Bert Yost. $79-245. 7 rooms, 3 with PB, 1 two-
bedroom and 1 three-bedroom suites. Breakfast and afternoon tea included
in rates. Types of meals: Full bkfst, wine, dinner and Dinner by reservation
only-limited to groups of 8 or more. Restaurant on premises.
Certificate may be used: Anytime, except holiday periods.

Windham

Albergo Allegria B&B

#43 Route 296, PO Box 267
Windham, NY 12496-0267
(518)734-5560 Fax:(518)734-5570
Internet: www.albergousa.com
E-mail: mail@albergousa.com

Circa 1892. Two former boarding houses were joined to create
this luxurious, Victorian bed & breakfast whose name means
"the inn of happiness." Guest quarters, laced with a Victorian
theme, are decorated with period wallpapers and antique furnishings. One master suite
includes an enormous
Jacuzzi tub. There are plenty
of relaxing options at
Albergo Allegria, including
an inviting lounge with a
large fireplace and over-
stuffed couches. Guests also
can choose from more than 300 videos in the innkeeper's
movie collection. Located just a few feet behind the inn are the
Carriage House Suites, each of which includes a double
whirlpool tub, gas fireplace, king-size bed and cathedral ceil-

ings with skylights. The innkeepers came to the area originally to open a deluxe, gourmet restaurant. Their command of cuisine is evident each morning as guests feast on a variety of home-baked muffins and pastries, gourmet omelettes, waffles and other tempting treats. The inn is a registered historic site.

Innkeeper(s): Marianna Leman, Leslie Leman. $99-269. 21 rooms with PB, 8 with FP, 8 with WP, 9 suites. Breakfast included in rates. Types of meals: Full gourmet bkfst.

Certificate may be used: Mid-week, Sunday-Thursday, non-holiday.

Woodstock

Enchanted Manor of Woodstock

23 Rowe Rd
Woodstock, NY 12401
(845)679-9012
Internet: www.enchantedmanorinn.com
E-mail: enchantedmanorinn@gmail.com

Enjoy elegant accommodations amid eight scenic acres in Woodstock, New York. Step out onto the six-level deck to watch deer and geese. The soothing sound of a waterfall adds ambiance to a relaxing soak in the six-person hot tub or swim in the saltwater pool. Schedule a healing Swedish massage after a workout in the onsite gym or personalized yoga class. Select a guest room in the main house or the cozy cottage with a propane-fueled pot belly stove. Start each day with a rejuvenating breakfast. The innkeepers are happy to accommodate vegetarian and vegan diets. The town is a wellness and artistic hub with a Zen monastery, Shakespeare festival, drumming circles, craft fairs, cross-country skiing and a film festival.

Innkeeper(s): Claudia Hirsch, Rolan Hirsch. $170-335. 4 rooms with PB.

Certificate may be used: Sunday-Thursday, November-April.

North Carolina

Asheville

Abbington Green B&B
46 Cumberland Circle
Asheville, NC 28801-1718
(828) 251-2454 (800) 251-2454 Fax:(828)251-2872
Internet: www.abbingtongreen.com
E-mail: info@abbingtongreen.com

Circa 1908. Experience a bit of Britain only half-a-mile from downtown Asheville, North Carolina. The historic home surrounded by mature trees has been preserved to award-winning quality. A gardener's delight, the inn features a boxwood

parterre with a tiered fountain, an Oriental garden with a path of stepping stones, and an informal shade garden. One of the common rooms offer a solid brass chandelier and the sun shines through original windows to light an English decor. Highlights of the eight guest rooms include king-size beds, whirlpool tubs, and working fireplaces. True luxury can be found in the five-room Eaton Square Suite with a private entry, furnished porch, and kitchen with china and crystal. Two suites are dog-friendly. Home-grown herbs and local, organic ingredients are used in the daily breakfast that feels more like a lovely brunch with friends. Sit at one of two large tables beside the handmade oak mantel in the dining room.

Innkeeper(s): Valerie Larrea. $169-425. 8 rooms with PB, 8 with FP, 8 with WP, 4 total suites, including 1 two-bedroom suite. Breakfast included in rates. Types of meals: Full bkfst, veg bkfst, early coffee/tea, 24-hour beverage service and ice machine.

Certificate may be used: January only, no weekends.

ASIA Bed and Spa
128 Hillside Street
Asheville, NC 28801
(828) 255-0051
Internet: www.ashevillespa.com
E-mail: info@ashevillespa.com

Stay in your robe all weekend at an inn where relaxation is the key objective. Wake up early with the sunrise or sleep late; breakfast is on your schedule. Feel stress lift from your shoulders at the Zen-inspired Tatami Porch and Japanese Strolling Garden. Snuggle by the gas fireplace in your room or soak in a tub scented with bath salts. Combine the benefits of hot and cold in the Finnish sauna and outdoor shower for two.

Couples massages are performed in the separate onsite suite next to the Meditation Garden. Leave with glowing skin after a facial using Eminence Organics products. Rates are based on all-inclusive packages with spa services. Room only rates are available during the week and occasionally on weekends. Plan a girls' getaway, unwind with your bridal party prior to your big day, or just get away for a healthy retreat. A walk to the heart of Asheville in just 10 minutes.

Innkeeper(s): Ryn McKenna, Jon Winter. $175-300. 5 rooms.

Certificate may be used: Jan. 1-Feb. 28, excluding weekends and holidays.

Oakland Cottage B&B
74 Oakland Road
Asheville, NC 28801
(828)994-2627 (866)858-0863 Fax:(828)994-0316
Internet: www.OaklandCottage.com
E-mail: info@VacationInAsheville.com

Circa 1910. Oakland Cottage B&B is a large historic home near downtown Asheville, North Carolina. Enjoy conversation on the front porch or back deck. The interior common areas are open, warm and inviting with a gas fireplace. A guest kitchen and laundry facilities are available to use. Guest rooms and spacious two-room suites are nicely decorated. A hearty breakfast is served in the main dining room. The entire cottage may be reserved with or without full services. Discounted tickets to the nearby Biltmore Estate are sold onsite. Whether traveling on a family vacation, a romantic getaway or a weekend with girlfriends, this B&B is a perfect setting.

Innkeeper(s): Mary Bridges, Jim. $105-150. 5 rooms with PB, 3 two-bedroom suites. Breakfast included in rates. Types of meals: Full bkfst.

Certificate may be used: January-March, Sunday-Thusday. Cannot be combined with any other discounts. Based on rack rates only.

Balsam

Balsam Mountain Inn
68 Seven Springs Drive
Balsam, NC 28707
(828)456-9498 (855)224-9498
Internet: www.balsaminn.net
E-mail: info@balsammountaininn.net

Circa 1905. This inn, just a quarter mile from the famed Blue Ridge Parkway, is surrounded by the majestic Smoky Mountains. The inn was built in the Neoclassical style and overlooks the scenic hamlet of Balsam. The inn is listed in the National Register of Historic Places and is designated a Jackson

County Historic Site. It features a mansard roof and wrap-around porches with mountain views. A complimentary full breakfast is served daily, and dinner also is available daily.

Innkeeper(s): Merrily Teasley. $125-175. 50 rooms with PB, 8 suites. Breakfast included in rates. Types of meals: Full bkfst, early coffee/tea, picnic lunch and dinner. Restaurant on premises.

Certificate may be used: Sunday-Thursday, November-June and September, excluding holiday periods.

Banner Elk

1902 Turnpike House

317 Old Turnpike Rd Northwest
Banner Elk, NC 28604-7537
(828) 898-5611 (888) 802-4487 Fax:(828)898-5612
Internet: www.1902turnpikehouse.com
E-mail: info@1902turnpikehouse.com

Circa 1902. Located at the foot of Beech Mountain in the high country near Daniel Boone's historic area, this restored farmhouse is also just minutes from Sugar and Grandfather Mountains. Spacious guest bedrooms feature down comforters and are appointed with an eclectic blend of antiques and family treasures. Enjoy an early morning cup of freshly brewed coffee on the covered front porch, or by the fireside when it's cool. Then gather for breakfast around a large farm table set with heirloom china, crystal and vintage sterling silver. Specialty juices, breads and meats accompany chef-prepared gourmet recipes such as Bananas Foster French Toast, Turnpike House Egg Casserole, Fresh Blueberry Pancakes, Ham and Three-cheese Omelets.

Innkeeper(s): Paul Goedhart, Cindy Goedhart. $89-144. 7 rooms with PB, 2 with WP. Breakfast and snacks/refreshments included in rates. Types of meals: Full gourmet bkfst, veg bkfst and early coffee/tea.

Certificate may be used: Sunday-Thursday.

Beech Alpen Inn

700 Beech Mountain Pkwy
Banner Elk, NC 28604-8015
(828)387-2252 (866)284-2770 Fax:(828)387-2229
Internet: www.beechalpen.com
E-mail: oceanreal@msn.com

Circa 1968. This rustic inn is a Bavarian delight affording scenic vistas of the Blue Ridge Mountains. The innkeepers offer accommodations at Top of the Beech, a Swiss-style ski chalet with views of nearby slopes. The interiors of both properties are inviting. At the Beech Alpen, several guest rooms have stone fireplaces or French doors that open onto a balcony. Top of the Beech's great room is a wonderful place to relax, with a huge stone fireplace and comfortable furnishings. The Beech Alpen Restaurant serves a variety of dinner fare.

Innkeeper(s): Steve Raymond. $79-159. 25 rooms with PB, 4 with FP. Breakfast included in rates. Types of meals: Cont, early coffee/tea and gourmet dinner. Restaurant on premises.

Certificate may be used: Sunday-Thursday, Jan. 3-Dec. 14.

Beaufort

Langdon House

135 Craven St
Beaufort, NC 28516-2116
(252)728-5499
Internet: www.langdonhouse.com
E-mail: innkeeper@coastalnet.com

Circa 1734. With Colonial Federal design and generous hospitality this 1734 house is Beaufort's oldest running bed and breakfast. Relax on either of the two-story porches with hammocks and rockers. Sit by the fire in the sitting room with polished heartpine flooring. An 1800s Estey organ highlights the parlor. Each first-floor guest bedroom reflects the traditional ambiance of the inn with antique furnishings and decor. Hallmark candlelight breakfasts are served at the huge dining room table on the second floor. Two courses, fresh fruit and yogurt and a house specialty alongside delectable accompaniments are sure to please. Personal preferences and dietary restrictions are gladly accommodated. Stroll through the landscaped country-style garden.

Innkeeper(s): Jimm Prest, Lizzet Prest. $108-238. 4 rooms with PB, 1 conference room. Breakfast and snacks/refreshments included in rates. Types of meals: Full gourmet bkfst, veg bkfst and early coffee/tea.

Certificate may be used: December to February, only includes one breakfast, this offer excludes Master Suite.

Black Mountain

Red Rocker Inn

136 N Dougherty St
Black Mountain, NC 28711-3326
(828) 669-5991 (888) 669-5991
Internet: www.redrockerinn.com
E-mail: info@redrockerinn.com

Circa 1896. Voted as the best B&B in Asheville, Black Mountain and all of Western North Carolina for the past six years, this three-story inn sits on one acre of pristinely landscaped grounds. Located just 14 miles east of Asheville and the famous Biltmore Estate, discover why the Atlanta Journal named this inn one of its "Top 12 Favorites in the Southeast." Elegant, air-conditioned guest bedrooms exude an inviting ambiance. Many feature fireplaces and whirlpool tubs. Each morning sit down to a heaping Southern breakfast that is sure to satisfy. Stroll through gorgeous gardens with a view of the mountains or relax in front of a roaring fire. Red rockers line the expansive wraparound porch, a perfect spot to enjoy tea and hand-dipped macaroons. Special dining packages are available year-round which include homemade specialties and award-winning desserts.

Innkeeper(s): Doug Bowman, Jenny Bowman. $105-220. 17 rooms with PB, 4 with FP, 5 with WP. Breakfast, afternoon tea, snacks/refreshments included in rates. Breakfast buffet complimentary to house guests and available to others at $12.00 each. Includes egg casseroles, hot baked goods, home made granola, cheese grits, specialty pancakes and french toasts, bacon, sausage, fresh fruit and other Southern favorites included in rates. Types of meals: Full bkfst, veg bkfst, early coffee/tea, wine, gourmet dinner and Sadie's Tea Room - Private parties by reservation for afternoon tea parties. Restaurant on premises.

Certificate may be used: Feb. 1 to March 15, Sunday-Thursday; Nov. 15 to Dec. 20, Sunday-Thursday.

Brevard

The Inn at Brevard

315 E Main St
Brevard, NC 28712-3837
(828)884-2105 Fax:(828)885-7996
Internet: www.theinnatbrevard.com
E-mail: brevard@theinnatbrevard.com

Circa 1885. Furnished with 17th and 18th century decor, this renovated Antebellum mansion is listed in the National Register. The Inn at Brevard is located in the mountains of Western North Carolina in Transylvania County, known as the Land of Waterfalls. Feel refreshed by the relaxed elegance of this southern B&B with a pond as well as herb and flower gardens. Stay in a guest room or suite in the main house, some feature fireplaces and ball and claw tubs. Cabin-style rooms are available in the annex. Breakfast is bountiful, with entrees plated individually and side dishes served family style. Dinner at the inn is open to the public. Enjoy the Brevard Music Center adjoining Pisgah National Forest in the valley of the French Broad River, easily accessible from Blue Ridge Parkway.

Innkeeper(s): Howard Yager, Faye Yager. $99-225. 15 rooms with PB, 4 with FP, 1 with WP, 2 suites, 3 conference rooms. Breakfast included in rates. Types of meals: Full gourmet bkfst, veg bkfst, early coffee/tea, gourmet lunch, picnic lunch, afternoon tea, snacks/refreshments, wine, gourmet dinner, room service and Special occasion desserts and cakes. Restaurant on premises.

Certificate may be used: Jan.1-May 15, Nov. 1-Dec. 30; $165/night Annex, $175/night Main House, does not include breakfast or tax.

Cape Carteret

Harborlight Guest House

332 Live Oak Drive
Cape Carteret, NC 28584
(252)393-6868 (800)624-VIEW
Internet: www.harborlightnc.com
E-mail: info@harborlightnc.com

Circa 1963. This three-story home rests on a peninsula just yards from Bogue Sound and the Intracoastal Waterway. In-room amenities might include a massive whirlpool tub, a claw-foot tub or fireplace, and each of the guest suites feature a beautiful water view. The decor is done in a modern, coastal style. Multi-course, gourmet breakfasts begin with fresh juices, coffee, tea and an appetizer, perhaps a stuffed mushroom. From there, guests enjoy a fresh fruit dish followed by a creative entree. All of which is served in suite or deckside. Museums, an aquarium, historic sites, Hammocks Beach State Park and harbor tours are among the attractions. Fort Macon State Park affords guests an opportunity to view a restored Civil War fort. Popular beaches and horseback riding are just minutes away.

Innkeeper(s): Leah Evans. $110-300. 7 rooms, 5 with FP, 6 with HT, 7 suites, 1 conference room. Breakfast included in rates. Types of meals: Full gourmet bkfst, early coffee/tea and picnic lunch.

Certificate may be used: Nov. 1-Feb. 28, Sunday-Thursday, excluding holidays. Only certain suites available for this special.

Gibsonville

Burke Manor Inn

303 Burke Street
Gibsonville, NC 27249
(336)449-6266 (888)679-1805 Fax:(133)644-71240
Internet: www.burkemanor.com
E-mail: info@burkemanor.com

Circa 1906. Blending the warmth of exceptional hospitality with prestigious service, this historic Victorian bed & breakfast inn features luxurious surroundings, quality reproductions and a comfortable atmosphere. Lavish suites include upscale amenities for the leisure and business traveler alike. Breakfast reflects the quality of food that has given the inn's restaurant a reputation for fine dining. Play tennis, then swim in the heated pool or soak tired muscles in the hot tub. The 3.5 acres provide a peaceful setting for beautiful garden weddings. It is an easy walk from the inn to downtown sites and shops.

Innkeeper(s): Lil Lacassagne, Lori Lacassagne. $139-309. 8 rooms, 9 with PB, 1 suite, 2 conference rooms. Breakfast and snacks/refreshments included in rates. Types of meals: Full gourmet bkfst, veg bkfst, early coffee/tea and room service.

Certificate may be used: Anytime, Sunday-Thursday. Some blackout dates and restrictions apply or Anytime, Last Minute-Based on Availability.

Grover

The Inn of the Patriots Bed and Breakfast Hotel

301 Cleveland Avenue
Grover, NC 28073
(704) 937-2940 Fax:(888)217-3470
Internet: www.theinnofthepatriots.com
E-mail: enjoyandrelax@theinnofthepatriots.com

Indulge your taste buds at this inn that houses the Presidential Culinary Museum. Owned by a former White House Chef, the inn offers a three-course breakfast as a daily exercise in euphoria. Cooking classes with dinner are available every Wednesday and Saturday for those wishing to learn how to create gourmet entrees themselves. The museum features china designs from more than 20 first ladies, a tour of the old underground servant quarters, and sponsors an annual Easter Egg Roll. Five guest rooms are filled with eclectic accents that add surprises to every corner. Marvel at the 1879 tile floor in The Colonel Cleveland Room bathroom. Full-sized sapling trees and a water fountain bring a sense of the outdoors to the Nature and Earth Room. Find sailors love letters and other treasures in the desk of the Oceanicus Blue Dreams room. Nearby Kings Mountain National Military Park preserves a major patriot victory during the Revolutionary War and includes a 1.5 mile battlefield trail.

Innkeeper(s): Marti and Stormy Mongiello. Call for rates. 5 rooms, 2 with FP, 3 with HT. Breakfast included in rates.

Certificate may be used: Anytime, subject to availability.

Hendersonville

Echo Mountain Inn

2849 Laurel Park Hwy
Hendersonville, NC 28739-8925
(828) 693-9626 (888) 324-6466
Internet: www.echoinn.com
E-mail: frontdesk@echoinn.com

Circa 1896. Echo Mountain Inn is the perfect getaway for a special occasion or a family get together. It is nestled in the Blue Ridge Mountains, about three miles between Jump Off Rock scenic overlook and downtown Hendersonville. Combining the character of an historic landmark with the comfort and charm of a Southern inn guests are offered spectacular

views from the warm and inviting sun porch, living room and library/game room. The morning sun greets each guest in the dining room where weekday deluxe continental and weekend country buffet breakfasts are served. Every guest room is named to reflect its particular decor and charm, complete with private heat/air, wireless internet and TV. Some have a wood burning fireplace and most provide an overlooking view of the valley of Hendersonville. Summer pleasures include a swim in the outdoor pool or a game of shuffleboard while winter evenings can be spent in front of a cozy fire. The inn serves as a great launching base for local shopping and antiquing and outdoor activities such as hiking, biking, rafting and golf. Echo Mountain Inn's cheerful staff will make your stay at Echo Mountain Inn a relaxing and memorable one.

Innkeeper(s): Greg, Stephanie . $85-195. 32 rooms with PB, 8 with FP, 1 with HT, 4 suites, 2 conference rooms. Breakfast included in rates. Types of meals: Cont plus and early coffee/tea.

Certificate may be used: January-September, November-December, Sunday-Thursday. Holidays, holiday weeks and special events excluded.

Hertford

1812 on The Perquimans B&B Inn

385 Old Neck Road
Hertford, NC 27944
(252)426-1812

Circa 1812. William and Sarah Fletcher were the first residents of this Federal-style plantation home, and the house is still in the family today. The Fletchers were Quakers and the first North Carolina residents to offer to pay the way for workers who wished to return to Africa. The farm rests along the banks of the Perquimans River, and the grounds retain many original outbuildings, including a brick dairy, smokehouse and a 19th-century frame barn. In the National Register of Historic Places, the inn is appropriately appointed with antiques highlighting the restored mantels and woodwork. The inn is a lovely, pastoral retreat with bikes and canoeing available.

Innkeeper(s): Peter Rascoe, Nancy Rascoe. $80-85. 4 rooms. Breakfast included in rates. Types of meals: Cont plus and Full Plantation Breakfast available for $5 per person.

Certificate may be used: All year, except for weekends in April, May, September, October and Easter weekend or Christmas Eve or night.

Highlands

Colonial Pines Inn Bed and Breakfast

541 Hickory St
Highlands, NC 28741
(828)526-2060 (866)526-2060
Internet: www.colonialpinesinn.com
E-mail: sleeptight@colonialpinesinn.com

Circa 1937. Secluded on a hillside just half a mile from Highlands' Main Street, this inn offers relaxing porches that boast a mountain view. The parlor is another restful option, offering a TV, fireplace and piano. Rooms, highlighted by knotty

pine, are decorated with an eclectic mix of antiques. The guest pantry is always stocked with refreshments for those who need a little something in the afternoon. For breakfast, freshly baked breads accompany items such as a potato/bacon casserole and baked pears topped with currant sauce. In addition to guest rooms and suites, there are two cottages available, each with a fireplace and kitchen.

Innkeeper(s): Chris Alley, Donna Alley. $95-165. 8 rooms, 5 with PB, 1 with FP, 2 two-bedroom suites, 1 cottage, 1 guest house. Breakfast, afternoon tea and snacks/refreshments included in rates. Types of meals: Full gourmet bkfst, veg bkfst and early coffee/tea.

Certificate may be used: Monday-Wednesday during May, June or September excluding holidays. Anytime, Last Minute-Based on Availability.

Inn At Half-Mile Farm

214 Half Mile Dr
Highlands, NC 28741
(828)526-8170 (800)946-6822 Fax:(828)526-2625
Internet: www.halfmilefarm.com
E-mail: stay@halfmilefarm.com

Circa 1870. Spread across 14 scenic acres with fields, forests, streams, two stocked ponds and a six-acre lake, this country inn exudes a casual elegance. Inn at Half-Mile Farm is located in Highlands, North Carolina, at the southern end of the Blue Ridge Mountains near Asheville. Atlanta is a two-hour drive. Enjoy wine and appetizers while relaxing on the landscaped courtyard or patio. Swim in the outdoor pool, go fly fishing or whitewater rafting on Chattooga River. Simple yet luxurious accommodations feature guest bedrooms, suites and cabins with an assortment of amenities that may include a fireplace, jetted tub, deck, fresh flowers and thick robes. Savor a hearty breakfast before exploring the area. Special and packages are usually available.

Innkeeper(s): Kate. $160-550. 23 rooms with PB, 18 with FP, 22 with WP, 3 cabins. Breakfast, snacks/refreshments, hors d'oeuvres and wine included in rates. Types of meals: Full gourmet bkfst, veg bkfst, early coffee/tea and picnic lunch.

Certificate may be used: Sunday-Wednesday; not valid on weekends or during the month of October.

Maggie Valley

Misty Mountain Ranch B&B

561 Caldwell Dr
Maggie Valley, NC 28751
(828)926-2710 (888)647-8922 Fax:(828)926-2710
Internet: www.mistymtnranch.com
E-mail: info@mistymountainranch.com

Circa 2001. For a fun getaway this bed & breakfast is a relaxing home away from home. Recently built on two acres, the ranch features tongue and groove pine construction. Sip Karen's homemade mountain apple wine and laugh at Peter's jokes in the library. Themed guest suites are comfortable and spacious with generous amenities. Enjoy a hearty breakfast in the dining room each morning. Weather permitting, cookouts with hot dogs and marshmallows are held at Murphy's Fire Pit. Fish for rainbow trout in the stocked pond.

Innkeeper(s): Karen . $99-175. 6 rooms, 5 with FP, 6 suites, 1 conference room. Breakfast, snacks/refreshments and Cabins do not include breakfast or snacks included in rates.

Certificate may be used: January-May, Sunday-Thursday, subject to availability. Not valid on holidays.

Mills River

Bed & Breakfast on Tiffany Hill

400 Ray Hill Road
Mills River, NC 28759
(828)290-6080
Internet: www.BBonTiffanyHill.com
E-mail: vacation@BBonTiffanyHill.com

Circa 2009. Newly constructed and purpose built, a casual elegance blends with Southern hospitality spanning six gorgeous acres. Located in the foothills of Western North Carolina, it is easy to explore the waterfalls of Dupont State Park, hike Pisgah Forest, tour along the Blue Ridge Parkway and visit the popular Biltmore Estate. Bed & Breakfast on Tiffany Hill in Mills River boasts upscale amenities and comfort for business or leisure. A 24-hour complimentary guest pantry provides snacks and beverages. Upscale suites feature a decor that reflects the southern towns they are named after. Select an ADA accessible room, one with a fireplace or a large soaking tub. Vegetarian breakfasts can be served upon request. Gather informally each afternoon for wine and appetizers. The innkeepers will gladly assist with trip planning.

Innkeeper(s): Selena Einwechter. $185-235. 5 suites. Breakfast, snacks/refreshments and wine included in rates. Types of meals: Full gourmet bkfst, veg bkfst, early coffee/tea, picnic lunch and hors d'oeuvres.

Certificate may be used: Monday-Thursday in January, March or August (Excludes Carriage House Suites).

Mount Airy

Sobotta Manor Bed and Breakfast

347 West Pine Street
Mount Airy, NC 27030
(336)786-2777
Internet: www.sobottamanor.com
E-mail: sobottamanor@aol.com

Circa 1932. Feel surrounded by a casual elegance at Sobotta Manor Bed and Breakfast in Mount Airy, North Carolina, just ten miles from the Blue Ridge Parkway. Built in 1932 and recently renovated, this stately Tudor-style mansion offers romantic accommodations in the Yadkin Valley, now known for its vineyards. Gather for the social hour and sip a glass of local wine with appetizers. A variety of newspapers are available to read in the parlor and afternoon treats are also provided. The B&B has a complete concierge service. Enjoy a pleasant night's rest in one of the well-appointed guest bedrooms with upscale amenities. Linger over a lavish three-course gourmet breakfast in the European-inspired dining room overlooking the formal English gardens, in the intimate nook or on an open-air porch.

Innkeeper(s): Thurman Hester, Robin Hester. $139-149. 4 rooms with PB. Breakfast and snacks/refreshments included in rates. Types of meals: Full gourmet bkfst, early coffee/tea, wine and Every day starts off with a leisurely but gourmet three-course breakfast served in the European inspired dining room overlooking the formal gardens. Different dining venues such as the cozy breakfast nook or the open-air porches provide for the option for privacy or for conversation with fellow guests.

Certificate may be used: December-March, Sunday-Thursday. Holidays and special events excluded.

New Bern

Harmony House Inn

215 Pollock St
New Bern, NC 28560-4942
(252)636-3810 (800)636-3113
Internet: www.harmonyhouseinn.com
E-mail: innkeeper215@yahoo.com

Circa 1850. Long ago, this two-story Greek Revival was sawed in half and the west side moved nine feet to accommodate new hallways, additional rooms and a staircase. A wall was then built to divide the house into two sections. The rooms are decorated with antiques, the innkeeper's collection of handmade crafts and other collectibles. Two of the suites include a heart-shaped Jacuzzi tub. Offshore breezes sway blossoms in the lush garden. Cross the street to an excellent restaurant or take a picnic to the shore.

Innkeeper(s): Ed Kirkpatrick, Sooki Kirkpatrick. $109-175. 10 rooms with PB, 2 with WP, 3 total suites, including 1 two-bedroom suite, 2 conference rooms. Breakfast, snacks/refreshments and wine included in rates. Types of meals: Full bkfst, veg bkfst and early coffee/tea.

Certificate may be used: Year-round, Sunday-Thursday. Weekends November-February on a space available basis, excluding holidays and special events.

Sparta

Harmony Hill Bed & Breakfast

1740 Halsey Knob Rd
Sparta, NC 28675
(336)209-0475
Internet: www.harmonyhillbnb.com
E-mail: innkeeper@harmonyhillbnb.com

Feel immediately welcome by a sign stating "Come Sit on Our Porch." Have a seat and enjoy the sweeping field and mountain views, then contemplate the story of how after moving the entire building to the top of the hill, the innkeepers restored the inn to include original floors, wavy glass windows, and an old doorbell. The bed and breakfast houses a library and a music room with a piano. Close the shutters or enjoy the view from the Jacuzzi tub in the Peach Bottom Room. You can plan a girlfriend getaway or mother-daughter weekend in the Baker's Ridge Room with two antique twin beds. Find all the amenities of home in the separate Carriage House Suite with a kitchen, living room, dining room, and private deck. Pancakes or oven-baked omelets can be served in the dining room or al fresco in the gazebo. Consider reserving the grounds for a storybook outdoor wedding. The inn is close to wineries, golf courses, and New River State Park.

Innkeeper(s): Jim Halsey, Barbara Halsey. $140-195. 6 rooms with PB, 1 suite, 1 cottage.

Certificate may be used: January-March, Sunday-Thursday, subject to availability.

Sylva

Mountain Brook Cottages

208 Mountain Brook Rd
Sylva, NC 28779-9659
(828)586-4329
Internet: www.mountainbrook.com
E-mail: mcmahon@mountainbrook.com

Circa 1931. Located in the Great Smokies, Mountain Brook in western North Carolina consists of 14 cabins on a hillside amid rhododendron, elm, maple and oak trees. The resort's 200-acre terrain is criss-crossed with brooks and waterfalls, contains a trout-stocked pond and nature trail. Two cabins  are constructed with logs from the property, while nine are made from native stone. They feature fireplaces, full kitchens, porch swings and some have Jacuzzi's.

Innkeeper(s): Gus, Michele, Maqelle McMahon. $100-150. 12 cottages with PB, 12 with FP, 4 with HT. Types of meals: Early coffee/tea.

Certificate may be used: Feb. 1 to Oct. 1, Nov. 1 to Dec. 20, holidays excluded.

Tryon

1906 Pine Crest Inn and Restaurant

85 Pine Crest Lane
Tryon, NC 28782-3486
(828)859-9135 (800)633-3001 Fax:(828)859-9136
Internet: pinecrestinn.com
E-mail: iloveinns@pinecrestinn.com

Circa 1906. Once a favorite of F. Scott Fitzgerald, this inn is nestled in the foothills of the Blue Ridge Mountains. Opened in 1917 by famed equestrian Carter Brown, the inn offers guests romantic fireplaces, gourmet dining and wide verandas that offer casual elegance. The Blue Ridge Parkway and the famous Biltmore House are a short drive away. Rooms are available in the Main Lodge and cottages. Original buildings include a 200-year-old log cabin, a woodcutter cottage and a stone cottage. Elegant meals are served in a Colonial tavern setting for full breakfasts and gourmet dinners.

Innkeeper(s): Carl Caudle. $89-299. 35 rooms with PB, 29 with FP, 2 with HT, 16 with WP, 8 total suites, including 2 two-bedroom suites and 1 three-bedroom suite, 10 cottages, 2 cabins, 3 conference rooms. Breakfast, afternoon tea, snacks/refreshments and Complimentary Port & Sherry in the evenings included in rates. Types of meals: Full gourmet bkfst, veg bkfst, Sun. brunch, early coffee/tea, gourmet lunch, picnic lunch, hors d'oeuvres, wine, gourmet dinner and room service. Restaurant on premises.

Certificate may be used: Anytime subject to availability excluding October, holidays and special events.

Valle Crucis

The Baird House

1451 Watauga River Road
Valle Crucis, NC 28691
(828) 297-4055 (800) 297-1342
Internet: www.bairdhouse.com
E-mail: bairdhouse@charter.net

Circa 1790. Warm hospitality has been offered since 1790 at this Colonial Farmhouse sitting on 16 secluded acres of riverfront coupled with rolling hills, wooded pastures and cool mountain breezes. The front porch rocking chairs invite relaxation and conversation. Enjoy sodas and homemade treats from the bottomless cookie jar. Fully restored, the hand-planed hardwood and other original details are accented by antiques, family heirlooms and a contemporary country decor. Several of the spacious guest bedrooms in the main house and carriage house feature gas log or wood-burning fireplaces, whirlpool baths, a balcony or wraparound porch. A continental breakfast is available before a hearty meal that may include creamy style eggs, hashbrown casserole, hot biscuits, thick hickory smoked bacon, butter pecan coffee cake, fresh granola and fruit cups. Step outside the front door to swim, fish or tube on the river. Linville Falls, Grandfather Mountain, golf and ski resorts provide a variety of local activities.

Innkeeper(s): Deede Hinson, Tom Hinson. $139-179. 7 rooms with PB, 4 with FP, 3 with HT, 1 two-bedroom suite. Breakfast and snacks/refreshments included in rates. Types of meals: Country bkfst and early coffee/tea.

Certificate may be used: Anytime, subject to availability.

The Mast Farm Inn

2543 Broadstone Road
Valle Crucis, NC 28691
(828) 963-5857 (888) 963-5857 Fax:(828) 963-6404
Internet: www.themastfarminn.com
E-mail: reserve@themastfarminn.com

Circa 1812. Listed in the National Register of Historic Places, this 18-acre farmstead includes a main house and ten outbuildings, one of them a log cabin built in 1812. The inn features a

wraparound porch with rocking chairs, swings and a view of the mountain valley. Fresh flowers gathered from the garden add fragrance throughout the inn. Rooms are furnished with antiques, quilts and mountain crafts. In addition to the inn rooms, there are seven cottages available, some with kitchens. Before breakfast is served, early morning coffee can be delivered to your room. Organic home-grown vegetables are featured at dinners, included in a contemporary regional cuisine.

Innkeeper(s): Danielle Deschamps Stabler & Ken Stabler. $125-450. 15 rooms, 8 with PB, 4 with FP, 3 with HT, 7 cottages, 2 guest houses. Breakfast included in rates. Types of meals: Full gourmet bkfst, veg bkfst, early coffee/tea, picnic lunch, snacks/refreshments, wine and gourmet dinner. Restaurant on premises.

Certificate may be used: May and September only.

Warrenton

Ivy Bed & Breakfast

331 North Main Street
Warrenton, NC 27589
(252)257-9300 (800)919-9886 Fax:(252)257-1802
Internet: www.ivybedandbreakfast.com
E-mail: info@ivybedandbreakfast.com

Circa 1903. Open year-round, this Queen Anne Victorian B&B is located near Lake Gaston and Kerr Lake. It is an easy stroll to quaint downtown shops and an old-fashioned drug store and soda fountain. The one-acre grounds include an English-style box garden with sitting area and fountain. Pat's Porch has inviting rockers and wicker chairs. Evening social hour with appetizers and beverages is hosted in Carter Williams Parlour with a vintage grand piano. Named after the ladies who have lived here, guest bedrooms feature heart pine floors, antiques and Waverly window and bed treatments. Stay in a room with a Jacuzzi and canopy bed or a clawfoot tub and brass bed. The Ivy Suite adjoins two rooms with a connecting bathroom. An incredible three-course candlelit breakfast is served in the Nannie Tarwater Dining Room.

Innkeeper(s): Ellen Roth, Jerry Roth. $100-120. 4 rooms, 3 with PB, 1 with WP, 1 two-bedroom suite, 1 conference room. Breakfast and A full 3-course candlelit breakfast of your choosing is served at a time that fits your schedule included in rates. Types of meals: Full gourmet bkfst, veg bkfst and early coffee/tea.

Certificate may be used: Anytime, subject to availability.

Waynesville

GrandView Lodge

466 Lickstone Road
Waynesville, NC 28786
(828)456-5212 (800)730-7923
Internet: www.grandviewlodgenc.com
E-mail: stay@grandviewlodgenc.com

Circa 1890. Sheltered on three acres in a mountain cove, this newly remodeled historic farm-style home is located near Waynesville, North Carolina. Sit on porch rockers, breathe deep the sweet fresh air and let the peacefulness of the Great Smoky Mountains refresh you. Locally family-owned for more than 75 years, great pleasure is taken in providing a wonderful experience with cherished memories. Country-style guest rooms feature custom-made log beds and some rooms have a fireplace. The Colonel Love room is pet-friendly. The two-bedroom, two-bath cottage includes a kitchen, living and dining area and Jacuzzi. A gourmet breakfast is always a satisfying way to start each day, and the Sunday Country Buffet is too good to miss. Catered dining events are popular in this delightful setting.

Innkeeper(s): Tom. $79-119. 9 rooms with PB, 3 with FP, 1 cottage, 1 conference room. Breakfast included in rates. Types of meals: Country bkfst, veg bkfst and Sunday brunch.

Certificate may be used: Anytime, subject to availability.

West Jefferson

Meadowsweet Gardens Inn

502 Golf Course Rd.
West Jefferson, NC 28694
(919)619-2215 (919)619-2268
Internet: www.meadowsweetgardens.com/
E-mail: debbierpatterson@gmail.com

Travel to a lovely town in the Blue Ridge Mountains for a quaint escape in this old farmhouse built with local resources including chestnut and oak from the original property. A mountain stream bubbles to a quiet pond.while butterflies flit through the gardens. The mountains offer a colorful backdrop especially during the fall months and you can sit on a rocking chair on the upstairs porch with a book from the Garden or Pioneer rooms. All three guest rooms have a double bed and include breakfast. This bed and breakfast is a lovely spot for a garden wedding because you can say your vows under the arbor and have your first dance in the gazebo. Watch cheese being made at the Ashe County Cheese Factory. Sample Appalachian grape wines at New River Winery. The natural beauty of the area inspires many artists and numerous galleries can be found in West Jefferson. Be sure to bicycle along New River to be immersed in the scenery.

Innkeeper(s): Debbie Patterson, Ken Jones. $90-115. 3 rooms with PB.

Certificate may be used: Sunday-Thursday, November-April.

Williamston

Big Mill Bed & Breakfast

1607 Big Mill Rd
Williamston, NC 27892-8032
(252) 792-8787
Internet: www.bigmill.com
E-mail: info@bigmill.com

Circa 1918. Originally built as a small arts and crafts frame house, the many renovations conceal its true age. The historic farm outbuildings that include the chicken coop, smokehouse, pack house, tobacco barns and potato house, were built from on-site heart pine and cypress trees that were felled and floated down the streams of this 250-acre woodland estate. The Corncrib guest bedroom is in the pack house that originally housed mules. Each of the guest bedrooms feature climate control, stenciled floors, faux-painted walls, hand-decorated tiles on the wet bar and a private entrance. The suite also boasts a stone fireplace and impressive view. The countryside setting includes a three-acre lake with bridges, fruit orchard, vegetable and flower gardens. Eighty-year-old pecan trees planted by Chloe's parents provide nuts for homemade treats as well as shade for the inn.

Innkeeper(s): Chloe Tuttle. $95-155. 4 rooms with PB, 1 with FP, 2 suites, 1 conference room. Breakfast and We offer catered candlelight dinners under the grapevine or in your room included in rates. Types of meals: Cont plus, veg bkfst, early coffee/tea, picnic lunch, gourmet dinner and Catered candlelight meals delivered to your room or on your private patio. Picnic lunches for your outings.

Certificate may be used: Weekdays, December and February, January any day, subject to availability, excludes all holidays, applies to nightly rates only. Cannot be combined with any other offers.

Wilmington

C.W. Worth House B&B

412 South 3rd Street
Wilmington, NC 28401-5102
(910) 762-8562 Fax:(910)763-2173
Internet: www.worthhouse.com
E-mail: relax@worthhouse.com

Circa 1893. This beautifully detailed three-story Queen Anne Victorian boasts two turrets and a wide veranda. From the outside, it gives the appearance of a small castle. The inn was renovated in 1995, and it retains many of the architectural details of the original house, including the paneled front hall. Victorian decor is found throughout the inn, including period antiques. The Rose Suite offers a king four-poster bed, sitting room and bath with a clawfoot tub and separate shower. Guests are treated to gourmet breakfasts. Freshly baked muffins and entrees such as eggs Florentine, rosemary and goat cheese strata and stuffed French toast are served. A second-story porch overlooks the garden with dogwood, ponds and pecan trees.

Innkeeper(s): Margi Erickson, Doug Erickson. $154-194. 7 rooms with PB, 1 with WP. Breakfast and snacks/refreshments included in rates. Types of meals: Full gourmet bkfst, early coffee/tea and wine.

Certificate may be used: November-March, Sunday-Thursday, excluding holidays.

Graystone Inn

100 S 3rd St
Wilmington, NC 28401-4503
(910)763-2000 (888)763-4773 Fax:(910)763-5555
Internet: www.graystoneinn.com
E-mail: contactus@graystoneinn.com

Circa 1906. If you are a connoisseur of inns, you'll be delighted with this stately mansion in the Wilmington Historic District and in the National Register. Recently chosen by American Historic Inns as one of America's Top Ten Romantic Inns, towering columns mark the balconied grand entrance. Its 14,000 square feet of magnificent space includes antique furnishings, art and amenities. A staircase of hand-carved red oak rises three stories. Guests lounge in the music room, drawing room and library. A conference room and sitting area are on the third floor, once a grand ballroom. The elegant guest rooms are often chosen for special occasions, especially the Bellevue, which offers a King bed, sofa and handsome period antiques with a 2-person soaking tub and shower.

Innkeeper(s): Rich Moore, Marcia Moore. $169-359. 9 rooms with PB, 7 with FP, 1 conference room. Breakfast included in rates. Types of meals: Full gourmet bkfst and early coffee/tea.

Certificate may be used: Nov. 1-March 31, Sunday-Thursday, holidays excluded.

Windsor

The Inn at Gray's Landing

401 S King St
Windsor, NC 27983-6721
(252) 794-2255 (877) 794-3501 Fax:(252)794-2254
Internet: www.grayslanding.com
E-mail: innkeepers@grayslanding.com

Circa 1790. Experience classic Southern tradition at this historic Georgian Colonial B&B that is furnished with Victorian period antiques and reproductions. The Inn at Grays Landing Bed & Breakfast is surrounded by cotton, corn and tobacco fields in the historic district of Windsor, North Carolina. This small town sits on the banks of the Cashie River and is a short drive to the Outer Banks. Stroll by the English side garden then sit on the porch and look out on magnolias and crepe myrtles. Stay in a guest room or suite with a canopy, sleigh or brass bed and a spa, steam or rain shower, Jacuzzi or clawfoot tub. After a satisfying breakfast explore the many regional activities. Ask about the special weekend getaway package offered.

Innkeeper(s): Lynette Mallery. $79-139. 5 rooms with PB, 1 with WP, 2 suites, 1 conference room. Breakfast and Sunday brunch included in rates. Types of meals: Full bkfst, veg bkfst, early coffee/tea, wine, Dinners on Thursday and Friday nights by reservation. Back Porch Bar/Restaurant on premises.

Certificate may be used: Sunday-Thursday, January-April.

Winston-Salem

The Augustus T. Zevely Inn

803 S Main St
Winston-Salem, NC 27101-5332
(336)748-9299 (800)928-9299 Fax:(336)721-2211
Internet: www.winston-salem-inn.com
E-mail: reservations@winston-salem-inn.com

Circa 1844. The Zevely Inn is the only lodging in Old Salem. Each of the rooms at this charming pre-Civil War inn have a view of historic Old Salem. Moravian furnishings and fixtures permeate the decor of each of the guest quarters, some of which boast working fireplaces. The home's architecture is reminiscent of many structures built in Old Salem during the second quarter of the 19th century. The formal  dining room and parlor have wood burning fireplaces. The two-story porch offers visitors a view of the period gardens and a beautiful magnolia tree. A line of Old Salem furniture has been created by Lexington Furniture Industries, and several pieces were created especially for the Zevely Inn.

Innkeeper(s): Linda Anderson. $95-235. 12 rooms with PB, 3 with FP, 1 suite. Breakfast and snacks/refreshments included in rates. Types of meals: Full bkfst, early coffee/tea, afternoon tea, Continental breakfast during the week and full breakfast on the weekends. Coffee, tea and ice water throughout the day.

Certificate may be used: January-February, Sunday-Thursday, Subject to availability.

North Dakota

Mountain

221 Melsted Place

8735 130th Ave., NE
Mountain, ND 58262
(701) 993-8257 Fax:(701)993-8257
Internet: www.melstedplace.com
E-mail: 221melpl@polarcomm.com

Circa 1910. This handsome gabled estate is comprised of unique cast concrete blocks and offers three stories with a wide porch, stained and mullioned windows, and inside, a grand staircase. Elegantly furnished guest accommodations feature antiques. The mansion is popular for tours because of its history and beauty. Candlelight dining, first-class service and many other amenities are making 221 Melsted a popular romantic destination for couples. There's a Victorian spa, and the innkeepers can arrange other activities including a private limousine tour of the countryside, berry picking expedition or an evening playing torch light croquet. The area has Icelandic heritage, and each August, the Deuce Icelandic Festival is held.

Innkeeper(s): Lonnette Kelley. $80-120. 4 suites, 1 conference room. Breakfast included in rates. Types of meals: Full gourmet bkfst, early coffee/tea, picnic lunch, afternoon tea, snacks/refreshments and gourmet dinner.

Certificate may be used: Anytime, subject to availability.

One Majestic Place

12588 88th St. N.E.
Mountain, ND
(701) 402-2148 (888) 518-6570
Internet: www.onemajesticplace.com
E-mail: retreat@onemajesticplace.com

Circa 2010. Snowmobile yourself into this beautiful hand-crafted cabin complete with a rock fireplace and hot tub - or drive in with the whole family. It is directly on the North Dakota State Snowmobile Trail and offers 80 acres of nature paths, scenic picnic spots and views overlooking the Red River Valley. You can also bring friends with tents and have your own retreat or book a silent retreat complete with spiritual counselor. There is a retreat center on the property as well.

Innkeeper(s): Staci Jenson. $111-177. 2 rooms, 1 with PB, 1 with FP, 1 with HT, 1 cabin. No meals included in rates, Restaurant located 3 miles away and grocery shopping nearby.

Certificate may be used: January-March, Sunday-Thursday, subject to availability.

Ohio

Alexandria

WillowBrooke Bed 'n Breakfast

4459 Morse Road
Alexandria, OH 43001
(740)924-6161 (800)722-6372
Internet: www.willowbrooke.com
E-mail: wilbrk@aol.com

Circa 1980. There are no worries at this English Tudor Manor House and Guest Cottage located in a secluded 34-acre wooded setting. Furnished in a traditional decor, spacious guest bedrooms and romantic suites offer extensive amenities that pamper and please like feather beds or pillowtop mattresses, candlelight, whirlpool tubs, kitchens and balconies or patios. Families are welcome to stay in the Garden Suite or Guest House. For breakfast, choose from three juices along with French toast and strawberries, scrambled eggs and ham. Enjoy year-round use of the outdoor hot tub, and browse the gift shop for glass oil candles and crystal table accessories.
Innkeeper(s): Sandra Gilson. $115-270. 5 rooms, 6 with PB, 3 with FP, 3 suites, 1 cottage, 1 guest house. Breakfast included in rates. Types of meals: Full gourmet bkfst and early coffee/tea.
Certificate may be used: Monday-Thursday, subject to availability, excludes October.

Ashtabula

Gilded Swan B&B

5024 West Ave
Ashtabula, OH 44004
(440)992-1566 (888)345-7926
Internet: www.gildedswan.com
E-mail: gsinfo@roadrunner.com

Circa 1902. Romantic interludes and memorable moments are easily experienced at this lavish Queen Anne Victorian in a Lake Erie harbor town. Painstakingly restored, the B&B is furnished with cherished family heirlooms and antiques. Comfortable guest bedrooms and suites boast welcoming decor, canopy beds, whirlpool tubs, a fireplace and pillow chocolates. In the elegant dining room, a sumptuous breakfast may include raspberry-stuffed French toast and grilled sausage links. Afternoon snacks are also offered. Centrally located, the inn is within easy access to wine country, Cleveland's museums, Pennsylvania's attractions and Amish country.
Innkeeper(s): Elaine Swanson. $75-105. 4 rooms, 2 with PB, 1 with FP. Breakfast and snacks/refreshments included in rates. Types of meals: Full gourmet bkfst, early coffee/tea, picnic lunch and afternoon tea.
Certificate may be used: Anytime, subject to availability.

Berlin

Donna's Premier Lodging B&B

5523 Twp Rd 358 East Street
Berlin, OH 44610
(330) 893-3068 (800) 320-3338
Internet: www.donnasofberlin.com/?iloveinns
E-mail: info@donnasb-b.com

Circa 1991. Staying here for any reason is a pleasure. Come for the perfect romantic getaway, a respite from everyday cares or just because. Every season is a great time to visit. See glistening snow-covered hills and experience the holiday season. Travel country roads in spring and glimpse new life on Amish farms. Catch the many summer festivals with out-of-this-world local foods or take in the awe-inspiring colorful displays of autumn. Accommodations range from gorgeous villas and suites to secluded cedar cabins in the woods with cascading waterfalls, fireplaces and Jacuzzis. Indulge in a full-course breakfast in bed before beginning the day's adventures. Special touches may include a couples' massage, sleigh and carriage rides, gift baskets and much more. Gracious and friendly staff go out of their way to make each visit memorable. Donna's is conveniently located close to gift shops and attractions in Berlin, Ohio.
Innkeeper(s): Donna Marie Schlabach. $99-369. 6 rooms, 17 with PB, 17 with FP, 17 with HT, 3 suites, 5 cottages, 9 cabins. Breakfast, Coffee, Tea, Cocoa and Popcorn included in rates. Types of meals: Country bkfst, veg bkfst, picnic lunch, snacks/refreshments and In-room gourmet meals available.
Certificate may be used: November-May, Sunday-Thursday, Honeymoon/Anniversary Villa only. Anytime, Last minute-based on availability.

Bucyrus

HideAway Country Inn

1601 SR 4
Bucyrus, OH 43302
(419) 562-3013 (800) 570-8233 Fax:(419)562-3003
Internet: www.HideAwayInn.com
E-mail: innkeeper@hideawayinn.com

Circa 1938. Experience a refreshing getaway while staying at this remarkable inn. Because of the inn's outrageous service, even the business traveler will feel rejuvenated after embarking on a rendezvous with nature here. Exquisite guest suites feature private Jacuzzis, fireplaces and amenities that pamper. Savor a leisurely five-course breakfast. Enjoy fine dining in the restaurant, or ask for an intimate picnic to be arranged. A productive conference room instills a personal quiet and inspires the mind.
Innkeeper(s): Snobilee Bloomfield . $79-290. 12 rooms with PB, 7 with FP, 1 with HT, 10 with WP, 10 total suites, including 2 two-bedroom suites, 2

guest houses, 2 conference rooms. Breakfast, A Full Hearty Breakfast is served daily. If you would like to leave very early and a take-it-with- you or brown bag breakfast is ready to go included in rates. Types of meals: Full gourmet bkfst, veg bkfst, Sun. brunch, early coffee/tea, gourmet lunch, picnic lunch, afternoon tea, snacks/refreshments, hors d'oeuvres, wine, gourmet dinner, room service, Enjoy Breakfast, Lunch or Dinner in the fine dining atmosphere of the on-site restaurant and or choose from the menu and have it delivered to your room in a Picnic Basket. Enjoy wine and spirits in the fully inclusive wine cellar and martini bar. Restaurant on premises.

Certificate may be used: Sunday-Thursday, excluding holidays and group events.

Cedarville

Hearthstone Inn & Suites

10 S Main St
Cedarville, OH 45314-9760
(937) 766-3000 (877) 644-6466
Internet: www.hearthstoneinn.com
E-mail: Please call our toll-free number

Circa 2001. Blending regional themes with small-town hospitality, this country inn hotel with an upscale bed and breakfast ambiance is family-owned and non-smoking. Enjoy old-fashioned friendliness, generous service and impeccable cleanliness. Relax on the wraparound porch or on the leather sofa by the huge Ohio River rock hearth in the Fireplace Lounge with Queen Anne decor. Browse through the historical displays and the cottage gift shop. Pleasant guest bedrooms and Jacuzzi suites feature pampering amenities. Hand-hewn beams beneath the second-floor balcony and mural art accent the Breakfast Commons where a Supreme Selections morning buffet is served. The inn is conveniently located right on the Ohio to Erie Bike Trail.

Innkeeper(s): Stuart & Ruth Zaharek. $109-169. 20 rooms with PB, 2 with HT, 2 suites, 1 conference room. Breakfast included in rates. Types of meals: Cont plus.

Certificate may be used: November-January, Sunday-Wednesday; April-May, Sunday-Wednesday. Last minute subject to availability (same day, anytime).

Cleveland

Stone Gables Bed and Breakfast

3806 Franklin Blvd
Cleveland, OH 44113
(216) 961-4654 (877) 215-4326
Internet: stonegables.net
E-mail: stonegablesbnb@yahoo.com

Circa 1883. Historic Mansion Row on the west side is where to find this Queen Anne Stick-style inn that was renovated and opened as a B&B in 2001. The grand elegance of the past mingles fine antique furnishings with modern comforts. Quiet public areas enhance intimate gatherings. Tastefully decorated suites and guest bedrooms feature special touches. Two of the romantic rooms boast oversize whirlpool/showers for two. Savor culinary favorites like dark chocolate waffles with Frangelica cream and hot fudge or carrot cake waffles, eggs Benedict and fresh fruit. Colorful flower displays come from the cutting garden that is enclosed with an embellished iron fence. A spa and sauna are fitting ways to relax and rejuvenate after a day of sightseeing.

Innkeeper(s): Richard Turnbull . $125-190. 5 rooms, 1 with PB, 2 with HT, 2 suites. Breakfast and snacks/refreshments included in rates. Types of meals: Full gourmet bkfst and early coffee/tea.

Certificate may be used: November-March, subject to availability, weekdays only.

Danville

The White Oak Inn

29683 Walhonding Rd, SR 715
Danville, OH 43014
(740)599-6107 (877)908-5923
Internet: www.whiteoakinn.com
E-mail: info@whiteoakinn.com

Circa 1915. Large oaks and ivy surround the wide front porch of this three-story farmhouse situated on 13 green acres. It is located on the former Indian trail and pioneer road that runs along the Kokosing River, and an Indian mound has been discovered on the property. The inn's woodwork is all original white oak, and guest rooms are furnished in antiques. Visitors often  shop for maple syrup, cheese and handicrafts at nearby Amish farms. Three cozy fireplace rooms and two cottages provide the perfect setting for romantic evenings.

Innkeeper(s): Yvonne Martin, Ian Martin. $145-240. 12 rooms with PB, 6 with FP, 3 with WP, 2 cottages, 1 conference room. Breakfast and snacks/refreshments included in rates. Types of meals: Country bkfst, veg bkfst, early coffee/tea, gourmet dinner and Romantic dinner baskets delivered to rooms.

Certificate may be used: Sunday-Thursday, except holidays.

Geneva On The Lake

Eagle Cliff Inn

5254 Lake Road East
Geneva On The Lake, OH 44041
(440)466-1110 Fax:(440)466-0315
Internet: www.eaglecliffinn.com
E-mail: beachclub5@roadrunner.com

Circa 1880. Catering to adults, this recently renovated 1880 Victorian inn graces one acre of the Strip in the state's first resort village. It is listed in the National Register, noted as significantly reflecting the dominant recreation history of Geneva On The Lake. Enjoy the relaxed atmosphere while sitting on white wicker cushioned chairs and rockers or a porch swing. Elegantly functional guest bedrooms and a suite offer views of the Strip and lake. The cottages are situated privately in the back. Savor a satisfying daily breakfast. Magnificent sunsets are best viewed from the inn's easy beach access. Sip a local wine from famed Ashtabula County while chatting by the fireplace. Visit the nearby Jenny Munger Museum.

Innkeeper(s): LuAnn Bunch, Michelle & Peggy. $115-159. 7 rooms, 6 with PB, 2 total suites, including 1 two-bedroom suite, 3 cottages. Breakfast, afternoon tea and snacks/refreshments included in rates. Types of meals: Full bkfst, veg bkfst and early coffee/tea.

Certificate may be used: mid-May through mid-October, Sunday-Thursday, excludes holidays.

The Lakehouse Inn

5653 Lake Road E
Geneva On The Lake, OH 44041
(440)466-8668 Fax:(440)466-2556
Internet: www.thelakehouseinn.com
E-mail: inquiries@thelakehouseinn.com

Circa 1940. In a quaint lakefront location, this inn offers a variety of accommodations that boast a nautical/country decor. Stay "bed and breakfast style" in standard guest bedrooms or Jacuzzi suites with fireplaces, DVD players, microwaves and refrigerators. Renovated cottages include a living room, fully equipped kitchen, bath and one or two bedrooms. The secluded Beach House features a living and dining area, kitchen, Jacuzzi bath, two-person shower, spacious bedroom and outdoor deck. Enjoy the central air and heat as well as panoramic views of Lake Erie and the Geneva Marina.

Innkeeper(s): Andrea Bushweiler. $139-389. 8 rooms with PB, 4 with FP, 4 with WP, 3 two-bedroom suites, 3 cottages, 1 guest house, 1 conference room. Breakfast included in rates. Types of meals: Full bkfst, veg bkfst, early coffee/tea, snacks/refreshments and wine. Restaurant on premises.

Certificate may be used: November-April, Sunday-Thursday, subject to availability.

Georgetown

Bailey House

112 N Water St
Georgetown, OH 45121-1332
(937)378-3087
Internet: www.baileyhousebandb.com
E-mail: baileyho@frontier.com

Circa 1830. The stately columns of this three-story Greek Revival house once greeted Ulysses S. Grant, a frequent visitor

during his boyhood when he was sent to buy milk from the Bailey's. A story is told that Grant accidentally overheard that the Bailey boy was leaving West Point. Grant immediately ran through the woods to the home of Congressman Thomas Hamer and petitioned an appointment in Bailey's place which he received, thus launching his military career. The inn has double parlors, pegged oak floors and Federal-style fireplace mantels. Antique washstands, chests and beds are found in the large guest rooms.

Innkeeper(s): Nancy Purdy. $65-70. 4 rooms, 1 with PB, 2 with FP. Breakfast included in rates. Types of meals: Full bkfst and early coffee/tea.

Certificate may be used: Anytime, subject to availability.

Logan

Inn & Spa At Cedar Falls

21190 State Route 374
Logan, OH 43138
(740)385-7489 (800)653-2557 Fax:(740)385-0820
Internet: innatcedarfalls.com
E-mail: info@innatcedarfalls.com

Circa 1987. This sophisticated inn, complete with traditional rooms along with separate cottages and cabins, was construct-

ed on 75 acres adjacent to Hocking Hills State Parks and one-half mile from the waterfalls. The kitchen and dining rooms are in a 19th-century log house. Accommodations in the two-story

barn-shaped building are simple and comfortable, each furnished with antiques. There are six fully equipped log cabins and twelve cozy cottages available, each individually decorated. The cabins include a kitchen and living room with a gas-log stove; some have a whirlpool tub. The cottages feature under-the-counter refrigerators, gas-log stoves and whirlpool tubs. There also is a meeting room equipped with a wood-burning stove. Verandas provide sweeping views of woodland and meadow. The grounds include organic gardens for the inn's gourmet dinners, and animals that have been spotted include red fox, wild turkey and white-tail deer.

Innkeeper(s): Ellen Grinsfelder & Terry Lingo. $125-345. 5 cabins, 26 with PB, 19 with FP, 15 with WP, 12 cottages, 1 conference room. Breakfast, snacks/refreshments and Homemade cookies in the room on arrival included in rates. Types of meals: Full gourmet bkfst, veg bkfst, early coffee/tea, gourmet lunch, picnic lunch, wine, gourmet dinner, room service, Picnic lunch, Cheese and fruit trays, Picnic dinner and Brown bag lunch. Restaurant on premises.

Certificate may be used: Year-round, Sunday-Thursday only, except holidays.

Miamisburg

English Manor B&B

505 E Linden Ave
Miamisburg, OH 45342-2850
(937)866-2288
Internet: www.englishmanorohio.com
E-mail: englishmanorohio@yahoo.com

Circa 1924. This is a beautiful English Tudor mansion situated on a tree-lined street of Victorian homes. Well-chosen

antiques combined with the innkeepers' personal heirlooms added to the inn's polished floors, sparkling leaded-and-stained-glass windows and shining silver, make this an elegant retreat. Breakfast is served in the formal dining room. Fine restaurants, a water park, baseball, air force museum and

theater are close by, as is The River Corridor bikeway on the banks of the Great Miami River.

Innkeeper(s): Julie Chmiel, Larry Chmiel. $89-125. 5 rooms, 3 with PB, 1 total suite, including 2 two-bedroom suites, 1 conference room. Breakfast included in rates. Types of meals: Full gourmet bkfst, veg bkfst, early coffee/tea, picnic lunch, afternoon tea and dinner.

Certificate may be used: Sunday-Thursday all year, upon availability.

Millersburg

Hannah's House Bed & Breakfast

5410 County Road 201
Millersburg, OH 44654
(330) 893-2368
Internet: www.hannahshouseretreat.com
E-mail: info@hannahshouseretreat.com

Circa 1997. Spanning five acres with a rock waterfall and spacious patio area, this premier B&B in Holmes County boasts a Victorian style. Guest bedrooms and suites overlook a wooded valley. Select a room with a natural gas fireplace or a stay in a suite on the main floor with a Jacuzzi for two, as well as kitchen, dining and sitting areas and a patio entrance. Hannah's House Bed & Breakfast in Berlin, Ohio provides a hot and hearty breakfast each morning. Ask about specials and packages available. Browse in the local Amish Country Leather Shop for quality items to keep or give as gifts.

Innkeeper(s): Barbara. $90-215. 5 rooms with PB, 1 with FP, 2 with WP, 2 suites. Breakfast and Sparkling Grape Juice included in rates. Types of meals: Full bkfst.

Certificate may be used: November-April, Sunday-Thursday (All rooms must be consecutive nights stay). Not valid on holidays or holiday weekends, subject to availability.

Mount Vernon

The Russell-Cooper House

115 E Gambier St
Mount Vernon, OH 43050-3509
(740)397-8638 Fax:(740)397-3839
Internet: www.russell-cooper.com
E-mail: innkeeper@russell-cooper.com

Circa 1829. Dr. John Russell and his son-in-law, Colonel Cooper, modeled a simple brick Federal house into a unique Victorian. Its sister structure is the Wedding Cake House of Kennebunk, Maine. There is a hand-painted plaster ceiling in the ballroom and a collection of Civil War items and antique medical devices. Woodwork is of cherry,  maple and walnut, and there are etched and stained-glass windows. Hal Holbrook called the town "America's Hometown."

Innkeeper(s): Tom Dvorak. $65-100. 6 rooms with PB, 1 conference room. Breakfast and snacks/refreshments included in rates. Types of meals: Full gourmet bkfst.

Certificate may be used: November-March, Sunday-Thursday, subject to availability and 24 hrs. advance notice.

Painesville

Fitzgerald's Irish B&B

47 Mentor Ave
Painesville, OH 44077-3201
(440)639-0845
Internet: www.FitzgeraldBB.com
E-mail: fitzbb@gmail.com

Circa 1937. Warm Irish hospitality is extended at this 1937 French Tudor home situated in the historic district. It was recently restored as a landmark of craftsmanship with its castle-like design, unusual turret, slate roof, ornate staircase, hardwood floors and elaborate 11-foot fireplace. Watch satellite TV in the sitting room, play games and relax by the fire in the large gathering room. Lounge on the sun porch overlooking the park-like grounds and frequent birds. Air-conditioned guest bedrooms include pleasing amenities. Sleep on a four-poster or sleigh bed. The third-floor Bushmills Room features a microwave, refrigerator, VCR, CD player, Jacuzzi tub and Roman shower. Savor a full breakfast on weekends and holidays and a generous continental breakfast during the week. Popular trails and beaches of the Great Lakes region are nearby.

Innkeeper(s): Debra Fitzgerald, Tom Fitzgerald. $105-150. 4 rooms with PB. Breakfast included in rates. Types of meals: Full Breakfast on weekends and Continental Plus on weekdays.

Certificate may be used: Sunday-Thursday, Nov. 1-April 29, for the Mayo and Dublin rooms only. Holidays excluded.

Rider's 1812 Inn

792 Mentor Ave
Painesville, OH 44077-2516
(440)354-8200 Fax:(440)350-9385
Internet: www.ridersinn.com
E-mail: ridersinninfo@yahoo.com

Circa 1812. In the days when this inn and tavern served the frontier Western Reserve, it could provide lodging and meals for more than 100 overnight guests. Restored in 1988, the pub features an original fireplace and wavy window panes. Most of the inn's floors are rare, long-needle pine. A passageway in the cellar is said to have been part of the Underground Railroad. An English-style restaurant is also on the premises. Guest rooms are furnished with antiques. Breakfast in bed is the option of choice.

Innkeeper(s): Elaine Crane & Gary Herman. $90-110. 10 rooms, 9 with PB, 1 suite, 3 conference rooms. Breakfast included in rates. Types of meals: Full bkfst, veg bkfst, Sun. brunch, early coffee/tea, lunch, picnic lunch, afternoon tea, wine, dinner and room service. Restaurant on premises.

Certificate may be used: Sunday-Friday, year round, not valid on Saturdays.

Stockport

Stockport Mill

1995 Broadway Avenue
Stockport, OH 43787
(740)559-2822 Fax:(740)559-2236
Internet: www.stockportmill.com
E-mail: mill@stockportmill.com

Stay at this century-old restored grain mill on the Muskingum River for a truly authentic historic experience combined with everything desired for a romantic getaway, business retreat or stress-free change of pace. Each of the four floors offers an assortment of common areas and accommodations. Browse the main lobby, an inviting library and the gift gallery showcasing local craftsman and artists. The Massage Therapy Room was the original grain bin. Themed guest bedrooms are named and decorated as a tribute to the local region and its prominent people. Stay in a luxurious suite with a two-person whirlpool spa and private balcony. Riverview Rooms feature clawfoot tubs, southern views of the river and private terraces. Ask about special packages and scheduling events at the Boathouse Banquet Hall.

Innkeeper(s): Dottie Singer. Call for rates. Call inn for details. Types of meals: Cont, lunch, picnic lunch, snacks/refreshments, hors d'oeuvres, dinner and room service. Restaurant on premises.

Certificate may be used: Anytime, November-March, subject to availability, suites only (2nd or 3rd floor). Does not include Valentines Day or holidays.

Strasburg

The Garver House

410 N. Wooster Ave.
Strasburg, OH 44680
(330)878-4113
Internet: www.garverhousebnb.com
E-mail: stay@garverhousebnb.com

Circa 1902. This inn is a showcase of historic workmanship with original wood floors that feature a different border design in each room. Rooms are colored by the sun shining through five original stained glass windows. In the garden young goldfish swim in a restored stone and cement pool. Spend a romantic weekend in the lavender and black Strasburg Suite with large soaking tub and electric fireplace. Add a side-by-side ensuite couple's massage for extra relaxation. Join other guests in the dining room each morning for pumpkin pancakes or a breakfast strata. Celebrate a special anniversary with a three or five-course candlelight dinner on the sun porch. Step back in time by watching a movie at the oldest drive-in theater in the state. Look for that perfect find at local antique store then travel the Ohio and Erie Canal via bicycle or canoe. The inn is close to many Amish cultural and historical destinations.

Innkeeper(s): Natalie Cline, Al Cline. $100-110. 3 rooms with PB. Types of meals: Full bkfst.

Certificate may be used: November-April, Sunday-Thursday, subject to availability.

Oklahoma

Guthrie

Guthrie Inns
202 W. Harrison
Guthrie, OK 73044
(405)282-1000 Fax:(405)293-9585
Internet: guthrieinns.com
E-mail: guthrieinns@coxinet.net

Two historic buildings are combined to create a charming experience for travelers to Guthrie, Oklahoma. Nestled in the heart of the historic downtown area, the Pollard Inn and the Harrison House Bed and Breakfast offer all master bedroom suites with queen beds, king beds, or two beds. Guests enjoy the privacy of en suite bathrooms and the old world ambiance of rooms decorated with antiques. Breakfast is a complimentary, delectable five-course event served at Megan's in the Pollard Inn. Walk to art galleries, antique shops, and wine bars or take in a show at the Pollard Theatre which focuses on creative storytelling. The city of Guthrie boasts one of the largest historic districts in the National Register and is home to a unique assortment of museums including the Oklahoma Frontier Drugstore Museum, the Oklahoma Sports Hall of Face Guthrie Annex, and the Owens Art Place Museum.

Innkeeper(s): Michelle Ladd. $129-169. Call inn for details.

Certificate may be used: July-August, January-February, subject to availablity.

Rollins Creek Old West Town & Bed and Breakfast
3131 N Anderson Rd
Guthrie, OK 73044
(405) 293-3131
Internet: www.rollinscreek.com
E-mail: info@rollinscreek.com

Circa 2003. Historic Guthrie is known as The Bed and Breakfast Capital of Oklahoma. You will be sleeping and eating a fine country breakfast in the rustic Boarding House and you can spend your evening playing cards in the Paradise Saloon that is located in Rollins Creek Old West Town. Your view from the balcony of Rollins Creek Bed and Breakfast overlooks Old West Town that pulls you back in to the 1880s Old West when the Outlaws roamed the area known as "Cowboy Flats".

Innkeeper(s): Connie & Colin Coffey. $125-150. 3 rooms, 1 with PB, 1 conference room. Breakfast included in rates. Types of meals: Country bkfst.

Certificate may be used: Anytime, subject to availability.

Muskogee

Historic Hayes House
555 N 12th St
Muskogee, OK 74401-5914
(918)682-4652 (888)647-3622
Internet: www.historichayeshouse.com
E-mail: historichayeshouse@yahoo.com

This stately inn was built to be the Oklahoma governor's mansion and holds the history of speeches delivered from the front balcony. The elegant home had only a short brush with fame as the owner did not win the election. Nevertheless, guests today can pretend to be important politicians in the Governor's or First Lady's Suites with antique furniture and goose down comforters. Each guest room has a private bathroom with a whirlpool tub for two and lounging robes and slippers. Start the day with eggs, breakfast meat, and fruit with Devonshire cream, then spend the afternoon sunning by the pool. If you are a bride to be, you can invite 150 of your closest friends and family to witness your wedding on the manicured lawn beside the koi pond. The innkeepers are happy to assist in planning your special day. Specials include a romance package and a candlelit five-course dinner.

Innkeeper(s): James Holder. Call for rates. 2 suites, 1 cottage.

Certificate may be used: November-March, subject to availability.

Norman

Montford Inn
322 W Tonhawa St
Norman, OK 73069-7124
(405) 321-2200 (800) 321-8969 Fax:(405)321-8347
Internet: www.montfordinn.com
E-mail: innkeeper@montfordinn.com

Circa 1994. Although this inn was built just a few years ago, the exterior is reminiscent of a country farmhouse, with its covered front porch lined with rockers. The interior is a mix of styles, from the decidedly Southwestern Chickasaw Rancher room to the romantic Solitude room, which includes a king-size bed canopied in Battenburg lace. Each of the guest rooms has a fireplace. The gourmet breakfasts are arranged and presented artfully, featuring succulent egg dishes, freshly baked breads and fruit smoothies.

Innkeeper(s): William Murray, Phyllis and Ron Murray. $99-239. 16 guest houses with PB, 16 with FP, 2 with HT, 10 with WP, 6 suites, 6 cottages. Breakfast, snacks/refreshments and wine included in rates. Types of meals: Full gourmet bkfst and early coffee/tea.

Certificate may be used: June-Aug. 15.

Oklahoma City

The Grandison Inn at Maney Park

1200 N Shartel Ave
Oklahoma City, OK 73103-2402
(405) 232-8778 (888) 799-4667 Fax:(405)232-5039
Internet: www.grandisoninn.com
E-mail: innkeeper@grandisoninn.com

Circa 1904. This spacious Victorian has been graciously restored and maintains its original mahogany woodwork, stained glass, brass fixtures and a grand staircase. Several rooms include a Jacuzzi, and all have their own unique decor. The Treehouse Hideaway includes a Queen bed that is meant to look like a Hammock and walls that are painted with a blue sky and stars. The Jacuzzi tub rests beneath a skylight. The home is located north of downtown Oklahoma City in a historic neighborhood and is listed in the National Register.

Innkeeper(s): Claudia Wright, Bob Wright. $99-199. 8 rooms with PB, 4 with FP, 7 with WP. Breakfast and snacks/refreshments included in rates. Types of meals: Cont plus, early coffee/tea, wine, room service, In-room dinners, Picnic Basket, Cheese and Cracker Tray, Full Breakfast - Weekends Only and Off-Site Catering Available.

Certificate may be used: Sunday-Thursday or Anytime, Last Minute-Based on Availability.

Oregon

Ashland

Albion Inn

34 Union Street
Ashland, OR 97520-2958
(541) 488-3905 (888) 246-8310
Internet: www.albion-inn.com
E-mail: info@albion-inn.com

Circa 1905. One block off the main street, this inn is an oasis of peace, quiet, and beauty in the historic Hargadine District. This modest farmhouse has grown over the years with architecturally harmonious additions and was transformed into a bed and breakfast in 1990. To better serve theatre-goers to Ashland's world-famous Oregon Shakespeare Festival, guest rooms include private bathrooms and two courtyard suites were added by the rose garden. Watch satellite TV in the downstairs den that also has an extensive collection of games and puzzles. Read the newpaper and magazines or use the guest computer in the living room. Fine art hangs throughout the inn. A delicious, organic breakfast always starts with a fresh fruit smoothie and a fruit parfait, then fresh baked goods. The hot main course alternates between a savory meal one day and a sweeter meal the next. Mention special dietary needs when booking and Cyd will cook you a special meal.

Innkeeper(s): Cyd Ropp, Gary Ropp. $99-174. 5 rooms with PB, 1 with FP, 1 conference room. Breakfast, snacks/refreshments, wine, Fresh cookies daily. Cashews, fresh and dried fruit, sweets, sherry and unlimited tea bar included in rates.

Certificate may be used: Anytime, November-March, subject to availability.

Astoria

Franklin Street Station Bed & Breakfast

1140 Franklin Ave
Astoria, OR 97103-4132
(503)325-4314 (800)448-1098
Internet: www.astoriaoregonbb.com
E-mail: franklinststationbb@yahoo.com

Circa 1900. Sit out on the balcony and take in views of the Columbia River and beautiful sunsets from this 1900 Victorian-style inn. Ornate craftsmanship and antique furnishings, right down to the clawfoot bathtubs, transport visitors into the past. The six guest rooms are named Starlight Suite, Sweet Tranquility, the Hide-away, the Magestic, Magnolia Retreat and Enchanted Haven. The full breakfast includes dishes like fruit, waffles and sausage. The Flavel House Museum and Heritage Museum within walking distance, and the Astoria Column and Fort Clatsop are a short drive from the inn.

Innkeeper(s): Rebecca Greenway. $60-135. 6 rooms, 5 with PB, 1 with FP, 3 total suites, including 2 two-bedroom suites. Breakfast included in rates. Types of meals: Full bkfst and Coffee.

Certificate may be used: Oct. 15-Jan. 15, Sunday-Friday.

Grandview B&B

1574 Grand Ave
Astoria, OR 97103-3733
(503)325-0000 (800)488-3250
Internet: www.pacifier.com/~grndview/
E-mail: grandviewbedandbreakfast@usa.net

Circa 1896. To fully enjoy its views of the Columbia River, this Victorian house has both a tower and a turret. Antiques and white wicker furnishings contribute to the inn's casual, homey feeling. The Bird Meadow Room is particularly appealing to bird-lovers with its birdcage, bird books and bird wallpaper. Breakfast, served in the main-floor turret, frequently includes smoked salmon with bagels and cream cheese.

Innkeeper(s): Charleen Maxwell. $69-161. 10 rooms, 7 with PB, 3 with FP, 2 suites. Breakfast and snacks/refreshments included in rates. Types of meals: Full bkfst.

Certificate may be used: Nov. 1-May 17, holidays okay except two weekends in February may be excluded.

Carlton

The Carlton Inn B&B

648 W Main St
Carlton, OR 97111
(503)852-7506
Internet: www.thecarltoninn.com
E-mail: info@thecarltoninn.com

Circa 1915. Gracing the Wine Capital Region of Oregon in the Willamette Valley, this cottage-style inn is located in Carlton, and centrally located just one hour from Mt. Hood, Salem, Portland, the Columbia Gorge and the coast. Feel at home and relax by the wood-burning fireplace or sit on the shaded back porch overlooking the garden. Comfortable furnishings include American and European antiques and Amish craftsmanship. Accommodations feature central heat and air conditioning, wifi, private bathrooms, and aromatherapy bath products. The main floor Garden Room boasts a jetted tub and shower, or stay in one of upstairs guest rooms or spacious Yamhill-Carlton Suite that sleeps up to 3. Indulge in a freshly prepared gourmet breakfast made with local and organic ingredients; some of the vegetables and herbs are grown onsite. Breakfast-to-go is available for early departures. Linger over a second cup of Mud River Coffee before embarking on the day's adventures.

Innkeeper(s): Karen Choules. $139-235. 4 rooms with PB, 1 with WP, 1 suite. Breakfast and afternoon tea included in rates. Types of meals: Full bkfst, early coffee/tea and wine.

Certificate may be used: November-March, Sunday-Thursday, subject to availability.

Coos Bay

Old Tower House Bed & Breakfast

476 Newmark Ave
Coos Bay, OR 97420-3201
(541)888-6058
Internet: www.oldtowerhouse.com
E-mail: oldtowerhouse@yahoo.com

Circa 1872. Fully restored and listed in the National Register, Old Tower House Bed & Breakfast offers a delightful setting to relax and enjoy the Oregon coast. Located just a few yards from the ocean in Coos Bay, there are many beaches to explore as well as other activities and attractions. Visit Shore Acres Park and play on one of the top-rated Bandon Dunes golf courses. Browse through the movie collection in the enclosed sun porch. Stay in a guest bedroom in the main house or enjoy the spacious privacy in Ivy Cottage, the original carriage house and tack room. It features a sitting room, microwave and clawfoot tub. A continental breakfast is provided in the formal dining room of the main house or on the sunny veranda.

Innkeeper(s): Stephanie Kramer. Call for rates. Call inn for details. A gourmet breakfast is offered for an additional $9.50 per person or a Continental Breakfast is included in rates. Types of meals: Full gourmet bkfst.

Certificate may be used: December-April, Monday-Thursday, except holidays.

Cottage Grove

Apple Inn Bed and Breakfast

30697 Kenady Ln
Cottage Grove, OR 97424
(541) 942-2393 (800) 942-2393
Internet: www.appleinnbb.com
E-mail: kandh@appleinnbb.com

Circa 1973. Surrounded by more than 270 forested acres in Cottage Grove, Oregon, this inn offers the perfect visit to the Pacific Northwest. Located in the picturesque Willamette Valley near Eugene, there are two lakes, wineries and a 26-mile bike trail nearby. Guests are given a one-hour free guided walking or riding forest tour of the Tree Farm. Relax in the common room or on the large deck and soak in the hot tub. Thoughtful amenities and views of the garden or forest make the accommodations inviting retreats. Evening snack trays are provided with beverages and treats. Gather for a satisfying gourmet breakfast each morning made with recipes from the inn's cookbook. Personalized packages are available to make each stay most enjoyable.

Innkeeper(s): Kathe & Harry. $130-150. 2 rooms with PB, 1 with FP. Breakfast and snacks/refreshments included in rates. Types of meals: Full gourmet bkfst, veg bkfst, early coffee/tea, gourmet lunch and wine.

Certificate may be used: November -March, Monday -Thursday.

Enterprise

1910 Historic Enterprise House Bed & Breakfast

508 First South Street
Enterprise, OR 97828
(541)426-4238 (888)448-8825
Internet: www.enterprisehousebnb.com
E-mail: fcloud@pacifier.com

Circa 1910. Listed in the National Register, 1910 Historic Enterprise House Bed & Breakfast is an elegant three-story Edwardian/Queen Anne Victorian mansion. Located in Enterprise, Oregon along Hells Canyon Scenic Byway, Joseph and Wallowa Lakes are close by. The B&B sits on a hill overlooking Eagle Cap Mountains. Stroll through the orchards or walk to the local Terminal Gravity Brewery, a popular place for food and beer. Read by the fire on leather furnishings surrounded by a quiet and relaxed atmosphere in the living room. After a good night's rest in a guest bedroom or suite, indulge in a gourmet breakfast buffet made with family recipes in the garden-view dining room. Nearby Eagle Cap Wilderness offers numerous outdoor activities.

Innkeeper(s): Jack Burgoyne, Judy Burgoyne. $121-320. 5 rooms. Breakfast included in rates. Types of meals: Full gourmet bkfst, veg bkfst, early coffee/tea, picnic lunch, wine, dinner and Occasion dinners offered with advance notice.

Certificate may be used: Oct. 15-Nov. 15.

Fossil

Wilson Ranches Retreat Bed and Breakfast

16555 Butte Creek Rd
Fossil, OR 97830
(541)763-2227 (866)763-2227 Fax:(541)763-2719
Internet: www.wilsonranchesretreat.com
E-mail: npwilson@wilsonranchesretreat.com

Circa 1910. Amidst wide open spaces off a quiet country road in North Central Oregon, the Wilson Ranches Retreat Bed and Breakfast in Fossil is a 9,000-acre working cattle and hay ranch. Scenic and secluded, the retreat was designed for comfort and relief from stress. It sits in Butte Creek Valley in the John Day Basin surrounded by the Cascade Mountain Range. Bird watch from the large deck or relax in the living room Called the "best rest in Wheeler County," western-themed guest bedrooms are on the main floor and upstairs as well as two spacious accommodations in the daylight basement that are perfect for families. Hunger disappears after a hearty cowboy breakfast served on the handcrafted 11-foot knotty pine dining room table. Experience cattle drives, horseback rides, hikes, and four-wheel drive ranch tours.

Innkeeper(s): Phil & Nancy Wilson. $79-149. 6 rooms, 2 with PB, 1 with FP, 1 conference room. Breakfast included in rates. Types of meals: Country bkfst and early coffee/tea.

Certificate may be used: January and February, Monday-Thursday.

Grants Pass

Weasku Inn

5560 Rogue River Hwy
Grants Pass, OR 97527
(541)471-8000 (800)493-2758 Fax:(541)471-7038
Internet: www.weasku.com
E-mail: kirt@countryhouseinns.com

Circa 1924. Built as a secluded fishing lodge, this historic inn once hosted the likes of President Herbert Hoover, Zane Grey, Walt Disney, Clark Gable and Carole Lombard. It is said that after Lombard's death, Gable spent several weeks here lamenting the loss of his beloved wife. A complete restoration took place in the late 1990s, reviving the inn back to its former glory. The log exterior, surrounded by towering trees and 10 fragrant acres, is a welcoming site. Inside, crackling fires from the inn's rock fireplaces warm the common rooms. Vaulted ceilings and exposed log beams add a cozy, rustic touch to the pristine, airy rooms all decorated in Pacific Northwest style. Many rooms include a whirlpool tub and river rock fireplace, and several offer excellent views of the Rogue River, which runs through the inn's grounds. In addition to the inn rooms, there are riverfront cabins, offering an especially romantic setting. In the evenings, guests are treated to a wine and cheese reception, and in the mornings, a continental breakfast is served. The staff can help plan many activities, including fishing and white-water rafting trips.

Innkeeper(s): Kirt Davis. $150-329. 7 rooms, 17 with PB, 12 with FP, 3 with HT, 3 suites, 1 guest house, 12 cabins, 2 conference rooms. Breakfast, afternoon tea, snacks/refreshments, wine, Afternoon wine and cheese social and fresh coffee and tea available through the day included in rates. Types of meals: Cont plus, early coffee/tea, A selection of local wines and beers and micro brews available for purchase from the front desk.

Certificate may be used: Anytime, subject to availability.

Lincoln City

Brey House

3725 NW Keel Ave
Lincoln City, OR 97367
(541)994-7123 (877)994-7123
Internet: www.breyhouse.com
E-mail: sbrey@wcn.net

Circa 1941. The innkeepers at this three-story, Cape Cod-style house claim that when you stay with them it's like staying with Aunt Shirley and Uncle Milt. Guest rooms include some with ocean views and private entrances, and the Deluxe Suite offers a living room with fireplace, two baths and a kitchen. The Admiral's Room on the third floor has knotty pine walls, a skylight, fireplace and the best view.

Innkeeper(s): Shirley Brey. $90-160. 4 rooms with PB, 3 with FP, 2 suites. Breakfast included in rates. Types of meals: Full gourmet bkfst, early coffee/tea and snacks/refreshments.

Certificate may be used: September-June, Sunday-Friday. No Saturdays, no holiday weekends.

Monmouth

Airlie Farm

14810 Airlie Road
Monmouth, OR 97361
(503) 838-1500
Internet: www.airliefarminn.com
E-mail: airliefarm@aol.com

Circa 1910. Delightfully situated on 226 spectacular, scenic acres in Oregon, this tastefully remodeled 1910 farm home reminds you of a cozy, comforting, updated visit to Grandma's house with an eye to luxury. Walk through the informal gardens, pick luscious berries, listen to the fountain or watch the koi pond. Check out the new foals or get lucky and help deliver a new foal on this well known and active Quarter Horse Breeding farm. Relax before the fireplace and play the piano amid antiques and paintings. Snuggle into a guest room with a down comforter, private balcony or petite fireplace, slippers, candies, robes, heated towel racks and modern amenities. Savor a full gourmet breakfast on fine china. Willamette Valley boasts over 250 gracious wineries. Monmouth is home to WOU, one of the oldest universities west of the Mississippi. Recreational options are endless, including live theater, concerts, museums and onsite rides and riding lessons.

Innkeeper(s): Nancy Petterson, Joe Petterson. $95-120. 6 rooms, 2 with PB, 1 with FP, 1 total suite, including 1 two-bedroom suite, 1 three-bedroom suite and 1 four-bedroom suite, 1 conference room. Breakfast, afternoon tea, snacks/refreshments, and wine included in rates. Types of meals: Full gourmet bkfst, veg bkfst, early coffee/tea, lunch, picnic lunch, gourmet dinner and Gluten Free. Charge for High Tea.

Certificate may be used: Anytime, subject to availability.

Roseburg

Delfino Vineyards B&B

3829 Colonial Rd
Roseburg, OR 97470-9002
(541)673-7575
Internet: www.delfinovineyards.com
E-mail: info@delfinovineyards.com

The rocky hillsides of Roseburg, Oregon create the backdrop for this family-owned vineyard, tasting room and guest cottage amid 160 scenic acres. Taste the award-winning estate-grown wines while overlooking the lake, mountains and gorgeous landscape. Take a refreshing swim in the lap pool, or soak in the hot tub. To fully appreciate the warm country hospitality of the Umpqua Valley, stay in the air-conditioned one-bedroom guest cottage with a living room furnished with antiques. Delightful amenities include a fireplace and spa robes. Upon arrival, a complimentary bottle of Delfino Vineyards wine is provided. Request either a Breakfast Basket with fresh baked goods, seasonal fruit, local jams and roasted coffee or select the Pantry Basket with items needed to prepare breakfast when desired.

Innkeeper(s): Terri. Call for rates. 1 cottage. Types of meals: Cont plus, Home-baked cranberry scones or muffins, fresh seasonal fruit and local Oregon jams and fresh roasted coffee,.

Certificate may be used: January-March and October-November.

Scottsburg

Daybreak Haven B&B

395 Burchard Dr
Scottsburg, OR 97473
(541) 587-4205 (800) 376-6770 Fax:(541)587-4205
Internet: www.daybreakhaven.com/
E-mail: DaybreakHaven@msn.com

Circa 1995. Find peace at a cozy inn with numerous decks overlooking the Umpqua River. Head down the stairs to the private dock with access to a pontoon boat and prime fishing spots. You may be accompanied by one of three resident dogs; one who especially makes a point of spending time with guests. The home-style breakfast changes daily and tasty sweet treats are available all day long; remember that calories don't count when you are on vacation. Two comfortable guest suites have views of the river or garden and coffee makers for those who want a bit of caffeine as the day begins. Find a quiet corner off the living room to curl up with a book or choose from more than 1,000 DVDs to watch on the 65" plasma television. Take a piece of the inn home by purchasing one of the watercolors created by a local artist or ask to have a painting commissioned just for you.

Innkeeper(s): Shelley Ryan, Pat Ryan. $129-159. 2 rooms with PB, 1 with FP. Breakfast and snacks/refreshments included in rates. Types of meals: Country bkfst, veg bkfst, early coffee/tea, lunch, picnic lunch, hors d'oeuvres, wine and gourmet dinner.

Certificate may be used: November-February, Sunday-Thursday, excluding holidays, subject to availability.

Vida

McKenzie River Inn

49164 McKenzie Hwy
Vida, OR 97488-9710
(541)822-6260 Fax:(541)same# call 1st
Internet: www.mckenzieriverinn.com
E-mail: innkeeper@mckenzieriverinn.com

Circa 1933. Three acres of lush grounds and river frontage highlight the McKenzie River Inn B&B and Cabins in Vida, Oregon. Meander along trails that lead to hammocks, benches and picnic areas. Stay in a romantic suite or a guest bedroom on the second floor of the inn with a Jacuzzi tub. Spacious and private, the cabins offer a variety of accommodations that may include decks, whirlpool tubs and full kitchens. Breakfast caters to specialties such as vegetarian and allergy-free diets with delicious and satisfying dishes sure to please everyone. Many recipes include fresh fruit from the orchard. Ask about guided fly-fishing and rafting trips or eco-packages.

Innkeeper(s): Ellie de Klerk. $98-185. 6 rooms with PB, 2 with WP, 2 suites, 1 cottage, 2 cabins, 1 conference room. Breakfast and afternoon tea included in rates. Types of meals: Full gourmet bkfst, veg bkfst, early coffee/tea, picnic lunch, hors d'oeuvres, wine and Organic juices and fruit from own orchard.

Certificate may be used: Nov. 1-May 31.

Pennsylvania

Akron

Boxwood Inn Bed & Breakfast

1320 Diamond Street
Akron, PA 17501
(717)859-3466 (800)238-3466 Fax:(717)859-4507
Internet: www.theboxwoodinn.net
E-mail: innkeeper@theboxwoodinn.net

Circa 1768. Bordered by boxwood hedges and evergreens, Boxwood Inn Bed & Breakfast graces three acres of landscaped grounds. The backyard boasts a wooden bridge over a stream surrounded by holly bushes and lilac, weeping willow and magnolia trees. Relax on an Amish rocker on the front porch of this 1768 renovated stone farmhouse in Akron, Pennsylvania near the popular Lancaster County attractions. Elegant, tranquil and hospitable guest bedrooms are available in the main house. Pets and children are welcome in the Carriage House with a wood-burning fireplace, Jacuzzi, refrigerator and balcony. Start each day with a bountiful breakfast. Ask about gift certificates and specials offered.

Innkeeper(s): Betsy Fitzpatrick, Greg Fitzpatrick. $110-235. 5 rooms, 4 with PB, 1 with FP, 2 with WP, 1 cottage, 1 conference room. Breakfast and snacks/refreshments included in rates. Types of meals: Country bkfst, veg bkfst and early coffee/tea.

Certificate may be used: January 1 through February 29.

Bellefonte

The Queen, A Victorian B&B

176 East Linn St.
Bellefonte, PA 16823
(814)355-7946 (888)355-7999
Internet: www.thequeenbnb.com
E-mail: thequeenbnb@psualum.com

Circa 1885. Adorning the historic district, this Queen Anne Victorian bed and breakfast is open year-round. It is ornately decorated with collectibles and memorabilia. Relax on the terraced landscaped grounds with a patio, waterfall and perennial gardens. Experience a taste of the past in the parlor with a Victrola, player piano, and stereoptic viewers. The foyer is accented with a fireplace. After a restful night's sleep in a tastefully appointed guest bedroom linger over a gourmet breakfast in the spacious dining room with vintage glassware and linens. Pastries and fruit accompany Creme Brulee French Toast, Eggs Benedict, Grecian Omelet or waffles with fresh-picked berries. A refrigerator and microwave are available to use anytime.

Innkeeper(s): Nancy Noll, Curtis Miller. $99-229. 7 rooms, 4 with PB, 3 with FP, 1 suite, 1 guest house. Breakfast, afternoon tea and snacks/refreshments included in rates. Types of meals: Full gourmet bkfst, veg bkfst, early coffee/tea and Flexible breakfast time.

Certificate may be used: Anytime, subject to availability.

Canadensis

Brookview Manor Inn

4534 Route 447
Canadensis, PA 18325
(570) 595-2451 (800) 585-7974 Fax:(570)595-7154
Internet: www.brookviewmanor.com
E-mail: innkeepers@thebrookviewmanor.com

Circa 1901. By the side of the road, hanging from a tall evergreen, is the welcoming sign to this forest retreat on six acres  adjoining 250 acres of woodland and hiking trails. The expansive wraparound porch overlooks a small stream. There are brightly decorated common rooms and eight fireplaces. Ten guest rooms include two with Jacuzzis and two deluxe suites. The carriage house has three additional rooms. One of the inn's dining rooms is surrounded by original stained glass, a romantic location for the inn's special six-course dinners prepared by an award-winning New York chef now on staff.

Innkeeper(s): Gaile Horowitz, Marty Horowitz. $130-250. 10 rooms with PB, 6 with FP, 2 with WP, 2 two-bedroom suites, 1 conference room. Breakfast included in rates. Types of meals: Full gourmet bkfst, veg bkfst, wine, gourmet dinner, Restaurant on premise,international cusine and Bar and lounge on premise. Restaurant on premises.

Certificate may be used: Sunday to Thursday, subject to availability, not on holiday or special event weeks.

Carlisle

Pheasant Field B&B

150 Hickorytown Rd
Carlisle, PA 17015-9732
(717)258-0717 (877)258-0717
Internet: www.pheasantfield.com
E-mail: stay@pheasantfield.com

Circa 1800. Located on 10 acres of central Pennsylvania farmland, this brick, two-story Federal-style farmhouse features wooden shutters and a covered front porch. Rooms

include a TV and telephone. An early 19th-century stone barn is on the property, and horse boarding is available. The Appalachian Trail is less than a mile away. Fly-fishing is popular at Yellow Breeches and Letort Spring. Dickinson College and Carlisle Fairgrounds are other points of interest.

Innkeeper(s): Dee Fegan. $117-219. 8 rooms with PB, 1 with FP, 2 with WP, 1 cottage, 1 conference room. Breakfast and snacks/refreshments included in rates. Types of meals: Full bkfst and early coffee/tea.

Certificate may be used: January and March.

Chadds Ford

Pennsbury Inn

883 Baltimore Pike
Chadds Ford, PA 19317-9305
(610)388-1435 (888)388-1435 Fax:(610)388-1436
Internet: www.pennsburyinn.com
E-mail: info@pennsburyinn.com

Circa 1714. Originally built with Brandywine Blue Granite rubble stone and later enlarged, this country farmhouse with hand-molded Flemish Bond brick facade is listed in the National Historic Register. Retaining its colonial heritage with slanted doorways, wooden winder stairs and huge fireplaces, it boasts modern conveniences that include complimentary wireless Internet. There are elegant public sitting areas such as the parlor, music room, library with an impressive book collection and breakfast in the garden room. Comfortable guest rooms feature antiques, feather beds and unique architectural details. The eight-acre estate boasts formal gardens with a fish pond and a reflection pool in a serene woodland setting.

Innkeeper(s): Cheryl Grono, Chip Grono. $105-230. 7 rooms, 6 with PB, 5 with FP, 2 suites, 3 conference rooms. Breakfast, afternoon tea and snacks/refreshments included in rates. Types of meals: Full gourmet bkfst, veg bkfst, early coffee/tea, gourmet lunch, picnic lunch and hors d'oeuvres.

Certificate may be used: January-February; Sunday-Thursday in March and July-August, no holidays. Last Minute anytime (less than 24 hours), subject to availability.

Chambersburg

Lillie's Garden Bed and Breakfast

65 Norland Ave.
Chambersburg, PA 17201
(717) 261-6593
Internet: www.lilliesgarden.com
E-mail: lillie@lilliesgarden.com

Historic downtown Chambersburg and pastoral farmland are both convenient to this Dutch Colonial inn across from Wilson College. You'll feel like you are staying with old friends when you ask for stories about the numerous family heirlooms on display. Settle in a wingback chair with a good book in the privacy of your room or just snuggle under a comforting quilt on a queen size bed or two twin beds. In the morning, enjoy a full breakfast at a table for two in the breakfast room. Spend a relaxing evening telling stories with other guests at a table in the backyard or in the spacious living room. Small pets are welcome. Honeymoon and babymoon packages include thoughtful gift baskets. The bed and breakfast is within half-an-hour of four major Civil War battlefields for exploring or challenge yourself to a game of golf on a championship course or take it easy on a nine-hole course without water hazards or blind spots.

Innkeeper(s): Lillie Raimo. $97-159. 4 rooms, 3 with PB. Types of meals: Full bkfst, veg bkfst and early coffee/tea.

Certificate may be used: Sunday-Thursday, January-March, excluding holidays. Subject to Availability.

Choconut

Addison House B&B

Rural Route 267
Choconut, PA 18818
(570)553-2682
Internet: www.1811addison.com
E-mail: gloria@1811addison.com

Circa 1811. Addison House was built by one of Choconut's earliest settlers, an Irish immigrant who purchased the vast homestead for just under a dollar an acre. The early 19th-century house is built in Federal style, but its interior includes many Victorian features, from the rich decor to the hand-carved marble fireplaces. A creek rambles through the 260-acre property, and guests will enjoy the secluded, wilderness setting. In the guest rooms, fluffy comforters top antique beds and floral wallcoverings add to the country Victorian ambiance. Breakfasts begin with items such as fresh berries with cream, followed by a rich entree. The innkeepers are happy to help guests plan their days. The area offers a multitude of outdoor activities, as well as historic sites, antique shops, covered bridges and much more.

Innkeeper(s): Dennis McLallen, Gloria McLallen. $75-110. 4 rooms, 1 suite. Breakfast included in rates. Types of meals: Full gourmet bkfst, early coffee/tea and afternoon tea.

Certificate may be used: Anytime, subject to availability.

Cornwall

Cornwall Inn

50 Burd Coleman Rd
Cornwall, PA 17016
(717)306-6178 (866)605-6563
Internet: www.cornwallinnpa.com
E-mail: innkeeper@cornwallinnpa.com

Circa 1820. This lovely historic inn offers suites that include one with a romantic four poster bed and 14-foot-high ceiling and another with stained glass windows. If you're traveling to the area, staying here will be more than a night's lodging and will provide you with an experience of the area and its culture as well. Take your camera to breakfast because you'll want to photograph the beautifully presented morning entrees. The inn also specializes in weddings and events, and the staff is skilled and experienced in all that is needed to create an outstanding party or business meeting. Cornwall Inn has transformed its historic structure into a memorable lodging offering for those visiting the area and belies the building's original life as a company store and local jail.

Innkeeper(s): Lynee Porter. $125-185. 5 rooms, 4 with FP, 2 with WP, 5 total suites, including 2 two-bedroom suites, 1 conference room. Breakfast and snacks/refreshments included in rates. Types of meals: Full gourmet bkfst, veg bkfst, Sun. brunch, early coffee/tea, gourmet lunch, picnic lunch, afternoon tea, hors d'oeuvres, wine, gourmet dinner and room service.

Certificate may be used: Sunday-Thursday.

Danielsville

Filbert Bed & Breakfast

3740 Filbert Drive
Danielsville, PA 18038
(610) 428-3300
Internet: filbertbnb.com
E-mail: filbertbnb@aol.com

Circa 1800. Feel refreshed in the quiet country setting of this restored 1800 Queen Anne Victorian on six acres in Danielsville, Pennsylvania. Adorning the foothills of Blue Mountains between Lehigh Valley and the Pocono Mountains, The Filbert Bed & Breakfast is a warm and welcoming B&B open all year. Relax on the 60-foot porch, play games or watch movies in the large sitting room or gather for conversation in the greeting parlor. Air-conditioned guest suites boast hardwood floors and antiques. Savor a bountiful breakfast in the dining room before embarking on the day's adventures. Massage and skin care appointments are available from a certified therapist and licensed cosmetologist.

Innkeeper(s): Kathy Lorah- Silfies, Terry Silfies. $100-200. 5 total suites, including 1 two-bedroom suite. Breakfast and snacks/refreshments included in rates. Types of meals: Country bkfst, early coffee/tea, picnic lunch, Country Tea, Italian Dinners and Courtyard Menues,Party Menues.

Certificate may be used: March-November, subject to availability, Anytime, Last Minute-Based on Availability.

Danville

Abigail House Bed & Breakfast

12 Center Street
Danville, PA 17821
(570)284-4677 (157)059-45815
Internet: www.abigailhousedanville.com
E-mail: info@abigailhousedanville.com

Originally the home of Danville philanthropist, Abigail Geisinger, the inn was fully renovated in 2012. The downtown business district is a short distance away from this brick bed and breakfast. With a nod to the iron heritage of the area, each guest room has an iron-cast bed. Write a traditional letter home using the antique desk or set up your lap top and use the complimentary WiFi. Sleep late without the intrusion of the sun by lowering the darkening shades. Four friends will be comfortable in the Kelly Room or spend a romantic weekend in the Abigail Room. Store leftovers in the mini-fridge in your room and reheat them as a midnight snack in the dining room. Enjoy a gourmet breakfast served on china each morning before relaxing on the porch with a good book. Catch the brass ring on the Grand Carousel at Knoebels Amusement Park or play a game of golf on one of the four local courses.

Innkeeper(s): Carla Leighow, John Leighow. $135-175. 5 rooms, 4 with PB, 1 with FP, 2 with WP. Breakfast, afternoon tea and All day complimentary beverages included in rates. Types of meals: Full gourmet bkfst, Guests also have 24/7 access to the dining room, furnished with tables, chairs, microwave and and all-day complimentary beverages from our beverage center.

Certificate may be used: November-March, subject to availability.

Dillsburg

Blair Mountain Bed and Breakfast

231 W. Ridge Road
Dillsburg, PA 17019
(717) 571-9342 Fax:(717)432-9322
Internet: www.blairmtn.com/
E-mail: Blairmtn@Comcast.Net

Circa 1767. A bit of history blends with the quiet of a wooded setting at this restored farmhouse just minutes from central Pennsylvania attractions and shopping. Four unique guest rooms offer themed decor and a king or queen-size bed. Laura's Dream Suite feels more like a luxurious studio apartment than a guest room with lush drapes, a romantic fireplace, private sitting area, two-person Jacuzzi and walk-in shower. Awaken to the aroma of breakfast coming from the dining room; indulge in sweet potato pancakes, quiche or Baked Apple Bette. Floor-to-ceiling windows look out over the woods from the Common Room setting the scene for an intimate elopement or small wedding ceremony. Use the two-tiered deck and a tent for a family reunion full of activities and merriment. Year-round adventure can be found at Roundtop Mountain Resort four miles from the inn. Visit during the famous Carlisle Car Show or sample wines at a York County vineyard.

Innkeeper(s): John Yergo, Tracie Yergo. $109-209. 4 rooms with PB, 1 with FP, 2 with WP, 1 suite, 1 conference room.

Certificate may be used: September, no weekends.

Eagles Mere

Crestmont Inn

180 Crestmont Dr
Eagles Mere, PA 17731
(800)522-8767 Fax:570-525-3534
Internet: www.crestmont-inn.com
E-mail: info@crestmont-inn.com

Circa 1914. Enjoy outdoor activities all year-round at this romantic country inn gracing a high peak of the Endless Mountains in the Victorian village of Eagles Mere, Pennsylvania. Surrounded by the serenity of nature, historic accommodations include a variety of amenities for business and leisure. Stay in a luxury guest room or suite with antique furnishings, two-person whirlpool tub, and comfortable beds. Wake up and sip early-morning coffee on the porch, or sleep in and linger over a hearty breakfast. Fine dining is available onsite in the Fouquet Room or in the more casual setting of the fireside Woodlands pub. Hiking trails and miles of walking paths are just outside the door. Privileges to the local country club, golf course, lake and beach are provided. Weddings, special events and corporate retreats are popular here.

Innkeeper(s): Tony Faulkiner, Melissa Faulkiner. $120-250. 15 rooms with PB, 2 with FP, 4 with WP, 3 two-bedroom suites. Breakfast and snacks/refreshments included in rates. Types of meals: Country bkfst, early coffee/tea, wine, dinner, Restaurant with two dining rooms and a lounge. Specials may include prime sirloin, scallops & gnocchi, filet mignon, crab cakes, pan seared duck breast and or Ahi tuna. Restaurant on premises.

Certificate may be used: Monday-Thursday, Anytime, subject to availability.

East Berlin

Bechtel Victorian Mansion B&B Inn

400 W King St
East Berlin, PA 17316
(717)259-7760 (800)579-1108
Internet: www.BechtelVictorianMansion.com
E-mail: info@bechtelvictorianmansion.com

Circa 1897. The town of East Berlin, near Lancaster and 18 miles east of Gettysburg, was settled by Pennsylvania Germans prior to the American Revolution. William Leas, a wealthy banker, built this many-gabled romantic Queen Anne mansion, now listed in the National Register. The inn is furnished with an abundance of museum-quality antiques and collections. Rooms are decorated in country Victorian style with beautiful quilts and comforters, lace, dolls and teddy bears.

Innkeeper(s): Richard Carlson, Carol Carlson. $120-190. 6 rooms with PB, 2 suites. Breakfast included in rates. Types of meals: Full bkfst, early coffee/tea and snacks/refreshments.

Certificate may be used: December-August, Sunday-Thursday, except special events, subject to availability.

Ephrata

1777 Americana Inn

301 West Main Street
Ephrata, PA 17522
(717)721-9268
Internet: www.1777americanainn.com
E-mail: info@1777americanainn.com

Circa 1777. Travel to Lancaster County to stay in an inn with a storied history as a private residence, millinary shop, stage-coach stop, hotel, restaurant, and doctor's office. The bright and airy Garden Window guest room looks out over the English garden and courtyard or you could spend a quiet evening cuddling by the gas fireplace in the Tranquility Cottage with country white-washed walls. Soak in the private sunken Jacuzzi tub in the Rustic Hideaway for a honeymoon or anniversary celebration; with a personal porch, living room, and queen pillow top bed with a white picket headboard, you may never want to leave. Stay in touch using the wireless Internet tablet provided in each guest room. Discover beautiful surprises around every corner of the manicured lawns or simply sit under the pergola enjoying the day. Experience the Amish culture at the Amish Village. There are seven wineries within 30 miles of the bed and breakfast.

Innkeeper(s): Steve Trapp, Wendy Trapp. $117-277. 6 rooms with PB, 2 with FP, 4 with WP, 2 cottages. Breakfast and snacks/refreshments included in rates. Types of meals: Full bkfst.

Certificate may be used: November-March, subject to availability.

Erwinna

Golden Pheasant Inn on the Delaware

763 River Rd
Erwinna, PA 18920-9254
(610) 294-9595 (800) 830-4474 Fax:(610)294-9882
Internet: www.goldenpheasant.com
E-mail: sally@goldenpheasant.com

Circa 1857. The Golden Pheasant is well established as the location of a wonderful, gourmet restaurant, but it is also home to six charming guest rooms decorated by Barbara Faure. Four-poster canopy beds and antiques decorate the rooms, which offer views of the canal and river. The fieldstone inn was built as a mule-barge stop for travelers heading down the Delaware Canal. The five-acre grounds resemble a French-country estate, and guests can enjoy the lush surroundings in a plant-filled greenhouse dining room. There are two other dining rooms, including an original fieldstone room with exposed beams and stone walls with decorative copper pots hanging here and there. The restaurant's French cuisine, prepared by chef Michel Faure, is outstanding. One might start off with Michel's special pheasant pate, followed by a savory onion soup baked with three cheeses. A mix of greens dressed in vinaigrette cleanses the palate before one samples roast duck in a luxurious raspberry, ginger and rum sauce or perhaps a sirloin steak flamed in cognac.

Innkeeper(s): Sally Falls. $200-300. 4 rooms with PB, 1 with FP, 1 suite. Breakfast included in rates. Types of meals: Cont plus, early coffee/tea, picnic lunch, snacks/refreshments, gourmet dinner and room service. Restaurant on premises.

Certificate may be used: Sunday-Thursday, excluding holidays.

Fairfield

The Fairfield Inn 1757

15 West Main Street (Rt. 116 West)
Fairfield, PA 17320
(717)642-5410 Fax:(717)642-5920
Internet: www.thefairfieldinn.com
E-mail: fairfieldinn1757@aol.com

Circa 1757. Rich in history, this authentic American treasure has been a continuously operating tavern, restaurant and inn for 180 years and its origins as the Mansion House of the town's founder date back 245 years. Tour the Gettysburg battlefield then retreat to the hospitality and refinement expected from a small luxury hotel yet enjoyed at this inn. Sip a hot beverage by one of the eight fireplaces. Squire Miller's Tavern offers conversation and libations. Renovated guest bedrooms and suites boast air conditioning and cable television. The Mansion House Restaurant serves an imaginative menu of classically prepared and artistically presented dishes. A patio garden is bordered with privacy hedges and filled with flowers. Cooking classes, special dinners and holiday activities are among the many events planned throughout the year.

Innkeeper(s): John G. Kramb. $99-225. 6 rooms with PB, 2 with FP, 4 with WP, 2 suites, 1 conference room. Breakfast included in rates. Types of meals: Full bkfst, Sun. brunch, lunch, picnic lunch, snacks/refreshments, wine and dinner. Restaurant on premises.

Certificate may be used: Anytime, November-March, subject to availability, may not be combined with any other discounts, vouchers, coupons or gift certificates.

Gettysburg

James Gettys Hotel

27 Chambersburg St
Gettysburg, PA 17325
(717)337-1334 (888)900-5275 Fax:(717)334-2103
Internet: www.jamesgettyshotel.com
E-mail: info@jamesgettyshotel.com

Circa 1803. Listed in the National Register, this newly renovated four-story hotel once served as a tavern through the Battle of Gettysburg and was used as a hospital for soldiers. Outfitted with cranberry colored awnings and a gold painted entrance, the hotel offers a tea room, nature store and gallery on the street level. From the lobby, a polished chestnut staircase leads to the guest quarters. All accommodations are suites with living rooms appointed with home furnishings, and each has its own kitchenette. Breakfasts of home-baked scones and coffee cake are brought to your room.

Innkeeper(s): Stephanie Stephan. $140-250. 12 rooms, 1 with FP, 1 with WP, 12 suites. Breakfast included in rates. Types of meals: Cont.

Certificate may be used: Monday-Thursday, excluding holidays and special events, Jan. 1-Dec. 30.

Keystone Inn B&B

231 Hanover St
Gettysburg, PA 17325-1913
(717)337-3888
Internet: www.keystoneinnbb.com
E-mail: Keystoneinn@comcast.net

Circa 1913. Furniture maker Clayton Reaser constructed this three-story brick Victorian with a wide-columned porch hugging the north and west sides.

Cut stone graces every door and window sill, each with a keystone. A chestnut staircase ascends the full three stories, and the interior is decorated with comfortable furnishings, ruffles and lace.

Innkeeper(s): Michael Day, Marjorie Day. $119-175. 8 rooms, 6 with PB, 1 with WP, 2 two-bedroom suites. Breakfast and snacks/refreshments included in rates. Types of meals: Full bkfst and early coffee/tea.

Certificate may be used: November-April, Monday-Thursday.

The Gaslight Inn

33 E Middle St
Gettysburg, PA 17325
(717) 337-9100 Fax:(717)337-1100
Internet: www.thegaslightinn.com
E-mail: info@thegaslightinn.com

Circa 1872. Gaslights illuminate the brick pathways leading to this 130-year-old Italianate-style, expanded farmhouse. The inn boasts two elegant parlors separated by original pocket doors, a spacious dining room and a first-floor guest room with wheelchair access that opens to a large, brick patio. An open switchback staircase leads to the second- and

third-floor guest rooms, all individually decorated in traditional and European furnishings. Some of the rooms feature covered decks, fireplaces, whirlpool tubs and steam showers for two. Guests are invited to enjoy a hearty or heart-healthy breakfast and inn-baked cookies and brownies and refreshments in the afternoon. Winter weekend packages are available and carriage rides, private guides and a variety of activities can be arranged with the help of the innkeepers.

Innkeeper(s): Mike Hanson, Becky Hanson. $131-186. 9 rooms with PB, 6 with FP, 2 with HT. Breakfast and snacks/refreshments included in rates. Types of meals: Full gourmet bkfst and early coffee/tea.

Certificate may be used: Dec. 1-March 31, Sunday-Thursday, no holidays.

Gordonville

Osceola Mill House

313 Osceola Mill Rd
Gordonville, PA 17529
(717)768-3758 (800)878-7719 Fax:(717)768-7539
Internet: www.lancaster-inn.com
E-mail: osceolamill@frontiernet.net

Circa 1766. In a quaint historic setting adjacent to a mill and a miller's cottage, this handsome limestone mill house rests on the banks of Pequea Creek. There are deep-set windows and wide pine floors. Guest

bedrooms and the keeping room feature working fireplaces that add to the warmth and charm. Breakfast fare may include tasty regional specialties like locally made Pennsylvania Dutch sausage, and Dutch babies- an oven-puffed pancake filled with fresh fruit. Amish neighbors farm the adjacent fields, their horse and buggies enhance the picturesque ambiance.

Innkeeper(s): Patricia Ernst, Ron Ernst. $110-190. 5 rooms with PB, 4 with FP, 1 cottage. Breakfast included in rates. Types of meals: Country bkfst, veg bkfst and snacks/refreshments.

Certificate may be used: January-March, Sunday-Thursday, subject to availability, excludes holidays and special events, cannot be combined with any other offers, discounts or gift certificates.

Hanover

The Beechmont B&B Inn

315 Broadway
Hanover, PA 17331-2505
(717)632-3013 (800)553-7009 Fax:(717)632-2769
Internet: www.thebeechmont.com
E-mail: innkeeper@thebeechmont.com

Circa 1834. Feel welcomed by centuries of charm at this gracious Georgian inn, a witness to the Battle of Hanover, the Civil War's first major battle on free soil. A 130-year-old magnolia tree shades the flagstone patio and wicker furniture invites a lingering rest on the front porch. The romantic Magnolia Suite features a marble fireplace, whirlpool tub and Queen canopy bed. The inn is noted for its sumptuous breakfasts.

Innkeeper(s): Kathryn White, Thomas White. $119-169. 7 rooms with PB, 4 with FP, 1 with WP, 3 suites. Breakfast and snacks/refreshments included in rates. Types of meals: Full gourmet bkfst and early coffee/tea.

Certificate may be used: Sunday-Thursday, Dec. 1-March 31, no holidays.

Intercourse

Carriage Corner

3705 E Newport Rd.
Intercourse, PA 17534-0371
(717)768-3059 (800)209-3059
Internet: www.carriagecornerbandb.com
E-mail: innkeeper@carriagecornerbandb.com

Circa 1979. Located in the heart of Amish farmland, this two-story Colonial rests on a pastoral acre. Homemade, country breakfasts are served, often including innkeeper Gordon Schuit's special recipe for oatmeal pancakes. A five-minute walk will take guests into the village where they'll find Amish buggies traveling down the lanes and more than 100 shops displaying local crafts, pottery, quilts and furniture, as well as art galleries. The innkeepers can arrange for dinners in an Amish home, buggy rides and working Amish farm tours. Longwood Gardens, Hershey's Chocolate World and Gettysburg are also nearby.

Innkeeper(s): Gordon Schuit, Gwen Schuit. $68-94. 5 rooms with PB, 1 conference room. Breakfast included in rates. Types of meals: Full bkfst and early coffee/tea.

Certificate may be used: December-February, excluding holiday weekends. March-April, November, Sunday-Wednesday, excluding special events. Anytime, Last Minute-Based on Availability.

The Inn & Spa at Intercourse Village

3542 Old Philadelphia Pike, POB 598
Intercourse, PA 17534
(717)768-2626 (800)664-0949
Internet: www.inn-spa.com
E-mail: innkeeper@inn-spa.com

Circa 1909. Located in historic Intercourse, Pennsylvania, near Lancaster this winner of the iLoveInns.com Top 10 Romantic Inns of 2009 caters to couples. Relax on white wicker furniture on the front porch as the Amish pass by in horse-drawn carriages. The Intercourse Village Inn & Spa offers guest rooms in the two-story 1909 Victorian main house. The Homestead Suites are in more modern buildings with gas-burning fireplaces, refrigerators and microwaves. The Summer House Suite stands alone and boasts a heart-shaped whirlpool. A gourmet five-course breakfast is served by candlelight in the formal dining room of the main house on fine English china. Visit the town's craft, quilt and antique shops or tour the candle and pretzel factories. Hershey is only an hour away and Gettysburg an hour and a half.

Innkeeper(s): Ruthann Thomas. $149-399. 9 rooms, 9 with FP, 3 with WP, 9 total suites, including 6 two-bedroom suites. Breakfast included in rates. Types of meals: 5-course Full Breakfast.

Certificate may be used: December-August, Monday-Wednesday only. Valid only for Grand Suites. Subject to availability, cannot be combined with any other offers.

Jim Thorpe

The Inn at Jim Thorpe

24 Broadway
Jim Thorpe, PA 18229
(570)325-2599 (800)329-2599 Fax:(570)325-9145
Internet: www.innjt.com
E-mail: reservations@innjt.com

Circa 1849. Step into a landmark treasure in the heart of a historic town. Modern amenities blend seamlessly with the old world charm of this inn in the National Register of Historic Places. Soak in a whirlpool tub or relax by the fire in your suite. Burn calories in the exercise room or bike through the surrounding mountains; bike storage is available on-site, then treat yourself to a hot stone massage or lavender wrap. Consider hosting a corporate retreat or meeting. High speed Internet access is available. Choose a flame-grilled specialty off the menu of the hip Broadway Grille and Pub. Be sure to ask about packages for mid-week getaways, romance, or adventure. The quaint town offers shops, galleries, live music, and restaurants within walking distance of the inn. Enjoy the natural beauty of the area by going river rafting, kayaking, skiing, or hiking. Mauch Chunk Museum and the Old Jail Museum provide an interesting way to learn about the area.

Innkeeper(s): David Drury. $103-399. 51 rooms with PB, 9 with FP, 14 with WP, 16 total suites, including 3 two-bedroom suites, 2 conference rooms. Breakfast included in rates. Types of meals: Full bkfst, veg bkfst, early coffee/tea, lunch, snacks/refreshments, wine, dinner, room service, Full service restaurant, the Broadway Grille & Pub is located just downstairs. Open from 7 am till the wee hours.

Certificate may be used: Sunday-Thursday excluding holidays, excludes August and October, not valid on packages, cannot be combined with other offers.

Lancaster

A New Beginning Bed & Breakfast

1400 East King Street
Lancaster, PA 17602
(717) 393-5935
Internet: www.anewbeginningbb.com
E-mail: info@anewbeginningbb.com

Circa 1912. Located in the heart of Pennsylvania Dutch Country in Lancaster, this historic home has been restored with its original chestnut woodwork and updated to offer modern technology like Wifi. Sit in the fireside parlor and play games or watch a movie. Tour the Amish countryside, shop the outlet malls, visit a museum and enjoy Hershey Park. Stay in an inviting air-conditioned guest room or the spacious two-room Country Suite. The Serenity Room boasts a whirlpool tub. Linger over a hearty breakfast in the formal dining room or on the front porch. It includes homemade granola and cereals, yogurts, breads and pastries that complement gourmet and classic entrees and made-to-order eggs accompanied by locally cured meats. Afternoon tea and treats are provided on weekends and indulge in refreshments each evening before retiring.

Innkeeper(s): Al Ricci, Denise Ricci. $90-125. 4 rooms with PB, 1 with WP,

1 two-bedroom suite. Breakfast, afternoon tea and snacks/refreshments included in rates. Types of meals: Full gourmet bkfst, veg bkfst, early coffee/tea, Weekends 4:00 pm tea and goodies. Restricted and gluten free diets upon request.

Certificate may be used: Jan. 1-April 30.

Lovelace Manor Bed and Breakfast

2236 Marietta Pike
Lancaster, PA 17603
(717) 399-3275
Internet: www.lovelacemanor.com
E-mail: hostess@lovelacemanor.com

Circa 1882. Gracing the heart of Amish Country in Lancaster, Pennsylvania, Lovelace Manor Bed and Breakfast remains an exceptional historic example of a Second Empire Victorian home. Luxury linens, all-season fireplaces, flat screen TVs with a video library, and complimentary wifi are just a few of the amenities offered and a full, hearty breakfast is served each morning in the dining room. Refreshments such as coffee, tea and cookies are available to guests 24 hours a day. All second-floor guest rooms are air-conditioned and include private en suite bathrooms with eco-friendly amenities. The grounds are certified as both a Wildlife Habitat and a Bird-Friendly Habitat. In fact, there is an aviary tucked away on a garden path for guests to enjoy. With a balanced combination of antique, traditional and modern furnishings, Lovelace Manor B&B in Lancaster is the perfect place to experience the elegance of yesterday with the comforts of today.
Innkeeper(s): Lark McCarley, Michael McCarley. $125-190. 4 rooms with PB, 4 with HT, 3 guest houses. Breakfast included in rates. Types of meals: Full gourmet bkfst, early coffee/tea, afternoon tea, snacks/refreshments and wine.

Certificate may be used: November-March, Sunday-Thursday, subject to availability.

Lebanon

Berry Patch B&B

115 Moore Rd
Lebanon, PA 17046
(717)865-7219 Fax:(717) 865-6119
Internet: www.berrypatchbnb.com
E-mail: bunny@berrypatchbnb.com

Circa 1999. Experience Pennsylvania Dutch hospitality at this newly built log home situated on 10 acres outside a quaint small town, yet close to the many nearby attractions. An old country ambiance is enhanced by antiques and Victorian charm. A foyer and parlor provide lots of comfy sitting areas. An extensive Strawberry Patch and Friends doll collection can be visited in the loft museum. All the guest bedrooms and suites feature fireplaces and are laptop accessible. Most offer two-person Jacuzzis and some have a private entrance and a patio. The hearty breakfast menu varies, but includes fresh fruit, hot main dishes and homemade breads. Strawberry pancakes are a house specialty. Browse the gift shop where Strawberry Patch jam and other foods, as well as t-shirts and collectibles are for sale. Stroll through the Strawberry Rose garden, or enjoy the veranda.
Innkeeper(s): Charlie Yinger, Bunny Yinger. $129-199. 7 rooms with PB, 7 with FP, 4 with WP, 1 cottage, 1 conference room. Breakfast and snacks/refreshments included in rates. Types of meals: Full gourmet bkfst, veg bkfst, early coffee/tea, picnic lunch and wine.

Certificate may be used: November-March, subject to availability, excluding holidays, good only for Loft rooms.

Lititz

The Lititz House B&B

301 N Broad St
Lititz, PA 17543
(717)626-5299 (800)464-6764
Internet: www.lititzhouse.com
E-mail: stay@lititzhouse.com

Circa 1904. Experience small-town charm at this 1904 bed and breakfast situated in the heart of downtown in Pennsylvania Dutch Country in Lancaster County. It is mingled with elegant touches for enjoyment and comfort. The first floor has been redecorated with Scandinavian teak, glass and leather furniture on area rugs. Relax in the second-floor sitting room. Air-conditioned guest bedrooms and a two-bedroom suite with private entrances are tasteful and inviting. Let your taste buds rejoice in the elegant gourmet breakfast. Sit on the wraparound front porch rockers, the landscaped decks or the backyard swing amid the flower garden with a fountain.
Innkeeper(s): Heidi Lucier, John Lucier. $95-169. 5 rooms with PB, 1 two-bedroom suite. Breakfast, hors d'oeuvres and wine included in rates. Types of meals: Full gourmet bkfst, veg bkfst, early coffee/tea and snacks/refreshments.

Certificate may be used: January-April, subject to availability.

Mercersburg

The Mercersburg Inn

405 S Main St
Mercersburg, PA 17236-9517
(717)328-5231 (866)MBURG01 Fax:(717)328-3403
Internet: www.mercersburginn.com
E-mail: lisa@mercersburginn.com

Circa 1909. Situated on a hill overlooking the Tuscorora Mountains, the valley and village, this 20,000-square-foot Georgian Revival mansion was built for industrialist Harry Byron. Six massive columns mark the entrance, which opens to a majestic hall featuring chestnut wainscoting and an elegant double stairway and rare scagliola (marbleized) columns. All the rooms are furnished with antiques and reproductions. A local craftsman built the inn's four-poster, canopied king-size beds. Many of the rooms have their own balconies and a few have fireplaces. Thursday through Sunday evening, the inn's chef prepares noteworthy, elegant dinners, which feature an array of seasonal specialties.
Innkeeper(s): Lisa & Jim McCoy. $140-325. 17 rooms with PB, 3 with FP, 2 with WP, 1 cottage, 2 conference rooms. Breakfast included in rates. Types of meals: Full gourmet bkfst, veg bkfst, picnic lunch, wine and gourmet dinner. Restaurant on premises.

Certificate may be used: Sunday-Thursday, excludes holidays. Only available for Superior and Extravagant rooms.

Mount Joy

Olde Square Inn

127 E Main St
Mount Joy, PA 17552-1513
(717) 653-4525 Fax:(717)653-0976
Internet: www.oldesquareinn.com
E-mail: info@oldesquareinn.com

Circa 1910. Gracing the historic square in Mount Joy, Pennsylvania, this stately red brick masterpiece has been recently renovated and is conveniently located near the heart of Amish country. It is an easy walk to great restaurants, the coffee house and the train station. The surrounding areas of Hershey, Lancaster, York and Gettysburg, are all within a half hour's drive. Rich in heritage as well as activities, ask about local events that may be happening. Take a wine-tasting tour, visit art galleries or shop the markets. Relax on the grand porch, patio or in the fireside sitting room. Enjoy a refreshing swim in the seasonal in-ground pool. Accommodations in the Carriage House are handicap accessible as well as being family and pet friendly. Select an inviting room with a fireplace and a whirlpool tub. Gather each morning in the dining room for a hearty breakfast made with local produce, farm-fresh eggs, meats, fruit, homemade breads and sweet treats.
Innkeeper(s): Georgie. $139-260. 6 rooms with PB, 6 with FP, 2 with WP, 1 cottage. Breakfast included in rates. Types of meals: Full bkfst and early coffee/tea.
Certificate may be used: November-March. Does not include the day before a holiday, the holiday itself or the day after a holiday.

The Victorian Rose Bed & Breakfast

214 Marietta Ave
Mount Joy, PA 17552-3106
(717)492-0050 (888)313-7494
Internet: www.thevictorianrosebandb.com
E-mail: victorianrosebb@juno.com

Circa 1897. Central to Hershey and Gettysburg battlefield, The Victorian Rose in Mount Joy is an elegant but comfortable place from which to explore beautiful Lancaster County. Enjoy the stately guest rooms and a number of elegant areas including the library and a formal living room. Guests are treated to innkeeper Doris Tyson's home-baked treats for breakfast, and to her homemade candies at other times. Pennsylvania Dutch Country is just 12 miles from the inn.
Innkeeper(s): Doris L. Tyson. $90-95. 4 rooms, 3 with PB. Breakfast included in rates. Types of meals: Country bkfst, Breakfast can be tailored to specific guest requirements, medical, religious and personal preference. Please let innkeeper know at time of reservation.
Certificate may be used: November-May, excluding holidays. Subject to availability.

North East

Grape Arbor Bed and Breakfast

51 East Main St
North East, PA 16428-1340
(814)725-0048 (866)725-0048 Fax:(814)725-5740
Internet: www.grapearborbandb.com
E-mail: grapearborbandb@aol.com

Circa 1832. Two side-by-side brick Federal mansions with Victorian embellishments have been restored to preserve their antiquity yet provide today's conveniences. Built in the early 1830s as private homes, their history includes having served as a stagecoach tavern, primary school, and possibly a stop on the Underground Railroad. Watch videos, play games or read a book by the fire in the library. Socialize over hors d' oeuvres in the parlor. Elegant guest bedrooms and suites are named for local varieties of grapes and feature antiques, reproductions, data ports, VCRs and fine toiletries. Two main breakfast dishes, pastries and breads, a hot or cold fruit sampler, juice and freshly ground coffee are enjoyed in the formal Dining Room or the light and airy Sun Porch. A guest refrigerator is stocked with beverages and homemade treats are always available.
Innkeeper(s): Dave Hauser, Peggy Hauser. $95-175. 8 rooms with PB, 4 with FP, 5 suites. Breakfast and snacks/refreshments included in rates. Types of meals: Full gourmet bkfst and early coffee/tea.
Certificate may be used: November-March, excludes holidays and Wine Trail Events. Anytime, Last Minute-Based on Availability.

Philadelphia

Gables B&B

4520 Chester Ave
Philadelphia, PA 19143-3707
(215)662-1918 Fax:(215)662-1918
Internet: www.gablesbb.com
E-mail: gables@gablesbb.com

Circa 1889. Located in the University City section, this red-brick Queen Anne Victorian has three stories and offers off-street parking. Chestnut and cherry woodwork, a grand entry hall and sitting rooms furnished with antiques make this a popular site. A wraparound porch overlooks the inn's gardens of perennials, roses, dogwood and Japanese cherry and magnolia trees. The Christmas Room has mahogany antiques and a queen four-poster bed, while the Tower Room has a working fireplace and a settee tucked into the turret. Another room offers a soaking tub and sun porch. This inn received Philadelphia Magazine's four-heart award and the "Best of Philly 1996" award as an urban getaway.
Innkeeper(s): Don Caskey, Warren Cederholm. $125-200. 10 rooms, 8 with PB, 2 with FP. Breakfast included in rates. Types of meals: Full bkfst.
Certificate may be used: January-February, Sunday-Thursday, no holidays, subject to availability.

Silverstone Bed & Breakfast

8840 Stenton Ave
Philadelphia, PA 19118-2846
(215)242-3333 (800)347-6858 Fax:(215)242-2680
Internet: www.silverstonestay.com
E-mail: silverstonestay@gmail.com

Circa 1850. Italian masons built this Victorian Gothic mansion with silvery stone from the Appalachian Mountains in 1877. Adorning historic Chestnut Hill inside the Philadelphia Metro area of Pennsylvania, this central location in is perfect for walking to local shops and restaurants. Select one of the well-appointed and spacious guest bedrooms or suites. For longer stays, short-term furnished apartments are available. After a satisfying breakfast visit Lancaster's Amish Country or take a day trip to Washington, D.C. or New York City. Laundry facilities and a private guest kitchen are provided. Silverstone Bed & Breakfast offers fresh herbs and vegetables from the garden.

Innkeeper(s): Yolanta Roman. $115-155. 3 rooms with PB, 2 with HT, 1 two-bedroom and 1 three-bedroom suites. Breakfast, Guests may use kitchen to drink coffee and tea or prepare meals included in rates. Types of meals: Full bkfst, veg bkfst, early coffee/tea, Guests may use kitchen any time to drink coffee and tea or cooked meals.

Certificate may be used: July and January only.

Pine Grove Mills

The Chatelaine Bed & Breakfast

347 W. Pine Grove Rd.
Pine Grove Mills, PA 16868
(814) 238-2028 (800) 251-2028 Fax:(814)308-9573
Internet: www.chatelainebandb.com
E-mail: kkeeper0@comcast.net

Circa 1841. Pass by the border of heirloom perennials and a welcoming signpost, through the double canopy of stately pine to this vintage farmhouse. A formal yet comfortable sitting room features deep sofas, chairs and luxurious hassocks. Distinctive antiques furnish elegantly decorated guest bedrooms and a suite. Generous amenities include robes, soda, ice and glasses. Enjoy cordials from bedside decanters. A breakfast feast is a lighthearted, whimsical affair in the dining room amidst an extensive china collection. Take a break from the B&B's peaceful serenity to visit nearby historic sites.

Innkeeper(s): Amanda McQuade, Mae McQuade. $115-400. 4 rooms with PB, 2 with FP, 1 two-bedroom suite, 1 conference room. Breakfast, afternoon tea and snacks/refreshments included in rates. Types of meals: Full gourmet bkfst, veg bkfst, early coffee/tea and Grill or hibachi available to cook-out on the patio or at Whipple's Dam just 5 miles away. Bring utensils and cooler for food storage.

Certificate may be used: November-March, subject to availability.

Pottsville

The Maid's Quarters Bed & Breakfast

402 S. Centre Street
Pottsville, PA 17901
(484) 223-9497
Internet: www.themaidsquartersbedandbreakfast.com
E-mail: maidsquarters_1829@yahoo.com

Circa 1829. Stay in the heart of Pottsville, Pennsylvania, at a historic Victorian inn. The very first tenant installed the mezuzot in 1831; there are currently six mezuzot with a Hebrew verse from the Torah on doorposts in the bed and breakfast. Sit at a table for two for a gourmet breakfast of omelets, quiche, or French toast. Snuggle in a plush robe by the private ensuite fireplace. You can reserve a seat or schedule an intimate gathering in the onsite tearoom then walk to unique shops and local restaurants. For brew fans, take a tour and sample the beer at Yuengling, the oldest brewery in the country. Learn about local history at The Schuylkill County Historical Society or journey underground at Crystal Cave, the most popular natural attraction in the state. Then go white-water rafting, hike part of the Appalachian Trail, or join a hawk watch tour. Spend an evening watching a performance at the Schuylkill Ballet Theater or Sovereign Majestic Theater.

Innkeeper(s): Allyson Chryst. $85-135. 3 rooms, 1 with PB, 3 with FP, 1 suite. Breakfast, afternoon tea, snacks/refreshments and wine included in rates. Types of meals: Full gourmet bkfst, veg bkfst, Sun. brunch, early coffee/tea, lunch, room service, freshly baked cookies on arrival and on-site tearoom available by reservations only.

Certificate may be used: Anytime, excluding holidays and special events.

Red Lion

Red Lion Bed & Breakfast

101 S Franklin St
Red Lion, PA 17356
(717) 244-4739 (888) 280-1701
Internet: www.redlionbandb.com
E-mail: staywithus@redlionbandb.com

Circa 1920. Explore one of the more popular regions of the state while staying at this unpretentious and quiet three-story brick, Federal-style home. Snuggle up next to the fireplace in the living room with a book from the well-stocked collection of reading material. Sip a cool iced tea on the enclosed sun porch or outside garden patio. Half of the six quaint and comfortable guest bedrooms offer a full bath and queen-size bed. Twin beds and cots are also available for families or groups traveling together. Breakfasts are substantial with quiche, pancakes, stuffed French toast, fresh baked rolls and muffins served alongside fruit or granola. The town has antique and craft shops and is within a 45-minute drive of vineyards, the Amish country of Lancaster, Hershey and the Gettysburg Battlefield.

Innkeeper(s): George Sanders, Danielle Sanders. $85-109. 6 rooms, 3 with PB, 1 conference room. Breakfast included in rates. Types of meals: Full bkfst.

Certificate may be used: January-February and July-August.

Reinholds

Brownstone Colonial Inn

590 Galen Hall Rd
Reinholds, PA 17569-9420
(717)484-4460 (877)464-9862 Fax:(717)484-4460
Internet: www.brownstonecolonialinn.com
E-mail: info@brownstonecolonialinn.com

Circa 1759. Early German Mennonite settlers built this sandstone farmhouse in the mid eighteenth century. It graces seven scenic acres amidst Amish countryside. Feel relaxed and pampered at this fully restored inn. Guest bedrooms and a suite boast random-width plank floors, locally handcrafted period-authentic furniture, sleigh or pencil post beds and antique Shaker peg boards. Enjoy a hearty country breakfast in the homestead's original smokehouse with brick floor, ceiling beams and open hearth fireplace. Start the day with fresh juices, homemade pastries and jams, a hot entree and fruits grown on-site. Stroll by the flower and gardens, or walk the nearby nature trails. An abundance of outlet and antique malls as well as historical and cultural sites are minutes away.

Innkeeper(s): Brenda & Mark Miller. $89-119. 4 rooms with PB, 1 two-bedroom suite. Breakfast, afternoon tea and snacks/refreshments included in rates. Types of meals: Country bkfst and early coffee/tea.

Certificate may be used: Monday-Thursday.

Ronks

Candlelight Inn B&B

2574 Lincoln Hwy E
Ronks, PA 17572-9771
(717)299-6005 (800)772-2635 Fax:(717)299-6397
Internet: www.candleinn.com
E-mail: candleinn@aol.com

Circa 1920. Located in the Pennsylvania Dutch area, this Federal-style house offers a side porch for enjoying the home's acre and a half of tall trees and surrounding Amish farmland. Guest rooms feature Victorian decor. Three rooms include a Jacuzzi tub and fireplace. The inn's gourmet breakfast, which might include a creme caramel French toast, is served by candlelight. The innkeepers are professional classical musicians. Lancaster is five miles to the east.

Innkeeper(s): Tim Soberick, Heidi Soberick. $90-179. 7 rooms with PB, 3 with FP, 3 with HT, 3 with WP. Breakfast and snacks/refreshments included in rates. Types of meals: Full gourmet bkfst.

Certificate may be used: December-April, excluding holidays, Sunday-Thursday.

Somerset

Quill Haven Country Inn

1519 North Center Ave
Somerset, PA 15501-7001
(814)443-4514 (866)528-8855 Fax:(814)445-1376
Internet: www.quillhaven.com
E-mail: quill@quillhaven.com

Circa 1918. Set on three acres that were once part of a chicken and turkey farm, this historic Arts & Crafts-style home offers guest rooms, each individually appointed. The Bridal Suite includes a four-poster wrought iron bed and sunken tub in the bath. The Country Room includes a decorative pot-bellied stove. Antiques, reproductions and stained-glass lamps decorate the rooms. Guests are treated to a full breakfast with items such as baked grapefruit or apples, homemade breads and entrees such as stuffed French toast or a specialty casserole of ham, cheese and potatoes. Guests can spend the day boating or swimming at nearby Youghiogheny Reservoir, take a whitewater-rafting trip, bike or hike through the scenic countryside, ski at one of three ski resorts in the area or shop at antique stores, outlets and flea markets. Frank Lloyd Wright's Fallingwater is another nearby attraction.

Innkeeper(s): Carol & Rowland Miller. $99-120. 4 rooms with PB. Breakfast and snacks/refreshments included in rates. Types of meals: Full bkfst and early coffee/tea.

Certificate may be used: March-September, subject to availability.

South Sterling

French Manor

50 Huntingdon Drive
South Sterling, PA 18445
(570)676-3244 (877)720-6090 Fax:(570)676-8573
Internet: www.thefrenchmanor.com
E-mail: info@thefrenchmanor.com

Circa 1932. In a storybook setting this country inn and restaurant sits atop Huckleberry Mountain with views of the northern Poconos. Built by local craftsman and artisans of German and Italian descent, the impressive architecture of this fieldstone chateau includes an imported Spanish slate roof, Romanesque arched entrance and cypress interior. Luxuriously romantic accommodations offer a generous variety of upscale amenities. Manor house guest rooms boast period furnishings. The unique two-story Turret Suite boasts a living room and private staircase to the bedroom. Stay in a fireplace or Jacuzzi suite in the adjacent La Maisonneuve Building with private wrought-iron balconies. Savor breakfast in the elegant dining room with a forty-foot vaulted ceiling and twin fireplaces. Schedule an appointment with the in-house massage therapist after hiking or biking the miles of trails on the grounds.

Innkeeper(s): Bridget, Genevieve. $190-375. 19 rooms with PB, 13 with FP, 13 with WP, 14 total suites, including 1 two-bedroom suite, 2 conference rooms. Breakfast, afternoon tea, snacks/refreshments, Midweek "Enchanted Evenings" package includes full breakfast and gourmet candlelight dinner and a picnic lunch included in rates. Types of meals: Full gourmet bkfst, veg bkfst, picnic lunch, hors d'oeuvres, wine, gourmet dinner, room service and Spa lunch available upon request. Restaurant on premises.

Certificate may be used: Midweek in March and April, subject to availability.

Starlight

The Inn at Starlight Lake

PO Box 27
Starlight, PA 18461-0027
(570)798-2519 (800)248-2519 Fax:(570)798-2672
Internet: www.innatstarlightlake.com
E-mail: sari@innatstarlightlake.com

Circa 1909. Escape city stress and be rejuvenated at the peacefully pleasant and informal setting of The Inn at Starlight Lake in northeastern Pennsylvania. Relax on the front porch of this  country retreat with gorgeous views of the tranquil and clear Starlight Lake surrounded by rolling hills and woods. This historic 1909 inn boasts year-round hospitality and thoughtful details families appreciate. Play ping pong or billiards in the game room, watch a movie in the sunroom and sip a glass of wine with appetizers in the Stovepipe Bar. Use the tennis court, swim in the lake, ride a bike or try the trails by foot, snowshoe or cross-country skis. Accommodations are warm and inviting with a satisfying made-to-order breakfast included each morning. Lunch and dinner are offered in the lakeside dining room for an extra charge.

Innkeeper(s): Sari Schwartz. $85-255. 23 rooms, 19 with PB, 1 with FP, 1 suite, 3 cottages. Breakfast included in rates. Types of meals: Full bkfst, Sun. brunch, early coffee/tea, lunch, picnic lunch, snacks/refreshments, wine and dinner. Restaurant on premises.

Certificate may be used: September-May excluding holidays, subject to availability.

Terre Hill

The Artist's Inn & Gallery

117 E Main St
Terre Hill, PA 17581
(717)445-0219 (888)999-4479
Internet: www.artistinn.com
E-mail: Relax@Artistinn.com

Circa 1848. Four-course breakfasts and warm and inviting guest rooms are offered at this Federal-style inn. Watch Amish buggies clip clop by from the Victorian veranda and listen to the chimes from the church across the way. Then plan your day with the help of innkeepers Jan and Bruce, avid adventurers who cross-country ski and explore the area's best offerings to share insights with guests. There's an art gallery with works by the resident artist. Guest accommodations are inviting with antiques, gas fireplaces, hardwood floors and decorative painting, wallpapers and borders. The Rose Room offers a Jacuzzi bath. The Garden Suite offers a whirlpool bath for two, massage shower, fireplace, king-size featherbed, private balcony and sitting room. Breakfasts feature breads such as scones or muffins, fruit parfaits, crepes or egg dishes and a luscious dessert -perhaps a pie, cake or tart.

Innkeeper(s): Jan Garrabrandt, Bruce Garrabrandt. $115-260. 5 rooms with PB, 4 with FP, 3 with WP, 2 two-bedroom suites, 2 cottages. Breakfast and snacks/refreshments included in rates. Types of meals: Full gourmet bkfst, veg bkfst, early coffee/tea and We will happily cater to celiac guests.

Certificate may be used: Sunday-Thursday, November-April. Holidays excluded.

Valley Forge

The Great Valley House of Valley Forge

1475 Swedesford Road
Valley Forge, PA 19355
(610) 644-6759
Internet: www.greatvalleyhouse.com
E-mail: pattye@greatvalleyhouse.com

Circa 1690. This 300-year-old Colonial stone farmhouse sits on four acres just two miles from Valley Forge Park. Boxwoods line the walkway, and ancient trees surround the house. Each of the three antique-filled guest rooms is hand-stenciled and features a  canopied or brass bed topped with handmade quilts. Guests enjoy a full breakfast before a 14-foot fireplace in the "summer kitchen," the oldest part of the house. On the grounds are a swimming pool, walking and hiking trails and the home's original smokehouse.

Innkeeper(s): Pattye Benson. $104-129. 3 rooms with PB, 1 conference room. Breakfast and Full Gourmet Breakfast included in rates. Types of meals: Full gourmet bkfst, veg bkfst, early coffee/tea. Lunch, dinner, weekend brunch or dietetic needs available with prior arrangement

Certificate may be used: Nov. 1-April 30, both nights must be Sunday-Thursday, excludes holidays.

White Horse

Stoltzfus Bed and Breakfast at the Fassitt Mansion

6051 Old Philadelphia Pike
White Horse, PA 17527
(717) 442-0453
Internet: www.stoltzfusbandb.com
E-mail: stoltzfusbandb@gmail.com

Circa 1845. This historic inn was built originally to host lavish parties and also served as a stop on the Underground Railroad. Now owned by an innkeeper who grew up Amish, there are antique furnishings that grace large guest rooms with fireplaces. Sunlight beams through 11-foot windows in those rooms with 12-foot ceilings and the impressive four-poster king-size bed in the Masters Chamber is a balm to weary travelers. The Freedom Room holds a secret compartment in the closet that sheltered 32 slaves over the years. Locally grown ingredients and free range eggs are used to create full country breakfasts with Amish extras such as peanut butter spread, smearkase, and shoofly pie. Watch horse and buggies trot by as you breath fresh country air on the front porch and consider reserving the entire inn to host family reunion activities on the two-acre lawn. The Ultimate Amish Experience Package including dinner for two in an Amish home is available with a stay of two nights or more.

Innkeeper(s): Ginger Stoltzfus, Sam Stoltzfus. $99-139. 6 rooms, 5 with PB, 4 with FP, 1 cottage. Breakfast and snacks/refreshments included in rates. Types of meals: Full gourmet bkfst and veg bkfst.

Certificate may be used: November-March, subject to availability.

Rhode Island

Newport

Adele Turner Inn

93 Pelham St
Newport, RI 02840
(401) 848-8011 (888) 820-8011 Fax:(401)845-0336
Internet: www.adeleturner.com
E-mail: info@adeleturner.com

Circa 1855. Architecturally significant, this recently restored inn is listed in the National Register. Named one of iLoveInns.com's Top 10 Most Romantic Inns in 2002, it is located in an historic residential neighborhood and sits on the country's first gaslit street. Two fireplaces highlight the elegant parlor, where afternoon tea is served. Books and videos are also available there. Well-appointed guest rooms and suites reflect regional themes and events. Encounter period furnishings and fireplaces, with some rooms boasting two-person whirlpool tubs. Ask for the Harborview Spa which includes French doors leading to a rooftop deck with private hot tub and panoramic harbor view. In the parlor, a breakfast buffet begins a delicious meal followed by a hot entree. Complimentary wine, cheese and fresh fruit are offered on Saturdays.

Innkeeper(s): Cheryl Schatmeyer, Harry Schatmeyer, Jr. $149-359. 11 rooms with PB, 11 with FP, 1 with HT, 3 with WP, 3 suites. Breakfast and afternoon tea included in rates. Types of meals: Full gourmet bkfst.

Certificate may be used: July 1-Sept. 30 weekdays only. Anytime from November-June 30.

Beech Tree Inn

34 Rhode Island Ave
Newport, RI 02840-2667
(401)847-9794 (800)748-6565
Internet: www.beechtreeinn.com
E-mail: cmquilt13@cox.net

Circa 1897. This inn's location in historic Newport offers close access to the famous local mansions, and the turn-of-the-century home is within walking distance of the harbor. Most of the guest rooms include a fireplace. Special furnishings include canopy or poster beds, and suites offer the added amenity of a whirlpool tub. The innkeepers provide a breakfast feast, and guests enjoy made-to-order fare that might include eggs, pancakes, waffles, omelettes, ham, bacon and more. Snacks, such as freshly baked cookies, are always on hand to curb one's appetite.

Innkeeper(s): Cindy Mahood. $99-359. 4 rooms, 8 with PB, 5 with FP, 3 with HT, 5 with WP, 1 suite. Breakfast, afternoon tea and snacks/refreshments included in rates. Types of meals: Full bkfst and early coffee/tea.

Certificate may be used: Anytime, November-March, subject to availability.

Belle View Inn

22 Freebody Street
Newport, RI 02840
(401) 849-8211 (800) 722-6354 Fax:(401) 619-1578
Internet: www.belleviewinn.com
E-mail: innkeeper@belleviewinn.com

Circa 1900. Stay at this Grand Victorian bed and breakfast that is elegant, centrally located and reasonably priced. Write out postcards to home while sitting at the umbrella table on the outside deck or relax on a front porch rocker. Stay in one of the spacious and romantic two-bedroom guest suites with four-poster beds, sitting rooms and views of the historic Tennis Hall of Fame grass courts. Start each day with a complimentary deluxe continental breakfast. Prestigious Bellevue Avenue is one block away while Cliff Walk, Newport Beach, Newport Harbor, Salve Regina University, downtown Newport and several Newport mansions are just three blocks away.

Innkeeper(s): Lorna Zaloumis, Anthony Zaloumis. $110-329. 2 rooms, 2 with HT, 2 suites. Breakfast and snacks/refreshments included in rates. Types of meals: Cont.

Certificate may be used: November-December, May, Sunday-Thursday, excluding holidays, subject to availability.

Gardenview Bed & Breakfast

8 Binney St
Newport, RI 02840-4304
(401)849-5799 Fax:(401)845-6675
Internet: www.gardenviewbnb.com
E-mail: gardenview8@hotmail.com

Circa 1978. Sitting in a quiet neighborhood not far from the beaches, mansions and famous Ocean Drive, this Saltbox home has a comfortable country colonial decor. The common room is an inviting place to play games. Browse through local menus and brochures in the cozy sitting area. Full afternoon tea is served (for an extra charge) in the sunroom overlooking the gardens. Stay in the Garden Room or the Sun-Lit Suite. Fresh flowers, turndown service, French lace curtains, whirlpool tubs and a fireplace enhance the intimate ambiance. A hearty country breakfast is served in the fireside dining room amid antiques. Homemade granola and fresh fruit accompany chocolate orange scones or other sweet treats. Entrees may include pecan waffles, chocolate coconut pancakes or an egg dish. The large yard boasts a fish pond and a waterfall.

Innkeeper(s): Mary and Andrew Fitzgerald. $125-195. 2 rooms, 1 with PB, 1 suite. Breakfast included in rates. Types of meals: Country bkfst, veg bkfst, early coffee/tea and afternoon tea.

Certificate may be used: November-April, subject to availability, excludes holidays. Some weekends require 3-night minimum stay.

Hydrangea House Inn

16 Bellevue Avenue
Newport, RI 02840
(401)846-4435 (800)945-4667 Fax:(401)846-6602
Internet: www.hydrangeahouse.com
E-mail: hydrangeahouseinn@cox.net

Circa 1876. Well-known for it impeccable service, elegant furnishings, rich warm colors, luxurious fabrics and masterful faux painting, this New England inn is a delightful place to stay. Beach towels are provided for soaking up the sun on the roof deck. After an incredible night's rest, join the first or second seating for a gourmet breakfast in the formal dining room. Start with the special blend Hydrangea House Coffee that complements the signature raspberry pancakes, home-baked breads, granola, seasoned scrambled eggs in puff pastry or other tempting recipes that will provide enough energy for the whole day. Ask about special packages available.

Innkeeper(s): Grant Edmondson, Dennis Blair. $265-475. 9 rooms with PB, 9 with FP, 7 with HT, 7 with WP, 7 suites. Breakfast and afternoon tea included in rates. Types of meals: Full gourmet bkfst and early coffee/tea.

Certificate may be used: November-April with Sunday-Wednesday check-ins.

The Burbank Rose B&B

111 Memorial Blvd W
Newport, RI 02840-3469
(401)849-9457 (888)297-5800
Internet: www.burbankrose.com
E-mail: theburbankrose@yahoo.com

Circa 1850. The innkeepers of this cheery, yellow home named their B&B in honor of their ancestor, famed horticulturist Luther Burbank. As a guest, he probably would be taken by the bright, flowery hues that adorn the interior of this Federal-style home. Rooms, some of which afford harbor views, are light and airy with simple decor. The innkeepers serve afternoon refreshments and a substantial breakfast buffet. The home is located in Newport's Historic Hill district and within walking distance of shops, restaurants and many of the seaside village's popular attractions.

Innkeeper(s): Brian Cole. $79-250. 5 rooms with PB, 3 suites. Breakfast and Continental breakfast included in rates. Types of meals: Cont.

Certificate may be used: Anytime, based on availability. Excluding weekends May-November. Continental breakfast only.

The Victoria Skylar Bed and Breakfast

107 Second St.
Newport, RI 02840
(401) 855-8701 (866) 756-7445
Internet: victoriaskylar.com
E-mail: victoriaskylarbb@aol.com

Circa 1892. Open year-round with seasonal specials and packages available, this historic Victorian luxury cottage graces the quiet neighborhood of Point District in Newport, Rhode Island. Romantic, relaxing and elegant suites boast separate linens on four-poster beds, central air conditioning, fireplaces, Godiva chocolates, fresh flowers, Evian and San Pellegrino bottled waters and Italian-tiled baths with Crabtree and Evelyn

toiletries and some Jacuzzis. Savor a gourmet breakfast on china and crystal in the candlelit dining room. Afternoon refreshments are enjoyed in the formal garden amid award-winning roses and perennials. Sip evening sherry or brandy in the fireside parlor. It is a short walk one block to the harbor, shopping and restaurants.

Innkeeper(s): Anne S. Coulton. $229-269. 4 rooms with PB, 1 two-bedroom suite. Breakfast, snacks/refreshments and wine included in rates. Types of meals: Full gourmet bkfst, veg bkfst, early coffee/tea, picnic lunch and afternoon tea.

Certificate may be used: Anytime excluding, May 24-28, July 4-7, July 26-28, Aug. 2-5, Aug. 9-12, Spet. 6-9, Nov. 27-30 and Dec. 23-Jan. 7.

Victorian Ladies Inn

63 Memorial Blvd
Newport, RI 02840-3629
(401)849-9960
Internet: www.victorianladies.com
E-mail: info@victorianladies.com

Circa 1851. Innkeepers Cheryl and Harry have created a comfortable and welcoming atmosphere at this restored three-story Victorian inn and cottage. Intimate and inviting, this traditional New England bed & breakfast features spacious guest bedrooms furnished with period pieces, fine reproductions, rich fabrics and wallcoverings. Linger over a gracious breakfast in the dining room. Stroll through the award-winning gardens, walk over the small bridge and gaze at the koi pond. Relax in the living room while planning activities for the day. Walk to nearby beaches, the Colonial town, famed mansions, cliff walk and harbor front.

Innkeeper(s): Cheryl Schatmeyer, Harry Schatmeyer, Jr. $129-289. 11 rooms with PB, 5 with FP. Breakfast included in rates. Types of meals: Full gourmet bkfst and veg bkfst.

Certificate may be used: July 1-Sept. 30 weekdays only. Anytime from November-June 30.

Providence

Edgewood Manor B&B

232 Norwood Ave
Providence, RI 02905
(401) 781-0099 Fax:401 467 6311
Internet: www.providence-lodging.com
E-mail: edgemanor@aol.com

Circa 1905. Built as a private home, this 18-room Greek Revival Colonial mansion has served as a convent, an office, a rooming house and is now restored as an magnificent bed and breakfast. An elegant era is reflected in the coffered, beamed and domed-foyer ceilings, leaded- and stained-glass windows, hand-carved mantels and blend of Victorian and Empire decor. Romantic guest bedrooms feature Jacuzzi tubs and wood-burning fireplaces. Savor a satisfying gourmet breakfast served in the dining room or on the patio. The inn is within walking distance to Narragansett Bay and Roger Williams Park and Zoo, with 230 acres of magnificent gardens, sculptures and historic buildings.

Innkeeper(s): Joy Generali. $129-329. 20 rooms, 18 with PB, 3 with FP, 9 with HT. Breakfast included in rates. Types of meals: Full gourmet bkfst, afternoon tea, wine and cheese hour on Friday and Saturday Eves.

Certificate may be used: Monday-Thursday only, not valid May 15-Nov. 15.

Westerly

Grandview B&B

212 Shore Rd
Westerly, RI 02891-3623
(401)596-6384 (800)447-6384
Internet: grandviewbandb.com
E-mail: grandviewbandb@verizon.net

Circa 1910. An impressive wraparound stone porch highlights this majestic Shingle Victorian inn, which also boasts a lovely ocean view from its hilltop site. The inn features 9 guest rooms, a family room with cable TV, a spacious living room with a handsome stone fireplace, and a sun porch where visitors enjoy a hearty breakfast buffet. Antiquing, fishing, golf, swimming and tennis are found nearby as are Watch Hill, Mystic and Newport. The Foxwoods and Mohegan Sun casinos also are nearby.

Innkeeper(s): Patricia Grande. $115-140. 7 rooms, 4 with PB, 1 suite. Breakfast included in rates. Types of meals: Cont plus and early coffee/tea.

Certificate may be used: November-April, Sunday-Thursday, subject to availability.

Wyoming

Stagecoach House Inn

1136 Main St
Wyoming, RI 02898
(401)539-9600 (888)814-9600
Internet: www.stagecoachhouse.com
E-mail: info@stagecoachhouse.com

Circa 1796. Meticulously restored, this historic 1796 Colonial with Victorian decor is an inviting South County country inn. Relax on the front porch overlooking garden shrubs and trees that reflect the original landscaping. Sit by the large fireplace in rocking chairs and listen to the player piano in the lobby. Air-conditioned guest bedrooms and suites feature remote control fireplaces and whirlpool tubs. The honeymoon suite boasts a two-person Jacuzzi and double shower. French doors lead onto the upper deck with a view of the Wood River and horseshoe waterfall. A family suite has two adjoining rooms and a ground-level room is handicapped accessible. A deluxe continental breakfast is served daily.

Innkeeper(s): Deb and Bill Bokon. Call for rates. 12 rooms. Breakfast included in rates. Types of meals: Cont plus.

Certificate may be used: November-March, Sunday-Thursday subject to availability, holidays excluded, standard room only.

South Carolina

Conway

The Moore Farm House Bed and Breakfast

3423 Highway 319 E
Conway, SC 29526
(843) 365-7479
Internet: www.themoorefarmhouse.com
E-mail: info@TheMooreFarmHouse.com

Circa 1914. Warm southern hospitality has been extended here for more than 100 years. Feel refreshed and recharged by the nostalgic ambiance amid contemporary amenities. Munch on fresh-baked cookies upon arrival. Hot and cold beverages are available any time. Select a book from the well-stocked library or play billiards. Select and watch a movie in the living room. Guest rooms on the second floor boast chocolates, all-natural Sassy Goat Milk Soap and some rooms feature whirlpool soaking tubs. Gather in the dining room to linger over a gourmet breakfast that includes delicious twists on classic favorites and signature entrees designed by a highly acclaimed executive chef. Explore the local sights of the historic Waccamaw River town of Conway, South Carolina. This B&B is just 15 miles from famous Myrtle Beach. Ask about events packages and specials offered.

Innkeeper(s): Harry Pinner, Cathy Pinner. $119-159. 4 rooms.

Certificate may be used: Anytime, November-March, subject to availability.

Georgetown

Mansfield Plantation B&B Country Inn

1776 Mansfield Rd
Georgetown, SC 29440-6923
(843)546-6961 (866)717-1776 Fax:(843) 546-1367
Internet: MansfieldPlantation.com
E-mail: mightymansfield@aol.com

Circa 1800. Listed in the National Register, and featured in Mel Gibson's movie, The Patriot, Mansfield Plantation is a perfect respite for those in search of romance and history in a natural, secluded setting. The large dining room and sitting rooms are furnished with the owner's collections of 19th-century American antiques that include paintings, china, silver, furniture and gilt-framed mirrors. Accommodations include three guesthouses, each decorated in a romantic style and boasting fireplaces, hardwood floors, high ceilings, comfortable furnishings and collectibles. The vast grounds (900 private acres), shaded by moss-draped oaks, provide ideal spots for relaxing. Enjoy aza-

lea and camellia gardens, as well as views of the surrounding marshlands. Guests can relax in hammocks or swings, watch for birds or enjoy a bike ride. Boating on the Black River is another possibility. Guests may bring their own boats or rent canoes or kayaks nearby. Among the plantation's notable historic features are a schoolhouse, kitchen, winnowing house, slave village and chapel, all of which predate the Civil War.

Innkeeper(s): Kathryn Green. $150-200. 8 rooms with PB, 8 with FP, 3 guest houses, 1 conference room. Breakfast included in rates. Types of meals: Full gourmet bkfst, veg bkfst, early coffee/tea, picnic lunch and afternoon tea.

Certificate may be used: Anytime, subject to availability.

The Shaw House B&B

613 Cypress Ct
Georgetown, SC 29440-3349
(843)546-9663
Internet: www.iloveinns.com/the-shaw-house-id17760.html

Circa 1972. Near Georgetown's historical district is the Shaw House. It features a beautiful view of the Willowbank marsh, which stretches out for more than 1000 acres. Sometimes giant turtles come up and lay eggs on the lawn. Guests enjoy rocking on the inn's front and back porches and identifying the large variety of birds that live here. A large screened porch extends over the rice fields. A Southern home-cooked breakfast often includes grits, quiche and Mary's heart-shaped biscuits.

Innkeeper(s): Mary Shaw, Joe Shaw. $100. 3 rooms with PB. Breakfast included in rates. Types of meals: Full bkfst, early coffee/tea and snacks/refreshments.

Certificate may be used: Sunday-Friday, anytime available.

Lancaster

Kilburnie, the Inn at Craig Farm

1824 Craig Farm Road
Lancaster, SC 29720
(803)416-8420 Fax:(803)416-8429
Internet: www.kilburnie.com
E-mail: johannes@kilburnie.com

Circa 1828. The area's oldest surviving antebellum home, this Greek Revival was saved from demolition, moved to this 400-acre estate and extensively restored. Listed in the National Register, its historic and architectural significance is seen in the intricate details found in the public rooms. Experience Southern hospitality accented by European charm in a quiet and secluded setting with a classic elegance. Each guest bedroom and suite boasts a fireplace, as do two bathrooms. An unsurpassed two-course breakfast may include fresh-baked bread and muffins, a fruit appetizer of Poached Pears with Blueberries or Southern Pecan Peaches and a main entree of Oven-Shirred Eggs or Herbed Goat Cheese Omelette. Relax on one of the piazza rockers after a stroll on the nature path through the wildlife backyard habitat with bridges spanning the woodlands.

Innkeeper(s): Johannes Tromp. $150-200. 5 rooms with PB, 5 with FP, 1 suite, 1 conference room. Breakfast included in rates. Types of meals: Full gourmet bkfst.

Certificate may be used: Anytime, Sunday-Thursday, except holidays.

Landrum

The Red Horse Inn

45 Winstons Chase Court
Landrum, SC 29356
(864)909-1575 Fax:(864)895-4968
Internet: www.theredhorseinn.com
E-mail: theredhorseinn@aol.com

Circa 1996. Sweeping mountain views, pastoral vistas and endless sky offer the perfect setting for a romantic getaway or refreshing vacation. The Red Horse Inn on almost 190 acres in Landrum, South Carolina, offers intimate cottages and luxurious guest bedrooms that feature fireplaces, whirlpool tubs and generous upscale amenities. After a delightful breakfast, enjoy the many local sites and scenic attractions nearby.

Innkeeper(s): Mary Wolter, Roger Wolters. $175-320. 12 rooms, 6 with PB, 6 with FP, 6 with WP, 6 cottages, 1 conference room. Breakfast included in rates. Types of meals: Full gourmet bkfst, early coffee/tea and picnic lunch.

Certificate may be used: November-January, Monday-Thursday, subject to availability. Not valid on holidays or weekends stays.

Moncks Corner

Rice Hope Plantation Inn Bed & Breakfast

206 Rice Hope Dr
Moncks Corner, SC 29461-9781
(843)849-9000
Internet: www.ricehope.com
E-mail: louedens@gmail.com

Circa 1840. Resting on 285 secluded acres of natural beauty, this historic mansion sits among oaks on a bluff overlooking the Cooper River. A stay here is a visit to yesteryear, where it is said to be 45 short minutes and three long centuries from downtown Charleston. Formal gardens boast a 200-year-old camellia and many more varieties of trees and plants, making it a perfect setting for outdoor weddings or other special occasions. Nearby attractions include the Trappist Monastery at Mepkin Plantation, Francis Marion National Forest and Cypress Gardens.

Innkeeper(s): Jamie Edens. $85-165. 5 rooms with PB, 1 conference room. Breakfast included in rates. Types of meals: Full bkfst and early coffee/tea.

Certificate may be used: Sunday-Thursday.

Mount Pleasant

Plantation Oaks Inn

1199 Long Point Rd
Mount Pleasant, SC 29464
(843) 971-3683
Internet: www.plantationoaksinnbandb.com
E-mail: info@plantationoaksinnbandb.com

Circa 1987. Surrounded by 300-year-old oak trees, this log exterior inn is ready to treat guests to true Southern hospitality near Charleston. The full breakfast changes daily and Sunday mornings feature cream cheese and chive scrambled eggs and pan-seared rib-eye steak. A wall of windows brings the morning sun into the breakfast room filled with tables for two. All guest rooms are on the second floor and were named to celebrate the rich culture of the South. Comfortable queen beds are located in the Magnolia, Indigo, Palmetto, and Cotton rooms; or relax on the king bed in the Plantation Room. Complimentary parking and Wi-Fi access are included. Exposed beams and a stone fireplace add a rustic ambiance while the leather sofa invites guests into the living room. Sit outdoors and enjoy views of the enchanting tidal creek or spend a day at a local beach using the inn's beach chairs and towels with the Sun and Fun Special.

Innkeeper(s): Phyllis Walterhouse, Steve Walterhouse. $99-155. 5 rooms with PB. Breakfast included in rates. Types of meals: Full bkfst.

Certificate may be used: November-February, weekdays only.

Orangeburg

Thee Matriarch Inn, Meeting and Special Events Venue

1170 Fischer St
Orangeburg, SC 29115
(803) 937-4271
Internet: www.theematriarch.com/
E-mail: info@theematriarch.com

Southern charm and a romantic aura radiate from this inn, event, and meeting space in Orangeburg, South Carolina. Innkeeper Rachelle has a background in fashion and interior design and has restored the home with hardwood floors and lush fabrics. Experience another part of the world in The Out of Africa room with fun animal prints while the black, white, and red sitting room of The Jazz It Up Suite will put anyone in a celebratory mood. The bed and breakfast is available for weddings, holiday parties, cocktail receptions, poetry readings, church retreats, and more. RSVPs can be handled through the inn's website. Everyone is welcome to enjoy Chef Fred's culinary masterpieces at lunch or dinner on the first Friday of every month. The inn invites local chefs and caterers to showcase their talents in a social setting on the third Tuesday of the month. Both of these monthly events allow guests to mingle with locals and new friends.

Innkeeper(s): Rachelle Jamerson-Holmes, Chef Fred Holmes. Call for rates. 3 rooms, 2 with PB, 2 with FP, 1 with HT, 1 with WP, 1 total suite, including 1 two-bedroom suite and 1 three-bedroom suite. Breakfast included in rates.

Certificate may be used: Anytime, subject to availability.

Union

The Inn at Merridun

100 Merridun Pl
Union, SC 29379-2200
(864)427-7052 (888)892-6020 Fax:(864)429-0373
Internet: www.merridun.com
E-mail: info@merridun.com

Circa 1855. Nestled on nine acres of wooded ground, this Greek Revival inn is in a small Southern college town. During spring, see the South in its  colorful splendor with blooming azaleas, magnolias and wisteria. Sip an iced drink on the inn's marble verandas and relive memories of a bygone era. Soft strains of Mozart and Beethoven, as well as the smell of freshly baked cookies and country suppers, fill the air of this antebellum country inn. In addition to a complimentary breakfast, guest will enjoy the inn's dessert selection offered every evening.

Innkeeper(s): Peggy Waller . $99-135. 5 rooms with PB, 3 conference rooms. Breakfast and Evening dessert included in rates. Types of meals: Full gourmet bkfst, gourmet lunch, picnic lunch, afternoon tea, gourmet dinner and luncheons.

Certificate may be used: Jan. 15-Nov. 15, Monday-Thursday.

South Dakota

Deadwood

Black Hills Hideaway B&B

11744 Hideaway Rd.
Deadwood, SD 57732
(605)578-3054 (877)500-4433
Internet: www.enetis.net/~hideaway
E-mail: hideaway@enetis.net

Circa 1976. Guests enjoy the privacy of 67 wooded acres and views of mountain peaks at this bed & breakfast. The eight guest rooms are tucked into a mountain chalet-style home with cathedral ceilings and natural wood interior. The home is located on what was a wagon trail in the late 19th century. The decor is comfortable and there's a huge brick fireplace to enjoy. Each guest room has its own theme, including Western and European themes with antiques. Most rooms have a fireplace, deck and whirlpool or hot tubs. The innkeepers also offer a housekeeping cabin south of Pactola Lake. The home is about 40 miles from Mt. Rushmore and the Crazy Horse Monument. A gold mine, the Passion Play, Spearfish Canyon and other attractions are nearby. Deadwood, a historic national landmark, is 7 miles away.

Innkeeper(s): Ned Bode, Kathy Bode. $129-189. 8 rooms with PB, 7 with FP, 3 with HT, 4 with WP. Breakfast and snacks/refreshments included in rates. Types of meals: Full bkfst, early coffee/tea and dinner.

Certificate may be used: Sept. 16-May 15, Sunday-Thursday, subject to availability.

Rapid City

Coyote Blues Village

23165 Horseman's Ranch Rd
Rapid City, SD 57702
(605)574-4477 (888)253-4477 Fax:(605)574-2101
Internet: www.coyotebluesvillage.com
E-mail: info@coyotebluesvillage.com

Circa 1996. Experience genuine European style with the Streich family from Switzerland in their 9,000-square-foot, two-story European cabin, resting on 30 acres of woodlands in the Black Hills of South Dakota. Four uniquely themed rooms provide style to fit any taste, from "jungle" to "Oriental." Relax in the hot tub just outside the room on the private patio and breathe in the fresh pine scent that fills the crisp air. Rise each morning with the sweet aroma of freshly baked goods from the Swiss Specialty Bakery downstairs. Enjoy breakfast in the dining room or on the deck before an excursion in town.

Innkeeper(s): Christine Streich, Hans-Peter Streich. $75-155. 10 rooms with PB, 4 with HT, 1 with WP, 1 two-bedroom suite, 1 conference room.

Breakfast and snacks/refreshments included in rates. Types of meals: Full gourmet bkfst, veg bkfst, early coffee/tea, gourmet lunch, gourmet dinner, Dinner and lunch and vegetarian by request.

Certificate may be used: September-May, subject to availabilty, last minute, subject to availabilty.

Hisega Lodge

23101 Triangle Trail
Rapid City, SD 57702
(605) 342-8444
Internet: www.hisegalodge.net
E-mail: info@hisegalodge.net

Circa 1909. Listen to the bubbling creek and let the smell of pine refresh the senses at this serene retreat in Rapid City, South Dakota. Each of the nine comfortable guest rooms has a private bath and private entrance. Guests are treated to a gourmet breakfast every morning. Sit in the large sunlit library, socialize with new friends in the great room, relax on a rocking chair on the porch, or play with feisty Guinness, the lodge cat. Hisega Lodge has been hosting guests for more than 100 years and is the oldest lodge in the Black Hills. Renovations over the years deliver modern conveniences. Gather 10-20 friends for an unforgettable mystery party with dinner, dessert, and lodging. Enjoy the outdoors by hiking or fishing right on the lodge property. The inn is centrally located near many attractions including Mount Rushmore, Custer State Park, Deadwood, hiking and winter sports in the Black Hills, and Sturgis, home of the famous motorcycle rally.

Innkeeper(s): Carol Duncan, Kenn Duncan. $99-169. 9 rooms with PB. Breakfast and a big fresh-baked cookie when you check in included in rates. Types of meals: Happy to provide picnic lunches or full dinners upon request. Just arrange a day ahead.

Certificate may be used: November-February, Sunday-Thursday, excluding holidays, subject to availability.

Tennessee

Gatlinburg

Creekwalk Inn and Cabins at Whisperwood Farm

166 Middle Creek Road and Highway 321
Gatlinburg, TN 37722
(423)487-4000 (800)962-2246
Internet: www.creekwalkinn.com
E-mail: info@creekwalkinn.com

Circa 1984. Swim or fish in the trout-stocked Cosby Creek while staying at this B&B outside Gatlinburg, Tennessee in the Great Smoky Mountains. Creekwalk Inn and Cabins at Whisperwood Farm in Cosby offers the setting of a log home on a private estate with 3000 feet of water frontage. Firewood is available for outdoor campfires and a guitar is available for strumming and singing along. Beverage service is provided all day. Stay in a guest bedroom with a cathedral ceiling and assorted amenities that may include a creek or meadow view, Jacuzzi, fireplace, robes, balcony or a private outdoor hot tub in a bamboo thicket. Honeymoon and family cabins are also available. Savor a daily gourmet breakfast before exploring the scenic area. The wedding chapel and reception lodge are popular romantic venues.

Innkeeper(s): Janice Haynes, Tifton Haynes. $139-310. 5 rooms, 4 with FP, 2 with HT, 4 with WP, 2 two-bedroom suites, 1 cottage, 10 cabins, 2 conference rooms. Breakfast and Tea and coffee beverage service available 24 hours/day self service. Cabins do not include breakfast included in rates. Types of meals: Full gourmet bkfst, veg bkfst, early coffee/tea, gourmet lunch, picnic lunch, Private chef available with 24 hours notice, private dinners by reservation, fresh fruit and juice served with full gourmet breakfast, vegetarian meals by request, guests may bring own wine and guest refrigerator.

Certificate may be used: Sunday-Thursday, except month of October. No holiday weeks or special event weeks.

Kingston

Whitestone Country Inn

1200 Paint Rock Rd
Kingston, TN 37763-5843
(865)376-0113 (888)247-2464 Fax:(865)376-4454
Internet: www.whitestoneinn.com
E-mail: moreinfo@whitestoneinn.com

Circa 1995. This regal farmhouse sits majestically on a hilltop overlooking miles of countryside and Watts Bar Lake. The inn is surrounded by 360 acres, some of which borders a scenic lake where guests can enjoy fishing or simply communing with nature. There are eight miles of hiking trails, and the many porches and decks are perfect places to relax. The inn's interior

is as pleasing as the exterior surroundings. Guest rooms are elegantly appointed, and each includes a fireplace and whirlpool tub. Guests are treated to a hearty, country-style breakfast, and dinners and lunch are available by reservation. The inn is one hour from Chattanooga, Knoxville and the Great Smoky Mountains National Park.

Innkeeper(s): Paul Cowell, Jean Cowell. $150-280. 21 rooms with PB, 21 with FP, 21 with WP, 2 conference rooms. Breakfast included in rates. Types of meals: Full bkfst, picnic lunch and dinner. Restaurant on premises.

Certificate may be used: Jan. 1-March 31, Sunday-Thursday.

Monteagle

Monteagle Inn

204 West Main Street
Monteagle, TN 37356
(931)924-3869 Fax:(931) 924-3867
Internet: www.monteagleinn.com
E-mail: suites@monteagleinn.com

Circa 1997. Offering European elegance and comfort, this recently renovated inn is classical in style and design. Adjacent to the courtyard, a large wood-burning fireplace accents the great room that showcases a 1923 baby grand piano family heirloom. Guest bedrooms boast a variety of comfortable furnishings and amenities. Choose a four-poster, iron or sleigh bed with soft linens. Many include balconies. The two-bedroom Cottage boasts a fully equipped kitchen, front porch, dining and living rooms. Enjoy a homemade breakfast in the dining room. The garden gazebo is surrounded by year-round color, designed by a local horticulturist and a prominent landscape architect. Ask about romance and anniversary packages.

Innkeeper(s): Jim Harmon. $160-265. 13 rooms with PB, 1 conference room. Breakfast and snacks/refreshments included in rates. Types of meals: Full gourmet bkfst, veg bkfst, Sun. brunch, early coffee/tea, gourmet lunch, picnic lunch, hors d'oeuvres, wine, gourmet dinner and Full Mountain Gourmet Breakfast.

Certificate may be used: January-March, Sunday-Tuesday.

Mountain City

Historic Prospect Hill B&B Inn

801 W Main St (Hwy 67)
Mountain City, TN 37683
(423) 727-0139 (800) 339-5084
Internet: www.prospect-hill.com
E-mail: inn@prospect-hill.com

Circa 1889. This three-story shingle-style Victorian manor garners a great deal of attention from passersby with its appealing architecture and commanding hilltop location. Romantic rooms offer tall arched windows, 11-foot ceilings and spectacular views. Fashioned from handmade bricks, it was once home to Major Joseph Wagner, who, like many of his neighbors in far northeastern Tennessee, served on the Union side. The restored home features five guest rooms. A 1910 oak Craftsman dining set complements the oak Stickley furniture (circa 1997) that decorates the living room. Fireplaces, whirlpools and stained glass add luxury to the guest rooms. Prospect Hill boasts views of the Appalachian and Blue Ridge Mountains. From the front window, guests can see three states: Tennessee, Virginia and North Carolina. The inn is within an hour of the Blue Ridge Parkway, Appalachian Trail and Roan and Grandfather mountains, the Virginia Creeper Trail and 25 minutes from Boone, NC.

Innkeeper(s): Judy & Robert Hotchkiss. $99-235. 6 rooms, 5 with PB, 4 with FP, 1 three-bedroom suite, 1 cottage, 1 conference room. Breakfast and snacks/refreshments included in rates. Types of meals: Full gourmet bkfst, veg bkfst, early coffee/tea, Snacks in the room and meals not provided at cottage—couples may at at inn (fee).

Certificate may be used: Sunday-Thursday, not valid on NASCAR weekends or Oct. 1-25. Will accept at last minute (no more than 24 hours ahead booking) B&B rooms only.

Newport

Christopher Place - An Intimate Resort

1500 Pinnacles Way
Newport, TN 37821-7308
(423)623-6555 (800)595-9441 Fax:(423)613-4771
Internet: www.christopherplace.com
E-mail: stay@christopherplace.com

Circa 1975. 2009 Winner - Travelers' Choice for Romance. Christopher Place is an incomparable resort secluded in the scenic Smoky Mountains near Gatlinburg, in Newport, Tennessee. This award-winning inn was created especially for romantic retreats, unforgettable honeymoons, and special events. Surrounded by more than 200 acres with incredible views, the inn's interior, as well as the hospitality and service has earned it four-diamonds for more than a decade and the iLoveInns 2009 Travelers' Choice for Romance award. Enjoy numerous activities and amenities. Swim, play tennis, go hiking, visit the sauna, shoot pool in the billiard room or just sit amid the beautiful vistas from a rocking chair on the veranda. Start each relaxing day with a full service breakfast and experience four-course gourmet meals in the formal dining room. More casual dining is offered in Marston's Library Pub.

Innkeeper(s): Marston Price. $165-330. 9 rooms, 8 with PB, 2 with FP, 5 with HT, 5 with WP. Breakfast and snacks/refreshments included in rates. Types of meals: Full gourmet bkfst, veg bkfst, early coffee/tea, picnic lunch, wine, gourmet dinner and room service. Restaurant on premises.

Certificate may be used: Monday-Thursday, November-May.

Red Boiling Springs

Armours Hotel

321 E Main St
Red Boiling Springs, TN 37150-2322
(615) 699-2180
Internet: www.armourshotel.com
E-mail: armourshotel@yahoo.com

Circa 1924. As Tennessee's only remaining mineral bathhouse, this two-story, National Historic Register house is tucked away in the rolling hills of the Cumberland Plateau. Whether resting in one of the 23 antique-furnished guest rooms, listening to the babbling creek from the second-floor veranda, strolling under covered bridges, or simply enjoying the sunrise in a rocking chair on the porch before breakfast, tranquillity awaits each guest. Spend the afternoon in the gazebo with your favorite book from the library next door, or get in a game of tennis at the park across the street before dinner.

Innkeeper(s): Dennis Emery, Debra Emery. $69-129. 13 rooms with PB, 2 two-bedroom suites, 1 conference room. Breakfast and dinner included in rates. Types of meals: Country bkfst, veg bkfst, early coffee/tea, lunch, snacks/refreshments, hors d'oeuvres and Luncheons and dinners for up to 80 people with arrangements made in advance. Restaurant on premises.

Certificate may be used: Anytime, subject to availability.

Sevierville

Bluff Mountain Inn

1887 Bluff Mountain Rd
Sevierville, TN 37876-7397
(865)908-0321 (888)559-0321 Fax:(865)774-3308
Internet: www.bluffmountaininn.com
E-mail: rick@bluffmountaininn.com

For an intimate ceremony or elaborate gala with 200 guests', celebrate a beautiful inn wedding in the Great Smoky Mountains. Let Rick, a professional photographer, and Rhonda, a certified wedding planner, coordinate a memorable ceremony and charming reception on the five-acre estate in Sevierville, Tennessee. The bride and bridesmaids can relax in plush robes while getting ready in the Bridal Suite. Couples can say "I Do" in the chapel, under the pergola, or on the lawn. After the ceremony, celebrate with guests inside the hall with scenic views of the mountains and gorgeous fireplace or dance under the stars in the open air pavilion. At the end of the evening, the new bride and groom can relax in the Jacuzzi tub in the Honeymoon Suite. Other wedding guests will find many lodging options nearby, some within walking distance. With many wedding packages available, every couple is sure to find the right fit for them.

Innkeeper(s): Rick King, Rhonda King. Call for rates. 2 rooms, 2 with FP, 2 with HT, 2 with WP, 2 suites, 1 conference room.

Certificate may be used: Anytime, subject to availability.

Texas

Boerne

Paniolo Ranch Bed & Breakfast Spa

1510 FM 473
Boerne, TX 78006
(830)324-6666 (866)726-4656 Fax:(830)324-6665
Internet: www.paniloranch.com
E-mail: paniolo@paniloranch.com

Circa 2002. Paniolo Ranch Bed & Breakfast Spa is a hundred-acre ranch And romantic resort retreat in Boerne, Texas. Surrounded by Texas Hill Country, Hawaiian spa luxuries blend with Lone Star sensibilities to offer total relaxation. Swim in the pool overlooking the lake and hills, soak in the hot tub under the stars or pick fruit and veggies from the orchard and garden. Sophisticated amenities highlight the wide variety of upscale accommodations that include a generous in-room breakfast. Stay in a room with a covered porch and hot tub or lakeside patio. Browse for items to take home in one of the three gift shops and be sure to experience one of the treatments from the extensive spa menu.

Innkeeper(s): C'ne. $230-295. 4 cottages with PB, 4 with HT, 1 two-bed-room suite, 1 conference room. Breakfast and snacks/refreshments included in rates. Types of meals: Full bkfst, veg bkfst, early coffee/tea, lunch, picnic lunch, wine, dinner and room service.

Certificate may be used: Sunday-Thursday only.

Cat Spring

BlissWood Bed and Breakfast Ranch

13300 Lehmann Legacy Ln
Cat Spring, TX 78933
(713)301-3235
Internet: www.blisswood.net
E-mail: carol@blisswood.net

Surrounded by a tranquil country setting, this working ranch graces more than 650 acres, located just one hour west of Houston. Exotic animals abound from American bison and Corriente cattle to llamas and camels. Picnic at the gazebo looking out on Enchanted Lake, ride a horse across the meadows and creeks, try catch and release bass fishing or sit by a pond watching ducks, swans and geese glide by. A seven-circuit labyrinth is in the Mystical Forest. A variety of accommodations include the two-story Texas Farmhouse, Log Cabin or Lehmann House with a clawfoot, antique tin or Jacuzzi tub. The Dog Trot House includes a pool, deck, patio and fireplace. Stay in the secluded Writer's Cabin secluded among the live oaks. Enjoy the smoke-free environment and a deluxe continental breakfast.

Innkeeper(s): Carol Davis. $149-419. 20 rooms, 15 with PB, 3 with FP, 1

with HT, 2 with WP, 8 cottages, 10 guest houses, 2 cabins. Breakfast included in rates. Types of meals: Cont, veg bkfst, gourmet lunch, picnic lunch, wine and gourmet dinner.

Certificate may be used: Sunday-Thursday or anytime at last minute based on availability. No holidays or antique week.

Cypress

Seventh Heaven Bed and Breakfast

19870 Cypress Church Rd.
Cypress, TX 77433
(281)256-2130
Internet: www.stayat7.com
E-mail: nicole@stayat7.com

Enjoy country luxury on ten-and-a-half acres in Cypress, Texas. A gourmet breakfast is included and the inn offers a unique all-inclusive package with soda, wine, beer, and dinner ingredients in the common fridge. The soothing sounds of a stone waterfall pour into the outdoor pool beside the relaxing hot tub. Take a kayak out in of the three ponds and fish for bass, tilapia, and catfish. Both the bedroom and bathroom can be lit by a romantic glow from the two-sided fireplace in the Heavenly Haven room. A family of six can be comfortable in the large Green Hill Suite with a king-size bedroom, living area with pullout sofa, and small room with twin bunk beds. All guest rooms have down pillows, luxurious bathrobes, Jacuzzi tubs, and water and snack baskets. Located only 25 miles from downtown Houston, guests can easily take a day trip or just drive to the city for dinner.

Innkeeper(s): Nicole Mass. $139-199. 6 rooms with PB, 1 with FP, 5 with WP, 1 suite.

Certificate may be used: October- January, Sunday-Thursday, subject to availability.

Denison

Inn of Many Faces Victorian Bed & Breakfast

412 West Morton Street
Denison, TX 75020
(903)465-4639
Internet: www.innofmanyfaces.com
E-mail: innofmanyfaces@gmail.com

Circa 1897. Resplendently sitting in the middle of towering pecan trees on two wooded acres, this restored Queen Anne Victorian provides rest and relaxation. A collection of whimsical faces are displayed throughout the house and gardens reflecting its name, Inn of Many Faces. Themed guest bedrooms offer spacious accommodations. The Katy Room is a romantic retreat dressed in toile that boasts a fireplace, Jacuzzi tub and shower. The Texoma room features a plush king-size bed, fireplace and sitting area with two-person Jacuzzi and shower. All the rooms include a large gourmet breakfast with fresh fruit, baked entree, breakfast meats and breads. The B&B is located four short blocks from antique shops and art galleries on Main Street and near Lake Texoma for boating, fishing and golfing.

Innkeeper(s): Donna Ferchak. $119-149. 4 rooms with PB, 2 with FP, 3 with WP, 1 conference room. Breakfast and snacks/refreshments included in rates. Types of meals: Full gourmet bkfst, veg bkfst and early coffee/tea.

Certificate may be used: Anytime, subject to availability.

Fort Worth

MD Resort Bed & Breakfast

601 Old Base Road
Fort Worth, TX 76078
(817) 489-5150 (866) 489-5150 Fax:(817)489-5036
Internet: www.mdresort.com
E-mail: innkeeper@mdresort.com

Circa 1999. Stay at a home away from home at this antique-filled country lodge and working ranch on 37 T-shaped acres. Enjoy a large meeting room, living room with big screen TV, game room and limited access to the full kitchen. Each of the guest bedrooms is decorated in a theme, such as German, Western, Victorian or safari, to name just a few. A full home-cooked breakfast will satisfy the heartiest of appetites. A completely furnished barn apartment also is available. The large spa and swimming pool are especially refreshing interludes after a nature walk. Lunch and dinner are served by reservation. A laundry room is accessible when needed.

Innkeeper(s): Caty Manning. $109-499. 15 rooms, 12 with PB, 1 with FP, 6 with WP, 4 total suites, including 1 two-bedroom suite, 1 guest house, 1 cabin, 1 conference room. Breakfast and Breakfast served in main lodge dining area at 9 AM each day included in rates. Types of meals: Country bkfst, lunch, picnic lunch, snacks/refreshments, dinner, room service, Romantic In-Room Ribeye Steak Dinner for two = $100, includes salad, baked potato, bread and specialty dessert. Restaurant on premises.

Certificate may be used: Sunday-Thursday, except on holidays or TMS (Texas Motor Speedway) weekends. Cannot be combined with any other offers.

Texas White House B&B

1417 8th Ave
Fort Worth, TX 76104-4111
(817)923-3597 (800)279-6491 Fax:(817)923-0410
Internet: www.texaswhitehouse.com
E-mail: txwhitehou@aol.com

Circa 1910. A spacious encircling veranda shaded by an old elm tree, graces the front of this two-story home located within five minutes of downtown, TCU, the zoo and many other area attractions. The inn's parlor and living room with fireplace and gleaming hardwood floors are the most popular spots for relaxing when not lingering on the porch. Guest rooms are equipped with phones and television, and early morning coffee is provided before the inn's full breakfast at a time convenient to your personal schedule. Suites include hot tub, sauna and fireplace. Baked egg casseroles and freshly made breads are served to your room or in the dining room. The owners are Fort Worth experts and keep abreast of cultural attractions and are happy to help with reservations and planning. The inn is popular with business travelers — secretarial services are available, etc. — during

the week and appealing to couples on weekends.

Innkeeper(s): Grover & Jamie McMains. $129-249. 5 rooms with PB, 1 with FP, 2 suites, 1 conference room. Breakfast and snacks/refreshments included in rates. Types of meals: Full gourmet bkfst, early coffee/tea and room service.

Certificate may be used: Sunday-Thursday, no holidays. Nights must be consecutive; May 1-Aug. 31. Anytime, Last Minute-Based on Availability.

Galveston

Villa Bed & Breakfast

1723 25th Street
Galveston, TX 77550
(409)766-1722 (866)618-1723
Internet: www.thevillabedandbreakfast.com
E-mail: lindawaldren@msn.com

Circa 1914. Gracing the Silk Stocking Historic District in Galveston, Texas, this Mediterranean-style B&B has been fully restored and offers modern amenities amid antique furnishings. Villa Bed & Breakfast is an inviting place to stay with a nostalgic ambiance and a pleasant courtyard sitting area that also has a barbecue pit. Relax or watch a movie in the fireside living room. Snacks are provided. Select a gracious guest room on the second floor that may feature a Jacuzzi or balcony. Indulge in a three-course gourmet breakfast in the dining room. Located just four blocks from the beach, the Trolley stop is on the nearby corner.

Innkeeper(s): Linda Waldren. $99-199. 3 rooms with PB, 2 with WP, 1 conference room. Breakfast, snacks/refreshments and wine included in rates. Types of meals: Full gourmet bkfst and early coffee/tea.

Certificate may be used: November-March, subject to availability. No weekends or holidays.

Houston

Robin's Nest

4104 Greeley St
Houston, TX 77006-5609
(713) 528-5821 (800) 622-8343 Fax:(713)528-6727
Internet: www.therobin.com
E-mail: robin@therobin.com

Circa 1898. Robin's Nest adorns the museum and arts district, known as The Montrose, in Houston, Texas. This circa 1898  two-story Queen Anne Victorian is much like an intimate European hotel but with a touch of funky American flair. Relax on the wraparound porch or in the parlor. Upstairs there is a tea/coffee station. Inviting guest bedrooms offer a sweet respite from the day's adventures. Whirlpool suites boast private entrances and porches. Murder mystery parties and weddings are popular events at this bed and breakfast inn. Situated near downtown theaters and gourmet restaurants, Galveston and Johnson Space Center are about an hour away.

Innkeeper(s): Robin Smith, Dinora Martinez. $99-240. 9 rooms with PB, 2 with WP, 4 total suites, including 1 two-bedroom suite, 1 conference room. Breakfast included in rates. Types of meals: Full gourmet bkfst, veg bkfst, early coffee/tea and late risers: always something in the kitchen. Help yourself.

Certificate may be used: Sunday-Thursday, Anytime, based on availability.

Ingram

Roddy Tree Ranch & Guest Cottages

820 Texas 39
Ingram, TX 78025
(830)367-2871 (800)309-9868 Fax:(830)367-2872
Internet: www.roddytree.com
E-mail: cabins@roddytree.com

Circa 1940. Experience the rustic elegance of these cedar and rock cottages on fifty tranquil acres along the Guadalupe River in Texas Hill Country. The campground resort ambiance and dude ranch-like setting are perfect for peaceful getaways or family vacations. Stay in a nicely decorated one-to-four bedroom cottage with antique furnishings, climate control, fully equipped kitchens, video library and barbecue grills. Some include a porch, deck, fireplace, living room or sitting area. A covered pavilion boasts a jukebox and picnic tables. Swim in the pool or in the river, fish in the catch and release pond, play badminton, volleyball or horseshoes and go for a nature walk. Take out a canoe or paddleboat. Kids love the playscape and playground area. Browse through nearby shops. Visit San Antonio and the Alamo within an hour's drive.

Innkeeper(s): Keith Asbury, Gretchen Asbury. $100-300. 16 cottages with PB, 8 with FP, 1 conference room. Types of meals: Full gourmet bkfst, veg bkfst, picnic lunch and room service.

Certificate may be used: September-May (off-season), Sunday-Thursday, subject to availability.

Jefferson

McKay House

306 E Delta St
Jefferson, TX 75657-2026
(903) 665-7322 (800) 468-2627
Internet: www.mckayhouse.com
E-mail: innkeeper@mckayhouse.com

Circa 1851. For more than 15 years, the McKay House has been widely acclaimed for its high standards, personal service and satisfied guests.
Both Lady Bird Johnson and Alex Haley have enjoyed the gracious Southern hospitality offered at the McKay House. The Greek
Revival cottage features a front porch with pillars. Heart-of-pine floors, 14-foot ceilings and documented wallpapers complement antique furnishings. A full "gentleman's" breakfast is served in the garden conservatory by the gable fireplace. Orange French toast, home-baked muffins and shirred eggs are a few of the house specialties. In each of the seven bedchambers you find a Victorian nightgown and old-fashioned nightshirt laid out for you. History abounds in Jefferson, considered the "Williamsburg of the Southwest."

Innkeeper(s): Hugh Lewis & Darla McCorkle. $66-149. 7 rooms with PB, 5 with FP, 1 two-bedroom suite, 1 cottage, 1 conference room. Breakfast, snacks/refreshments, hors d'oeuvres and wine included in rates. Types of meals: Full gourmet bkfst, veg bkfst, early coffee/tea, lunch, picnic lunch, dinner and room service.

Certificate may be used: Sunday-Thursday, not including spring break or festivals/holidays; space available, reserved one week in advance please.

The Hale House Inn

702 S Line St
Jefferson, TX 75657-2224
(903)665-9955 Fax:(903)665-7616
Internet: www.thehalehouseinn.com
E-mail: mystay@thehalehouseinn.com

Circa 1880. Relaxation comes easy at The Hale House Inn Bed & Breakfast, an historic Greek Revival with Victorian accents and antiques. Take a short stroll to downtown Jefferson, Texas, originally known for being a bustling riverport. Relax on a southern-style veranda, two porches and a gazebo amid flowers and shade trees. Enjoy refreshments and treats in either parlor, one with a fireplace and the other with a big-screen TV and DVD player. Afternoon snacks are available in the library. Themed guest rooms boast a variety of pleasing choices. Stay in a room that overlooks the park or gardens. One room has a fireplace and most feature a clawfoot tub and shower. Indulge in a hearty Texas Gentleman's breakfast in the dining room, side porch, or gazebo.

Innkeeper(s): Timm Jackson, Karen Jackson. $99-14944. 6 rooms with PB, 1 with FP, 1 conference room. Breakfast and snacks/refreshments included in rates. Types of meals: Country bkfst, early coffee/tea, afternoon tea and Texas Gentleman's Breakfast.

Certificate may be used: Sunday-Thursday, excluding spring break, local festivals and holidays. On space available basis when reserved one week in advance.

Lumberton

Book Nook Inn

10405 Cooks Lake Rd.
Lumberton, TX 77657
(409)225-9106
Internet: www.booknookinn.com

A sprawling lawn surrounds this inn on the edge of the Big Thicket National Preserve. Outdoor activities are plentiful as guests can hike and canoe on the preserve, fish the stocked pond or swim in the crystal clear pool. As nighttime falls, sit on the wrap-around porch as the stars twinkle, curl up with a book from the extensive library, or stretch out on the stair step seating in the movie room. Business travelers will find the tranquil guest rooms well-appointed with high-speed Wi-Fi, desk space, and private bathrooms. Couples can find romance in the Yellow Room with a whirlpool tub and views of the garden. Connect with other guests in the dining room each morning or elect to have a full breakfast served in the privacy of your guest room. Beverages and snacks are always available. The inn is one hour from Houston and convenient to the entire Golden Triangle of Texas.

Innkeeper(s): David Hearne, Stacie Hearne. $85-105. 4 rooms, 4 with WP, 1 cottage.

Certificate may be used: Sunday-Thursday; subject to availability. No holidays.

Mineola

Munzesheimer Manor

202 N Newsom St
Mineola, TX 75773-2134
(903)569-6634 (888)569-6634 Fax:(903)569-9940
Internet: www.munzesheimer.com
E-mail: innkeeper@munzesheimer.com

Circa 1898. Let time stand still while staying at this historic 1898 Victorian home that was built entirely with pine and cedar. Its classic features include many bay windows, large rooms with high ceilings and original fireplaces with mantles. Sip lemonade on the spacious wraparound porch with wicker furniture and rockers. Relax in one of the two inviting parlors. Choose an upstairs guest bedroom in the main house or an adjacent ground-floor cottage room with a private entrance. The pleasing accommodations feature central heat and air conditioning and American and English antiques. Soak in a claw-foot tub with bath salts before sleeping in a vintage nightgown or nightshirt. A gourmet breakfast is served on china and silver in the formal dining room.

Innkeeper(s): Bob & Sherry Murray. $110-120. 7 rooms with PB, 3 with FP, 3 cottages. Breakfast included in rates. Types of meals: Full bkfst and early coffee/tea.

Certificate may be used: January-December, Monday-Thursday and will offer room upgrade if available.

Mission

Indian Ridge Bed and Breakfast

209 West Orange Grove Road
Mission, TX 78574
(956)519-3305 Fax:956-583-6557
Internet: www.indian-ridge-bb.com
E-mail: equipuppy@sbcglobal.net

Circa 1980. Set in the Rio Grande, this inn, with its wraparound porch, 20 acres of ponds, big trees and wildlife, gives guests an opportunity to go back to the future and enjoy a relaxing and inspirational getaway. Choose from a variety of rooms that feature whirlpool tubs, including the Safari Suite and the Flutterby. Two rooms are spacious enough to accommodate children or girlfriend getaways. Bring your appetite and take time to browse the list of possibilities for breakfast when you check in. The World Birding Center and Bentsen Rio Grande Valley State Park are nearby and you can enjoy birding from the inn's property as well. The innkeeper will set up blinds to help photographers shoot pictures of the abundant variety of birds. There is a swimming pool with underwater floodlights that light up streams of water that shoot up from the pool in the evening.

Innkeeper(s): Suzanne Herzing. $95-175. 5 rooms with PB, 1 with FP, 2 with WP, 1 two-bedroom suite. Breakfast, Expanded Continental (coffee, tea, juice, fresh fruit, pastries, cereals, frozen breakfast options like stuffed bagels, sausage & egg biscuits, etc.) included with booking. Gourmet breakfasts available for additional charge. Evening glass of wine or beer provided as gift to guests included in rates. Types of meals: Full gourmet bkfst, veg bkfst, picnic lunch, wine and expanded continental breakfast included. Gourmet breakfasts and other meals for additional charge.

Certificate may be used: Anytime, excluding holidays and weekends.

Muenster

Elm Creek Manor

2287 FM 2739
Muenster, TX 76252
(940) 759-2100 (877) 356-2733
Internet: www.elmcreekmanor.com
E-mail: info@elmcreekmanor.com

The convenient North Texas location of this luxury B&B resort adds to the ease of escape. Old World ambiance and European elegance are surrounded by 14 acres of rolling hills with towering pecan trees lining the banks of two creeks. Relax on a front porch rocker, nap in a hammock or walk the nature trails. Gather in the library, the back veranda with a fountain or under the vine-covered arbor by the swimming pool for the daily cocktail hour. Stay in an amazing guest bedroom, suite or cottage featuring upscale amenities. The second-floor Austrian Suite boasts a fireplace, whirlpool tub, two-person shower and private porch. The fairy-tale Asace cottage boasts a cedar deck and fenced hot tub. Breakfast is served in the manor house dining room.

Innkeeper(s): Susie, Mgr.. $229-279. 6 rooms with PB, 2 with FP, 2 with HT, 4 with WP, 2 suites, 2 cottages, 2 guest houses, 1 conference room. Breakfast, hors d'oeuvres and wine included in rates. Types of meals: Full gourmet bkfst, veg bkfst, early coffee/tea, gourmet lunch, picnic lunch, snacks/refreshments and gourmet dinner.

Certificate may be used: August-September and January. No weekends or holidays.

New Braunfels

Acorn Hill Bed & Breakfast

250 School House
New Braunfels, TX 78132-2458
(830)907-2597 (800)525-4618 Fax:(830)964-5486
Internet: www.acornhillbb.com
E-mail: acornhill@acornhillbb.com

Circa 1910. Enjoy wandering the five scenic acres of gardens and fields while staying at this year-round bed & breakfast with a log house that was originally a school and themed cottages conveniently located only five minutes from the Guadalupe River and downtown Gruene. Overlook the hills from a porch rocker. Play the converted pump organ and make calls from an antique phone booth. Suites and cottages feature fireplaces and some boast Jacuzzi tubs. Indulge in an all-you-can-eat multi-course breakfast buffet in the log house dining room. Swim in the in-ground pool or soak in the relaxing hot tub. Browse through the antique and gift shop for treasures to take home. Barbecue pits and picnic tables are provided throughout the grounds. The Victorian Garden is an ideal setting for weddings.

Innkeeper(s): Richard Thomas, Pam Thomas. $100-175. 6 rooms with PB, 6 with FP, 3 suites, 3 cottages, 1 conference room. Breakfast included in rates. Types of meals: Country bkfst, veg bkfst, early coffee/tea and picnic lunch.

Certificate may be used: Nov. 1-March 1, Sunday-Thursday.

Firefly Inn

120 Naked Indian Trail
New Braunfels, TX 78132-1865
(830) 905-3989
Internet: www.fireflyinn.com
E-mail: info@fireflyinn.com

Circa 1983. Romance the Texas Hill Country in New
Braunfels, Canyon Lake, Gruene near the Guadalupe River. The
Country Victorian decor and quality handcrafted furniture provide comfort and style. Each guest suite offers several spacious
rooms, including a kitchen. To add to the pampering, an excellent breakfast is delivered to the door each morning, ready to
satisfy. Spectacular views can be seen from the private deck or
porch overlooking the meadows. Picnic tables in the courtyard,
small ponds with waterfalls and a hot tub surrounded by
mountain hills and fresh air are pleasurable treats to enjoy. A
small intimate wedding in the gazebo is complete with a pastor
available to perform the ceremony.

Innkeeper(s): Jack Tipton, Kathy Tipton. $100-175. 4 cottages, 4 suites.
Breakfast included in rates. Types of meals: Full bkfst.

Certificate may be used: Sept. 15-February, Sunday-Thursday, excluding
holidays and special events.

Gruene Mansion Inn

1275 Gruene Rd
New Braunfels, TX 78130-3003
(830)629-2641 Fax:(830)629-7375
Internet: www.gruenemansioninn.com
E-mail: frontdesk@gruenemansioninn.com

Circa 1872. Overlook the Guadalupe River from the porches of
this Victorian mansion located on three acres in Hill Country,
adjacent to the state's oldest dance hall. The inn has been designated a Historic Landmark and is listed in the National
Register. The Mansion, barns, corn crib, carriage house and
other outbuildings have all been refurbished to offer quiet and
private guest bedrooms, cottages and guest houses. A rustic
Victorian elegance is the ambiance and style of decor that
blends antiques, fine fabrics and wall coverings. Savor breakfast
entrees that boast a Mexican flair and flavor. For a day trip, visit
the Alamo, 30 miles away.

Innkeeper(s): Judi Eager, Cecil Eager, Jackie Skinner. $165-299. 31 rooms,
30 with PB, 2 two-bedroom suites, 1 cottage, 1 conference room. Breakfast
included in rates. Types of meals: Full bkfst and snacks/refreshments.

Certificate may be used: January, February and September; Sunday-Thursday
for Sunday Hauses only.

Lamb's Rest Inn

1385 Edwards Blvd
New Braunfels, TX 78132-4055
(830)609-3932 (888)609-3932 Fax:(830)620-0864
Internet: www.lambsrestinn.com
E-mail: info@lambsrestinn.com

Circa 1970. Between Austin and San Antonio on the
Guadalupe River, stands this inn with large decks that overlook
the river. Peace and tranquility are at the heart of guests' experience at the Lambs Rest, where they can hear the sounds of
birds and wildlife during the day and draw up close to the
crackling fire at night. Two large decks and a garden terraced to
the river invites relaxation with fountains, ponds, herb gardens,
large oaks and giant cypress trees. The six accommodations

include one suite and one cottage. A full gourmet breakfast is
served in the dining room or on the veranda overlooking the
river. Breakfast fare includes such delights as Orange Frosty
Frappe, Vancluse Eggs with asparagus and red pepper sauce,
cheese grits, sausage, and a variety of homemade breads and
biscuits served with the inn's special honeys, jams and sauces.
During the spring and summer, Bluebonnets and other Texas
wildflowers abound in nearby breathtaking fields. Between the
quiet Comal River and the rapids of the Guadalupe River,
guests can enjoy a variety of water sports including kayaking,
rafting, canoeing, tubing and fly-fishing.

Innkeeper(s): Alyson. $135-250. 6 rooms with PB, 6 with FP, 1 two-bed-
room suite, 1 cottage. Breakfast included in rates. Types of meals: Full
gourmet bkfst and early coffee/tea.

Certificate may be used: Sept. 15-March 1, excluding holidays, Sunday-
Thursday in Mulberrie Court, Grapes Inn or Quilly's Antiques.

Rockport

Anthony's By The Sea

732 S Pearl St
Rockport, TX 78382-2420
(361)729-6100 (800)460-2557 Fax:(361)729-2450
Internet: www.anthonysbythesea.com
E-mail: info@anthonysbythesea.com

Circa 1997. This quiet, casual retreat is hidden away beneath
huge oak trees, near the ocean in an area known as the Texas
Riviera. Choose from comfortably furnished single rooms or
suites with private baths and sitting areas. Separate guest house
has a fully equipped kitchen, spacious living area and sleeps up
to six, making it ideal for families and small groups. A sparkling
pool and covered lanai provide the most popular areas for relaxing or enjoying the gourmet breakfasts. Located within walking
distance of Rockport Beach, a variety of water activities are available, as well as local shopping, restaurants and museums.

Innkeeper(s): Smitty & Beth. $105. 6 rooms, 4 with PB, 1 suite, 1 guest
house, 1 conference room. Breakfast included in rates. Types of meals: Full
gourmet bkfst and early coffee/tea.

Certificate may be used: Anytime, November-March, subject to availability.

San Antonio

Brackenridge House

230 Madison
San Antonio, TX 78204-1320
(210) 271-3442 (877) 271-3442 Fax:(210)226-3139
Internet: www.brackenridgehouse.com
E-mail: brackenridgebnb@aol.com

Circa 1901. As the first bed and breakfast in San Antonio's
historic King William District, the Brackenridge House Bed and
Breakfast has been pampering guests for 20 years. Each of the
guest rooms is individually decorated. Clawfoot tubs, iron beds
and a private veranda are a few of the items that guests might
discover. Several rooms include kitchenettes. Many of San
Antonio's interesting sites are nearby. The San Antonio Mission
Trail begins just a block away, and trolleys will take you to the
Alamo, the River Walk, convention center and more.
Coffeehouses, restaurants and antique stores all are within
walking distance. Ideal for romantic getaways, family reunions
or just for fun escapes.

100 years in historic King William, 2 blocks from the River and 5 blocks from downtown San Antonio.

Innkeeper(s): Lily and Roland Lopez. $109-300. 5 rooms with PB, 3 suites. Breakfast included in rates. Types of meals: Full gourmet bkfst and early coffee/tea.

Certificate may be used: Monday-Thursday, June-September; January and February no holidays, last minute based on projected availability.

Christmas House B&B

2307 McCullough
San Antonio, TX 78212
(210)737-2786 (800)268-4187 Fax:(210)734-5712
Internet: www.christmashousebnb.com
E-mail: stay@christmashousebnb.com

Circa 1908. Located in Monte Vista historic district, this two-story white inn has a natural wood balcony  built over the front porch. The window trim is in red and green, starting the Christmas theme of the inn. (There's a Christmas tree decorated all year long.) Guest rooms open out to pecan-shaded balconies. The Victorian Bedroom offers pink and mauve touches mixed with the room's gold and black decor. The Blue & Silver Room is handicap accessible and is on the first floor. Antique furnishings in the inn are available for sale.

Innkeeper(s): Penny. $85. 3 rooms with PB. Breakfast and snacks/refreshments included in rates. Types of meals: Full bkfst, veg bkfst and early coffee/tea.

Certificate may be used: Sunday-Thursday, not on holidays or during Fiesta.

Inn on the Riverwalk

129 Woodward Pl
San Antonio, TX 78204-1120
(210) 225-6333 (800) 730-0019 Fax:(210)271-3992
Internet: www.innontheriverwalksa.com
E-mail: innkeeper@innontheriverwalksa.com

Circa 1916. Located in a restored river home, the inn is encircled by an iron fence and shaded by a tall pecan tree. There are gables and a wraparound porch. Inside are polished pine floors and tall ceilings. Antiques, Jacuzzi tubs, fireplaces and private porches are among the guest room offerings. A third-floor penthouse offers French doors opening to a private balcony. There is a large Jacuzzi and King-size bed. Stroll to the Riverwalk for scenic shopping, restaurants and entertainment. The Convention Center is four blocks away.

Innkeeper(s): Tina Gonzales. $89-350. 14 rooms with PB, 2 with FP, 5 with HT, 2 with WP, 3 two-bedroom suites. Breakfast, snacks/refreshments and Breakfast is served each morning from 8:30-9:30 AM. Complimentary snacks are always available in the breakfast area included in rates. Types of meals: Full bkfst.

Certificate may be used: Sunday-Thursday. PLEASE call and confirm blackout dates (Feb. 13-15, Dec. 25-31st and others). Certificate MUST be acknowledged by Inn when making reservation.

San Marcos

Anna Lee's Viola Street Inn

714 Viola St.
San Marcos, TX 78666
(512)392-6242 Fax:(512)392-6244
Internet: violastreetinn.com
E-mail: violastreetinn@gmail.com

Circa 1902. A large front porch with wicker furniture and a swing greets guests of this Texas Folk Victorian Style inn. Whether visiting a student at Texas State University or vacationing in San Marcos, this bed and breakfast with four suites will be a comfortable place to relax. Hardwood floors and a luxurious decor grace each accommodation and you can feel like a movie star in the dressing room of the Hillside Hideaway with chandeliers and wrap-around mirrors. Snuggle by the candle-lit fireplace in the first floor Gypsy Spirit suite or sink into a sofa in the blue-hued Gathering Room and curl up with a book in the Library. The backyard is a hidden gem with stone patios and a hot tub large enough for eight under a canopy of oak trees. The town square and restaurants for every fancy are within a few blocks. Austin and San Antonio are less than an hour away.

Innkeeper(s): Melinda McKissack. $95-160. 4 rooms.

Certificate may be used: December & January.

Crystal River Inn and Day Spa

326 W Hopkins St
San Marcos, TX 78666-4404
(512)396-3739 (888)396-3739 Fax:(512)396-6311
Internet: www.crystalriverinn.com
E-mail: info@crystalriverinn.com

Circa 1883. Tall white columns accent this Greek Revival inn that features a fireside dining room with a piano and wet bar. Innkeepers encourage a varied itinerary, including sleeping until noon and having breakfast in bed to participating in a hilarious murder mystery. Rock the afternoon away on the veranda or curl up by the fireplace in a guest bedroom by the headwaters of crystal-clear San Marcos River. Clawfoot tubs, four-poster and canopied beds add to the pleasing ambiance. Shop at the state's largest outlet mall that features more than 200 designer stores.

Innkeeper(s): Mike Dillon, Cathy Dillon. $110-175. 12 rooms with PB, 4 with FP, 4 two-bedroom suites, 1 cabin, 1 conference room. Breakfast included in rates. Types of meals: Full gourmet bkfst, early coffee/tea, lunch, picnic lunch and dinner.

Certificate may be used: Sunday-Thursday, year-round, except for holiday weeks (Thanksgiving, Memorial Day, July 4th, etc.).

Seguin

Mosheim Mansion

409 North Austin Street
Seguin, TX 78155
(830)372-9905
Internet: www.mosheimmansion.com
E-mail: info@mosheimmansion.com

Circa 1898. Mosheim Mansion graces the Seguin historic district, just three blocks from town square. This luxury bed and breakfast is just 30 minutes from San Antonio and one hour from Austin. Stroll among the gardenia and hibiscus blooms in the gardens or under a palm tree by the fountain. Sit with a snack or beverage on the two-story porch. Complimentary wine is offered at check-in. A guest refrigerator and a microwave are provided for guest use. Stay in a guest room or a suite that features a double whirlpool tub and a fireplace as well as upscale amenities. Linger over a satisfying breakfast each morning before exploring the surrounding areas. Room services are available. Ask about scheduling spa amenities.

Innkeeper(s): Carol Hirschi. $89-259. 6 rooms with PB, 3 with FP, 4 with WP, 2 conference rooms. Breakfast, snacks/refreshments, wine, Full breakfast, Snacks, Beverages including homemade cookies and To-order breakfast served during window of several hours so guests can eat when they want included in rates. Types of meals: Full gourmet bkfst, veg bkfst, early coffee/tea, gourmet lunch, afternoon tea, hors d'oeuvres, gourmet dinner, room service and Anything other than a full breakfast from menu or complimentary snacks and wine must be arranged in advance. Private dinners in room or fireside in a private dining room available if arranged in advance.

Certificate may be used: Sunday-Thursday excludes holidays and special events. Can be used on weekends only with special permission of innkeeper. Reservations required, subject to availability.

Shiner

The Old Kasper House Bed & Breakfast

219 N Avenue C
Shiner, TX 77984
(361) 594-4336 Fax:(361) 594-4533
Internet: www.oldkasperhouse.com/
E-mail: oldkasperhouse@aol.com

Walk through the white picket fence and get away from the hustle and bustle of city life with a reenergizing stay in Shiner, Texas. You'll be stepping back in time as you admire the period furnishings and decorations in the Victorian-style bed and breakfast. The romantic Royal Suite covers the entire second floor of the Main House with a sitting room, breakfast area, private bath, and reading nook. Start a new life as husband and wife in the one-bedroom Honeymoon Cottage. Families will love the two-bed rustic Marenka's Cottage. Two more cottages with multiple guest rooms round out the accommodations at this inn. Every room has a basket of morning treats so breakfast is on your schedule. Walk to the Spoetzl Brewery, the state's oldest independent brewery and proud producers of Shiner Bock. Watch an amateur play at the historic Gaslight Theater and make time to learn more about the town's legacy at the Wolters Memorial Museum.

Innkeeper(s): Cynthia Martinez. $99-150. 13 rooms with PB, 1 with FP, 1 with HT, 2 cottages. Basket of Breakfast Items included in rates.

Certificate may be used: November-March, subject to availability.

Smithville

Katy House Bed & Breakfast

201 Ramona St.
Smithville, TX 78957-0803
(512)237-4262 (800)843-5289 Fax:(512)237-2239
Internet: www.katyhouse.com
E-mail: bblalock@austin.rr.com

Circa 1909. Shaded by tall trees, the Katy House's Italianate exterior is graced by an arched portico over the bay-windowed living room. Long leaf pine floors, pocket doors and a graceful

stairway accent the completely refurbished interior. The inn is decorated almost exclusively in American antique oak and railroad memorabilia. A 1909 caboose is being restored to be used as a guest room. Historic Main Street is one block away with a fine collection of antique shops. Guests usually come back from walking tours with pockets full of pecans found around town. Smithville was the hometown location for the movie "Hope Floats."

Innkeeper(s): Bruce Blalock, Sallie Blalock. $95-160. 5 rooms with PB, 4 with FP, 1 with WP, 1 suite, 2 cottages. Breakfast and snacks/refreshments included in rates. Types of meals: Full bkfst, early coffee/tea, picnic lunch and Fresh baked cookies available each evening.

Certificate may be used: Sunday-Thursday, except holidays.

Wimberley

Serenity Farmhouse Inn & Spa

251 Circle Dr
Wimberley, TX 78676-9145
(512)847-8985 (888)882-8985
Internet: www.serenityfarmhouseinn-spa.com
E-mail: serenity@anvilcom.com

Circa 2001. Perfect for a romantic getaway or rejuvenating vacation, Serenity Farmhouse Inn & Spa graces 20 scenic acres in Wimberley, surrounded by Central Texas Hill Country. Relax in the gazebo hot tub and swim in the chemical-free pool after enjoying the walking trails. This elegant country retreat boasts cottages that feature heart-shaped Jacuzzis for two, stacked rock fireplaces and fresh flowers. The vintage and whimsical dÃ©cor is accented by hand-painted furniture. Some include intimate private patios and kitchens. Schedule a body massage and other spa services. Ask about specials and packages. Personal chef services for gourmet meals, and wine, cheese and fruit trays are available for pre-order.

Innkeeper(s): Suzy West. Call for rates. 9 rooms, 7 with PB, 6 with FP, 6 with HT, 1 with WP, 2 total suites, including 1 two-bedroom suite, 4 cottages, 1 guest house, 2 conference rooms. No meals included except with Spa specialties included in rates. Types of meals: Full gourmet bkfst, picnic lunch, Personal Chef services are available for gourmet lunches and dinners. Wine and cheese and fruit trays are available upon request. Must be pre-ordered.

Certificate may be used: Sunday-Thursday subject to availability.

Utah

Kamas

Woodland Farmhouse Inn

2602 E State Road # 35
Kamas, UT 84036-9660
(435) 783-2903
Internet: woodlandfarmhouseinn.com
E-mail: innkeeper@woodlandfarmhouseinn.com

Circa 1897. Feel refreshed at this high altitude country farm-house on two acres in the fertile Uintah Mountain Valley of the Provo River just 25 minutes east of Park City, Utah and one hour east of Salt Lake City. Experience the friendly, relaxed atmosphere, comfortable furnishings with upscale amenities, and natural beauty. Soak in the outdoor hot tub on a quiet, starry night. Stay in a romantic guest suite in the historic main inn or spacious luxury accommodations in the South House. The Bunkhouse offers a more rustic and sturdy ambiance for families, fishermen and hunters. Savor a hearty home-style breakfast before embarking on the day's adventures. Recreational activities are plentiful. Explore the scenic area on snowshoes in the winter or ski at one of the first-class resorts nearby. Hike, bike run and rock climb the scenic trailheads of Mirror Lake in the summer.

Innkeeper(s): Sheri Marsing. $109-189. 6 total suites, including 3 two-bedroom suites and 1 three-bedroom suite, 1 cottage, 1 guest house. Breakfast and Upon request we will prepare a sack lunch ($8ea) that can withstand a snowmobile's vibration included in rates. Types of meals: Country bkfst, veg bkfst, Sun. brunch, early coffee/tea, We serve a full, hot country breakfast and "Cooks Choice". When possible we will take requests from our website menu.
Certificate may be used: Off season Tuesday night special, March 31-April 30 and October 1-December 15.

Park City

Old Town Guest House

1011 Empire Ave
Park City, UT 84060
(435)649-2642 Fax:(435)649-3320
Internet: www.oldtownguesthouse.com
E-mail: Dlovci@cs.com

Circa 1901. Centrally located, this historic inn is perfect for hikers, skiers and bikers to enjoy all that the mountains offer. Experience convenience and affordability accented with adventure and inspiration. Some of the comfortable guest bedrooms and suites feature lodge-pole pine furnishings and a jetted tub or fireplace. A Park City Breakfast is included and sure to please hungry appetites. The innkeepers' motto of "play hard, rest easy" is pleasantly fulfilled. Assistance is offered in making the most of any stay. Refuel with afternoon snacks and relax in the hot tub.

Innkeeper(s): Deb Lovci . $99-259. 4 rooms with PB, 1 with FP, 1 two-bedroom suite. Breakfast, afternoon tea and snacks/refreshments included in rates. Types of meals: Full bkfst, veg bkfst, early coffee/tea and Hearty Mountain Breakfast served each morning. Afternoon Snacks with Tea and Hot Chocolate.
Certificate may be used: Sunday-Thursday, Subject to availability. Not good during special events: Sundance Film Festival, etc.

Parowan

Victoria's Bed & Breakfast

94 North 100 East
Parowan, UT 84761
(435)477-0075 (866)477-9808 Fax:(435)477-0079
Internet: www.utahretreat.com
E-mail: info@utahretreat.com

Circa 1870. Revel in the gorgeous views of the surrounding mountains while staying at this 1870 Victorian home that sits at the base of Brian Head Ski Resort. Furnished with antiques that are easy to fall in love with, and each one is available to purchase and take home. Comfortable guest bedrooms and a suite feature pretty colors and pleasing amenities. Take the private entrance to Rhett's Room with a fireplace and double-headed shower. Aunt Pitty Pat's Suite features a soft green and blue dÃ©cor with a sitting room. A hearty breakfast boasts favorites like homemade biscuits with country gravy, hash browns, sausage, bacon, muffins, cereal and yogurt. Winter sports are popular as well as hiking, biking, fishing and hunting. Stroll the well-maintained gardens and lawns and relax on the wraparound veranda.

Certificate may be used: Anytime, April 20-May 31 and Sept. 5-Nov. 15; Monday-Thursday, Nov. 16-April 19 and June 2-Sept. 4. Anytime, last minute-based on availability.

Salt Lake City

Ellerbeck Mansion B&B

140 North B St
Salt Lake City, UT 84103-2482
(801)355-2500 (800)966-8364 Fax:(801)530-0938
Internet: www.ellerbeckbedandbreakfast.com
E-mail: ellerbeckmansion@qwestoffice.net

Circa 1892. Pleasantly located in the city's downtown historic district, this Victorian inn has been renovated for modern comfort and lovingly restored with original moldings, hardwood floors and stained glass. Impressive fireplaces can be found in the splendid main floor and upstairs galleries as well as in several of the six guest bedrooms. Different seasonal motifs adorn the bedrooms, so every day is a holiday in Christmas Wishes, complete with a sleigh bed. Autumn Winds and Spring Breeze can serve as an ideal suite for families. Enjoy a continental breakfast that is delivered to each room at an agreed-upon time. After exploring the local sites and nearby attractions, the turndown service, evening chocolates and complimentary soft drinks are welcome additions.

Innkeeper(s): Debbie Spencer. $99-189. 6 rooms with PB, 3 with FP, 1 conference room. Breakfast and snacks/refreshments included in rates. Types of meals: Full bkfst.

Certificate may be used: Monday-Wednesday excludes black-out periods and holidays. Cannot be used with any other discount or coupons.

Torrey

SkyRidge Inn Bed and Breakfast

1090 E. SR 24
Torrey, UT 84775
(435)425-3222 Fax:(435)425-3222
Internet: www.skyridgeinn.com
E-mail: info@skyridgeinn.com

Circa 1994. Located on 75 acres, this gabled, three-story territorial style inn offers views of Capitol Reef National Park, Dixie National Forest and Torrey Valley. Antiques, art and upscale furnishings fill the rooms.  Some guest chambers feature a hot tub, jetted tub and private deck. Breakfast is served in the dining room overlooking forested Boulder Mountain. Wilderness tours via horseback or four-wheel drive may be arranged. The natural arches, sheer canyon walls and multi-colored cliffs and domes of Capitol Reef National Park are five minutes away. Guests are welcome to pick fruit from the Park's ancient orchards during summer and fall.

Innkeeper(s): Kimball Langton, Irene Langton. $109-164. 6 rooms with PB, 2 with HT. Breakfast included in rates. Types of meals: Full gourmet bkfst and early coffee/tea.

Certificate may be used: November-January, Monday-Thursday.

Vermont

Barnard

Maple Leaf Inn

5890 ROUTE 12
Barnard, VT 05031
(802)234-5342 (800)51-MAPLE Fax:(802)234-6456
Internet: www.mapleleafinn.com
E-mail: innkeeper@mapleleafinn.com

Circa 1994. The Maple Leaf Inn is the classic New England
bed and breakfast located in Barnard, Vermont near
Woodstock. Enjoy views of Silver Lake and the Green
Mountains from this Victorian-style farmhouse situated on 16
acres accented with maple and birch trees. Relax in one of the
many common areas of this intimate B&B. Books and international artifacts highlight the library that boasts comfortable
seating. Gather for late-night refreshments in the elegant parlor.
Generous upscale amenities are provided in the spacious guest
bedrooms that feature a pillow library and individually controlled heat and air-conditioning. Candlelit tables for two are
set up in the dining room for a romantic breakfast.
Innkeeper(s): Mike Boyle, Nancy Boyle. $160-290. 7 rooms with PB.
Certificate may be used: March-August, Sunday-Wednesday.

The Fan House

PO Box 294
Barnard, VT 05031
(802)234-6704
Internet: www.TheFanHouse.com
E-mail: swidness@aol.com

Circa 1840. Sitting on two acres with birch trees and perennial
gardens this renovated bed and breakfast was built in 1840 and
maintains a history full of lore and legend. Furnished and decorated in a sophisticated minimalist style, old pine floors reside
comfortably with artwork and heirloom Gobelin tapestries from
around the world. Relax by the fire in the living room. Elegant
air-conditioned guest bedrooms and a two-bedroom suite feature fine Anichini linens, down comforters and wraparound
bath sheets. Savor a leisurely hand-crafted breakfast in the dining room. Nap in a hammock, enjoy a private yoga session and
schedule an in-room massage. Take a three-minute walk to
swim in Silver Lake. The river below the ravine separates the
grounds from 55,000 acres of wilderness known as The
Chateauguay. Hike the Appalachian Trail.
Innkeeper(s): Sara Widness. $160-240. 3 rooms with PB, 1 with FP, 1 two-
bedroom suite, 1 conference room. Breakfast and wine included in rates.
Types of meals: Country bkfst, veg bkfst, early coffee/tea and gourmet dinner.
Certificate may be used: November, March-April subject to availability, Non
holiday, Sunday-Thursday only.

Bennington

South Shire Inn

124 Elm St
Bennington, VT 05201-2232
(802)447-3839 Fax:(802)442-3547
Internet: www.southshire.com
E-mail: relax@southshire.com

Circa 1887. Built in the late 1800s, this inn boasts a
mahogany-paneled library, soaring 10-foot ceilings, and three of
the guest rooms include one of the home's original fireplaces.
Guest rooms feature antiques and Victorian décor. Rooms in
the restored carriage house include both a fireplace and a
whirlpool tub. Guests are pampered with both a full breakfast,
as well as afternoon tea. Local attractions include the
Bennington Museum, antique shops, craft stores, covered
bridges and skiing.
Innkeeper(s): George Goeke, Joyce Goeke. $110-225. 9 rooms with PB, 7
with FP, 1 suite. Breakfast and afternoon tea included in rates. Types of
meals: Full bkfst, veg bkfst and early coffee/tea.
Certificate may be used: Sunday-Thursday, Nov. 1-May 31, excluding holidays
and special events.

Brandon

Brandon Inn

20 Park St
Brandon, VT 05733-1122
(802) 247-5766 (800) 639-8685
Internet: www.brandoninn.com
E-mail: stay@brandoninn.com

Circa 1786. Listed in the National Register, this historic four-
story Dutch Colonial boasts Victorian influence. It also offers
modern technology like wifi and the commitment to environmentally friendly practices. The gorgeous setting in the Green
Mountains and the romantic ambiance has made it a popular
wedding destination as well as the town centerpiece. Dining
rooms, a pub and ballroom enhance every event. Open all year,
there are activities for every season. Sit and read on the front
closed-in porch or swim in the outdoor pool. The living room
includes a large screen television. Air-conditioned guest rooms
provide a variety of sleeping configurations or stay in a spacious
Jacuzzi suite. A bountiful country breakfast is made by the
award-winning culinary chef. Take day trips from the local area
of Brandon, Vermont to experience New England and explore
the scenic countryside.
Innkeeper(s): Sarah Pattis, Louis Pattis. $99-200. 39 rooms with PB, 2 with
WP, 1 conference room. Full country breakfast included in rates. Types of meals:

Full bkfst, early coffee/tea, wine, Dinner available by prior request on some dates in season. Chef owned Inn and catering available for private functions.

Certificate may be used: Anytime, subject to availability.

Lilac Inn

53 Park St
Brandon, VT 05733-1121
(802)247-5463 (800)221-0720 Fax:(802)247-5499
Internet: www.lilacinn.com
E-mail: innkeeper@lilacinn.com

Circa 1909. For some, the scenery is enough of a reason to visit Vermont. For those who need more, try the Lilac Inn. The restored inn's beautiful furnishings, polished woodwork and fireplaces add to the ambiance. Canopy beds dressed with fine linens, flowers, whirlpool tubs and sitting areas grace the guest rooms. A full, gourmet breakfast is included in the rates. The inn is a popular

site for unforgettable romantic weddings. The landscaped, two-acre grounds include ponds, a gazebo and hundreds of perennials and annuals. Flowers decorate the ground's stone walls.

Innkeeper(s): Shelly & Doug Sawyer. $150-335. 9 rooms with PB, 3 with FP, 1 with WP, 4 conference rooms. Breakfast and three-course cooked to order gourmet breakfast included in rates. Types of meals: Full gourmet bkfst, early coffee/tea, snacks/refreshments, hors d'oeuvres, wine, gourmet dinner and room service. Restaurant on premises.

Certificate may be used: Anytime, subject to availability.

Bristol

Russell Young Farm Bed & Breakfast

861 Russell Young Rd.
Bristol, VT 05443
(802) 453-7026 (877) 896-7026
Internet: www.russellyoungfarm.com
E-mail: relax@russellyoungfarm.com

Circa 1870. Seventy acres of pasture and woods surround this Vermont farmhouse in Jerusalem. Every season offers spectacular views of the Green Mountains and a variety of scenic activities. Russell Young Farm Bed & Breakfast boasts a private one-half acre swimming pond fed by a mountain stream and springs. Soak in the outdoor hot tub after hiking, skiing or sledding. Relax in the second-floor Sunroom. The entire first floor is handicapped accessible. Sit by the huge stone fireplace in the Great Room. Front porch rockers and a telescope invite stargazing. The self-serve bar features a guest refrigerator stocked with beverages. Stay in the ADA-compliant Shalmansir Room or in one of the second-floor guest bedrooms, all with towel warmers and pleasing amenities. Savor a country breakfast made with local, Vermont-made products and seasonal ingredients.

Innkeeper(s): Glenn LaRock. $130-165. 3 rooms with PB. Breakfast and snacks/refreshments included in rates. Types of meals: Country bkfst, veg bkfst and early coffee/tea.

Certificate may be used: Dec. 2-Dec. 20 and Jan. 3-Jan. 31, subject to availability.

Chelsea

Windswept Acres

16 Windswept Lane
Chelsea, VT 05038
(802) 685-3842
Internet: www.windsweptacres-vt.com
E-mail: doc@windprod.com

Circa 1815. Drive up the country lane to a pastoral retreat filled with ponds and pastures. Accommodations are available for every style. Reserve a comfortably appointed room in the Main House. The Sugar House provides the opportunity for a true rustic vacation with an outhouse and views of the lower pond; the cabin is available year-round for those with a real adventurous spirit. RVs and campers are also welcome at a special site just for them with electric hookup, water hookup, and grey-water disposal. Go swimming, fishing, or canoeing in one of the two ponds. Sunbathe on a sandy beach far away from the ocean. Breathe the fresh Vermont air during a hike through 55 acres. Laze away the day on a hammock then feed the ducks or visit the horses at the Hooved Animal Sanctuary. The small town of Chelsea, Vermont, has the distinction of having two commons and a historic district listed in the National Register.

Innkeeper(s): Doc Gordon, Sara Gordon. $105-115. 4 rooms, 1 cabin. Types of meals: Cont plus, early coffee/tea, picnic lunch, snacks/refreshments. Call for specifics.

Certificate may be used: June-August, Monday-Thursday, subject to availability.

Chester

Hugging Bear Inn & Shoppe

244 Main St
Chester, VT 05143
(802)875-2412 (800)325-0519
Internet: www.huggingbear.com
E-mail: inn@huggingbear.com

Circa 1850. Among the 10,000 teddy bear inhabitants of this white Victorian inn, several peek out from the third-story windows of the octagonal tower. There is a teddy bear shop on the premises and children and adults can borrow a bear to take to bed with them. Rooms are decorated with antiques and comfortable furniture. A bear puppet show is often staged during breakfast.

Innkeeper(s): Georgette Thomas.
$110-185. 5 rooms with PB. Breakfast included in rates. Types of meals: Country bkfst and early coffee/tea.

Certificate may be used: Available all nights except for Christmas-New Year week and the last 2 weeks of February and September-October.

Danby

Silas Griffith Inn

178 South Main Street
Danby, VT 05739
(802)293-5567 (888)569-4660
Internet: www.silasgriffith.com
E-mail: stay@silasgriffith.com

Circa 1891. Rolling meadows and views of the Tacomic and Green Mountains surround this country inn gracing more than 10 acres with flower gardens accenting the grounds. Relax on a porch rocker, swim in the seasonal inground pool, and soak in the spa in the gazebo. Common rooms in the manor house include the large living room, media room and music room. People and pet friendly, stay in an air-conditioned guest room or suite on the second or third floor with Victorian period furnishings and a gas fireplace. Most have private entrances with sitting porches. Savor a home-cooked breakfast full of made-to-order classic foods. Be sure to make dinner reservations at Emma's, the fireside restaurant in the carriage house, serving New England fare Thursday through Sunday. Danby, Vermont is near the many shopping opportunities in Manchester and Rutland.

Innkeeper(s): Brian Preble, Catherine Preble. $99-299. 10 rooms with PB, 10 with FP, 1 two-bedroom suite, 2 conference rooms. Breakfast included in rates. Types of meals: Full bkfst, veg bkfst, dinner, BYOB. Dinner reservations require 24 hours advance notice. We specialize in local foods and and many of the vegetables are from our own gardens. Restaurant on premises.

Certificate may be used: Anytime Nov. 1-June 30, Monday-Thursday only for July 1-Oct. 30, subject to availability, excludes package events, cannot be combined with any other offer. Package events are weekend retreats where the guest receives all meals as part of their package.

Essex Junction

The Essex, Vermont's Culinary Resort & Spa

70 Essex Way
Essex Junction, VT 05452-3383
(802) 878-1100 (800) 727-4295 Fax:(802)878-0063
Internet: www.vtculinaryresort.com
E-mail: info@vtculinaryresort.com

Circa 1989. Set on 18 acres between the vistas of the Green Mountains and the splendor of Lake Champlain in Essex Junction, Vermont, this destination resort offers a plethora of amenities and activities. The full-service spa, salon, fitness center, cooking classes in the J.K. Adams and Chef's Kitchens of Cook Academy, and two award-winning restaurants with an extensive award-winning wine list perfectly complement the inviting and distinctive accommodations. This is a popular pet- and family-friendly choice as well as a favorite for group/corporate events and romantic wedding destinations for dozens of happy couples tying the knot each year. The Essex boasts a recipe for relaxation unlike any other resort in New England.

Innkeeper(s): Jim Glanville . $189-699. 120 rooms with PB, 50 with FP, 16 with WP, 30 total suites, including 2 two-bedroom suites, 8 conference rooms. Types of meals: Full gourmet bkfst, veg bkfst, Sun. brunch, early cof-

fee/tea, gourmet lunch, picnic lunch, snacks/refreshments, hors d'oeuvres, wine, gourmet dinner and room service. Restaurant on premises.

Certificate may be used: November-July, Sunday-Thursday.

Fair Haven

Marble Mansion Inn

12 W. Park Place
Fair Haven, VT 05743
(802) 265-4556 Fax:(802) 278-8055
Internet: www.marblemansioninn.com
E-mail: reservations@marblemansioninn.com

Circa 1867. Experience the glamour of the 1800s in this three-story Vermont marble bed and breakfast in Fair Haven, Vermont. Relatives of Revolutionary War hero Ethan Allen built this exquisite French Second Empire home with 12-foot high ceilings, Georgian style plaster crown moldings, herringbone pattern wood floors and fireplaces with hand carved mantles. It was the first house in town to have electricity. Marvel at the unique peacock wallpaper in the Jane Austen Room. Relax in the pink and silver J. R. R. Tolkien Room. All five guest rooms are named after classic authors. The inn offers an expanded continental breakfast and afternoon tea. Many festivals and events are hosted on the village green right outside the doors of the bed and breakfast. Walk to quaint shops and restaurants in the business district. Explore the Vermont Marble Museum, Pember Museum of Natural History or Hubbardton Battlefield Museum. Lake Bomoseen, the largest in the state, is a short 12-mile drive from the inn.

Innkeeper(s): The Parke Family . $90-140. 12 rooms, 11 with PB, 4 with FP, 1 conference room. Breakfast, afternoon tea and Afternoon tea at 4pm on request included in rates. Types of meals: Full gourmet bkfst, veg bkfst, early coffee/tea, snacks/refreshments and A superb restaurant (The Fair Haven Inn) is only a 5 minute walk and serves Greek American cuisine specializing in fish/seafood.

Certificate may be used: November-March, subject to availability.

Fairlee

Silver Maple Lodge & Cottages

520 US Rt 5 South
Fairlee, VT 05045
(802)333-4326 (800)666-1946Internet: www.silvermaplelodge.com
E-mail: scott@silvermaplelodge.com

Circa 1790. This old Cape farmhouse was expanded in the 1850s and became an inn in the '20s when Elmer & Della Batchelder opened their home to guests. It became so successful that several cottages, built from lumber on the property, were added. For 60 years, the Batchelder family continued the operation. They misnamed the lodge, however, mistaking silver poplar trees on the property for what they thought were silver maples. Guest rooms are decorated with many of the inn's original furnishings, and the new innkeepers have carefully restored the rooms and added several bathrooms. A screened-in porch surrounds two sides of the house. Three of the cottages include working

fireplaces and one is handicap accessible.

Innkeeper(s): Scott Wright, Sharon Wright. $79-119. 16 rooms, 14 with PB, 3 with FP, 8 cottages. Breakfast included in rates. Types of meals: Cont.

Certificate may be used: Sunday-Thursday, Oct. 20-Sept. 20.

Ludlow

Echo Lake Inn

PO Box 154
Ludlow, VT 05149-0154
(802)228-8602 (800)356-6844 Fax:(802)228-3075
Internet: echolakeinn.com
E-mail: echolkinn@aol.com

Circa 1840. An abundance of year-round activities at an ideal location in the state's central mountain lakes region make this authentic Victorian inn a popular choice. Built as a summer hotel in 1840, its rich heritage includes visits from many his-

toric figures. Relax in the quiet comfort of the living room with its shelves of books and a fireplace or gather for refreshments in The Pub. The assortment of guest bedrooms, suites and condos ensure perfect accommodations for varied needs. Some boast two-person Jacuzzi tubs and fireplaces. Dining is a treat, with the fine country restaurant highly acclaimed for its excellent food, attentive service and casual ambiance. Tennis, badminton and volleyball courts are adjacent to the large swimming pool. Take out a canoe or rowboat from the dock on crystal-clear Echo Lake or fly fish the Black River.

Innkeeper(s): Laurence V. Jeffery. $89-380. 23 rooms with PB, 2 two-bedroom and 1 three-bedroom suites. Breakfast included in rates. Types of meals: Full bkfst, veg bkfst, early coffee/tea, wine, gourmet dinner and room service. Restaurant on premises.

Certificate may be used: April 1-Sept. 20, Oct. 20-Dec. 12, Jan. 1-March 31, Sunday-Thursday, non-holiday.

Manchester

Wilburton Inn

River Road (off Historic Route 7A)
Manchester, VT 05254
(802)362-2500 (800)648-4944 Fax:(802)362-1107
Internet: www.wilburton.com
E-mail: wilburtoninn@gmail.com

Circa 1902. Shaded by tall maples, this grand Victorian estate sits high on a hill overlooking the Battenkill Valley, set against a majestic mountain back-

drop. In addition to the three-story brick mansion, there are four villas and a five-bedroom house. Carved mahogany paneling, Oriental carpets and leaded-glass windows are complemented by carefully chosen antiques. Besides accommodations, the Teleion Holon Holistic Retreat offers yoga, workshops, vegetarian meals and healing treatments. Spanning 20 acres in Manchester, Vermont enjoy the three tennis courts, a pool,

green lawns, sculptured gardens and panoramic views. Country weddings are a Wilburton Inn specialty. Enjoy dining on New American cuisine in a setting of classic elegance.

Innkeeper(s): Georgette Levis. $135-315. 35 rooms with PB, 9 with FP, 4 with WP, 4 guest houses, 5 conference rooms. Breakfast included in rates. Types of meals: Full gourmet bkfst, afternoon tea, snacks/refreshments, wine, gourmet dinner and room service. Restaurant on premises.

Certificate may be used: March-April, cannot be combined with any other discounts.

Montpelier

Betsy's B&B

74 E State St
Montpelier, VT 05602-3112
(802)229-0466 Fax:(802)229-5412
Internet: www.BetsysBnB.com
E-mail: BetsysBnB@comcast.net

Circa 1895. Within walking distance of downtown and located in the state's largest historic preservation district, this Queen Anne Victorian with romantic turret and carriage house features lavish Victorian antiques throughout its interior. Bay windows, carved woodwork, high ceilings, lace curtains and wood floors add to the authenticity. The full breakfast varies in content but not quality, and guest favorites include orange pancakes.

Innkeeper(s): Jon Anderson, Betsy Anderson. $85-160. 12 rooms with PB, 5 two-bedroom suites. Breakfast included in rates. Types of meals: Full bkfst.

Certificate may be used: Nov. 1-April 30, holiday weekends excluded.

Northfield

The Northfield Inn

228 Highland Ave
Northfield, VT 05663-5663
(802)485-8558
Internet: www.TheNorthfieldInn.com
E-mail: TheNorthfieldInn@aol.com

Circa 1901. A view of the Green Mountains can be seen from this Victorian inn, which is set on a mountainside surrounded by gardens and overlooking an apple orchard and pond. The picturesque inn also affords a view of the village of Northfield and historic Norwich University. Rooms are decorated with antiques and Oriental rugs, and bedrooms feature European feather bedding and brass and carved-wood beds. Many outdoor activities are available on the three-

acre property, including croquet, horseshoes, ice skating and sledding. Visitors may want to take a climb uphill to visit the Old Slate Quarry or just relax on one of the porches overlooking the garden with bird songs, wind chimes and gentle breezes.

Innkeeper(s): Aglaia Stalb. $95-179. 12 rooms with PB, 2 suites. Breakfast and snacks/refreshments included in rates. Types of meals: Full bkfst.

Certificate may be used: November-April, Monday-Thursday as available. Holiday and special events excluded.

Poultney

Bentley House B&B

399 Bentley Ave
Poultney, VT 05764
(802)287-4004
Internet: www.thebentleyhouse.com
E-mail: bentleyhousebb@comcast.net

Circa 1895. This three-story peaked turret Queen Anne inn is located next to Green Mountain College. Stained glass, polished woodwork and original fireplace mantels add to the Victorian atmosphere, and the guest rooms are furnished with antiques of the period. A sitting room adjacent to the guest rooms has its own fireplace.

Innkeeper(s): Pam Mikkelsen, Rich Mikkelesen. $105-145. 5 rooms with PB. Breakfast included in rates. Types of meals: Full bkfst.

Certificate may be used: November-March, subject to availability.

Proctorsville

Golden Stage Inn

399 Depot St
Proctorsville, VT 05153
(802) 226-7744 (800) 253-8226
Internet: www.goldenstageinn.com
E-mail: innkeeper@goldenstageinn.com

Circa 1788. The Golden Stage Inn was a stagecoach stop built shortly before Vermont became a state. It served as a link in the Underground Railroad and was the home of Cornelia Otis

Skinner. Cornelia's Room still offers its original polished wide-pine floors and view of Okemo Mountain, and now there's a four-poster cherry bed, farm animal border, wainscoting and a comforter filled with wool

from the inn's sheep. Outside are gardens of wildflowers, a little pen with two sheep, a swimming pool and blueberries and raspberries for the picking. Breakfast offerings include an often-requested recipe, Golden Stage Granola. Home-baked breakfast dishes are garnished with Johnny-jump-ups and nasturtiums from the garden. Guests can indulge anytime by reaching into the inn's bottomless cookie jar. The inn offers stay & ski packages at Okemo Mountain with 24 hours advance notice, and it's a 20 minute drive to Killington access.

Innkeeper(s): Michael Wood, Julie-Lynn Wood. $155-279. 8 rooms with PB, 1 with FP, 2 two-bedroom suites. Breakfast, afternoon tea, snacks/refreshments, Two course breakfast is entirely homemade and using local ingredients whenever possible included in rates. Types of meals: Full gourmet bkfst, veg bkfst, early coffee/tea, homemade, wholesome breakfasts, bottomless cookie jar, all day coffees,tea, hot chocolate, Saturday night chocolate cake and winter weekends bring homemade soups and hot apple cider in afternoons.

Certificate may be used: April-June, November.

Quechee

Inn at Clearwater Pond

984 Quechee-Hartland Road
Quechee, VT 05059
(802)295-0606 (888)918-4466 Fax:(802)295-0606
Internet: innatclearwaterpond.com
E-mail: innatclearwaterpond@gmail.com

Circa 1800. Right down the road from Woodstock, VT is a bit of paradise; close to town but nestled in the country. Set amongst hills and old country roads, the Inn at Clearwater Pond offers simplicity and understated elegance. This hidden gem also offers romance, beauty and a bit of adventure, as well. Lift off from the backyard for a thrilling hot air balloon flight and soar over the spectacular Quechee Gorge, enjoy a crystal clear pond and swim in fresh drinking water. Indulge in a massage performed in the comfort and privacy of your room. Guests can stay in shape, even while vacationing, in the spacious and well-equipped workout room. The Inn will arrange for most outdoor equipment rentals or dining reservations. Appreciate nature as you hike along the Waterfall Trail, Mt. Tom or the Appalachian Trail. The accommodations are sophisticated, spacious and so very comfortable. Awaken each morning to the aroma of a delicious breakfast, served fireside in the romantic dining room with soft music and candlelight. Relax, unwind and savor simple pleasures of country life as you enjoy the panorama of distant views from the lush back lawn of this outstanding bed and breakfast.

Innkeeper(s): Christine DeLuca. $175-295. 5 rooms with PB, 1 with FP, 1 suite, 1 cottage. Breakfast and snacks/refreshments included in rates. Types of meals: Full gourmet bkfst, veg bkfst, early coffee/tea, gourmet lunch, picnic lunch, afternoon tea, hors d'oeuvres, wine, gourmet dinner, Private cocktail parties, Picnic lunches and Catered weddings and special events.

Certificate may be used: Anytime subject to availability. May not be available holidays, special local events and fall foliage.

Reading

Bailey's Mills B&B

1347 Bailey's Mills Rd
Reading, VT 05062
(802)484-7809 (800)639-3437 Fax:(802)484-0014
Internet: www.baileysmills.com
E-mail: info1@baileysmills.com

Circa 1820. This Federal-style inn features grand porches, 11 fireplaces, a "good-morning" staircase and a ballroom on the third floor. Four generations of Baileys lived in the home, as

well as housing mill workers. There also was once a country store on the premises. Guests can learn much about the home and history of the people who lived here through the innkeepers. Two of the

guest rooms include a fireplace, and the suite has a private solarium. There's plenty to do here, from exploring the surrounding 48 acres to relaxing with a book on the porch swing or in a hammock. If you forgot your favorite novel, borrow a book from the inn's 2,200-volume library.

Innkeeper(s): Barbara Thaeder. $120-199. 3 rooms with PB, 2 with FP, 1 suite. Breakfast included in rates. Types of meals: Full bkfst and early coffee/tea.

Certificate may be used: November-May, Sunday-Thursday or call anytime for last-minute openings.

Richmond

The Richmond Victorian Inn

191 East Main Street
Richmond, VT 05477-0652
(802)434-4410 (888)242-3362 Fax:(802)434-4411
Internet: www.richmondvictorianinn.com
E-mail: innkeeper@richmondvictorianinn.com

Circa 1850. This Queen Anne Victorian, with a three-story tower, is accented with green shutters, a sunburst design, fish scale shingles and a gingerbread front porch. The Tower Room is filled with white wicker, delicate flowered wallpaper and an antique brass bed. The Gold Room features a Queen-size bed and a Jacuzzi, while the Pansy Room features an antique bed, white walls and a stenciled pansy border. There are hardwood floors and leaded-glass windows throughout. From the tree-shaded porch, enjoy the inn's lawns and flower gardens after a full breakfast.

Innkeeper(s): Frank Stewart, Joyce Stewart. $139-189. 6 rooms with PB. Breakfast and snacks/refreshments included in rates. Types of meals: Full gourmet bkfst, veg bkfst, early coffee/tea and afternoon tea.

Certificate may be used: Nov. 1-April 30, Sunday-Thursday, non-holidays. subject to availability. May not be combined with other promotions.

Rochester

Liberty Hill Farm

511 Liberty Hill
Rochester, VT 05767-9501
(802) 767-3926 Fax:(802)767-6056
Internet: www.libertyhillfarm.com
E-mail: beth@libertyhillfarm.com

Circa 1825. A working dairy farm with a herd of registered Holsteins, this farmhouse offers a country setting and easy access to recreational activities. The inn's location, between the

White River and the Green Mountains, is ideal for outdoor enthusiasts and animal lovers. Stroll to the barn, feed the calves or climb up to the hayloft and read or play with the kittens. Fishing, hiking, skiing and swimming are popular pastimes of guests, who are treated to a family-style dinner and full breakfast, both featuring many delicious homemade specialties.

Innkeeper(s): Robert Kennett, Beth Kennett. $210. 7 rooms. Breakfast, dinner, Dinner at 6 PM and Breakfast at 8 am included in rates. Types of meals: Full bkfst and early coffee/tea.

Certificate may be used: Jan. 1-May 20 Sunday-Thursday; anytime, last minute-based on availability.

Stowe

Bears Lair Inn

4583 Mountain Rd
Stowe, VT 05672
(800)659-6289 (800)821-7891 Fax:(802)253-7050
Internet: www.bearslairinn.com
E-mail: bearslairinn@gmail.com

Circa 1980. Stowe needs no introduction to its famous outdoor resort facilities. The Bears Lair Inn is perfectly situated to take advantage of these activities in every season of the year. Cross-country ski trails leave right from the front door, and during the warm months, a 5.3-mile bike and walking path winds through some of Vermont's most splendid scenery, crossing wooden bridges and working farms. The inn resembles a Swiss chalet, while the interior decor has a homey, country feel. Some guest rooms feature canopy, brass or sleigh beds; others boast a spa. If the night is star filled, an outdoor hot tub makes a fun nightcap. In the morning, a light breakfast of fresh fruit, homemade muffins and cereal is followed by a more substantial one of waffles with homemade raspberry sauce, apple-cinnamon pancakes, or eggs Benedict. During the summer you'll enjoy this in the patio garden. The center of Stowe is only a stroll away along the recreation path. Here you can browse through the numerous antique and craft shops.

Innkeeper(s): Carolyn Cook, Bill Cook. $129-269. 10 rooms, 8 with PB, 2 with FP, 2 suites. Breakfast included in rates. Types of meals: Full gourmet bkfst and veg bkfst.

Certificate may be used: Jan. 3-Sept. 14, Oct. 15-Dec. 20, Sunday-Thursday, not valid President's week.

Vergennes

Strong House Inn

94 W Main St
Vergennes, VT 05491-9531
(802)877-3337 Fax:(802)877-2599
Internet: www.stronghouseinn.com
E-mail: innkeeper@stronghouseinn.com

Circa 1834. This Federal-style home boasts expansive views of the Green Mountains and the Adirondack range. The inn's 14 guest rooms offer amenities such as private baths, fireplaces, private balconies, and wireless access. A delectable country breakfast is served each morning and snacks and goodies are available throughout the day. Families attending events at Middlebury College will find the Strong House Inn to be a perfect home

base, just a short drive away. Nearby Lake Champlain offers boating and fishing, and golfing, hiking, skiing and some of the finest cycling in Vermont are all part of the area's myriad of outdoor activities. Innkeeper Mary Bargiel is an avid gardener and decorates the grounds with flowers and herb gardens. During the Winter, Quilters flock from all over the country to attend Mary's famous quilting retreats. The Inn also hosts special events, weddings, and luncheons and sets a perfect backdrop for your next event!

Innkeeper(s): Hugh Bargiel, Mary Bargiel. $120-340. 14 rooms with PB, 4 with FP, 1 suite, 1 conference room. Breakfast and snacks/refreshments included in rates. Types of meals: Country bkfst and early coffee/tea.

Certificate may be used: Nov. 1-May 15, Sunday-Thursday, subject to availability.

Waitsfield

Mad River Inn

Tremblay Rd, PO Box 75
Waitsfield, VT 05673
(802)496-7900 (800)832-8278 Fax:(802)496-5390
Internet: www.madriverinn.com
E-mail: madriverinn@madriver.com

Circa 1860. Surrounded by the Green Mountains, this Queen Anne Victorian sits on seven scenic acres along the Mad River.

The charming inn boasts attractive woodwork throughout, highlighted by ash, bird's-eye maple and cherry. Guest rooms feature European feather beds and include the Hayden Breeze Room, with a King brass bed, large windows TV and A/C, and the Angelina Mercedes Room with a four-poster bed and picturesque views. The inn sports a billiard table, gazebo, organic gardens and a hot tub overlooking the mountains. Guests can walk to a recreation path along the river.

Innkeeper(s): Luc Maranda, Karen Maranda. $115-165. 8 rooms with PB. Breakfast and afternoon tea included in rates. Types of meals: Full gourmet bkfst.

Certificate may be used: Midweek only, non-holiday or foliage season. Jan. 5 to Sept. 20, Oct. 25-Dec.15.

Warren

West Hill House

1496 West Hill Rd
Warren, VT 05674-9583
(802) 496-7162
Internet: www.westhillbb.com
E-mail: innkeepers@westhillbb.com

Circa 1856. West Hill House boasts a great location in Warren, Vermont, on a quiet and scenic country road, just a mile from the Sugarbush Ski Area and next to the Sugarbush Golf Course. The nine-acre grounds include four ponds, meadows, perennial gardens, a uniquely designed gazebo and winter mountain views. All rooms offer a Jacuzzi and/or steam bath and there are gas fireplaces in all of the bedchambers. A delicious cooked breakfast is served each morning and

coffee, tea, hot chocolate and homemade cookies are always available. Candlelight dinners are available for six or more guests by prior arrangement. Weddings at this B&B accommodate up to 80 guests and can be held in the house and on the garden terrace, or in the marvelous barn.

Innkeeper(s): Peter MacLaren, Susan MacLaren. $140-275. 9 rooms with PB, 9 with FP. Breakfast and all day refreshments included in rates. Types of meals: Full bkfst, early coffee/tea, snacks/refreshments, wine, beer and single malt scotch bar.

Certificate may be used: April-June, Oct. 20-Dec. 18, Sunday-Thursday, subject to availability.

West Dover

Deerfield Valley Inn

PO Box 1834
West Dover, VT 05356
(802)464-6333 (800)639-3588 Fax:(802)464-6336
Internet: www.deerfieldvalleyinn.com
E-mail: deerinn@sover.net

Circa 1885. Built as a country house in 1885 at the foothills of the Green Mountains, the inn is listed in the National Register and features the original wax-rubbed ash encasements and millwork. It was converted into one of the first inns in Mount Snow and new wings have been added. Sit by the fire in the living room. Enjoy a light afternoon tea. Intimate yet spacious guest bedrooms boast pleasant furnishings and decor. Sleep in the canopy bed in Room 5 with a sitting area and wood-burning fireplace. A bountiful, hearty breakfast is served in the pleasant dining room. The picturesque area offers many year-round activities. Golf packages are available.

Innkeeper(s): Doreen Cooney. $100-200. 9 rooms with PB, 5 with FP. Breakfast and snacks/refreshments included in rates. Types of meals: Country bkfst and veg bkfst.

Certificate may be used: Mid March-mid September and mid October-mid December anytime subject to availabilty; Mid December-mid March Sunday to Thursday only, non-holidays.

Williston

Catamount B&B

592 Governor Chittenden Rd
Williston, VT 05495
(802)878-2180 (888)680-1011 Fax:(802)879-6066
Internet: www.catamountoutdoor.com
E-mail: eric@catamountoutdoor.com

Circa 1796. This huge Federal Colonial Revival inn on 500 acres has been in the McCullough family since 1873. In its early years, the elegant homestead sponsored many grand balls, and today the home exudes a sense of rich family history. The inn is the oldest standing building in Williston, and it has been a Williston landmark for more than 200 years. It is located on the family farm where the family owns and operates a recreation center that includes many outdoor activities. The grounds have one of the finest mountain bike facilities available. It has a professionally designed trail network that includes flat, rolling and steep trails that range from single-track to wide. And it has an acre of groomed ice for ice skating and a tree-free sledding hill. Guests who stay in the inn's three guest bedrooms (including one suite) enjoy a hearty continental breakfast each morning with courses such as homemade muffins, seasonal fruits, cereals, coffee and tea and sometimes waffles.

Innkeeper(s): Lucy McCullough, Jim McCullough. $95-145. 3 rooms, 1 with PB, 1 suite, 1 conference room. Breakfast included in rates. Types of meals: Cont plus, veg bkfst and early coffee/tea.

Certificate may be used: June 1-Labor Day, Sunday-Thursday; Anytime, Columbus Day-May 1; Anytime, Last Minute-Based on Availability.

Windham

A Stone Wall Inn

530 Hitchcock Hill Road
Windham, VT 05359
(802) 875-4238 (888)450-5070 Fax:802-875-4329
Internet: www.astonewallinn.com
E-mail: sleepwithus@astonewallinn.com

A Stone Wall Inn is an architecturally stunning and award-win-ning inn surrounded by the Vermont wilderness. Reminiscent of tree houses for adults, the buildings have creative and unique nooks and rooms both inside and out. There are no telephones or televisions in the guest rooms and cell phone service is minimal giving guests the opportunity to truly escape from the real world. Eco-friendly buildings use no fossil fuels for heat. Enjoy the views from the common and private decks of the Long House or let rays of sunshine awaken you in the Cloud Room. Sit near the picture window in the Pondview Rooms to view one of the three ponds. Reserve the separate Corner House with four guest rooms as a vacation rental for a group. Bring your pets with you and let them frolic on the lawns and woodland paths or just sit by the fountain powered by solar energy or relax in the pool or hot tub.

Innkeeper(s): Sean Longtin. Call for rates. 10 rooms, 8 with PB, 1 with FP, 2 with WP, 1 guest house, 1 conference room. Breakfast, afternoon tea and snacks/refreshments included in rates. Types of meals: Cont plus, veg bkfst and early coffee/tea.

Certificate may be used: March-August, November-December, subject to availability.

Woodstock

Applebutter Inn

Happy Valley Rd
Woodstock, VT 05091
(802)457-4158 (800)486-1734 Fax:(802)457-4158
Internet: www.applebutterinn.com
E-mail: aplbtrn@comcast.net

Circa 1854. Gracious hospitality and comfort are equally enjoyed at this elegant 1854 country home. Authentically restored, this Federal gabled inn listed in the National Register boasts original wide pine floors, Oriental rugs and rare antiques. Relax by the fire in the Yellow Room or browse through the extensive book collection. Play the Mason & Hamlin grand piano in the Music Room. Several of the spacious and romantic guest bedrooms feature fireplaces. The Cameo Room also has a separate entrance. Sleep well on an 18th century pencil-post bed in the King David Room with a private porch. Sit in the morning sun of the breakfast room and savor a gourmet meal highlighted by Barbara's own applebutter. Play croquet on the expansive lawn, or sit on the porch with afternoon tea and fresh-baked cookies. Located in the tranquil hamlet of Taftsville, seasonal activities and fine dining are close by.

Innkeeper(s): Michael Pacht, Barbara Barry. $95-195. 6 rooms with PB, 4 with FP, 1 conference room. Breakfast, afternoon tea and pastries included in rates. Types of meals: Full gourmet bkfst, veg bkfst, early coffee/tea and snacks/refreshments.

Certificate may be used: November-April, Sunday-Thursday excluding holiday weeks, subject to availability.

Charleston House

21 Pleasant St
Woodstock, VT 05091-1111
(802)457-3843 (888)475-3800
Internet: charlestonhouse.com
E-mail: charlestonhousevermont@comcast.net

Circa 1835. This authentically restored brick Greek Revival town house, in the National Register, welcomes guests with shuttered many-paned windows and window boxes filled with pink blooms. Guest rooms are appointed with period antiques and reproduc-tions, an art collection and Oriental rugs. Some of the rooms boast four-poster beds, and some feature fireplaces and Jacuzzis. A hearty full breakfast starts off the day in the can-dlelit dining room, and the innkeepers serve afternoon refreshments, as well. Area offerings include winter sleigh rides, snow skiing, auctions, fly fishing, golfing and summer stock theater, to name a few.

Innkeeper(s): Dieter Nohl, Willa Nohl. $135-290. 9 rooms with PB, 3 with FP, 4 with WP. Breakfast included in rates. Types of meals: Full gourmet bkfst.

Certificate may be used: November-March, subject to availability.

Virginia

Cape Charles

Cape Charles House

645 Tazewell Ave
Cape Charles, VA 23310-3313
(757)331-4920
Internet: capecharleshouse.com
E-mail: stay@capecharleshouse.com

Circa 1912. A local attorney built this 1912 Colonial Revival home on the site of the town's first schoolhouse. The Cape Charles House is the recipient of the Governor's Award for

Virginia Bed and Breakfast Hospitality. Oriental rugs cover lovingly restored hardwood floors. The owners have skillfully combined antiques, heirlooms, artwork, fabrics and collections. Spacious guest bedrooms are named after historically significant townspeople. The premier Julia Wilkins Room features a whirlpool tub/shower and balcony. Gourmet breakfasts served in the formal dining room may include favorites like fresh mango-stuffed croissants in an egg custard with grated nutmeg and orange liqueur. Enjoy late afternoon wine and cheese as well as tea and sweets. Visit the historic Victorian village and swim the quiet bay beach. Bikes, beach towels, chairs and umbrellas are available.

Innkeeper(s): Bruce & Carol Evans. $140-200. 5 rooms with PB. Breakfast, afternoon tea and snacks/refreshments included in rates. Types of meals: Full gourmet bkfst, veg bkfst, early coffee/tea and wine.

Certificate may be used: November-March, Sunday-Thursday.

Charlottesville

Alexander House Inn & Hostel

1205 Monticello Road
Charlottesville, VA 22902
(434) 327-6447
Internet: alexanderhouse.us
E-mail: booking@alexanderhouse.us

Circa 1912. Enjoy these comfortable, affordable and smoke-free accommodations located in Charlottesville, Virginia. The setting is informal and relaxed with a home-like and personal feel. Sit on the deck, patio or covered front porch. The landscaped back yard is accented with flower and herb gardens. The inn has a living room with sofas, a computer and wifi. There is also a sunny dining room and kitchen. Stay in one of the inn's private guest rooms or in the large coed room in the hostel. Access to a light breakfast using local, fair-trade and organic products is included. Bike rentals are available for exploring the area. Be sure to visit some of the many historic sites nearby, including Jefferson's Monticello. Environmental sustainability is practiced here and local business is promoted as part of a commitment to the surrounding and global community.

Innkeeper(s): Sky, Kayde, Vera, Jesse, Misty, Raven, and Flame. $75-100. 3 rooms, 1 guest house. Unprepared breakfast items (bread, butter, jam, fruit and coffee and tea) and kitchen facilities available at all times included in rates. Types of meals: Cont, Local baked Bread, with butter and local jam, fresh fruit and and fair trade coffee and tea are available at all times. Kitchen facilities also available.

Certificate may be used: Sunday-Thursday.

The Inn at Monticello

Rt 20 S, 1188 Scottsville Rd
Charlottesville, VA 22902
(434)979-3593 (877)735-2982
Internet: www.innatmonticello.com
E-mail: stay@innatmonticello.com

Circa 1850. Thomas Jefferson built his own home, Monticello, just two miles from this gracious country home.

The innkeepers have preserved the historic ambiance of the area. Rooms boast such pieces as four-poster beds covered with fluffy, down comforters. Some of the guest quarters have private porches or fireplaces. Breakfast at the inn is a memorable gourmet-appointed affair. Aside from the usual home-made rolls, coffee cakes and muffins, guests enjoy such entrees as pancakes or French toast with seasonal fruit, egg dishes and a variety of quiche. The front porch is lined with chairs for those who wish to relax, and the grounds feature several gardens to enjoy.

Innkeeper(s): Bob Goss, Carolyn Patterson. $195. 5 rooms with PB, 2 with FP, 1 cottage. Breakfast and afternoon tea included in rates. Types of meals: Full gourmet bkfst and early coffee/tea.

Certificate may be used: Sunday-Thursday, January-February, no holidays.

Clifton Forge

Firmstone Manor

6209 Longdale Furnace Rd
Clifton Forge, VA 24422-3618
(540)862-0892 (800)474-9882
Internet: www.firmstonemanor.com
E-mail: firmstonemanor@aol.com

Circa 1873. Built by the ironmaster of the Longdale Furnace Company, this Victorian is located in the historic district named for the firm. The home boasts many unusual original features, including a wraparound porch with a built-in gazebo and a view onto a walking wedding maze. There are more than 12 acres and a budding orchard to enjoy as well as views of the surrounding Shenandoah Valley and  the Allegheny Mountains from all the rooms. Large guest bedrooms are elegantly appointed with ceiling fans and most have fireplaces. Civil War sites, museums, children's activities, shopping, lakes and state parks are in the area. Stay on-site and relax in a hammock under a 150-year-old tree with a good book and the sounds of a stream in the background.

Innkeeper(s): Barbara Jarocka. $90-130. 6 rooms with PB, 1 suite, 2 cottages. Breakfast and snacks/refreshments included in rates. Types of meals: Full gourmet bkfst, veg bkfst, early coffee/tea, lunch, picnic lunch, afternoon tea, wine, gourmet dinner, Breakfast in bed, bonfire cook outs and outside grill for guest use.

Certificate may be used: Anytime, Subject to availability.

The Red Lantern Inn

314 Jefferson Ave
Clifton Forge, VA 24422
(540) 862-2027 (540) 862-2027
Internet: www.theredlanterninn.com
E-mail: theredlanterninn@gmail.com

Circa 1913. A completely renovated 100-year-old building can be a home away from home for the whole family in Clifton Forge. Reserve all seven bedrooms for a reunion or a single guest room for a weekend getaway. Put the kids in a room with two twin beds and close the door for a quiet, comfortable night in a queen or king-size bed. Small pets can join the fun for an additional fee. Cook old favorites or create something new in the fully-equipped kitchen; pots, pans, plates, glasses, and utensils are all ready for use. Complimentary coffee, tea, and hot chocolate add to the homey feel of the inn. Concoct a tasty beverage at the bar in the media room while watching favorite shows on the big screen television or sit out under the stars on the courtyard or curl up with a book on the glassed-in second floor porch. The inn is close to hiking, fishing, and sightseeing in the Alleghany Highlands.

Innkeeper(s): Jo Ann Carter Gideons. Call for rates. 9 rooms.

Certificate may be used: November-March, subject to availability.

Culpeper

Fountain Hall B&B

609 S East St
Culpeper, VA 22701-3222
(540)825-8200 (800)298-4748
Internet: www.fountainhall.com
E-mail: visit@fountainhall.com

Circa 1859. The well-appointed, oversized guest bedrooms and suites offer comforts galore. Some feature a private porch, whirlpool tub, plush robes and sweeping views of neighboring farms. Enjoy a leisurely breakfast of just-baked flaky croissants with butter and jam, fresh fruits, yogurt, hot and cold cereals and beverages. The surrounding area is steeped in rich American history, and the meticulously landscaped grounds feature seasonal gardens and a lawn groomed for croquet and bocce ball.

Innkeeper(s): Steve Walker, Kathi Walker. $125-200. 6 rooms with PB, 2 suites. Breakfast and snacks/refreshments included in rates. Types of meals: Cont plus and early coffee/tea.

Certificate may be used: Nov. 15-March 31, Sunday to Thursday, Rooms are limited, please mention certificate in advance of placing reservation.

Edinburg

Hockman House Bed & Breakfast

16388 Old Valley Pike
Edinburg, VA 22824-3529
(540)984-8889
Internet: www.hockmanhousebb.com
E-mail: hmhbb@shentel.net

Circa 1868. The Hockman Manor House Bed & Breakfast spans more than four wooded acres in the Shenandoah Valley in Edinburg, Virginia. Sitting on the north fork of the Shenandoah River with views of George Washington National Forest and the Massanutten Mountains, this B&B is surrounded by scenic beauty. A canoe is available and the front porch is perfect for watching the sunset with refreshments. Two large decks also provide incredible vistas. Built in 1868, this Italianate home is designated a Virginia Historic Landmark. Guest bedrooms and a suite with a fireplace and private deck offer comfort and gracious living. A certified massage therapist can be arranged in advance. Start each day with a bountiful family-style breakfast.

Innkeeper(s): Pat Sylvester, Charlie Sylvester. $95-145. 5 rooms, 3 with PB, 1 with FP, 1 suite. Breakfast, snacks/refreshments and wine included in rates. Types of meals: Full gourmet bkfst, veg bkfst and early coffee/tea.

Certificate may be used: November-March, subject to availability.

Fredericksburg

The Richard Johnston Inn

711 Caroline St
Fredericksburg, VA 22401-5903
(540) 899-7606
Internet: www.therichardjohnstoninn.com
E-mail: info@therichardjohnstoninn.com

Circa 1770. Voted one of the country's best 15 inns by Inn Traveler, this unique, upscale 18th-century Colonial sits in the heart of the historic district within walking distance to shops and restaurants. History is found in every nook and cranny of this inn, built by John Tayloe who was one of the original signers of the Declaration of Independence. Elegant furnishings highlight the tastefully decorated guest bedrooms and suites that feature private baths and comfortable beds covered with 360 count sheets, fluffy pillows and comforters. Savor breakfast with settings of fine china, crystal, silver and linens in the Federal-style dining room. Innkeeper Bonnie's cookbook is available to bring the inn's flavor and recipes home.

Innkeeper(s): Lindi Calegari. $125-225. 9 rooms with PB, 2 suites. Breakfast included in rates. Types of meals: Full gourmet bkfst.

Certificate may be used: January-February, Sunday-Thursday, subject to availability.

Goshen

The Hummingbird Inn

30 Wood Lane
Goshen, VA 24439-0147
(540)997-9065 (800)397-3214
Internet: www.hummingbirdinn.com
E-mail: stay@hummingbirdinn.com

Circa 1853. This early Victorian villa is located in the Shenandoah Valley against the backdrop of the Allegheny Mountains. Both the first and second floors offer wraparound verandas. The rustic den and one guest room comprise the oldest portions of the inn, built around 1780. Dinners are available by advance reservation (Friday and Saturday). An old

barn and babbling creek are on the grounds. Lexington, the Virginia Horse Center, Natural Bridge, the Blue Ridge Parkway and antiquing are all nearby.

Innkeeper(s): Patty Harrison, Dan Harrison. $149-179. 5 rooms with PB, 5 with FP, 2 with WP. Breakfast and snacks/refreshments included in rates. Types of meals: Country bkfst, veg bkfst, wine, 24 hr coffee/tea bar, picnics and lunch to-go.

Certificate may be used: Sunday-Thursday, October and holidays excluded, subject to availability.

Harrisonburg

By the Side of the Road

491 Garbers Church Rd
Harrisonburg, VA 22801
(540)801-0430 (866)274-4887 Fax:n/a
Internet: www.bythesideoftheroad.com
E-mail: stay@bythesideoftheroad.com

Built in 1790, this Flemish Bond brick home sits in the heart of historic Shenandoah Valley in Harrisonburg, Virginia. By the Side of the Road is a peaceful country retreat just minutes from the excitement of city life with Blue Ridge Parkway and Skyline Drive close by. The bed and breakfast boasts extensive gardens with perennials bordering the walkway and edible flower and herb gardens. Luxurious accommodations include oversized whirlpool

or clawfoot tubs, fireplaces, feather beds and other upscale amenities. The spacious yet intimate cottages are perfect for feeling pampered. Breakfast is delivered to the door. The delightful Main House suites feature 15-inch brick walls that ensure privacy. Gather in the Common Room for the morning meal served on vintage china and sterling flatware.

Innkeeper(s): Janice Fitzgerald, Dennis Fitzgerald. $179-289. 7 rooms, 7 with FP, 4 with WP, 7 total suites, including 2 two-bedroom suites, 3 cottages. Breakfast and snacks/refreshments included in rates. Types of meals: Full gourmet bkfst, veg bkfst, early coffee/tea, picnic lunch and breakfast baskets delivered to your cottage door.

Certificate may be used: Anytime, except October and May, for Manor House only.

Kilmarnock

Kilmarnock Inn

34 Church Street
Kilmarnock, VA 22482
(804)435-0034 Fax:(804)435-0042
Internet: www.kilmarnockinn.com
E-mail: innkeeper@kilmarnockinn.com

Circa 1884. Situated between Chesapeake Bay and the Rappahannock River in Kilmarnock, Virginia, the historic main house of the Kilmarnock Inn was owned by only one family before being purchased and turned into an inn. The seven cottages were designed and named to reflect the rich presidential heritage of Virginia. The Wilson features an inviting foyer with the first floor serving as the welcoming area. A dining room, parlor, sitting room, study/computer room, and fully equipped kitchen with bar adjacent to the front desk are open for use anytime. The Washington, Jefferson, Monroe, Harrison, Taylor, and Tyler Cottages as well as Madison, the honeymoon cottage, each has its own bathroom and offers a variety of numerous amenities from fireplaces and Jacuzzis to decks overlooking the landscaped courtyard.

Innkeeper(s): Amanda. $150-250. 16 rooms with PB, 6 with FP, 5 with WP, 4 suites, 7 cottages, 1 conference room. Breakfast included in rates. Types of meals: Full gourmet bkfst, Sun. brunch, early coffee/tea, snacks/refreshments and wine.

Certificate may be used: Anytime, subject to availability.

Locust Dale

The Inn at Meander Plantation

2333 North James Madison Hwy.
Locust Dale, VA 22948-9701
(540)672-4912 (800)385-4936 Fax:(540)672-0405
Internet: www.meander.net
E-mail: inn@meander.net

Circa 1766. This historic country estate was built by Henry Fry, close friend of Thomas Jefferson who often stopped here on his way to Monticello. The mansion is serenely decorated with elegant antiques and period reproductions, including four-poster beds. Healthy gourmet breakfasts are prepared by Chef Suzie. Enjoy views of the Blue Ridge Mountains from the rockers on the back porches. Ancient formal boxwood gar-

dens, surrounding natural woodlands, meadows, pastures and Robinson River frontage are part of Meander Conservancy, offering educational programs and back-to-nature packages.

Innkeeper(s): Suzie Blanchard, Suzanne Thomas. $120-200. 8 rooms with PB, 5 with FP, 4 suites, 1 conference room. Breakfast included in rates. Types of meals: Full bkfst, early coffee/tea, lunch, picnic lunch, snacks/refreshments and gourmet dinner.

Certificate may be used: Year-round, Sunday-Thursday, excluding holidays and October.

Luray

Allstar Lodging

803 E. Main St.
Luray, VA 22835
(540) 843-0606 (866) 780-7827
Internet: www.allstarlodging.com
E-mail: allstar@allstarlodging.com

Select from rustic to luxurious vacation homes, cottages and cabins in the scenic Shenandoah Valley, Page County and Luray, Virginia area. Choose locations with preferred amenities that may include mountain views, river or fishing pond access, near George Washington National Forest, pet-friendly or secluded. Some also feature Internet, hot tubs, canoes, bikes, swimming pools and campfire pits. Pre-arranged concierge services can provide catering, massage, flowers, candles, gift baskets, outdoor adventures, boat rentals and horseback riding. Specials and seasonal rates are often available. Allstar Lodging offers a personal touch to ensure the perfect romantic getaway, family reunion, or business retreat with the desired necessities as well as indulgent extra touches that will pamper and relax.

Innkeeper(s): Carlos Ruiz. $85-250. 40 rooms.

Certificate may be used: Sept. 6-May 27, Sunday-Thursday, excludes holidays.

The Cottage at Ravens Roost Farm

1129 Stonyman Rd
Luray, VA 22835
(540)843-0776
Internet: www.ravensroostluray.com
E-mail: ravens.roost@hotmail.com

Circa 1750. Enjoy a stay at a quaint country cottage near the picturesque Shenandoah Valley National Park. The cottage has sliding doors that go out to the patio where a romantic dinner can be served under the starry night sky. A stunning view offers rolling hills and old Virginia farms along with the majestic Blue Ridge Mountains. It is the perfect place for a honeymoon, romantic getaway for two, or a place to unwind from a busy lifestyle. The inn is minutes from the National Parks and Luray caverns where you can experience the many outdoor attractions of hiking, canoeing, kayaking or white water rafting just minutes away. The outdoor enthusiast will find plenty of caverns to explore at Luray. Treat yourself with a wine tasting at one of the local wineries, or visit the area's many art galleries, Civil War historical sites, and live theater performances. The self-pampering cottage has all the latest in amenities. The cottage has a simple, but homey style uniquely its own capturing the serenity of country life. There's a fully furnished kitchen and a complete breakfast. The farm allows guests to pick garden fresh herbs and vegetables when in season for meals. Stables and horseback riding is available and amenities include a flat screen satellite televi-

son with free wireless internet access, central heat/air, comfy king size bed with comforter and a jetted bath tub/shower.

Innkeeper(s): Betsy Maitland, Edgar Allan Poe. $175-185. 1 cottage with PB. Breakfast included in rates. Types of meals: Full bkfst and select herbs and vegetables from our gardens in season.

Certificate may be used: December-February, Sunday-Thursday, excluding holidays, subject to availability.

Lynchburg

Carriage House Inn B&B

404 Cabell St
Lynchburg, VA 24504-1217
(434)846-1388 (800)937-3582
Internet: www.TheCarriageHouseInnBandB.com
E-mail: info@TheCarriageHouseInnBandB.com

Circa 1878. Gracing more than one acre in the Daniels Hill Historic District, this 1878 red brick Italianate mansion proudly welcomes leisure and business travelers after a meticulous four-year restoration and renovation. Carriage House Inn Bed & Breakfast is located in Lynchburg, Virginia in the foothills of the Blue Ridge Mountains along the banks of the James River. Enjoy refreshments in the formal parlor or on the wraparound front porch. Guest bedrooms and suites are named for members of the Watts family, the home's first owners. Soak in an original clawfoot tub and schedule a massage or body treatment with a certified therapist. Amenities include Egyptian cotton towels, fine linens, coal-burning fireplaces, robes, slippers and turndown service with water and chocolates. Linger over a three-course gourmet breakfast before taking a scenic bike ride.

Innkeeper(s): Kathy Bedsworth, Mike Bedsworth. $179-329. 6 rooms, 5 with PB, 2 suites, 1 conference room. Breakfast, snacks/refreshments, hors d'oeuvres, wine, 4-course breakfast featuring a signature dish each month and Snacks and wine for arrivals between 4-5PM included in rates. Types of meals: Full gourmet bkfst, veg bkfst, early coffee/tea, Many excellent restaurants are nearby several within walking distance, Brunch or teas can be arranged in our Event Center and 4-course breakfast featuring monthly specials.

Certificate may be used: January-April, June-July, November-December, cannot be combined with any other discount, offer or voucher.

Federal Crest Inn

1101 Federal St
Lynchburg, VA 24504-3018
(434)845-6155 (800)818-6155 Fax:(434)845-1445
Internet: www.federalcrest.com
E-mail: inn@federalcrest.com

Circa 1909. The guest rooms at Federal Crest are named for the many varieties of trees and flowers native to Virginia. This handsome red brick home, a fine example of Georgian Revival architecture, features a commanding front entrance flanked by columns that hold up the second-story veranda. A grand staircase, carved woodwork, polished floors topped with fine rugs and more columns create an aura of elegance. Each guest room offers something special and romantic, from a mountain view to a Jacuzzi tub. Breakfasts are served on fine china, and the first course is always a freshly baked muffin with a secret message inside.

Innkeeper(s): Ann & Phil Ripley. $145-230. 5 rooms, 4 with PB, 4 with FP, 1 with WP, 2 total suites, including 1 two-bedroom suite, 1 conference room. Breakfast, afternoon tea and snacks/refreshments included in rates. Types of meals: Full gourmet bkfst, veg bkfst and early coffee/tea.

Certificate may be used: Jan. 2-Dec. 30, Sunday-Thursday.

Madison

Ebenezer House Bed and Breakfast

122 Seville Road, Rt. 621 west
Madison, VA 22727
(540) 948-3695 (877) 514-2510
Internet: www.theebenezerhousebb.com
E-mail: doris.webb@ezermail.com

Circa 1901. Gracing the foothills of the Blue Ridge
Mountains this recently renovated country chalet was originally Ebenezer Methodist Church before being dismantled
and moved to its present location on two wooded acres. The
decor is accented by an eclectic collection of family antiques
and paintings. Relax over refreshments upon arrival. The
Great Room with a wood-burning stove includes a formal living room, library and game table. Early morning coffee, tea
and juice is available in the upstairs TV room. The formal dining room opens to a downstairs deck with a goldfish pond. A
country buffet breakfast made with organic ingredients can be
enjoyed in either of those areas. Fox-hunting and beagling are
popular activities. Hike Shenandoah National Park and visit
nearby historic sites and battlefields.

Innkeeper(s): Alan Webb,Doris Webb. $99-149. 3 rooms, 1 with PB.
Breakfast, afternoon tea, snacks/refreshments and wine included in rates.
Types of meals: Full gourmet bkfst and early coffee/tea.

Certificate may be used: Anytime, November-March, subject to availability.

Middleburg

Briar Patch Bed & Breakfast Inn

23130 Briar Patch Lane
Middleburg, VA 20117
(703) 327-5911 (866) 327-5911 Fax:(703)327-5933
Internet: www.briarpatchbandb.com
E-mail: info@briarpatchbandb.com

Circa 1805. Leave stress behind when staying at this historic
farm that sits on 47 rolling acres of land that once was where
the Civil War's Battle of the Haystacks was fought in 1863.
Located in the heart of horse, antique and wine country, it is
just 20 minutes from Dulles Airport and 45 minutes from
Washington, DC. Overlook the Bull Run Mountains while sitting on the front porch. Antique-filled guest bedrooms in the
main house are named after the flowers and feature canopy or
four-poster beds. Two rooms can adjoin to become a suite. A
separate one-bedroom cottage includes a fully equipped
kitchen, dining area and living room. Breakfast is provided in
the large kitchen or outside patio. Swim in the pool or soak in
the year-round hot tub.

Innkeeper(s): Henriette Buell, Tricia Brennan. $95-285. 9 rooms, 3 with PB,
3 with FP, 3 two-bedroom suites, 1 cottage. Breakfast included in rates.
Types of meals: Full breakfast on weekends and Continental on weekdays.

Certificate may be used: Monday-Thursday.

Nellysford

The Mark Addy

56 Rodes Farm Dr
Nellysford, VA 22958-9526
(434)361-1101
Internet: www.mark-addy.com
E-mail: info@mark-addy.com

Circa 1837. It's not hard to understand why Dr. John Everett,
the son of Thomas Jefferson's physician, chose this picturesque, Blue Ridge Mountain setting for his home. Everett
expanded the simple, four-room farmhouse already present into
a gracious manor. The well-appointed guest rooms feature double whirlpool baths, double showers or a clawfoot tub. Beds are
covered with vintage linens, feather pillows and cozy, down
comforters. There are plenty of relaxing possibilities, including
five porches and a hammock set among the trees.

Innkeeper(s): Leslie Tal, Rafael Tal. $99-229. 10 rooms with PB, 4 with FP,
2 with WP, 1 suite, 1 conference room. Breakfast included in rates. Types of
meals: Full gourmet bkfst, veg bkfst, early coffee/tea, gourmet lunch, picnic
lunch, wine and gourmet dinner. Restaurant on premises.

Certificate may be used: Monday-Thursday year-round except October.

New Church

The Garden and The Sea Inn

4188 Nelson Road
New Church, VA 23415-0275
(757)824-0672 (800)824-0672
Internet: www.gardenandseainn.com
E-mail: innkeeper@gardenandseainn.com

Circa 1802. The Garden and Sea Inn adorns five acres with
woods and wildlife, as well as landscaped gardens. Located

near Chincoteague and
Assateague Islands and the
Chesapeake Bay in New Church,
Virginia, this historic Victorian
B&B is the perfect setting for
year-round relaxation. Sit on the
patio or on the wicker-accented
porch. A swing beckons by one of
the ponds or nap in a hammock.
Swim in the heated pool and enjoy the shade of the adjacent
gazebo. Afternoon refreshments are served in the parlor. Air-
conditioned guest rooms and a suite are delightful retreats.
Many boast whirlpool tubs and some include a fireplace.
Whether an early riser or sleeping in, a bountiful breakfast will
be available in the dining room. Sample popular German specialties as well as traditional classic dishes.

Innkeeper(s): Thomas and Dorothee Renn. $95-225. 9 rooms with PB, 3
with FP, 8 with WP, 2 suites, 1 conference room. Breakfast and
snacks/refreshments included in rates. Types of meals: Full gourmet bkfst,
early coffee/tea, gourmet dinner and room service.

Certificate may be used: Sunday-Thursday, April-June, October-November.

New Market

Jacob Swartz House

574 Jiggady Rd
New Market, VA 22844-2030
(540)740-9208
Internet: www.jacobswartz.com
E-mail: virginia@jacobswartz.com

Gracing the rolling hills of the scenic Shenandoah Valley in New Market, Virginia, this remote and historic guest cottage provides peaceful privacy at the end of a tree-lined lane overlooking the North Fork of the Shenandoah River. Relax on the screened porch, river-bluff terrace with a wood-burning fire pit, and delightful gardens. An intimate living room features a wood-burning stove that adjoins the dining area and well-stocked kitchen. The lower level master bedroom boasts an all-season electric fireplace and skylights. There is also a loft bedroom and a sun room with movies, books, games and puzzles. Linger over a sumptuous breakfast served at a mutually designated time in the main house or in the cottage.

Innkeeper(s): Virginia D. Harris. $125-150. 2 rooms. Breakfast and dessert included in rates.

Certificate may be used: February-March; Tuesday, Wednesday or Thursday, subject to availbility.

Orange

Mayhurst Inn

12460 Mayhurst Ln
Orange, VA 22960
(540) 672-5597 (888) 672-5597
Internet: www.mayhurstinn.com
E-mail: mayhurstbandb@aol.com

Circa 1859. Romance and relaxation await at this stunning 1859 plantation mansion. Meticulously restored to offer the best of contemporary comforts, it has retained yesterday's enchantment. Enjoy wine and cheese upon arrival. Ascend the four-story oval staircase to the fanciful cupola. Stately guest bedrooms boast double whirlpool tubs, fine linens, original Italian marble fireplaces, antique furnishings and period decor. Satisfying plantation  breakfasts are served in front of the fireplace in the dining room, on the rear veranda or on the brick courtyard. Wander the 37 acres with summer kitchen, smokehouse and schoolhouse still standing amongst 200-year-old trees. Generals Lee, Jackson and Hill were guests when the Army's Northern Virginia Corps III headquartered here. Visit local wineries, three presidential homes and several major Civil War battlefields, all within 25 miles.

Innkeeper(s): Jack & Pat North. $179-249. 8 rooms with PB, 8 with FP, 2 with WP, 2 two-bedroom suites, 1 cottage, 1 conference room. Breakfast, snacks/refreshments, hors d'oeuvres, wine and Special diets accommodated included in rates. Types of meals: Full gourmet bkfst, veg bkfst, early coffee/tea, picnic lunch and lunches/dinners available through several caterers. Dining room seats 30. Special diets can be accommodated.

Certificate may be used: Sunday-Thursday, January-March 31 and July 5-Aug. 31.

Pearisburg

Inn at Riverbend

125 River Ridge Drive
Pearisburg, VA 24134
(540) 921-5211 Fax:(540)921-2720
Internet: www.innatriverbend.com
E-mail: stay@innatriverbend.com

Circa 2003. Expansive views of the New River and the surrounding valley are incredibly breathtaking while staying at this contemporary bed and breakfast. Enjoy refreshments in front of the stone fireplace in a great room with a wall of French doors and windows. Two levels of huge wraparound decks offer an abundance of space to appreciate the scenic beauty and assortment of birds. Watch a movie or gather as a group in the TV/meeting room. Luxury guest bedrooms are delightful retreats that have access to decks or terraces and feature pressed linens, specialty personal products, stocked refrigerators, and other generous amenities. Several rooms boast whirlpool tubs. After a three-course breakfast, sample some of the area's many outdoor activities. The Appalachian Trail is only two miles away.

Innkeeper(s): Janet & Jimm Burton. $190-264. 7 rooms with PB, 3 with WP, 1 conference room. Breakfast and snacks/refreshments included in rates. Types of meals: Full gourmet bkfst, veg bkfst, early coffee/tea, lunch, picnic lunch, wine and dinner.

Certificate may be used: November-April, Sunday-Thursday.

Stanardsville

The Lafayette Inn

146 E. Main St
Stanardsville, VA 22973
(434)985-6345
Internet: www.thelafayette.com
E-mail: info@thelafayette.com

Circa 1840. Rich with a local legacy, this historic landmark was built in 1840 and stands as a stately three-story Federalist red brick building in downtown Stanardsville, Virginia. Huge porches are accented with white colonnades. Surrounded by scenic beauty, Shenandoah National Park is just 10 minutes away. The Lafayette Inn features romantic, well-appointed guest bedrooms and suites with generous amenities to make each stay most comfortable. Dicey's Cottage, the original two-story slave quarters, provides spacious privacy, Jacuzzi tubs, gas fireplaces, a kitchenette and a deck. A country-style breakfast is served in the coffee and tea house, transformed daily from being the Tavern where lunch and dinner are available. There is much to see and experience in the area. Take a tour of local vineyards, shop for pottery or visit nearby Monticello. Ask about special packages offered.

Innkeeper(s): Alan Pyles, Kaye Pyles. $139-199. 6 rooms, 2 with PB, 5 suites, 1 cottage. Breakfast and Sunday Brunch is optional included in rates. Types of meals: Country bkfst, Inn guests can reserve a "Taste of the Lafayette Inn" dinner for Monday through Wednesday evenings - 7:00 PM seating (advanced reservations required) and $50 per person. Special 3-course $25.00 Prix Fixe dinner by reservation on Sunday-Thursdays. Advance reservations required. Regular restaurant menu available on Friday and Saturday.

Certificate may be used: Monday-Thursday.

Staunton

Anne Hathaways Cottage

950 W. Beverley Street
Staunton, VA 24401
(540) 885-8885 Fax:(540)885-8885
Internet: anne-hathaways-cottage.com
E-mail: juliette@anne-hathaways-cottage.com

Circa 2008. Travel to an English thatched cottage without leaving the United States at the Anne Hathaways Cottage. The Great Room has tall ceilings and exposed wood beams and maintains a cozy feel with a warm fireplace. Celebrate Shakespeare in Juliet's, Romeo's, or William's Room. The three guest rooms offer queen-size beds with crewel comforters, private baths, free WiFi, and flat screen televisions. A full breakfast is served on Fridays and Saturdays with an extended continental breakfast the rest of the week. The resident felines are happy to greet other furry friends at this pet-friendly bed and breakfast. Host an event for 50 people in the Great Room or 130 in the lush gardens. This country bed and breakfast is eight blocks away from downtown Staunton. Browse through the many antique shops in town and the surrounding area and be sure to explore the traditional rural buildings at the Frontier Culture Museum. It's a short 15 minutes to the Blue Ridge Parkway for a scenic hike.

Innkeeper(s): Juliette Swenson. $99-159. 3 rooms with PB, 1 with FP, 1 conference room. Types of meals: Full bkfst, veg bkfst, early coffee/tea, snacks/refreshments, wine and gourmet dinner.

Certificate may be used: Sunday-Thursday, November-April and June-September, holiday weekends and Valentine's Day excluded.

Staunton Choral Gardens

216 W. Frederick St.
Staunton, VA 24401
(540)885-6556
Internet: www.stauntonbedandbreakfast.com
E-mail: StauntonBandB@Comcast.net

Circa 1915. Stay in the heart of the Shenandoah Valley at this wonderfully restored, gracious Sam Collins brick inn and 150-year-old award-winning Carriage House, a large, luxurious two-story private suite, in historic downtown Staunton, Virginia. Guest bedrooms feature upscale amenities that include wireless high-speed Internet service, lush featherbed-topped mattresses and central air conditioning. A fireplace, refrigerator and microwave are also available in some rooms. Enjoy thoughtful touches of fresh flowers, candies, and personal products. Savor multi-course breakfasts and afternoon refreshments. Relax in one of the three gardens. A large goldfish pond and fountain accent the courtyard garden; there is ample seating in the shade garden and a roof-covered swing welcomes rainy-day pleasures at Staunton Choral Gardens. A kennel area is available.

Innkeeper(s): Carolyn Avalos. $105-200. 6 rooms with PB, 2 with FP, 2 two-bedroom and 1 three-bedroom suites, 1 cottage, 2 guest houses. Breakfast, afternoon tea and snacks/refreshments included in rates. Types of meals: Full gourmet bkfst, early coffee/tea, picnic lunch and room service.

Certificate may be used: Last minute, subject to availabilty.

Tappahannock

Essex Inn

203 Duke St
Tappahannock, VA 22560
(804) 443-9900 (866) ESSEXVA
Internet: www.EssexInnVA.com
E-mail: info@EssexInnVA.com

Circa 1850. Authentically restored to its original splendor, this 1850 Greek Revival mansion is furnished with period antiques, reproductions and family heirlooms that reflect an old-world elegance. The Essex Inn is located one block from the Rappahannock River in the heart of the Tappahannock downtown historic district. Relax in the private brick courtyard, screened-in porch or the sunroom. The Music Room, with a baby grand piano, and the library have an inviting fireplace. A butler's pantry includes a microwave, refrigerator, coffee and ice maker as well as wine, beer and snacks. Spacious guest bedrooms in the main house boast fireplaces. The servants' quarters are now indulgent suites with custom amenities. Savor the specialty recipes Melody creates for incredible three-course breakfasts before exploring scenic Virginia.

Innkeeper(s): Bob McGee, Janice McGee. $175-205. 8 rooms with PB, 8 with FP, 4 suites. Full gourmet breakfast, early coffee/tea and afternoon snacks and beer/wine included in rates.

Certificate may be used: Anytime, subject to availability.

Washington

Caledonia Farm - 1812 B&B

47 Dearing Rd (Flint Hill)
Washington, VA 22627
(540)675-3693 (800)BNB-1812
Internet: www.bnb1812.com
E-mail: rphilipirwin@gmail.com

Circa 1812. This gracious Federal-style stone house on the National Register is beautifully situated on 115 forever protected acres adjacent to Shenandoah National Park. It was built by  a Revolutionary War officer, and his musket is displayed over a mantel. The house, a Virginia Historic Landmark, has been restored with the original Colonial color scheme retained. All rooms have working fireplaces, air conditioning and provide views of stone-fenced pastures and the Blue Ridge Mountains. The innkeeper is a retired international broadcaster.

Innkeeper(s): Phil Irwin. $140. 2 rooms, 2 with FP, 2 total suites, including 1 two-bedroom suite, 1 cottage, 1 conference room. Breakfast and snacks/refreshments included in rates. Types of meals: Full gourmet bkfst.

Certificate may be used: Anytime, subject to availability, except weekends.

Fairlea Farm Bed & Breakfast

636 Mt Salem Ave., PO Box 124
Washington, VA 22747-0124
(540)675-3679
Internet: www.fairleafarm.com
E-mail: longyear@shentel.net

Circa 1960. View acres of rolling hills, farmland and the Blue Ridge Mountains from this fieldstone manor house. Rooms are decorated with crocheted canopies and four-poster beds. Potted plants and floral bedcovers add a homey feel. The stone terrace is set up for relaxing with chairs lined along the edge. As a young surveyor, George Washington laid out the boundaries of the historic village of Little Washington, which is just a 5-minute walk from Fairlea Farm, a working sheep and cattle farm.

Innkeeper(s): Susan Longyear, Walt Longyear. $195-220. 4 rooms with PB, 1 suite. Breakfast and afternoon tea included in rates. Types of meals: Full gourmet bkfst and early coffee/tea.

Certificate may be used: December-February, Suite only, No holidays or Saturdays.

Waynesboro

Iris Inn

191 Chinquapin Dr
Waynesboro, VA 22980-5692
(540)943-1991 (888)585-9018 Fax:(540)942-2093
Internet: www.irisinn.com
E-mail: innkeeper@irisinn.com

Circa 1991. Feel embraced by the natural beauty and tranquil setting of this romantic modern retreat on 12 wooded acres in the Blue Ridge Mountains of Waynesboro, Virginia. Sit on a porch at the Iris Inn and be surrounded by the scenic Shenandoah National Forest. A three-story stone fireplace and expansive hand-painted mural depicting local flora and fauna highlight the great room. Read or use the computer in the loft library and enjoy the breeze from the third-floor lookout tower. Indulge in the bottomless cookie jar and beverages upon checking in. Stay in a guest room or suite that features a whirlpool or hot tub, gas fireplace, kitchenette and private access to outdoor decks that overlook the Shenandoah Valley. After a hearty breakfast explore the nearby cultural hub of Charlottesville or take a tour of Jefferson's Monticello.

Innkeeper(s): David Lanford, Heidi Lanford. $149-319. 15 rooms with PB, 8 with FP, 7 with HT, 3 with WP, 1 conference room. Breakfast included in rates. Types of meals: Full bkfst, veg bkfst, early coffee/tea, picnic lunch, snacks/refreshments and wine.

Certificate may be used: Jan. 1-March 31, Nov. 15-Dec. 31, Sunday-Thursday, excluding holidays and special events.

White Stone

Flowering Fields B&B

232 Flowering Field
White Stone, VA 22578-9722
(804)435-6238 Fax:(804)435-6238
Internet: www.floweringfieldsbandb.com
E-mail: floweringfieldsbandb@gmail.com

Circa 1790. Flowering Fields Bed & Breakfast sits in White Stone near the mouth of the Rappahannock River before it flows into the Chesapeake Bay. This tranquil B&B is hidden away in the waterfront area known as the Northern Neck of Virginia and is known to be "where southern hospitality begins." Families will enjoy the game room with a pool table or watching movies by the fire in the gathering room. Refreshing lemonade is on the welcome table in the large foyer in the summertime. Browse through the library's extensive collection of health, diet and cookbooks as well as paperbacks to read. Formal but inviting and comfortable guest bedrooms include sitting areas. Linger over a relaxing and delicious breakfast accented with the inn's famous blue crab crabcakes. Activities are endless in this scenic and central location.

Innkeeper(s): Susan Moenssens. $75-125. 5 rooms with PB, 1 conference room. Breakfast, snacks/refreshments, Afternoon Tea on request, Lemonade on welcoming table in summer months, soft drinks, candies, fruits and coffee & tea 24/7. included in rates. Types of meals: Full gourmet bkfst, veg bkfst, early coffee/tea, afternoon tea, Full breakfast featuring crabcakes & specialty omelettes, fresh fruits and blueberry pancakes. special diets and requests accommodated. Special Rates for Continental Breakfast. $75 weekdays and $100 weekends.

Certificate may be used: January-April.

Washington

Bellingham

Tree Frog Night Inn

1727 Mt Baker Highway
Bellingham, WA 98226
(360) 676-2300
Internet: www.treefrognight.com
E-mail: inn@treefrognight.com

Circa 2010. Sustainably built with clay and lime walls, this eco inn on five lush acres of majestic cedars, gardens and creeks boasts beautiful art, tile, fabric and craftwork by local artisans. Located near downtown Bellingham, Washington and all the outdoor activities of Whatcom County, relax amid the secluded country feel. Enjoy wine or juice upon arrival. There is a full line of spa services and an infrared sauna. Luxury king suites feature fireplaces, down bedding, radiant heat floors, Blu-ray players, iPod docks, wifi, cotton robes, hair dryers, fresh flowers, kitchenettes, handmade soaps, and baths with a double tiled shower or jetted tub. Linger over a gourmet, organic breakfast, then sit on the private hardwood decks and watch birds and wildlife. The adjacent Cedar Tree House retreat center and vacation rental is perfect for small events and weddings.
Innkeeper(s): Kara Black, Kurt Yandell. $120-185. 2 rooms, 2 with FP, 1 with HT, 1 with WP, 2 suites, 1 cottage. Breakfast, brunch, Sunday brunch and wine included in rates. Types of meals: Full gourmet bkfst, veg bkfst, picnic lunch, snacks/refreshments, Organic, homegrown and local foods.
Certificate may be used: November-March excluding weekends or anytime last minute-Based on Availability. Cannot be combined with any other discounts.

Camano Island

The Inn at Barnum Point

464 S Barnum Rd
Camano Island, WA 98282-8578
(360)387-2256 (800)910-2256
Internet: www.innatbarnumpoint.com
E-mail: barnumpoint@camano.net

Circa 1991. The Inn at Barnum Point is a Cape Cod-style B&B located on the bay on Camano Island, Washington. Enjoy listening to the water lap at the shoreline, watching deer in the orchard and sneaking a kiss under an heirloom apple tree. The newest accommodation is the 900-square-foot Shorebird Room with deck, fireplace and soaking tub overlooking Port Susan Bay and the Cascade Mountains.
Innkeeper(s): Carolin Barnum Dilorenzo. $125-225. 3 rooms with PB, 3 with FP. Breakfast included in rates. Types of meals: Full gourmet bkfst and early coffee/tea.
Certificate may be used: Anytime, Subject to availability.

Dayton

The Purple House

415 E Clay St
Dayton, WA 99328-1348
(509)382-3159 (800)486-2574
Internet: www.purplehousebnb.com
E-mail: info@purplehousebnb.com

Circa 1882. History buffs will adore this aptly named bed & breakfast, colored in deep purple tones with white, gingerbread trim. The home, listed in the National Register, is the perfect  place to enjoy Dayton, which boasts two historic districts and a multitude of preserved Victorian homes. Innkeeper Christine Williscroft has filled the home with antiques and artwork. A highly praised cook, Christine prepares the European-style full breakfasts, as well as mouthwatering afternoon refreshments. Guests can relax in the richly appointed parlor or library, and the grounds also include a swimming pool.
Innkeeper(s): Christine Williscroft. $95-135. 4 rooms, 2 with PB, 1 with FP, 1 suite. Breakfast and afternoon tea included in rates. Types of meals: Full gourmet bkfst, early coffee/tea, picnic lunch and dinner.
Certificate may be used: Sunday-Thursday, February-June, $95 per room only.

Friday Harbor

Harrison House Suites

235 C St
Friday Harbor, WA 98250-8098
(360)378-3587 (800)407-7933 Fax:(360)378-2270
Internet: www.harrisonhousesuites.com
E-mail: innkeeper@harrisonhousesuites.com

Circa 1905. Providing abundant hospitality in a scenic hilltop setting with spectacular views of the Pacific Northwest, this historic Craftsman retreat is located in Friday Harbor, Washington, a premier destination on San Juan Island. Complimentary bikes and kayaks invite exploration of the local area with easy access to the ferry landing just 1½ blocks away. Browse through the reading and video library collection for less active moments. Stay in a spacious guest suite that may include a fireplace, whirlpool tub, well-stocked kitchen, private deck, grill and hot tub. Gather in the relaxing cafe or request in-room service for a four-course gourmet breakfast made with recipes from the inn's own cookbook. Afternoon tea and treats are always pleasurable interludes. Special dinners, catering, packages and other thoughtful extras are available.

Innkeeper(s): Anna Maria de Freitas, David Pass. $135-405. 5 rooms with PB, 3 with FP, 5 with HT, 3 with WP, 2 two-bedroom and 1 three-bedroom suites, 1 cottage, 1 conference room. Breakfast and snacks/refreshments included in rates. Types of meals: Full gourmet bkfst, veg bkfst, early coffee/tea, gourmet lunch, picnic lunch, gourmet dinner, room service and Group/Event Catering.

Certificate may be used: October-May, excluding holidays and weekends.

Grandview

Cozy Rose Inn
1220 Forsell Rd
Grandview, WA 98930
(509)882-4669 (800)575-8381 Fax:(509)882-4234
Internet: www.cozyroseinn.com
E-mail: stay@cozyroseinn.com

Circa 1908. Enjoying Washington's wine country from the privacy of your own luxurious suite is only part of the unforgettable experience that awaits at this delightful country inn, which combines a Cape Cod and farmhouse-style design with French Country decor. Walk through family vineyards and orchards to be renewed in a relaxing six-acre setting. Each romantic, villa-style suite includes a private bath, fireplace, stereo, refrigerator, microwave and a separate entrance with a private deck overlooking vineyards and orchards. Some also include a Jacuzzi. The Suite Surrender boasts an incredible view and includes Italian furniture, Jacuzzi tub, walk-in tiled shower and flat screen satellite TV/DVD/VCR. Feel truly pampered by a full candlelight breakfast that may include huckleberry pancakes, delivered to each suite. After a day of sightseeing, biking or golfing, soak in the Under The Stars hot tub. Make friends with the two pet llamas, Chocolate and Stubborn.

Innkeeper(s): Mark Jackson, Jennie Jackson. $99-229. 5 rooms, 5 with FP, 5 suites. Breakfast included in rates. Types of meals: Country bkfst and veg bkfst.

Certificate may be used: November-February, Monday-Wednesday. No holidays or special event weekends. Rack rate only and consecutive nights only. Upgrade upon check in only if available.

Greenbank

Guest House Log Cottages
24371-SR 525, Whidbey Island
Greenbank, WA 98253
(360)678-3115 (800)997-3115
Internet: www.guesthouselogcottages.com
E-mail: stay@guesthouselogcottages.com

Circa 1925. These storybook cottages and log home are nestled within a peaceful forest on 25 acres. The log cabin features stained-glass and criss-cross paned windows that give it the feel of a gingerbread house. Four of the cottages are log construction. Ask for the Lodge and enjoy a private setting with a pond just beyond the deck. Inside are two Jacuzzi tubs, a stone fireplace, king bed, antiques and a luxurious atmosphere.

Innkeeper(s): Peggy Walker, Doug Creger. $125-350. 6 cottages with PB,

6 with HT. Breakfast included in rates. Types of meals: Full bkfst and early coffee/tea.

Certificate may be used: Monday-Thursday, Oct. 15-April 15.

Leavenworth

Haus Rohrbach Pension
12882 Ranger Rd
Leavenworth, WA 98826-9503
(509)548-7024 (800)548-4477
Internet: www.hausrohrbach.com
E-mail: info@hausrohrbach.com

Circa 1975. Situated on 13 1/2 acres overlooking the village, Haus Rohrbach offers both valley and mountain views and is at the entrance to Tumwater Mountain cycling and hiking trails. Leavenworth is two minutes away. Private fireplaces and whirlpools for two are features of each of three suites. Sourdough pancakes and cinnamon rolls are specialties of the house. Guests often take breakfast out to the deck to enjoy pastoral views that include grazing sheep and a pleasant pond. In the evening, return from white-water rafting, tobogganing, skiing or sleigh rides to soak in the hot tub.

Innkeeper(s): Carol Wentink, Mike Wentink. $105-200. 10 rooms, 8 with PB, 3 with FP, 3 with WP, 3 suites, 1 cottage, 1 conference room. Breakfast included in rates. Types of meals: Full bkfst, early coffee/tea, lunch, picnic lunch, snacks/refreshments and dinner.

Certificate may be used: Jan. 7-May 7, Sept. 10-Oct. 31, Sunday-Thursday. Holiday and festival times are excluded.

Mazama

Mazama Country Inn
15 Country Road
Mazama, WA 98833-9700
(509)996-2681 (800)843-7951 Fax:(509)996-2646
Internet: www.mazamacountryinn.com
E-mail: info@mazamacountryinn.com

Circa 1985. Escape to this country inn, a quiet retreat in the small town of Mazama, secluded in the beauty of Washington's North Cascades. Relax amid log beams and cedar siding in comfortable guest rooms with breathtaking views. Gather with a hot beverage by the huge Russian fireplace in the great room. Stay in deluxe accommodations with a Jacuzzi tub and gas stove. There is a room for every budget with an assortment of amenities. Vacation homes are available nearby for more space and privacy, with fully equipped kitchens and linens provided. During winter, an inclusive three-meal option is offered to inn guests with a hearty breakfast, pack-your-own lunch to go and a family-style dinner. The inviting setting includes a fitness center, sauna, hot tub, swimming pool, tennis courts and an onsite restaurant. Enjoy a variety of local activities.

Innkeeper(s): Mary Milka. $80-170. 18 rooms with PB, 8 with FP, 3 with WP, 20 cabins. Types of meals: Full bkfst, lunch, picnic lunch and gourmet dinner. Restaurant on premises.

Certificate may be used: Anytime, except holidays and holiday weekends.

Newport

Inn at the Lake

581 S. Shore Diamond Lake Rd
Newport, WA 99156
(509)447-5772 (877)447-5772 Fax:(509)447-0999
Internet: www.innatthelake.com
E-mail: info@innatthelake.com

Circa 1993. A vacation paradise, this Southwestern-style home offers resort amenities. A family room boasts a gas-log fireplace, VCR, books and games. The large entertainment deck overlooks tiered gardens and ponds. Luxurious waterfront suites boast spacious privacy, fireplaces, double Jacuzzis and lake views. Stay in the romantic Peach Penthouse Suite with a roof-top deck and two-person swing. Breakfast is found in each room's refrigerator, ready to enjoy when desired. Fish for rainbow trout from the dock, or rent a canoe. Play volleyball on the grass beach before a refreshing swim. Winter sports also are in abundance.
Innkeeper(s): Blaine & Virginia Coffey. $95-159. 5 rooms, 1 with FP, 5 suites. Breakfast and snacks/refreshments included in rates. Types of meals: Cont plus, veg bkfst, afternoon tea and room service.
Certificate may be used: Sunday-Thursday, Nov. 1-April 30, except holidays.

Olga

Sand Dollar Inn

445 Point Lawrence Rd
Olga, WA 98279
(360) 376-5696
Internet: www.sdollar.com
E-mail: sanddollar@rockisland.com

Circa 1920. Whether arriving by car or by ferry, it will be easy to relax amid the breathtaking beauty and peaceful tranquility of the San Juan Islands while staying at this delightful inn overlooking Buck Bay on Orcas Island in Olga, Washington. Outstanding views are enjoyed from the balcony deck. Sweeping vistas of the water, Lopez Island and the Olympic Mountains are seen from the inviting upstairs guest rooms. Sleep soundly then wake fully rested to gather in the Sunroom for a hearty breakfast before exploring the scenic area. Hike the miles of trails in Moran State Park and enjoy the refreshing pleasures of the nearby fresh water lakes. Take a day trip to Seattle for a taste of city life and to experience the many attractions found there.
Innkeeper(s): Ann Sanchez. $100-135. 3 rooms with PB. Breakfast included in rates.
Certificate may be used: Anytime, Subject to availability.

Port Angeles

Five SeaSuns Bed & Breakfast

1006 S Lincoln St
Port Angeles, WA 98362-7826
(360)452-8248 (800)708-0777 Fax:(360)417-0465
Internet: www.seasuns.com
E-mail: info@seasuns.com

Circa 1926. Take a respite from the rush of today at this restored, historic home that reflects the 1920s era of sophistication with a sense of romance and refinement. Guest bedrooms depict the seasons of the year and are furnished with

period antiques. Pleasing amenities include whirlpool or soaking tubs, balconies and water or mountain views. Artfully presented gourmet breakfasts are served by candlelight with fine china and silver. Relax on the porch or wander the picturesque gardens that highlight the estate-like grounds. Explore nearby Olympic National Park and the Ediz Hook Coast Guard Station. The Underground History Walk is ten blocks. Visit the Makah Indian Museum 75 miles away.
Innkeeper(s): Jan Harbick, Bob Harbick. $115-165. 5 rooms with PB, 1 suite, 1 cottage. Breakfast, afternoon tea and snacks/refreshments included in rates. Types of meals: Full gourmet bkfst, veg bkfst and early coffee/tea.
Certificate may be used: November-April, excluding holiday weekends, subject to availability.

Puyallup

Hedman House A Bed & Breakfast

502 9th Street SW
Puyallup, WA 98371-5855
(253)848-2248 (866)433-6267
Internet: www.hedmanhouse.com
E-mail: contact@hedmanhouse.com

Circa 1907. It is just 15 minutes to Puget Sound from this traditional 1907 farmhouse that is furnished with antiques and boasts original fir woodwork. It has been lovingly well-maintained with careful attention to details. Relax on a swing or rocking chair on the covered front porch. Read, listen to music or watch a movie by the fire in the living room. After a restful sleep in one of the comfortable guest bedrooms, gather for breakfast in the dining room or al fresco in the courtyard. Lounge in the yard and enjoy a soak in the spa.
Innkeeper(s): Normajean Hedman, Neil Hedman. $105-145. 3 rooms with PB. Breakfast included in rates. Types of meals: Full bkfst and early coffee/tea.
Certificate may be used: January-February, Sunday-Thursday, subject to availability.

Seattle

Chittenden House Bed and Breakfast

5649 47th Ave SW
Seattle, WA 98136
(206)935-0407 Fax:(206)932-5328
Internet: www.chittendenhouse.com
E-mail: info@chittendenhouse.com

Circa 1926. Take advantage of the many scenic sights of the Northwest while staying at Chittenden House Bed and Breakfast in West Seattle, Washington near Alki Beach and Lincoln Park. Serene and quiet, relax in the sun room, on the back deck with a view of Puget Sound or sit on the brick patio in the garden. Intimate guest bedrooms at this European-style B&B include pleasing amenities. Soak in a clawfoot or English slipper tub. The downstairs suite boasts a living room and kitchen. Wake up and savor a delicious breakfast in the dining room or kitchen. Visit the Space Needle and experience Pike Place Market. Tour the aquarium and local museums. Take a day trip to Mount Rainier or a ferry ride to Bainbridge Island.

Innkeeper(s): Marcia Chittenden. $99-144. 3 rooms with PB, 1 two-bedroom suite. Breakfast, afternoon tea and snacks/refreshments included in rates. Types of meals: Full bkfst, veg bkfst and early coffee/tea.

Certificate may be used: January-March, Tuesday-Wednesday.

Inn Of Twin Gables

3258 14th Ave W
Seattle, WA 98119-1727
(206)284-3979 (866)466-3979 Fax:(206)284-3974
Internet: www.innoftwingables.com
E-mail: info@innoftwingables.com

Circa 1915. Situated in the Queen Anne Hill district in Seattle, Washington, Inn of Twin Gables is an Arts and Crafts home built in 1915. Feel welcomed and comfortable at this B&B that makes personal attention a high priority. Gather by the fireplace in the living room, read a book in the enclosed sun porch or sit on a garden bench and watch the sunset. A mini refrigerator is provided for guest use. Guest bedrooms boast fresh flowers and pressed cotton linens. The adjoining North and East Rooms can become a suite for four. A generous gourmet breakfast is served daily in the formal dining room with a variety of popular specialty entrees. Visit nearby Pike Place Market, Pioneer Square and Seattle Center.

Innkeeper(s): Katie Frame. $100-220. 3 rooms with PB. Breakfast, afternoon tea, Tea is offered upon arrival and the pot for hot water can be set up in the dining room to be available when requested included in rates. Types of meals: Full gourmet bkfst, veg bkfst, early coffee/tea, Sumptuous hot gourmet breakfast with kitchen garden herbs in the formal dining room at 8:30 every morning. Before 8:00 AM, a continental breakfast can be arranged. Dietary restrictions accommodated if possible. For special consideration, or if you are unable to attend breakfast please let the innkeeper know the day before.

Certificate may be used: Sunday-Thursday, October-May, except holidays, subject to availability.

Soundview Cottage B&B

17600 Sylvester Rd SW
Seattle, WA 98166-3266
(206) 244-5209
Internet: www.seattlecottage.net
E-mail: annie@soundviewcottage.com

Perched on a hill overlooking the gorgeous waters of Puget Sound in Seattle, Washington, Soundview Cottage B&B offers a self-contained, private guest house built in the Craftsman style. The cottage features a fully equipped kitchen and dining area. The living room boasts an electric woodstove and an entertainment media center with an extensive video library. Watch the sunset over the Olympic Mountains. Soak in the outdoor hot tub on the deck with sweeping vistas. After a peaceful night's sleep in a king bed, a variety of breakfast foods are provided to create a classic gourmet feast. Hike Mount Rainier, cruise the harbor in Elliott Bay or visit the many city sites and attractions.

Innkeeper(s): Anne Phillips. $150-200. 1 guest house with PB. Breakfast included in rates. Types of meals: Includes a wide assortment of breakfast food which guests can prepare at their leisure.

Certificate may be used: November, January-March, no weekends.

Three Tree Point Bed & Breakfast

17026 33rd Ave SW
Seattle, WA 98166-3116
(206)669-7646 (888)369-7696 Fax:(206)242-7844
Internet: www.3treepointbnb.com
E-mail: whislers@comcast.net

Circa 1993. Overlooking the shoreline of Three Tree Point on Puget Sound, this contemporary northwest retreat sits on a quiet hillside with panoramic vistas of Mount Rainier and the Olympic Mountains. The Suite with French doors, and the Cottage with a river rock fireplace, each feature a living room, dining area, full kitchen and patio with views of the water. A variety of foods and ingredients are provided and restocked for a daily breakfast that can be prepared and enjoyed when desired. A barbecue, laundry facilities, spa hot tub, and pampering amenities add to the luxury. Take a walk on the beach or hike the historic Indian Trails.

Innkeeper(s): Penny Whisler. $150-250. 2 rooms, 1 with FP, 1 suite, 1 cottage. Breakfast, afternoon tea and snacks/refreshments included in rates. Types of meals: Full bkfst.

Certificate may be used: Anytime, Sunday-Thursday, excluding June-September, December and holidays, subject to availability.

Seaview

Shelburne Inn

4415 Pacific Way
Seaview, WA 98644
(360)642-2442 (800)INN1896 Fax:(360)642-8904
Internet: www.theshelburneinn.com
E-mail: frontdesk@theshelburneinn.com

Circa 1896. Established in 1896, the Shelburne Inn is the oldest continuously operating hotel in Washington and is listed in the National Register. A beautiful wooden former church altar is the front desk of this historic hotel. The entire inn is thoughtfully appointed in antiques and fine furnishings. Art nouveau stained-glass windows were rescued from an  1800's church torn down in Morecambe, England, and now shed light and color in the dining room, pub and throughout many of the guest bedrooms. Each morning savor the renowned innkeeper's full gourmet breakfast. Just a 10-minute walk from the ocean, the inn graces Seaview on the Long Beach Peninsula, a 28-mile stretch of seacoast that includes bird sanctuaries, lighthouses, historic centers and national parks.

Innkeeper(s): David Campiche, Laurie Anderson. $139-199. 15 rooms with PB, 2 suites, 1 conference room. Breakfast included in rates. Types of meals: Full gourmet bkfst, lunch, gourmet dinner, room service and Coffee & Tea service all day in lobby. Restaurant on premises.

Certificate may be used: Midweek, October-May, excluding holidays.

Tacoma

Branch Colonial House

2420 North 21st St
Tacoma, WA 98406
(253)752-3565 (877)752-3565
Internet: www.branchcolonialhouse.com
E-mail: stay@branchcolonialhouse.com

Branch Colonial House sits perched above the historic Old Town District of Tacoma, Washington, overlooking Puget Sound. Relax on the front porch before exploring the scenic Pacific Northwest. This delightful bed and breakfast features Colonial Revival architecture and a romantic ambiance. Stay in a luxury, upscale guest room or suite with modern amenities, robes, a fireplace and a jetted or cast iron soaking tub. Browse local shops, tour museums, go to the zoo and visit the aquarium. It is an easy drive to the many city attractions in Seattle with the splendid majesty of Mount Rainier in the background.

Innkeeper(s): Robin Korobkin. Call for rates. Call inn for details. Breakfast included in rates. Types of meals: Full gourmet bkfst, veg bkfst, early coffee/tea and snacks/refreshments.

Certificate may be used: Sunday-Thursday, subject to availability. Blackout dates do apply, call ahead to confirm. Rooms available: Branch, Prospect and Sunroom.

Chinaberry Hill B&B - A Luxury Urban B&B Experience

302 Tacoma Ave N
Tacoma, WA 98403
(253)272-1282
Internet: www.chinaberryhill.com
E-mail: chinaberry@wa.net

Circa 1889. In the 19th century, this Queen Anne was known as far away as China for its wondrous gardens, one of the earliest examples of landscape gardening in the Pacific Northwest. The home, a wedding present from a husband to his bride, is listed in the National Register. The innkeepers have selected a unique assortment of antiques and collectibles to decorate the manor. The house offers two Jacuzzi suites and a guest room, all eclectically decorated with items such as a four-poster rice bed or a canopy bed. There are two lodging options in the Catchpenny Cottage, a restored carriage house steps away from the manor. Guests can stay either in the romantic carriage suite or the Hay Loft, which includes a bedroom, sitting room, clawfoot tub and a unique hay chute. In the mornings, as the innkeepers say, guests enjoy "hearty breakfasts and serious coffee." Not a bad start to a day exploring Antique Row or Pt. Defiance, a 698-acre protected rain forest park with an aquarium, gardens, beaches and a zoo. Seattle is 30 minutes away.

Innkeeper(s): Cecil Wayman, Yarrow Waymen. $139-245. 5 rooms with PB, 1 with FP, 3 with WP, 2 two-bedroom suites, 1 cottage, 1 guest house. Breakfast and snacks/refreshments included in rates. Types of meals: Full gourmet bkfst and early coffee/tea.

Certificate may be used: November, January-March, Monday-Wednesday. Seven days prior to reservation. Excludes holidays and special events.

Plum Duff House

619 North K Street
Tacoma, WA 98403
(253)627-6916 (888)627-1920 Fax:(253)272-9116
Internet: www.plumduff.com
E-mail: plumduffhouse@gmail.com

Circa 1900. Friendly and casual with a relaxing ambiance and genuine hospitality, Plum Duff House in the North Tacoma district in Washington was built in 1901 in the Victorian style. Antiques, country and modern furnishings mix in an appealing and inviting way. Relax by the fire in the living room or gather in the enclosed sun porch for a game of chess or browse for a book off the shelf. Snacks and beverages are available at any time. Stay in a comfortable guest bedroom or a suite that boasts a fireplace and Jacuzzi tub. After a satisfying breakfast explore the Great Pacific Northwest. Take day trips to Seattle, Puget Sound, Mt. Rainier and the Olympic Peninsula.

Innkeeper(s): Peter Stevens, Robin Stevens. $100-150. 4 rooms with PB, 1 with FP, 1 with WP, 1 two-bedroom suite. Breakfast included in rates. Types of meals: Full bkfst.

Certificate may be used: November-March, Sunday-Thursday, last minute, subject to availability, no holidays.

Walla Walla

The Maxwell House Bed and Breakfast Inn

701 Boyer Avenue
Walla Walla, WA 99362
(509)529-4283
Internet: www.themaxwellhouse.com
E-mail: inn@themaxwellhouse.com

Circa 1913. The Maxwell House, a charming 100 year old Craftsman home, is located in a delightful neighborhood. Shady trees line the streets of this quiet neighborhood, a prime distance from the downtown area restaurants, tasting rooms, and Whitman College. Carefully decorated rooms that delight your senses invite you to relax and settle in for a wonderful stay. Delectable meals, pleasant hospitality and comfortable ambiance will put The Maxwell House as a memory to be returned to again and again.

Innkeeper(s): Penny Maxwell Bingham. $160-165. Call inn for details. Types of meals: Full bkfst and early coffee/tea.

Certificate may be used: April-November, midweek.

West Virginia

Charleston

Brass Pineapple B&B

1611 Virginia St East
Charleston, WV 25311-2113
(304) 344-0748 (866) 344-0748
Internet: www.brasspineapple.com
E-mail: info@brasspineapple.com

Circa 1910. Original oak paneling, leaded and stained glass are among the architectural highlights at this smoke-free inn that

graces the historic district near the Capitol Complex. Guest bedrooms feature thoughtful amenities including terry robes and hair dryers as well as technology for business needs. A full breakfast consisting of tea, juices,

fruit, muffins, waffles, quiche, basil tomatoes and cottage fries, is served in the dining room. Dietary requirements can be met upon request.

Innkeeper(s): Lisa, Vicky, Cheryl. $129-179. 6 rooms with PB, 1 suite. Breakfast, afternoon tea, snacks/refreshments and hors d'oeuvres included in rates. Types of meals: Full gourmet bkfst, veg bkfst, early coffee/tea and picnic lunch.

Certificate may be used: Anytime, subject to availability.

Landgraff

Elkhorn Inn & Theatre

30767 Coal Heritage Rd (Route 52)
Landgraff, WV 24829
(304)862-2031 (800)708-2040 Fax:(304)862-2031
Internet: www.elkhorninnwv.com
E-mail: elisse@elkhorninnwv.com

Circa 1922. Named for the trout-filled Elkhorn Creek that runs behind the inn, this historic Italianate brick building with archways and a balcony on the Coal Heritage Trail has been lovingly restored by Dan and Elisse. Period antiques and 1930s furnishings complement an international art collection. Paintings, prints, ceramics, stained glass, sculpture and textiles are for sale. Stay in a guest bedroom or suite with handmade vintage quilts, clawfoot tubs and bubble baths. A family suite with two adjoining rooms is available. Alto Grande Coffee, offered exclusively at the inn, accompanies a continental breakfast. Located near Pinnacle Rock State Park and Panther State Forest, there are ATV and bike trails on Burke Mountain. McDowell County is also a popular hunting and fishing area.

Innkeeper(s): Elisse Clark, Dan Clark. $99-198. 13 rooms, 3 with PB, 1 two-bedroom suite. Breakfast included in rates. Types of meals: Cont, veg bkfst, Sun. brunch, early coffee/tea, lunch, afternoon tea, snacks/refreshments, hors d'oeuvres, wine, gourmet dinner, Weddings, dinner parties, buffet dinner parties and other special events.

Certificate may be used: Anytime, subject to availability, not valid Oct. 1-10.

Wisconsin

Appleton

Franklin Inn on Durkee

310 North Durkee
Appleton, WI 54911
(920)993-1711 (888)993-1711
Internet: www.appleton-wisconsin.com
E-mail: info@franklinstreetinn.com

Circa 1894. Experience an elegant setting and unique international themes amid lush woodwork and fine furnishings at this
restored Queen Ann Victorian with beautiful landscaping. Relax
in spacious common areas. Guest rooms and suites boast
whirlpools, fireplaces pillow-top beds and wifi. In the dining
room, gourmet breakfasts are presented underneath an antique
chandelier or enjoy dining al fresco on the porch or more privately, in-room. The convenient location is in the historic district of downtown Appleton, Wisconsin, only blocks away from
the highlights of Fox Valley: the Performing Arts Center, History
Museum at the Castle, Trout Museum of Art, Lawrence
University, City Park and Fox River Trail. Popular events hosted
at the inn include a murder mystery party, small wedding or
shower, girlfriend getaway, scrapbook event or retreat.
Innkeeper(s): Ron and Judy Halma. $99-219. 4 rooms with PB, 2 with FP, 2
with WP, 2 total suites, including 1 three-bedroom suite, 1 conference room.
Breakfast and snacks/refreshments included in rates. Types of meals: Full
gourmet bkfst, veg bkfst, early coffee/tea, room service and Innkeeper has
published a cookbook. Breakfast menus are created using these recipes.
Certificate may be used: Last minute based on projected availability for 2 for
1 overnight accommodations in the lovely Petit Chateau Suite or Sea Breeze
Suites. Reservations required; holidays, holiday weeks and special event
weekends excluded.

Ashland

Second Wind Country Inn

30475 Carlson Road
Ashland, WI 54806
(715)682-1000
Internet: www.secondwindcountryinn.com
E-mail: catchyourbreath@secondwindcountryinn.com

Circa 2004. Encompassing 35 magnificent acres, this non-
smoking log and timber lodge offers an incredible view of
Lake Superior's Chequamegon Bay area. Relax in the gathering room with a Northwoods lodge decor or on one of the
outdoor decks. Three guest suites feature a luxurious
ambiance and whirlpool tubs. The Bear Den is handicap
accessible. The Northern Lights Loft includes a kitchenette
with refrigerator and microwave. Wake up after a restful sleep
and enjoy a home-cooked breakfast. Gather for a late-night

bonfire and evening treats. Browse the Second Wind
Mercantile for gifts to bring home.
Innkeeper(s): Mark Illick, Kelly Illick. $89-159. 3 rooms, 3 with WP, 3 total
suites, including 1 three-bedroom suite, 1 conference room. Breakfast and
Sunday brunch included in rates. Types of meals: Country bkfst, early
coffee/tea and snacks/refreshments.
Certificate may be used: October 15-May 15, subject to availability.

Bayfield

Old Rittenhouse Inn

301 Rittenhouse Ave
Bayfield, WI 54814-0584
(715)779-5111 (800)779-2129 Fax:(715)779-5887
Internet: www.rittenhouseinn.com
E-mail: gourmet@rittenhouseinn.com

Circa 1892. Two historic Queen Anne mansions, a guest house
and a private cottage comprise this elegant Victorian inn and
gourmet restaurant just a few blocks from downtown. Under

massive gables, a wrap-
around veranda is filled
with white wicker furni-
ture, geraniums and petu-
nias. The inn boasts 22
working fireplaces amidst
antique furnishings. Well-
appointed guest bedrooms
and luxury suites offer a variety of romantic amenities that may
include whirlpools as well as views of Madeline Island and Lake
Superior. The two-story Fountain Cottage is just uphill. For
breakfast indulge in baked muffins served with Rittenhouse
Jams, Jellies and a cup of coffee accompanied by dishes such as
Wild Bayfield Blueberry Crisp or Moonglow Pears Poached in
White Zinfandel.
Innkeeper(s): Jerry, Mary, Mark, Wendy, and Julie Phillips. $99-349. 26
rooms with PB, 19 with FP, 17 with WP, 7 total suites, including 2 two-bedroom suites, 2 cottages, 2 guest houses. Breakfast, Continental Breakfast
included in room rate and Full Breakfast available for $8.50/houseguest and
$11.50/person for walk ins included in rates. Types of meals: Full gourmet
bkfst, gourmet lunch, snacks/refreshments, wine, gourmet dinner, room service, Weddings, Reunions and catered special events. Restaurant on premises.
Certificate may be used: Nov. 1 to May 14, Wednesday and Thursday.

Birchwood

Cobblestone Bed & Breakfast

319 S Main St
Birchwood, WI 54817-8826
(715)354-3494 (800)659-4883 Fax:(715)354-9850
Internet: www.cobblestonebedandbreakfast.com
E-mail: cobblestone@centurytel.net

Circa 1912. An Old English-style lamp lights the cobblestone walkway to the porch of this historic country manor in Birchwood, Wisconsin. Each season offers delightful reasons to visit this enchanting inn. Fragrant blossoms of flower and fruit trees scent the spring air. Lazy days of summer include strolls to the beach for a refreshing dip. Sit on the front porch swing with a beverage and admire the colorful fall leaves. Winter sports are popular at nearby Christie Mountain and the Great North Woods trails. Relax after a gourmet breakfast amid simple comfort and peaceful elegance. Browse the gift shop for local fine arts and craftsmanship. The Four Corners area is centrally located between Rice Lake, Spooner, Ladysmith and Hayward.

Innkeeper(s): Mary Lou Campion. $89-175. 7 rooms, 3 with PB, 3 with FP, 1 with WP, 1 two-bedroom suite. Breakfast, afternoon tea and snacks/refreshments included in rates. Types of meals: Full gourmet bkfst and early coffee/tea.

Certificate may be used: Sunday-Thursday, Nov. 1-May 15; excluding Ladies/Gents room & English Garden Suite and Feb 17-24.

Cambridge

Oscar H. Hanson House

303 E. North Street
Cambridge, WI 53523
(608)423-4379
Internet: www.ohhanson.com
E-mail: info@ohhanson.com

Circa 1883. Experience the romance with in-room breakfast service, fireplaces, stained glass, spacious showers, and claw-foot soaking or Jacuzzi tubs in an eco-friendly environment.

Innkeeper(s): Duke Mihajlovic, Mary Jane Mihajlovic. Call for rates. 4 rooms.

Certificate may be used: November-April, Sunday-Thursday. (excluding Holidays and Holiday eves).

Camp Douglas

Sunnyfield Farm B&B

N6692 Batko Rd
Camp Douglas, WI 54618
(608)427-3686 (888)839-0232
Internet: www.sunnyfield.net
E-mail: soltvedt@mwt.net

Circa 1899. Scenic bluffs and rich land surround this 100-year-old, three-story farmhouse boasting 10-foot ceilings. Lovingly restored, the original hardwood floors and hand-carved oak woodwork reside easily with brass ceiling tiles and family heirlooms. Guest bedrooms feature a country decor with handmade quilts and stenciling. The Rose Room has an adjoining room that is perfect for families or groups. A private studio apartment on the third floor offers a cozy yet spacious suite with living room, kitchen and sky windows for stargazing. Wake up to a complete country breakfast served in the spacious dining room. Three of the 160 acres are manicured lawns to enjoy. Wisconsin Dells is just 30 minutes away.

Innkeeper(s): Susanne Solvedt, John Soltvedt. $80-120. 4 rooms, 2 with PB. Breakfast included in rates. Types of meals: Country bkfst and early coffee/tea.

Certificate may be used: November-April, anytime, subject to availability.

Cedarburg

The Washington House Inn

W 62 N 573 Washington Ave
Cedarburg, WI 53012-1941
(262)375-3550 (800)554-4717 Fax:(262)375-9422
Internet: www.washingtonhouseinn.com
E-mail: info@washingtonhouseinn.com

Circa 1886. This three-story cream city brick building is in the National Register. Rooms are appointed in a country Victorian style and feature antiques, whirlpool baths and fireplaces. The original guest registry, more than 100 years old, is displayed proudly in the lobby, and a marble trimmed fireplace is often lit for the afternoon wine and cheese hour. Breakfast is continental and is available in the gathering room, often including recipes from a historic Cedarburg cookbook for items such as homemade muffins, cakes and breads.

Innkeeper(s): Wendy Porterfield. $145-275. 34 rooms with PB, 3 suites, 1 conference room. Breakfast included in rates. Types of meals: Cont plus and snacks/refreshments.

Certificate may be used: Sunday-Thursday only on rooms $172 and up, no holidays or festival dates.

Elkhorn

Ye Olde Manor House

N7622 US Hwy 12
Elkhorn, WI 53121
(262)742-2450 Fax:(262)742-2425
Internet: www.yeoldemanorhouse.com
E-mail: innkeeper@yeoldemanorhouse.com

Circa 1905. Located on three tree-shaded acres, this country manor house offers travelers all the simple comforts of home. The guest rooms, living room and dining room are decorated with a variety of antiques and comfortable furniture that inspires a family atmosphere. One room offers a porch and views of Lauderdale Lakes. The B&B offers a full gourmet breakfast each morning.

Innkeeper(s): Karen Fulbright-Anderson, John Anderson. $125-200. 8 rooms with PB, 1 two-bedroom suite, 1 conference room. Breakfast, snacks/refreshments, wine and High tea can be provided for an additional fee with prior notice included in rates. Types of meals: Full gourmet bkfst, veg bkfst, early coffee/tea and Afternoon tea is available for an additional charge. Vegan and gluten free meals are happily prepared upon request.

Certificate may be used: Monday-Thursday, anytime based on availability.

Ellison Bay

Bayview Resort and Harbor, Inc.

12037 Cedar Rd. P.O. Box 73
Ellison Bay, WI 54210
(920)854-2006
Internet: www.bayviewresortandharbor.com
E-mail: info@bayviewresortandharbor.com

Located in the heart of Ellison Bay featuring two fishing piers, a swim raft, private sand beach and much more. Twelve modern and spacious units offer water views and complete with all of the comforts of home for up to 8 people. An ideal setting for family vacations, reunions and romantic getaways.

Innkeeper(s): Kevin Roberts. $145-395. 8 cabins.

Certificate may be used: November, subject to availability. Must call and advise that you have the certificate when making reservation.

Green Bay

The Astor House B&B

637 S Monroe Ave
Green Bay, WI 54301-3614
(920)432-3585 (888)303-6370 Fax:(920)436-3145
Internet: www.astorhouse.com
E-mail: info@astorhouse.com

Circa 1888. Located in the Astor Historic District, the Astor House is completely surrounded by Victorian homes. Guests have their choice of five rooms, each uniquely decorated for a range of ambiance, from the Vienna Balconies to the Marseilles Garden to the Hong Kong Retreat. The parlor, veranda and many suites feature a grand view of City Centre's lighted church towers. This home is also the first and only

B&B in Green Bay and received the Mayor's Award for Remodeling and Restoration. Business travelers should take notice of the private phone lines in each room, as well as our wireless high-speed Internet access.

Innkeeper(s): Greg Robinson, Barbara Robinson. $120-159. 5 rooms with PB, 4 with FP, 3 suites. Breakfast included in rates. Types of meals: Cont plus.

Certificate may be used: Sunday-Thursday, subject to availability. Excludes special events like holidays and Packer Football Games. May be used only for rooms with whirlpool and fireplace.

Green Lake

McConnell Inn

497 S Lawson Dr
Green Lake, WI 54941-8700
(920)294-6430 (888)238-8625
Internet: www.mcconnellinn.com
E-mail: info@mcconnellinn.com

Circa 1901. This stately home features many of its original features, including leaded windows, woodwork, leather wainscoting and parquet floors. Each of the guest rooms includes beds covered with handmade quilts and clawfoot tubs. The grand, master suite comprises the entire third floor and boasts 14-foot

vaulted beam ceilings, Victorian walnut furnishings, a Jacuzzi and six-foot oak buffet now converted into a unique bathroom vanity. Innkeeper Mary Jo Johnson, a pastry chef, creates the wonderful pastries that accompany an expansive breakfast with fresh fruit, granola and delectable entrees.

Innkeeper(s): Mary Jo Johnson, Scott Johnson. $80-190. 5 rooms with PB, 2 with FP, 2 with WP, 1 suite. Breakfast included in rates. Types of meals: Full gourmet bkfst and early coffee/tea.

Certificate may be used: November-April, excluding holidays, subject to availability, Anytime, Last Minute-Based on Availability.

Hazel Green

Wisconsin House Stagecoach Inn

Main & Fairplay Streets
Hazel Green, WI 53811-0071
(608)854-2233 (877)854-2233
Internet: www.wisconsinhouse.com
E-mail: ken@wisconsinhouse.com

Circa 1846. Located in southwest Wisconsin's historic lead mining region, this one-time stagecoach stop will delight antique-lovers. The spacious two-story inn once hosted Ulysses S. Grant, whose home is just across the border in Illinois. One of the inn's guest rooms bears his name and features a walnut four-poster bed. Don't miss the chance to join the Dischs on a Saturday evening for their gourmet dinner, served by reservation only.

Innkeeper(s): Ken Disch, Pat Disch. $75-125. 8 rooms, 6 with PB, 2 two-bedroom suites. Breakfast included in rates. Types of meals: Full gourmet bkfst, early coffee/tea, snacks/refreshments and gourmet dinner.

Certificate may be used: Monday-Thursday, May-October anytime, rooms with shared baths only. Other months all rooms available.

Hazelhurst

Hazelhurst Inn

6941 Hwy 51
Hazelhurst, WI 54531
(715)356-6571
Internet: www.hazelhurstinn.com
E-mail: hzhrstbb@frontier.com

Circa 1969. Situated in the scenic Northwoods, this country inn graces 18 wooded acres that are adjacent to the Bearskin State Trail. Outdoor enthusiasts appreciate the hiking, swimming, fishing, golfing, hunting, snowmobiling, cross-country skiing, horseback riding, boating and the many other activities the area offers. Enjoy a hearty breakfast each morning after a peaceful night's rest in a comfortable guest bedroom. Families are welcome here. Soak up the view from the sitting room or just relax by the fire.

Innkeeper(s): Sharon Goetsch. $75-90. 4 rooms, 3 with PB. Breakfast included in rates. Types of meals: Country bkfst.

Certificate may be used: Anytime, subject to availability.

Hustler

Fountain Chateau Bed & Breakfast Inn

202 E. Main Street,
Hustler, WI 54637
(608)427-3787 (877)427-3719
Internet: www.fountainchateau.com
E-mail: innkeeper@fountainchateau.com

Circa 1922. Friendly service, wholesome food and delightful accommodations are available year round amid scenic tranquility. The peaceful setting includes a deck, book library, fitness room and a piano. Historic Fountain Chateau Bed & Breakfast in Hustler, Wisconsin is near popular bike trails and the water sports at Castle Rock Lake. Wisconsin Dells is a 30-minute drive. Stay in a themed guest room with robes, slippers and other pleasing amenities. Some of the rooms boast baths with pedestal sinks and walk-in showers. This B&B is handicap and wheelchair accessible. A hearty breakfast buffet menu served in the Harmony Bistro Restaurant satisfies every palate. Ask about specials and packages offered.

Innkeeper(s): Susanne Soltvedt. $100-159. 8 rooms with PB, 1 two-bedroom suite, 1 conference room. Breakfast and afternoon tea included in rates. Types of meals: Full gourmet bkfst, veg bkfst, Sun. brunch, early coffee/tea, room service, Jazz Sunday Brunch every 1st and 3rd Sunday in each month. Contact Innkeeper for details. The Harmony Bistro Restaurant is on site. Guests are offered a 4oz. glass of wine, snack and refreshments provided upon request for a small fee. Meals are provided for group meetings and also list of other Fine Dining Reataurants in the area.
Certificate may be used: Sept. 10-May 30, Sunday-Thursday.

Lodi

Victorian Dreams Bed and Breakfast

115 Prairie Street
Lodi, WI 53555
(608)592-0362
Internet: www.victoriandreamsbnb.com
E-mail: innkeeper@victoriandreamsbnb.com

Circa 1897. Two adjacent Victorian homes charm guests with a carved grand staircase, stained glass windows, antique ash wood and oak fireplaces, and original light fixtures. Seven opulent guest rooms have queen beds and private bathrooms. Step into the cozy alcove in Abigail's Oasis for a relaxing soak in a whirlpool tub for two. Spread out in the two-room Josephine's Jewel with a table and wingback chairs that are perfect for those that wish to have breakfast delivered to the room. Candles add a warm ambiance to the full breakfast served in the dining room each morning. Chat with other guests at the evening reception or take a glass of wine to the wrap-around porch to enjoy the sounds of the night. Truly relax on your getaway with a couples massage in your room. Visit nearby antique and specialty shops or stroll through 16 acres of beauty at the Olbrich Botanical Gardens.

Innkeeper(s): John Stevens, Cindy Stevens. $109-229. 7 rooms, 4 with FP, 6 with WP, 7 suites. Breakfast, wine and Wine and Cheese included in rates. Types of meals: Full bkfst, veg bkfst, early coffee/tea and room service.
Certificate may be used: November- January, excluding holidays, subject to availability. Not valid in Ella's Veranda Suite.

Madison

Arbor House, An Environmental Inn

3402 Monroe St
Madison, WI 53711-1702
(608)238-2981
Internet: www.arbor-house.com
E-mail: arborhouse@tds.net

Circa 1853. Nature-lovers not only will enjoy the inn's close access to a 1,280-acre nature preserve, they will appreciate the innkeepers' ecological theme. Organic sheets and towels are offered for guests as well as environmentally safe bath products. Arbor House is one of Madison's oldest existing homes and features plenty of historic features, such as romantic reading chairs and antiques, mixed with modern amenities and unique touches. Five guest rooms include a whirlpool tub and three have fireplaces. The Annex guest rooms include private balconies. The innkeepers offer many amenities for business travelers, including value-added corporate rates. The award-winning inn has been recognized as a model of urban ecology. Lake Wingra is within walking distance as are biking and nature trails, bird watching and a host of other outdoor activities. Guests enjoy complimentary canoeing and use of mountain bikes.

Innkeeper(s): John Imes, Cathie Imes. $150-230. 8 rooms with PB, 3 with FP, 1 suite, 1 conference room. Breakfast included in rates. Types of meals: Full bkfst.
Certificate may be used: November-April, Sunday-Thursday, excluding holidays (John Nolen and Cozy Rose guest rooms only).

Speckled Hen Inn Bed & Brkfst

5525 Portage Rd
Madison, WI 53704-2756
(608) 244-9368 (877) 670-4844 Fax:(608)244-1666
Internet: www.speckledheninn.com
E-mail: innkeeper@speckledheninn.com

Circa 1989. Fifty acres of woodlands, meadows and marshes are surrounded by 2,000 more acres of green space at this Dane County bed and breakfast. The Speckled Hen Inn B&B offers easygoing elegance and country charm in Madison, Wisconsin. Gather in one of the two large lounge areas, or watch a movie in the home theater with a complimentary beverage. Read in the enclosed gazebo, on a porch or balcony. Guest bedrooms and suites are spacious, romantic retreats, some with a fireplace. Several feature whirlpool tubs and one room boasts a clawfoot tub. Linger in the sunny breakfast room or candlelit dining room over a multi-course breakfast made with Wisconsin cheese, produce and locally roasted coffee beans.

Innkeeper(s): Patricia Fischbeck, Robert Fischbeck. $150-240. 5 rooms with PB, 4 with FP, 4 with WP. Breakfast and snacks/refreshments included in rates. Types of meals: Full gourmet bkfst, early coffee/tea and wine.
Certificate may be used: Nov. 1-April 30, Sunday-Thursday only. Holidays excluded. Subject to availability.

Milwaukee

Schuster Mansion Bed & Breakfast

3209 W. Wells Street
Milwaukee, WI 53208
(414)342-3210 Fax:(414)344-3405
Internet: www.schustermansion.com
E-mail: welcome@schustermansion.com

Circa 1891. Schuster Mansion Bed and Breakfast, built on the elite West side of Milwaukee, Wisconsin is a multi-level mansion with Victorian and Edwardian antique furnishings and dÃ©cor. This historic mansion with red sandstone, red brick and ornamental red terra cotta trim was designed with Richardson Romanesque architecture and Queen Anne, Flemish, Gothic, Shingle and Colonial influences. Gather for conversation or a quiet read in one of the parlors. Stay in a guest room or suite that features a themed decor. After breakfast, visit the art museum, Boerner Botanical Gardens, the Schlitz Audubon Nature Center and other nearby attractions. Weddings and special events are popular at this romantic and opulent setting.

Innkeeper(s): Rick Mosier, Laura Sue Mosier. $110-189. 6 rooms, 4 with PB, 1 with WP, 1 two-bedroom and 3 three-bedroom suites. Breakfast and snacks/refreshments included in rates. Types of meals: Full gourmet bkfst, veg bkfst and room service.

Certificate may be used: Oct. 15-March 15 excluding Nov. 24-25, Dec. 23-25, Dec. 31-Jan. 1, Feb. 13-14.

Osceola

St. Croix River Inn

305 River St, PO Box 356
Osceola, WI 54020-0356
(715) 294-4248 (800) 645-8820
Internet: www.stcroixriverinn.com
E-mail: innkeeper@stcroixriverinn.com

Circa 1908. Timeless elegance is imparted at this meticulously restored stone house that blends old world charm with new world luxuries. Indulge in dramatic vistas from this gorgeous

setting on the bluffs of the river. A comfortable ambiance embraces this inn where complimentary coffee is always found in the sitting room. There is also a wine and beverage bar. Select a book or game from the entertainment closet. Videos and CDs are also available for use in the private suites that all feature a fireplace and a hydromassage tub. A sumptuous breakfast served to each room is highlighted with spectacular views of the water.

Innkeeper(s): Ben Bruno. $135-250. 7 rooms, 7 with PB, 7 with FP, 7 with WP, 7 suites. Breakfast and snacks/refreshments included in rates. Types of meals: Full gourmet bkfst, veg bkfst, early coffee/tea, picnic lunch, hors d'oeuvres, wine and gourmet dinner.

Certificate may be used: Nov. 30 to April 30, Sunday-Thursday, excluding holidays.

Reedsburg

Parkview B&B

211 N Park St
Reedsburg, WI 53959-1652
(608)524-4333 Fax:(608)524-1172
Internet: www.parkviewbb.com
E-mail: info@parkviewbb.com

Circa 1895. Tantalizingly close to Baraboo and Spring Green, this central Wisconsin inn overlooks a city park in the historic district. The gracious innkeepers delight in tending to their

guests' desires and offer wake-up coffee and a morning paper. The home's first owners were in the hardware business, so there are many original, unique fixtures, in addition to hardwood floors, intricate woodwork, leaded and etched windows and a suitors' window. The downtown business district is just a block away.

Innkeeper(s): Tom Hofmann, Donna Hofmann. $89-115. 4 rooms, 2 with PB, 1 with FP. Breakfast and snacks/refreshments included in rates. Types of meals: Full gourmet bkfst, veg bkfst and early coffee/tea.

Certificate may be used: Sunday-Thursday, May 1-Oct. 31, holidays not included, anytime remainder of year.

Sheboygan Falls

The Rochester Inn

504 Water Street
Sheboygan Falls, WI 53085-1455
(920)467-3123 (866)467-3122
Internet: www.rochesterinn.com
E-mail: info@rochesterinn.com

Circa 1848. This Greek Revival inn is furnished with Queen Anne Victorian antiques, wet bars and four-poster beds. The most romantic offerings are the 600-square-foot suites. They include living rooms with camel back couches and wing back chairs on the first floor and bedrooms with double whirlpool tubs on the second floor. Sheboygan Falls is one mile from the village of Kohler.

Innkeeper(s): Jacci O'Dwanny. $99-174. 6 rooms with PB, 5 with HT, 5 with WP, 5 two-bedroom suites. Breakfast included in rates. Types of meals: Full gourmet bkfst, veg bkfst, early coffee/tea, afternoon tea and snacks/refreshments.

Certificate may be used: November-April, based on regular rates, excluding holidays. Subject to Availability.

Sparta

Justin Trails Resort

7452 Kathryn Ave
Sparta, WI 54656-9729
(608) 269-4522 (800) 488-4521
Internet: www.justintrails.com
E-mail: donna@justintrails.com

Circa 1920. Guests frequently mention how calm and peaceful the energy is at Justin Trails Resort. Log cabins, a cottage and suites in a 1920 Foursquare greet you with fireplace, large whirlpool bathtub, porch, balcony or patio for relaxing outdoors. Each is furnished with a refrigerator, coffee maker, microwave, DVD player. Several have 250 channel satellite hookup on the television. Set off on a stroll/walk or hike on the 200 acres with groomed trails on organic land that has not been treated with pesticides since 2008. Three ponds, a rock outcropping, 2 disc golf courses, 53 species of birds to watch and 10 miles of trails can entertain you for days. Summer or winter there is plenty of privacy in the hills and valleys of this outdoor paradise. A full country breakfast is served in The Lodge or delivered and served to your cabin or suite. The menu includes Justin Trails handcrafted granola, plain yogurt sweetened with maple syrup, fresh fruit or fruit compote, Justin Trails muffins or scones, choice of orange, apple or cranberry juice, choice of hot beverage and your choice of an entree of scrambled organic eggs, pancakes or French toast.

Innkeeper(s): Don Justin, Donna Justin. $115-350. 6 rooms, 3 suites, 1 cottage, 2 cabins, 1 conference room. Breakfast included in rates. Types of meals: Full bkfst and veg bkfst.

Certificate may be used: Year round, Monday-Thursday, except holidays.

Sturgeon Bay

Garden Gate Bed & Breakfast

434 N 3rd Ave
Sturgeon Bay, WI 54235
(920) 217-3093 (877) 743-9618
Internet: doorcountybb.com
E-mail: stay@doorcountybb.com

Circa 1890. Sturgeon Bay's Garden Gate Bed & Breakfast exudes a romantic Victorian elegance. The historic inn's oak-paneled foyer features a stairwell with hand-turned spindles. An antique oak fireplace mantle with Doric columns and a beveled oval mirror is a focal point. Gracious verandas beckon relaxation. Guest rooms offer quilt-covered beds and entertainment centers. Nine-panel pocket doors accent the dining room where a delightful daily breakfast is served with soft music by candlelight. Early risers can enjoy coffee and tea first. Ask about specials available. Located in Sturgeon Bay, Wisconsin in Door County, this area is home to a wide variety of outdoor activities and amusements.

Innkeeper(s): Robin Vallow. $115-155. 4 rooms with PB, 4 with FP, 1 with WP. Breakfast included in rates. Types of meals: Full gourmet bkfst, early coffee/tea and snacks/refreshments.

Certificate may be used: Monday-Thursday only.

The Reynolds House B&B

111 S. 7th Ave
Sturgeon Bay, WI 54235
(920)746-9771 (877)269-7401 Fax:(920)746-9441
Internet: www.reynoldshousebandb.com
E-mail: hahull@reynoldshousebandb.com

Circa 1900. A three-story, red-roofed Queen Anne Victorian house, the Reynolds House Bed and Breakfast is painted in two shades of teal and yellow with white trim on its balustrades and brackets. Leaded-glass windows and a stone veranda that wraps around the front of the house are features. Rooms are cheerfully decorated and

offer antique beds, attractive bed coverings and wallpapers. Tucked under the gable, the Winesap Suite includes a whirlpool, sitting room and fireplace. The innkeeper's kitchen garden furnishes fresh herbs to accent breakfast dishes, as well as flowers for the table.

Innkeeper(s): Heather Hull. $80-200. 4 rooms, 5 with PB, 3 with FP, 2 with WP, 1 suite. Breakfast and snacks/refreshments included in rates. Types of meals: Full gourmet bkfst and early coffee/tea.

Certificate may be used: November-April, subject to availability.

White Lace Inn

16 N 5th Ave
Sturgeon Bay, WI 54235-1795
(920) 743-1105 (877) 948-5223
Internet: www.WhiteLaceInn.com
E-mail: Romance@WhiteLaceInn.com

Circa 1903. The romantic White Lace Inn is composed of four beautifully restored Victorian houses connected by meandering garden paths. This Sturgeon Bay bed and breakfast has inviting rooms and suites with fine antiques and ornate Victorian or canopy beds. Suites include oversized whirlpool baths, fireplaces, white linens, down comforters and many other amenities. Often the site for romantic anniversary celebrations, a favorite suite has a two-sided fireplace, magnificent walnut Eastlake bed, English country fabrics and a whirlpool. Lemonade or hot chocolate and cookies are offered upon arrival. In the morning, the delectable offerings include items such as cherry apple crisp and creamy rice pudding. Year-round activities invite frequent visits - the Festival of Blossoms, the Lighthouse Walk, Cherry Festival and the Classic Wooden Boat event, for instance. Take museum and gallery strolls, and enjoy the area's great restaurants.

Innkeeper(s): Dennis Statz, Bonnie Statz. $70-235. 18 rooms with PB, 15 with FP, 12 with WP, 5 suites, 4 guest houses. Breakfast and snacks/refreshments included in rates. Types of meals: Full bkfst, early coffee/tea and Special dietary needs can be accommodated with advance notice.

Certificate may be used: Sunday-Thursday, November-April excluding holidays and some other restrictions, at "high season" rate.

Viroqua

Viroqua Heritage Inn B&B's

217 & 220 E Jefferson St
Viroqua, WI 54665
(608)637-3306 (888)443-7466
Internet: www.herinn.com
E-mail: info@herinn.com

Circa 1890. It is easy to relax at this handsome 1897 three-story English Tudor Revival inn with gables and leaded windows in Viroqua, Wisconsin. Find a quiet hideaway on the sunporch, or wander in the garden by the pond. The trellis bench is an inviting spot for meditation. A favorite accommodation is the two-room suite with its own enclosed porch and pocket doors. Ask for a guest bedroom with a whirlpool tub or fireplace. The inn sometimes features murder mystery weekends. A full breakfast is served on weekends, and an expanded continental breakfast is offered during the week.

Innkeeper(s): Nancy Rhodes. $85-135. 8 rooms, 6 with PB, 2 with FP, 1 with WP. Breakfast included in rates. Types of meals: Full bkfst, early coffee/tea and All organic breakfast.

Certificate may be used: Anytime, November-April, subject to availability.

Wales

Pedal'rs Inn Bed and Breakfast

101 James Street
Wales, WI 53183
(262)968-4700
Internet: www.pedalrsinn.com
E-mail: info@pedalrsinn.com

Circa 1895. Just as the name suggests, cycle enthusiasts will enjoy the setting and thoughtful amenities of Pedal'rs Inn Bed and Breakfast in Wales, Wisconsin. Trail passes are for sale from the Concierge service, covered bike storage is provided and a two-way 10-mile radio is available to use. For those who prefer to relax without wheels, lawn and board games offer fun entertainment, or sit on the veranda. Explore the Archive Room for artifacts from the house and gather in one of the two parlors for conversation. Most of the guest bedrooms feature a fireplace and either a whirlpool jetted or soaker tub. On weekdays an American-style full breakfast is served. On weekends savor a four-course gourmet breakfast in the formal dining room.

Innkeeper(s): Dee Nierzwicki. $95-145. 4 rooms with PB, 3 with FP, 2 with WP. Breakfast included in rates. Types of meals: Full gourmet bkfst, veg bkfst, early coffee/tea, picnic lunch and wine.

Certificate may be used: January-March, Sunday-Thursday, excluding holidays.

Waupaca

Cleghorn Bed & Breakfast

N2080 Cleghorn Rd
Waupaca, WI 54981
(715)258-5235 (800)870-0737 Fax:(715)258-5235
Internet: www.cleghornbnb.com
E-mail: lyerkes@charter.net

Circa 1985. Three acres surround this country house with a log facade. The inn boasts interiors of barn-board walls and  Amish furnishings and quilts. For instance, there are some hand-crafted bedsteads including a four-poster. A large stone fireplace in the living room and woodland views from the dining room enhance the country setting. Dutch pancakes with apple topping and maple butter is a favorite breakfast item. Nearby are antique shops, art galleries, streams for canoeing and back roads for cycling.

Innkeeper(s): Bob Yerkes, Linda Yerkes. $89-125. 3 rooms with PB, 2 with FP. Breakfast included in rates. Types of meals: Full bkfst and early coffee/tea.

Certificate may be used: Sept. 1 to June 15, Sunday-Thursday and Nov. 1 to May 1, subject to availability, last minute based on projected availability.

Crystal River Inn B&B

E1369 Rural Rd
Waupaca, WI 54981-8246
(715)258-5333 (800)236-5789 Fax:(715)258-5310
Internet: www.crystalriver-inn.com
E-mail: cri@crystalriverbb.com

Circa 1853. The stately beauty of this historic Greek Revival farmhouse is rivaled only by its riverside setting. Each room features a view of the water, garden, woods or all three. A Victorian gazebo, down comforters and delicious breakfasts, with pecan sticky buns, a special favorite, add to guests' enjoyment. A recent addition to the inn's offerings include a newly restored historic cottage. With luxurious decor it includes two bedrooms, a living room with fireplace and private porches. It may be reserved singly or together. Exploring the village of Rural, which is in the National Register, will delight those interested in bygone days. Recreational activities abound, with the Chain O'Lakes and a state park nearby.

Innkeeper(s): Deb Benada, Robert Benada. $69-149. 7 rooms, 5 with PB, 4 with FP, 2 cottages, 1 conference room. Breakfast and snacks/refreshments included in rates. Types of meals: Full bkfst and early coffee/tea.

Certificate may be used: mid-September to mid-May, subject to availability, not valid for Little House on the Prairie.

Whitewater

Victoria-On-Main B&B

622 W Main St
Whitewater, WI 53190-1855
(262)473-8400
Internet: victoriaonmainbb.com
E-mail: viconmain@sbcglobal.net

Circa 1895. This graceful Queen Anne Victorian, shaded by a tall birch tree, is in the heart of Whitewater National Historic District, adjacent to the University of Wisconsin. It was built for Edward Engebretson, mayor of Whitewater. Yellow tulip and sunny daffodils fill the spring flower beds,  while fuchsias and geraniums bloom in summertime behind a picket fence. The inn's gables, flower-filled veranda and three-story turret feature a handsome green tin roof. Each guest room is named for a Wisconsin hardwood. The Red Oak Room, Cherry Room and Bird's Eye Maple Room all offer handsome antiques in their corresponding wood, Laura Ashley prints, antique sheets, pristine heirloom-laced pillowcases and down comforters. A hearty breakfast is sometimes served on the wraparound veranda, and there are kitchen facilities available for light meal preparation. Whitewater Lake and Kettle Moraine State Forest are five minutes away.

Innkeeper(s): Nancy Wendt. $85-95. 3 rooms, 1 with PB, 1 with FP. Breakfast included in rates. Types of meals: Full bkfst and early coffee/tea.

Certificate may be used: June-September and January, Sunday-Thursday.

Wisconsin Dells

Bowman's Oak Hill Bed and Breakfast

4169 State Hwy 13
Wisconsin Dells, WI 53965
(608)253-5638 (888)253-5631
Internet: bowmansoakhillbedandbreakfast.com
E-mail: bowmansoakhillbb@aol.com

Circa 1969. Thirteen acres of country peacefulness surround this estate with lawns, gardens, fields and a cottage ranch home built in the 1960s. This smoke-free, adult retreat is "where comfort comes with your key." Relaxation is easy on the front porch wicker furniture or three-season sun porch. Sit in wing-backed chairs and watch a movie from the video library in the living room. Afternoon and evening snacks and refreshments are offered. Air-conditioned guest bedrooms boast family heirloom furniture, sitting areas and cozy robes. Fresh fruit smoothies are a house specialty for breakfast that includes a hot egg dish and warm baked goods or pancakes. An outdoor covered swing and sitting areas provide romantic settings. Walk in the woods, play croquet or a game of horseshoes.

Innkeeper(s): David Bowman, Nancy Bowman. $100-185. 6 rooms with PB, 4 with FP, 3 with WP, 3 cottages. Breakfast and snacks/refreshments included in rates. Types of meals: Full gourmet bkfst, veg bkfst and early coffee/tea.

Certificate may be used: November-May excluding all holidays, Sunday-Thursday, subject to availability, Anytime, Last Minute-Based on Availability.

Wyoming

Cody

Mayor's Inn Bed & Breakfast

1413 Rumsey Ave
Cody, WY 82414
(307) 587-0887
Internet: www.mayorsinn.com
E-mail: reserve@MayorsInn.com

Circa 1909. Considered the town's first mansion, this stylish two-story, turn-of-the-century home was built for Cody's first elected mayor. A romantic Victorian ambiance is achieved with warm hospitality, antiques, soft lighting, chandeliers and splendid wall and ceiling papers. The parlor inspires nostalgia. The guest bedrooms feature either a brass bed and clawfoot tub, a lodge pole pine bed, jetted tub and western art, or an open, sunny room with double shower. The suite boasts a fresh water hot tub and CD player. Offering private seating, breakfast is served in both of the dining rooms. The Carriage House is a cottage with a fully equipped kitchen.

Innkeeper(s): DaleLee Delph. $90-215. 5 rooms, 4 with PB, 1 with HT, 1 with WP, 1 cottage. Breakfast included in rates. Types of meals: Full bkfst and early coffee/tea.

Certificate may be used: November-April, subject to availability.

Robin's Nest Bed & Breakfast

1508 Alger Ave
Cody, WY 82414
(307) 527-7208 (866) 723-7797
Internet: robinsnestcody.com/
E-mail: RBerry@RobinsNestCody.com

Circa 1930. Gracing a quiet neighborhood in historic Cody, Wyoming, about one hour from 2 of the 5 Yellowstone National Park entrances, non-smoking accommodations are within walking distance to the many local attractions from museums at the Buffalo Bill Historical Center to rodeos, gun fights, horseback riding, outdoor concerts, swimming golf and more. Relax on the back porch or deck, nap in the hammock or play the piano in the library. Many items on display are available for purchase including artwork, vintage photography and hand-woven Indian basketry. Stay in an upstairs guest room with a large soaking tub or a spacious suite. Indulge in a sumptuous breakfast each morning that may include the signature favorite, Bob's Upside Down Cream Cheese Stuffed Praline Toast. There is an assortment of special packages offered and pets are accepted with advance approval.

Innkeeper(s): Robin Berry. $89-155. 4 rooms with PB. Breakfast included in rates. Types of meals: Full bkfst.

Certificate may be used: November-March, subject to availability.

Newcastle

EVA-Great Spirit Ranch B&B

1262 Beaver Creek Rd
Newcastle, WY 82701
(307)746-2537
Internet: www.eva-ranch.webs.com
E-mail: ispillane@hotmail.com

Circa 1984. Amidst spectacular scenery of mountains and woods, guests will find this modern log home. Although the home is new, it rests on what was an old stagecoach route. A century-old barn is located on the property, as well as ruins of a 19th-century bunkhouse. The interior features hardwood floors and high ceilings, and the guest rooms are comfortably furnished in a modern style. There are two rooms with private baths and two adjoining rooms with a shared bath. Irene offers spring and fall hunting packages, where guests can search for deer, elk and wild turkey on the 525-acre property and adjacent Bureau of Land Management and state lands. The vast acreage borders Black Hills National Forest in South Dakota.

Innkeeper(s): Irene Ward. $65-90. 4 rooms, 2 with PB. Breakfast included in rates. Types of meals: Full bkfst.

Certificate may be used: Sept. 15-May 15, Sunday-Saturday. Bed & breakfast stay only. Hunting packages and Romantic Getaways excluded.

Canada

British Columbia

Duncan

Jacquie Gordon's Bed and Breakfast
2231 Quamichan Park Place
Duncan, BC V9L 5E9
(250)746-7736
Internet: www.jacquiegordon.com
E-mail: jacquiegordon@shaw.ca

Mature gardens surround this heritage home on a quiet cul-de-sac in the Cowichan Valley. Guests are welcomed by the scent of forget-me-nots, cherries, and rhododendrons. A floor-to-ceiling stone fireplace centers the social room. A large window brings the sun into the breakfast room. Choose a hearty hot breakfast or light continental fare each morning. Four people can comfortably sleep in the second floor Vista Room with a queen bed and two twin beds. A quiet getaway for two can be found in the first floor Heritage Room with authentic carved furniture from the 1920s. Listen for the sound of birds as you relax on the patio. The inn is a short drive from the shops in downtown Duncan and the working marinas and quaint village of Cowichan Bay. A dozen wineries dot the countryside for your tasting pleasure. Celebrate nature with a hike through the BC Forest Discovery Centre, a 100-acre open air museum.
Innkeeper(s): Jacquie Gordon. $105-135. 2 rooms with PB.
Certificate may be used: Sunday-Thursday.

Whistler

Golden Dreams B&B
6412 Easy St
Whistler, BC V0N 1B6
(604) 932-2667 (800) 668-7055
Internet: www.goldendreamswhistler.com
E-mail: ann@goldendreamswhistler.com

Circa 1986. Experience the many secrets of great B&B stays at this established inn. Surrounded by mountain views and the beauty of nature, this West Coast home features a private guest living room with wood fireplace where the innkeepers share their knowledge of the locale. Thick Terry robes, duvets and sherry decanters are provided in the guest bed rooms, which have Black bear, Wild West and Rainforest themes. After a wholesome breakfast, valley trail and bus stop are just outside. Whistler village and skiing are only one mile away. Relax in the hot tub and enjoy house wine and snacks. A large BBQ sundeck and guest kitchen are convenient amenities. Town Plaza village condos are also available for families. Discount skiing, sight-seeing passes and airport transport booking services are available.

Innkeeper(s): Ann and Terry Spence. $95-175. 3 suites, 1 guest house. Breakfast, afternoon tea and snacks/refreshments included in rates. Types of meals: Full gourmet bkfst, veg bkfst and early coffee/tea.
Certificate may be used: Sunday-Thursday, April 1-Dec. 15, Must be pre-approved. Anytime, Last Minute-Based on Availability.

Victoria

Prancing Horse Retreat
573 Ebadora Lane
Victoria, BC V0R 2L0
(250)743-9378 (877)887-8834
Internet: www.prancinghorse.com
E-mail: stay@prancinghorse.com

Circa 1998. Breathtaking scenery and a spectacular setting surround this premier mountain-top retreat with fantastic views of the Olympic Mountains. This red-roofed Victorian villa boasts a turret with stained-glass windows and luxury accommodations. Indulge in a deluxe suite that features fresh flowers, Aveda bath products and Bernard Callebaut Chocolate. Luxury suites also include double soaker tubs, fireplaces and private decks. Savor a gourmet breakfast that is accented by just-squeezed orange juice and champagne in the dining room or on the spacious patio overlooking the valley. Colorful gardens with terraced rocks lead to a multi-tiered deck with a gazebo and hot tub.
$100-210. 7 total suites, including 1 two-bedroom suite. Breakfast included in rates. Types of meals: Full gourmet bkfst and early coffee/tea.
Certificate may be used: Anytime, November-March, subject to availability.

New Brunswick

Sackville

Marshlands Inn
55 bridge Street
Sackville, NB E4L 3N8
(506)536-0170 (180)056-11266
Internet: www.marshlands.nb.ca
E-mail: info@marshlands.nb.ca

Circa 1854. One of Canada's most popular country inns, this 1854 pre-confederation home is surrounded by eight acres of marshland, lawns and gardens. Open year-round, it is rich in history, and has hosted many social, political and royal dignitaries. The inn consists of the main house and the carriage house. Relax with refreshments on one of the two large verandas. In the evening gather for hot chocolate and ginger snaps by the fire in one of the parlors accented by original artwork and easy chairs. Inviting guest bedrooms and a suite are furnished with antiques and boast clawfoot tubs. Enjoy fine dining in the upscale restaurant and shop for Canadian glass in the Blue Willow Antiques onsite store.

Innkeeper(s): Lucy Dane, Barry Dane. $89-129. Call inn for details.

Certificate may be used: Sunday-Thursday, November-March, subject to availability. May-October at innkeepers discretion.

Ontario

Kingston

Hotel Belvedere

141 King St E
Kingston, ON K7L 2Z9
(613)548-1565 (800)559-0584 Fax:(613)546-4692
Internet: www.hotelbelvedere.com
E-mail: reserve@hotelbelvedere.com

Circa 1880. Hotel Belvedere began its life as a private mansion, built in the Georgian style of architecture. Eventually, it was transformed into a hotel and then into a boarding house. Thankfully, it has been restored and refurbished back to its original state. The interior boasts the fine woodwork, carved mantels and marble floors one expects in a grand mansion. Elegant guest rooms are decorated in period style with antiques, and beds are dressed with fine white linens. In warm weather, the innkeepers serve a continental breakfast on the private terrace. Guests can enjoy the morning fare in their room or in front of a warm fire in the living room. Secluded three hours from Toronto along the shores of Lake Ontario, Kingston is a charming site for a getaway. Historic homes, museums and dinner cruises are among the offerings in town. The town once served as the capital of Canada.

Innkeeper(s): Donna Mallory, Ian Walsh. $119-259. 20 rooms with PB, 2 suites, 1 conference room. Breakfast included in rates. Types of meals: Cont plus and early coffee/tea.

Certificate may be used: Nov. 1-March 31 on Friday, Saturday, Sunday.

Ottawa

Auberge McGee's Inn

185 Daly Ave
Ottawa, ON K1N 6E8
(613)237-6089 (800)262-4337 Fax:(613)237-6201
Internet: www.mcgeesinn.com
E-mail: contact@mcgeesinn.com

Circa 1886. Gracing historic Sandy Hill, this restored Victorian mansion offers luxurious and peaceful getaways. It was built for John McGee, Canada's Fourth Clerk of the Privy Council. The portico is reminiscent of his Irish roots featuring pillars that were common in Dublin architecture. Well-appointed guest bedrooms and suites are comfortable and include generous amenities as well as modern conveniences. Some boast fireplaces and Jacuzzis. Sitting in the heart of the city, walk to nearby Byward Market and Parliament Hill. Visit the many museums or the popular Rideau Center.

Innkeeper(s): Jason Armstrong, Judy Armstrong, Sarah Armstrong, Ken Armstrong. $90-198. 14 rooms with PB, 3 with FP, 3 with WP, 3 suites. A full breakfast including apple juice, orange juice, yogurt, fruit salad, muffins,

croissants and various cereals and Eggs Benedict or Omelet; different fruit crepes each day and on occasion French Toast included in rates. Types of meals: Full bkfst, veg bkfst, early coffee/tea and afternoon tea.

Certificate may be used: January, March and April, subject to availability.

Quebec

Montreal

Auberge Le Pomerol

819 de Maisonneuve East.
Montreal, QC H2L 1Y7
(514)526-5511 (800)361-6896 Fax:(514)523-0143
Internet: www.aubergelepomerol.com
E-mail: info@aubergelepomerol.com

Circa 1913. In the heart of the city, this century-old house exudes warmth and finesse. The ultra-contemporary decor enhances the calm ambiance. Sit by the fireplace and relax in the cozy lounge area, or at the end of the day enjoy a complimentary snack in a corner of the kitchen. The inn's 27 guest bedrooms offer urban comfort and style with an abundance of pleasing amenities including high speed Internet access, a flatscreen TV with cable and many have a whirlpool bath, a fridge, a little lounge or a working space. Linger over a healthy breakfast that is delivered right to your door. There's a meeting room perfect for business needs. Ask about the Romance Package that includes a luxury room with whirlpool bath and sparkling wine, or add a touch of gourmet dining with a six-course dinner at the Les Temps Nouveaux restaurant. A concierge is always available. There's a parking lot and transportation is easily accessible. Many local events and festivals offer lively entertainment.

Innkeeper(s): Daniel Racine. $105-185. 27 rooms with PB, 27 with HT, 9 with WP, 1 conference room. Breakfast, afternoon tea, snacks/refreshments and Continental breakfast delivered to the room included in rates. Types of meals: Cont and early coffee/tea. Restaurant on premises.

Certificate may be used: Nov. 22-Dec. 22, Jan. 2-Jan. 31, not valid Friday and Saturday.

Inns of Interest

African-American History

Deacon Timothy Pratt Bed & Breakfast Inn C.1746
. . . . Old Saybrook, Conn.
The Historic Peninsula Inn & Spa
. . . . Gulfport, Fla.
Washington Plantation . . . . Washington, Ga.
1851 Historic Maple Hill Manor B&B
. . . . Springfield, Ky.
The Alexander House Booklovers B&B
. . . . Princess Anne, Md.
Munro House B&B and Spa . . . . Jonesville, Mich.
Oakland Cottage B&B . . . . Asheville, N.C.
10 Fitch . . . . Auburn, N.Y.
Arbor View House B&B . . . . East Marion, N.Y.
Rider's 1812 Inn . . . . Painesville, Ohio
The Signal House . . . . Ripley, Ohio
Kilpatrick Manor Bed & Breakfast
. . . . Niagara Falls,
Post House Country Inn / Burke House Inn
. . . . Niagara On The Lake,
The Fairfield Inn 1757. . . . . Fairfield, Pa.
The Great Valley House of Valley Forge
. . . . Valley Forge, Pa.
Rockland Farm Retreat . . . . Bumpass, Va.
Firmstone Manor . . . . Clifton Forge, Va.
Mayhurst Inn . . . . Orange, Va.
Lilac Inn . . . . Brandon, Vt.
Elkhorn Inn & Theatre . . . . Landgraff, W.Va.

Animals

Pearson's Pond Luxury Inn & Adventure Spa
. . . . Juneau, Alaska
Abineau Lodge Bed and Breakfast
. . . . Flagstaff, Ariz.
Casa De San Pedro . . . . Hereford, Ariz.
Lodge at Sedona-A Luxury Bed and Breakfast Inn
. . . . Sedona, Ariz.
Grand Living Bed and Breakfast
. . . . Williams, Ariz.
Hotel Charlotte . . . . Groveland, Calif.
The Inn at Schoolhouse Creek
. . . . Mendocino, Calif.
Black Forest B&B Lodge & Cabins
. . . . Colorado Springs, Colo.
Romantic RiverSong Inn . . . . Estes Park, Colo.
Sundance Trail Guest Ranch
. . . . Red Feather Lakes, Colo.
A Meadow House . . . . Lakeville, Conn.
Cedar Mountain Farm . . . . Athol, Idaho
Greyhouse Inn B&B . . . . Salmon, Idaho
Scottish Bed and Breakfast
. . . . Bremen, Ind.
First Farm Inn . . . . Petersburg, Ky.
1851 Historic Maple Hill Manor B&B
. . . . Springfield, Ky.
Country Ridge B&B . . . . Opelousas, La.
The Inn at Restful Paws . . . . Holland, Mass.
Inn on The Horse Farm . . . . Sudbury, Mass.
Gramercy Mansion . . . . Stevenson, Md.

Greenville Inn at Moosehead Lake
. . . . Greenville, Maine
Maple Hill Farm B&B Inn . . . . . . Hallowell, Maine
Silent Sport Lodge . . . . Wolverine, Mich.
Hawkesdene House B&B Inn and Cottages
. . . . Andrews, N.C.
Chimney Hill Estate Inn . . . . Lambertville, N.J.
HideAway Country Inn . . . . Bucyrus, Ohio
Orchard House. . . . . Granville, Ohio
Stone Crest Cellar B&B . . . . South Beach, Ore.
Pennsbury Inn . . . . Chadds Ford, Pa.
The Inn at Barley Sheaf Farm
. . . . Holicong, Pa.
Berry Patch B&B . . . . Lebanon, Pa.
Willowgreen Farm B&B . . . . Summerside,
The Shaw House B&B . . . . Georgetown, S.C.
BlissWood Bed and Breakfast Ranch
. . . . Cat Spring, Texas
MD Resort Bed & Breakfast . . . . Fort Worth, Texas
Indian Ridge Bed and Breakfast
. . . . Mission, Texas
Katy House Bed & Breakfast
. . . . Smithville, Texas
Southwind . . . . Wimberley, Texas
Woodland Farmhouse Inn . . . . . . Kamas, Utah
Bridgewater Inn and Cottage
. . . . Bridgewater, Va.
The Cottage at Ravens Roost Farm
. . . . Luray, Va.
The Garden and The Sea Inn
. . . . New Church, Va.
Golden Stage Inn . . . . Proctorsville, Vt.
Inn at Clearwater Pond. . . . . Quechee, Vt.
Arlington's River Rock Inn
. . . . Arlington, Wash.
Tree Frog Night Inn . . . . Bellingham, Wash.
Heritage Farm Museum & Village
. . . . Huntington, W.Va.
EVA-Great Spirit Ranch B&B
. . . . Newcastle, Wyo.

Barns

Fensalden Inn . . . . Albion, Calif.
Deer Crossing Inn . . . . Castro Valley, Calif.
Black Forest B&B Lodge & Cabins
. . . . Colorado Springs, Colo.
A Meadow House . . . . Lakeville, Conn.
Roseledge Country Inn & Farm Shoppe
. . . . Preston, Conn.
Greyhouse Inn B&B . . . . Salmon, Idaho
Corner George Inn . . . . Maeystown, Ill.
Sonora Gardens Farmstead . . . . Nauvoo, Ill.
Pinehill Inn. . . . . Oregon, Ill.
First Farm Inn . . . . Petersburg, Ky.
1851 Historic Maple Hill Manor B&B
. . . . Springfield, Ky.
Country Ridge B&B . . . . Opelousas, La.
Inn on The Horse Farm . . . . Sudbury, Mass.
Maple Hill Farm B&B Inn . . . . . . Hallowell, Maine
Brannon-Bunker Inn . . . . Walpole, Maine

Inn at Harbour Ridge . . . . Osage Beach, Mo.
Hawkesdene House B&B Inn and Cottages
. . . . Andrews, N.C.
The Mast Farm Inn . . . . Valle Crucis, N.C.
Big Mill Bed & Breakfast . . . . . . Williamston, N.C.
Inn at Glencairn . . . . Princeton, N.J.
HideAway Country Inn . . . . Bucyrus, Ohio
Inn & Spa At Cedar Falls . . . . Logan, Ohio
McKenzie River Inn. . . . . Vida, Ore.
Pennsbury Inn . . . . Chadds Ford, Pa.
Filbert Bed & Breakfast. . . . . Danielsville, Pa.
The Inn at Barley Sheaf Farm
. . . . Holicong, Pa.
Berry Patch B&B . . . . Lebanon, Pa.
Willowgreen Farm B&B . . . . Summerside,
MD Resort Bed & Breakfast . . . . . Fort Worth, Texas
Indian Ridge Bed and Breakfast
. . . . Mission, Texas
Woodland Farmhouse Inn . . . . Kamas, Utah
Bridgewater Inn and Cottage
. . . . Bridgewater, Va.
The Hummingbird Inn. . . . . Goshen, Va.
Stonewall Jackson Inn B&B . . . . . Harrisonburg, Va.
The Cottage at Ravens Roost Farm
. . . . Luray, Va.
Rosebelle's Victorian Inn. . . . . Brandon, Vt.
Silas Griffith Inn. . . . . Danby, Vt.
Cobble House Inn . . . . Gaysville, Vt.
Phineas Swann B&B Inn . . Montgomery Center, Vt.
Inn at Clearwater Pond. . . . . Quechee, Vt.
Arlington's River Rock Inn
. . . . Arlington, Wash.
Justin Trails Resort . . . . Sparta, Wis.
Heritage Farm Museum & Village
. . . . Huntington, W.Va.
EVA-Great Spirit Ranch B&B
. . . . Newcastle, Wyo.

Boats

A Meadow House . . . . Lakeville, Conn.
Stonecroft Country Inn. . . . . Ledyard, Conn.
The Historic Peninsula Inn & Spa
. . . . Gulfport, Fla.
Bayfront Marin House Bed & Breakfast
. . . . Saint Augustine, Fla.
First Farm Inn . . . . Petersburg, Ky.
1851 Historic Maple Hill Manor B&B
. . . . Springfield, Ky.
The Alexander House Booklovers B&B
. . . . Princess Anne, Md.
Harbour Towne Inn on The Waterfront
. . . . Boothbay Harbor, Maine
Hartstone Inn . . . . Camden, Maine
Greenville Inn at Moosehead Lake
. . . . Greenville, Maine
Silent Sport Lodge . . . . Wolverine, Mich.
The Historic Afton House Inn
. . . . Afton, Minn.
Spicer Castle Inn . . . . Spicer, Minn.
Notleymere Cottage . . . . Cazenovia, N.Y.

Kilpatrick Manor Bed & Breakfast
. . . . Niagara Falls,
McKenzie River Inn. . . . . Vida, Ore.
Berry Patch B&B . . . . Lebanon, Pa.
Magnolia House Inn . . . . Hampton, Va.
Fountain Chateau Bed & Breakfast Inn
. . . . Hustler, Wis.

Bordellos

Hotel Charlotte. . . . . Groveland, Calif.
The Groveland Hotel at Yosemite National Park
. . . . Groveland, Calif.
1859 Historic National Hotel, A Country Inn
. . . . Jamestown, Calif.
Peri & Ed's Mountain Hide Away
. . . . Leadville, Colo.
Villa OneTwenty . . . . Newport, R.I.

Castles

French Manor. . . . . South Sterling, Pa.

Churches & Parsonages

All Seasons Inns . . . . Eureka Springs, Ark.
Alpenhorn Bed & Breakfast . . . Big Bear Lake, Calif.
Washington Plantation . . . . Washington, Ga.
Old Church House Inn . . . . Mossville, Ill.
Christopher's B&B . . . . Bellevue, Ky.
Country Ridge B&B . . . . Opelousas, La.
The Parsonage Inn . . . . East Orleans, Mass.
Reynolds Tavern . . . . Annapolis, Md.
Parsonage Inn . . . . Saint Michaels, Md.
Silent Sport Lodge . . . . Wolverine, Mich.
Deutsche Strasse (German Street) B&B
. . . . New Ulm, Minn.
10 Fitch . . . . Auburn, N.Y.
Sunny's Roost Bed & Breakfast
. . . . Lewiston, N.Y.
HideAway Country Inn . . . . Bucyrus, Ohio
Post House Country Inn / Burke House Inn
. . . . Niagara On The Lake,
Berry Patch B&B . . . . Lebanon, Pa.
Villa OneTwenty . . . . Newport, R.I.
Bridgewater Inn and Cottage
. . . . Bridgewater, Va.
Phineas Swann B&B Inn . . Montgomery Center, Vt.
Estabrook House . . . . Saint Johnsbury, Vt.
Fountain Chateau Bed & Breakfast Inn
. . . . Hustler, Wis.

Civil War

A Meadow House . . . . Lakeville, Conn.
Washington Plantation . . . . Washington, Ga.
Mason House Inn and Caboose Cottage of
Bentonsport
. . . . Bentonsport, Iowa
The Steamboat House Bed and Breakfast
. . . . Galena, Ill.
Old Church House Inn . . . . Mossville, Ill.
Chestnut Street Inn. . . . . Sheffield, Ill.
1851 Historic Maple Hill Manor B&B
. . . . Springfield, Ky.
Stockade Bed & Breakfast . . . . . . Baton Rouge, La.
The General Rufus Putnam House
. . . . Rutland, Mass.
1862 Seasons On Main B&B . . . Stockbridge, Mass.
Munro House B&B and Spa . . . . . Jonesville, Mich.
Deutsche Strasse (German Street) B&B

. . . . New Ulm, Minn.
The Dickey House B&B . . . . Marshfield, Mo.
Southern Hotel. . . . . Sainte Genevieve, Mo.
Fairview Inn & Sophia's Restaurant
. . . . Jackson, Miss.
1847 Blake House Inn Bed & Breakfast
. . . . Asheville, N.C.
The Inn at Brevard. . . . . Brevard, N.C.
Harmony House Inn . . . . New Bern, N.C.
C.W. Worth House B&B. . . . . . Wilmington, N.C.
HideAway Country Inn . . . . Bucyrus, Ohio
Rider's 1812 Inn. . . . . Painesville, Ohio
Pheasant Field B&B . . . . Carlisle, Pa.
Pennsbury Inn . . . . Chadds Ford, Pa.
The Fairfield Inn 1757. . . . . Fairfield, Pa.
James Gettys Hotel . . . . Gettysburg, Pa.
Keystone Inn B&B . . . . Gettysburg, Pa.
The Beechmont B&B Inn . . . . Hanover, Pa.
Berry Patch B&B . . . . Lebanon, Pa.
Red Lion Bed & Breakfast . . . . . . Red Lion, Pa.
Villa OneTwenty . . . . Newport, R.I.
Chesnut Cottage B&B. . . . . Columbia, S.C.
Historic Prospect Hill B&B Inn
. . . . Mountain City, Tenn.
McKay House . . . . Jefferson, Texas
The Hale House Inn . . . . Jefferson, Texas
Bridgewater Inn and Cottage
. . . . Bridgewater, Va.
Firmstone Manor . . . . Clifton Forge, Va.
The Hummingbird Inn. . . . . Goshen, Va.
Magnolia House Inn . . . . Hampton, Va.
By the Side of the Road . . . . . . Harrisonburg, Va.
Stonewall Jackson Inn B&B. . . . Harrisonburg, Va.
The Cottage at Ravens Roost Farm
. . . . Luray, Va.
Mayhurst Inn . . . . Orange, Va.
Inn at Riverbend . . . . Pearisburg, Va.
Essex Inn. . . . . Tappahannock, Va.
Sugar Tree Inn . . . . Vesuvius, Va.
Iris Inn . . . . Waynesboro, Va.
Lilac Inn. . . . . Brandon, Vt.
Cobble House Inn . . . . Gaysville, Vt.

Cookbooks Written by Innkeepers

"By Request, The White Oak Cookbook"
The White Oak Inn . . . . Danville, Ohio
"Favorite Recipes of Whitestone Country Inn"
Whitestone Country Inn . . . . Kingston, Tenn.

Farms and Orchards

Fool's Cove Ranch B&B. . . . . Kingston, Ark.
Lodge at Sedona-A Luxury Bed and Breakfast Inn
. . . . Sedona, Ariz.
Apple Blossom Inn B&B. . . . . . . Ahwahnee, Calif.
The Inn at Schoolhouse Creek
. . . . Mendocino, Calif.
Featherbed Railroad Company B&B
. . . . Nice, Calif.
Albert Shafsky House Bed & Breakfast
. . . . Placerville, Calif.
A White Jasmine Inn . . . . Santa Barbara, Calif.
Carriage Vineyards Bed and Breakfast
. . . . Templeton, Calif.
Howard Creek Ranch . . . . Westport, Calif.
Wicky-Up Ranch B&B . . . . Woodlake, Calif.

Black Forest B&B Lodge & Cabins
. . . . Colorado Springs, Colo.
Connecticut River Valley Inn
. . . . Glastonbury, Conn.
A Meadow House . . . . Lakeville, Conn.
Stonecroft Country Inn. . . . . Ledyard, Conn.
Roseledge Country Inn & Farm Shoppe
. . . . Preston, Conn.
Washington Plantation . . . . Washington, Ga.
Sonora Gardens Farmstead . . . . Nauvoo, Ill.
Chestnut Street Inn. . . . . Sheffield, Ill.
Arbor Hill Inn . . . . La Porte, Ind.
The Landmark Inn at The Historic Bank of Oberlin
. . . . Oberlin, Kan.
First Farm Inn . . . . Petersburg, Ky.
1851 Historic Maple Hill Manor B&B
. . . . Springfield, Ky.
Gilbert's B&B. . . . . Rehoboth, Mass.
Inn on The Horse Farm. . . . . Sudbury, Mass.
The Alexander House Booklovers B&B
. . . . Princess Anne, Md.
Gramercy Mansion . . . . Stevenson, Md.
Hartstone Inn . . . . Camden, Maine
Greenville Inn at Moosehead Lake
. . . . Greenville, Maine
Maple Hill Farm B&B Inn. . . . . . . Hallowell, Maine
Grand Victorian Bed & Breakfast Inn
. . . . Bellaire, Mich.
Kingsley House . . . . Saugatuck, Mich.
Grey Hare Inn Vineyard B&B
. . . . Traverse City, Mich.
Silent Sport Lodge . . . . Wolverine, Mich.
Spicer Castle Inn . . . . Spicer, Minn.
Plain & Fancy Bed & Breakfast
. . . . Ironton, Mo.
The Inn of the Patriots Bed and Breakfast Hotel
. . . . Grover, N.C.
The Mast Farm Inn . . . . Valle Crucis, N.C.
Big Mill Bed & Breakfast . . . . . Williamston, N.C.
Brass Heart Inn . . . . Chocorua, N.H.
Inn at Ellis River . . . . Jackson, N.H.
Chimney Hill Estate Inn . . . . . . Lambertville, N.J.
Whistling Swan Inn . . . . Stanhope, N.J.
The Black Range Lodge. . . . . Kingston, N.M.
Halcyon Farm Bed & Breakfast
. . . . Amsterdam, N.Y.
Agape Farm B&B and Paintball
. . . . Corinth, N.Y.
HideAway Country Inn . . . . Bucyrus, Ohio
Orchard House. . . . . Granville, Ohio
Kilpatrick Manor Bed & Breakfast
. . . . Niagara Falls,
McKenzie River Inn. . . . . Vida, Ore.
Pennsbury Inn . . . . Chadds Ford, Pa.
Filbert Bed & Breakfast. . . . . Danielsville, Pa.
The Inn at Barley Sheaf Farm
. . . . Holicong, Pa.
Berry Patch B&B . . . . Lebanon, Pa.
Red Lion Bed & Breakfast . . . . . . Red Lion, Pa.
Willowgreen Farm B&B . . . . Summerside, Pa.
Villa OneTwenty . . . . Newport, R.I.
Bridgewater Inn and Cottage
. . . . Bridgewater, Va.
Rockland Farm Retreat . . . . Bumpass, Va.
Firmstone Manor . . . . Clifton Forge, Va.
The Hummingbird Inn. . . . . Goshen, Va.
The Cottage at Ravens Roost Farm

. . . . Luray, Va.

Mayhurst Inn . . . . Orange, Va.

Phineas Swann B&B Inn . . Montgomery Center, Vt.

Golden Stage Inn . . . . Proctorsville, Vt.

Inn at Clearwater Pond. . . . . Quechee, Vt.

Liberty Hill Farm . . . . Rochester, Vt.

A Stone Wall Inn . . . . Windham, Vt.

Tree Frog Night Inn . . . . Bellingham, Wash.

Justin Trails Resort . . . . Sparta, Wis.

Heritage Farm Museum & Village

. . . . Huntington, W.Va.

French & Indian War

The Inn of the Patriots Bed and Breakfast Hotel

. . . . Grover, N.C.

Gardens

Pearson's Pond Luxury Inn & Adventure Spa

. . . . Juneau, Alaska

Cliff Cottage Inn - Luxury B&B Suites & Historic
Cottages

. . . . Eureka Springs, Ark.

Casa De San Pedro. . . . . Hereford, Ariz.

Lodge at Sedona-A Luxury Bed and Breakfast Inn

. . . . Sedona, Ariz.

The Heritage Inn . . . . Snowflake, Ariz.

Grand Living Bed and Breakfast

. . . . Williams, Ariz.

Brewery Gulch Inn . . . . Mendocino, Calif.

The Inn at Schoolhouse Creek

. . . . Mendocino, Calif.

A White Jasmine Inn . . . . Santa Barbara, Calif.

Carriage Vineyards Bed and Breakfast

. . . . Templeton, Calif.

Romantic RiverSong Inn . . . . Estes Park, Colo.

Avenue Hotel, A Victorian B&B

. . . . Manitou Springs, Colo.

Connecticut River Valley Inn

. . . . Glastonbury, Conn.

A Meadow House . . . . Lakeville, Conn.

Stonecroft Country Inn. . . . . Ledyard, Conn.

Deacon Timothy Pratt Bed & Breakfast Inn C.1746

. . . . Old Saybrook, Conn.

B&B at Taylor's Corner . . . . Woodstock, Conn.

Lily Creek Lodge. . . . . Dahlonega, Ga.

Washington Plantation . . . . Washington, Ga.

The Hancock House . . . . Dubuque, Iowa

Blue Belle Inn B&B . . . . Saint Ansgar, Iowa

Beall Mansion, An Elegant B&B

. . . . Alton, Ill.

Sonora Gardens Farmstead . . . . Nauvoo, Ill.

Chestnut Street Inn. . . . . Sheffield, Ill.

Cincinnati's Weller Haus B&B

. . . . Bellevue, Ky.

First Farm Inn . . . . Petersburg, Ky.

1851 Historic Maple Hill Manor B&B

. . . . Springfield, Ky.

Country Ridge B&B . . . . Opelousas, La.

Chatham Old Harbor Inn . . . . Chatham, Mass.

Gabriel's at the Ashbrooke Inn

. . . . Provincetown, Mass.

Inn on The Horse Farm. . . . . Sudbury, Mass.

Great Oak Manor . . . . Chestertown, Md.

The Inn at Mitchell House . . . . . . Chestertown, Md.

The Alexander House Booklovers B&B

. . . . Princess Anne, Md.

Gramercy Mansion . . . . Stevenson, Md.

Harbour Towne Inn on The Waterfront

. . . . Boothbay Harbor, Maine

Hartstone Inn . . . . Camden, Maine

The Brewster Inn . . . . Dexter, Maine

Greenville Inn at Moosehead Lake

. . . . Greenville, Maine

Prairieside Suites Luxury B&B

. . . . Grand Rapids, Mich.

Huron House Bed & Breakfast

. . . . Oscoda, Mich.

Kingsley House . . . . Saugatuck, Mich.

Silent Sport Lodge . . . . Wolverine, Mich.

Spicer Castle Inn . . . . Spicer, Minn.

The Dickey House B&B . . . . Marshfield, Mo.

Inn at Harbour Ridge . . . . Osage Beach, Mo.

Fairview Inn & Sophia's Restaurant

. . . . Jackson, Miss.

Hawkesdene House B&B Inn and Cottages

. . . . Andrews, N.C.

The Inn at Brevard. . . . . Brevard, N.C.

The Inn of the Patriots Bed and Breakfast Hotel

. . . . Grover, N.C.

Colonial Pines Inn Bed and Breakfast

. . . . Highlands, N.C.

Sobotta Manor Bed and Breakfast

. . . . Mount Airy, N.C.

1906 Pine Crest Inn and Restaurant

. . . . Tryon, N.C.

The Mast Farm Inn . . . . Valle Crucis, N.C.

Big Mill Bed & Breakfast . . . . . . Williamston, N.C.

Adair Country Inn and Restaurant

. . . . Bethlehem, N.H.

Coppertoppe Inn & Retreat Center

. . . . Hebron, N.H.

Cabernet Inn . . . . North Conway, N.H.

A Grand Inn-Sunset Hill House

. . . . Sugar Hill, N.H.

Wakefield Inn. . . . . Wakefield, N.H.

Main Street Manor Bed and Breakfast

. . . . Flemington, N.J.

Whistling Swan Inn . . . . Stanhope, N.J.

Touchstone Inn, Spa & Gallery

. . . . Taos, N.M.

B Street House Bed and Breakfast

. . . . Virginia City, Nev.

10 Fitch . . . . Auburn, N.Y.

Berry Hill Gardens B&B. . . . . Bainbridge, N.Y.

Notleymere Cottage . . . . Cazenovia, N.Y.

Arbor View House B&B . . . . East Marion, N.Y.

The Edward Harris House B&B Inn

. . . . Rochester, N.Y.

HideAway Country Inn . . . . Bucyrus, Ohio

Gambier House . . . . Gambier, Ohio

Orchard House. . . . . Granville, Ohio

Inn & Spa At Cedar Falls . . . . Logan, Ohio

Kirkwood Inn. . . . . Mason, Ohio

Kilpatrick Manor Bed & Breakfast

. . . . Niagara Falls,

Post House Country Inn / Burke House Inn

. . . . Niagara On The Lake,

Albion Inn . . . . Ashland, Ore.

McKenzie River Inn. . . . . Vida, Ore.

Pheasant Field B&B . . . . Carlisle, Pa.

Pennsbury Inn . . . . Chadds Ford, Pa.

The Inn at Barley Sheaf Farm

. . . . Holicong, Pa.

Berry Patch B&B . . . . Lebanon, Pa.

The Artist's Inn & Gallery

. . . . Terre Hill, Pa.

Villa OneTwenty . . . . Newport, R.I.

Edgewood Manor B&B . . . . Providence, R.I.

Custer Mansion B&B . . . . Custer, S.D.

Historic Prospect Hill B&B Inn

. . . . Mountain City, Tenn.

McKay House . . . . Jefferson, Texas

The Hale House Inn . . . . Jefferson, Texas

Indian Ridge Bed and Breakfast

. . . . Mission, Texas

Woodland Farmhouse Inn . . . . Kamas, Utah

Bridgewater Inn and Cottage

. . . . Bridgewater, Va.

The Hummingbird Inn. . . . . Goshen, Va.

Magnolia House Inn . . . . Hampton, Va.

By the Side of the Road . . . . Harrisonburg, Va.

The Garden and The Sea Inn

. . . . New Church, Va.

Colonial Manor Inn . . . . Onancock, Va.

Mayhurst Inn . . . . Orange, Va.

Essex Inn. . . . . Tappahannock, Va.

Sugar Tree Inn . . . . Vesuvius, Va.

Colonial Gardens. . . . . Williamsburg, Va.

Lilac Inn . . . . Brandon, Vt.

Rosebelle's Victorian Inn. . . . . Brandon, Vt.

Silas Griffith Inn. . . . . Danby, Vt.

Phineas Swann B&B Inn . . Montgomery Center, Vt.

Golden Stage Inn . . . . Proctorsville, Vt.

Inn at Clearwater Pond. . . . . Quechee, Vt.

White House of Wilmington . . . . . Wilmington, Vt.

A Stone Wall Inn . . . . Windham, Vt.

Tree Frog Night Inn . . . . Bellingham, Wash.

Plum Duff House . . . . Tacoma, Wash.

Cobblestone Bed & Breakfast

. . . . Birchwood, Wis.

Fountain Chateau Bed & Breakfast Inn

. . . . Hustler, Wis.

Justin Trails Resort . . . . Sparta, Wis.

Glacier Viewing

Pearson's Pond Luxury Inn & Adventure Spa

. . . . Juneau, Alaska

Matanuska Lodge. . . . . Sutton, Alaska

Gold Mines & Gold Panning

Pearson's Pond Luxury Inn & Adventure Spa

. . . . Juneau, Alaska

Casa De San Pedro. . . . . Hereford, Ariz.

Lodge at Sedona-A Luxury Bed and Breakfast Inn

. . . . Sedona, Ariz.

Deer Crossing Inn . . . . Castro Valley, Calif.

Hotel Charlotte. . . . . Groveland, Calif.

The Groveland Hotel at Yosemite National Park

. . . . Groveland, Calif.

1859 Historic National Hotel, A Country Inn

. . . . Jamestown, Calif.

Albert Shafsky House Bed & Breakfast

. . . . Placerville, Calif.

Black Forest B&B Lodge & Cabins

. . . . Colorado Springs, Colo.

Winter Park Chateau . . . . Winter Park, Colo.

Lily Creek Lodge. . . . . Dahlonega, Ga.

Greyhouse Inn B&B. . . . . Salmon, Idaho

The Black Range Lodge. . . . . Kingston, N.M.

McKenzie River Inn. . . . . Vida, Ore.

Custer Mansion B&B . . . . Custer, S.D.

Cobble House Inn . . . . Gaysville, Vt.
Echo Lake Inn . . . . Ludlow, Vt.

Hot Springs

Mount View Hotel & Spa . . . . Calistoga, Calif.
Rainbow Tarns B&B at Crowley Lake
. . . . Crowley Lake, Calif.
A White Jasmine Inn . . . . Santa Barbara, Calif.
Vichy Hot Springs Resort & Inn
. . . . Ukiah, Calif.
Winter Park Chateau . . . . Winter Park, Colo.
River Park Inn . . . . Green Cove Springs, Fla.
Greyhouse Inn B&B . . . . Salmon, Idaho
The Inn on Crescent Lake . . Excelsior Springs, Mo.
McKenzie River Inn . . . . Vida, Ore.
Custer Mansion B&B . . . . Custer, S.D.
Bridgewater Inn and Cottage
. . . . Bridgewater, Va.
Firmstone Manor . . . . Clifton Forge, Va.
The Hummingbird Inn . . . . Goshen, Va.

Inns Built Prior to 1800

1600 1830 Quince Tree House
. . . . Sandwich, Mass.
1690 The Great Valley House of Valley Forge
. . . . Valley Forge, Pa.
1704 Farmstead Bed and Breakfast
. . . . Eliot, Maine
1714 Pennsbury Inn . . . . Chadds Ford, Pa.
1720 Roseledge Country Inn & Farm Shoppe
. . . . Preston, Conn.
1730 Joy House Inc., B&B . . . . Dennis Port, Mass.
1731 B&B at Taylor's Corner
. . . . Woodstock, Conn.
1734 3 Liberty Green B&B . . . . . . Clinton, Conn.
1734 Langdon House . . . . Beaufort, N.C.
1736 Inn at Glencairn . . . . Princeton, N.J.
1737 Reynolds Tavern . . . . Annapolis, Md.
1739 The Ruffner House . . . . Luray, Va.
1740 Connecticut River Valley Inn
. . . . Glastonbury, Conn.
1740 Inn at Lower Farm. North Stonington, Conn.
1740 Lamb and Lion Inn . . . . . . Barnstable, Mass.
1740 The Inn at Barley Sheaf Farm
. . . . Holicong, Pa.
1743 High Acres Bed and Breakfast
. . . . North Stonington, Conn.
1743 The Inn at Mitchell House
. . . . Chestertown, Md.
1746 Deacon Timothy Pratt Bed & Breakfast Inn
C.1746
. . . . Old Saybrook, Conn.
1750 The General Rufus Putnam House
. . . . Rutland, Mass.
1750 Peace With-Inn Bed & Breakfast
. . . . Fryeburg, Maine
1750 The Cottage at Ravens Roost Farm
. . . . Luray, Va.
1757 The Fairfield Inn 1757
. . . . Fairfield, Pa.
1759 Brownstone Colonial Inn
. . . . Reinholds, Pa.
1761 Elk Forge Bed & Breakfast Inn, Spa, Events, Tea Room & Shop
. . . . Elkton, Md.
1761 Harpswell Inn . . . . Harpswell, Maine
1763 Blackberry River Inn . . . . . . Norfolk, Conn.
1763 Casa de Solana, B&B Inn

. . . . Saint Augustine, Fla.
1766 Seven South Street Inn
. . . . Rockport, Mass.
1766 Osceola Mill House . . . . Gordonville, Pa.
1766 The Inn at Meander Plantation
. . . . Locust Dale, Va.
1767 Blair Mountain Bed and Breakfast
. . . . Dillsburg, Pa.
1768 Boxwood Inn Bed & Breakfast
. . . . Akron, Pa.
1769 The Inn at Millrace Pond
. . . . Hope, N.J.
1770 The Parsonage Inn . . . . . East Orleans, Mass.
1770 The Richard Johnston Inn
. . . . Fredericksburg, Va.
1774 Gibson's Lodgings . . . . Annapolis, Md.
1774 Inn at Valley Farms B&B and Cottages
. . . . Walpole, N.H.
1777 1777 Americana Inn . . . . Ephrata, Pa.
1778 Brass Heart Inn . . . . Chocorua, N.H.
1780 Hotel Saint Pierre . . . . . New Orleans, La.
1780 Birch Hill Bed & Breakfast
. . . . Sheffield, Mass.
1780 The Dowds' Country Inn
. . . . Lyme, N.H.
1783 The Towers B&B . . . . Milford, Del.
1784 Maple House Bed & Breakfast
. . . . Rowe, Mass.
1785 The Ergemont Village Inn
. . . . South Egremont, Mass.
1785 1785 Inn & Restaurant
. . . . North Conway, N.H.
1786 Brandon Inn . . . . Brandon, Vt.
1788 Golden Stage Inn . . . . Proctorsville, Vt.
1789 By the Side of the Road
. . . . Harrisonburg, Va.
1790 Silvermine Tavern . . . . Norwalk, Conn.
1790 Southern Hotel . . . . . . Sainte Genevieve, Mo.
1790 The Baird House . . . . Valle Crucis, N.C.
1790 The Inn at Gray's Landing
. . . . Windsor, N.C.
1790 The Maples at Warner . . . . . . Warner, N.H.
1790 Flowering Fields B&B . . . . White Stone, Va.
1790 Silver Maple Lodge & Cottages
. . . . Fairlee, Vt.
1790 The Putney Inn . . . . Putney, Vt.
1791 St. Francis Inn . . . . . . Saint Augustine, Fla.
1791 Sedgwick Inn . . . . Berlin, N.Y.
1792 Bridges Inn at Whitcomb House
. . . . West Swanzey, N.H.
1792 1792 Filigree Inn . . . . Canandaigua, N.Y.
1793 Cove House . . . . Kennebunkport, Maine
1794 Historic Merrell Inn . . . . . . South Lee, Mass.
1794 The Whitehall Inn . . . . New Hope, Pa.
1795 Shaker Meadows . . . . . . New Lebanon, N.Y.
1795 Living Spring Farm B&B
. . . . Mohnton, Pa.
1796 Catamount B&B . . . . Williston, Vt.
1797 Applebrook B&B . . . . Jefferson, N.H.
1799 Dr. Jonathan Pitney House
. . . . Absecon, N.J.

Literary Figures Associated With Inns

Jack London
Vichy Hot Springs Resort & Inn
. . . . Ukiah, Calif.

D.H. Lawrence
Vichy Hot Springs Resort & Inn
. . . . Ukiah, Calif.

Mark Twain/Samuel Clemens
Vichy Hot Springs Resort & Inn
. . . . Ukiah, Calif.

Louisa May Alcott
Hawthorne Inn . . . . Concord, Mass.

Ralph Waldo Emerson
Hawthorne Inn . . . . Concord, Mass.

Nathaniel Hawthorne
Hawthorne Inn . . . . Concord, Mass.

Henry Beston
Inn at the Oaks . . . . Eastham, Mass.

Ralph Waldo Emerson
Emerson Inn By The Sea . . . . Rockport, Mass.

Nathaniel Hawthorne
Emerson Inn By The Sea . . . . Rockport, Mass.

Llama Ranches

Grand Living Bed and Breakfast
. . . . Williams, Ariz.
Black Forest B&B Lodge & Cabins
. . . . Colorado Springs, Colo.
A Meadow House . . . . Lakeville, Conn.
1851 Historic Maple Hill Manor B&B
. . . . Springfield, Ky.
Maple Hill Farm B&B Inn . . . . Hallowell, Maine
Hawkesdene House B&B Inn and Cottages
. . . . Andrews, N.C.
Chimney Hill Estate Inn . . . . Lambertville, N.J.
Orchard House . . . . Granville, Ohio
Woodland Farmhouse Inn . . . . Kamas, Utah
Mayhurst Inn . . . . Orange, Va.
Phineas Swann B&B Inn . . Montgomery Center, Vt.
Inn at Clearwater Pond . . . . Quechee, Vt.
Justin Trails Resort . . . . Sparta, Wis.

Log Cabins/Houses

Matanuska Lodge . . . . Sutton, Alaska
Abineau Lodge Bed and Breakfast
. . . . Flagstaff, Ariz.
Grand Living Bed and Breakfast
. . . . Williams, Ariz.
Ocean Wilderness Inn . . . . Sooke,
Alpenhorn Bed & Breakfast . . . Big Bear Lake, Calif.
Knickerbocker Mansion Country Inn
. . . . Big Bear Lake, Calif.
Black Forest B&B Lodge & Cabins
. . . . Colorado Springs, Colo.
Highland Haven Creekside Inn
. . . . Evergreen, Colo.
Wild Horse Inn Bed and Breakfast
. . . . Fraser, Colo.
A Meadow House . . . . Lakeville, Conn.
Cedar Mountain Farm . . . . Athol, Idaho
1851 Historic Maple Hill Manor B&B
. . . . Springfield, Ky.
Sweet Dreams Inn Victorian B&B
. . . . Bay Port, Mich.
Silent Sport Lodge . . . . Wolverine, Mich.
Spicer Castle Inn . . . . Spicer, Minn.
1906 Pine Crest Inn and Restaurant
. . . . Tryon, N.C.
The Mast Farm Inn . . . . Valle Crucis, N.C.
Elaine's, A B&B . . . . Cedar Crest, N.M.
Log Country Inn - B&B of Ithaca

. . . . Ithaca, N.Y.
HideAway Country Inn . . . . Bucyrus, Ohio
Heartland Country Resort. . . . Fredericktown, Ohio
Inn & Spa At Cedar Falls . . . . Logan, Ohio
Weasku Inn . . . . Grants Pass, Ore.
McKenzie River Inn. . . . . Vida, Ore.
Pennsbury Inn . . . . Chadds Ford, Pa.
Berry Patch B&B . . . . Lebanon, Pa.
BlissWood Bed and Breakfast Ranch
. . . . Cat Spring, Texas
Roddy Tree Ranch & Guest Cottages
. . . . Ingram, Texas
Woodland Farmhouse Inn . . . . Kamas, Utah
Bridgewater Inn and Cottage
. . . . Bridgewater, Va.
Woodruff Inns and Shenandoah River Cabin Escapes
. . . . Luray, Va.
Mayhurst Inn . . . . Orange, Va.
The Inn at Burg's Landing . Anderson Island, Wash.
Arlington's River Rock Inn
. . . . Arlington, Wash.
Guest House Log Cottages . . . . . Greenbank, Wash.
Justin Trails Resort . . . . Sparta, Wis.
Heritage Farm Museum & Village
. . . . Huntington, W.Va.

Movie Locations

The Majestic
Shaw House B&B Inn . . . . Ferndale, Calif.
Holiday Inn
Village Inn & Restaurant . . . . Monte Rio, Calif.
Isaac's Storm
C.W. Worth House B&B. . . . . . Wilmington, N.C.
Consenting Adults
Rice Hope Plantation Inn Bed & Breakfast
. . . . Moncks Corner, S.C.

National Historic Register

Cliff Cottage Inn - Luxury B&B Suites & Historic
Cottages
. . . . Eureka Springs, Ark.
Lodge at Sedona-A Luxury Bed and Breakfast Inn
. . . . Sedona, Ariz.
The Heritage Inn . . . . Snowflake, Ariz.
Grand Living Bed and Breakfast
. . . . Williams, Ariz.
Mount View Hotel & Spa . . . . Calistoga, Calif.
Hotel Charlotte. . . . . Groveland, Calif.
The Groveland Hotel at Yosemite National Park
. . . . Groveland, Calif.
Vichy Hot Springs Resort & Inn
. . . . Ukiah, Calif.
The Bross Hotel B&B. . . . . Paonia, Colo.
A Meadow House . . . . Lakeville, Conn.
Stonecroft Country Inn. . . . . Ledyard, Conn.
Deacon Timothy Pratt Bed & Breakfast Inn C.1746
. . . . Old Saybrook, Conn.
Roseledge Country Inn & Farm Shoppe
. . . . Preston, Conn.
B&B at Taylor's Corner . . . . . . Woodstock, Conn.
The Towers B&B. . . . . Milford, Del.
River Park Inn. . . . . Green Cove Springs, Fla.
The Historic Peninsula Inn & Spa
. . . . Gulfport, Fla.
Bayfront Marin House Bed & Breakfast
. . . . Saint Augustine, Fla.
St. Francis Inn . . . . Saint Augustine, Fla.

Beach Drive Inn . . . . Saint Petersburg, Fla.
Tybee Island Inn. . . . . Tybee Island, Ga.
Washington Plantation . . . . Washington, Ga.
Mont Rest . . . . Bellevue, Iowa
Mason House Inn and Caboose Cottage of
Bentonsport
. . . . Bentonsport, Iowa
The Hancock House . . . . Dubuque, Iowa
The Mandolin Inn . . . . Dubuque, Iowa
Beall Mansion, An Elegant B&B
. . . . Alton, Ill.
The Steamboat House Bed and Breakfast
. . . . Galena, Ill.
Corner George Inn . . . . Maeystown, Ill.
Arbor Hill Inn . . . . La Porte, Ind.
The Landmark Inn at The Historic Bank of Oberlin
. . . . Oberlin, Kan.
Cincinnati's Weller Haus B&B
. . . . Bellevue, Ky.
1851 Historic Maple Hill Manor B&B
. . . . Springfield, Ky.
College Club. . . . . Boston, Mass.
The Beach Rose Inn . . . . Falmouth, Mass.
Old Mill on The Falls Inn . . . . Hatfield, Mass.
Winterwood at Petersham . . . . . Petersham, Mass.
Historic Merrell Inn . . . . South Lee, Mass.
1862 Seasons On Main B&B . . . Stockbridge, Mass.
Inn on The Horse Farm. . . . . Sudbury, Mass.
Gramercy Mansion . . . . Stevenson, Md.
The Brewster Inn. . . . . Dexter, Maine
Maine Stay Inn & Cottages . Kennebunkport, Maine
Terrace Inn & Restaurant . . . . Petoskey, Mich.
The Historic Afton House Inn
. . . . Afton, Minn.
Classic Rosewood - A Thorwood Property
. . . . Hastings, Minn.
Nicolin Mansion Bed & Breakfast
. . . . Jordan, Minn.
Spicer Castle Inn . . . . Spicer, Minn.
Eagle's Nest. . . . . Louisiana, Mo.
Fairview Inn & Sophia's Restaurant
. . . . Jackson, Miss.
Olive Branch Inn at the Lindley House
. . . . Bozeman, Mont.
Wright Inn & Carriage House
. . . . Asheville, N.C.
The Inn at Brevard. . . . . Brevard, N.C.
Colonial Pines Inn Bed and Breakfast
. . . . Highlands, N.C.
1906 Pine Crest Inn and Restaurant
. . . . Tryon, N.C.
The Mast Inn . . . . Valle Crucis, N.C.
C.W. Worth House B&B. . . . . . Wilmington, N.C.
Wakefield Inn. . . . . Wakefield, N.H.
Bottger Mansion of Old Town
. . . . Albuquerque, N.M.
B Street House Bed and Breakfast
. . . . Virginia City, Nev.
Notleymere Cottage . . . . Cazenovia, N.Y.
Rosewood Inn . . . . Corning, N.Y.
The Turret House B&B . . . . Dryden, N.Y.
Wells House . . . . Greenport, N.Y.
The Edward Harris House B&B Inn
. . . . Rochester, N.Y.
Eagle Cliff Inn . . . . Geneva On The Lake, Ohio
Rider's 1812 Inn. . . . . Painesville, Ohio
The Grandison Inn at Maney Park

. . . . Oklahoma City, Okla.
Albion Inn . . . . Ashland, Ore.
Pennsbury Inn . . . . Chadds Ford, Pa.
The Fairfield Inn 1757 . . . . Fairfield, Pa.
James Gettys Hotel . . . . Gettysburg, Pa.
Berry Patch B&B . . . . Lebanon, Pa.
The Priory . . . . Pittsburgh, Pa.
French Manor. . . . . South Sterling, Pa.
Adele Turner Inn . . . . Newport, R.I.
Villa OneTwenty . . . . Newport, R.I.
Edgewood Manor B&B . . . . . . Providence, R.I.
Custer Mansion B&B. . . . . Custer, S.D.
Historic Prospect Hill B&B Inn
. . . . Mountain City, Tenn.
Pecan Street Inn . . . . Bastrop, Texas
McKay House . . . . Jefferson, Texas
Mosheim Mansion . . . . Seguin, Texas
Katy House Bed & Breakfast
. . . . Smithville, Texas
Ellerbeck Mansion B&B. . . . . Salt Lake City, Utah
Hockman House Bed & Breakfast
. . . . Edinburg, Va.
Magnolia House Inn . . . . Hampton, Va.
Mayhurst Inn . . . . Orange, Va.
Lilac Inn. . . . . Brandon, Vt.
Rosebelle's Victorian Inn. . . . . Brandon, Vt.
Silas Griffith Inn. . . . . Danby, Vt.
Estabrook House . . . . Saint Johnsbury, Vt.
Charleston House. . . . . Woodstock, Vt.
Fountain Chateau Bed & Breakfast Inn
. . . . Hustler, Wis.
Victorian Dreams Bed and Breakfast
. . . . Lodi, Wis.
Schuster Mansion Bed & Breakfast
. . . . Milwaukee, Wis.
The Rochester Inn. . . . . Sheboygan Falls, Wis.
Franklin Victorian Bed & Breakfast
. . . . Sparta, Wis.
White Lace Inn . . . . Sturgeon Bay, Wis.

Old Mills

A Meadow House . . . . Lakeville, Conn.
Silvermine Tavern. . . . . Norwalk, Conn.
Sylvan Falls Mill. . . . . Rabun Gap, Ga.
Old Mill on The Falls Inn . . . . Hatfield, Mass.
Historic Merrell Inn . . . . South Lee, Mass.
Silent Sport Lodge . . . . Wolverine, Mich.
Big Mill Bed & Breakfast . . . . . Williamston, N.C.
Asa Ransom House. . . . . Clarence, N.Y.
Pennsbury Inn . . . . Chadds Ford, Pa.
Berry Patch B&B . . . . Lebanon, Pa.
Bridgewater Inn and Cottage
. . . . Bridgewater, Va.
The Hummingbird Inn. . . . . Goshen, Va.
Stonewall Jackson Inn B&B . . . . Harrisonburg, Va.
The Cottage at Ravens Roost Farm
. . . . Luray, Va.
Sugar Tree Inn . . . . Vesuvius, Va.

Oldest Continuously Operated Inns

All Seasons Inns . . . . Eureka Springs, Ark.
Lodge at Sedona-A Luxury Bed and Breakfast Inn
. . . . Sedona, Ariz.
1859 Historic National Hotel, A Country Inn
. . . . Jamestown, Calif.

The Inn at Schoolhouse Creek
. . . . Mendocino, Calif.
Vichy Hot Springs Resort & Inn
. . . . Ukiah, Calif.
Peri & Ed's Mountain Hide Away
. . . . Leadville, Colo.
Avenue Hotel, A Victorian B&B
. . . . Manitou Springs, Colo.
Florida House Inn . . . . Amelia Island, Fla.
St. Francis Inn . . . . Saint Augustine, Fla.
Mason House Inn and Caboose Cottage of
Bentonsport
. . . . Bentonsport, Iowa
Gabriel's at the Ashbrooke Inn
. . . . Provincetown, Mass.
Emerson Inn By The Sea . . . . Rockport, Mass.
Reynolds Tavern . . . . Annapolis, Md.
Harbour Towne Inn on The Waterfront
. . . . Boothbay Harbor, Maine
Greenville Inn at Moosehead Lake
. . . . Greenville, Maine
Khardomah Lodge. . . . . Grand Haven, Mich.
Terrace Inn & Restaurant . . . . Petoskey, Mich.
Classic Rosewood - A Thorwood Property
. . . . Hastings, Minn.
Loganberry Inn . . . . Fulton, Mo.
Southern Hotel. . . . . Sainte Genevieve, Mo.
1906 Pine Crest Inn and Restaurant
. . . . Tryon, N.C.
The Mast Farm Inn . . . . Valle Crucis, N.C.
A Grand Inn-Sunset Hill House
. . . . Sugar Hill, N.H.
Wakefield Inn. . . . . Wakefield, N.H.
Stirling House Bed & Breakfast
. . . . Greenport, N.Y.
McKenzie River Inn. . . . . Vida, Ore.
The Fairfield Inn 1757. . . . . Fairfield, Pa.
The Great Valley House of Valley Forge
. . . . Valley Forge, Pa.
The Bellevue House . . . . Block Island, R.I.
Adele Turner Inn . . . . Newport, R.I.
Custer Mansion B&B . . . . Custer, S.D.
Robin's Nest . . . . Houston, Texas
McKay House . . . . Jefferson, Texas
Federal Crest Inn. . . . . Lynchburg, Va.
Colonial Manor Inn . . . . Onancock, Va.
Rosebelle's Victorian Inn. . . . . Brandon, Vt.

On the Grounds of a U.S. National Memorial

Bayfront Marin House Bed & Breakfast
. . . . Saint Augustine, Fla.
Fountain Chateau Bed & Breakfast Inn
. . . . Hustler, Wis.

Plantations

Washington Plantation . . . . Washington, Ga.
1851 Historic Maple Hill Manor B&B
. . . . Springfield, Ky.
Country Ridge B&B . . . . Opelousas, La.
Mansfield Plantation B&B Country Inn
. . . . Georgetown, S.C.
Rice Hope Plantation Inn Bed & Breakfast
. . . . Moncks Corner, S.C.
The Inn at Meander Plantation
. . . . Locust Dale, Va.
Mayhurst Inn . . . . Orange, Va.

Ranches

Lodge at Sedona-A Luxury Bed & Breakfast Inn
. . . . Sedona, Ariz.
Grand Living Bed and Breakfast
. . . . Williams, Ariz.
The Inn at Schoolhouse Creek
. . . . Mendocino, Calif.
Carriage Vineyards Bed and Breakfast
. . . . Templeton, Calif.
Howard Creek Ranch . . . . Westport, Calif.
Romantic RiverSong Inn . . . . Estes Park, Colo.
Sundance Trail Guest Ranch
. . . . Red Feather Lakes, Colo.
A Meadow House . . . . Lakeville, Conn.
Cedar Mountain Farm. . . . . Athol, Idaho
1851 Historic Maple Hill Manor B&B
. . . . Springfield, Ky.
Wilson Ranches Retreat Bed and Breakfast
. . . . Fossil, Ore.
BlissWood Bed and Breakfast Ranch
. . . . Cat Spring, Texas
MD Resort Bed & Breakfast. . . . . Fort Worth, Texas
Hasse House Ranch . . . . Mason, Texas
Fountain Chateau Bed & Breakfast Inn
. . . . Hustler, Wis.

Revolutionary War

Washington Plantation . . . . Washington, Ga.
Hawthorne Inn. . . . . Concord, Mass.
Historic Merrell Inn . . . . South Lee, Mass.
Gibson's Lodgings . . . . Annapolis, Md.
Reynolds Tavern . . . . Annapolis, Md.
The Inn of the Patriots Bed and Breakfast Hotel
. . . . Grover, N.C.
1906 Pine Crest Inn and Restaurant
. . . . Tryon, N.C.
Inn at Glencairn . . . . Princeton, N.J.
Whistling Swan Inn . . . . Stanhope, N.J.
Pennsbury Inn . . . . Chadds Ford, Pa.
Berry Patch B&B . . . . Lebanon, Pa.
The Great Valley House of Valley Forge
. . . . Valley Forge, Pa.
Villa OneTwenty . . . . Newport, R.I.
McKay House . . . . Jefferson, Texas
Mayhurst Inn . . . . Orange, Va.
Phineas Swann B&B Inn . . Montgomery Center, Vt.

Schoolhouses

Grand Living Bed and Breakfast
. . . . Williams, Ariz.
The Inn at Schoolhouse Creek
. . . . Mendocino, Calif.
Vichy Hot Springs Resort & Inn
. . . . Ukiah, Calif.
A Meadow House . . . . Lakeville, Conn.
B&B at Taylor's Corner . . . . Woodstock, Conn.
Bayfront Marin House Bed & Breakfast
. . . . Saint Augustine, Fla.
The Roosevelt Inn. . . . . Coeur D'Alene, Idaho
Old Sea Pines Inn . . . . Brewster, Mass.
HideAway Country Inn . . . . Bucyrus, Ohio
Berry Patch B&B . . . . Lebanon, Pa.
Custer Mansion B&B . . . . Custer, S.D.
Mayhurst Inn . . . . Orange, Va.
Fountain Chateau Bed & Breakfast Inn
. . . . Hustler, Wis.

Heritage Farm Museum & Village
. . . . Huntington, W.Va.

Stagecoach Stops

Fensalden Inn . . . . Albion, Calif.
Hotel Charlotte. . . . . Groveland, Calif.
1859 Historic National Hotel, A Country Inn
. . . . Jamestown, Calif.
Albert Shafsky House Bed & Breakfast
. . . . Placerville, Calif.
Melitta Station Inn . . . . Santa Rosa, Calif.
Tidewater Inn . . . . Madison, Conn.
Mason House Inn and Caboose Cottage of
Bentonsport
. . . . Bentonsport, Iowa
Maple House Bed & Breakfast
. . . . Rowe, Mass.
Historic Merrell Inn . . . . South Lee, Mass.
Harbour Towne Inn on The Waterfront
. . . . Boothbay Harbor, Maine
Maple Hill Farm B&B Inn. . . . . . Hallowell, Maine
Sweet Dreams Inn Victorian B&B
. . . . Bay Port, Mich.
Southern Hotel. . . . . Sainte Genevieve, Mo.
Wakefield Inn. . . . . Wakefield, N.H.
Whistling Swan Inn . . . . Stanhope, N.J.
Hacienda Vargas . . . . Algodones, N.M.
Kirkwood Inn. . . . . Mason, Ohio
Rider's 1812 Inn. . . . . Painesville, Ohio
McKenzie River Inn. . . . . Vida, Ore.
The Fairfield Inn 1757. . . . . Fairfield, Pa.
The Great Valley House of Valley Forge
. . . . Valley Forge, Pa.
Phineas Swann B&B Inn . . Montgomery Center, Vt.
Golden Stage Inn . . . . Proctorsville, Vt.
Wisconsin House Stagecoach Inn
. . . . Hazel Green, Wis.
EVA-Great Spirit Ranch B&B
. . . . Newcastle, Wyo.

Still in the Family

Vichy Hot Springs Resort & Inn
. . . . Ukiah, Calif.
Black Forest B&B Lodge & Cabins
. . . . Colorado Springs, Colo.
Romantic RiverSong Inn . . . . Estes Park, Colo.
Angels' Watch Inn . . . . Westbrook, Conn.
Cedar Mountain Farm. . . . . Athol, Idaho
Sonora Gardens Farmstead. . . . . Nauvoo, Ill.
Harbour Towne Inn on The Waterfront
. . . . Boothbay Harbor, Maine
Spicer Castle Inn . . . . Spicer, Minn.
The Mast Farm Inn . . . . Valle Crucis, N.C.
Big Mill Bed & Breakfast . . . . . . Williamston, N.C.
Touchstone Inn, Spa & Gallery
. . . . Taos, N.M.
Brae Loch Inn. . . . . Cazenovia, N.Y.
Inn & Spa At Cedar Falls . . . . Logan, Ohio
McKenzie River Inn. . . . . Vida, Ore.
Willowgreen Farm B&B . . . . Summerside,
Hasse House Ranch . . . . Mason, Texas
Golden Stage Inn . . . . Proctorsville, Vt.
Catamount B&B . . . . Williston, Vt.
Justin Trails Resort . . . . Sparta, Wis.

Taverns

Lodge at Sedona-A Luxury Bed and Breakfast Inn

. . . . Sedona, Ariz.
Fensalden Inn . . . . Albion, Calif.
Hotel Charlotte. . . . . Groveland, Calif.
1859 Historic National Hotel, A Country Inn
. . . . Jamestown, Calif.
A Meadow House . . . . Lakeville, Conn.
Silvermine Tavern. . . . . Norwalk, Conn.
The Historic Peninsula Inn & Spa
. . . . Gulfport, Fla.
Bayfront Marin House Bed & Breakfast
. . . . Saint Augustine, Fla.
Historic Merrell Inn . . . . South Lee, Mass.
Reynolds Tavern . . . . Annapolis, Md.
Chapman Inn . . . . Bethel, Maine
Southern Hotel. . . . . Sainte Genevieve, Mo.
A Grand Inn-Sunset Hill House
. . . . Sugar Hill, N.H.
The Tilton Inn and Onions Pub & Restaurant
. . . . Tilton, N.H.
Halcyon Farm Bed & Breakfast
. . . . Amsterdam, N.Y.
HideAway Country Inn . . . . Bucyrus, Ohio
Rider's 1812 Inn. . . . . Painesville, Ohio
Pennsbury Inn . . . . Chadds Ford, Pa.
The Fairfield Inn 1757. . . . . Fairfield, Pa.
James Gettys Hotel . . . . Gettysburg, Pa.
Berry Patch B&B . . . . Lebanon, Pa.
Villa OneTwenty . . . . Newport, R.I.
The Garden and The Sea Inn
. . . . New Church, Va.

Train Stations & Renovated Rail Cars

Grand Living Bed and Breakfast
. . . . Williams, Ariz.
Mount View Hotel & Spa . . . . Calistoga, Calif.
Featherbed Railroad Company B&B
. . . . Nice, Calif.
Melitta Station Inn . . . . Santa Rosa, Calif.
Winter Park Chateau . . . . Winter Park, Colo.
Deacon Timothy Pratt Bed & Breakfast Inn C.1746
. . . . Old Saybrook, Conn.
Mason House Inn and Caboose Cottage of
Bentonsport
. . . . Bentonsport, Iowa
Arbor Hill Inn . . . . La Porte, Ind.
1906 Pine Crest Inn and Restaurant
. . . . Tryon, N.C.
Berry Patch B&B . . . . Lebanon, Pa.
Red Lion Bed & Breakfast . . . . Red Lion, Pa.
Katy House Bed & Breakfast
. . . . Smithville, Texas
Bridgewater Inn and Cottage
. . . . Bridgewater, Va.
Cape Charles House . . . . Cape Charles, Va.
Firmstone Manor . . . . Clifton Forge, Va.
Estabrook House . . . . Saint Johnsbury, Vt.
Fountain Chateau Bed & Breakfast Inn
. . . . Hustler, Wis.
Pedal'rs Inn Bed and Breakfast
. . . . Wales, Wis.
Elkhorn Inn & Theatre . . . . Landgraff, W.Va.

Tunnels, Caves, Secret Passageways

Cliff Cottage Inn - Luxury B&B Suites & Historic
Cottages

. . . . Eureka Springs, Ark.
Casa De San Pedro. . . . . Hereford, Ariz.
Lodge at Sedona-A Luxury Bed and Breakfast Inn
. . . . Sedona, Ariz.
Grand Living Bed and Breakfast
. . . . Williams, Ariz.
American Historic Bed and Breakfast
. . . . Kelowna,
Albert Shafsky House Bed & Breakfast
. . . . Placerville, Calif.
The Steamboat House Bed and Breakfast
. . . . Galena, Ill.
Sweet Dreams Inn Victorian B&B
. . . . Bay Port, Mich.
Munro House B&B and Spa . . . . . Jonesville, Mich.
1906 Pine Crest Inn and Restaurant
. . . . Tryon, N.C.
10 Fitch . . . . Auburn, N.Y.
The Turret House B&B . . . . Dryden, N.Y.
Arbor View House B&B . . . . East Marion, N.Y.
HideAway Country Inn . . . . Bucyrus, Ohio
Gambier House . . . . Gambier, Ohio
Rider's 1812 Inn. . . . . Painesville, Ohio
Pennsbury Inn . . . . Chadds Ford, Pa.
Berry Patch B&B . . . . Lebanon, Pa.
The Great Valley House of Valley Forge
. . . . Valley Forge, Pa.
Stoltzfus Bed and Breakfast at the Fassitt Mansion
. . . . White Horse, Pa.
Villa OneTwenty . . . . Newport, R.I.
Custer Mansion B&B . . . . Custer, S.D.
Bridgewater Inn and Cottage
. . . . Bridgewater, Va.
Firmstone Manor . . . . Clifton Forge, Va.
Stonewall Jackson Inn B&B . . . . . Harrisonburg, Va.
Iris Inn . . . . Waynesboro, Va.
White House of Wilmington . . . . . Wilmington, Vt.
Fountain Chateau Bed & Breakfast Inn
. . . . Hustler, Wis.

Underground Railroad

Roseledge Country Inn & Farm Shoppe
. . . . Preston, Conn.
Mason House Inn and Caboose Cottage of
Bentonsport
. . . . Bentonsport, Iowa
The Steamboat House Bed and Breakfast
. . . . Galena, Ill.
Inn at Aberdeen . . . . Valparaiso, Ind.
Historic Merrell Inn . . . . South Lee, Mass.
The Alexander House Booklovers B&B
. . . . Princess Anne, Md.
Halcyon Farm Bed & Breakfast
. . . . Amsterdam, N.Y.
10 Fitch . . . . Auburn, N.Y.
Maxwell Creek Inn Bed & Breakfast
. . . . Sodus, N.Y.
HideAway Country Inn . . . . Bucyrus, Ohio
Rider's 1812 Inn. . . . . Painesville, Ohio
Kilpatrick Manor Bed & Breakfast
. . . . Niagara Falls,
Post House Country Inn / Burke House Inn
. . . . Niagara On The Lake,
Pheasant Field B&B . . . . Carlisle, Pa.
Pennsbury Inn . . . . Chadds Ford, Pa.
The Fairfield Inn 1757. . . . . Fairfield, Pa.
The Great Valley House of Valley Forge

. . . . Valley Forge, Pa.
Stoltzfus Bed and Breakfast at the Fassitt Mansion
. . . . White Horse, Pa.
Villa OneTwenty . . . . Newport, R.I.
Lilac Inn. . . . . Brandon, Vt.
Rosebelle's Victorian Inn. . . . . Brandon, Vt.
Cobble House Inn . . . . Gaysville, Vt.
Golden Stage Inn . . . . Proctorsville, Vt.

Unusual Architecture

All Seasons Inns . . . . Eureka Springs, Ark.
Cliff Cottage Inn - Luxury B&B Suites & Historic
Cottages
. . . . Eureka Springs, Ark.
Casa De San Pedro. . . . . Hereford, Ariz.
Lodge at Sedona-A Luxury Bed and Breakfast Inn
. . . . Sedona, Ariz.
The Heritage Inn . . . . Snowflake, Ariz.
Deer Crossing Inn. . . . . Castro Valley, Calif.
Brewery Gulch Inn . . . . Mendocino, Calif.
A White Jasmine Inn . . . . Santa Barbara, Calif.
Bissell House . . . . South Pasadena, Calif.
Avenue Hotel, A Victorian B&B
. . . . Manitou Springs, Colo.
Winter Park Chateau . . . . Winter Park, Colo.
A Meadow House . . . . Lakeville, Conn.
Roseledge Country Inn & Farm Shoppe
. . . . Preston, Conn.
The Towers B&B. . . . . Milford, Del.
Bayfront Marin House Bed & Breakfast
. . . . Saint Augustine, Fla.
Sylvan Falls Mill. . . . . Rabun Gap, Ga.
Washington Plantation . . . . Washington, Ga.
Blue Belle Inn B&B . . . . Saint Ansgar, Iowa
Hansen House Mansion, The Centennial Houses of
Lincoln Park
. . . . Chicago, Ill.
The Steamboat House Bed and Breakfast
. . . . Galena, Ill.
The Landmark Inn at The Historic Bank of Oberlin
. . . . Oberlin, Kan.
Serenity Bed and Breakfast Inn
. . . . Wichita, Kan.
1851 Historic Maple Hill Manor B&B
. . . . Springfield, Ky.
HH Whitney House on the Historic Esplanade
. . . . New Orleans, La.
The Inn at Restful Paws . . . . Holland, Mass.
Clamber Hill Inn & Restaurant
. . . . Petersham, Mass.
Gibson's Lodgings . . . . Annapolis, Md.
The Alden House Bed & Breakfast
. . . . Belfast, Maine
Lord Camden Inn . . . . Camden, Maine
The Brewster Inn. . . . . Dexter, Maine
Greenville Inn at Moosehead Lake
. . . . Greenville, Maine
Grand Victorian Bed & Breakfast Inn
. . . . Bellaire, Mich.
Terrace Inn & Restaurant . . . . Petoskey, Mich.
Spicer Castle Inn . . . . Spicer, Minn.
The Dickey House B&B . . . . Marshfield, Mo.
Fairview Inn & Sophia's Restaurant
. . . . Jackson, Miss.
Wright Inn & Carriage House
. . . . Asheville, N.C.
C.W. Worth House B&B . . . . Wilmington, N.C.

Inns of Interest

Coppertoppe Inn & Retreat Center
. . . . Hebron, N.H.
A Grand Inn-Sunset Hill House
. . . . Sugar Hill, N.H.
The Black Range Lodge. . . . . Kingston, N.M.
Touchstone Inn, Spa & Gallery
. . . . Taos, N.M.   ·
Hilltop House. . . . . Amenia, N.Y.
Notleymere Cottage . . . . Cazenovia, N.Y.
The Turret House B&B . . . . Dryden, N.Y.
Arbor View House B&B . . . . East Marion, N.Y.
The Sheldon Mansion Inn Bed and Breakfast
. . . . Granville, N.Y.
The Edward Harris House B&B Inn
. . . . Rochester, N.Y.
Rollins Creek Old West Town & Bed and Breakfast
. . . . Guthrie, Okla.
The Queen, A Victorian B&B
. . . . Bellefonte, Pa.
Pennsbury Inn . . . . Chadds Ford, Pa.
Berry Patch B&B . . . . Lebanon, Pa.
The Priory . . . . Pittsburgh, Pa.
The Great Valley House of Valley Forge
. . . . Valley Forge, Pa.
Villa OneTwenty . . . . Newport, R.I.
Edgewood Manor B&B . . . . Providence, R.I.
Custer Mansion B&B . . . . Custer, S.D.
Historic Prospect Hill B&B Inn
. . . . Mountain City, Tenn.
Cape Charles House . . . . Cape Charles, Va.
Firmstone Manor . . . . Clifton Forge, Va.
Hockman House Bed & Breakfast
. . . . Edinburg, Va.
Magnolia House Inn . . . . Hampton, Va.
Federal Crest Inn. . . . . Lynchburg, Va.
Mayhurst Inn . . . . Orange, Va.
Anne Hathaways Cottage . . . . Staunton, Va.
Essex Inn. . . . . Tappahannock, Va.
Lilac Inn. Brandon, Vt.
Rosebelle's Victorian Inn. . . . . Brandon, Vt.
Silas Griffith Inn . . . . Danby, Vt.
Cobble House Inn . . . . Gaysville, Vt.
A Stone Wall Inn . . . . Windham, Vt.
Tree Frog Night Inn . . . . Bellingham, Wash.
Cobblestone Bed & Breakfast
. . . . Birchwood, Wis.
Heritage Farm Museum & Village
. . . . Huntington, W.Va.
Elkhorn Inn & Theatre . . . . Landgraff, W.Va.

Unusual Sleeping Places

In a water tower
John Dougherty House . . . . Mendocino, Calif.
In a caboose
Featherbed Railroad Company B&B
. . . . Nice, Calif.
In a bank
The Landmark Inn at The Historic Bank of Oberlin
. . . . Oberlin, Kan.
In a trading post
Hacienda Vargas . . . . Algodones, N.M.
On or next to an archaeological dig site
The White Oak Inn . . . . Danville, Ohio

War of 1812

A Meadow House . . . . Lakeville, Conn.
The Inn at Mitchell House . . . . . Chestertown, Md.

Kilpatrick Manor Bed & Breakfast
. . . . Niagara Falls,
Post House Country Inn / Burke House Inn
. . . . Niagara On The Lake,

Waterfalls

Pearson's Pond Luxury Inn & Adventure Spa
. . . . Juneau, Alaska
Casa De San Pedro. . . . . Hereford, Ariz.
Lodge at Sedona-A Luxury Bed and Breakfast Inn
. . . . Sedona, Ariz.
The Heritage Inn . . . . Snowflake, Ariz.
Deer Crossing Inn . . . . Castro Valley, Calif.
Hotel Charlotte. . . . . Groveland, Calif.
Vichy Hot Springs Resort & Inn
. . . . Ukiah, Calif.
A Meadow House . . . . Lakeville, Conn.
Lily Creek Lodge. . . . . Dahlonega, Ga.
Sylvan Falls Mill. . . . . Rabun Gap, Ga.
Old Mill on The Falls Inn . . . . . . Hatfield, Mass.
Greenville Inn at Moosehead Lake
. . . . Greenville, Maine
Terrace Inn & Restaurant . . . . Petoskey, Mich.
Nicolin Mansion Bed & Breakfast
. . . . Jordan, Minn.
Colonial Pines Inn Bed and Breakfast
. . . . Highlands, N.C.
1906 Pine Crest Inn and Restaurant
. . . . Tryon, N.C.
The Mast Farm Inn . . . . Valle Crucis, N.C.
Cabernet Inn . . . . North Conway, N.H.
10 Fitch . . . . Auburn, N.Y.
Inn & Spa At Cedar Falls . . . . Logan, Ohio
Hannah's House Bed & Breakfast
. . . . Millersburg, Ohio
Kilpatrick Manor Bed & Breakfast
. . . . Niagara Falls,
Post House Country Inn / Burke House Inn
. . . . Niagara On The Lake,
McKenzie River Inn. . . . . Vida, Ore.
Woodland Farmhouse Inn . . . . Kamas, Utah
Bridgewater Inn and Cottage
. . . . Bridgewater, Va.
Sugar Tree Inn . . . . Vesuvius, Va.
Iris Inn . . . . Waynesboro, Va.
Phineas Swann B&B Inn . . Montgomery Center, Vt.
Arlington's River Rock Inn
. . . . Arlington, Wash.
Second Wind Country Inn . . . . Ashland, Wis.

Who Slept/Visited Here

Jesse James
All Seasons Inns . . . . Eureka Springs, Ark.
Lillian Russell
Bayview Hotel . . . . Aptos, Calif.
Clark Gable
Gold Mountain Manor Historic B&B
. . . . Big Bear, Calif.
Carole Lombard
Gold Mountain Manor Historic B&B
. . . . Big Bear, Calif.
Gram Parsons
Joshua Tree Inn. . . . . Joshua Tree, Calif.
President William McKinley
Cheshire Cat Inn & Spa. . . . . . Santa Barbara, Calif.
Mark Twain (Samuel Clemens)
Vichy Hot Springs Resort & Inn

. . . . Ukiah, Calif.
Jack London
Vichy Hot Springs Resort & Inn
. . . . Ukiah, Calif.
Theodore Roosevelt
Vichy Hot Springs Resort & Inn
. . . . Ukiah, Calif.
Ulysses Grant
Vichy Hot Springs Resort & Inn
. . . . Ukiah, Calif.
Robert Louis Stevenson
Vichy Hot Springs Resort & Inn
. . . . Ukiah, Calif.
The Carnegies
Florida House Inn . . . . Amelia Island, Fla.
John D. Rockefeller
Florida House Inn . . . . Amelia Island, Fla.
Ulysses S. Grant
Florida House Inn . . . . Amelia Island, Fla.
Jefferson Davis
Washington Plantation . . . . Washington, Ga.
Louis Armstrong
Hotel Saint Pierre. . . . . New Orleans, La.
Tennessee Williams
Hotel Saint Pierre. . . . . New Orleans, La.
Anthony Edwards
Classic Rosewood - A Thorwood Property
. . . . Hastings, Minn.
Calvin Coolidge
Lehmann House B&B . . . . Saint Louis, Mo.
Theodore Roosevelt
Lehmann House B&B . . . . Saint Louis, Mo.
William H. Taft
Lehmann House B&B . . . . Saint Louis, Mo.
F. Scott Fitzgerald
1906 Pine Crest Inn and Restaurant
. . . . Tryon, N.C.
Ernest Hemmingway
1906 Pine Crest Inn and Restaurant
. . . . Tryon, N.C.
Cary Grant
The Mulburn Inn . . . . Bethlehem, N.H.
Barbara Hutton
The Mulburn Inn . . . . Bethlehem, N.H.
Woolworth Family
The Mulburn Inn . . . . Bethlehem, N.H.
Big Nose Kay
Plaza Hotel . . . . Las Vegas, N.M.
Billy the Kid
Plaza Hotel . . . . Las Vegas, N.M.
Teddy Roosevelt
Notleymere Cottage . . . . Cazenovia, N.Y.
Herbert Hoover
Weasku Inn . . . . Grants Pass, Ore.
Zane Grey
Weasku Inn . . . . Grants Pass, Ore.
Walt Disney
Weasku Inn . . . . Grants Pass, Ore.
Clark Gable
Weasku Inn . . . . Grants Pass, Ore.
Carole Lombard
Weasku Inn . . . . Grants Pass, Ore.
Lillian Hellman
The Inn at Barley Sheaf Farm
. . . . Holicong, Pa.

Marx Brothers
The Inn at Barley Sheaf Farm
. . . . Holicong, Pa.

S.J. Perlman
The Inn at Barley Sheaf Farm
. . . . Holicong, Pa.

Buffalo Bill Cody
The Inn at Jim Thorpe . . . . Jim Thorpe, Pa.

Thomas Edison
The Inn at Jim Thorpe . . . . Jim Thorpe, Pa.

John D. Rockefeller
The Inn at Jim Thorpe . . . . Jim Thorpe, Pa.

Dwight D. Eisenhower
Swann Hotel . . . . Jasper, Texas

General George Patton
Swann Hotel . . . . Jasper, Texas

Alex Haley
McKay House . . . . Jefferson, Texas

Lady Bird Johnson
McKay House . . . . Jefferson, Texas

Thomas Jefferson
The Inn at Meander Plantation
. . . . Locust Dale, Va.

Elizabeth Taylor
Residence Bed & Breakfast . . . . Lynchburg, Va.

Gerald Ford
Residence Bed & Breakfast . . . . Lynchburg, Va.

Georgia O'Keeffe
Residence Bed & Breakfast . . . . Lynchburg, Va.

President Calvin Coolidge
Echo Lake Inn . . . . Ludlow, Vt.

Henry Ford
Echo Lake Inn . . . . Ludlow, Vt.

Thomas Edison
Echo Lake Inn Ludlow, Vt.

Martin Sheen
Justin Trails Resort . . . . Sparta, Wis.

World War II

The Goose & Turrets B&B . . . . Montara, Calif.
River Park Inn . . . . Green Cove Springs, Fla.
Adair Country Inn and Restaurant
. . . . Bethlehem, N.H.
HideAway Country Inn . . . . Bucyrus, Ohio
Villa OneTwenty . . . . Newport, R.I.

INN EVALUATION FORM

Please copy and complete for each stay and mail to the address shown. Since 1981 we have provided this evaluation form to millions of travelers. Also visit iLoveInns.com to review all the inns you've visited or the iPhone application InnTouch.

Name of Inn: _____

City and State: _____

Date of Stay: _____

Your Name: _____

Address: _____

City/State/Zip: _____

Phone: (__ __ __) __ __ __ – __ __ __ __

E-mail: _____

Please use the following rating scale for the next items.
1: Poor.   2: Fair.   3: Average.   4: Good.   5: Outstanding.

Service	1	2	3	4	5
Condition	1	2	3	4	5
Cleanliness	1	2	3	4	5
Room Comfort	1	2	3	4	5
Location	1	2	3	4	5
Overall	1	2	3	4	5

Comments on Above: _____

_____

_____

_____

_____

MAIL THE COMPLETED FORM TO:
American Historic Inns, Inc.
PO Box 669
Dana Point, CA 92629-0669
(949) 481-7276
www.iLoveInns.com

iLoveInns.com

PO Box 669
Dana Point
California
92629-0669
(949) 481-7276
Fax (949) 481-3796
www.iLoveInns.com

Order Form

Date: __ __ / __ __ / __ __   Shipped: __ __ / __ __ / __ __

Name: _____

Street: _____

City/State/Zip: _____

Phone: (__ __ __) __ __ __ – __ __ __ __   E-mail: _____

QTY.	Prod. No.	Description	Amount	Total
_____	AHI25	Bed & Breakfasts and Country Inns	$24.95	_____
		Subtotal		_____
		California buyers add 7.75% sales tax		_____
		Shipping and Handling		
		PRIORITY (3-5 days): $5.60 for 1-2 books. 3 Books UPS $9 - 2ND-DAY AIR: $20.00.		_____
		TOTAL		_____

❑ Check/Money Order   ❑ Discover   ❑ Mastercard   ❑ Visa   ❑ American Express

Account Number __ __ __ __ __ __ __ __ __ __ __ __ __ __ __ __   Exp. Date __ __ / __ __

Security Code _____

Name on card _____

Signature _____

Or

Order Online At store.iLoveInns.com

www.iLoveInns.com

- More than 19,000 bed & breakfasts and country inns.
- Color photos and room descriptions.
- Use our easy Innfinder Search to quickly access inns near your destination.
- Online room availability, booking and guest reviews.
- Search for inns in our "Buy-One-Night-Get-One-Night-Free" program.
- Or use our Advanced Search to look for inns that meet your specific needs.
- See our specially selected Featured Inns.
- Learn about bed & breakfast hot spots across the country.
- Find out where the top inns are, including our famous picks for the Top 10 Most Romantic Inns.
- Expert articles highlighting our unique inns.
- Mobile friendly.

iPhone + B&Bs =

InnTouch
from iLoveInns.com

a free application for the
iPhone that helps you
get InnTouch with your
favorite bed and breakfasts

Now you can find your favorite bed and breakfast
getaway spot right on your iPhone.

Looking for a romantic getaway at a great little
boutique inn or bed and breakfast?

iLoveInns.com presents your guide to America's
best and most romantic inns right on your iPhone
or iPod touch.

Download InnTouch today at the App Store.